The Gu

comprising
The Guns of Normandy
and
The Guns of Victory

GEORGE G. BLACKBURN

Robinson
LONDON

Constable Publishers
3 The Lanchesters
162 Fulham Palace Road
London W6 9ER
www.constablerobinson.com

This combined paperback edition first published in the UK
by Robinson, an imprint of Constable & Robinson Ltd 2000

Second Impression

The Guns of Normandy first published in Canada
by McClelland & Stewart Inc. 1995
Copyright © George G. Blackburn 1995
The Guns of Victory first published in Canada
by McClelland & Stewart Inc. 1996
Copyright © George G. Blackburn 1996

A copy of the British Library Cataloguing in
Publication Data is available from the British Library.

ISBN 1-84119-210-4

Printed and bound in the EU

The Guns of Normandy

A Soldier's Eye View, France 1944

Dedicated to all who served in Normandy, and to all who loved them and lived for months on end in dreadful suspense, particularly mothers and wives who, like my dear Grace, never knew when the doorbell rang that there wouldn't be a telegram beginning "We regret to inform you . . . ."

ENGLISH

Alderney

CHANNEL

GUERNSEY

Sark

ISLANDS

JERSEY

C O T E N T I N

Cherbourg

Baie

Carentan

Arromanches les Bai

Sommervieu

Bayeux

N

St. Lô

Caumont

O

R

La Vire R.

N

Golfe de St.-Malo

Vire

St. Malo

Avranches

Mortain

CHANNEL

la Seine

Dieppe

Offranville

1 Sept

1 Sept

1 Sept

31 Aug

Le Havre

Rouen

31 Aug

SEINE

Trouville

RIVER

Forêt
de la Lande

Bourgthéroulde

Courseulles-
sur-Mer

Bernières-sur-Mer

St. Aubin-sur-Mer

26 Aug

26 Aug

27 Aug

Elbeuf

Ouistreham

25 Aug

Buron

11 July

24 Aug

25 Aug

Brionne

Authie

Caen

24 Aug

Carpiquet

Faubourg de Vaucelles

Lisieux

Thiberville

24 Aug

Boisney

Caen to Point 122
(See detailed map)

Verrières

N

D

Y

Point 122

La Dives River

23 Aug

Orne R.

Bretteville-sur-Laize

Odon R.

Le Laize R.

M

A

23 Aug

Orbec

Livarot

23 Aug

Friardel

Falaise

21 Aug

22 Aug

Vimoutiers

"MACZUGA"

Hill 262

Tran

Bretteville-sur-Laize
to Falaise
(See detailed map)

Chambois

Argentan

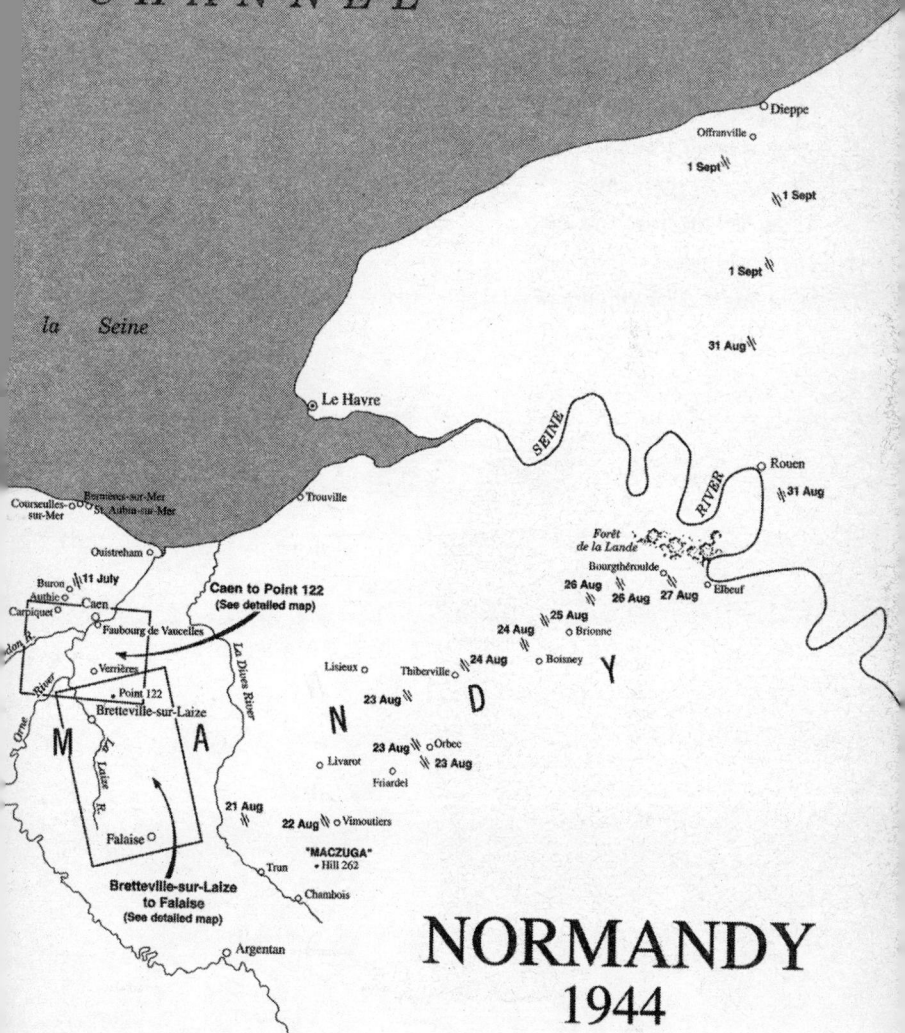

NORMANDY
1944

| 0 | | 10 | | 20 | | 30 mi |

| 0 | 10 | 20 | 30 | 40 | 50 km |

4 RCA gun positions ....

Ubique means that warnin' grunt
The perished linesman knows,
When o'er his strung and sufferin' front
The shrapnel sprays his foes,
And when the firin' dies away
The husky whisper runs
From lips that haven't drunk all day
"The guns, thank God, the guns."

– Rudyard Kipling

CONTENTS

PART SIX - AUGUST 12-13
2ND DIVISION OUTFLANKS ENEMY POSITIONS

PART SEVEN - AUGUST 14-23
RENEWING ATTACK TO ENTRAP THE GERMAN ARMY

PART EIGHT - AUGUST 24-SEPTEMBER 5
BEING WELCOMED AS LIBERATORS

MAPS

INTRODUCTION

---　✳　---

THIS WAS TO BE SIMPLY THE STORY OF ONE REGIMENT OF 25-pounders in Normandy engaged in what may have been the most intense clash of arms on any front in World War II, written in such a way as to allow our grandchildren to relive those awful days when the fate of Europe and the course of history, as it concerns the thrust of democracy across this earth, hung in the balance.

However, to make understandable the crucial role of the guns and the awesome concentrations they were called upon to fire day after day, rising to insane levels along Verrières Ridge south of Caen in late July, it has been necessary to describe in some detail the terrible problems confronting the frontline troops and the artillery forward observation officers (FOOs) and crews who shared their lot in every attack and counter-attack.

And since no one can properly appreciate the valour and judge the effectiveness of the frontline soldiers, and the gunners who supported them, who does not fully appreciate the unparalleled severity of the fighting in Normandy, an earnest effort has been made to capture the high tension overlaying every minute of every hour of every day for weeks on end, when massive opposing forces were committed to endless offensive operations designed to overwh_
and destroy each other in a bloodbath that was pur_
unabated fury for almost three months, with neither s_

any flexibility of manoeuvre – the Allies confined by the perimeters of the bridgehead, and the enemy denied any planned withdrawal by their Führer.

However, locating material describing what it was like at the cutting edge of 1st Canadian Army from the middle of July until the end of August – in effect the fighting from Caen to Falaise that entrapped the German armies in Normandy – was very difficult. No one has succeeded in accurately describing the ferocity of the battles for Verrières Ridge and beyond. And perhaps no one ever will, for few who served with the rifle companies of the infantry battalions, including artillery FOOs and their crews, managed to survive more than a few days.

Some were casualties within hours of joining units, and, of the few who survived to see it through all the way with a rifle company, none seemingly have been able or willing to write of it. During my interviews with them – many of which were conducted right after the war ended, when battle experiences should still have been alive and clear – I discovered that for those who had survived the worst of it, memories of Normandy were blurred and disordered bits and pieces. While retaining vivid impressions, they recalled few details and resorted to generalities when they tried to describe them.

Over and over I heard, "gawdawful . . . terrifying . . . completely demoralizing . . . bloody hell . . . scared shitless," and other combinations of four-letter words favoured by soldiers, but when pressed for details their responses were embarrassingly sparse.

And beyond having no recall of what happened from hour to hour for days on end, some could not even remember having been in an attack where I personally knew they had been. This I found difficult to believe until I tried filling in diary notes of my own memories of later battles in the Rhineland and found myself lost in the same impenetrable fog, unable to account for more than a few hours of the days I had been involved, and what little I could recall had the quality of a nightmare.

Obviously the same combination of exhaustion and terror that makes it difficult to think or see clearly in the shattering confusion and roar of battle (when a man functions only from habit, drill, and discipline), makes it equally difficult to retain coherent, detailed memories, in much the same way the conscious mind is able to recall only a few disconnected details and a general impression of horror on waking up from a nightmare. And so I could only piece together a composite picture, made up of the fragmentary memories of some who survived in humble thankfulness those awful days, and place these back to back with the frightful casualty statistics.

The official record-keepers of those times were of no help; they seem to have been entirely disinterested in recording such matters. Beyond brief references to the weather, there is little recognition of the conditions under which the fighting soldier existed, which, more often than not, were dreadful. While extremely useful in authenticating personal notes and diaries, none of the sparse unit diaries or post-battle intelligence reports make any serious attempt to describe what was entailed in simply staying alive during those terrible days and nights.

This deficiency in the material set down at the time by those responsible for preserving historical records (on which all official and unofficial histories would be based) has led to inaccurate, irresponsible conclusions bordering on outright dishonesty – even in the works of our own official historians – regarding the training and fighting qualities of Canadian officers and men in World War II. And these inaccuracies – insulting to the memory of all those Canadians who died facing the enemy while the official record-keepers sheltered miles to the rear – are being perpetuated by British and American writers and even built upon by some domestic revisionists.

Far from accurately portraying the ferocity of the deadly clashes in battles of attrition reminiscent of World War I, the war historians tend to give the impression that it was some sort of game, played out by cunning generals, with the outcome hinging on the level of "aggressiveness" shown by one side or the other – most particularly on that of the "junior commanders."

It is irritating to the point of enraging to read critical analyses of the shortcomings of men and officers engaged at the spearhead of operations by critics with not a single day of frontline experience. Well-rested, well-fed, safe and secure, writing within the relaxed atmosphere of their homes or offices, with no responsibility for men's lives resting on their decisions, they are sickeningly arrogant. Clearly, when all the sinister mystery is removed from any battlefield as to what the enemy has over there beyond those trees, or among the silent rubble of that village, or in the dead ground just over that ridge, any fool can decide what should have been done and the best way of doing it.

And there is something particularly obscene about the works of historians who conduct coldblooded analyses and write without emotion of the accomplishments of units and the "fighting qualities" of men while never giving any indication they recognize and understand the frailty of the human spirit and the resolve of all men, regardless of training or background, when forced to live for days without end in a continuing agony of fear, made manageable only by the numbing effects of extreme fatigue.

I think I would have keeled over in shock had I come across one historian, purporting to describe the battles on the road to Falaise, who once acknowledged that those battles (like those in every major operation extending over several weeks) were not fought by alert, well-rested, well-fed, healthy men, but by men suffering utter exhaustion, from heat and dysentery and the neverending itching induced by lice and sand fleas, from never being allowed to stretch out and get a night's sleep, and from continuously living with grinding tension arising from the irrepressible dread of being blown to pieces or being left mangled and crippled.

Everyone tends to forget just how awful some aspects were. I had to be reminded of my bout with disturbed bowels by an ex-major of the Royal Regiment of Canada. His recall of one man's dysentery-induced expulsion aroused my own memories of the convulsive cramps and feverish, shuddering ague brought on by that damnable scourge that struck the Canadian Army around Verrières before the drive down the Falaise road began, which worsened as time went on to the point where it came close to putting some units out of action when supplies of medicine to treat it ran out. Yet dysentery, if mentioned at all by historians, is touched on only in passing, as though of no more consequence than some minor irritating inconvenience like lice or mosquitoes.

What a hellish nightmare it must have been for foot-soldiers with dysentery just to drag themselves over hill and dale, let alone dash here and there for cover when on the attack, and then dig in on the objective to meet the inevitable counter-attack. I wondered then and I wonder still how men found the will to move out from cover and risk death and crippling wounds day after day until they were wounded or killed. I saw them do it when they were so stunned by fatigue they scarcely flinched when an 88-mm whacked an airburst above them. And I saw them do it shortly after some opening rounds of a fire plan fell short, causing a few, overwrought with tension, to cry like babies.

Armchair strategists writing of those days – whether British, American, or Canadian – have all spent too much time wondering why they were so slow getting down past Falaise to meet up with the Americans. They should have spent more time wondering how men ever summoned up the necessary moral courage and physical stamina to get there at all.

Those base-wallahs who since the war have dared to criticize the Canadians for not closing the Falaise Gap sooner – inferring from what seems to have been slow daily progress a general lack of aggressiveness – were obviously not around at the time to see and experience what it was like for the troops at the cutting edge of the Canadian army. And while lack of first-hand experience in a writer may be forgiven, no such tolerance can be extended to those pretending to be historians who purposely ignore the evidence provided by the awful casualty rate among the Canadian divisions, which on the road to Falaise and beyond rose to twice the American rate and two and a half times the British rate (a rate the British considered unsustainable, causing them to set up a new category, "Double Intense," for measuring the intensity of battle).

By mid-August the nine 2nd Cdn Division infantry battalions were 1,900 short of establishment in their fighting strength of 5,040.

As in World War I, some staff officers and field commanders, to escape criticism, blamed the fighting men for failures. Thus we have the ridiculous declaration by Lt-General Charles Foulkes, CO of 2nd Division, that "at Falaise and Caen, we found that when we bumped into battle-experienced German troops, we were no match for them."

"Bumped into"? Foulkes's infantry brigades were never out of contact with the best troops Hitler ever assembled, from when 2nd Division entered battle, south of Caen, to Falaise and beyond. And it was the German elite SS units that were shredded, defeated, and herded to their destruction in the Falaise pocket – not the other way around!

But historians have lent status to such myths, thus guaranteeing their perpetuation by writers following behind, while largely ignoring the fact that the greatest failure in Normandy was the tanks, not the heroes who manned them. Except for a few "Fireflies," created by the British by replacing the 75-mm guns on Sherman tanks with the high-velocity 17-pounders, Allied tanks (American Shermans and British Churchills and Cromwells) were totally outclassed.

Every man in every armoured division, from the Officer Commanding down to the lowliest driver, within hours of arriving in Normandy, was aware that in any confrontation with German tanks, few Allied tanks would live to fight another day. For instance, Panthers could sit back at one and a half kilometres, and Tigers at two and a half kilometres, and knock out Shermans, while the 75-mm gun of the Shermans couldn't penetrate the frontal armour of those German tanks at any range. If this bred caution in armoured units moving up, who could blame them? Yet no high-ranking officer, from Eisenhower down through Montgomery and Bradley to Army and Corps commanders, or back up through the Combined Allied General Staffs, has accepted blame or been held responsible for putting at risk the whole invasion by sending men to their doom in under-gunned, under-armoured tanks. The fact some Shermans were upgraded with 17-pounders before the invasion proves that someone high up realized the extent of the problem, but a conspiracy of silence was imposed at the highest levels of the military and political powers.

It is a matter of record that in 1944 a well-informed civilian – Richard Stokes, a British MP – on many occasions from March to August asked questions in the House of Commons in an attempt to make the government aware of the inferior fire-power of Allied tanks. But all he gained was scornful laughter from incredulous government benches, and outright false statements from Prime Minister Churchill, who, on March 16 and again on July 20, 1944, assured the House: "The next time that the British Army takes the field in country suitable for the use of armour, they will be found to be equipped in a manner at least equal to the forces of any other country in the world."

Incredibly, even as the planners recognized the bridgehead in Normandy might be wiped out before it was properly established, and fully understood the crucial role tanks must play in ensuring its survival, no Allied army commander demanded tanks be upgraded to at least the level of the bastard Sherman "Fireflies," which, though more lightly armoured than German tanks, at least matched them in firepower. As it was, most historians agree the initial landings were saved from devastating attacks by superior German Panzers only by Hitler's interference. The Führer held Rommel's strategic reserves of armour too far from the coast to allow their fast deployment against the landing forces during the hours of darkness, the only time they could safely move up hidden from the deadly Typhoon rocket attacks.

Suppression of the facts may have been justified at the time to prevent demoralization of the Allied armies, but the irrefutable fact that our tankmen were equipped with grossly inferior weapons with which to push through the German Panthers and Tigers on the road to Falaise should not have been ignored by our historians. To have done so is inexcusable.

At any rate, my own awareness of the insulting criticisms of the Canadian soldier in World War II provided the necessary incentive to finish this book, begun back in the summer of 1945 when I was first given the opportunity to research the story of my regiment while stationed in Holland shortly after the war ended. Using personal notes and diaries, official war diaries on deposit at Canadian Army Records at Acton, London, and conducting dozens of interviews, especially with surviving original members of the Regiment who had signed up in September 1939, I wrote the first 132-page core manuscript. And in my attempt to bring to life those far-off days it was always necessary to draw heavily on personal experience, for no one can really describe the experience of another person.

Any reader looking for adventure, must look elsewhere. Even as I made mental notes, and wrote down my thoughts during action for the book I intended to write some day if I survived, I was fully aware that if misery and fear failed to dominate my documentation, it would be in danger of becoming chauvinistic and therefore false. My narrative might stir poignant memories of comradeship and unselfish acts, and sometimes recognize acts of courage – even great courage – but never should it develop in the fashion of an adventure story, for the simple reason that a story that deals honestly with war can never be an adventure story. It may be gripping and even melodramatic in a horrible sort of way, but never, never an adventure story.

In the foreword of his remarkable book *All Quiet on the Western*

Front, about life for the German front-line soldier in World War I, author Erich Maria Remarque said it so well: "Death is not an adventure to those who stand face to face with it." With unique precision and clarity, those few words deny the existence of any romance in the killing ground of a battle front.

The truth of this is known to every man who has survived close shelling or bombing, cowering with painful tightness of breath and panting, waiting for the next instant when he'll be blown to oblivion, or has felt the utter nakedness and vulnerability to those bullets from hidden gun muzzles when at last he is called upon to abandon his safe cover and go forth with trembling legs into the open in the attack.

The regiment of 25-pounders, from whose perspective the struggle for Normandy is viewed in this book, is 4th Field RCA, whose batteries were ordered to mobilize the same day Hitler's legions invaded Poland, on September 1, 1939, two days before Britain and France declared war. And the Regiment was largely up to strength, by voluntary enlistments, when eight days later the Parliament of Canada proclaimed the nation at war with the German Reich.

The Regiment's first year was passed in Canada in makeshift accommodation, including hastily converted stables and pigsties in the exhibition grounds of Ottawa and Toronto. The soldiers were garbed, at least for the first few months, in ill-fitting, shabby, moth-eaten 1914-18 uniforms that were not always complete, forcing some to wear their light civilian shoes on parade and fill out their attire with civilian garments when issued a tunic but no breeches, or breeches but no tunic. Early training, while approached with enthusiasm, was conducted mainly on obsolete equipment such as World War I 18-pounder guns or 4.5-inch howitzers. And sometimes there was no equipment at all, as in the case of troop deployments when trucks could not be rented from local merchants and gunners were forced to walk about among logs set in the ground representing guns, carrying placards representing vehicles (invariably drawing indignant inquiries from civilian passersby curious to know "Why the hell is the Army on strike?").

Canada's embryonic war industries, which at their maturity would turn out a flood of guns, vehicles, ships, planes, and hundreds of other essential items for her own forces and those of her allies — at such a rate that an army division of twenty thousand could be equipped in a week – was, until the summer of 1940, held back by Britain's reluctance to release blueprints and patents of their tools of war for manufacture outside the British Isles. Not until some 224,000 bedraggled British soldiers and 112,000 of their French and Belgian comrades returned to England without guns and vehicles, having abandoned them all at Dunkirk as they made their way to the little boats that had come to rescue them, did Churchill issue his earnest appeal to North America: "Give us the tools and we will finish the job."

On September 5, 1940, the Regiment arrived in Aldershot, England, without weapons or vehicles, expecting to be issued new 25-pounders so they might join in the defence of the realm against the imminent invasion by German hordes fresh from their Blitzkrieg strikes that had brought Western Europe to its knees.

Instead each battery received forty rifles and fifteen cartridges per rifle, mildly consoled by the knowledge they were infinitely better off than nearby units of the Home Guard (the civilian army of men too old or unfit for regular military service), who were equipped with iron-tipped pike poles made by local blacksmiths that would not have been out of place in Oliver Cromwell's army of the seventeenth century.

The first week of October — with the nation standing-to at maximum alertness — the Regiment was equipped with wooden-wheeled French 75-mm guns of 1898 vintage, and seven shells per gun. All of which would have been very funny if the island had not been in such peril, standing alone, with only what help the Commonwealth could then provide, against the combined might of Germany and Italy.

But if Britain's claim that it was prepared to "fight on the beaches . . . on the landing grounds . . . in the fields . . . in the streets . . . and on the hills," was, in the summer and fall of 1940, largely without substance, the threat of invasion by Hitler was real enough. German records would one day reveal that Hitler scheduled "Sealion," as it was known, for September 21, and only postponed it with four days to go when Göring's Luftwaffe failed to knock out the RAF and gain full dominance of the skies over the English Channel, a prerequisite for the success of a cross-Channel sea-borne invasion.

On October 12 Hitler rescheduled the invasion for April 1941. But some time over the winter he decided he must first conquer Russia, and on June 22 he turned his armies of three million men and 3,580 tanks eastwards, to the profound relief of all charged with the defence of Britain, including the men of 4th Field, who, having been re-equipped early in 1941 with some less-old British 75-mm guns with pneumatic tires, had become part of "the last line of defence of the City of London" and were awaiting the invasion with some anxiety, even as they took pride in Churchill's statement that "If you Canadians were to leave England, I would not sleep at night."

By September 1941 the Regiment had its full complement of new 25-pounders and the "quads" to tow them about, and from then until the spring of 1944, when not doing garrison duty along the Sussex and Kentish coasts, officers and other ranks underwent intensive training, frequently under the critical eyes and guidance of "the apostles of the gospel according to Larkhill," as British Instructors in Gunnery from the Royal School of Artillery at Larkhill were sometimes known.

During those two and a half years, equipment (particularly radio transmitters) improved remarkably, and modifications to the fire-control system of field guns placed incredible firepower for dealing with "targets of opportunity" in the hands of British Commonwealth forward observation officers or FOOs (captains and the subalterns substituting for them). The new firepower was of a speed and mass not available even to the field marshalls and five-star generals of other nations, allowing concentrations of shells of unbearable intensity to be brought down on targets from the twenty-four guns of a regiment within three or four minutes of their being called for by a FOO, and very little longer when the combined fire of all seventy-two guns of the division, or the 216 guns of the corps, was required.

However, until Normandy 1944 – apart from living on the fringes of the German bombing raids on England, including the 1940-41 blitz of London, doing anti-invasion garrison duty along the vulnerable coasts of Sussex and Kent, and contributing to the 1942 Dieppe Raid a small contingent of three officers and twenty other ranks (of whom three were killed and the others taken prisoner, one to escape later back to England) – the war had largely passed the 4th Field Regiment by.

After Dieppe, with 2nd Division infantry battalions having to rebuild, some of them completely (Essex Scottish having only 52 of the 521 who went on the raid return to England, and the Royal Regiment of Canada, with whom the 4th Field lads landed, leaving all but 65 of their 554 officers and men of their assaulting companies dead on the beach or in captivity), other Canadian divisions (1st and 5th) were chosen to join the Allied invasions of Sicily and Italy in the summer of 1943.

And when it came time to select a Canadian division to join two British divisions and three American divisions in assaulting the beaches of Normandy on June 6, 1944, 3rd Division got the nod.

The Regiment, along with the rest of 2nd Division, was left encamped in the fields of Kent among the great masses of men and materials assembled in the southern counties near the Channel ports, waiting their turn to cross over to France and build up the forces in the bridgehead to a level where a breakout might be attempted.

There were rumours that 2nd Division was to go on D plus 7 (seven days after D-Day); then it was D plus 14, and this might have been authentic, but on June 19 (D plus 13) a great gale started to blow in the Channel, wrecking much of the Mulberry artificial harbour installations they'd put together on the beaches, and causing delays in shipping schedules.

Then on D plus 20, the Regiment is placed on six hours' notice, meaning that six hours after the order is received it will move with guns and vehicles to the "marshalling area" from whence it will proceed to the boats.

According to the BBC there is vicious fighting in the area north of Caen . . .

PART ONE: JULY 1-10

Off to War After Years of Training

I

TO FRANCE VIA LONDON

✳

IT IS THE NIGHT OF JULY 1, 1944 – TWENTY-FIVE DAYS SINCE
the invasion of Normandy began – and still 4th Field Regiment,
along with the rest of 2nd Canadian Division, is left stewing in restless indolence here in Kent.

You've just come back with a boisterous truckload of gunners
and NCOs off a five-hour pass to Margate . . . or was it Deal? At any
rate, it was a little coastal town near Dover, identifiable by an
unusual pub located below grade in a crypt-like cellar (called The
Crypt, you think), where, for much of those five hours, you helped
somebody celebrate his birthday with many too many gin-and-
lemons. And now you want only to find the officers' marquee tent,
flop down on your bedroll, and flake out for a long and peaceful
night's sleep.

This will be the seventy-third night you have slept on the ground
in this tent you share with the other subalterns and captains of the
Regiment; you should know where it's located. But the night is so
black with the promise of rain, it takes an age to find, and then only
with the help of a considerate NCO. When finally you locate your
bedroll, the desire to lie down fully clothed and drift off among the
dissembling fumes that enshroud your head is irresistible. But even
in your state of vague awareness, in the dim light shed by a heavily

shaded petrol lantern hissing at the far end of the tent, you are conscious of an unusual amount of activity for this hour of the night. This you could easily ignore, but to your utter disgust two of your closest buddies since your earliest days in the Regiment – Lieut. Len Harvey and Lieut. Jack Cameron – inexplicably become insufferable pests, even resorting to kicking the soles of your boots to wake you. And it seems nothing will deter them. Even when you threaten physical assault, they refuse to leave you alone until you accept their advice to get up, shaking your head, and start packing up your bedroll and the rest of your belongings for a trip to the continent.

Once aware they are not joking – that they, along with everybody else in the marquee, really are packing up – the prospect of taking off for France produces a certain sobering effect. But it's only temporary. By the time you have followed the others down to the dark vehicle park and stowed away your gear in your truck, you're more than ready to climb aboard and pass into blessed oblivion for the several hours you expect it will take to get to where you are going – a matter of speculation until you assemble with the rest of the Regiment in a shadowy, dark mass to listen to a distant voice, recognizable as that of the Commanding Officer, Lt.-Colonel C. M. "Bud" Drury, extend a *bon voyage* as he reveals the Regiment is proceeding tonight to London and the East India docks where it will board ships for Normandy.

After referring to the many long years of training, leading up to this day, the CO wishes all ranks well and ends by declaring a general amnesty for those serving sentences for recent transgressions – stating most emphatically that all members of the Regiment are leaving for France with "a clean slate," and a chance to prove they are good soldiers.

As you return to your vehicle, you mull over the profound meaning this last announcement must have for one particular gunner, who, for reasons known only to himself, in recent days absolutely refused to accept that part of his sentence for "field punishment" that involved marching about the detention square for a specified period each day in full marching order, his big pack loaded with sand. While he'd dressed and equipped himself for the task each day, when ordered to march he had simply sat down and refused to budge. However, Sergeant of the Guard "Lefty" George Phillips, one of your Able Troop gun sergeants, refused to be defeated by such mulish behaviour. According to fellow sub-altern Leslie "Hutch" Hutcheon, the duty officer yesterday, Phillips, a husky, athletic man of boundless energy, simply leaned down and, grasping the webbing behind the gunner's neck, proceeded to drag the recalcitrant man round and round the dusty, gritty square on the seat of his pants for the required period of time. Surely the guard must now be as relieved as the guarded that this charade is over.

Calculating it will be dawn before you reach London, travelling at the regular after-dark convoy speed of seven and a half miles an hour, you settle down in your truck for a good long snooze. But this is not to be. Before the convoy moves off, you get a message from your battery commander, Major Gordon Wren, that you are to climb on a motorbike and spend the night riding herd on the convoy.

In your hazy state, this is the last thing on earth you should be doing. Even with all senses sharply alert and fully functioning, it is extremely dangerous riding a motorbike at night on narrow roads and through blacked-out towns and villages crowded in by stone walls and hedges, among shadowy, lurching vehicles and guns – at times barely crawling, while at other times clanking along at break-neck speed, only to be brought up short without warning, to a shuddering, jolting stop. And just to top things off, as the convoy is pulling out of Waldershare Park, it starts to rain.

You decide there is only one way to survive this night, and that's to get in behind one gun and stay there, concentrating on the glow of its white muzzle-cover, faintly lit by the reflected light of its tiny bulb. And that is what you do, though it is not without its hazards as the muzzle continually moves in close to your face and then away again – sometimes so close you have to move your head sideways to escape it, and sometimes so far away you lose sight of it in the foggy drizzle – a nerve-wracking rhythm of speeding up and slowing down, as drivers struggle to accommodate the eternal accordion motion. The regimental diary will record "many minor vehicle casualties" this night. And shortly after 4:00 A.M., during a twenty-minute halt, the shocking news is passed up the column: Gunner G.W. "Doc" Sparling, a most popular 26th Battery dispatch rider, has just been killed by a Regimental Headquarters vehicle trying to regain its position in the column.

By dawn the convoy is passing through a densely built-up area of metropolitan London. During a pause a milkman, dropping off his clinking bottles at a front door near the street, calls out, "Good luck, lads!" and you are reminded that this is not just another convoy on the way to a training exercise.

Later, when the city is waking up and you are passing through the East End, where the worst of the bombing raids of '40 and '41 struck, and which now lies on the centre-line of doodle-bug alley, ladies come out of war-scarred rowhouses whenever the convoy slows down, to pass little cakes and cookies into the back of trucks, or toss them up to sergeants standing with their heads and shoulders up through the roof-hatches of the quads* pulling the guns.

And whenever the convoy stops for more than a moment, they run out with teapots and milk and fill as many of the gunners' cups as they can reach. The speed with which the tea and cookies are produced at the briefest of halts, makes it clear you are not the first convoy of troops to receive such royal treatment passing here on the

---

* Humpbacked gun tractors, generally known as "quads," short for "quadrupeds," because all four wheels were power-driven.

way to the docks. There's no way they could have known you were coming, but they are prepared for you. This spontaneous generosity on the part of these people of modest means, who lived through the hell of the first blitz and are now living with the flying bombs, is incredible.*

At about 10:15 A.M., the Regiment pulls into an area laid waste by the earlier blitz, within sight of the cranes of the East India Docks. All ranks leave their vehicles and take up residence within the confines of a high wire-fence surrounding a marshalling compound, which reminds some of a recently levelled city dump, complete with acres of rolled brick rubble and cinders, devoid of all vegetation. A lot of green pup tents, floored with straw palliasses, sit in rows, each row carrying a number or letter.

As soon as all the motors are shut off, a voice, with an accent uncannily like the one affected by BBC news announcers, comes forth from Tannoy loudspeakers hanging on posts, instructing you to sort yourselves out: officers to that area, NCOs to this area, and other ranks over that way, where you are to choose a tent in which you can park your personal kit and eventually sleep. The Voice also draws attention to little, narrow, below-grade blast shelters distributed here and there throughout the compound, and offers advice on how to protect yourself against injury from the earth-quaking blast of a flying bomb. You are to assume the prone position, but ensure your chest and stomach are kept up and away from the earth.

The Voice is in the process of pointing out the existence of a couple of large marquee tents, sheltering a great many folding

---

* From June 13 to the end of 1944, flying bombs and rockets killed 7,533 and wounded almost 20,000 London civilians. In 1945, 1,705 more were killed and 3,836 wounded. Outside of London, along the route taken by the bombs, 1,097 were killed and 2,765 were wounded during 1944–45.

tables and a helter-skelter of folding chairs, to be used for messing and other purposes in case of rain, when it breaks into a mechanical drone closely resembling the Speaker of the House of Commons calling for order:

"Take cov-uh ... Take cov-uh ... Take cov-uh."

Immediately you are conscious of the unmistakable blabber of the ram-jet engine of a buzz bomb coming up the Thames. While no one questions the experience and advice of The Voice, everyone tries to move casually, not wishing to appear in an unseemly rush to get into a shelter. But when the raucous motor suddenly stops, and the little plane with the stubby wings starts plunging to earth, there is such a scramble for every shelter stairwell that all ranks suffer a legendary number of bruises, minor cuts, and abrasions to all parts of their anatomy. Some shelter openings are so jammed with humanity that dozens are caught outside almost standing upright when the horrendous explosion occurs. Fortunately it is some distance away, and no one is hurt from the blast. But you and many others decide that henceforth you will make for your pup tent and lie prone (face down with chest and stomach above the ground), convinced it is less hazardous than plunging into a throng of flailing hobnailed boots in one of those narrow shelters.

Shortly after this, Major Wren calls an Orders Group in one of the marquee tents to explain the routine. All ranks will be confined to the compound until the marching parties depart for the ships tomorrow afternoon. Vehicle loading will begin at 5:30 A.M.

The voice on the Tannoy speakers again starts droning, "Take cov-uh ... Take cov-uh ... Take cov-uh."

The Major continues to read from his notes, studiously ignoring the blabbering, stubby-winged plane, now clearly visible, flying low up the Thames and momentarily bathed in sunlight. But you are not hearing a word he is saying – the raucous sound of that pitiless monster, coming closer and closer with its lethal load, has captured your complete attention. It's flying so low it looks as if it may not clear a humpbacked bridge over a tributary of the Thames (River Lea) that empties into the main waterway close by. The bridge is jammed with noonday traffic crawling slowly over it, including a red double-decker bus moving from right to left. How awful it must be for the people on that bus, watching that thing coming at them. But it clears the bridge and bus with plenty to spare.

Now you realize it is headed straight this way. The Major stops talking, but still nobody moves. Suddenly it turns nose down, and its blabbering ceases. In the ominous silence, some scramble to get down on the ground beneath the flimsy tables, but most sit frozen, watching it plunge into the glittering surface of the water and explode, sending up a violent spume of water and black smoke that drifts slowly up and over the red bus on the bridge, still crawling along in the traffic as the muffled roar reaches you.

Immediately, the Major carries on, outlining the form and procedures that will maintain from now until the Regiment boards the ships for France. But in a few minutes, there's the sound of another buzz bomb coming. It's on a path almost identical to the last one, but when it comes over the bridge, it doesn't plunge into the river.

Obviously it's going to pass over the middle of the compound, and a distinct feeling of uneasiness spreads among all in the marquee. Still no one moves – no one wants to be the first to head for a shelter. Travelling at more than 400 miles an hour, in only a matter of seconds the thing is passing directly over the marquee and is momentarily out of sight. At that instant the guttural roar of the engine stops, and in the eerie silence there's a mad scramble to get down on the ground among a clutter of table legs, chair legs, and human legs.

You land in a spot at the rear of the marquee that provides an unobstructed view of the stubby-winged plane diving straight down among the buildings beyond the bombed-out acres, which means you are among the privileged few to witness a split-second phenomenon in the grey and sultry sky immediately above the spot where the buzz bomb disappeared: a ghostly, shimmering, dark grey concussion ring – not a smoke ring, but the air itself made visible by some freak of refracting light picking up the compressed ring of air, lasting only a brief moment as it expands, quivering, into oblivion, above a huge, roiling black cloud of debris and smoke rising hundreds of feet into the sky, accompanied by a reverberating boom.

And the actions and reactions of this first hour in the compound set the pattern of existence here, as the stuttering doodle bugs continue to come in day and night, some plunging down close by, others far enough away to raise only a dull boom. Some arrive close together, almost following on the tails of the ones before them, and others are up to twenty minutes apart.

Late in the afternoon you are told, by one who has been keeping track, that they are averaging about one every ten minutes. And while the sequence of sounds and action soon becomes familiar, and you learn to take maximum advantage of the peaceful intervals – even as you go about whatever you are doing with one ear always cocked for a faint burbling sound in the southeast sky – you know you'll never be able to say that you got used to them.

Each time you accommodate the instructions of The Voice, droning, "Take cov-uh . . . Take cov-uh . . . Take cov-uh" – meaning, "This one is headed this way and could be dangerous" – the anxiety rises within you, and you're no longer reluctant to hurry to stretch out on your palliasse in the pup tent. Each and every time a buzz bomb is heard coming this way, you experience two or three interminable minutes of painful tension and fear, developing into real chest-tightening terror when the stuttering motor grows louder and louder into a guttural growling directly overhead.

As you run out of things to do, you try to read the pamphlet they've issued you about France, but you can't concentrate on it; you'll read it on board ship. You try to get off some letters home, but you find you have nothing to say; you are not allowed to write about where you are or what's going on here, even if you wanted to. The buzz bombs have not only set the style of life in the compound, but are dominating your thinking as well.

While these hateful robots – significantly called "revenge weapons" by the Germans,* according to the London papers – are not capable of precision bombing, being designed rather to spread terror and destruction wherever they drop in the city, you cannot help admiring the high degree of accuracy so many of them are showing in making it to what must be a prime war target: the docks. Though a certain number are said to be tilting off course and crashing into the Channel or in the Kent countryside on the way to London, those making it here – through what must be the heaviest possible screen of fighter planes, ack-ack guns, and barrage balloons ever assembled – consistently come in over the same bend in the river, following the same narrow flight path, and shut down their motors and dive to earth within what appears to be no more than a square mile, enclosing much of the docking area. Not bad for pilotless craft after a flight of more than one hundred miles.

In the afternoon the final stages of waterproofing the vehicles is carried out, the oil topped up, and petrol tanks filled. Then "emergency rations" are issued to each man for use on arrival in France.

Once darkness falls it's off to sleep, for there is simply no place that can be blacked-out in the compound. However, this is no

---

* The first of the Germans' two instruments of terror, the flying bomb, was known in Germany as the v-1, for *Vergeltungswaffen-1*, or "Weapon of Revenge, Number One" (the v-2 rocket would come later). The unmanned aircraft was twenty-five feet long, carrying a ton of explosive in its warhead. It had a range of 155 miles and could outrun fighter planes that weren't already up and waiting, precisely positioned on standing patrol. Of the 8,000 launched against England (5,000 before the end of July 1944), 2,300 reached London, most of them during the first few weeks while defensive techniques were still being developed.

hardship; everyone is so tired, after being up all last night, that sleep comes easily. And though for light sleepers there may be wakeful moments induced by nearby booms, you are not conscious of a single explosion all night.

2

FAREWELL LEICESTER SQUARE

———————————— ✷ ————————————

REVEILLE ON JULY 3 IS AT DAWN, AND AT 5:00 A.M. THE DRIVERS start moving the vehicles and guns to the ships. With the daylight, the noise of the city returns, including those creaking sounds of a rusty dock crane on the Thames that became so irritating yesterday as the day wore on. It grates and squeals unceasingly under the weight of guns and heavily laden ammunition trucks being hoisted aboard ships.

For a while you amuse yourself by standing at the fence watching the early-morning traffic of civilian lorries and red double-decker buses crawling over that now-familiar distant bridge, spanning the only visible stretch of river. There is such a sense of unreality about all this, the perspective so bizarre, that you have to keep reminding yourself you actually are in London, wonderful London of so many memories of civilized living in civilized surroundings: of clean streets and Underground stations; of clean bedsheets and pillowcases in fresh-smelling hotel rooms with rugs on the floor and gleaming white-tiled bathrooms with white linen towels draped on steam-heated towel racks; and of white table-cloths in restaurants like Genarro's, where the major-domo, of courtly manners and a distinguished white *mostaccio*, nightly hands out red rosebuds to each lady guest arriving for a matchless, rich minestrone.

You find yourself reliving one particularly memorable leave in London, in November 1942, cosseted in the luxury of the Savoy Hotel, thanks to the generosity of Len Harvey, who insisted on lending you the money to accompany him on "a weekend to end all weekends" when it appeared that 4RCA (4th Field Regiment) was about to be warned for cross-channel action. Stony broke, you'd tried to turn down his offer, protesting that without a prolonged run of luck at poker it would take months to pay him back. He'd merely scoffed at your protests while making a telling argument: "What the hell. It's only money! Anyway, your bank account will build up fast from now on. You won't be spending any money where you're going!"

Incredible, that more than a year and a half ago all ranks in the Regiment were led to believe a wild rumour that you were about to go into action, simply because it coincided with an order from on high that the Regiment should "arrange for a maximum number to go on leave at once." Thus, wrapped in authenticity, the rumour was accepted as fact, and the feeling that this was your last chance to partake of civilized living enhanced the taste of every glorious hour.

Memories still glow: of Robert Morley in *The Man Who Came to Dinner* at the Savoy Theatre, of the sound of Geraldo's orchestra on the way to dinner after the show, of the swimming-pool-sized sunken bathtub and breakfast in bed in the hall of mirrors that was your bedroom – just the usual crumbly "scrambled" dried egg, soya links, and cold toast, but served with such élan from under silver covers by a waiter in a dinner jacket! Is it possible that life in all those familiar places in the West End is carrying on as usual? It certainly would seem so, if the traffic over that bridge can be taken as evidence. You picture the endless stream of black taxis, with their distinctive, blatting horns, jockeying for position among the chuckling red double-decker buses sailing almost nose-to-tail along Piccadilly, Regent Street, Oxford Street, and the Strand. And people strolling in parks and feeding the pigeons in their beloved Berkley, Leicester, and Trafalgar squares.

You wonder if the theatres are still open. Knowing how Londoners carried on during the first blitz, you feel certain they are – that audiences each night are gasping at the appearance of a swastika on the curtain before the second act of Ivor Novello's musical play *The Dancing Years*, which opened in 1938; that Sid Field, "the funniest man in the world," according to Bob Hope, is still standing each night at centre stage in top hat and tails, weaving and hiccoughing for a taxi, as he sings the song he's made famous, "I'm Gonna Get Lit Up When the Lights Go On in London"... And the Windmill? Surely that gallant burlesque house with its scantily clad girls is sustaining its unique reputation earned during the first blitz, and proudly displayed in big letters on its marquee, "We Never Closed."

During breakfast, consumed in relative comfort at tables in the marquee, albeit from mess tins, an air-raid siren in the middle distance winds up to its highest pitch and sustains the long, mournful whine of the "all clear" signal, the first heard since coming here.

It might have saved itself the trouble, however, for within a few minutes it is rising and falling in the familiar wailing waves that warn of an impending raid. And soon the first of today's crop of flying bombs is blattering up the Thames and over that traffic-covered bridge.

All day they come in, with only brief pauses in between, seemingly taking turns passing to the right, then to the left, and then directly over the compound, before cutting their engines and crashing out of sight beyond the buildings, but always sending up their towering, black clouds, followed by thunderous roars.

And while you are constantly grateful that they continue to fall elsewhere, you find yourself wincing for the poor souls who may have been living or working near those black clouds, since you became aware yesterday of the appalling consequences of each blasting roar. Through conversations with civilians passing outside the fence, you learned that every flying bomb falling into a residential street destroys half a city block of row-housing.*

No one has any regrets about leaving this grim place when at 3:30 P.M. "marching parties" start departing by bus for the docks to board grey freighters you are told are Liberty Ships. The 181 vehicles and 24 guns of the Regiment, as well as the 36 officers and 673 other ranks (including 59 attached personnel), are divided among three ships.

---

* Field Marshal Sir Alan Brooke, chief of the general staff, on this very day recorded in his war diary: "Flying bombs becoming more serious danger and likely to encroach on our war effort if we are not careful. . . . The threat is assuming dimensions which will require more drastic action." The next day, July 4, he faced the fact that our "fighter aircraft are not proving fast enough, and the guns are not hitting them." And the following day, his diary entry makes it clear the flying bombs were damaging the war effort: "The Germans fully realize that we are at present devoting nearly 50 per cent of our air effort to trying to stop these beastly bombs, added to which 25 per cent of London's production is lost through the results of these bombs." Not until the end of August, two months later, would the number of bombs reaching London be reduced to a trickle, averaging only twelve a day, with 80 per cent of those making it across the Channel being knocked down over Kent or Sussex. Fighter planes and barrage balloons would account for 32 per cent of them, but the majority (68 per cent) would be shot down by ack-ack gunners, who providentially were equipped with better radar and, most importantly, with shells carrying the new "proximity fuze," a Canadian–American invention of revolutionary design based on a British idea. A tiny radar set in the nose of each shell meant that shells passing close to, but missing, a buzz bomb received a triggering reflection and exploded at the appropriate moment. And as time went on, the Canadian Army would take a direct hand in closing down completely the V-1 attacks on London. While there was no way the men of 4RCA could have anticipated it, the unit was destined to move up the coast of France in September, clearing ports and overrunning the very sites from which these frightful missiles were being launched at the docks in July.

The ship to which your A Troop of 2nd Battery, and at least some part of regimental headquarters, has been assigned was built in less than four days, according to a member of the ship's crew. And this may well be true, since the record, you are told, for welding together prefabricated sections into a completely functioning Liberty Ship is eighty hours and thirty minutes. But when you do a walk-around survey of the ship, you find it hard to believe that anything so large could be put together in such a short time. While she's no *Queen Mary*, she still is 441 feet long (equal in length to almost one and a half football fields) and clearly capable of carrying some three hundred soldiers along with more than sixty assorted vehicles, guns, and limbers, with several trucks loaded with shells.

Big as she is, however, she's still a freighter, with no provision for passengers. Senior officers have cabin accommodation somewhere in the superstructure amidships, but all other passengers below the rank of major are ushered down a ladder-like companionway into a cargo hold, where they're to sleep in hammocks or on the deck beneath them. Since there are no portholes, the hold must be ventilated by a huge canvas tube, the top end of which is strung up above the open deck to catch the wind created by the movement of the ship, the rest of it snaking down the companionway like a giant, snuffling elephant trunk.

Tonight the ship will lie at anchor, and there will be 305 men in this hold that is rated to accommodate only 250. While there is no grumbling – everyone being very conscious of the fact that the day is not far off when this will appear in retrospect to be the very lap of luxury – you sincerely hope there'll be a good, strong breeze to drive some air down that tube.

Kit stowed, everybody returns to the open deck to watch the vehicle-loading still in progress – cranes lifting and lowering them into the gaping mouth of another hold of the ship. There are many ships at nearby quays, but what attracts speculation are several huge floating structures under construction among a forest of cranes across the way. Formed of concrete, the structures resemble windowless warehouses about four storeys high and the length of a city block. Later you'll learn, on seeing one being towed slowly across the Channel by an ocean-going tug, they are to be sunk off the Normandy beach to form the breakwater for the artificial port "Mulberry."

At supper you have your first experience with self-heating soup, delivered to the cargo hold quarters in cases of cans stencilled "Oxtail Soup."

According to instructions on the can, all you have to do to get hot soup is touch a tiny wick imbedded in a yellow blob of sealing wax on one end of the can with the glowing end of a lighted cigarette. But when you do, there is only a slight sputter and then nothing.

This is very disappointing to you and the four or five officers surrounding the test can on the steel floor, studying the holes you'd punched in the top to let out the steam. Everybody is getting a little testy from hunger. To be served nothing but a can of soup for supper is bad enough, but to have to drink it cold is the last straw. After following an improvised drill for a misfire, in good old artillery fashion, someone decides it has irrevocably "gone out," and picks up the can to examine it – only to let it drop in a hurry with suitable exclamatory remarks as he fans his fingers to cool them. The can is boiling, and when you rescue it, using a handkerchief as a potholder, and pour its contents into the waiting cups, you find it is absolutely delicious.

When you take the can apart to examine its innards, you find only a steel tube about the size of your index finger, running down from the top of the can, filled with absorbent cotton stained brown from the excessive heat of the chemical reaction that obviously started when the fuze opened a hole for the air to get in. What an invention! What a blessing this could be for front-line troops not in a position to light a fire or show a light! (That you'll never see another self-heating can in action is not something anyone would want to believe tonight.)

By early evening the ship is loaded, and with the sun still above the horizon, she begins to back up and turn around in the narrow basin. And as she slowly starts downriver, the dock workers who loaded her, and other workers on nearby quays, cheer lustily – some removing their caps to wave goodbye.

You feel so embarrassed you take off your beret and wave back at them, marvelling at their generous, brave hearts. After only two days, you're very glad to be leaving this place – the very bull's-eye of the principal target Hitler has set for his pilotless monsters. Those unsung heroes down on the dock have been there loading ships for days on end, ever since the doodle-bug scourge began three weeks ago, June 13 – carrying on without benefit of uniform or recognition of any kind. And they'll be there tomorrow, and the next day, and the day after that, while every ten minutes or so a mindless angel-of-death hums and blabbers over their heads, and they listen for it to cut out and dive down in nerve-wrenching silence to a towering, black, earth-quaking blast – never far away.

And the image of those men, waving and cheering the departing vessel, is still vivid next morning, when the harbour-master comes out in his plunging craft to where the ship is anchored in the misty Estuary to take off Col. Drury for a shore meeting of the senior officers of 2nd Division. Hailing the bridge with his megaphone, he tells the captain that just after his ship departed downriver last night, the dock where it had been loading all day was struck by a flying bomb and blown to bits.

All of July 4 and 5, the ship lies at anchor far out in the Thames Estuary, somewhere off Southend. When not occupied with "inspections of quarters" by the ranking officer on each vessel, accompanied by the ship's captain, or participating in "life-raft drills," or lining up for meals served off a hatch-cover on the open deck, the men are left to their own devices.

Many have brought along reading material, and card games are popular. Others pass the time writing letters home, which in turn provides work for troop officers who have been designated as censors – a task you find thoroughly distasteful; having to read the intimate thoughts of men written for the eyes of their loved ones, while you look for references to times and places which might be useful to the enemy.

But by far the most popular pastime is a giant crap game on a big hatch-cover, which began shortly after breakfast and seems destined to continue (apart from mealtimes) throughout the hours of daylight all the way to France. On a single roll of the dice, a huge pot, built up by the sheer numbers of gamblers, can be won or lost – not to mention countless side-bets among the onlookers waiting to get a turn with the dice.

Shortly after 7:00 P.M., your ship, along with the others, raises anchor and the convoy gets underway. You are told that the movement is so timed that the ships will be passing out of the Thames Estuary after dark, and through the straits of Dover around midnight. No one but designated subalterns will be allowed on deck after dark. Your shift starts at midnight.

Suddenly you are aware of an atmosphere of tension that wasn't there during the past two days. It's as though everyone now recognizes that 4th Field is finally – after all those years of training and endless rumours of going into action – on its way to war.

3

GATHERING FOR WAR

---------------------------- ✳ ----------------------------

IT IS SHORTLY AFTER MIDNIGHT ON JULY 6. THE DARK WATERS
of the Channel, seething leisurely past the side of the blacked-out
ship, are only lightly streaked with luminous froth from the mild
bow-wave the vessel is creating as it slowly and sedately slips west,
past Dover and the white cliffs lying ghostly and vague a few
hundred yards to starboard. It's as though the convoy bound for
Normandy, which pulled out of the Thames Estuary just before
dark last night, is hugging the coast in the hope of tiptoeing past the
giant guns over on the Pas de Calais.

All ranks are confined below decks and won't be allowed up until
0600 hours this morning. The reason given is that the ships may be
shelled as they pass through the Straits, and though the chances of
receiving a direct hit are slight, the hazards from shell splinters are
real enough. You are on deck only because you've been assigned to
stand guard from midnight until dawn at the companionway
leading up from the sleeping hold, to ensure that the order to
"remain below" is obeyed by all ranks. Before coming up on deck,
you were privileged, as one of the designated orderly officers, to
place your bedroll on the floor of the hold, conveniently near the
foot of the open, ladder-like companionway, where you wouldn't
have to stumble through a mass of prostrate forms and kits on the
way out. Thus you were the beneficiary of the freshest air coming

into the hold, being near the lower end of the giant canvas tube carrying air from the open deck. Still, you were relieved when the time came for your tour of duty on deck, and you feel truly sorry for anyone subject to claustrophobia down there.

Waiting your turn to go on duty, you found it impossible to sleep. All you could do was lie there in the inky darkness, on the throbbing steel floor, listening to a cacophony of deep and laboured breathing, snoring, throat-clearings, and periodic coughing spasms – all the while conscious of the irregular gushes of air down that quivering, snuffling fabric tube, dangling a couple of feet above your head. And with each passing hour, that tube became more a source of anxiety than comfort, as you mulled over the dismal thought that that primitive affair was actually the only means of catching the night breezes and ventilating an entire hold and 305 sets of ravenous lungs.

Now standing at the starboard rail of the ship, watching Dover slowly drift by, you speculate how big the splinters could be from 1,300-pound shells looped over by one of the 16-inch "Adolph" guns at Blanc Nez, or the 15-inch guns at Cap Gris-Nez. Only a few days ago you'd sat on the side of that hill rising up behind Dover, there, with fellow 4th Field subaltern Doug MacFarlane, watching shells from one of those cross-Channel guns send up giant geysers amidst a convoy like this, sailing with agonizing slowness past a burning freighter that had been hit and was drifting helplessly, laying down a long trail of black smoke across the sea. There'd been a "shell warning" by way of a siren in the same manner as for an air raid, and a most polite warden had invited you and Doug to make your way to a deep shelter in the hillside designed especially to withstand the frequent bombardments from across the Channel that over the years had reduced poor little Dover to a truly desolate condition. But after the warden had passed on down the road, you'd climbed up near the summit of the hill to the west of the town, feeling secure in the belief that Jerry was only after the ships and would leave Dover alone that day.

With your field-glasses, you'd been able to pick up the tiny flash on the horizon each time the gun fired from the French coast. And after about forty-five seconds, there'd been a fearful wail, rising quickly to an ugly, intimidating howl, just before a water-spout leapt towering out of the sea between the burning ship and the shore, and a monstrous roar rolled up the valley and over the land, echoing and re-echoing down the coast. There had been long waits between each shell, and you'd had to leave to go back to camp without knowing whether any more ships were hit. You calculate that just about now you are passing over the spot where that burning ship lay on D-Day.

Tonight there's much air activity on both sides of the Channel. Waves of bombers have been passing over towards the continent, and the flashing on the horizon and faint grumbling from the direction of Calais probably mean their targets are the launching sites for the V-1s reputed to be there. Now and then a buzz bomb blabbers overhead on its way to London, attracting a gaggle of searchlight beams and a torrent of ack-ack tracers above Kent that releases a myriad of twinkling explosions in the sky, ultimately producing a delayed crackling that comes to you in a spooky, muffled fashion. You imagine you know where those guns are sited, just north of Dover, in Waldershare Park, which from April 19 to July 2 was home under canvas for all 2nd Division artillery, including 4th Field.

It is strange knowing that you are now passing almost within sight of those lovely, green, rolling, parkland fields of the Earl of Guilford, having left there in the middle of the night five days ago to drive all the way up to London to board these ships.

But now, having travelled some 130 miles down the serpentine course of the Thames, out into the Estuary, and around through the North Sea into the mouth of the English Channel, you feel for the first time that you are well and truly launched on your way to France. And this feeling grows deeper as the white cliffs recede into the misty night and you are left alone with your thoughts of what you and all those men down in the hold are about to face in Normandy.

The news from France has maintained a positive bias, underlined by the front-page pictures of visits to the bridgehead by General Eisenhower the day after D-Day, and of Churchill and Smuts only four days later. But while reports have been generally sketchy, so as to provide no comfort or useful intelligence to the enemy, clearly the fighting in the bridgehead has become, if not a bloody stalemate, then the next thing to it: a battle of attrition. Since a week after D-Day, very little ground has been gained by any Allied formation.

You realize huge quantities of men and equipment must be built up before any breakout can be safely attempted, and your own 2nd Division – obviously earmarked months ago to carry out a leading role in such an operation, having been involved in countless training exercises involving "breaking out of a bridgehead" – is only now on its way to the continent. But even allowing for a lengthy build-up period, the inability of the powerful Allied forces already in the bridgehead to expand the perimeter to any remarkable degree after almost a month ashore, surely means that German resistance is formidable.

Undoubtedly there are rough times ahead for the Regiment – just how rough and just how well it will measure up, only time will tell. But of one thing you are certain, no artillery regiment in the history of war has ever entered battle better trained.

Mobilized in the first week of September 1939, it has been in constant training ever since – a matter of fifty-eight months. Regular "permanent force" artillery units might have recorded longer training periods between the wars, but there is a great difference in the intensity and quality of training when there is no war on the horizon and when a conflict is raging and a unit is expecting to be sent into action at any time.

Over the years, gunners, drivers, signallers, and motor mechanics have become so proficient at their jobs, you believe they could almost perform them with their eyes closed. And in the case of the drivers, this is closer to the truth than anyone could possibly imagine who has never ridden in the cab of a truck with one of them on a narrow, twisting, English road in the blackout. How often you marvelled at drivers wheeling recreational trucks full of gunners along winding mountain roads in Wales, through lashing rain and the swirling mists of a pitch-black night on the way back to Senneybridge artillery camp from an evening in Brecon or Merthyr Tydfyl.

How they managed to follow the road, with only the vaguest yellow glow escaping through a tiny nail-hole in each blacked-out headlight, especially on wet, stormy nights (which invariably they were in winter in Wales), you never could fathom. No matter how hard you stared through the windshield, or how intensely you concentrated, only the curling mist or the rain sheeting down immediately in front of the truck was visible to you. Never once during one of those drives could you make out anything of consequence of the road ahead. While the superman in the cab beside you – enlivened for the return trip by several pints of mild or bitter, but armed with some natural form of radar – would be carrying on as though it were daylight, gearing up and gearing down, wheeling around bends you couldn't even see, and all the while rattling off cheerful stories or singing at the top of his lungs along with the gang in the back.

The signallers have become so proficient that reliable communications by land lines or R Talk (radio telephony) – absolutely vital to the operation of artillery, but extremely difficult to come by – are now taken for granted.

Equally accepted as normal is the extraordinary speed with which the regimental surveyors and command-post staffs are able to get all six troops on "regimental grid," with all twenty-four guns parallel and accurately oriented with each other, awaiting the arrival of more accurate survey data from Division that will put the

Regiment on Divisional grid, and in time on "theatre grid" by still more accurate survey information from Corps, tying in the guns of the Regiment with all the other guns in the division, the corps, and the army.*

And of course the men who maintain and fire the guns, the very reason for the Regiment's existence, could hardly be better trained.

As early as the summer of 1942, 4RCA was judged the best artillery regiment in Britain by those gods of gunnery, Larkhill IGs (instructors in gunnery) of the Royal School of Artillery, following a competition in "crash action" on Salisbury Plain within sight of Stonehenge. And the flattering judgement was not without foundation, for crash actions not only have practical application in the rapid fire and movement of modern war, but being the fastest of all

---

*   "Grid" refers to the numbered grid lines overprinted on the large-scale military maps by which the position of each troop pivot gun (the right-hand gun of four) can be spelled out in eight-figure coordinates and plotted on the gridded paper of its own troop artillery board, allowing ranges between guns and targets, and switches from a zero line, to be measured and read off by command-post staffs for application to the guns. Getting the guns on "regimental grid" – establishing the position on the face of the planet of each "pivot gun" by using triangulation on distant identifiable aiming points such as church steeples – is carried out by the Regimental Survey Party. At the same time they ensure the guns are parallel on the zero line (a grid bearing, pointing along the axis of advance) by passing a reverse bearing from their director (survey instrument) to each troop director. Divisional Grid arrives later with more accurate survey data to be applied to the guns (in the case of the bearing on which they are laid) and to artillery boards where pivot-gun plots have to be adjusted. Finally the ultimate in survey data accuracy, starting from bronze "benchmarks" imbedded in rock, is brought forward across hill and dale by "chaining" and directors laid and relaid on survey flags. This establishes "theatre grid," ensuring all guns in all regiments, not only in Canadian Army, but throughout 21st Army Group, are accurately oriented with each other, so that any unit can join in a fireplan, or defensive fire, on any front within their range.

deployments, they put to the test all the training and discipline of all ranks. A troop, rolling down the road "on wheels," goes into crash action the moment the Gun Position Officer (GPO) receives over the radio the map reference of an unseen target miles away, with the order "Right ranging . . . Fire!"

To the GPO, who has been assiduously following his map to ensure he knows exactly where he is at any given moment, that message means: Get your guns deployed in the nearest field and put them on line to that target, using your map, your compass, the dial-sight of your pivot gun, and a local aiming point; and then give them the range so your pivot gun can get off a ranging round that will land on or near the target, which your troop commander can see and use to complete the ranging.

Every troop in the Regiment can routinely bring its guns into action and get off the first round within three to five minutes of receiving such a target while travelling along a road. (Three minutes if there is no unusual delay because of the terrain.)

This is no small feat when you consider that before drivers, gun sergeants, and gunners can engage in their teamwork of wheeling the guns onto their platforms and dropping their trails in position to receive the proper line (compass bearing) and elevation (range) from the GPO, he has to locate an open space in which to deploy them, with adequate "crest clearance" (muzzles not pointing at a line of trees or a bluff rising on the immediate front). Then he must find access to this location through the stone wall or hedge that is likely in the way, keeping an eye open for a culvert over the inevitable ditch that is adequate to carry such tonnages as he'll be leading over it. And all the while, he must constantly make sure he keeps himself oriented on the map in relation to the surface of the globe, so he can establish the position of his pivot gun within an accuracy of twenty-five yards.

For the gun crews, putting guns in action and firing has become second nature. And while the official "normal" rate of fire for a 25-pounder is three rounds per minute, and "intense" is five rounds,

4th Field gunners can easily achieve twelve to fifteen rounds per minute.

And then, over and beyond the expertise they've gained in gunnery and other matters military during their four and a half years of concentrated training, the men of the Regiment have developed an extraordinary capacity to take care of themselves in the most primitive and miserable conditions without losing heart.

Having learned first-hand, during your brief time as an enlisted man, the worth of an officer concerned about the welfare of his men, and having had it pounded into you by every instructor during officer's training that the welfare of the men always comes before your own, you had been most conscious of your responsibility when you first joined the Regiment. But concern soon turned to wonder, at the tough, resilient nature of gunners – veterans of endless manoeuvres, exercises, schemes, shoots, and training camps carried out in every kind of filthy weather, on every kind of bleak down, windy mountain, misty moor, and soggy cow-pasture. Even when dumped out into pelting rain in the gathering darkness of a gusty, winter night on Alfriston ranges, to set up guns, haul ammunition, lay signal wire, and bed down among the dripping, prickly gorse to await a dawn shoot, they always managed somehow to maintain their extraordinarily high morale.

And finally there's a reservoir of strength, built up over the years, that could never be expected of a less highly trained unit: the ability of men to carry out jobs different from those for which they originally were trained and to which they are regularly assigned. For instance, many drivers have become signallers, replacing signallers who in turn have become drivers, and so on. This is particularly true of members of the "carrier crews" of troop commanders, who must be able to take over any job at a forward observation post so as to be able to spell each other off during long periods of duty, or in an emergency take over any job left unattended through casualties.

It's hard to imagine any difficulty arising from terrain or weather, or any problem of a technical or mechanical nature connected with guns, vehicles, wireless sets, or other equipment, that hasn't been confronted and overcome on countless occasions during training schemes. In many respects the Regiment could be compared to a reliable, well-oiled machine, that has benefitted from the most up-to-date modifications and been run-in long enough to have all the bugs worked out of it.

It was not always thus. The stories of foul-ups, large and small, reaching back through the years are legion, and all ranks should be grateful they were not committed to battle in those first couple of years of inadequate equipment and training, but allowed to accumulate the superior training and equipment they now possess.

However, this opinion would not be common among the men down in the holds of these darkened ships tonight – at least not among the "originals" who enlisted in the first days of September 1939 and have been waiting ever since to get into action.

4

"COMIN' OUT WITH A NATCH!"

---- ✳ ----

AFTER BREAKFAST YOU GET A MESSAGE TO REPORT TO THE major on the upper deck that surrounds the central superstructure of the ship. You find him, with a few others of the privileged classes, in what appears to be a rather cramped ward room. At least you assume that's what it is from the used porcelain tea mugs on the tables. For a moment you lapse into fantasy, warmed by the thought that you've been asked up to this relatively civilized spot to share a cup of tea.

But Major Wren promptly puts such wild speculation to rest, making it quite clear you are here on business. First, he requires you to confirm the rumour that you were a newspaperman in Civie Street. Then he parks you at a table in front of a loudspeaker implanted in the cabin wall, hands you a pencil, places a pad of issue message-paper before you, and instructs you to take down the news bulletins from the BBC broadcast about to come on the radio, so that you can type out copies and distribute them among the troops.

When the broadcast comes on, you are relieved to find that it is delivered very slowly and deliberately in short chunks, at longhand dictation speed. This, however, proves most embarrassing to the Major, who assures everyone in the ward room that he never would have gone to all this trouble if he'd known that the announcer was going to talk at such a slow speed.

The way he fidgets about beside you, you can tell he wishes you'd disappear in a puff of smoke. Far from providing an active testimony to his initiative on behalf of the troops, you have turned out to be an embarrassment to him – and in full view of the CO too! While feeling equally foolish, you must persevere to the end, and eventually you type out several copies of the news bulletins containing references to places you'll soon come to know most intimately:

– Canadian troops in the Carpiquet area, west of Caen, yesterday beat back three heavy German armoured counter-attacks within five hours to hold the ground they had gained fighting the day before.

– Very heavy mortar fire was being directed on the Canadians from Carpiquet airfield, where some hangers still are 600 yards ahead of the Canadians, and from high ground further west. One officer described it as the "hottest spot in France."

– In the Canadian sector the Germans have tanks dug in on the high ground behind the airfield and are using them as artillery in support of panzers on the flat surface of the airfield itself.

– British troops on the Canadians' right flank are engaged in heavy fighting.... One report said patrols had established contact on the high ground between Carpiquet and Verson, establishing a solid three-mile knife into the German positions in front of Caen.

– RAF Lancasters and Halifaxes last night followed up their day raid on the "flying bomb" platforms in the Pas de Calais.

– Mosquitoes bombed a synthetic oil plant in the Ruhr.

– More flying bombs were used against Britain Tuesday night and yesterday. Three RAF fighter pilots each shot down three of them while on patrol.

After you've issued several copies for passing around the ship, you have no other duties and are free to enjoy the cruise. It's a lovely, warm, sunny day, and the Channel is remarkably smooth. The ship maintains a westerly course just off the coast of England, and a crew member tells you it will continue until the Isle of Wight, where it will swing south. You find a spot on the starboard side where you can sit and watch the coast go by . . . a wonderful chance to see one of the most interesting bits of coastline in the world. But the long night with very little sleep demands its price; no matter how hard you try, you can't keep your eyes open. And a moment after you've found a flat space on which to flop down, you're asleep.

When you awake, the ship is out of sight of land. The crap game is still in progress, and players and onlookers completely surround the hatch-cover. Late in the afternoon, bits of wood and other debris begin to appear on the waves, and once a body in battledress floats by and is left bobbing face down in the ship's wake.

At about 6:00 P.M. someone calls out, "Hey, there's France!" For a moment everyone around the hatch cover is silent as they stare at the low streak of grey on the horizon, as though sensing it is a historic moment. Then a hoarse voice yells, "Comin' out with a natch!" and they all turn back to the game.

Half an hour later, the ship's engines cease their heavy throbbing and are barely turning over as she edges her way towards an anchorage among the other ships closer to shore.

Slowly she and the rest of the convoy wheel around, in and out past ships at anchor: ships, ships, ships – Liberty ships, battleships, cruisers, destroyers, corvettes, minesweepers, torpedo boats, and landing craft. A few are moving, but most of them lie still, spread out like a great grey herd, covering the whole calm bay from the beaches to the horizon of the open Channel.* Only someone in a

---

*   Almost 7,000 ships were involved in Operation Overlord: 200 battleships, monitors, cruisers, and destroyers; 553 sloops, frigates, corvettes, patrol craft, gun boats, anti-submarine trawlers, motor torpedo boats, etc.; and 6,047 landing craft of five varieties, including LCVPs (Landing Craft Vehicle and Personnel) required for the artillery.

plane, like the pilot of the humming Spitfire patrolling above the basin, could ever get a complete overview of the armada suggested by the number of ships visible to you as yours weaves slowly between them, making for an anchorage you suspect is being allotted this very moment by that winking signal-light on a distant ship, to which the shutters on your own ship's lamp are now chattering and clacking in response.

You are still hoping she'll be allowed to drop anchor close enough to shore for you to see something interesting, when she's brought to rest so far out you can barely make out a line of unimpressive buildings, some barrage balloons (the kind used around London) floating over the beaches, and very little else. For those who expected intense activity, there is disappointment. It is all so quiet that the coarse, rusty, clattering chain letting down the anchor seems out of place.

The towering British battleship *Rodney*, whose nine 16-inch guns smashed the *Bismarck* back in 1941, and in the news since D-Day for its role in shelling enemy positions up to twelve miles inland, is sleeping close by. Over on the left, a minesweeper works a section of the sea close to shore. A few landing craft move between the ships, and a couple of motor launches, with miniature barrage balloons riding close-hauled only a few feet above their decks, cross and recross the bay. Barrage balloons of regular size and shape hang over the beach and some vessels are so high and dry they seem to have been purposely beached. With or without binoculars all eyes study the scene, the vast array of ships and the shore, but above all the shore. While the beach at this distance offers no indication of what took place there, let alone what is now going on farther inland, it is still fascinating. It is France!

5

SOMMERVIEU

❋

SLEEP THIS NIGHT IN THE HOLD IS RESTLESS TO SAY THE LEAST.
At one point the whole ship rattles from the blasting roar of the
great guns of the *Rodney*, bombarding, with methodical delibera-
tion, something far inland. Now and then the deck is splattered
with fragments of ack-ack shells sent up against marauding planes
attempting to attack the beach and ships. It is a monster barrage,
from more guns, you are told, than were assembled to protect
London during the Blitz.

Reveille on July 7 is at dawn. Two hours later, shortly after 6:00
A.M., a party of Royal Engineers, after attaching landing craft to
each side of the ship, comes on board to take charge of the off-
loading of equipment onto these smaller craft providing a shuttle-
service between the large ships and the beach. Starting up the
rattling winches on the ship's cranes, they remove the hatch covers.
Then winchmen, following the hand signals of a director, making
motions as though directing a symphony, pluck vehicles out of the
hold with steel nets, swinging them high above the deck, before
lowering them over the side into the gently heaving smaller craft,
officially known as LCVPs, or Landing Craft Vehicles and Personnel.
These scow-like, motorized steel boxes are designed to ride in
through shallow water until they beach themselves, at which time

they drop open their square noses to form ramps over which the vehicles can drive right onto the sand.

One by one, ammunition trucks, guns, limbers, gun tractors, armoured scout cars, van-like HUPs (Heavy Utility Personnel), Jeeps, 15-hundredweight trucks, and Bren gun carriers are raised from the hold as easily as toys from a children's "fish pond." And as each landing craft is loaded to capacity, personnel related to those vehicles climb over the ship's rail and scramble down a rope net, slung down the side of the ship, into the heaving landing-craft.

The sight of the first landing craft pulling away for the distant shore, loaded with recognizable faces and familiar vehicles, each of them displaying your regimental sign – a white "42" superimposed on a red-and-blue background, red on top and blue on the bottom – heightens a sense of anxiety that you realize has been building ever since you pulled out of Waldershare Park.

And it's not too difficult to pin down its origins. While no one knows precisely what lies ahead, all know the hour is close at hand when the guns will be in action, near enough the enemy to shell him, and therefore near enough to be shelled by him.

The question now foremost in everybody's mind is: "How will I stand up under fire?" While every man is entirely convinced he is part of one of the most highly trained artillery outfits in the history of war, having had four and a half years to prepare for this day, no one can tell how he will measure up in action, for no officer or man has ever fired a round in anger. So there is tension, anxiety, and a growing sense of urgency among all ranks.

In great contrast, there is a total lack of urgency among the Engineers. They approach their work as though this is an old routine for them. Obviously they've done many similar off-loadings along this stretch of Normandy coast (and perhaps at more than one bridgehead in the Mediterranean), and under conditions a great deal more trying than exist here on this calm summer day, with nothing flying around the ship but some gulls. But their unhurried, methodical, measured pace is a source of wonderment to all members of 4th Field, and of deep irritation to the more impatient characters on board, particularly those senior officers who feel it necessary to be transparently conscientious and are fidgeting in frustration up on the bridge as they survey the scene from on high. From the look in their eyes, you imagine their frustration comes from being unable to find a way of blaming it all on "the subalterns not taking over." And when, at precisely 10:00 A.M., the winches suddenly go silent, leaving a White Armoured Scout Car dangling high over the deck, Major Wren comes charging down to where you're standing at the open hatchway, inquiring fiercely:

"What the hell's the matter? Why have they stopped?"

You point down in the hold, and he almost falls in as he takes in the scene. The Engineers, grouped around a steaming pot on a hissing Primus stove, are brewing up their mid-morning cuppa. His comment comes straight from the heart:

"My God! Can you believe it!"

However, as with all expert tradesmen who never seem to hurry, but pile up accomplishments in effortless fashion, the Royal Engineers by late afternoon have emptied the ship with only one vehicle casualty, a 14th Battery truck dropped in the ocean when a chain breaks. The loss of a vehicle at this stage is still a matter of serious concern, but it provides Lieut. Ted Adams, an eternally laid-back character (ex-Royal Canadian Horse Artillery troop sergeant-major who'd enlisted as a gunner in 1939) a chance to exercise his sardonic wit while calming down his overwrought battery commander, who saw the vehicle drop and heard the splash. Rushing up to Ted at the rail, he starts spouting a stream of questions in anguished tones:

"Where did it go, Ted? Is it in the drink?"

Still contemplating the rush of bubbles rising from the bed of the ocean just beyond the landing craft, and thoughtfully stroking his reddish-blond "handlebar-hank" moustache, the phlegmatic Ted issues his immortal comment:

"I sure hope she's well waterproofed!"

Guffaws from onlookers relieve the unholy tension, and even Major James Wilson Dodds, the battery commander, breaks into a broad grin as he walks away.

At last your vehicle appears out of the hold, and as it's being lowered into the smaller craft, you climb over the rail and carefully make your way down the rope net. This is a new experience. You weren't on any of the specialized training schemes to which the majority of the officers and men had been exposed, and you become a little anxious watching others scramble down and dangle momentarily over the plunging landing craft. On the way down you have to suppress the image of failing to make the leap into the landing craft now grinding up and down on the side of the ship. But it turns out to be a piece of cake: you step off into the landing craft as she rises on the swell as easily as stepping off an elevator.

When your landing craft grounds onto the beach, the chains holding the ramp are released, and it splashes down directly in front of your vehicle into about a foot or so of water. Your driver, Gunner George Weston, starts his engine, but immediately the captain of the landing craft, who has appeared at the open mouth of the craft to check the depth of the water, gives the signal to cut the engines.

In the stillness that follows, he explains: "Might as well wait – tide's on its way out. In about fifteen or twenty minutes you'll be able to drive off onto dry sand – save a lot of trouble later on, not having to pull the wheels and clean the saltwater out of brake drums and the like."

While you are impatient to get moving and rather resent being held back by this guy, what he says makes sense. You settle down to wait, contemplating the featureless, broad expanse of sand between the outgoing tide and the low bluff, covered with coarse grass, forming the horizon ahead. When you try to establish your position on the map, you realize how difficult it must have been for those landing on D-Day to identify their allotted zones along the beach. Without the aid of the captain of the landing craft, identifying those rather ragged-looking buildings just there on your left front as Courseulles, and just a bit farther left, Bernières and St. Aubin, you wouldn't have a clue where you are landing.

The recent gale, which cluttered some beaches with debris, seems to have swept this one clean. But immediately to the left, no more than twenty-five yards away, lies a big LST (Landing Ship Tank), with so much of her bulk high and dry on the sand, you wonder if she'll ever get a tide high enough to float free.

The captain can't say for sure about this one, but that gale drove a lot of shipping ashore and wrecked much of the Mulberry artificial harbour, over on the right in the distance.

Weston, impatiently watching the line of drying sand, which is creeping towards the ramp as slowly as the second hand of a watch, is inclined to dwell on other things – mainly the endless flaming hours he and the other drivers and mechanics spent waterproofing these flaming vehicles for a flaming wet landing.

The whole thing reminds you of always arriving late at Sunday School picnics or your father's lodge picnics when you were a little boy. No matter how hard you urged your family to hurry, the thing was always in full swing when you arrived. The sound of a big drum, from over where the action was taking place, never failed to induce a sense of breathless excitement. But there was always that last-minute tremor in the knees, a feeling of reluctance to get involved in events already in motion, shaped by others – by those damned early birds. There was a moment when you almost wished you hadn't come. The only cure had been to get involved as fast as possible.

You look down – the tide has almost disappeared back under the lowered ramp. You turn to Weston:

"Okay, let's go."

"Yes, sir!"

In the silence surrounding the beach, the starter-gears grind coarsely round and round, and then there's the furious fanning roar of the engine that sits in the tin box between you. There's the familiar abrupt shifting of gears – this time to bull low, for that wet sand may be soggy, and then the HUP dips down the ramp and bumps off onto the soil of France. Immediately Weston cuts his wheels left, making an obvious detour to splash through a shallow puddle of stranded sea water, growling:

"After all that goddamned waterproofing, she's at least going to get her feet wet!"

After grinding up the sandy embankment, through a gap bull-dozed in the grassy-topped bluff, your vehicle is directed to a track leading inland to a road busy with tanks, Jeeps, dumptrucks, and ambulances. And just a short distance in from the sea, beyond a village called Graye-sur-Mer, you are directed to join other 4RCA trucks in a field where they have been halted to peel away as much waterproofing gunk as possible before proceeding southwest to a concentration area northeast of Bayeux, near the village of Sommervieu. It's about eight miles as the crow flies, but will be a much longer drive by the assigned route.

Everybody is much amused to learn that the first vehicle of the Regiment to touch down on French soil was that of non-combatant Curt Embleton, YMCA Auxiliary Services' supervisor. Curt's truck, always the last vehicle in regimental convoys, was the last loaded on the ship in London. Thus it was the first loaded onto the landing craft.

However, many unit vehicles haven't arrived, and at 8:00 P.M. there are some fifty vehicles and two hundred men missing when the Regiment pulls out for Sommervieu. Still, it can't be helped; the timing of all movement along the roads, here, is strictly controlled by the beachmasters. (The missing men and vehicles will not catch up until 5:30 A.M., having been held offshore on landing craft for five hours awaiting the tide.)

As the convoy pulls out onto a dirt road, leading south from the sea, everyone's attention is directed to a huge sign warning that no vehicle breakdown must be allowed to block traffic, and that if a breakdown occurs, the vehicle is to be pushed into the ditch and abandoned.

A dust-covered Provost Corps soldier, doing point duty at a crossroads, pumps his arm up and down, vigorously signalling the vehicles to get a move on. And large signs beside the road repeatedly make it clear that this is one of the most important roads in the world and must not be blocked for any reason.

As you pass mountains of petrol tins, ammunition cases, and Compo rations, stacked right out in the open, on both sides of the road, you can see why. It's obviously a principal lifeline for much of the Allied forces in the bridgehead, and will soon be the lifeline of the Regiment.

While evidence of hard fighting is everywhere in the villages along the beach – all badly scarred by D-Day bombardments from air and sea – inland, away from any buildings, the only sign that there was fighting through here is the odd burned-out tank, and here and there along the verges of the road a crude wooden cross stuck in the ground beside a sad mound of dusty earth.

Suddenly the vehicle in front speeds up, and the whole convoy starts moving along at a speed well above anything allowed back in England. As the inevitable accordion motion in the convoy comes into play, keeping up becomes a real problem, and the furious fanning in the tin box begins to sound strained. Weston hunches over the steering wheel, concentrating on holding the bouncing vehicle on the road. Not that much would happen if he failed to do so, there being no ditches of any real consequence and, most surprisingly, no fences of any kind for as far as you can see.

Even over the smell of engine fumes and dust roiling up around the convoy, a pungent odour of crushed grass fills the air as you roar by what, only a few days ago, must have been lush green meadows and pasturelands, but which are now the bleached, sandy colour of dead grass turning to dust.

Several Typhoons and Spitfires are lined up at the edge of a landing strip made of steel-mesh webbing rolled out over the turf like a giant carpet. Their bodies and wings are striped with three white bands (interspersed with black) to distinguish them as Allied aircraft for trigger-happy anti-aircraft gunners during these days of close support by the fighter-bombers. A pilot, wearing dark sunglasses, stands beside the road, watching the convoy go by. It may be his first hour in France too, but to you he appears a dashing figure, a perfect example of "an early bird."

After a few minutes the landscape changes. On both sides are the hedgerows mentioned in that radio newscast the Major had you copy down on board ship: ". . . the difficult *bocage* country . . . the dense hedgerows . . . heavy casualties . . . fanatic counterattacks . . . Canadians involved in intense fighting around Carpiquet airfield and Caen." You must be quite near those places, for the bridge-head on the map is so tiny that nothing can be far from the front line.

What's it really like to be shelled or mortar-bombed? You look at your driver: he could be dead tomorrow. What's it like to die, or get an arm or leg blown off? That you should turn out to be a coward is beyond consideration. But still, how do you know? You really were quite timid when you were little. Sometimes you've had the feeling that manhood is really only a pose men assume, while remaining boys at heart – particularly those lusty, life-hardened, male animals, who, in the eyes of their peers, are most likely to qualify as "real men."

But you must stop this line of thinking. Now is not the time for self-doubt. There is no turning back. If it really all has been just a pose, then you must continue the pose of being a man and a leader to the very end. Too many will be depending on you making the correct decisions and giving the correct orders – keeping your head when everything is turning into a bloody mess – to do otherwise. That's it, of course: just keep on playing the role of a mature, level-headed, cool man until you buy it, or it's all over, one way or another. Anything less is unthinkable.

Suddenly you are aware your vehicle is turning into an opening in a hedgerow, following the other vehicles as they park around the perimeter of the field. The furious fan is shut off, and there you are, parked for the night in a quiet green cow-pasture, well away from the fighting zones, shut off from the road and the rest of Normandy by a succession of high, thick hedges.

It's remarkably quiet. There's only a faint booming of heavy guns far away on the left, in the direction of Carpiquet or Caen, a sound reminiscent of those bass drums at those childhood picnics.

No sooner are camouflage nets draped across the vehicles from the hedgerows, and personal slit trenches dug, than irrepressible Bombardier Ron Hooper, goal-keeper on the regimental hockey team and fine all-round athlete, produces a softball he has taken pains to bring with him from England, and organizes a long-range game of catch with anybody who wants to join in. The game merely consists of looping towering pitches back and forth across the field in all directions, with Hooper keeping up a steady stream of bantering comments, loud whoops, and joyous laughter. It's really a nothing game, but in these circumstances, the whole thing is very pleasant to watch. You wonder if Hooper realizes what a wonderful job he's doing for morale, not just for those participating in the game, but for the whole Battery and Regiment. Surrounded by all this greenness untouched by war, and all this laughing and shouting, it's as though you are still in Kent.

Just as you dig out your box of "emergency rations" and start to explore its mysteries, which in its sparseness will constitute dinner tonight, a veritable storm of shouting arises around the field. And when you look, it seems all, including Hooper and his pitch-and-catch buddies, are stampeding towards the gateway, where a crowd is gathering around someone who has just arrived in a Jeep.

As you make your way over, you recognize the chubby face and sparkling, mischievous eyes of Padre Ray McCleary, who left the Regiment in the fall of '43 to become chief padre of 3rd Division, and cross the Channel with them on D-Day. What an extraordinary man! Within a couple of hours of 4th Field arriving in France, he manages to become aware of it, has located this obscure concentration area, and is visiting "his boys."

Everybody is crowding and jostling to get close to him, calling out greetings. And he, standing up in his Jeep, his face beaming with a smile from ear to ear, his eyes twinkling and dancing with that well remembered mixture of joy, merriment, and a slight pinch of devilment, is calling out names so rapidly it's as though he's calling the regimental roll. Except he doesn't just call out names – he attaches to most a pungent remark or a sly question showing he hasn't forgotten their scrapes and capers when he was with the outfit.

Unfortunately, he can't hang around; his division is involved in a big attack on Caen in the morning. By the time he has to leave, it seems the entire Regiment, officers and men, is assembled about him, shouting and laughing, reluctant to let him go. And it is obvious he feels the same way, for when he starts off, still standing upright, holding onto the Jeep's windshield reminiscent of Monty, he has his driver circle the field, waving all the time to "his boys," who cheer wildly until he turns out the gateway and disappears.

As the crowd disperses, and the men return to the vicinity of their vehicles and slit trenches, there's a lot of bantering back and forth – perhaps not quite of the "mountain-to-mountain" variety you recall hearing on schemes in Wales, but enough to clearly indicate that Bombardier Hooper's game of catch and the padre's visit have combined to dispel much of the tension that had grown stronger with each passing day, among the buzz bombs in London, on the ship coming over, and then on the drive inland today along roads of intense turmoil, past the refuse and scars of battle, and mountains of ammunition stacked up awaiting the deadly struggles still to come.

Just after 10:00 P.M., in the long, lingering twilight, the air begins to throb with the deep, wavering drone of hundreds of huge, four-engined RAF bombers, coming from England to bomb Caen and its northern outskirts preparatory to a dawn ground attack. The 3rd

British Division will attack on the left, 59th British in the centre, and 3rd Canadian Division on the right after clearing Carpiquet airfield. Wave after wave, in what seems like an endless stream, the Halifaxes and Lancasters roar in from the Channel on their way to laying waste the city.*

It is tremendously impressive. You are a good ten miles from the target area, but the ground shudders from the bombs roaring and flashing on the horizon and heavy ack-ack fire skitters up from enemy guns that appear very close.

Sommervieu lies close to the flight path of planes returning home to their English bases after delivering their bomb load, and the German ack-ack guns continue to try to knock them down as they circle west and north to the Channel. At least one is hit and is on fire as it makes for the Channel.

Among the group left behind this evening in several landing craft "standing off the beach for five hours waiting for the tide," Sgt. Bruce Hunt, 26th Battery Command Post Ack, has a grandstand view of the bombers going and coming, and witnesses the demise of one of them in the sea close by. In his diary, begun just before leaving Waldershare Park, he will write:

The most impressive demonstration of air power we have seen. The planes pass over us and disappear into enemy territory oblivious of the flak showered skyward to meet them. Their mission completed they emerge a mile or so west of us bound for Britain. For a considerable time the sky is a two-lane highway, with masses of aircraft approaching and returning from the target area. One plane dives into the sea on its homeward journey,

---

*   In this first attempt to employ heavy bombers of the strategic air force in a tactical role in Normandy, 2,560 tons of high explosive were dropped by 467 Lancasters and Halifaxes – 16 more and much bigger planes than were employed by the Germans during their infamous raid on Coventry, November 14, 1940.

striking the water with a great burst of flame. The crew, happily, parachutes into the Channel, while air-sea rescue boats travel at high speed to anticipate their arrival.

By the time the last of the planes is droning off in the distance, it is totally dark.

6

COMPO RATIONS

✳

SOON AFTER THE BOMBING ENDS, A MUFFLED ROAR OF GUNS begins in the south and east and goes on all night. At least, each time you awake and sit up in your shallow trench, the sky along the horizon is lit by ragged flashes accompanied by dull rumbling, and you sleep fitfully, for you're mildly afflicted with claustrophobia in your unfamiliar, gravelike abode.

At dawn (about 0420 hours), when the ground attack (Operation Charnwood) is to go in, the bombardment reaches a climax, as hundreds of guns, including those of the cruisers *Belfast* and *Emerald*, the monitor *Roberts*, and the 16-inch monsters of the battleship *Rodney*, open up on a variety of targets not covered by the aerial bombing.

In time you learn that the main part of Caen, lying west of the Orne River, the airfield at Carpiquet, and a series of villages – with names like Verson and Bretteville-sur-Odon, soon to become familiar to 2nd Division – have been taken. But throughout July 8 and 9, the guns of 4th Field remain limbered up in the calm, green pastures of Sommervieu. And when the last vestige of water-proofing gunk is removed from the vehicles, the daylight hours are largely occupied with learning how to deal with "Composite Ration Packs" – boxes of canned rations designed to allow men to mess in small syndicates, each syndicate heating up its own food.

This, evidently, will be the arrangement from now on, and individual boxes have been issued to each gun crew, carrier crew, command-post crew, and so on. But this presents certain problems in logistics. A daily menu, supplied with each box, provides for "breakfast, dinner, tea, and supper" for fourteen men for one day, or seven men for two days, or 3.5 men for four days. Even overlooking the fact there are no half-men in the syndicates, these multiples present puzzles in scheduling and rationing for the mathematically inclined in six-man gun crews, four-man carrier crews, and command posts with more than seven but fewer than fourteen men.

There are various types of Compo boxes, each identified by a letter of the alphabet (from A to E at least) stencilled on the box, each type containing a different variety of tinned food. And deliveries to the troops are not all of one type for one day and another the next, but are a mixture so that there is no telling what you will get next.

COMPOSITE RATION PACK
TYPE E
(14 men for one day)
Contents and Suggested Use

BREAKFAST	Tea	*	3 tins (2 tall, 1 flat—Tea, Sugar & Milk Powder)
	†Sausage (1 hr.)	2 tins
	Biscuit	1 tin
	Margarine	1 tin

(*Items marked thus are also to provide for other meals)

DINNER	†Haricot Oxtail (½ hr.)	12 tins
	†Vegetables (½ hr.)	2 tins
	†Pudding (1 hr.)	3 tins (2 large, 1 small)

TEA	Tea	— (*see above)
	Biscuit	— (*see above)
	Margarine	— (*see above)
	Sardines	8 tins

Please turn over

SUPPER	Cheese	1 tin
	Biscuit	— (*see above)
EXTRAS	Cigarettes	2 tins (1 round, 1 flat— 7 cigarettes per man)
	Sweets	2 tins (1 tall, 1 flat)
	Salt	— ⎰ packed in flat
	Matches	— ⎱ sweet tin
	Chocolate	1 tin (1 slab per man)
	Latrine Paper	
	Soap	1 tablet

DIRECTIONS

Tea, Sugar and Milk Powder.—Use a dry spoon and
    sprinkle powder on heated water and bring to boil,
    stirring well. 3 heaped teaspoonfuls to 1 pint of
    water.

†May be eaten hot or cold. To heat, place unopened tins
    in boiling water for the minimum period as indicated.
    Sausage and pudding cut into ½-inch slices, may be
    fried (using margarine) if preferred.

Please turn over

905. 27042/3744. 190M. 9/43. C.P. Ltd. Gp. 784

The various types of boxes have been shuffled and mixed up at some supply base to ensure variety even within units, and to head off any charges of favouritism that might result from delivery patterns of more popular types of boxes.

The virtues of such rations are easily recognized, particularly for isolated OP (observation post) carrier crews. But still a fourteen-man box means four-man crews eat the same grub for three and a half days, and if, through the luck of the draw, their next box carries the same letter of the alphabet (as it may well do), they'll eat the same thing for seven days. And who's to say they won't get the same box three times in a row, providing no change of menu for ten and a half days.

For a while at least there'll be a certain excitement in receiving a Compo box. Finding you've been given the one with the can of peaches is like winning a lottery.

Since everything is already cooked, the tins have only to be heated up. And though only a few syndicates, such as battery-command posts, have equipped themselves with little petrol Primus stoves, within hours of the need presenting itself, the sand-box stove comes into common use. This consists of a tin box (the bottom half of a hardtack tin) loaded with sand and saturated with petrol. The fumes rising from the sand are set alight, under the other half of the hardtack tin half-filled with water in which the unopened ration tins are set to heat. While very smoky and grossly energy-inefficient, sand-box stoves can't be blown out by wind, and their flickering flames are capable of staying alive through all but the heaviest rain.

A great deal of time is spent reading directions and experimenting with methods of heating the contents of cans of "M & V" (meat and vegetable stew), "Steak and Kidney Pudding" (a can lined with thick dough and filled with a solidified concoction posing as chopped beef and kidney), "Sultana Pudding" (resembling a dried-out fruit cake that can be sliced and eaten cold with slices of canned cheddar), and "Treacle Pudding" (a caramel-coated creation that is especially pleasant when warmed up). One thing you quickly learn is that if the contents of a can requires heating to be really palatable, then it must be heated through and through – something not easily accomplished in the case of the "Steak and Kidney Pudding," due, you suspect, to the efficient insulation provided by the thick mass of dough lining the tin and surrounding the glutinous mess within.

It won't be long before repetition destroys all enjoyment of these rations, but so far Compo meals have been in some ways superior to many past meals developed by the cooks from fresh rations. A notable exception was breakfast the first morning: pre-cooked bacon. Cold, it plopped out of the can in a sickly white, cylindrical blob. Heated, it turned into liquid grease, which when poured off left a pitiful residue of red strings representing the lean meat that had streaked the fused rashers.

In each box there are two tins of "Boiled Sweets" (hard candies that contain no sugar), small slabs of very hard and remarkably taste-less chocolate (one per man per day), and two tins of cigarettes, one flat and one round, allowing seven cigarettes per man per day.

But, unquestionably, the feature of Compo rations destined to be remembered beyond all others is Compo tea: tea made from tea leaves already mixed with powdered milk and powdered sugar. Directions say to "sprinkle powder on heated water and bring to the boil, stirring well, three heaped teaspoons to one pint of water."

Every possible variation in the preparation of this tea is being tried, but so far it always ends up the same way. While still too hot to drink, it is a good-looking cup of strong tea. Even when it becomes just cool enough to be sipped gingerly, it is still a good-tasting cup of tea, if you like your tea strong and sweet. But let it cool enough to be quaffed and enjoyed, and your lips will be coated with a sticky scum that forms across the surface, which if left undisturbed will become a leathery membrane that can be wound around your finger and flipped away like something made of gutta-percha.

The second night, Curt Embleton shows a movie in a nearby field. But much more spectacular than any movie is the nightly show put on by the ack-ack guns in the dark dome of the skies overhead, when Jerry planes come over to bomb the equipment and ammunition dumps scattered among the surrounding fields and the ships unloading at the beaches.

At first everyone is inclined to stand out in the open to watch the spectacular display of fireworks, there being no obvious risk from bombs, since the German planes drop their dazzling flares on drift-ing parachutes miles away over their prime targets. However, when, along with the ripping sounds at high altitudes, fragments of shells begin to shower down, signalled by ominous *thumps* on the ground and sharp *clinks* on the metal roofs of the vehicles, steel helmets come into vogue, and space under vehicles becomes choice real estate.

At least three planes go down in flames.

You were told by the captain of your landing craft that there are more ack-ack guns protecting the Normandy bridgehead than were in action for the protection of London at the height of the Blitz. This you can believe after hearing the fearful racket and watching the show they put on here each night.

And unlike the ack-ack displays you'd watched in England, these seem successful in knocking down many of the raiders or diverting them from their targets, as the general absence of derelict ships lying offshore or on the beaches where you landed would testify.*

----

* In one month after D-Day, 261 Allied vessels were destroyed or damaged by enemy action of all kinds, including air bombing, mines laid along the sea corridors by night raiders, remote-controlled motorboats filled with explosives, and one-man torpedoes. (These torpedoes sank only two minesweepers and one cruiser.) This compares with 606 vessels lost during the period through bad weather and "human error," out of a total of 6,800 vessels involved in Operation Overlord. Besides the 6,047 specially designed landing ships and landing craft in five varieties (more than half provided by the British), there were 200 battleships, monitors, cruisers, and destroyers (of which 143 were Royal Navy or Royal Canadian Navy), and 553 other fighting ships (sloops, frigates, patrol craft, gunboats, anti-sub trawlers, motor torpedo boats, etc.) of which 424 were provided by the Royal Navy and the Royal Canadian Navy, and 129 by the Americans. Not counted as fighting ships were a great number of British and Canadian landing craft, known as "floating artillery," that could have been classed as gunboats. These were landing craft carrying field guns, loaded in such a way as to allow some of them to drench the beach with high explosive shells just ahead of their assaulting infantry debouching from landing craft all around them. The principal landing craft were: LSTs (Landing Ship Tank), LCTs (Landing Craft Tank, smaller and of shallower draught), LCIs (Landing Craft Infantry), LCAs (Landing Craft Assault), and LCVPs (Landing Craft Vehicles and Personnel). These statistics are from Chester Wilmot's *The Struggle For Europe* (London: Collins, 1952), p. 180.

PART TWO: JULY 11-17

Introduction to
Battlefield Conditions

7

BURON

※

AT 0530 HOURS, JULY 10, MINIMUM RECCE PARTIES FROM EACH battery, led by the second-in-command of the Regiment (Major Gordon Savage) and the regimental survey officer (Capt. Len Harvey) are warned to be ready to move in half an hour to locate new gun positions. Three hours later, word comes for the recce parties to rendezvous at Buron, about four kilometres northwest of Caen. At 1900 hours the Colonel returns from a meeting with Brig. R. H. Keefler, CRA (Commander Royal Artillery) at 2nd Division Headquarters, with orders for the Regiment to begin the move forward at 2230 to Buron where the guns will be put in action.

Immediately battery and troop advance parties, each consisting of a subaltern and an ack (a highly trained technical assistant) are sent forward to lay out their allotted positions and plant their gun-marker flags to allow the regimental survey party to carry their survey work right up to the marker of each "pivot gun" (the right-hand gun of each troop of four). The survey party will, first, establish the pivot gun's position on the face of the planet in terms of the numbered "grid" overprinting on the large-scale 1/25,000 map; and, second, will pass to each "director" (survey instrument) set on a tripod in front of each troop position and oriented to an identifiable distant aiming point, a precise "grid bearing," so that when the guns arrive the troop will be ready to pass on to each gun for its "dial-sight" the "zero line" (a grid bearing arbitrarily drawn by Divisional Headquarters through the middle of the enemy front). Thus all guns will be in accurate relationship to each other on "Regimental Grid" and their barrels will be parallel to each other, as a starting point for setting ranges and switches to targets.

The advance parties are advised to take along mine detectors so they may check out their areas as they wait for the guns to arrive.

The regimental convoy gets under way on time, but the narrow roads are so clogged with traffic, it takes three hours to complete the move.

It is a time for mixed feelings. At last the guns are going into action, which is a matter of great satisfaction. But you are told the Regiment could find itself in an anti-tank role in its first position, as a last-ditch reserve against a breakthrough by German tanks.

This sounds a bit far-fetched, considering that Caen is now in our hands.* But the warning has to be taken seriously, and it adds to the anxiety induced by the night move over dark, unknown roads without any lights whatsoever, into forbidding territory from which the sounds of gunfire have been almost continuous for the past three days.

It's not only a black night, but the roads are very dusty, and visibility, always poor, sometimes reduces to zero when you are moving

---

* While the warning about a possible tank breakthrough, like everything else about the Buron gun position, would later be looked upon as nothing more than a way of easing the Regiment into battle conditions before it went into action for real, there were some legitimate grounds for worry. The British 43rd Wessex Division, involved in a right hook meant to carry them to the Orne River, south of Caen, attacking south and east from Carpiquet, through Verson over the Odon River to Eterville and Maltot, ran into some very sticky going from heavy German counter-attacks supported by Panther and Tiger tanks on the night of July 10, that continued well into the next day.

CAEN TO POINT 122
("OPERATION TOTALIZE")

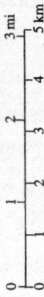

0 1 2 3 4 5 km
0 1 2 3 mi

4 RCA gun positions ....
Verrières Ridge ::::::::::::

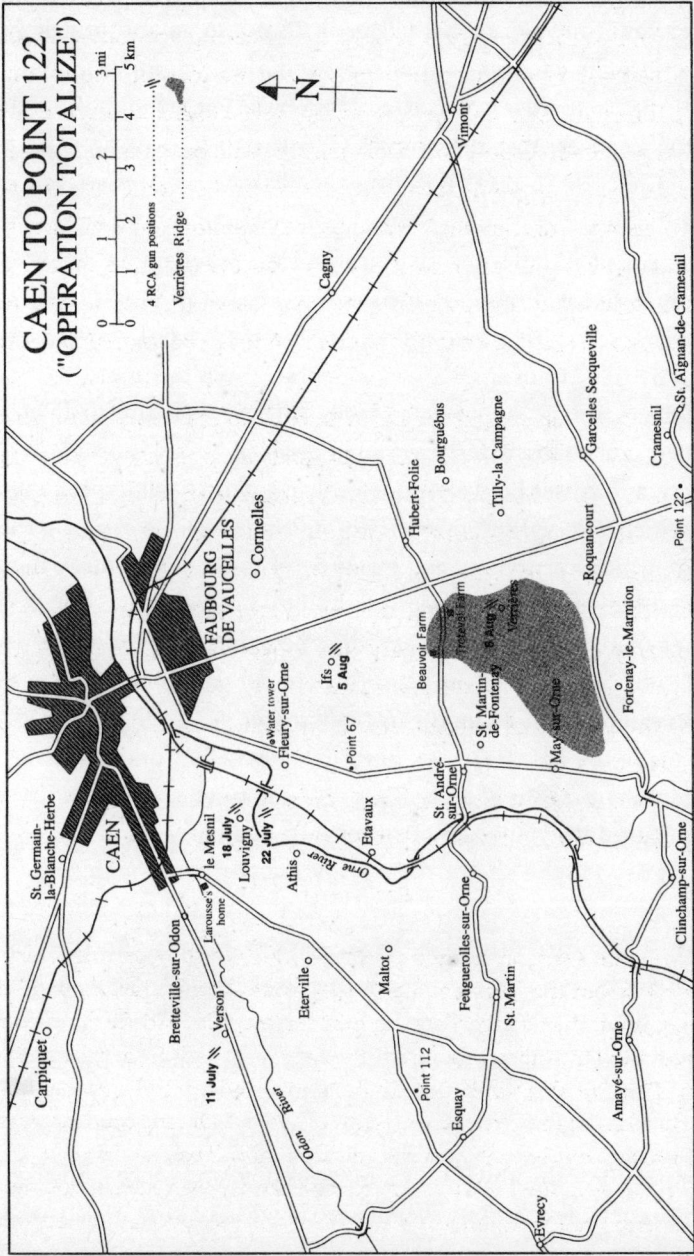

N

Carpiquet
St. Germain-la-Blanche-Herbe
CAEN
Bretteville-sur-Odon
Verson
11 July
le Mesnil
Larousse home
18 July
Louvigny
22 July
FAUBOURG DE VAUCELLES
Cormelles
Cagny
Hubert-Folie
Bourguébus
Tilly-la-Campagne
Garcelles Secqueville
Cramesnil
St. Aignan-de-Cramesnil
Water tower
Fleury-sur-Orne
Ifs
5 Aug
Point 67
Beauvoir Farm
Troteval Farm
St. Martin-de-Fontenay
5 Aug
Verrières
May-sur-Orne
Roquancourt
Fontenay-le-Marmion
Point 122
Athis
Elavaux
St. André-sur-Orne
Orne River
Clinchamp-sur-Orne
Maltot
Eterville
Feuguerolles-sur-Orne
St. Martin
Amayé-sur-Orne
Esquay
Point 112
Odon River
Évrecy

through the narrow streets of a derelict village. Once, as the convoy is crawling through such a village, it comes to an abrupt halt, and for a time the vehicles sit unmoving with their engines running.

As the dust settles, you can see over on the left, up in the direction of the beaches, that the nightly German air-raid is inspiring the usual fireworks display. Even over the idling truck engines, you can hear the furious pumping sounds of the rapid-firing ack-ack guns – hundreds of muzzles spewing heavenward thousands of white and red tracers, that climb almost leisurely, in endless streams through the wavering searchlight beams, disappearing at great heights where the skies are filled to overflowing with sparkling white bursts.

The reason for the halt becomes apparent as the first, huge, flatbed tank-transporter, carrying a disabled tank, looms up in the gloom and passes between your vehicle and the wall opposite with only inches to spare. For several minutes transports carrying their broken monsters whine and grind by in the dim and dusty night, sometimes scraping the wall of the building opposite. You don't count them as they appear and disappear, but as the minutes pass, and still they go by, you begin to wonder just how many active tanks can be left holding the front up there.

Finally the last one passes and the convoy gets underway again; and while it moves at a crawl most of the time, there are no more long halts until you reach Buron at 1:30 A.M., July 11.

Just beyond the village, the convoy stops on the road until guides from advance parties can lead each troop into its allotted area in the fields. They warn that mines have been turned up around here, and the fields have not been checked out completely. So vehicles are to play follow-the-leader, and the gun sergeants are to dismount and lead their gun tractors in on foot, making sure they follow existing tank tracks. In the dense gloom, with nobody allowed to use lamps-electric, tracks are difficult to see, but somehow all guns are dropped in position with their muzzles pointing south, and all gun tractors get safely back to the main road without blowing up, where they take off back to an area some distance away chosen as their "wagon lines."

After they've left, there is a lot of shouting by the gun position officers of each troop putting their guns on line. Standing with their acks, some fifty yards in front of the guns, working their director with the aid of wavering lamps–electric, they call out to each of their four guns in turn a reverse bearing in degrees and minutes so the gun-layer can set it on his dial sight and traverse his weapon left or right, until his sight is looking directly into the lighted lens of the director and he knows he is laid on the zero line.

But once all the guns in the Regiment have been "put on line" it is suddenly remarkably quiet. The air raid up along the beaches in the north is long since over, and neighbouring artillery tonight seems unusually inactive. Occasionally there are series of explosions in rapid succession, which you ascribe to enemy activity down in the south where fires are flaring on the horizon. But here, only the *clink* of picks and the *snitch-snitch* of shovels digging command posts, gun pits, and personal slit trenches can be heard.

Unquestionably all are conscious that for the first time they are actually within range of the enemy guns. No one seems inclined to talk, and when anyone does say something, he speaks softly, barely above a whisper. And the running patter of derogatory remarks about the army in general, and about the general in particular, that always arose between the gunners engaged in digging during training schemes in England, is totally absent.

Few offer any comment whatsoever. The one notable exception is a man who suddenly starts cursing with great feeling – all the more impressive because he curses quietly, almost under his breath. Questioned by his peers, he explains he was well on his way to completing the digging of his slit trench when he discovered he was uncovering a dead body.

On the way here, you passed through zones of foul odour, readily identifiable as coming from the rotting flesh of unburied dead horses and cows, killed in their stables or fields by shells and mortar bombs. But here, throughout the night, the air is filled with a most peculiarly repulsive odour you have never smelled before. And now and then, when the sultry air stirs, and the ghastly stench assails your nostrils at full strength, you can hardly keep from gagging.

Come daylight you discover the source: decaying bodies of men are everywhere. The sights on all sides are sickening. Obviously the Highlanders of Canadian 3rd Division came up against ferocious resistance from the SS defenders, and not just when they attacked two days ago, but also at some earlier date, for many of these bodies have been here a long time.*

When the battle moved on yesterday, German and Canadian dead were left strewn among the ruins of the village, and in and out of the nearby intricate German trench system that had made this, along with the nearby villages of Gruchy and Authie, a key strong point in the defence of Caen. The heat has done its work, and the indescribable, but unforgettable, stench from the bloated bodies of men surpasses the revolting odours of rotting animals in the nearby fields.

For the first time the men of the Regiment see dead Germans, and the sight induces only mild curiosity, as they study their steel

---

* The Canadians occupied Buron briefly on June 7, the day after D-Day, before being driven back to their startline by the first major enemy counter-attack by a regiment of 12th SS Hitlerjugend Division, under the command of one Kurt Meyer (who, in 1936, as a captain in Hitler's SS Liebstandarte, led the reoccupation of the Rhineland) bent on driving the Canadians back into the sea. Those swaggering, brainwashed young brutes under his command truly believed they could, and when they found they couldn't, they cried tears of frustration in the manner of young boys, which of course many of them were. See page 147 of *Overlord* by Max Hastings (New York: Simon & Schuster, 1984) quoting German Lt. Rudolph Schaaf of 1716th Artillery.

helmets with the two little lightning strokes side by side, signifying that they are SS. But it's another matter to look at the bodies in Canadian battledress, sprawled beside knocked-out vehicles, or huddled behind some bit of ground that had not been cover enough.*

In their diaries on this day, two 26th Battery sergeants make similar observations. Sgt. Bruce Hunt writes: "We see our first German dead. As these represent the ultimate in achievement to which our lives have been dedicated, it's strange the sight produces so little satisfaction; it would be even stranger, I suppose, if it did."

This contrasts with the anguish expressed by Sgt. Charles McEwan on seeing dead Canadians for the first time: "For most of us it was the first dead we had ever seen other than at a funeral, and it ended right then and there all the glory there is in war.

"The sight of dead Germans, no matter in what state of decomposition, does not bother us. But it really does something to you, way down inside, to see good Canadian boys – the pick of our country – lying sprawled across a slit trench or huddled up outside a

---

* At Buron, July 8, Highland Light Infantry had 262 casualties, 62 fatal. Canadian war correspondent Ross Munro, in his postwar book *Gauntlet to Overlord* (Toronto: Macmillan, 1945), would write of the fierce resistance of the Hitlerjugend, at Buron: "The 12th SS, full of young Nazis who had been taught for years to kill and knew little else, had been at grips with 3rd Division since the day after landing . . . Many were youths of seventeen and eighteen, steeped in the Nazi creed and trained through their boyhood for battle. Troops of this division carried out a criminal act on June 7, when they murdered 19 members of the Royal Winnipeg Rifles whom they had taken prisoner. The incident was carefully investigated and later General Crerar officially informed his troops of this murder. But many soldiers knew of this criminal act soon after it happened. The 12th SS was a marked division . . . it was annihilated in the Trun gap (the closing of the Falaise pocket), but it suffered extremely heavily at the hands of the Canadians in this attack on Caen."

burned-out Bren Gun Carrier where they had been shot down after bailing out of the blazing vehicle. It almost makes us sick to our stomachs. . . ."

And in still another diary, begun as a joint enterprise by two Baker Troop sergeants – Johnson and Foley – is found: "German and Allied dead are lying all around in and out of slit trenches. Many of them have been there for some time. They are bloated black and swollen, and the stench of decaying flesh is new and strange and sickening. When daylight breaks, the gruesome job of dragging the dead away from our guns has to be attended to. Quite an initiation. The Glengarians took quite a beating in a sunken road – ambushed."

Burial parties are formed to bury the German bodies in the immediate vicinity. This is allowable, but to bury Canadian bodies, you are advised, the padre must be present, not only to conduct a proper burial service, but also to see that reports are prepared consistent with regulations – and that "dog tags" and map references of the graves get back through the correct channels.

It is afternoon before the burial of the Canadians is undertaken. Over on the right, big guns are rumbling, but here there is only the sound of picks and shovels as the gunners dig shallow holes under the burning July sun to receive the stinking corruptions that once were men. You hear planes, with throttles wide open, high overhead, and a tremendous barrage opens up on ten German fighter planes heading for the ships and the beaches, flying line astern, weaving wildly to escape a profusion of black puffs growing around them. Five are hit and spin down smoking, and five white parachutes drift down in the distance. It's all over in a matter of seconds, but this remarkable display of ack-ack gunnery, the like of which no one has ever seen – not even during the Blitz in 1940 – is cheered lustily by the gunners.

A French civilian, returning to check out the condition of his home in Buron, is offered cans of stew and cigarettes. He in turn comes up with an ancient bottle of a very strong liquor he calls "Calvados."*

He warns that Calvados should be handled with care, and describes, with expressive pantomime, its disastrous effects on the first Canadians who arrived here, alleging that some at least were tipsy when they were hit by an SS counter-attack, with the dire consequences you can now observe about you.

Lieut. Louis Anthony Verdeil, 26th Battery ACPO, who is able to converse with him in French, learns of the deep hatred the people of occupied France have developed for the Boche. The man tells a fearful story of Gestapo savagery on D-Day against Frenchmen suspected of being members of the underground resistance movement.[†]

You take a break and visit the ruins of the village. Burned-out tanks, Bren carriers, and other vehicles lie here and there throughout the area. And strewn about the trenches is a clutter of German and Canadian equipment, including weapons of all kinds and live ammunition. One of the more curious items you come across lying in the front entry of a broken house is a sizeable case of German rifle ammunition – the brass cartridges as shiny and bright as though manufactured yesterday, but armed with bullets of hardwood, painted red, in place of regular steel-jacketed lead bullets.

------

* Taking its name from the region, Calvados is distilled from hard apple cider, at an alcoholic strength of seventy degrees, some 55 per cent stronger than the legal strength of forty-five degrees for brandy and Scotch.

† The Gestapo shot 87 of 88 men of the FFI (Free Forces of the Interior) held in the Caen prison on D-Day. Years after, the author became a friend of the 88th man, Marcellus Barjaud, who survived because he did not respond to the call by the German guard yelling, incorrectly, "Mario Barjaud." He was subsequently transferred with others to the infamous Frennes prison in Paris.

8

INTRODUCTION TO ETERVILLE
AND HILL 112

※

AS THE GUNS ARE BEING MOVED INTO POSITION AND READIED for action near Buron on the night of July 10–11, the three infantry battalions of 4th Brigade – the Royal Regiment of Canada (Royals), the Royal Hamilton Light Infantry (Rileys), and the Essex Scottish – which 4th Field will be supporting until the end of the war, are moving into reserve positions four thousand yards south, on the western outskirts of Caen.

From their positions in slit trenches and buildings, taken over from the Regina Rifles in St. Germaine-la-Blanche-Herbe, the Royals can see and hear a tank battle two or three miles to the southwest, which they observe with interest. By midnight, the horizon is grimly lit with the flames of half a dozen or more burning tanks, but they watch with a certain detachment, unaware that the distant battle, raging on throughout the night, is deciding who will possess the fields, the orchards, and a smashed village that within twenty-four hours will be their responsibility.

Desperately, the British are defending their new gains over the Odon against bitter counter-attacks by the SS and their frightful Tiger tanks, bent on wiping out the salient by driving them from Hill 112 and from Eterville, on its northeastern slope, which the Royals will take over tomorrow night.

The British first started fighting for their bridgehead over the

Odon and for domination of Hill 112 two weeks ago, on June 26, with an attack by 60,000 men of VIII Corps and 600 tanks, supported by 700 guns, including battleships anchored off the beaches.

In the opening attack of "Operation Epsom," designed to be the start of an encirclement of Caen through a right hook, they had moved south and east on a four-mile front, west of Carpiquet, towards the wooded ravines of the little Odon river. By the first night they'd gained three miles, but were locked in a struggle of awesome intensity that continued through the 27th and the 28th.

Finally, 11th Armoured Div, in the mud and rain, made it across the bloodstained stream, and on June 29, gained the summit of Hill 112, just in time to repulse a counter-attack by 9th and 10th SS Panzer Divisions of 2nd Panzer Corps.*

The commander of German 7th Army, Colonel-General Dollman, had attached so much importance to wiping out this salient over the Odon, that he'd collapsed and died on the second day of the battle in despair (some say by suicide), believing the British had the all-important heights firmly in their grasp and that he'd let his Führer down. But so tenuous had been the British hold on the hill that, later the same day, Gen. Dempsey, fearing his armour was at risk in the shallow bridgehead, had withdrawn all the tanks of 11th Armoured Division to the north bank of the Odon, allowing the enemy to regain Hill 112. In the four days of Operation Epsom, British 8th Corps lost 4,020 men.

Now, just ten days later, while Canadian 3rd Division and British 3rd Division are consolidating their gains in Caen, battalions of the 43rd Wessex Division are suffering another 2,000 casualties in renewed fighting for Hill 112 as they attempt to extend the Odon salient south and east, down to the Orne by way of Verson, Eterville, and Maltot.

---

* Newly arrived in France from having halted the Russian offensive at Tarnopol, 2nd Panzer Corps carried orders from Hitler to drive the Allies into the sea.

Initially, the dawn attack had gone well, following in behind the huge bombardment, and by 8:00 A.M. the 4th Dorsets had gained Eterville, and other units were well up Hill 112. But the Germans mounted such strong counter-attacks that the British were thrown on the defensive.

Successive battalion attacks by the Somersets and the 5th Duke of Cornwall's Light Infantry failed to gain the summit of 112, and they were forced to dig in on the northern slope of that dominating feature. And two attacks – one of brigade strength supported by M-10s (self-propelled 17-pounders), down the hill from Eterville to low-lying Maltot, about 1,300 metres farther south, had been shattered by the huge Tiger tanks of 2nd SS Panzer Corps and an extraordinarily intense bombardment by guns and mortars massed along the high ground east of the Orne that the Canadians would soon come to know as Verrières Ridge.*

By last light, July 10, the wheat fields between Eterville and Maltot and up the slopes of Hill 112 were dotted with blackened, burned-out Churchills and M-10s.

A vivid description of the severe conditions around Eterville position during the night of July 10 and throughout July 11 was recorded by the historian of the British 43rd Wessex Division:

> . . . Soon after dark the enemy penetrated Eterville, where hand-to-hand fighting with the Cameronians (who'd taken over from the 4th Dorsets) went on all night and continued till 8:00 A.M. when he finally withdrew leaving over a hundred dead. On the front of the 5th Dorset and 7th Somerset Light Infantry, a heavy counter-attack with tanks and infantry developed soon after dawn, only to be beaten back with huge loss, by our artillery, anti-tank and mortar fire.

All day (July 11) Tiger tanks, lying back beyond the crest,

---

* British writers refer to it as Bourguébus Ridge after the village they seized on the left flank during the second day of Operation Goodwood.

probed the forward defences in the open fields. The least movement brought down intense automatic fire. The mortaring went on without respite. It must be admitted that the German armour was less vulnerable than our own. If any of our Churchills appeared on the skyline, they were invariably hit and brewed up. The crest of the hill was littered with evidence to this effect. Meanwhile the constant stream of casualties continued to flow. It was only too clear that we had been forced on to the defensive."*

* From Second British Army Intelligence Summaries No. 3b, quoted in Report No. 58, Historical Section (G.S.) Canadian Army Headquarters, Dept. of National Defence, p. 45.

9

MOVING UP TO SUPPORT
THE SALIENT OVER ODON

※

THE REGIMENT IS NOT CALLED UPON TO FIRE A ROUND ALL DAY, and at 5:00 P.M. it is ordered to move forward to its first real position in action, in support of 4th Brigade infantry moving into the front line tonight. The 2nd Division is taking over from the British about 4,000 yards of the front, running from their positions along the northern slope of Hill 112, northeast to the 3rd Canadian Division, positions centred in Caen.

With the message to limber up and move comes a warning that the convoy may be subjected to some airbursts as it passes beyond Carpiquet on the way to the new positions. This causes concern, especially among the gun sergeants, who are required to stand with their heads and shoulders protruding through the hatch in the roof of their gun tractors when going into action. But nothing descends on the convoy, though Sgt. McEwan's diary will record "a fearful lot of shell-fire" falling to the right of the road on the way forward.

The move is through the smashed village of Carpiquet, past the badly holed and ragged airport, with strips of corrugated iron hanging forlornly from the steel skeletons of hangars. There, advance parties are waiting to lead the Regiment down a steep, chalky trail to an exceedingly dusty sunken road, leading southeast towards Verson and Eterville across a shallow, broad valley of open fields devoid of all buildings, trees, hedges, and even fences. An ideal place for tanks to do battle, you think in your ignorance of the reality of such matters. But nothing seems to have taken place here – at least no derelicts are visible, and until now the lush sugar beet fields have flourished undisturbed except for some widely spaced tank tracks slicing across them.

About a kilometre short of Verson, the Regiment is directed left, into positions in a beet field just off the sunken road.

The two troops of 2nd Battery are positioned unusually close together at the forward end of the positions, directly in front of and less than 100 yards from the muzzles of 14th Battery guns. The 26th is down the slope a little to the left rear. Never before have you seen all twenty-four guns of 4th Field deployed in such a small area, in total contravention of the most basic principle governing the deployment of guns, drilled into every gunner's head during training since Dunkirk: that batteries, troops, and individual guns must be dispersed as widely as practical so as to deny enemy bombers, strafing planes, and artillery the chance to hit a concentrated target.

However, the reason for this jamming up of the three battery positions becomes clear when it is pointed out by Major Gordon Savage, the second-in-command, who is here to watch the deployment, that the whole area allotted to 4th Field is under enemy observation from the distant high ground over the Orne down there on your left front. For this reason he's tried to get as much cover as possible for the troops by crowding them into this one corner of the valley, which bends back behind a bit of a rise with some bushes along the crest. While no troop can be completely hidden from the enemy here, this at least cuts down the amount of enemy high ground overlooking 4th Field.

He doesn't envy 5th and 6th Field, who'll be deploying over on our left, tomorrow, even more plainly in view than 4th Field. The digging is easy, and the guns and ammunition are put below grade with almost leisurely digging. British guns over on the right are rumbling away, but it is so peaceful here, it's as though you are on a training scheme in England. One gunner even remarks that this is just like Exercise Spartan (the largest of all British training schemes) with live ammunition. And as you watch great holes being excavated in the deep, fertile earth – including gun pits eighteen feet in diameter – you can't shake the feeling you are participating in an act of vandalism – an idea that first hit you as you directed the big quads, dragging heavy ammunition limbers and guns behind them, into position over the neat rows of sugar beets, crushing them to pulp.

But then an enemy shell lands with a terrific *crack* on Baker Troop position – just one, as though they are registering a target before it grows too dark. Fortunately it lands far enough away that no one is hurt, for it catches everybody standing upright. But it does make the shovels go faster, and goes a long way to restoring your own perspective of war and its priorities.

The valley opens to the southeast, sloping gently down towards the Orne some six kilometres away, where on the high ground, identifiable on the map as enemy territory just over the river at Fleury-sur-Orne, can be seen one of those peculiarly Norman, concrete water-towers. While directly south, over the road alongside the right of the gun position, the ground climbs gradually to a high point 3,600 metres away, its crest marked on the map by an oval contour 112.

As the Regiment digs gun pits, ammunition pits, command posts, and personal slit trenches, with the reddish glow of a rich sunset casting long, black shadows of guns and men across the beet fields, everyone is more than a bit anxious as to what the future holds for them. But no one has any idea that this will be the worst position the Regiment will ever occupy in action.

It is obvious to officers with maps, and to all who have eyes and can ask questions, that this natural amphitheatre overlooks the enemy-held high ground over the Orne, and that if you can see his position then he must be able to see yours equally well, if not better. Still, no one, no matter how long he stares apprehensively at the unforgettable water-tower standing sinister like a huge mushroom over there across the Orne, can imagine on this quiet, balmy evening what is to come, for no one can bring himself to believe the brass would place in jeopardy all seventy-two guns of the division by deploying them in full view of the enemy.

And even when things turn bad, it will be accepted without beefing, without blaming anybody, as the way war is: hell is to be expected, and the deployment of the guns within sight of the enemy must have been necessary because of the overcrowding in the confined bridgehead.

All six troop commanders are up with 4th Brigade, two with each battalion, but they won't occupy observation posts (OPs) as forward observation officers (FOOs) at the front until the infantry battalions take over from the British some 3,000 yards south of the guns around Eterville, the next village beyond Verson.

The guns aren't firing, though a "hostile mortar list" is received, with no fewer than 112 targets on it.

Just after dark, the field across the road fills with tanks coming back from the direction of Verson. And now and then the valley fills with a deep, reverberating roar of guns somewhere on the left rear. The consensus is that they are mediums (5.5-inch guns) engaged in counter-battery work – delivering 100-pound high explosive shells on suspected enemy gun and mortar positions.

IO

ETERVILLE

---------- ✳ ----------

SO INTENSE ARE THE GERMAN ASSAULTS ON ETERVILLE AND THE slopes of that infamous Hill 112, rising west of the village, that Gen. Montgomery, Commander-in-Chief of all Allied ground forces in Normandy, in replying this night of July 11 to congratulations from Churchill on the capture of Caen, is impelled to inform the Prime Minister:

"All today 9th and 10th SS Panzer Divisions have been attacking furiously to retake Pt. 112 to the northeast of Evrecy."*

This then is the situation into which the 4th Brigade is moving the night of July 11, when at 11:30 P.M. July 11 the three armoured White Scout Cars of the battery commanders (one for each battalion), and the six carriers of the troop commanders (two for each battalion) who will serve as forward observation officers, join a long line of troops trudging down through Venoix and Bretteville-sur-Odon towards Verson some five kilometres away. Here, they will cross a narrow stone bridge over the Odon and disperse to their allotted positions in and around Eterville in the salient.

After crossing, the Royals will continue straight on into the village of Eterville, a mile southeast of the Odon, to take over

---

* Winston Churchill, *Triumph and Tragedy* (Bantam Books, 1962), p. 26.

from the Glasgow Highlanders of 15th Scottish Division, who only this day relieved the 9th Cameronians. The Rileys will bear left beyond the Odon, moving forward to the reverse slope of a gentle hill just northeast of Eterville to take over from a battalion of the British Black Watch. On their left flank will be the Fusiliers Mont-Royal, of 6th Brigade, who are taking over from the Régiment de le Chaudière, just short of the road from Caen to Eterville. The Essex Scottish will relieve the Cameronians in their reserve position, just south of the Odon, at Rocrenil, about a mile north of Eterville.

From now on, whenever 4th Brigade is in the line, the CO of 4th Field will move with the infantry brigadier, serving as his "arty rep" (artillery representative), advising and laying on fire plans, involving not only 4th Field and the other two 2nd Division field regiments, but medium and heavy guns as necessary to thicken up support, or concentrate massive fire on enemy counter-attacking forces. Similarly, from now on, each of the three infantry battalion commanders will have one of the 4th Field battery commanders at his side morning, noon, and night.

However, it will be through the eyes of the six troop commanders – the FOOs – keeping the front under constant surveillance from OPs (observation posts) established in close contact with front-line company commanders, that the whole vast network of artillery representatives – leading back through the majors to the colonel, to the Brigadier CRA at Division, to the CCRA (Commander Corps Royal Artillery) at Corps Headquarters – will be kept in the picture. Normally FOOs are attached to specific companies in an operation, and as the battalion moves forward into the line, they move with them. But because it is the first time up for 4th Field FOOs, the FOOs of the British artillery unit supporting the three British battalions being relieved volunteer to guide them into their various positions. This might have worked out to everyone's benefit, except for the innovative method, invoked by the CO of 4th Field, of pairing up FOOs with their guides, resulting in only one

troop commander getting to where he is supposed to be. Both 2nd
Battery troop commanders, Capt. Stuart "Stu" Laurie, Able Troop,
and Capt. Gordon Hunter, Baker Troop, end up with the Rileys
instead of the Royals. Capt. "Sammy" Grange, Fox Troop, 26th
Battery, who customarily moves with the Essex Scottish, finds
himself with the Royals at Eterville, as does Capt. Britton "Brit"
Smith, of 14th Battery, who normally would be with the Rileys.
And the other 14th Battery troop commander, Capt. Jack
Thompson, ends up with the Essex Scottish. Only Capt. Reginald
Parker, Easy Troop, connects with a guide that takes him to his
correct battalion, the Essex Scottish.

To non-gunners, it might seem of little consequence which
troop commander goes with which battalion, since all the guns in
the Regiment are available and can be concentrated on targets by
any arty rep at any level. Nevertheless – as a matter of tradition,
training, and equitable employment of the FOOs – each battery has
been paired off with its own battalion for years now: 2nd Battery
with the Royals, 14th with the Rileys, and 26th with the Essex
Scottish. Thus in this first-ever move up to the front, when FOOs
are seemingly shuffled like a deck of cards, and only one of them
ends up with the correct battalion, confusion and anxiety are added
to an already confusing and anxious night.

Stu Laurie will remember the bewildering turmoil maintaining
at the rendezvous point in Bretteville-sur-Odon, where the 4th
Field captains are to be met by the guides from the British units
they are relieving:

The rendezvous is on the main street, with a great confusion of
troops and vehicles passing through. The place is on fire, and it is
being heavily shelled continuously. Finally "Bud" Drury [CO of
4th Field] says, "Find somebody and go with him!"

So we just grab hold of the first Englishman we find who is
there to take us where we're supposed to go. As it turns out, he's
a guide to where the RHLI are taking over, not to Eterville where

the Royals are headed. Just as we start off, this guy says he knows a shortcut, and as we go along this track we come to a little stone bridge over the river Odon. It's a very narrow bridge, only the width of one vehicle, and there's a great hole blown in the middle of it, so I get out in front of the carrier to try to guide it past the hole. All of a sudden the most god-awful mess of Moaning Minnies comes whirling at us. I dive under the carrier and promptly get run over.

Ryckman [Gunner George Ryckman] lets go of the brakes or something, and it rolls ahead. One track runs over one of my knees. Now, you know the track on a carrier is springy, but it is not that springy! [A universal carrier weighs four tons unloaded.] And I'm screaming bloody murder! So when Ryckman backs it off me and off the bridge, our guide decides we won't go this way; it's a little too tough to get across that bridge.

We go back around and up another way, up a long lane where I notice there are no leaves on the trees – they're all on the ground. The ground is covered with leaves though this is July. And for some reason they've been mounded up in random piles, one here and one there, all along the way. I wonder what the hell is this all about? And when I investigate one of the mounds, I find the body of an English soldier. Suddenly it all becomes clear: all these mounds are unburied dead men covered with leaves that floated down after being blown off the trees by shell-fire. Boy! They really had been plastered on their way in here. And at the moment we aren't doing too badly ourselves.*

Of that night, all FOOs, acks, signallers, and drivers of the six 4th Field carriers, interspersed between companies along the line of march of some two thousand walking troops, moving slowly up that forbidding road during the blackest midnight hours, will

---

*   Author interview.

remember above all else the fearful tension. Everyone moving through the sinister gloom past smashed buildings and derelict vehicles, lit only now and then by the flash of a mortar bomb, is subject to it.

At one point the column freezes in the obscene glare of a chandelier flare suspended from a little parachute, dropped by an enemy aircraft droning overhead, and everyone expects the worst. But the thing burns out without anything happening.

This is a new and frightening experience, moving up to the front at night. All are holding their breath, if not physically at least mentally, hoping the changeover can be effected without arousing the Germans and drawing heavy fire before they are settled in trenches.

Brit Smith will remember it as something of a nightmare, with the nervous system strained to the breaking point every now and then, when soldiers shift their packs and the muggy night is filled with an unholy rattling of enamelled tin cups, hanging from a strap on the outside of every small pack, clashing with equally resonant trenching-tools dangling beside them. When whole companies flop down on the road at the sizzle of a mortar bomb or the whine of an incoming shell, Brit is certain the "god-awful clattering is enough to wake every German within ten miles."

Then the racket of vehicles starting and stopping along the last mile to Eterville – when the Royals' column becomes entangled with the British vehicles moving out – is nothing short of horrifying to the ears of men who have been hoping to sneak into the front-line trenches without drawing enemy fire.

Years after, Royals' officers will recall how in the words of one, Robert Suckling, "the quiet of the night is made hideous with the noise of racing motors, clashing gears, and grinding trucks."

However, though there is some mortaring and shelling on the way in, and a lot more after the Royals get into position, the enemy never really takes advantage of the confusion to attack as he had the night before with such ferocity. It would seem the Germans on this front on the night of July 11 are simply too exhausted from all the attacks and counter-attacks in which they have been engaged during the last twenty-four hours in Maltot, on Hill 112, and particularly in Eterville.

II

YOUR FIRST ROUNDS FIRED

IN ANGER

------------------------ ✳ ------------------------

BACK AT THE GUNS, DURING THE NIGHT CAN BE HEARD THE other two 2nd Division regiments (5th and 6th Field) moving their guns into position down in the valley over on the left. And at dawn, looking down at them, it is obvious they are even more exposed to enemy observation than 4th Field. Each freshly dug pit is clearly visible, and camouflage nets, draped on poles above each gun in good old Alfriston Practice Ranges' style, in the same way they are tented over each 4th Field gun, would never confuse any enemy artillery observer.*

You find it impossible to shake the feeling that there's an irrational "Charge of the Light Brigade" quality about the positioning of 2nd Division guns. There are awkward questions from your

---

* 6th Field stuck it out for five days in the valley, miraculously losing only twelve men and one gun. Then, according to their Regimental History, after firing 250 rounds per gun on a fire plan on behalf of the British 43rd Division attack over on the right, that began 3:00 A.M. on July 17, two of their batteries "moved back over the hill behind RHQ, leaving the old positions rigged as real as our camouflage nets and wooden pieces could make it. The deception worked, for that morning Jerry gave it a real plastering which, we saw later, knocked out two 'guns' and enlarged the old E Troop Command Post considerably."

NCOs, such as "Who was the idiot that picked these positions for 4th Field, Sir?" And the line "Into the valley of death, into the mouth of hell" insists on going round and round in your head.

Still you cling to the belief that Brig. Bruce Matthews, 2nd Canadian Corps CCRA (Corps Commander Royal Artillery), and Brig. R. F. Keefler CRA 2nd Division, are not madmen, that they must have been forced to deploy the guns here because of a shortage of concealed positions within range of possible operations, due to the awesome accumulation of guns in the bridgehead.

Certainly, the sight of the entire division (seventy-two guns) arrayed in such a small area makes you realize the extent of the gigantic buildup that has been going on for a month, and which any day now will be unleashed for the break-out from the bridgehead, an operation for which 2nd Division trained so long in Britain.

Shortly after dawn on July 12, Stu Laurie, up at Eterville, three and a half kilometres southeast of here, reports his OP is being heavily shelled.

At 7:13 A.M. the Regiment fires its first "rounds in anger" on "an enemy infantry area."

At 8:30 A.M. the war diary records the Regiment is "on theatre grid," meaning the positions of your guns are now accurately fixed in relation to all other surveyed-in guns throughout the entire British–Canadian forces in Normandy, allowing all guns to be brought to bear on a single target, if so required, with equal accuracy at any time.

And at about 9:45 A.M. all ranks experience for the first time the nerve-wracking sensation of crouching in holes in the ground as the air is ripped around you and the earth shakes under you. Shells crash in, one after another, until it seems that they'll never stop – the smashes of sound shattering your wits and the shuddering concussions destroying all sense of equilibrium. And when every hole around here must have been hit except this one, it is suddenly quiet – so quiet the buzz of flies is noticeably loud.

Then the damage is assessed. You call over the Tannoy to the guns:

"Number One Gun, you all right?"

A pause, then a faint, "Okay."

"Number Two?

"Okay."

"Number Three?"

"Okay."

"Number Four?"

"Okay."

You can hardly believe it. No one was hit! And no equipment was lost. How utterly miraculous! Obviously slit trenches are the answer, but it is generally agreed that these "are not quite deep enough."

The Regiment's first casualty requiring evacuation is an OP signaller, Gunner Ernst Hodgkinson. Gun Sgt. Nick Ostapyck, of 14th Battery, was wounded slightly yesterday, but he was able to remain on duty. Others wounded today are 26th Battery Signal Sgt. Allan Lawson, Gunner Norman Coughlin, and Gunner Benjamin Parker.

Shelling continues spasmodically, and enemy planes bomb and strafe all positions from Verson up through the valley to Carpiquet aerodrome. Sgt. Bruce Hunt will record in his diary: "Had the distinction of being strafed. A worm's-eye view showed about eight 109s diving on the guns ... momentarily over the pits, firing all the while. Near misses registered all around us and shelling pretty continuous."

12

FOOS NEED RELIEF AFTER

ONLY TWO DAYS

✳

THE SHELLING THAT SEEMED SO BAD YESTERDAY IS WORSE today. Right after the Regiment opened up on some countermortar bombards this morning, the Germans retaliated with devastating accuracy, showering the gun positions with shells of all calibres more or less steadily for two hours, causing eighteen casualties, four of them fatal. Baker Troop suffered especially, losing two guns through direct hits. The shell that knocked out their Number Three gun killed Bombardier Ron Hooper and Gunner Mervin Bond instantly. Three other crew members were evacuated. One of them, Gunner Adrian Lennon, was wounded so severely he will not survive.

Miraculously, the crew of Number Two gun, the other gun disabled by a direct hit, escaped without a scratch.

During this hellish period, a heavy shell landed on Easy Troop Command Post, killing Gunner Norman Lockeyer, and wounding gunners Ray McLeod and John Weiss. Weiss produced a haunting image for buddies who set out to catch and restrain him, when he took off in panic from the wrecked command post, running a mindless pattern across the shell-torn field with jagged fragments of shell sticking out of his skull like horns.

Concussion from the same shell rendered the gun position officer, Lieut. Harold "Ali" Barber, temporarily unconscious, and burst the eardrums of Signaller Owen Hennessy, who eventually had to be evacuated.

Among the most unforgettable sights during these first days of action, is that of the MO (medical officer), still wearing the three-buckle overshoes he personally adopted as standard footwear on schemes in muddy old England, galloping across the dusty, sun-baked beet field from RHQ on his way to attend the wounded and dying at Baker and Easy troops even before there is any real break in the shelling.

An MO isn't supposed to go to the wounded; they are supposed to be brought to him at his regimental aid post by stretcher-bearers. But Dr. Burt Talmage Dunham is not one to let convention or custom inhibit his actions – as the sound of those ridiculous over-shoes, plop-plopping urgently past your command-post dugout while shells still scream and crash about the position, clearly attests. In the eyes of every man in 4th Field who witnessed his outsized courage and compassion today, he is a special kind of hero. And this is the man who told you one time in England that he was worried he might not show up too well in action – that he was, after all, on his way to becoming a baby specialist when, in a rash moment, he decided to enlist.

Days of the week, having no relevance to life here, have ceased to exist. Dates of the month, being only slightly more useful, threaten to disappear, and certainly will always be the subject of argument, even for those keeping diaries. But some dates will remain imprinted on the brain indelibly, such as July 13, 1944, the first time you are sent up as a FOO.

You only know it's the 13th because late in the day, when the German shelling slackens, you decide it's time you let your wife know you are okay using one of the preprinted cards they issued on the ship coming to France, anticipating conditions might not be conducive to letter-writing. All you have to do is address the card, check off the phrases you think appropriate, (such as "I am well,"

"Writing soon," and sign it, and it can start back to a base post-office through the supply chain, beginning with Sgt.-Maj. Tommy Mann when he brings up the rations tonight. However, dating the card presents a problem. Eventually a consensus of sorts establishes it is the 13th. And just as you launch into a detailed dissertation, pooh-poohing the bad-luck traditions of the date and listing all the good things that have happened to you on the 13th, the field telephone starts buzzing.

"Hutch" takes the message: You are to report to Battery Command Post, prepared to go up to the OP to relieve Capt. Laurie, who has exchanged battalions with Brit Smith. You are to check in with Major Wren at tactical headquarters of the Royal Regiment on the way up. Lieut. Bill Dunning, troop leader (assistant GPO) of Baker Troop, will be going up with you to relieve his troop commander, Capt. Gordon Hunter. You don't have to worry about rations and water; they will be in the carrier now on its way up from the wagon lines. You are to take an ack and a signaller up with you.

Conscious that all members of a carrier crew, other than the FOO, are volunteers (the risks being greater up there) you wonder what will happen now. Who could blame them if they chose not to volunteer for something that could prove even worse than the punishing existence they are enduring here. So when that pungent question, "Who wants to go up to the OP?" is posed, and for several seconds the only sound in the confined dugout is of deep breathing, you worry.

When at last two voices quietly announce they'll go, a wave of gratitude, without parallel, sweeps over you, humbling you as you realize two men have chosen to trust you and share with you the risks up there. Your heart goes out to Gunner Don Kirby, who'll be your signaller, and Gunner John Elder, who'll be your ack, as they fish out their kit from under GA, and extract what they want to take along.

Collecting your helmet and map board, hanging your binoculars around your neck, patting your compass and pistol to make sure they are in their cases on your web belt, and checking your pockets to ensure you've got extra smokes, matches, and lots of "Boiled Sweets," you set off for the battery command post. It's only a short way as the crow flies, just on the right along the sunken road. But not wanting to be caught more than diving distance from a hole when you hear the first whisper of an incoming shell, you lead your crew on a circuitous route, passing behind the gun pits as though on your way to the latrine.

As you stride briskly along, you're suddenly aware that your eyes, with no conscious direction from you, are darting here and there in the manner of an animal – searching, identifying, and measuring the distance to holes or folds in the ground in which you might possibly shelter, should the need arise. How quickly a man adopts techniques for survival once it's necessary. Only yesterday, for the first time in your life, you were forced to dive for shelter from shells and mortars, but already you have learned to tell in a split second – from the slightest whisper, crackle, or whine of mortar bomb or shell – if it's on line, and whether it will land close by or crash harmlessly beyond. Several times today you saw gunners standing bolt upright, watching 5th and 6th Field down in the valley taking their turns being shelled. And at one point, you made note that many kept their heads up to watch shells bursting black and ominous among the gun pits of friends in 26th Battery, less than 400 yards away to left rear.

Just short of the sunken road, you turn right and follow the lip of the field until you reach the dugout excavated in the deep bank next to the shallow ditch and road. Roofed over like your troop command post, with earth-covered corrugated-iron sheets from a hangar at Carpiquet aerodrome, it has been dug, and the earth mounded about in such a way, as to leave the grade-level turf of the lip of the field to serve as a table for the artillery boards. A shallow port, extending the full extent of this earthen table, some six feet long, has been left open for ventilation and light, and this, you note, can be closed off at night by a tarpaulin anchored with stones along the top of the dugout.

To look in, you are forced to kneel on the ground. Working with needle-pointed pencils on the gridded paper pinned to their artillery boards, plotting targets, measuring with arm and arc, and filling in long sheets of paper with neat columns of figures, are two CPO acks (Command Post Officer Assistants), one of them the garrulous Sgt. John Dunsmore. And standing behind them, where he can oversee the work, is Lieut. Gordon Lennox, the CPO.

When Lennox looks up at you wearily, you notice he's covered with dust. All of them are covered with dust – their hands, their faces, even their eyelids – and the wrinkles around their eyes and across their foreheads show up as sweaty, dark lines.

Immediately you realize why, as you follow the course of a truck that has come down off the Carpiquet aerodrome escarpment and is roaring towards the gun positions with a dust cloud billowing up behind it. As it passes within a few feet of where you are kneeling, the dust roils up and enshrouds the dugout and everybody in it. You try holding your breath until it settles, but with no wind it takes an age, and eventually you join the others in coughing and spitting sand.

When finally you can again see into the dugout, Lennox is grinning at you from ear to ear and chuckling in that unique staccato fashion he always manages when things are just too damned ridiculous for sensible comment. Then, as if to say, Look at what we have to work on under these frigging-awful conditions, he hands you up a list of map references under the heading: Hostile Mortar List. There are some forty targets on the list, and when you realize that they are working out the line, range, and angle of sight of all of them for both troops in the battery, you hasten to return it to him.

As he passes it on to the waiting acks, he volunteers: "They'll be sent to the troops on hostile-battery record forms as timed programs for harassing fire tonight. Let's hope some of the guns that have been plastering us are on it."

Dunsmore, who makes it a rule never to miss a chance to comment derisively on each and every situation as it arises, looks up grinning, as he wipes sand from his artillery board with his battledress sleeve. Then, baring his teeth and grinding them as though testing the sand content of his mouth, he starts to sing in a loud and raucous voice, affecting a Cockney accent:

"Ow, Ow, Ow – What a luvully waw!..."

However, he immediately loses his audience with the arrival of your carrier with its own dust cloud. You climb in front with the driver, Gunner W. "Buck" Saunders. Lieut. Bill Dunning, who has just arrived from Baker Troop, joins Kirby and Elder in one of the rear compartments on each side of the engine, which, in a Universal carrier, sits amidships dividing the main body-box in two. It must be a tight squeeze. Even when equipment is stowed cunningly by an experienced crew, it always appears to have been loaded helter-skelter, and whoever loaded this carrier was less than experienced.

But somehow they are able to jam themselves in among the clutter of remote-control cables, Compo rations, personal weapons, and a great confusion of small packs, tarpaulins, and extra batteries for the three radio sets: the main 19-set transmitter-receiver, the back-packing 18-set, and the little walkie-talkie 38-set.

As you move off, up the sunken road towards the village of Verson, you marvel at how smoothly a carrier rides. There is only a slight rocking as you pass over the railway crossing. The "bogie wheels," on which the track is suspended, are individually sprung, so that all the lumps and ruts in the worn and shell-pitted road are absorbed by the tracks bulging up and down.

It's been so long since you rode in a carrier it's like a brand-new experience. Although you were taught how to drive one during your officer's training, you seldom have been in one since, even during those big training schemes in England, which raises the whole question of your training for your current assignment with the infantry.

During the years of truly intensive training in England, while you received a solid grounding in the tactical application of artillery in support of the infantry and tanks, you were given no opportunity to work with the infantry as a Forward Observation Officer.

You are confident enough of your ability to handle all the technical work of a FOO – having received excellent training in the basic job of observing fire and correcting the guns onto targets of all kinds, through countless hours of practice on miniature smoke-table ranges, in addition to frequent opportunities to range real guns with live shells onto targets on the Alfriston and Senneybridge ranges. But you have no experience whatsoever working as a FOO with the infantry. On all major training schemes, involving the infantry and other arms of the service – sometimes extending over several days as in the case of the monster exercise Spartan – "Fooing" was always reserved exclusively for the elite troop commanders. Subalterns were kept fully occupied with all the problems of the guns, and seldom had time even to imagine what their captains might be involved in.

And now, only thirty-six hours after the Regiment has gone into action for the first time in direct support of the infantry in the line, you and another subaltern are on your way up to relieve two of these troop commanders.

As you approach the devastation that was once the village of Verson, you find yourself struggling to suppress the tension rising within you. While you think you have an idea what a front-line rifle company position might look like, deduced from seeing that cluster of abandoned infantry slit trenches and bodies lying about at that first gun position back at Buron, you haven't a clue what a battalion headquarters in action should look like. You worry you may not recognize it when you get to it.

Then, one after another, a succession of other silly worries rise up to plague you, until you realize they all spring from one general concern: unless you are careful, you are going to appear stupid in the eyes of the infantry. You tell yourself that all you can do is take things one step at a time, and maybe your inexperience won't show before you have learned the score.

You concentrate on the scene around you.

Verson has been pitifully smashed. As you pass through a tangle of dusty rubble, downed power-lines, and broken walls, you wonder where 4th Brigade Headquarters is located. On all sides are roofless, doorless, windowless, half-standing buildings, smelling of charred wood and the musty dust of ancient stables – overlaid by an all-pervasive acetic odour of souring apple cider leaking from punctured barrels, mixed with whiffs of a distinctive and repulsive odour which, from your Buron experience, you readily identify as rotting human flesh.*

The road you seek leads south from Verson through fields and hedges to Eterville, bearing off to the right, dipping down and passing over a watery ditch, which, according to your map, is the Odon River. The narrow stone bridge spanning this little stream, even in its chipped and scarred state, still exudes a certain charm, and the very fact it is still standing is remarkable. Besides escaping demolition by both sides, it has continued to withstand the passage of 40-ton Churchill tanks going and coming morning and night – to say nothing of 44-ton Panthers and the monster 68-ton Royal Tigers that must have been using it until a few days ago.

---

* Before Verson became a target for German shells and bombs, it was a special target for Allied bombardment as it was the headquarters of the 12th SS Hitlerjugend (Hitler Youth) Panzer Division. And Brigadeführer Fritz Witt, who preceded Kurt Meyer as division commander, was killed here by a British naval shell, June 16.

13

BATTALION TAC HEADQUARTERS
IN NORMANDY

※

FOR A SHORT WHILE YOU GRIND ALONG THE NARROW ROAD, lined with trees rising out of a thick hedgerow along its right side, with no sign of troops or equipment of any kind. The fierce sun, which has baked the yellowing wheat fields dry and dusty throughout the whole of this cloudless day, turns blood red on the western horizon, promising another blistering day tomorrow. As it is dropping out of sight beyond the British zone on the right, and the road is about to make a 90-degree turn to the left, having come up against a dense line of trees, you motion to Saunders to swivel the carrier through an opening in the corner of the field on the right, directly into the sun's blinding rays.

Just inside the gateway, you halt the carrier to look around. On your left there are some trenches dug up against a stone wall enclosing some woods. According to the map, the wall, enclosing the heavily treed grounds of a château, marks the northwest corner of the village of Eterville.

Your map reference for Battalion Tactical Headquarters of the Royal Regiment of Canada is this corner of this field, but you see nothing here that in your judgement would be worthy of that resounding title – not that you are qualified to make such a judgement, never having visited an infantry battalion headquarters before in your life.

For a moment your attention is drawn to an opening in the stone wall, where a giant German tank, which you believe is a Panther, points its long-barrelled gun right at you. There being no sign of damage to immobilize the awesome brute, it seems ready to crawl out of there at any moment, and the menace it exudes, even as it lies there dead, gives you the creeps.

You notice Dunning has dismounted and is walking towards someone in the far end of the trenches. When he bends down to talk to him, you recognize Major Wren. Those unprepossessing trenches are battalion tac headquarters after all!

Just as you are climbing out of the carrier, a penetrating voice – high-pitched and strident, but still authoritative in its clipped and rapid delivery – comes from the bush beyond the wall:

"Turn that carrier off . . . bring down mortar fire."

You turn to Saunders and give him a switch-off-engine signal. The rumbling engine dies, but immediately the voice from the bush orders, "Get that carrier out of there . . . bring down mortar fire."

You give Saunders the wind-it-up signal. He pushes the starter and the engine whirrs into life. But while you are looking around to see where you should send the vehicle, the voice from over the wall, like a broken record, orders, "Turn that carrier off . . . bring down mortar fire!"

Saunders looks at you, turns off the engine, and throws up his hands as though to say, "What the hell am I supposed to do?" You really don't know. Obviously the owner of that strident voice is losing, or has lost, touch with reality. But still it is clearly the voice of authority as it again orders, "Get that carrier out of there . . . bring down mortar fire!"

But then another, low-pitched, voice immediately behind you says quietly, "Don't let it worry you, sir. Have your driver park the carrier with those other vehicles down there."

When you turn, a battledress sleeve carrying the royal arms of a battalion sergeant-major is pointing past your ear towards a short line up of trucks about a hundred yards away in the field on the right.

Saunders needs no urging. With obvious satisfaction he winds up the carrier and wheels it away with a rocking flourish to a place of his own choosing. Assuming it won't be long before he'll be pulling out again for an OP, he parks the carrier out of sight on the far side of the tank, even as the voice from the bush is calling, "Turn that carrier off . . . bring down mortar fire!"

As you walk towards the trench-work with the Sergeant-Major, you ask, "Who the hell is that anyway?"

"The commanding officer, sir," he replies, and stalks briskly away from you as though he doesn't want to answer your next question.*

Dunning, who's been down on one knee talking to Major Wren in the trench, stands up when you approach, and informs you that Hunter and Laurie are on their way back to guide you up to your respective OPs.

At this point Wren advises, "You'd better go and find some cover while you're waiting. It can get pretty hot around here – their MO was killed today by a mortar bomb – direct hit on their First Aid Post."

As the meaning of his words "You'd better go and find some cover" sinks in, an unfamiliar wave of nausea surges through you.

Incredulous, Dunning says, "You mean we can't wait down in there with you?"

Fidgeting in some embarrassment, the Major explains, "They wouldn't like it – we're restricted to myself and one signaller. Actually, it can get pretty cramped in here when it's busy . . ."

You feel rage rising out of self-pity, but the conversation is cut off by the deadly swish of an incoming mortar bomb. You dive for the space between the German tank and the stone wall. As you hit the ground beside Dunning, you find you are actually in a shallow trench that someone started but gave up on after hitting a flinty, tightly packed mess of cinders and rock only about six inches

---

* Two days later, July 15, the commanding officer of the Royals was taken back to "B" Echelon, and never resumed command.

down. The way the conglomerate has been scratched and the soft parts torn away, it's as though someone had tried to scrape a hole with only a pocketknife and his bare hands.

The mortaring continues for several minutes. The German weapon is close enough that you can hear the hollow *plunk* each time it sends a missile swishing in over the trees, seemingly from just on the other side of the woods. And they must have this spot well taped, for the bombs are flashing very close, sending hot concussion waves through this narrow alleyway between the tank and the wall.*

Knowing that half your body is above ground is very unpleasant. While the wall behind you offers some protection, the latticework of tank tracks and bogey wheels right beside your head is not as reassuring, and during the bombardment all you can think is: It will all be over if one lands in here between the tank and the wall.

There's a brief lull, then the mortaring begins again. Another lull, and then once more the crashing explosions. Each time, you force your body down as flat as it will go, the rim of your helmet digging into the dirt and your nose touching the same little jagged crevice. You try to concentrate on that crevice, speculating on who scratched it. Whoever it was, you have complete empathy with the poor bugger. You can see him desperately scratching away in his vain attempt to get below grade. Did he manage to survive? Was he one of our boys, or was he a survivor from this tank?

But after a while you only have the wits to wonder one thing: Are you going to live through this? And when the horrendous crashing ceases and you become conscious of a bluebottle buzzing

---

* The very next day, July 14, the Royals discovered a German officer and a signaller hidden in a dugout just to the rear of the battalion area, only a hundred yards from the Verson–Eterville road. They were equipped with a wireless set netted in to their artillery – a "stay-behind party" purposely left there when the Germans retreated before the original British attack that took Eterville.

around you in the stillness of the gathering dusk, the sound is truly wonderful, for it means you are still alive.

During a lull, as the last light fades from the western sky, Hunter arrives back. He squeezes in beside you and Dunning, into what little space remains between the tank and the wall, just in time for another bombardment. When the flashing explosions finally cease, he declares this place is not fit for man or beast – and since Laurie probably won't get back until morning, now that it has grown dark, we should find a better hole for the night.

He reasons there are bound to be trenches dug near that line of vehicles down there in the field, and suggests, "The next time the mortaring stops, let's high-tail it down there and find one."

To you, this makes a lot of sense. You are more than ready to get out of here, for you are beginning to "get the wind up." With the deepening gloom, the flashing of the bombs as they land – lighting up everything for a fraction of a second, including the flinty rocks in front of your nose – seems to magnify their deadly menace and bring their hot breath even closer. So when the mortaring next ends and Hunter yells, "Okay, let's go," you and Dunning scramble to your feet.

Then just as you start running for the distant trucks, you hear a voice from the darkness on the right, sounding like the Royals' sergeant-major, shouting, "Wait! Don't go down there! They've orders to shoot without warning anything moving above ground after dark."

But by the time the significance of his words sinks in, you are completely committed to your desperate dash, pounding full-out after Hunter for those trucks now barely discernible in the dark, and the invisible slit trenches, which you must locate before the next basin of mortar bombs starts crashing down. When only a few yards from the first truck in the lineup, you think you spot a shadowy figure. Instantly there's the unmistakable *click-clack* of a .303 rifle bolt being cocked, as a sharp voice demands, "Halt! Who goes there?"

In that split second, you realize you've no idea what the password is for tonight. And Hunter apparently doesn't know either, for without replying he swerves sharply to the right to put the first big truck between him and the man with the rifle.

And you and Dunning pursue him at full gallop, round the rear of the truck and down the line, now more desperate than ever to find a hole, and wondering what you're going to do if you can't find one.

Suddenly Hunter seems to go down on his hands and knees, and, what is worse, he doesn't try to get up. But when you catch up to him, you see he hasn't fallen, but is standing in a slit trench. With tremendous relief, you jump in too, and a moment later Dunning comes tumbling in between you.

Each of you is desperately out of breath after that fearsome run, but when you hear the stealthy feet of the guards coming this way, you are forced to jam down in a mass of knees and elbows, while suppressing the need to heave and gasp for air, until they've passed out of earshot.

Obviously you have stirred up a hornet's nest among the guards, and confirmed their worst suspicions by running away from their challenge. Fortunately, they didn't follow precisely the drill of shooting anything moving above ground after dark and paused to challenge you – most probably because darkness had just fallen, and they weren't expecting any attempted enemy infiltration for some time. But from now until dawn, you know you are thoroughly and completely trapped in this hole, for these guards, and those who relieve them, will go on believing there are Germans hiding some-where in and around these trucks, and will be alert to every little sound and ready to fire at the slightest sign of movement.

As your breathing returns to normal, Dunning, in a whisper, questions the merits of "the stupid order" to shoot anything that moves after dark.

But Hunter, also whispering, explains that the Royals were warned by the British troops they relieved up here that Jerry patrols make a habit of infiltrating our lines after dark and raising hell in the rear. If our troops were allowed to move freely around above ground, there'd be no way of telling friend from foe in the dark. But this way you can assume that anything above ground is the enemy, and let him have it.

After this, conversation ceases. And soon the pleasure of finding this sanctuary begins to dissipate as you ponder your predicament: the three of you are jammed into a trench that's barely big enough for one. How on earth are you going to endure this the rest of the night?

That you managed to land in such a manner as to allow this bunty, five-foot slit to accommodate (albeit most uncomfortably) each of your six-foot frames, with all heads below ground, is quite incredible. But here you are: Hunter, with his back tight against the far end; you, with your back pressed against this end; and Dunning, squeezed down in the middle facing you – all jammed together in such a way that no man's bottom is in contact with the bottom of the trench, and each man's weight largely, but not entirely, suspended by pressure between a wide variety of parts of the anatomy.

For the most part you find these pressures are bearable, amounting to nothing worse than Dunning's knees jammed into your stomach. But the squatting position, reminiscent of a baseball catcher behind the plate, balancing on the balls of the feet, with bent-back toes eternally forcing your feet upwards towards your shins, induces an increasingly painful paralysis that becomes almost unbearable as the hours go by. And time passes with agonizing slowness. At one point, Dunning can't stand it any more. Declaring he must stretch to get the cramps out of his legs, even if it means getting shot in the process, he stands up, but as he moves he loosens some pebbles and the noise brings the two-man patrol to life. By the sound of their clicking rifle bolts and the clarity of their whispering, they're just on the other side of the nearest truck – no more than twenty or thirty feet away.

"Did you hear that?"

Click-clack.

"Yeh, something just over there!"

Click-clack.

From their agitated tone, you can tell they are very nervous, and their trigger fingers are bound to be equally nervous. So by the time their crunching boots have rounded the truck, Bill is down again, his knees back in your stomach. But in the brief time he was standing up, your position must have shifted slightly, for now you are pressed back against the end of the trench even harder than before, as he squeezes down to get as low as possible while the guards creep by and disappear in the gloom along the line of trucks.

The hours crawl by. Though three men squat together in bizarre intimacy, with their heads no more than eighteen inches apart, throughout an entire night, hours pass without one word being spoken. It's as though the repelling closeness you are forced to bear has made you desperate to place some barrier between you, even if it is no more than the coolness expressed by a refusal to converse.

You try to sleep, but it's next to impossible; you are too uncomfortable for more than fitful catnaps. And whenever you do doze off, it seems that that is the precise moment Jerry chooses to send over one of his heaviest baskets of mortar bombs. Fortunately the hours of darkness are mercifully few at this time of year in Normandy. (From last light about 10:30 P.M. British double-day-light saving time, to first light about 3:45 A.M.)

In the first vague light of dawn, you spot an empty trench not more than twenty feet away. Regardless of the risk, you have to get to it. You stand up as quietly as possible and wait for something approaching normal sensation to return to your tingling legs. Then, when you think your legs are operative, you scramble up and over and down into the empty trench, emulating a giant crab, but faster than any rabbit could have done it.

The trench is cold and clammy from the predawn mists, but it's incredibly roomy – and wonder of wonders, there's a blanket in the bottom. You roll up in it and in seconds are asleep. Almost immediately you are wakened by something sharp jabbing you in the back, and a faraway voice calling, "Stand to! Wake up! Stand to!"

As you squirm away from that painful jabbing and sit up, you realize it's a bayonet on the end of a rifle. But before you can gather your wits and put the blast on this outrageous tormentor, he's gone on to the next trench.

This is the last straw. And by the sounds emanating from the neighbouring trench, they think so too. Gord Hunter has obviously had all he can take. As he rises and starts climbing out of the hole, he roars, "To hell with this!" Spotting you, he calls, "Come on, we'll go back and see if Wren can rustle us up a cuppa tea – I could use one." He strides past you rather unsteadily, on legs that are probably more than half asleep, followed by Bill Dunning on equally rubbery legs. The thought of a nice strong, hot cup of tea makes you drool, and you scramble out to follow them. But then remembering why you were trapped in that hole all night, you call to him, "Wait – those trigger-happy buggers will all be standing to, waiting for us."

Without breaking stride, Hunter wheels left towards the hedgerow separating the field from the sunken road that runs from Verson to Eterville: "We'll go down the road then." And ploughing through a sparse section of the hedgerow, and stumbling down into the sunken road, he goes marching off up the dusty track at 145 paces to the minute, with you and Bill having to really push it to keep up.

Suddenly you feel wonderfully free in the refreshing, cool morning air. And as you reach the gateway at the corner and turn back into the field, you are delighted to see Stu Laurie has come back. He's kneeling down on the rim of the trench near Major Wren, whose head is barely visible above the low mounds of earth marking the trenches of tac headquarters. With everything strangely quiet – no mortars humming in and crashing about, no crazy, disembodied voices calling from the bushes over the stone wall – you get a chance to examine these holes in some detail.

U-shaped, the two trenches have been dug side by side, close against the stone wall. An earthen rectangular pillar, left in the middle of each excavation, serves as a table for map boards, telephones, radio sets, and clipboards loaded with paper. Each trench is just deep enough that, with the excavated dirt mounded up around the perimeter, a man can stand upright to study maps or talk on the phone with his head below grade. But they are entirely open to the sky and whatever nature or the enemy may choose to drop on them.

Whatever you imagined a battalion headquarters would look like, these crude, cramped, open pits surely aren't it. However, beauty is in the eye of the beholder, and with only Major Wren in one of the trenches at the moment, it appears quite spacious – outrageously spacious to Dunning, it seems. As he stands beside you, looking down at the Battery Commander talking to Stu, he nods his head at the trench and in a hoarse whisper, loud enough to be heard ten yards away, croaks, "Plenty of damned room in there for all of us last night if we'd been invited!"

Feeling equally mean – your legs still throbbing rheumatically – you venomously add in even less subdued tones, "Ah, but we were NOT invited, my friend, subalterns and captains being expendable, you see."

If the Major hears these pointed remarks, he's too weary to care, for he shows no reaction. Stu breaks off whatever he's been telling him and stands up. Smiling at you faintly by way of greeting, he abruptly turns away, and beckoning you to follow, makes for the gateway. Leading you out to where the road up from Verson makes its turn to the left, he points northeast up the track now clearly visible in the predawn glow and gives you the most extraordinarily explicit directions on how to get to A Company.

14

THE ORCHARD IN ETERVILLE

*

"IT'S VERY SIMPLE. JUST GO DOWN THAT LANE THERE UNTIL you come to a knocked-out 17-pounder with some dead soldiers lying around it. It's right beside a gate at the corner of a field full of dead cows. Turn in there and go diagonally across the field to the opposite corner, where you'll see three dead horses. There's a gate there, and as you leave the field bear to the right. Right there is the orchard where you'll find A Company. When you get there, report to the company commander, just so he knows you are there. His name is Major Whitley. Now I don't think there's any point in my going back up there to show you the way, do you? There's simply no way you could possibly make a mistake."

This is a bit of a disappointment. You'd counted heavily on him introducing you to the OP. All through the night, whenever you began to be a little concerned about occupying your first front-line position, you had been reassured by the thought that Stu would be leading you up and settling you in before leaving you on your own. But what he says seems so very sensible, and the pleading look in his eyes is so eloquent, you readily agree to make it on your own.

As your carrier creeps slowly down the narrow lane, dappled with the first dazzling rays of the rising sun filtering through the trees, you feel a surge of confidence after that miserable night. But it is short-lived. At the top of the lane, you come across the depressing sight of the battered anti-tank gun and the sad bodies in battledress sprawled around it.

Turning into the field, you thread your way through an entire herd of cows, all dead. Two legs on each cow point stiffly to the sky, held up by swelling bellies so grotesquely distended they must surely soon burst. In the shady far corner of the field, where horses would naturally be attracted to stand beneath a spreading tree in the heat of the day, stomping their hoofs and flicking away droning flies with their swishing tails, three poor beasts lie decaying, the flies now crawling unmolested over their bloody lacerations.

One of the horses lies directly in the laneway leading out of the field, and while it's obvious that other vehicles have had to pass over its mutilated head before this, still your empty stomach turns queasy when Saunders rolls a track over it following your hand signals to turn sharply around the corner and into the rear of the orchard.

There you halt the carrier to look around, expecting to see some soldiers in slit trenches. But you find only an empty, desolate orchard. It is positively eerie. There is not one living soul to be seen anywhere, and the whole orchard can be surveyed easily, for no foliage has been left on the trees – in fact, most of them are little more than blasted, limbless trunks. You're certain you haven't made a mistake, but check your map just to be sure. What on earth could have happened to them?

Mortar bombs start landing over on the left, among a fringe of trees at the rear of the yellow wheat fields that sweep forward along the flank of the position and across the front, dotted with black, burned-out Churchills and Shermans. You should get settled in somewhere fast.

As you hop out of the carrier and start walking up through the orchard, you wonder about the piles of branches lying here and there among the trees. It's as though the trees have just been pruned, and when you stop to examine one of the piles, you find the branches are freshly cut. Somebody has collected them quite recently.

Suddenly a chill runs down your spine as you realize you are staring directly into a pair of eyes watching you from a hole underneath the pile of branches you've been examining. Pulling yourself together – for immediately the meaning of the neatly collected piles becomes clear – you ask the owner of the eyes where to find A Company Headquarters. You reasonably expect that a head and shoulders will appear from the hole. But not even a helmeted head appears, only a hand, barely above ground level, with the index finger pointing in the direction of a grassy mound farther forward that looks like an old-fashioned root cellar. A muffled voice advises you, "Over there, in the German bunker."

Walking quickly towards the bunker, you glance around at the other little piles of branches to see if you can spot any stirrings under them induced by your presence. But the terrible menace that has turned these men into moles is stronger than curiosity, and though a whole company of infantry is dug in throughout this orchard somewhere, there is no sign of life.

Of all you've seen and experienced since coming up to the infantry, this is by far the most unnerving. And by the time you've found the entrance to the bunker (which, having been built by the Germans, faces south, away from the Allied guns and shells), you are ready to become a mole yourself.

Standing at the top of a shallow, earthen stairwell, shored up with well-weathered timbers that look as if they've been there a very long time, you call down, "Major Whitley!"

A scarecrow of a soldier appears in the opening at the foot of the stairs, and glaring up at you, growls, "Yes?"

"Major Whitley?" you inquire tentatively, hardly believing it is possible, for there is nothing about his dress to suggest he's an officer.

"Yes. Who are you?"

"I'm your new arty rep, taking over for Captain Laurie."

"Well, don't stand up there – unless you want to get your head blown off," he snarls. "You can talk just as well down here."

As you descend the stairs, you're not sure you like this guy. He's got a British accent, and you don't know yet if it's affected or real. (You can't stand Canadian officers who affect a phoney accent they believe sounds like an officer in the Guards.) But when at the foot of the stairs he reaches out and shakes your hand with a firm and honest grip, and smiles broadly at you, you're willing to give him the benefit of the doubt.

"Tom Whitley. Welcome aboard. Have to keep your head down up here if you want to stay alive ... constant shelling and mortaring, almost continuous, since we arrived ... and before that, I guess ... must have been, for when we took over from the Glasgow Highlanders up here, they were so stunned, our boys had to lead some of the poor buggers out of their holes by the hand ..."

For a moment he studies you from head to toe as though inspecting your dress, and then inquires, "Hear any bees buzzing around you up there just now?"

You admit you had heard some buzzing.

"Well," he chuckles, moving closer to you, "those aren't bees; those are bullets! Their snipers are trying to pick off our officers."

And with that he reaches over, grasps the left epaulette of your battledress blouse firmly with his right hand, and rips it out by the roots, almost pulling you off your feet.

"Got to get rid of everything that identifies you as an officer," he explains as he grabs your right epaulette and rips that out too.

As he hands you a bouquet of epaulettes, he flips your tie. "Get rid of that ... discard your web belt and holster ... put your compass in your pocket ... shove your pistol in your rear pocket ... and wear your binocs buttoned in the front of your battledress when you're not using them."

All of this is proclaimed in such an imperious way, with such total conviction (more in the manner of orders than advice), that you don't argue. In fact, you actually find yourself thanking him profusely, even as you ponder the frightening significance of his extreme agitation and outlandish appearance.

"You can't see anything to shoot at up here," he says. "Nature of the ground – falls away out of sight only a few hundred yards in front. Laurie holed up in a big shell hole – over there near the front of the position. I suggest you do the same. Just sit tight and keep your head down – we'll call you if we need you." Thus dismissed, you turn to go, but Jerry delays your departure. You flop down in the stairwell while shells crash in the orchard above, one at a time, a few seconds between each horrendous explosion and the scream of the next one coming in, as though he is using only one gun.

This bombardment – your first experience with the seemingly endless stream of shells and mortars of all calibres that will pour into this desolate acreage hour after hour, with only brief respites, during the next twenty-four hours – is awful. It gives you some idea what these poor guys have been going through up here. The tension that builds as the methodical shelling continues, on and on, relentlessly, is appalling. You've no way of knowing the calibre of the shells, but they're big ones, for the ground beneath your prone body shudders from their impact.

You visualize those poor guys out there in the orchard, crouching under their pitiful covers of brush, every man knowing that a direct hit means being blown to pieces. (This one coming in right now could be the one.) And they've been confined to those holes under this harrowing torture for more than two days now, in the hellish suspense of never knowing if this is their last moment on earth.

When the shelling finally ceases, the orchard reeks with the smell of cataclasmic violence that lingers along the ground after prolonged eruptions of high explosive. And as you make your way back to the carrier, which the crew has parked deep in the trees at the rear of the orchard, there are voices calling "Stretcher!" from over on the right, near the front of the position.

You proceed with all haste to get settled underground in the monster shell hole that Whitley referred to. Elder comes with you, carrying the remote control box and reeling out the control cable from the big No. 19 radio set in the carrier back in the orchard.

Easily located because of its size, the hole lies among the trenches of a forward platoon dug-in behind a low stone wall. Beyond the wall is a highway marking the extreme front edge of the Eterville salient, at the southeast corner of the village.

Of course, from the hole you can see nothing. But while Major Whitley may be correct that you can see nothing from *any* point up here, you have to check it out. Leaving Elder to wire up the remote control and test it, you go forward to peer over the wall, being careful to keep your head down, even crawling on hands and knees the last few feet, so as not to draw any more attention to this position than it's already receiving from Jerry.

Remembering Whitley's warning about snipers looking for officers, and binoculars being a dead giveaway, before you raise your head to look over the wall you remove from around your neck the personal camouflage netting that you've been using as a neckerchief, and drape it over your helmet, letting it fall over your face and shoulders.

This versatile little piece of lace curtain – a neckerchief in summer and a scarf in winter – dyed in random splotches of dusty, faded green and brown, not only disguises the recognizable silhouette of a soldier's head, but hides your white face and the tell-tale reflections of the sun off the lenses of your binoculars, while allowing you to see through them perfectly.

Not that you have much to use them on. Over the wall and across the road, tall yellow wheat covers the fields to the horizon, which is only three or four hundred yards distant because of the way the ground falls away and disappears down towards the Orne river about a mile farther on. Almost directly south, about the same distance, out of sight in a basin, is the village of Maltot. And on the left front, also hidden from view, about one and a half miles away, is the village of Louvigny.

Forward on the left front sit three blackened Churchill tanks, partially hidden by the tall wheat. Judging from the direction their guns are pointing, all three were headed for Maltot and were well-dispersed as they moved to the brow of the hill. But the long-barrelled 75-mm gun of a Panther or the 88-mm of a Tiger hidden among the trees of the orchards of Maltot had potted them just the same – long before they could close up to the effective range of their guns.

And over on the left, alongside the trees and just in the wheat field in front of the trees, are several Shermans. The ones with blackened hulls are obviously derelict, but those close to the trees could still be in service, judging by the way they are parked to take advantage of the shade, some with wilting, but recently cut, foliage covering gun and turret. And you recall that this morning just after dawn you heard tank tracks squeaking and squealing over this way.

For a few minutes you search the wheat to see if you can spot anything moving in it. It's certainly thick enough and tall enough to allow a patrol to sneak in close to your position without being seen, but it lies still and innocent in the glaring sun, now high in the sky. And as the minutes pass and it becomes increasingly hot and stuffy under your little camouflage netting, you finally bow to Whitley's judgement that nothing can be seen up here, and accept his advice to get in a hole, keep your head down, and wait for him to call.

By 6:00 A.M. you and Elder are ensconced in your shell hole, and are actively working on the problem of how to maintain the semblance of a sitting position on the slithering gravel walls of this funnel-like pit. Interest in this fades quickly, however, when the extreme vulnerability of the remote control cable becomes obvious on the very first bombardment after it is hooked up and functioning.

Elder, a tall, slender youth of even temperament – well-spoken, remarkably polite and considerate – is only nineteen, but before this day is out he will seem much older. And in the emotional sense, he in fact will have matured significantly. Just to pass the time crouching in the bottom of a hole, hour after hour, in these circumstances is quite bad enough – as the pitiful calls every now and then for a stretcher bear testimony – but Elder's job frequently requires him to move around above ground between enemy bombardments to repair the cable, which repeatedly is damaged by shell and mortar fragments.

It's a nerve-wracking business, for every time Elder scrambles out of the hole and goes dashing back through the broken trees with the cable running through his fingers to find where the shell or mortar fragment has cut it, he doesn't know how long he's got to splice it together and get back below ground before Jerry unloads his next lot.

It could be three minutes, five minutes, or even ten minutes. But then again it could be as little as one minute!

Sometimes, after locating the break, a lot of time is wasted locating the other end of the cable, which may have been blown some distance away. This happens to you on the only excursion Elder permits you to make on his behalf, when, after two particularly exhausting sorties in rapid succession, a third bombardment immediately cuts the line again.

And often the line is cut in several places and repairs take so long that he can't return in time and has to dive for whatever shelter is handy back in the orchard.

The first time he fails to return, the vicious, flashing blasts that rock the orchard seem to be worse and persist longer than usual. And you have visions of him having been caught running for shelter and getting shredded by the grass-cutting mortar bombs making up this lot. When it is over, you have to prepare yourself mentally before you can go out looking for him. But just as you are about to climb out of your hole, he comes crashing in unharmed.

The hole is big enough to accommodate both you and Elder sitting opposite each other on its slippery, gravel sides, both with your heads well below ground level. Normally the remote control box rests at the bottom between your feet, except when you hear Elder thumping this way on his returning gallop. At such times, you grab it up and tuck your feet up as high as you can, out of the way of those hobnailed boots on the end of those long, thrashing legs, as he jumps and slithers down in a cascade of gravel into an exhausted heap at the bottom, heaving and gasping for breath.

With little to talk about under such conditions, when survival is paramount and all normal subjects seem irrelevant and inconsequential, his description of what happened out there on his last scramble becomes a subject of great interest. Once, he shelters in the carrier with the signaller whose job it is to maintain the big radio set (which must operate twenty-four hours a day) and make sure the batteries are kept charged by the generator driven by a one-lung Chore Horse engine bolted to the rear of the vehicle. On another occasion when he runs out of time he dives under the carrier – a very close fit, he tells you.

Around noon, he returns with the news that he found Saunders in an abandoned trench right at the rear of the orchard. Not that Saunders was lost, but not having seen him since just after dawn, it is nice to know he is still all right.

And once when Elder's return is delayed until another lull in the firing, *you* have a story for *him*. While waiting for him to get back, your unease about occupying this giant shell hole, which until now has been firmly suppressed, bursts forth into your consciousness with almost painful clarity: This damned hole is just a big funnel, and with all this stuff falling around here, eventually something is bound to land in it.

This line of thinking is probably triggered by your wondering what kind of shell can have blown a hole this size. Was it a shell from one of the 16-inch guns of the battleship *Rodney*, standing off the coast and firing in here during the first of the British attacks?

Or was it excavated by a 300-pound missile from one of the 21-cm guns the Germans are reputed to have in Normandy?

While its spaciousness is very pleasant when the bombs are not dropping – its ample mouth providing a welcome target for a frantic signaller outrunning the whisper of a mortar bomb – its very size will inevitably be its ruin. Of this you are absolutely sure. And suddenly, you become conscious of a long, deep slit trench only a foot away from the lip of your shell hole. You noticed it was vacant when you first came here, but forgot about it, assuming the owner would be back. But now, as you think about it, you can't recall having seen anyone near it the whole time you've been here.

You decide to move in without delay. You place your eyeglasses, compass, and chinagraph pencil on the ledge of earth between the shell hole and the trench, and drop your map board over into it. Then, picking up the remote control box, you struggle up the slippery side of the hole and jump down into your new nest.

You are still bent over, settling the box into the far end of the trench, as far out of the way as possible from where Elder's feet are likely to land, when you hear it coming. It's only a faint, split-second, crackling whisper, but you know the sound of a shell dead-on for line and range. You jam down into the bottom of the trench just as it lands with a terrible crash in the shell hole, blowing blackened chips and brown flakes of stone and dirt all over your back and around your ears.

You turn and peer over the ledge, now swept clean of compass, eyeglasses, and pencil, down into the hole where you sheltered, from an hour after dawn until now. All footmarks and scars have been erased from its walls, leaving them so smooth they look as though they've been trowelled. And right in the precise, geometric centre of the cone at the bottom, a little wisp of blue-black smoke still curls upwards.

More shells follow – many of them, Elder tells you later – but you are oblivious to them, caught up in wonderment at the miracle of your deliverance. A delay of even one or two seconds in deciding whether to move and you would have been blown to eternity. And why the sudden compelling urge to remove yourself from a hole in which you'd been sheltering for many hours? When you are telling Elder about it, and mention the oddity of there having been only one shell, and he is correcting you, telling you there were the usual number in the bombardment, his manner is peculiarly gentle, as though he understands your bewilderment and shares your profound sense of awe. And this, surely, is natural enough, for he must know that had he returned on schedule he might have postponed the move, and then you would have died at the same instant together.

15

"ARE THOSE OURS?"

✳

UNDOUBTEDLY THE BATTERY COMMANDERS AND TROOP COMMAN-
ders were thoroughly briefed before they and the infantry moved in
here to take over from the British units.* But you, having received
no information on the tactical situation on your way up, can only
guess what has been going on up here from the shattered debris and
the stench of decaying flesh. Dozens of animals and more than fifty
German and British unburied bodies lie scattered about the immediate area. According to the map, the road just beyond the low stone
wall that marks the front of the position is a principal thoroughfare
leading from Evrecy, hidden away about eight kilometres on the
right, to Caen over on the left, some four kilometres northeast of
here, passing through the tiny hamlet of Le Mesnil on the way.

If that road wasn't dominated by German fire and you could
drive up the gently rising ground on your right about three kilometres, you would have the best view in any direction of the

---

* At the very least they would have been aware of the attempts by the
Germans to wipe out this bridgehead over the Odon, for even as the
Royals were being briefed on the morning of July 11 for their takeover up
there that night, the SS were in Eterville engaging the Cameronians in
such ferocious close fighting that one hundred of them would die in the
lanes, the churchyard, and the orchards of the village before they retired.

countryside around here, for you'd be on the crest of a broad hill of mostly open slopes, distinguished on the map by the figure 112 printed near an oval contour line at its summit, denoting its height above sea level in metres (about 373 feet). Obviously, whoever holds the summit dominates the countryside for miles around, including the village of Maltot, reputedly harbouring a nest of Tiger tanks, just out of sight in the valley down in front. And judging from the number of burned-out hulks of Shermans, Churchills, and self-propelled M-10 guns littering the wheat fields just across the road in front and up the slope on the right, the British made heroic efforts to do just that. But their efforts had been in vain, for their FDL (forward defended line) marked on your map board with a red chinagraph pencil, is only part-way up the northern slope, well down from the summit and the 112 contour line.

But what does the enemy hope to accomplish with his extraordinary expenditure of ammunition on Eterville and vicinity?

The fact this is a salient may be explanation enough, attracting showers of high explosive to ensure it is not used as a springboard for another Allied drive for the Orne. Or it could be that the Germans are engaged in a softening-up process, the prelude to a major attack designed to wipe out the salient.*

Whatever the enemy's intentions, the constant bombardment is having an effect. You are haunted by Major Whitley's description of the Highlanders' condition when relieved by the Royals, some of

---

* Historian of 2nd British Army (quoted in Report No. 58, Historical Section (G.S.) Canadian Army Headquarters, Dept. of National Defence, p. 45) unwittingly offers an explanation for the relentless bombardment of Eterville when he explains that Maltot had been made untenable to Allied attackers because of the number of German weapons sited just over the Orne on the dominant Verrières Ridge, including "not only a large number of flak guns (88's) defending the city of Caen, but a formidable concentration of multi-barrelled mortars. . . . At all events they were able to achieve with them something dear to the heart of the staff college

them having to be led out of their trenches by the hand after only a couple of days here. And you wonder about the condition of his own men after two and a half days of cowering in holes in the orchard under those flimsy mounds of brush. You are a witness to the fact that the commanding officer of the Royals back at tac head-quarters has lost touch with reality after the same length of exposure to the bombardment. And two of the best-trained, most highly motivated, self-possessed, and disciplined troop commanders in 4th Field asked for relief after only about thirty-six hours of it.

How much more can Whitley himself endure? Certainly he is showing signs of extreme physical and nervous exhaustion – his outsized preoccupation with snipers trying to pick off officers, for instance. When he leaned over to rip off your epaulettes, his eyes bulged so far out of his head they threatened to fall out on his cheeks, and they wore a fixed and angry stare.

From Whitley's bearing, you know he is the type of man who under normal conditions would be meticulous about his appear-ance. But now, sans epaulettes, sans tie, sans well-blancoed web belt and pistol holster – unwashed, unshaven, his tousled hair spilling down beneath the headband of his steel helmet, and his web anklets riding around backwards on the top rim of his boots – he certainly would confuse any German sniper trying to locate the company commander with his telescopic sights.

But in spite of all this, he's still very much in control of himself and his company, and you find his domineering manner and his snarling advice – proffered like royal decrees – strangely reassuring.

----

student, but so difficult to carry out in practice – denying a locality to the enemy through fire power; Maltot was that locality." Now, if true of Maltot, it should have been equally true of Eterville only a kilometre away and within range of all those same guns and mortars. Thus it would seem clear that the Germans' bombardment of Eterville and vicinity by guns, mortars, and sometimes planes, for eight days or more, was an attempt to use this "fire power" to render that village untenable.

In contrast, his second-in-command, Capt. Bob Rankin, almost bubbling with energy, shows no sign of being affected in any way by his experiences up here. At least not until mid-afternoon, when returning in his Jeep from Battalion with a load of small-arms ammunition, he chooses to "tweak the nose of the devil" in a most irrational way. With a perfectly good, hidden, route up from tac headquarters available to him (the same one you'd used to get here), he elects to emerge in no-man's-land somewhere down in the west end of Eterville. Roaring up the road in front of the position in full view of the enemy, he attracts a string of mortar bombs that land one after the other just behind the tail of his vehicle as he wheels it in and disappears in the orchard behind the bunker. The straining Jeep engine and the mortar bombs have barely stopped before you hear Major Whitley calling, "Foo! Foo!"

When you report to the bunker, he tells you that on his drive back Capt. Rankin located the observation post for the German mortars and can point it out to you. This sounds pretty exciting, until he tells you that it should be treated as a "Victor Target."

As you follow Rankin to the front of the position, you begin to think: surely Whitley was joking? You most certainly hope he was! Two hundred and sixteen guns on a German OP?

At the stone wall you expect Rankin to stop, but no, he vaults over it and positions himself in the middle of the sunlit road. And when you join him, facing southwest up the road towards the rising ground of Hill 112, dotted with burned-out Churchills and Shermans, he points out one of these derelicts about a thousand metres away, halfway up the slope, directly in line with the road. You expect he's going to use it as a reference point, but he assures you with the utmost conviction that the silent blackened hulk is the enemy OP.

Not wanting to prolong this conference out here in full view of the enemy, but terribly curious, you ask how he discovered that Jerry is occupying that tank?

His tone in replying suggests you must be stupid if you have to ask. "Didn't you see those mortar bombs landing right behind my Jeep all the way down the road?" he says. "Well, where the hell else could that OP be except right out there? So there's your Victor target. Go get it."

Of course you tell him a Victor target isn't possible, explaining it would involve every gun in the Corps – nine regiments of 25-pounders, plus the mediums, and perhaps a regiment of heavies. Surely he can see few targets would ever justify that.

He's unimpressed: "When they sent us up here, they promised us we would have the full support of the Corps artillery, and that we could call for a Victor target whenever we needed one."

You agree. Unquestionably that is true, but only when needed.

"Well," says he resignedly, "what in hell *can* you fire on it?"

You should tell him the truth, that it's only a one-gun target, but you don't dare, he might develop apoplexy. You assure him there'll be plenty of shells.

"Then get on with it," says he, and whirling around, as though he has suddenly lost interest in the whole business, he hops back over the wall and goes trotting back towards the bunker, leaving you feeling very much alone, very naked and very vulnerable.

Suppressing mightily the feeling you've been conned into a farcical situation by a bomb-happy man, you establish as quickly as possible the map reference of that damned tank, which is relatively easy, it being on the side of the hill in direct line with the road that bends right just before reaching it. You call over the wall to Elder, now jammed in a very small trench with the remote control he's managed to drag over here, "Able Troop target – map reference 985638 – right ranging – fire!"

All you want is to see one round. If it lands anywhere close to that damned tank, you'll go into "fire for effect" – maybe five rounds gunfire – enough to satisfy Whitley and Rankin that you've shelled the stupid thing. While you have to wait no more than a minute or so, it seems interminable out there on the road.

Estimating the range from gun to target at about 4,200 yards, you figure the shell will take about eight seconds to come up from the gun when it does fire.*

And when at last you hear Elder calling out the message he's received from the guns, it sounds like: "Shot – four thousand." Meaning, of course, the range at which the shot was fired.

You start counting to yourself, "Hippopotamus one, hippopotamus two, hippopotamus three . . ." Before you reach seven, there's a sizzling overhead, and before you can get your glasses up, *wham*, there it is, an orange flash in the middle of a violent puff of roiling smoke very close to the tank. As you do a running vault over the wall, you call to Elder, "Five rounds gunfire – fire!"

Kneeling down just inside the wall, waiting, it feels so safe and secure, you decide there's no way you're going to go out there again. Somehow they let you get away with it once, but luck like that can't last. Anyway, there's no point in making corrections if the fire is off the target; it's only a dead pile of scrap steel.

But when you hear the guns thumping, you've got to see those shells land, and the only way is to jump back out onto the road. You go down on one knee and get the tank in your glasses just in time to see the shells bursting all around it. No correction is needed – in fact you almost imagine a couple of rounds hit it, not that that would make any difference to the empty derelict.

Satisfied, you take the wall in a running leap back into the orchard and join Elder in his cramped trench.

When, after a minute, the firing stops, you immediately give the order "Repeat!" as though the target really means something. A head pokes up from a hole nearby and asks, "Are those ours?" When you assure him they are, he yells, "Give 'em hell, Foo!" This

---

* At Charge *III*, a 25-pounder shell, leaving the muzzle at 1,460 feet (or 488 yards) per second, takes 2.05 seconds to travel 1,000 yards.

seems to arouse others, and by the time the second bombardment is completed, you have come to realize that these are the first Allied shells these guys have heard being fired on their behalf since coming up here. This is confirmed by their platoon commander, an unusually tall and thin lieutenant, who, standing up for a brief moment and waving a long arm in your direction, introduces himself as Len Gage.

Apparently there has been a total lack of close-in targets, and harassing fire tasks are so far away and impersonal that all they've heard are hundreds of enemy shells and mortars seeking them out to kill or maim them. Now, for the first time hearing their shells working for them, they call out to each other and to you in a kind of ecstasy. Until now you've heard no sound of human voices among the trenches in the orchard except periodic calls for stretchers. Suddenly there is a veritable hum of voices.

Encouraged, you decide to invest another forty shells in a morale-boosting effort: "Ten rounds gunfire – repeat!"

The effect on the men of your random shelling of that silent tank might at first be described as "being beyond all expectations." But as things develop a more accurate description might be "astonishing," followed by "incredible – beyond belief," ending up "bizarre" – even "frightening."

A goodly number of A Company, particularly members of the nearby Gage platoon, shower you with compliments – some of them even getting out of their holes to come right over to your trench and call down at you, "Nice shootin', Foo!"

Over and over, you advise them to get back in their holes, that you've done nothing but shell a dead tank and the mortaring is bound to start again any minute. But they don't pay any attention to you; it's obvious they don't want to believe you. Right from the start of the shoot, the infantrymen seemed convinced that something good must come from all those reverberating roars out there in no-man's-land, where the 25-pounder shells were landing just beyond their view. So when the shelling stops and quiet reigns over this section of the front, they aren't at all surprised. And while you and Elder, with your remote control box and cable, scurry back to your own, less cramped trench near the big shell hole, they sit up above ground chatting.

Five minutes go by, then ten, then fifteen, and still no enemy mortars or shells. Half an hour of unnatural peace passes. By now it seems most of A Company have climbed out of their holes and gathered around stoves improvised out of empty hardtack tins cut in half and filled with sand saturated with petrol (from God knows where, maybe from a spare jerrycan on the Jeep) and are boiling water like mad for tea while simultaneously heating cans of meat-and-vegetable stew in it.

While your intellect roundly condemns these reckless activities, which now and then send tell-tale wisps of black smoke eddying skyward over the stone wall, your less highly disciplined stomach begins to growl noisily in appreciation of the delicious odours drifting your way. Neither you nor Elder has had anything to eat since yesterday afternoon, except for a few of those nutritionless, sugarless, hard candies known as "Boiled Sweets." He volunteers to go back to the carrier and see what he can rustle up. He's barely out of sight when Lieut. Gage carries over a mess tin loaded with steaming stew.

When you protest that you mustn't eat their food, explaining your signaller has just gone back to the carrier to get you something, he assumes you are lying and firmly insists you eat it, stating most emphatically, "You've bloody-well earned it!"

This is terribly embarrassing, and you tell him so. All you did was drop a few shells around a stupid, burned-out tank simply to humour a bomb-happy captain with too vivid an imagination, who chose as his *bête noire* one derelict tank out of all those derelicts lying about in the field and up the slope out there. It's all utterly ridiculous. Surely he can see that. And it's very dangerous for his troops to be wandering around above ground, so would he please get them back in their holes before Jerry starts shelling again.

Hunkering his tall frame down beside your trench so he can look you directly in the eye, Gage speaks with deep conviction: "Look, my friend, all I know is that from the time we came up here around midnight three days ago we've been shelled and mortared almost steadily. And whenever they left us alone for a few minutes, they shelled the troops next door. Now, ever since you worked them over out there, it's been quiet. And see those guys eating over there? They're having their first hot meal in three days. Now if your shelling didn't do this, what the hell did? You explain it."

Well, of course, you have no explanation. But you know there has to be one, and that it hasn't anything to do with you. It's as though you're sitting in the eye of a hurricane, waiting for the fury of the storm to resume.

Later you realize that if you'd carried that analogy of the lull before the storm to its logical conclusion, you might have come up with an explanation for the break in the shelling and mortaring: Jerry was preparing to attack.

16

THE GUNS

❋

IT COMES IN JUST AS THE SUN IS GOING DOWN, BEGINNING with a flurry of mortars, 88-mm airbursts, and a hail of machine-gun tracers lacing the orchard. The tracers are coming from the right front, but from some distance away, judging from the faintness of their staccato *bur-rup, bur-rup*s, barely distinguishable among the hammering Brens and mortar explosions over on the right. And it's clear the tracers, streaking mostly through the upper remnants of the trees, are originating from a point much lower than the orchard, probably from that skinny copse some 400 yards south of here, just east of the road you earlier studied while waiting for your rounds to land – a good forming-up point, providing a concealed route almost right up to the village.

On your map you find a DF (defensive fire) target marked precisely where you want to bring down fire. But when you pick up the remote microphone to call the guns, it's dead – the line again cut by a piece of mortar or shell. Scrambling out of your hole, you run crouched over as fast as you can back to the carrier and huddle down tight against its steel flank, just outside where Kirby is sheltering. Kirby's ears are covered with big, puffy earphones, and you have to tap him on the shoulder. When he uncovers his left ear, you give him the DF target number and the order "Fire!" for transmittal to the guns. In an incredibly short time of less than a minute, shells are rustling overhead, and a great furore of overlapping, roaring explosions starts rolling up from the area of the copse. But even as you relish the response of the guns, it dawns on you with a sickening shock that in the heat of the moment you forgot that only a brigadier and up is allowed to fire a DF target.*

God! What will they do to you? Something severe, unquestionably. Under present conditions, with so much at stake, they'll be ruthless. But surely they wouldn't go so far as to cashier an officer for this, would they? You force yourself to stop thinking about it. Later, you'll have time to worry – for now, there are more pressing matters.

You notice Kirby has an odd look on his face, and is shaking his head in bewilderment. Removing his earphones, he tells you there's a strange voice on the net calling for the guns to stop firing and hands you the earphones, with dangling mike attached, so you can listen.

Putting them on, you hear, "Hold your fire, we don't need it." Depressing the pressel switch on the mike, you demand, "Identify yourself. Who are you?" But the voice ignores your request, and keeps repeating: "Stop the artillery, we don't need your fire. Stop your fire, we don't need it," until all the required shells have been fired. Again and again you try to get him to say who he is, but he refuses to acknowledge you, either during the shoot or after. And

---

* DF targets are pre-selected "defensive fire" areas that seem most vulnerable to attack. All the technical work at the guns is done in advance, so that predicted fire (not needing correction by observation) will be forthcoming with maximum speed and accuracy. Scale and rate of fire on a DF task is three minutes "intense" for field regiments (five rounds per gun per minute, or 360 rounds per regiment), and three minutes "rapid" for medium and heavy regiments.

To prevent the enemy drawing fire by feints and thus learning the artillery defensive fire plan, only a brigadier or higher rank is allowed to fire a DF target.

you and Kirby are convinced he is a Jerry trying to disrupt the defensive fire.

The machine-gun fire doesn't die immediately, but by the time you have repeated the DF target a second time (having decided it can't get you into any more trouble than you're already in), nothing of any consequence is coming into the orchard. It's then that you sense someone is behind you. Turning around, you're amazed to find Stu Laurie there. He asks you where you've been dropping all that stuff, and you confess rather sheepishly that you were firing a DF task.

"Good gawd!" says he, "Which one?"

When you show him, he snorts, "That's not a DF task – that's an SOS task. It was a DF task, but they changed it."

Is he really sure?

"Of course!"

That would account for the speed of response by the guns to your call for fire. The guns always remain laid on the SOS target, considered the most likely route of an attack, when they are not otherwise engaged. The gun crews only have to load and fire when the SOS is called for, and it can be fired by a FOO. The relief that floods through you is so tremendous, you could hug Stu. Combined with the satisfaction at knowing your guns have just squelched an enemy attack of some consequence (no more tracers skitter through the trees, and the popping and chattering of small-arms fire down in the village seem to have stopped) and the realization you are now free to go back to the guns, where you'll be able to stretch out for a few hours' sleep, your happiness borders on elation.

But this dissipates quickly when you discover that the vehicle that brought up Stu and his crew a few minutes ago, and which was supposed to have taken you and your crew back to the guns, has, in all the noise and confusion, turned around and pulled out while you and Stu were talking. It being a HUP (a soft-skinned, van-like vehicle of glass and sheet metal), you can readily understand the reluctance of the driver (Gunner Weston) to hang around waiting with all that stuff flying around the orchard. At least your crew got on board before it pulled out.

But now you are faced with the choice of walking back or staying here another night. With darkness falling, there really is no choice. To try walking back in the dark would be inviting disaster from those trigger-happy Royals at tac headquarters. The sounds of those clicking rifle bolts still ring in your head. Was that really only last night?

Your disappointment at missing the chance to get back to the guns is leavened by the reassuring knowledge that Stu is now responsible for whatever Whitley and company may require during the night. You can crawl in a hole and sleep the whole night through.

And as you realize you're free of responsibility, you are at once conscious of outrageous, staggering fatigue. After last night, even half a slit trench will be luxury, and there is always the big shell hole. But as you start to explain to Stu how you've acquired a really nice big slit trench, preferable, you think, to the big shell hole he had been using, he tells you that at night Whitley invites him to share the far end of the company headquarters bunker, and he thinks there's room enough in there for you, too. This sounds wonderful. Enclosed, with a thick earthen roof overhead, it will be not only safe, but obviously warmer than an open trench, which, you have learned since coming to Normandy, can become very cold and clammy by early morning, regardless of how hot it has been during the day.

However, at the bunker, Stu leads you to a second entrance that you weren't aware of, facing southeast in the direction of Louvigny. It's not much more than a crawl space, about four or five feet high and four feet wide, obviously designed as an emergency escape route – a shallow, inclined tunnel apparently leading into the main part of the dugout. And the main dugout must be well-filled at the moment, for Stu, who settles in first, can only get far enough in to allow you to sit across the entrance, your back against one side and your feet against the other.

While your whole right side is exposed to the night air, and whatever the fates may choose to fling about here, the relaxing effect of extreme fatigue, combined with the psychological benefits of having a thick roof over your head and an old comrade beside you, overcomes any doubts you may have of your position. Even having to slap at the odd pesky mosquito suggests a modicum of normalcy, and you're surrendering to the sweetest of sleeps when Jerry starts lobbing over something of very large calibre – much heavier than anything he threw in here during the day.

They don't whine or wail like big shells, but sound more like giant mortar bombs. You only can guess that it's one of their larger-calibre Nebelwerfers firing their rocket-propelled mortar bombs (without their usual banshee-wailing devices), one bomb at a time instead of in six-bomb salvoes, thus extending their supply of heavier bombs.*

You can hear each one coming from a long way off, growing louder and louder – sounding remarkably like a bus humming towards you at high speed on a highway while you stand at the side of the road. But just as the sound suggests it's going by, it lands with a wicked flash and a horrendous roar that makes the ground shudder and sifts sand from the bunker ceiling. And now and then one lands so close, you feel a stunning compression rather than an

---

* At this time in Normandy all three brigades of 272 Nebelwerfers (known to the troops as "Moaning Minnies") were deployed opposite the Canadians and British south of Caen. These fearful multi-barrelled (six to ten barrels) rocket mortars came in three calibres:

	Projectiles	Range in Yards
150 mm	75 pounds	7,300
210 mm	248 pounds	8,600
300 mm	277 pounds	5,000

explosion. Some concussion waves are so strong, they actually lift you and shift you a little farther into the tunnel.

Despite this, you think you could sleep soundly if it weren't for the heels of Stu's boots scrunching and kicking you in the ribs. You're so tired nothing really matters any more, but he, cursed with alertness, having had several hours' sleep back at Carpiquet, is nervous as a cat. You can't see him in the blackness of the dugout except when it's lit momentarily by a flash of high explosive in the orchard outside, but he seems to be pointed head first into the tunnel, crouching on his hands and knees. And when one of those big "express buses" starts humming this way, his feet start "digging" involuntarily – ever more vigorously as the sound grows louder – the soles of his boots grinding and banging your left hip and lower ribcage until the humming ends with a stupendous explosion.

Fortunately, his "digging" lasts only a few seconds, but no sooner has an explosion brought an end to it, than another "bus" can be heard humming this way. Then, after some ten or fifteen of them, they cease for a while. During the lull, Stu silently digs you in the ribs with an elbow to get your attention, then pokes you urgently in the chest with what turns out to be a water-bottle full of Drambuie mixed with whisky. Gratefully you take a slug, then nudge him to take it back, as you listen to Tom Whitley's voice calling into the dark orchard, and hear distant voices, barely audible, replying.

"Number One Platoon?"

"Okay."

"Number Two Platoon?"

"Okay."

"Number Three Platoon?"

No answer.

"Number Three Platoon?"

"Stretcher!"

After that you doze off until the "buses" start coming again and Stu starts digging and booting you awake. And when the bombardment ends, there's an elbow in the ribs and the same wordless ritual with the breathtaking water-bottle, while outside in the dark stillness, the Major's voice can again be heard checking out his platoons. Once more there's a plaintive call of "Stretcher!" announcing another wounded man. And this goes on throughout the night, causing you to ponder the selfless courage of the stretcher-bearers, carrying wounded men back through the menacing shadows to the MO at the battalion aid post.*

Stretcher-bearers might be described as ordinary soldiers equipped with a limited supply of bandages, sulpha, and morphine, and a minimum of training in first aid. However, ordinary men they are not. They are men of extraordinary, outsized courage, not only providing succour to the wounded, but by their very presence providing vital reassurance to all who must remain here through the night, and who may, at any moment, have need of their services. And beyond all this, by their hour-to-hour exhibition of courageous service to their comrades, they are unwittingly setting a standard of conduct for their company and their battalion which few will match, and none is likely to surpass.

In a hazy half-awake, half-asleep condition, you pass the nightmarish hours, until finally it is daylight and Jerry moves his attention to the flanks and the rear areas for a while.

Well fortified by the frequent passing of the communion waterbottle throughout the night, you decide to make your way back on foot to tac headquarters, calling up a vehicle from the guns to meet you there.

Later you'll be told that Tiger tanks accompanied last night's attack and remained sitting on the flanks until well after dawn. But you neither see nor hear anything of them as you walk back through the first rays of the rising sun, past the fly-covered, mutilated dead

---

* On December 18, 1944, Pte. J. A. Smith was decorated with the Military Medal for his outstanding work at Eterville as a stretcher-bearer.

horses, through the field of dead cows, and down the shady lane past the bodies in battledress and German grey, their upturned faces turning black from the blistering heat of the past few days.

At first it is a pleasant change to be free of the confinement of that bunker tunnel. But soon you wish you'd waited for a vehicle, for the odours hanging in the air of rotting flesh of animals and men, freshly desecrated by last night's shelling, are intolerable.*

On arrival at Royals' tac headquarters, you discover your crew never made it beyond here last night. They arrived at about the same time as the German attackers were infiltrating through the village, and the Royals' sergeant-major drafted them to help defend the headquarters. Issued rifles and assigned holes close to the vehicles, they spent the night trying to spot and shoot Jerries out of trees on the perimeter of the field, where they'd placed themselves to shoot into the Royals' trenches.

On your way back to the guns with Weston in the HUP, which now sports a round bullet hole in the windshield directly in front of the passenger seat, you try sorting what you learned on your first tour of duty in an OP.

Even as you fight off nauseating waves of exhaustion from

---

*   Even after thirty years, Madame Restoux grimaced and wagged her head from side to side as she recalled for the author the day she and her family returned to their devastated farm at the southeast corner of Eterville on the road to Caen:

There were many, many dead Germans and Tommies lying around . . . and the 450 apple trees in our orchard were just so many sticks. Our first job was to bury our dead horses and thirty-five dead cows in the field behind the orchard. The smell was terrible. The bombardment must have been frightful . . . the ground through the orchard was covered with jagged pieces of metal, and when the metal collectors came with baskets, they collected a wagonload of copper and brass fuzes.

having been denied sleep for forty-eight hours, an overpowering sense of well-being surges through you – a mixture of relief, thankfulness, and pride that you came through it without coming apart at the seams. You now know that responding to the demands of the moment can mercifully keep a man from dwelling on survival. Sustained by a deep sense of belonging to a group and responsible for its collective safety – at least to the extent of holding your end up and conducting yourself in such a manner as not to bring danger to your comrades and disgrace to yourself – a man is encouraged to assume an aggressive spirit and posture. And while no sane man can escape suffering the agony of fear, you know that under certain conditions a terribly frightened man, quite illogically, will throw caution to the winds and give in to a burning desire to wreak vengeance on the enemy.

In a static position with no enemy in sight, however, survival is everything. You've survived to see the sun go down – but will you see it rise in the morning? You've survived to see the dawn – will you survive the day? Darkness has come again – will you survive the night? And so on. Is it possible it was only the day before yesterday you came up to the Royals, that fewer than forty-eight hours have passed while you were in that godforsaken acreage of Eterville? Is not some new scale required for measuring the passage of time when you are visiting hell; when every minute is concerned with survival and you spend your time counting the number of seconds between the sound of the distant thump of a smoking tube and the arrival of its roaring missile; when your reactions must be in split seconds if you are not to die, and your greatest pleasure comes from hearing the buzzing of a fly and knowing you're still alive after the last lot? Are sixty seconds of this the same as a minute back in Canada?

17

IGNORANCE WITHOUT BLISS

———————————— ✳ ————————————

WHEN YOU FIRST GO INTO ACTION, UNTIL BLESSED FATIGUE
dulls and stupefies them, your hyperalert senses dominate you. But,
though you live with an intense awareness of every sight, sound,
and smell, and every raw sensation that can be triggered in the body
and soul of a man, your physical horizons are extremely limited.
This is particularly true for members of OP crews up in the front
line, where it is vital to remain hidden from the enemy as you peer
out from a narrow hole in a wall, or from a trench with your eye
barely above ground-level. And your intelligence horizons, in the
military sense, are so limited as to be almost non-existent most of
the time.

Sometimes, back at the guns, when it's not too hectic, you can
pick up the BBC on a little walkie-talkie 38-set that operates on the
regular broadcast band. And, for what it's worth, there is each
morning a broadcast especially designed for the armed forces that
consists of bulletins covering this and other theatres of operations,
read a phrase at a time, with pauses, so they can be taken down and
relayed to the troops. Using what information these broad-brushed
generalities may reveal, and putting two and two together, it's
sometimes possible to make yourself believe you know what's
going on.

However, up in the front line – where you are forced to live in a hole day in and day out – regardless of rank, you're out of touch with everything and everybody except, perhaps, the occupants of those slit trenches right next to you. Having little or no access to official intelligence reports on the enemy, and not entrusted with even the slightest knowledge of Allied strategic plans and objectives beyond what is obvious even to the enemy, you have no way of knowing how the grand plan is unfolding and what they have in mind for you. And, of course, no one ever knows what the enemy is planning.

Thus, in addition to the overpowering sense of sinister menace lying over the front, all soldiers in a battle zone must learn to live in a dense fog of mystery.

Now and then the curtain can lift briefly on the broad picture, allowing you to experience a striking sense of relevance as you spot your own outfit and the units you're currently supporting, not buried among thousands of extras, but centre stage among the principal players. Such a moment arrives late in the afternoon of July 15, when, shortly after returning to the guns from Eterville, you are shown a copy of the first intelligence summary issued by RCA Headquarters at 2nd Division.

It's as if it had been researched especially to answer those particular questions you'd come to dwell on during the last weary hours before dawn this morning: Are they thick on the ground out there? Are they SS fanatics or regular Wehrmacht? Is it possible the chilling rumour about the Tiger tanks is correct and there actually is a herd of those reputedly invincible monsters at Maltot, just out of sight over the crest, down there in the valley in front of your Eterville orchard?

14 July 44

SECRET

RCA 2Cdn Inf Div Intelligence Summary #1

Part 1

On the division front, the main force continues to be 1 SS Panzer (Adolf Hitler) Division, whose fwd elements (1st Panzer Grenadiers) are disposed southeast of line Eterville–Le Mesnil. This regiment (the equivalent of a Canadian brigade in numbers) appears to be supported by the 102nd Heavy Tank Battalion (general headquarters troops) which is thought to have 25 Tigers; and the Werfer Lehr Regiment – 15-Centimetre Rocket Projectors (Moaning Minnies), strength unknown.

Their divisional artillery is thought to be concentrated in reserve about Fontenay-le-Marmion. 12 SS Panzer Division (Hitler youth division), that held this area before arrival of 1 SS, seems definitely to have withdrawn its broken remnants.

In front of the British 43rd Division (on 2nd Canadian Div's right flank just west of Eterville) responsibility for that sector appears to have been taken . . . by the 9th and 10th SS Panzer Divisions . . .

But to you, the appropriateness of the next paragraph is positively uncanny, providing a direct answer to questions that haunted you last night, as to why the Germans are maintaining their incessant bombardment of the Eterville salient, and whether that was just a fighting patrol in force last evening, or what it seemed to be, a serious attack that might have overrun Eterville if your deluge of shells had not descended on them so promptly because of the pre-arranged SOS target?

LE BON REPOS is held in considerable strength, as is MALTOT, and the orchard east of it. And the enemy is reported to be attempting to regain Pt. 112 (the hill just 2,000 metres west of ETERVILLE). In the same way the enemy is well dug-in in the orchard at 0166 (LOUVIGNY) and is attempting to regain ETERVILLE.

Anchored in FAUBERG DE VAUCELLES (a suburb of Caen) he appears determined to keep us away from the west bank of the Orne for as long as possible.

After digesting all this and more, and after studying the Counter Battery Intelligence Summary for the twenty-four-hour period ending at 6:00 P.M. last night – which identified by map reference on the Canadian front no fewer than sixty-three hostile batteries of 88-mm guns, 150-mm howitzers, and Nebelwerfers (Moaning Minnies) – you feel that you really have been put in the picture. But when evening comes, you realize nothing has changed at all; you're still completely ignorant of what is going on at every point on the compass, even only a few hundred yards away in the British zone, where it appears something big is underway.*

---

* Ignorance of what other neighbouring formations were going through from day to day in any battle zone was not restricted to those of lowly rank. Sir Brian Horrocks, Commander of British XXX Corps, in the introduction to his book *Corps Commander*, wrote: "Looking back I realize now that I was so involved with XXX Corps battles that I literally knew nothing about the operations of the Canadians, Poles and certain other British corps which fought from time to time on our left flank. My only contact with them came during the first phase of the Battle of the Reichswald, when I was under Canadian Command." Sir Brian Horrocks and Eversley Belfield, *Corps Commander* (Toronto: Griffin House), p. xv.

Just after dark, a massive artillery barrage opens up from over on the right and to the rear, involving hundreds of guns. And for some time, the sky over the dark crests in the west and north is lit with jagged flashes running back and forth across the whole horizon, much like summer heat-lightning. And the illusion of lightning is enhanced by the heavy, muffled thunder of big guns, beyond the thumping and cracking of medium and field guns just over the hill to the west.*

And even when the guns complete their firing, back along the crest in the northwest, strange lights continue wavering, reminiscent of car lights in peacetime slashing through fog as the vehicle comes over the crest of a hill. These lights are of course much broader and stronger, producing an eerie, misty scene around you as they light up the clouds of low-lying smoke drifting in from the now silent gun positions in the west. The smoke mixes with clouds of dust swirling up from the nearby sunken road, thoroughly congested with silent, marching men, tanks with deep engines and squeaking tracks, carriers dragging anti-tank guns, and armoured half-tracks and lorries moving up past the guns.

What the attack is meant to accomplish you don't even try to guess, but you're glad 4th Field Regiment guns aren't involved, for the attack has attracted German counter-battery fire on the British gun lines, and with some effect it appears.

Several fires begin to glow on the horizon – one not far away on the right, where it seems some kind of ammo dump, or a lorry loaded with ammunition, has been hit. Whatever it is, it puts on quite a show, glowing colourfully for a moment, then flaring up like fireworks, cracking and popping with spectacular vari-coloured, Roman-candle effects – rising up, falling off, and rising up again – accompanied by sporadic, heavier explosions that scatter hissing,

---

* Four hundred guns were involved, including those of battleships in the Channel.

flubbering chunks of ragged metal far and wide over the gun positions, that sound viciously lethal and persuade all 4th Field onlookers to seek shelter below ground.

In the morning you learn the strange lights on the horizon were diffused beams of British searchlights, purposely tipped horizontally to reflect off low-lying clouds and so light the battlefield – the first time this has ever been tried in war. The wavering effect was caused by the clouds of dust and smoke, mixing with ground mists. Officially known as "Movement Light," it already has acquired the more expressive nicknames "Artificial Moonlight" and "Monty's Moonlight."

In daylight there's a lot more two-way traffic past the guns, which includes a long parade of the big van-like ambulances, marked with large red crosses, hurrying up towards some forward casualty clearing point, disregarding your sign, SLOW! DUST MEANS DEATH, and raising a great cloud of it. Of course this attracts the usual number of German shells, which routinely fall short of the road onto 4th Field gun positions. On their way back, the ambulances move more slowly, but you suspect it's not due to concern about dust, but rather an attempt to be as gentle as possible with the bundles of pain wrapped in blankets within.

Answers to inquiries of the marching troops going by suggest the attack was successful, but from the amount of firing still going on in the southwest, it is obvious the outcome is still in doubt. The sound and fury of it all is impressive, but it seems strangely irrelevant.*

The war diary of 4th Field will report that July 16 is largely

---

* Such is the density of the blanket of security spread over operations that it will be long after the event before you learn there is any connection between the forthcoming operations involving 2nd Canadian Corps and this two-corps British attack (the third attempt to expand the Odon bridgehead with slight gains at terrible cost, reminiscent of the ghastly struggles for insignificant territorial gains in the First War). Attempts by

taken up engaging hostile batteries and counter-mortar tasks, along with "observed shoots, mainly Mike targets." And mention will be made of an air-raid tonight on the area just ahead of the guns lit up as bright as day by chandelier flares drifting on little parachutes, before the bombs start to drop: "At 2255 hours enemy aircraft were over bombing and strafing. Heavy at Verson – very little on actual positions."

Nothing is said in the diary of the build-up of ammunition for an upcoming big push, though this evening the Regiment received seven hundred rounds at each gun, which must be dug in before the regular nightly visit from Jerry planes.

Troop Sgt.-Maj. Mann, bringing up the rations, narrowly escapes serious wounding or death when a shell lands beside his Jeep and a shell fragment scratches his back and another dents his helmet.

XII Corps to seize Evrecy and the struggle by XXX Corps to secure the Noyers area are timed to draw German strength away from zones east of the Orne, adjacent to Caen and south of the city, where British and Canadians are to go forth on joint operations "Goodwood" and "Atlantic" on July 18, the heaviest strike against the perimeter of the bridgehead to date.

18

WHAT A SILLY PLACE TO
PARK A TANK

❄

WHEN THE FATE OF BRITAIN AND THE COMMONWEALTH, AND
thus of the whole world, was truly uncertain after the fall of
France, when, for months on end, disaster followed disaster in rapid
succession on land and sea in Europe, North Africa, and throughout the Far East, all the pacific preaching of the 1920s and 30s that
war was an idiot's delight faded from social consciousness in the
face of the desperate urgency to fight and win or accept enslave-
ment or death in concentration camps. So it comes as a bit of a
shock this evening of July 16 when old doctrinaire thoughts are
drawn from the recesses of the subconscious simply by the sight of
one of our tanks doing lonely vigil in a railway cutting nearby.

Just as the sun is setting, you venture forth on a solitary walk
away from the gun position (the only time you have taken such a
risk since coming here) to try to locate a barrel of cold apple
cider, the existence of which you became aware this morning
during a bizarre encounter with an itinerant Don R (or despatch
rider). You had been squatting over a latrine hole dug in the ditch
beside the road, when this passing Don R spotted you and did a
most spectacular roll off his motorbike down into the ditch beside
you. When he discovered you weren't bent over in the ditch
sheltering from enemy mortaring, but were rather "doing your

business," as he quaintly put it, he shrugged his shoulders philo-
sophically, brushed himself off, and grinning good-naturedly
confessed that this was the second time this morning he'd made
the same mistake.

He explained that with the noise of the motorbike, along with
the muffling effect of his crash helmet and the rush of air past its ear
holes, it was impossible to hear the sound of approaching mortar
bombs. So he had been carefully noting reactions of men along the
road, and when they dived for cover, he rolled off the bike.

Before taking leave of you, he removed a water-bottle from one
of his saddlebags and insisted you try its contents. Thus you were
introduced to Norman cider. Instantly an unquenchable love affair
with that musty, acetic drink was born. Here was a wonderful substitute for that wretched, chlorinated, tepid substance currently
being passed off as water – and you vowed never to pass up the
chance to fill up as many water-bottles as possible whenever in the
future you came across an unpunctured barrel of this marvellous
beverage.

And now this evening, with all the shelling and mortaring this
area has been experiencing, you know you are being foolish departing any distance from the gun position and its sheltering trenches.
But from the moment you were given a swig of that delicious, cool,
musty nectar by that kindly Don R, and he'd told you he got it out
of a barrel "just up the road," you had been unable to suppress the
dream of locating the source, drinking your fill, and bringing back
a clutch of water-bottles full for the Command Post gang.

And you do find it, at the back of a little brick building at the
railway crossing only a few hundred yards south along the narrow,
dusty, sunken road leading to Verson from Carpiquet.

It's when you are turning to go back to the guns, having drunk
all you could and filled all your water-bottles, that you spot the
Sherman, sitting right on the tracks a short distance east of a crossing, with its gun pointing towards Caen, and the thought flashes

to mind: What a silly place to park a tank. What if a train were to come along?

Instantly, of course, you remember where you are. There will be no train. All sane enterprise by normal people has been abandoned in these regions before the juggernaut of war. The thought lingers as you walk back to the guns: the whole world has abandoned its normal functioning to permit thousands of men to smash each other into submission or death in these fields of sugar beets and wheat. Most of the industrial might of Europe, North America, and Asia, for years now, has been dedicated to designing and producing the means by which masses of men can rage against each other in juvenile, cowboys-and-Indians fashion, right here in these fields, to decide who will run the world.

For the very first time since you donned a uniform, you realize that this is all you are now good for, having studied, trained, and practised for it for years.

And you're in good company. The best brains in government and industry have been engrossed for years in designing the most effective weapons and the most efficient methods of making and delivering them. The concentrated might of the Allied nations has been entirely focused on exploiting the most advanced technology and encouraging dedicated men and women in the teeming millions to work exhausting shifts, all for the purpose of equipping the men in this sugar beet field to overcome similarly equipped Germans in the wheat fields down the road.

Will it be believable to future generations that waging war was once the prime purpose of the world, when the needs of battle took precedence over everything else?

It's all so horribly simple-minded. You can feel, as much as you can see, that you are on the extreme cutting edge, the very culminating point of all this concentrated effort and astronomical expenditures of money. But far from being exhilarated by the idea, you are repelled that at this advanced period of history, wholesome, mature, cultivated people – including some of the best-informed and most talented people – should still be required to live like brutes, fight like brutes, and die like brutes in order to stamp out brutishness and restore civilized order to the world.

19

LIFE IN A TANK

———————— ✳ ————————

TANKS OF THE DESERT RATS (7TH BRITISH ARMOURED DIVISION)
use the wheat fields across the sunken road from the gun position
as an overnight parking lot, or "laager" as they say. Each morning
before first light, they move up the road towards Verson to defensive
positions with the British infantry holding the northern slope of
Hill 112 just to the right of Eterville. Exactly where they are able to
hide so many tanks up there is a mystery. But having tried without
much success, when you were up at Eterville, to spot the tanks of
the Fort Garry Horse (10th Armoured Regiment) that crawl up
each morning from wherever they laager to positions in the trees to
the left of the village, you realize it is possible.

And each evening at last light, the Desert Rats tanks come rumbling, squealing, and clinking back down the road again to curl
around in a circle in the wheat field for the night. To the gunners,
this seems a strange way to run a war – much like closing up shop
for the night and going home. What about the poor infantry? They
can't just "put up the shutters" and go to bed when it grows dark.
Aren't they being left vulnerable to a night attack by enemy tanks?
Still, until this evening no one has had the opportunity, let alone
the temerity, to question the tactics of this famous veteran division,
the pride of Monty's 8th Army, which outmanoeuvred and out-
fought Rommel's panzers in North Africa.

Just as the sun is going down, the *snip-snip* of bullets passing through the gun positions from the field across the road becomes more frequent than usual. Seemingly providing positive evidence of a sniper, long suspected of being hidden over there in one of those patches of grain still standing, uncrushed by the nightly invasions of tank tracks, it is decided he should be winkled out once and for all. Though an organized walk into the sunset in extended-line by most of the 2nd Battery gunners, carrying small arms at the ready, doesn't turn up a sniper, it does provide the gunners with a chance to chat with the tankmen, who arrive back at their laager just as the sniper-search is being abandoned in the gathering dusk. And from the British veterans they gain new perspectives, not only of tanks and the brave men who man them, but of themselves.

Tanks, being almost blind in the dark, are not only useless offensively at night, but are vulnerable to attacks by infantry carrying the hand-held anti-tank weapon known as the Panzerfaust, the German counterpart to the British Piat and the American Bazooka.

They also learn that maintenance of tanks is more easily carried out after dark behind the front, since it involves refuelling and delivery of fresh ammunition from soft-skinned lorries. And the crews of tanks, jammed into the confined space of their "bake ovens" for hours on end, are in even more need of "maintenance" than their vehicles.

Gunners, cowering in open slit trenches under bombardments of shells and mortars, might envy the tank men the protection of their mobile steel fortresses, but apparently just existing in a tank for up to sixteen hours at a stretch is such a trying experience that men must be given relief from it as often as possible. While tank commanders attempt to position their steel cocoons under trees or in the shade of buildings, few positions are that perfect, and in these days of air temperatures rising above 90 degrees Fahrenheit (32°C), and endless glaring sun, the metal by noon is too hot to touch. With five sweating men confined within the crowded space of a tank – three in the turret and two below – the hot, humid air can become foul.

Toilet facilities are non-existent, and expended cartridge cases have to serve as chamber pots, passed around among the crew and emptied out the hatch over the side. And through every minute of the day, that same confined space is filled with the perpetual, mostly unintelligible gabble of multiple, overlapping voices of signallers, with every kind of accent, spilling out of the earphones hanging around the neck of the tank commander.

But of all the information the gunners pick up, the most revealing and interesting is not about the tanks and the men in them, but their assessment of the intensity of the fighting here in Normandy. According to these veterans of North Africa and Italy, this is by far the worst they have ever encountered, and they have never seen artillery gun lines shelled like they have been here. Their actual words, which will be quoted and requoted throughout the Regiment, are: "We've never seen anything as bad as this before. The artillery isn't supposed to have to take it like this. The guns are never placed forward in full view of the enemy like they are here."

Their confirmation that this is a crazy, unusual position for guns, and the revelation that what they've been going through here is "the worst," far from having a demoralizing effect actually causes everyone's spirit to rise in a burst of pride. If what you've all been going through is "the worst," then you haven't been doing too badly under the circumstances.

20

THE HEAT IS AWFUL –
BUT GOD BLESS THE CZECHS

———————————— ✳ ————————————

DESPITE THE FACT THAT DAY AFTER CLOUDLESS DAY, TEM-
peratures stay in the high eighties Fahrenheit – around thirty
degrees Celsius – (as measured by an ammunition thermometer
stuck in a shaded recess between bags of cordite propellant in one of
the brass 25-pounder cartridges at Number One Gun), rising to
God-knows-what levels in the sun, soldiers in Normandy wear
woollen uniforms.

And even though for most there's no escape from the broiling
sun from sunrise to sunset, except in the dead, sultry air trapped in a
covered hole in the ground, Canadian and British soldiers wear
long underwear – not the thin, cotton Balbriggans with short
sleeves purveyed in more civilized times, but scratchy, thick
woollen longjohns, with legs extending to the ankles and sleeves to
the wrists.

The battledress, a British invention, clearly designed to combat
their own cool, damp weather, retain maximum body heat when
worn, according to regulations, tightly buttoned at the neck and
wrists, shirred and belted in at the waist, and gathered, folded, and
buttoned under anklets at boot-top level. And it is a telling
comment on British weather and temperatures that, during all the
years of training in Britain, no distinction was ever made between
summer and winter in the matter of uniform. Battledress was worn

throughout the moderate summers with little discomfort, and when combined with long underwear in winter, it was a source of great comfort to the wearer, as much when in residence in partially heated, draughty Nissen huts and clammy, unheated quarters of requisitioned houses, as when out on schemes in bone-chilling rain and fog on the South Downs or Welsh Hills.

Even here in Normandy, after the sun goes down and the chill of night descends, those confined to open trenches are grateful for all that wool surrounding them, which never seems excessive in the swirling mists that usually form around 3:00 A.M. But each day, with the sun beating down on uncovered slit trenches and gun pits, those on duty swelter, even after removing battledress blouses. While those off duty, trying to sleep under the blazing sun in open, sandy holes below grade – cut off from whatever little breeze may be stirring, bathed in sweat and itching – toss and turn and scratch and each day lose a little more of their vitality.

You have not experienced heat like this since leaving Canada, and you'd almost forgotten what a heat wave was like. But now memories are aroused of other hot days, when people alleviated their discomfort with cold drinks and light meals of salads and fruit. And your personal fantasy is the image and sound of cold water pouring freely and endlessly out of a tap.

The reality, however, is Compo rations, which, like the battle-dress, were designed for cold weather: meat-and-vegetable stew, steak-and-kidney pie (with its thick, soggy dough), sultana pudding and treacle pudding, all of them having to be served piping-hot to be at all palatable.

And in place of cold drinks, you have the choice of hot, sweet Compo tea, or warm, heavily chlorinated water from your water-bottle.

Oddly, no one as yet suffers from heat prostration, perhaps because they are issuing salt tablets, to be taken daily to replace the salt lost through perspiration. And it could be said the excessive heat today is responsible for actually saving a man from death.

As Gunner M. A. Killingbeck comes off the radio set in the armoured car this morning, and Kirby, his replacement, climbs up out of their slit trench – which they dug together and use alternately – on the far side of the vehicle, the sun is high in the sky and it's clear that this is going to be another scorcher. One look at that sun-drenched hole, and Killingbeck decides he can't face another day trying to sleep in a bed of sweat under the blazing sun. Enemy shelling be damned, he'll take his chances under the armoured car in the shade, reasoning that while he's above grade he'll be partially screened from shell fragments and grass-cutting mortars by the car's tires and a pile of small haversacks (stuffed with items for daily maintenance, razor, towel, handkerchiefs, socks, etc.), stored by members of the command post under the rim of the car where they are readily accessible.

However, Killingbeck doesn't tell anybody that he has changed his abode. So when Jerry starts shelling the Regiment (choosing to start off the morning by plastering Able Troop) and drops one directly into Killingbeck's trench with a terrible crash, everybody huddling in the troop command post dugout, only six feet away on the other side of the car, is certain he has bought it.

But even before the shelling stops, to everyone's relief he tumbles down into the command post, unhurt and profoundly grateful that the blazing sun had prompted him to not lie down in that trench just moments before the shell arrived. The full extent of his luck is revealed only after the shelling ceases, however, and an inspection carried out. Not only is his trench torn apart, but all the kit behind which he lay under the vehicle is riddled. Splinters ripped all four tires on the armoured car (GA), and there are holes in almost everything around and under the vehicle, including the jerrycan used for carrying bulk water for washing, tea, and all other purposes. Cans of Compo rations, clothing, small packs, and a tarpaulin are full of holes.

And in your small pack there is evidence of the lethal wickedness of the tiniest fragment of high-explosive shell. At first you think it somehow escaped damage, but when you open it, you find your socks have been turned into balls of tightly wound woollen yarn. And unwinding one of the balls, you find a tiny, ragged shell splinter inside no larger than a pea. Then you notice the end of your razor is dented and a bit of the chrome burred away, as though the tiny pea, deflected by the razor, became a buzzsaw within your pack, cutting, unravelling, and rolling up the yarn of your socks – in almost an instantaneous operation.

While everyone is still marvelling at Killingbeck's escape, he discovers, just under the front of the vehicle, inches from where his head lay, a clean, deep hole where a sizeable dud shell buried itself.

This dud and Killingbeck's fortuitous, life-saving move from his trench join a rising number of miraculous-escape-from-death stories involving members of the Regiment – most of them attributable to the high proportion of dud shells landing on the gun positions.

Over the past couple of days, on making the rounds of the gun crews, you've been shown several neat round holes in the earth in gun pits and at the end of slit trenches, drilled by 88-mm shells that failed to explode only inches from the occupants.

Despite Killingbeck's adventure, the record for the closest brush with death from a dud in this Carpiquet valley position is still being claimed by Easy Troop for Gunner C. J. Hillis, who on July 15 had the soles of his feet burned by a dud shell as it bored a hole in the side of the trench in which he was sleeping.

To excavate a dud 88-mm for examination is a major operation, since their extremely high muzzle velocity (2,400 feet per second, as compared to 1,485 for a 25-pounder at Charge III) imbeds them several feet down in the soft earth. One hole, drilled no more than six inches from the sleeping head of Gunner James Beatty, in the end of the slit trench he'd excavated in the side of a gun pit, is so deep that even when measured with a pole nine feet long the bottom can't be reached.

A couple of shells have been dug out and examined, however, and both had markings on them to show they were manufactured in Czechoslovakia. And for this reason, there is throughout 4th Field (as undoubtedly there must be in 5th and 6th Field over on the left, who've been receiving their share of duds) a truly warm feeling towards those unsung Czech heroes who are risking death from their Nazi masters each time they sabotage a fuze on a high-explosive shell to save the life of an Allied soldier. If only they could know the gratitude for their efforts, which without a shadow of a doubt have saved dozens of gunners from death or disablement in just the three regiments here in this valley.

Sgt. W. Elliott accurately voices the feeling abroad in this shell-torn valley, when, as he is showing you still another fresh hole punched by a dud near where he was sheltering, he declares earnestly, "God bless the Czechs!"

To which Sgt. Nick Ostapyck, Lieut. Ted Adams, and you must add a fervent "amen" this evening. You'd gone over to visit Ostapyck and Adams after spotting them during a lull in proceedings, standing out in front of their 14th Battery guns, staring and pointing in the direction of that distant mushroom water-tower across the Orne in enemy territory – so prominent and sinister and suspected by all of harbouring a Jerry artillery observer. You are lined up side by side, with Ostapyck in the middle, staring down across the valley, speculating on "who the hell was the idiot responsible for a whole division of guns being placed in this natural amphitheatre facing the enemy," when there is an earth-quaking thud on the very ground on which you all are standing, followed immediately by the horrible *ee-ee-ow* screech of an incoming 88-mm shell.

When you look down, there, between the toes of Ostapyck's boots, is a fresh round hole in the earth where still another impotent shell has buried itself. Once again, because a Czechoslovakian man or woman has sabotaged a fuze, in place of three mangled bodies lying on the ground, three men walk away unharmed. Ah yes, God bless the Czechs!

21

THREE–MAN SHIFTS AROUND
THE CLOCK

※

AS EARLY AS THE THIRD DAY HERE, THE REGIMENT BEGAN TO adopt a mode of living to suit the situation, and to make noticeable amendments to drills and practices that were preferred, if not obligatory, during the long years under the critical eyes of IGs (Instructors In Gunnery) in England.

So far, most of the firing required of the guns is designed either to harass the enemy or to cool down his guns and mortars, which continue to plaster infantry positions up ahead and each gun position back here.

Hostile batteries frequently attract the attention of the Flying OP, who zooms in low over the gun positions in his little plane to undertake a shoot using the Regiment. And he promotes a good deal of satisfaction among all ranks when his target is "active enemy mortars" and he is able to report "shoot effective."

The nature of the targets and the type of response required are such that they allow gun crews to be split into two shifts of three men each – one shift working under the gun sergeant and the other under his bombardier. Of course for any fire plan or heavy firing program *all* members of the crew will be awake and on the gun.

Similar arrangements are in vogue in all command posts: the gun position officer, one ack, and a signaller on one shift; and the troop

leader (GPO's second-in-command), another ack, and another signaller on a second shift. Thus the guns are serviced around the
clock.

Camouflage nets, invariably erected on their poles over the guns
during all training exercises in England (not to do so might well
have earned a bowler hat* for the subaltern in charge), have been
taken down and will not be used again because of their proclivity to
catch fire in the dry atmosphere during periods of sustained firing.

No one would now think of sleeping above ground, and roofs of
earth as thick as possible (at least two feet thick) have been added to
all command posts, with the use of corrugated iron sheets scav-
enged from the ragged Carpiquet hangars by thoughtful ammunition numbers in the wagon lines back on the aerodrome.

Men spend almost all their time below ground. And when
anyone has to move above ground, he makes sure he's never very far
away from a hole. Most men have dug their personal trenches
somewhere close to their place of duty, and holes dot the ground
around troop and battery command posts. Gun crews have dug
theirs into the rim of their gun pit or down in a corner of it.

Each day existing slit trenches are dug deeper, and there's a
favourite saying that "anyone digging deeper than nine feet will be
considered a deserter." (Some appear to be headed there.) And new
trenches appear daily as changing tastes in design and different
theories on the direction in which they should be running to
provide maximum protection to the occupant, are put into practice. (A trench running east–west presents a narrower target to
shells coming from the south, doesn't it?) Some have dug so many
holes it's almost as if they were doing penance or presenting alms to
the god of war in appeasement.

Morale is exceptionally good and a spirit of comradeship exists
that would be difficult to surpass – though the men's vitality is

---

* Symbol of civilian life to which the officer, discharged as unsuitable
officer material, would return.

ebbing, partly because of the scorching heat and partly because everyone has difficulty sleeping in holes that bounce and are filled with dust every time the guns fire. And though you do your best to ignore it, you are always tense under enemy observation, always conscious that the next one coming this way may have your name on it.

Everyone goes about his business with an ear cocked for the first faint hum of an enemy shell or mortar. And there are clenched fists and curses when now and then, without warning, the little Air OP plane coasts in with its engine shut down, the rustle of air aroused by its wings sounding for all the world like a mortar bomb looping in, sending everyone diving headlong into holes.

One Bofors 40-mm anti-aircraft gun has been assigned to each troop in the Regiment and henceforth will travel with you. While the Allies are supposed to have complete air superiority over the bridgehead, apart from that big RAF bombing raid preceding the taking of Caen, enemy planes have been more in evidence. On two different days large flights of enemy fighters have swept up the valley before zooming over the escarpment, where lies Carpiquet aerodrome, and disappearing. The first flock of ME 109s on July 12 strafed everything in sight, but with little effect as far you could discern. Again, two days later, fifteen of them roared full-throttle up the valley, weaving back and forth, but not firing at anything – they were either on reconnaissance or headed for the coast to attack ships unloading on the beaches. On neither occasion were any Allied fighters visible, but the considerable number of Bofors throughout the valley, sounding like men shingling a hollow roof – *bunka, bunka, bunka* – spewed streams of tracers at them. They shot down at least two, adding further to the growing prestige of the light anti-aircraft gunners.

Daytime efforts of the ack-ack gunners have been impressive, but at night their guns are now silent. The NCO in charge of your attached Bofors explains they are under strict orders not to fire, since they might hit "night fighters" – radar-equipped Beaufighters up on standing patrol, being directed onto the enemy bombers by mobile radar stations scanning the dark heavens from the ground. While he, like you, has never heard the rattle of Beaufighter guns up there any night, his superiors have assured him they'll knock down every Jerry plane "on their way home." (He can't explain why they don't knock them down on their way here.) And so when, each night around 11:00 P.M., the enemy bombers, a few at a time, come droning overhead and go about their business of bombing nearby targets in maddeningly leisurely fashion, the men on the Bofors grind their teeth in frustration.

On the night of the 14th, enemy planes dropped no fewer than ten chandelier flares over the gun positions, lighting up every trench and gun pit as bright as day, causing a period of great anxiety as everybody braced themselves for the worst. But no bombs were dropped. The next night, around 11:00 P.M., they came back, dropped their flares, and bombed Verson just up ahead of your guns. But nothing landed on the gun positions. Then again just before 11:00 P.M. on the 16th, Jerry bombers hummed in very low over the guns as everyone held their breath. But they dropped their flares and most of their bombs on Verson, only a few smaller anti-personnel bombs landing out ahead of the guns.

Tonight just before 11:00 P.M., following the now normal drill, everyone settles down in holes with the thickest roofs of earth to await the sound of the approaching enemy planes. As always at this hour the whole bridgehead seems to be quiet and waiting. Minutes pass slowly as almost half an hour goes by, and it seems that tonight they aren't coming. Then at about 11:30 a faint drone can be heard in the distance, growing louder and louder until the sound of the air whistling past their wings, like a low wind, can be heard distinctly as they pass unseen at low altitude over the guns.

Immediately several poppings are heard, and glaring white flares float directly over the Regiment, lighting up gun pits and command posts with breathtaking brightness. This is it. On other nights, the flares floated just to the right or to the left of the position. But tonight they hang with ominous intimacy directly overhead. Totally unmolested, the droning planes circle around. They take their time. One feels them turning, getting into just the right position to attack.

Then, with motors humming in a fast dive, a plane comes in, and roars away, a shrill whistle growing to a shriek and a monstrous *currump!* This is followed in rapid succession by more earth-quaking blasts, each louder than the one before, until the ultimate in sound and concussion – felt rather than heard – as two bombs straddle the guns. Then, an awful silence with only the sound of heavy breathing and muttered prayers to be heard in the bottoms of holes. (Yes, prayers are uttered and later men will frankly admit it without embarrassment.)

You can hear him off in the distance wheeling around, getting into position to attack again. (To each troop it seems they're the only one being attacked, and by one plane.) This time it's anti-personnel bombs, vicious, lightly fuzed little affairs that explode so close together it's just one prolonged *r-r-r-ipp*, as they send showers of grass-cutting fragments across the positions, leaving the field swept clean of every last blade of vegetation and covered with blackened rings.

On his last run across the position, strafing with his machine guns, he causes one casualty. A bullet ricochets off a rock in front of your command post and comes in through a narrow, horizontal slit left open to oversee the guns. It bounces off the corrugated-iron ceiling with a wicked flash momentarily lighting up the dugout, and imbeds its pointed nose in driver-signaller Bill Walkden's back, with just enough force to penetrate tunic and skin.

Then, as if to add insult to injury, the departing plane drops a ten-foot streamlined aluminum case, resembling a fish, in which the anti-personnel bombs were carried. It comes down with a weird fluttering sound, landing with a hollow *thunk* on Able Troop's position.

When finally the attack is over and the damage is assessed, it's found to be unbelievably light. Though a string of six 30-foot-wide craters have been excavated in a line across Able Troop, back across 14th Battery and RHQ over the road, there were only four casualties, and very little damage to equipment. One 14th Battery gun (Sgt. Hill's) has been knocked out, some ammunition blown up, and Sgt.-Maj. Flynn's Jeep left burning. Even a wooden tripod for a director (survey instrument) left fifty yards in front of your guns – where it might be used to check the parallelism of the guns – survives. At dawn Bombardier Hossack asks you to accompany him out there to bear witness that it's still standing, within three or four feet of the lip of a monster crater.

Later you learn that Douglas "Mac" MacFarlane, Baker Troop GPO, had his hand slashed by a fragment from a bomb dropped on Eterville, where he was relieving Hunter, thus becoming 4th Field's first officer casualty.

PART THREE: JULY 18–24

Supporting Operations
Goodwood and Atlantic

22

GREATEST AIR–ARMADA
ATTACK IN HISTORY

＊

IT IS GENERALLY BELIEVED THAT THE BREAK–OUT FROM THE bridgehead, so long visualized during training of 2nd Division in England, will occur just as soon as Monty decides everything is in place; that the Canadians, with their high reputation from the First World War still intact, will be among the leading assault forces; and that the fire-power Monty will bring to bear on behalf of the assault will dwarf El Alamein.

And so on the morning of July 18, 1944, it seems that the day has come. The integrated operations of "Goodwood" by the British and "Atlantic" by the Canadians – taking place simultaneously, shoulder to shoulder, principally on the other side of the Orne pointing towards Verrières Ridge and some twenty miles beyond to Falaise – have all the marks of the long-awaited break-out.

In Operation Goodwood, the centrepiece attack, three armoured divisions of British 8th Corps (the 11th, the Guards, and the 7th) will thrust south out of the shallow eastern corner of the bridgehead beyond the Orne, down past Faubourg-de-Vaucelles, the industrial suburb of Caen on the east bank of the Orne, passing along a corridor blasted by more than three thousand planes, the greatest air armada ever assembled for direct support of a ground attack.

The left flank of the attack will be protected by the 3rd British Infantry Division, while the Canadians, in Operation Atlantic, will deal with the Germans on the right flank. The 3rd Canadian Infantry Division will clear the east bank of the Orne down through the industrial suburbs of Caen (Colombelles, Faubourg-de-Vaucelles, and Cormelles), after which 5th Brigade of 2nd Division will cross the Orne at Caen to clear the bank down to Fleury-sur-Orne, which sits directly opposite the village of Louvigny, which must be taken by 4th Brigade.

The crack British tank divisions are expected to overpower any resistance remaining in the fortified villages south of Caen, secure Verrières Ridge, and exploit a break-out towards Falaise if the opportunity opens up. That these forces might fail to break their lines wide open and fall short of releasing an irresistible, liberating, tidal wave across France and the rest of Europe, is not even a consideration.

And the thousands of Allied soldiers, who at dawn will watch the bombing of Faubourg-de-Vaucelles and the fortified villages south of Caen – a bombing of enemy front-line positions, gun lines, and reserve positions without parallel in the history of war – will believe they are watching a hole being literally blown through the German army.

At about 4:45 A.M. the faint hum of the great armada of bombers coming from England can be heard in the sky north of Caen. Quickly it grows in intensity until you are enveloped in the throbbing roar of a huge flock of bombers lumbering in from the coast. They are not little specks high in the sky leaving vapour trails, as they appeared over Sussex and Kent on their way to raids on enemy-occupied Europe, but great four-engined machines, flying in from the northwest at a moderate height, plainly visible in all detail to the troops on the ground.

After years of listening to sparse reports by the BBC of bombing raids on occupied Europe, usually no more than bare-bones bulletins (such as "Several industrial targets in the Ruhr, including Essen, received the attention of our bombers last night"), leaving

VII CORPS

I CORPS

II CANADIAN CORPS

Canal

Ranville

Hérouville

Colombelles

3 CDN

CAEN

2 CDN

le Mesnil

Escoville

7TH

GDS

Giberville

11TH

3 BRIT

Louvigny

VAUCELLES

Eterville

Touffreville

Sannerville

Fleury-sur-Orne

Orne R.

Basse

Cormelles

Etavaux

Point 67

Ifs

St. André-
sur-Orne

Emieville

Bras

Four

Cagny

Beauvoir
Farm

Hubert-Folie

St. Martin-de-
Fontenay

Troteval
Farm

Bourguébus

Frénouville

May-sur-Orne

Verrières

Tilly-la Campagne

La Hogue

Fortenay-
le-Marmion

Roquancourt

Vimont

Garcelles
Secqueville

Secqueville-la-Campagne

Falaise

Cramesnil

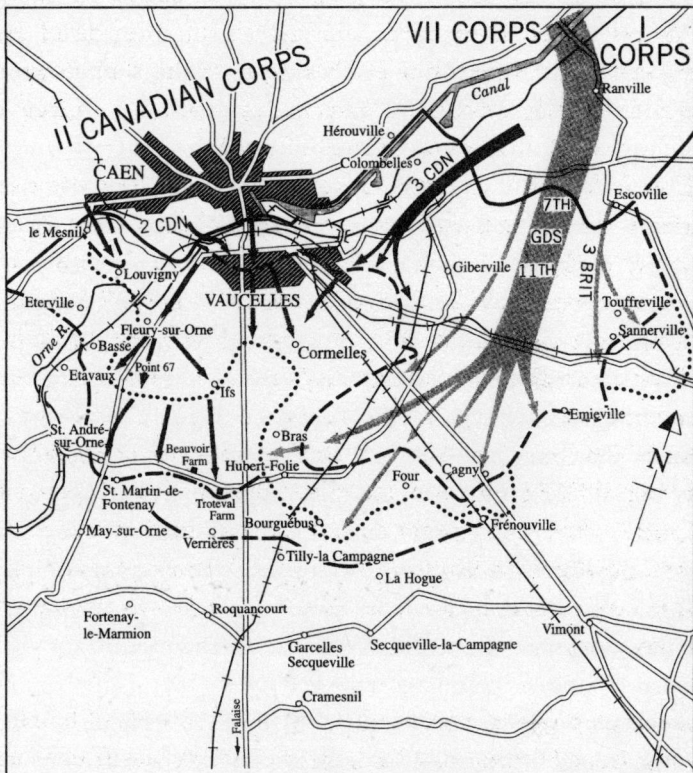

OPERATIONS GOODWOOD & ATLANTIC
(OBJECTIVES OF SPRING)

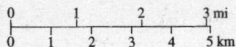

```
0        1        2        3 mi
0    1   2   3   4   5 km
```

British army movements ....

Canadian army movements ....

Front line - dawn July 18th ....

Front line - midnight July 18/19 ....

Front line - midnight July 19/20 ....

Front line - midnight July 20/21 ....

Front line - morning July 25 (Operation Spring) ....

everything to your imagination, you are about to have a grandstand view of a very large raid, the largest ever in direct support of ground forces.

As you watch the first planes turning east, lining up their run across Caen, the whole thing seems unreal, almost incongruous. RAF raids have always been at night, and your mind can't associate the obscenities of bombing destruction with this bright, beautiful, sunlit morning. But when suddenly the sky around the first planes reaching Caen is polluted with cracking, black puffs, and seconds later big bombs are tumbling down among the factory smokestacks of Faubourg-de-Vaucelles, creating earth-shaking concussions that jar your gun position five miles distant and send dense clouds of dust and debris roiling up hundreds of feet in the air, the reality is clear enough.

Soon the dust blocks out the factory smokestacks and church steeples, but not before you see a spire topple.

One Liberator, the sun glinting off it as it moves across Caen, tips over and goes down in flames. Another can be seen smoking as it swings overhead on its way back to the coast. In a few minutes all the flak disappears from the sky as the German guns are either blinded by smoke and dust or knocked out by the neutralizing fire that is now being laid on them by fifteen field regiments, twelve medium regiments, three heavy regiments, and three regiments of heavy ack-ack guns.

Now the planes streaming unmolested over their targets drop their bombs in seemingly routine fashion, wheeling around and heading back to England as though on a giant conveyor belt. For three hours the huge planes maintain a constant pulsing roar as they flow in from the coast to add their awful contributions to the thundering rumble. As the attack continues, on and on, and thick smoke and dust clouds drift across the front, all at the guns cease watching.

During the first forty-five minutes, 1,023 four-engined RAF Lancasters and Halifaxes are to drop more than five thousand tons of high explosive on factory suburbs marked by Pathfinder flares. Then 400 medium bombers of 9th U.S.A. Airforce are to scatter thousands of fragmentation bombs on the corridor of the attack. Six hundred Liberators will then hit targets east and south of the city designed to interrupt communications and snuff out counter-attacks. Finally, more than a thousand fighter-bombers will fly countless sorties over roads, farms, and villages far behind the enemy lines to prevent the Germans from moving up tanks or guns.

When the bombing ends at 7:45 A.M., almost eight hundred guns will begin laying down concentrations between the Orne river and Troarn, a village east of Caen. The Orne and Troarn are eight kilometres apart, the approximate width of the corridor down which the three British armoured divisions are to plunge.

The infantry of 2nd Division will not be involved until late in the day, when 4th Brigade will clear the right flank on this side of the river down to the village of Louvigny, so that 5th Brigade may cross the Orne after dark at Caen to begin clearing the far bank, south to Fleury-sur-Orne opposite Louvigny. The opening attack, the first by any battalion of 2nd Division since the disastrous Dieppe raid, will be by the Royal Regiment, now in reserve to the left rear of Eterville.

At first light Major Jack Anderson, acting battalion commander, and his company commanders go forward on reconnaissance to a cluster of ancient farm buildings held by 8th Recce near the hamlet of Le Mesnil and just short of the road running east from Eterville to Caen, which will be the startline for their attack. From here they sneak forward to study the ground over which they must pass on their way to taking their objectives: the village of Louvigny and its château, which is some fifteen hundred yards away down on the Orne, well screened by a tremendous orchard and grounds enclosed by a seven-foot-high stone wall.

However, they can see little of all this, for visibility is limited by a towering dust cloud drifting this way from the bombing of Caen's suburbs. Fortunately, the owner of the fourteenth-century manor farm held by 8th Recce, Jules Hollier-Larousse, is both a captain in the local Resistance and mayor of Louvigny, capable of providing the most minute detail on the layout of village and château grounds, and the best routes there.

23

LOUVIGNY

✳

THE PLAN DEVELOPED BY THE ACTING CO OF THE ROYALS CALLS for Major Jim Fairhead's D Company to take the orchard and château just north of Louvigny, and Tom Whitley's A Company to follow through to clear the village itself. After this, B Company will pass through the village and take up a position to shut off counter-attacks from upriver.

Capt. D. S. "Tim" Beatty is in command of B Company since Major J. F. Law was wounded two days ago in a bombing attack, though Beatty himself has only just come back from a casualty clearing station, sporting a dressing on a head wound caused by a shell fragment that pierced his helmet in Eterville three days ago. Major Ralph Young's C Company is to establish a firm base on the high open ground overlooking Louvigny, from where a squadron of tanks of the Fort Garry Horse (10th Armoured Regiment) will blow holes in the seven-foot-high stone wall bounding the orchard on three sides so that Major Fairhead's company can debouch into the orchard.

The three field regiments of 2nd Division, including 4th Field, will fire heavy concentrations of shells on the orchard, the village, and the woods between the château and a nearby railway bridge over the Orne; after which the village of Athis, from whence reinforcements for a counter-attack might come, will receive the full attention of the guns. Other support will be forthcoming from a company of 4.2-inch mortars and medium machine guns of the Toronto Scottish, as well as from the battalion's own 3-inch mortars.

The startline, the Eterville–Caen road as it runs past Larousse's farm through Le Mesnil, will be secured by the 8th Recce Regiment.

At 6:00 P.M., while the hot July sun still glares high above the crest of Hill 112 over to the west, the divisional fire plan opens up on Louvigny and vicinity, and the men and officers of the Royals, accompanied by 2nd Battery FOOs (Laurie and Hunter) and their carrier crews, leave the shelter of the broken walls of barns and houses along the road through Le Mesnil.

Crossing the highway, the companies walk in arrowhead formation through the unharvested, yellowing wheat, down across the fields towards the flashing roar of shells now furiously lashing the big apple orchard about a thousand yards away, enshrouding it in smoke and partially hiding the main objectives – the château and the village of Louvigny just beyond on the bank of the River Orne.

Able Troop Commander Stu Laurie, who, with his carrier and crew goes in with a leading company, will recall every foot of the way of this, his first attack:

They just start off on foot, walking across the wheat field, and immediately machine-gun fire begins to pour in – mostly through the wheat. Jesus! You wouldn't think you could miss having a foot taken off or at least wounded! But nothing like that happens. They keep on walking right along, and we're with them, until we get stuck – not in a ditch or a hole, but on a hump of earth!

I won't go on the road, though there is a very good road running all the way down on the right to the objective. I won't let Ryckman drive the carrier up on it, for I think it could be mined. So we are driving along in the fields, and God it's rough –

up and down, up and down. Suddenly we get stuck right out in the middle of the field, bottomed out on a bump-up in the land, with everybody firing at us – small-arms fire coming at us like hell! And they start shelling us too. It's a miracle we get out of it intact.

Just then somebody asks me if I can't do something about all the ammunition coming our way. So I get the Regiment on the blower to bring down the guns on a target, but they say, "Sorry, the Colonel's got the guns – no use – don't bother."

So we just march on ahead with shells and mortars coming our way like crazy. And that's when 4th Brigade Tac Headquarters behind us is hit. Set up in the field just about 600 yards back, they are getting plastered. That's when Gunner Walter Chater, the CO's Don R, is killed, and Brig. Sherwood Lett, the commander of 4th Brigade, is wounded.

Then a whole bevy of wounded Germans come through on the way back . . . slits in their chests . . . bubbling blood . . . all kinds of walking wounded . . . ten or twelve of them. One officer with them is wearing a steel helmet – all the rest are hatless . . . staggering along in terrible shape, all wounded so badly . . . from our fire plan I guess.

Just then our friend Rankin (Captain Bob of A Company) comes roaring down the road in a carrier, running right over towards the headquarters they've just captured. And as we watch, his whole carrier just goes boom up in the air, and a great cloud of black smoke comes out of it . . . run over a mine, of course. Just went roaring through and that was goodbye to him and everybody else in that carrier.

In the meantime I keep asking for the guns. I desperately want them, for I know precisely where the German fire is coming from. I can keep my head up, for while they are really pouring it into Brigade behind us, we have been moving out of it as we move forward.

But no, the Regiment is still being fired by the Colonel. So I say to myself, "To hell with this, if I can't get the guns I'll go operate on my own." It's then I cross over the road on the right and go up the hill – quite a decent hill – with a young lieutenant of the Royals. And that young man is really high! I don't mean drunk, just uptight with tension, yelling and screaming at the Germans to "Come out, you bastards!" as we walk together through the wheat and brush with Ryckman wheeling the Carrier along behind us.

And, by gawd, we start digging snipers out of ditches and slit trenches around there. There are lots of trenches up there and when we go up to them, there they are, right down in the bottom of the trench, hiding. They seem only too glad to be taken prisoner. Obviously they were left behind to do this: just fire across the wheat fields until we arrived.*

A Company, with Lieut. Len Gage's platoon leading, clears about half the village before being held up by heavy machine-gun fire from the south end at last light. Then, "it being considered bad practice to try house-clearing in the dark," Whitley pulls his company back into the orchard opposite the village until morning.

The Germans mount no counter-attack, though they occupy nearby Athis and Maltot in considerable strength, including a nest of their fearsome Tiger tanks. Unquestionably the pressure still being exerted by the two British corps, in their attacks that began three days ago over on the right beyond Hill 112, has affected the German capacity to reinforce Louvigny and mount counter-attacks. And the shelling by 4th Field guns directed on the Athis flank by the CO may have been decisive.

As time goes on and more details become known, 4th Field will take some pride in the role played by their colonel who assumed

---

* Author interview.

command of 4th Brigade when Brig. Lett was wounded in the middle of the attack.*

As in all battles, no one is allowed more than a skimpy view of the struggle while it is in progress, and the outcome is not clear until the next morning, when B Company resumes the attack on the village and finds the enemy have pulled out during the night.

Only then is it clear Louvigny was won in the orchard and the château grounds, where the worst fighting took place. Some of it was truly hand-to-hand combat, one of the Royals strangling his foe with his bare hands when his Sten gun jammed just as he jumped through the hole blown in the stone wall and found himself face to face with him. There, in the relatively confined orchard of the château, while inflicting heavy casualties on the defenders and taking 55 prisoners, the Royals suffered most of their 111 casualties, 34 of them fatal, including 4 officers killed and 2 wounded.

The bitter harvest of war revealed next morning will remain forever a vivid memory for Lieut. Bob Suckling:

I was a platoon commander in D Company, but after five days in Eterville (under almost continuous bombardment that inflicted 92 casualties on the Royals) I may have appeared a bit unstable, and not to be trusted. Anyway, I was LOB [left out of battle] overnight during the attack on Louvigny.†

Next morning when I'm bringing up the D Company LOBs

---

* For his "skill and resourcefulness" in guiding the Brigade, and his "personal courage" in bringing down observed fire "while exposed to enemy snipers, mortar and shell-fire," Lt.-Col. C. M. Drury was awarded a DSO.

† "Left out of battle" is a term covering infantrymen sent back to a rear battalion area for a short rest, usually only a day or night. The term most accurately describes those routinely selected to remain out of the attack to ensure a continuity of experience and command. If the company commander (a major) is in the attack, his second-in-command (a captain) is

and we are passing Jack Anderson, the Acting CO, on the road, he asks, "How many are you?"

I tell him, "Twenty."

And he says, "Not enough!"

And he certainly is right. When I find D Company, there are only seventeen men left, out of perhaps eighty or ninety, and they are under command of Sgt. Tryon of the Support Company's 3-inch Mortar Platoon. My company commander, Jim Fairhead, is dead, and so is a fellow lieutenant by the name of Moulder. If I wasn't in a state of shock before, I certainly am now.

A little while later I learn that two other platoon commanders and Bob Rankin, Tom Whitley's 2IC, also died in the attack — and Tim Beatty, another company commander, and a Lieut. Downie were wounded.*

LOB; and if the platoon commander (a lieutenant) is in the attack, his sergeant is LOB. Because lieutenants are particularly vulnerable, a percentage are always LOB. Also, a number of privates, depending on the strength of companies, are designated LOB for the same reason: to make sure there'll be a nucleus on which to build another company.

*   Author interview.

24

TRICOLOUR RAISED ON RUBBLE
OF TOWN HALL

✳

ABOUT 10:00 P.M. ON JULY 18, YOU RECEIVE ORDERS AT THE guns to prepare to move. A short time later the quads come up and the guns are winched out of the pits and limbered up.* All vehicles are then lined up along the forward edge of the position close to the Verson road, Able Troop leading. There you wait for the order to move to a position near Louvigny.

For half an hour you wait, and as it get closer to 11:00 P.M. – the hour the Jerry bombers have been arriving nightly – you begin to worry that if you don't get off this position soon, the Regiment is going to get clobbered. And with all the equipment and personnel above ground, it could be a disaster. The memory of that string of bombs coming down across this very ground last night is still horribly vivid, and you find yourself sighing a great deal as you wait.

But 11:00 P.M. comes and goes and no Jerry planes arrive. You conclude that tonight he's too busy across the Orne and in the suburbs of Caen to bother with the guns back here. And judging by the fires glowing on the horizon, the muffled explosions, the continuous rumbling of distant guns and the whine of motors, which you assume are tanks, he's being kept very busy indeed.

---

* Gun trails were hooked to ammunition limbers, which in turn were hooked to the quads.

However, when the order finally does come to move up through Verson and you pull out on the road, a number of blinding-white chandelier flares burst into life and float smoking over the village. For a while, in spite of the clouds of dust your trucks are raising, you can see the terrible destruction in that poor village as the convoy picks its way over the torn roads, partially clogged here and there with rubble and burned-out vehicles.

Over the grinding truck motors, you hear the drone of the German bombers directly overhead, and for what seems an age you hold your breath, expecting that at any moment their bombs or machine-gun bullets will come ripping down on the convoy. When the throb of their engines fades away without anything happening, you pull yourself together to make what use you can of the obscene light they've left hanging over you, to read the way ahead and spot your progress along the route marked on your map board in black chinagraph pencil.

To your profound relief the planes don't come back. Evidently the Orne crossings, including one by the Black Watch from the racetrack in Caen, have the attention of the German planes tonight. When the flares burn out, they leave everything even darker than before.

It is very slow going, with several stops to make sure you are still following the right route. Once you are close to Le Mesnil you are directed right by a Don R doing "point duty" along what seems to be a farm track across open fields towards Louvigny, and you are able to move at a good pace.

Just after the track has met the road, and the convoy is passing between an orchard on the left and the looming walls of old stone buildings of Louvigny crowding the road on the right, white tracer bullets flicker across the road in front of your vehicle towards the orchard. They're German of course, for Stens and Brens don't use tracers. Immediately you halt the convoy and, jumping down, pass the order back along the line of vehicles for everyone to get out and into the ditch with their small arms.

As you crouch in the ditch, straining your eyes and ears and wondering how on earth you are going to get the Regiment out of this predicament, three or four dark figures run out of the orchard on the left and clatter across the road, disappearing among the buildings on the right, no more than twenty-five yards away. For a moment, as they are outlined against the reddish glow from burning Caen, you are able to make out the unmistakable silhouette of German pot helmets. Then, with startling intimacy and clarity, out of the darkness of the orchard, a voice shouts, "Get those vehicles out of the way − I've got casualties here!"

Instantly you recognize that slightly snarling, slightly nasal, and more-than-slightly imperious voice you'd heard so often in the darkness of that wretched orchard in Eterville only four days ago. Major Whitley's voice is hoarse with fatigue, and there is a strident, desperate note in it, but it still rings with authority, completely unsubdued by whatever has been the experience of A Company tonight. While it's disconcerting to know you are passing in front of the infantry, the sound of that familiar voice is encouraging. The guns are not up here alone, the Royals are distributed in and around here somewhere.

You wish you could be of assistance to him, but you've got your own problems. If the Germans still hold the village, and this seems clearly to be the case, then the gun positions beyond the village to which you are leading the Regiment are in no-man's-land!

The only sensible thing to do is to turn the convoy around and go back to the old position. But there is no way to turn the vehicles here, jammed between stone walls and ditches. Even if it were possible to manhandle the guns and limbers about, and inch the quads around, it would take all night.

You hear a motorbike coming this way, and wonder if it's friend or foe. As he materializes out of the gloom, you see the silhouette of a friendly crash helmet, and climb up out of the ditch to meet him. When the motor is shut off, you recognize the voice of Bill Murdoch, the regimental orderly officer. Normally Bill's a guy who strives to be blasé, regardless of how bizarre or outrageous the situation. But tonight, as you hold a low-voiced conference with him, it's obvious the situation has really got to him, for he is very subdued.

"Looks like the village hasn't been taken yet," you whisper.

"That's pretty obvious."

"But aren't our positions beyond the village, by the river?"

"Yes."

"My God, Bill, what are we supposed to do? If we could turn everything around and go back ... but it's impossible."

"Well," he says, "they didn't shoot at me on the way back here just now. Anyway, you haven't any choice – you can't turn them round."

Of course it's true – you have no choice. And so the sooner you get out of here the better, for there's nothing more vulnerable than an artillery regiment on wheels with its guns limbered up. But knowing what must be done in no way reduces your anxiety from having to lead the Regiment forward into that dark void up ahead, which any second now may erupt into a flashing, lethal hailstorm of bullets.

Standing beside Bill, staring down that sinister road, you wish to God you were anywhere else in the world but here. And you can tell he's thinking the same way. For a moment he just sits there. Then, standing up, with one foot searching for the motorbike's cranking pedal, he declares in a hoarse whisper, "Okay, let's get the hell out of here."

But before he kicks the bike into life, he seems to remember why he came back to meet you in the first place:

"Oh, just one thing. When we get to where you leave the road, the Number Ones will have to get out and lead the guns in on foot – the position is full of frigging great bomb craters and we'll lose a gun or two for sure if we're not careful. Look for a hole in the fence – crossing the ditch will be tricky. Anyway, follow me."

With that he kick-starts the bike and it comes to life with an indecent roar. Without waiting for you to get the order to "mount" passed back along the line of the ditch and everybody back into their vehicles, he pulls away and disappears in the gloom ahead.

Though you curse his impatience, he has unwittingly provided you with something to dwell on in place of the grim spectre of a German ambush as you get the convoy underway and try to catch up with him.

Actually, the convoy barely gets rolling before the road converges with another, and right there, in front of a tall wayside shrine, barely visible in the murk, Murdoch is waiting and pointing to a field on the right. So far so good! You've made it without attracting a shot.

A sense of relief flows through you as your vehicle dips down and bounces into the field over the rough culvert of fenceposts the advance party has lain across the ditch. While fully aware that the Regiment is still vulnerable as it deploys in no-man's-land, responsibility for its fate is dividing and devolving onto a great many other shoulders of varying rank and seniority, as it splits into six distinct communities known as "troop gun positions." From this moment on, you are responsible only for your own troop.

Now if the Germans will just leave you alone until you're dug in . . . It's soft earth, but the night is hot and humid, and the air is saturated with the foul odours produced by rotting, bloated cattle somewhere nearby. On the left, near where a railway bridge over the Orne should be, mortar bombs flash and crash periodically. Otherwise the area is spookily peaceful, with only the sound of shovelling to be heard in the immediate vicinity.

Just as you are coming to believe the Germans must have been pulling back out of the village when you saw them scuttling across the road in front of your vehicle, there's the distinctive *bur-rup bur-rup* of a Schmeisser among the dark buildings over the fence and across the road behind you. Tracers streak out, but to the rear, away from the guns, towards the orchard behind the village as before.

In the silence that follows, a voice asks, "Is that a Jerry?" When he's assured that it is, the tempo of the shovelling can be heard to rise markedly on all sides.

Now and then throughout the night, during lulls in the mortar bombardment of the collapsed railway bridge over on the left, a Schmeisser *bur-rups* in the village, but never are its shots directed towards the gun position.

The first target shortly after dawn on July 19, for which no explanation is offered, is on this side of the river, just to the right of the village, at the ridiculously low range of 1,200 yards from the pivot gun of Able Troop, on the extreme right of the regimental position. Even using Charge I to gain maximum elevation for the gun muzzles, you will barely manage to clear the trees bordering the field and lining the riverbank along the front of the position, screening you from enemy territory on this side of the river, and to some extent the other side of the river. Actually, the trees are so close you have the gun sergeants open the breeches of their guns and look up through their barrels to make sure they can't see any tree branches before they load and fire. Shortly after, you have them do the same thing again when the SOS target is called only a thousand yards away on the other side of the river, beyond the broken bridge.

As the sun climbs in the sky, the lack of sleep begins to hit you, but you must remain alert. Information is sketchy; there's a rumour the Royals have occupied the whole of Louvigny. This would seem to be true, for Moaning Minnies begin to crash sporadically among the buildings and beyond, in what must be the château grounds. Then you get a report that when the Royals moved into the village at first light, they found the enemy had withdrawn during the night, which would explain why the Germans didn't attack the guns. If they were committed to withdrawing even before the guns came in last night, it would make little sense to men armed with Schmeissers to challenge the big guns in a duel.

In the daylight the village is a pitiful sight. Ragged buildings, torn and gutted by fire from yesterday's bombing and shelling and now damp with dew, give off a wretched, acrid smell of charred wood, joining the sickening odours coming from the dead cattle. Directly behind the guns, buildings in various states of ruin face the field from the other side of a roadway that is a tangle of rubble and drooping wires. Lying on the roadway just over the fence from your command post is a huge clock-tower, its face and hands largely intact, just as they were when it toppled down yesterday morning from the blast of a bomb that wrecked the building it graced, unquestionably the town hall.

As you stand at the fence, contemplating the terrible price Norman towns are paying for their liberation, a man of aristocratic bearing appears from the direction of the crossroads and its wayside Calvary. Following him closely is a boy, carrying, like a banner on a long staff, a large flag of France.

The man manages to march with great dignity, even as he picks his way through rubble strewn here and there in his path. The silent little parade attracts the attention of all eyes still awake and on the gun position. The man's solemn dignity is so studied, and the boy's attempt to emulate him while carrying the oversized flag so incongruous, the whole thing would in normal times be humorous. But this morning it is not; it is damned impressive.

When they reach the remains of the town hall, the man stops and directs the boy to plant the flag near the remnants of a doorway. And as the boy climbs up on the rubble and tries to fix the staff in a crack, the man makes gestures to plant it higher – still higher. When finally both are satisfied, the boy returns to the man's side, and together, standing rigidly at attention, they salute the flag.

Another bit of France is free.

The man, you'll learn later, is Jules Hollier-Larousse, mayor of Louvigny, and his flag-bearer is his son, Thierry, brought back from school in Paris before the invasion to act as a courier for the FFI (Free French of the Interior). Very small for his age – looking twelve rather than seventeen years old – Thierry was never suspected by the Germans, though he bore them a deep hatred and had a strong desire for revenge.

One afternoon before the invasion, a squad of Germans had roared into the yard of the Larousses' ancient farmhouse and demanded they reveal the hiding place of an illicit transmitter their directional-finders had established was right there.

Just minutes earlier a family friend, Leon Dumis, another captain in the Resistance, had moved the transmitter to Château Louvigny, a couple of miles away. When the Germans couldn't find it, they lined up father, mother, and boy with their hands against a wall and told them they would remain there until 6:00 P.M. If by then the transmitter had not come on the air it would be proof that they were the culprits, and they would be shot.

Thierry's mother at one point spat at the feet of one of the guards, who in response jammed her savagely against the wall and threatened to kill her. This was when Thierry swore he'd have his revenge if he survived.

And the Larousses had all been allowed to live, because Dumis, at his new location, had gone on the air just before six, and the German signaller in the nearby truck reported this fact to the officer in charge.

Later, as the Allied invading forces drew near their farm and the Germans ordered them to remove themselves from the battle zone, the Larousses became for a time refugees, sometimes living in the fields. Eventually the family managed to cross over into Allied territory, where father and son were able to help the Canadians by supplying information on the location of German positions.

Once, Thierry, using as an excuse the need to cut hay for their horse, went out into no-man's-land with a scythe, and until he had noted the location of the German trenches he studiously ignored the calls and waving arms of the Canadians on one side and Germans on the other as they tried to warn the "stupid child" to come in.

On another occasion some Canadians spotted a German Luger pistol in his back pocket and were lining him up for execution as a spy when a neighbour identified him as the son of the mayor of Louvigny. They allowed him to keep his Luger, and he rewarded them later by using it to release some of their buddies from a German marching them down a road near the farm. Another time near Athis, he saw German tanks churning across the Orne by way of a long-forgotten Roman ford that had become useable with the lower water level caused by the destruction of a dam downstream. He brought this crucial information to an artillery unit north of the farm. Until then, the Allies had no idea how the Germans got their tanks back and forth over the Orne without a bridge.

The day after the Chaudières overran the Larousse farm on July 10, they were relieved by the Fusiliers Mont-Royal. That day Thierry and his father returned. Immediately his father dug up in the garden a dozen bottles of prime Calvados he had saved from all he had systematically poured on the ground the day France fell to ensure the Germans would never have it. Though the soldiers were warned it was very strong – almost 50 per cent stronger than whisky – they overindulged. So all lay stretched out on the floor of the living room, dead to the world, when from an upstairs window Thierry spotted Germans poking around in the barnyard and looking in the long line of stable doors. Rushing downstairs, he went from one snoring form to another until he was able to get one on his feet. Leading the staggering soldier with a Bren outside to a vantage point along a high wall that separated garden from barnyard, he pointed down at the Germans investigating the stables. By then there were half a dozen.

The soldier tried to get a bead on them, steadying his Bren on the top of the wall, but he was wavering so much it was difficult. By the time his aim was steady enough, seventeen Germans had gathered in the barnyard cul-de-sac. He emptied a full magazine into them – then another.

25

IN THE DISTANCE THE
SKIRL OF PIPES

✳

AS FAR AS 2ND DIVISION IS CONCERNED IT'S A 5TH BRIGADE show today (July 19). During the night, while 4th Field was digging in here at Louvigny, west of the Orne, the Black Watch crossed the river up at the Caen racetrack, and the rest of the brigade followed. Le Régiment de Maisonneuve are to attack down this way to clear the east bank to the village of Fleury-sur-Orne only about half a mile away, directly across the river from the guns, which by now may have been outflanked by the British armoured divisions.

Before noon, the gunners are preparing ammunition for a heavy fire plan to begin at 1300 hours with a creeping barrage of eighteen lifts on a frontage of 1,200 yards.* It will involve all 2nd Division guns and four medium regiments of 2nd AGRA (Army Group Royal Artillery).

The barrage, designed to carry the Maisonneuves 2,000 yards south from their startline on the outskirts of the factory area of Caen, takes two hours to fire. Because of the unique position of the

---

* A barrage is a belt of fire moving ahead of the advancing troops. A creeping barrage is the usual type used in support of the infantry. The fire of the units taking part in it remains in the same relative positions throughout and the whole barrage advances together in steps, or "lifts," one line at a time (usually 100 yards apart) at a pace designed to conform

guns relative to the axis of the barrage, the "lifts," which normally take shells farther away from the guns, are really switches in line to the right, with continuous slight reductions in ranges, bringing the shells closer to the guns as the infantry sweep down the river, from the left along the high ground past the menacing water-tower across from your guns.

By afternoon, ranges to targets are increasing, and while the Maisies are consolidating in Fleury, the guns engage in some heavy divisional concentrations on behalf of the Calgary Highlanders, who pass through Fleury at 5:15 P.M. on their way to taking Point 67, a bald hill about two hundred feet higher than Louvigny and plainly visible some two thousand yards away through a gap in the line of trees skirting the front of Able Troop gun position.

Just about the time the Highlanders should be arriving at Point 67, Baker Troop Sgt.-Maj. "Rod" Williams arrives at your command post in such haste he starts a minor avalanche of sand and gravel down the crude earthen stairs of the dugout. Even before his slipping, sliding descent has ended, he is begging – nay, demanding – that you come out with your field-glasses and map to range on some Germans he's spotted dashing about on a hill across the river.

When you clamber outside to look, fully expecting that whatever he saw will long since have disappeared, you are astonished to see, less than fifteen hundred yards away, three or four crouching figures begin to run hell-for-leather up the slope away from you.

Even with the naked eye you can identify them by their baggy

---

with the rate of advance of the troops it is supporting. In an infantry attack it will rarely be faster than 100 yards in three minutes, and in difficult country it can be as slow as 100 yards in five or six minutes. For an armoured attack the barrage will move at 100 yards or more a minute. The width of the barrage is dictated by the number of guns available. The fire of field guns is arranged along each line at 25-yard intervals, and for the mediums, 50 yards.

camouflaged smocks belted-in at the waist. Before they reach the crest, you have them in your field-glasses. Sharply outlined against the sky, those bent-over, leg-churning men seem so shockingly close that for an instant you are back on the Alfriston practice ranges in Sussex watching British soldiers, dressed in captured field-grey uniforms, illustrate German infantry tactics for the officers of 2nd Division and the Home Guard. Clearly visible are their potlike, distinctly German helmets and those peculiar, corrugated cans (holding respirators) bouncing on their rumps as they scurry up and over the hill to the southwest. No sooner have they disappeared than two more small groups – about a hundred yards apart – rise up and start a similar gallop up the slope.

By now it's obvious that significant numbers are involved in this strange manoeuvre. You study the map and try to figure it out. Just how far along could our troops have advanced? Are those Jerries moving into position to hit the Calgary Highlanders from the flank, or have they been driven off the hill by the advancing Highlanders and in the process of withdrawing to a defensive line from which they'll almost immediately emerge in a blazing counter-attack – as had been strikingly illustrated by those Limey soldiers that day in 1943 in that natural amphitheatre on the South Downs?

By now the Sergeant-Major is frantic with impatience: "What in hell are WE waiting for, SIR?" Then, interpreting your lengthy study of the map and apparent indecisiveness as the inability to establish a map reference for that hill over there, he inquires loudly, "Why can't WE engage them over open sights, SIR?"

While you agree it's very tempting, you point out the risk is too great. The Highlanders could appear right in the target area as you are firing, in fact they might be there already, out of sight. We simply don't know where they are and have no way of finding out.

Using the map you try to explain all this to the very frustrated Sergeant-Major, but he can't keep his eyes off that hill across the river, even though it is now completely empty of all movement.

At last, convinced a great opportunity has been lost through your timidity, he turns away, and muttering deeply under his breath stalks off in the direction of Baker Troop, wagging his head in disappointment and disgust.

As you make your way back to the command post dugout, you think you must be going batty, for over the racket of mortaring across the river, you could swear you hear the faint skirl of bagpipes.*

An ammo count at 8:30 P.M. reveals that in the past twenty-four hours more than five hundred rounds per gun have been fired. At dusk the guns take part in divisional concentrations on behalf of the Black Watch attacking the village of Ifs. By midnight they have the village and are being counter-attacked. Then it's the Calgary Highlanders' turn. Throughout the night the guns are mainly on harassing fire, and whenever you have need to leave your candle-lit dugout to answer a call of nature, the darkness along the ridge over the river is filled with flashes and rumbles. But the main concern of the gunners becomes the digging-in of 350 rounds per gun dumped by Army Service – the first instalment of 1,000 rounds per gun, which they say is to be the normal complement for guns of 2nd Division from now on.

By now it is clear the British armoured attack has bogged down without gaining the high ground overlooking the line of advance, and the heavy dumping of ammunition can mean only one thing: extraordinary demands are about to be made on the guns in support

---

* Reginald Roy's book *The Canadians in Normandy* (Toronto: Macmillan, 1984), p. 77, describing the attack by the Calgary Highlanders to clear "the hill which had permitted the enemy to overlook Louvigny" confirms this: "Eager for battle and with at least one piper playing 'The Advance' as the men swept across the fields of grain and up the slopes of their objective, the Highlanders encountered mostly enemy snipers and mortar fire."

of the infantry heading for Verrières Ridge. While the usual state of ignorance persists, there are convincing rumours the tanks have taken an awful beating. One story, delivered with the Compo rations last night by Troop Sgt.-Maj. Mann, and reputedly from an eyewitness, inspires the image of wheat fields covered with burning British tanks.

Anyone with the inclination to speculate must assume that when the tanks quit attacking, as soon they must to cut their losses, the poor bloody infantry of 2nd Division will have to take over. And the word "bloody" may well become something more than a rude description of the men who must walk across those open fields and up that sloping ground. When three British crack armoured divisions – their right flank secured by 2nd Canadian Corps and preceded by the greatest aerial bombardment ever undertaken in support of ground forces – were unable to subdue the German fire dominating those open slopes of Verrières Ridge, clearly every yard will be bought dearly by infantry battalions.

26

OF MURDER TARGETS AND
BODY ARMOUR

✳

AT NOON ON JULY 20, THREE HOURS BEFORE THE ATTACK BY 6th Brigade with Essex Scottish attached, the villages of St. André-sur-Orne and St. Martin-de-Fontenay, sitting cheek-by-jowl down on the right from Verrières Ridge, are subjected to a "murder target" shelling by all field guns of 2nd and 3rd divisions and all the mediums and heavies of three AGRAS. In just three minutes, 59 tons of shells (60 per cent more than were fired during the Battle of Waterloo) are sent screaming and crashing into the twin hamlets by six regiments of 25-pounders firing 1,728 rounds, nine medium regiments firing 648 100-pound shells, and two regiments of 7.2-inch heavies firing 48 200-pound monsters.

A German artillery officer, captured at an OP on the hill eight hundred yards north of St. Martin, is much impressed by the concentrated fire that descended on him shortly before he was taken prisoner. According to Intelligence, the German "feels all troops in the area are very shaken. Seven years in army – through Stalingrad fight – first-class soldier – has never experienced anything like our artillery concentrations."[*]

Those ravaged interlocking villages of St. Martin and St. André

---

[*]   2nd Cdn Corps OP "Atlantic," file 225C2.012 (D7), National Archives of Canada.

are the objective of the Queens' Own Cameron Highlanders of Canada as they attack south along the river; while the South Saskatchewan Regiment – with the Essex Scottish in close support – attack up the slope in the centre to consolidate on the ridge at a point just over the crest; and the Fusiliers Mont-Royal thrust along the left flank bordering the Caen–Falaise highway towards Verrières, some 3.5 kilometres south of their startline at the village of Ifs.

Scheduled for noon, the attack is postponed in the hope that the black, lowering clouds will clear away, allowing the rocket-firing Typhoons to engage on call hull-down tanks as they are encountered on the ridge. And it's not until 3:00 P.M., with the cloud cover even blacker, that the infantry, accompanied by some tanks of the Sherbrooke Fusiliers, move out panting in the sultry heat behind a thunderous program of timed concentrations involving various combinations of the guns that had fired the murder target.

About halfway between Ifs and Verrières, in an otherwise bald landscape of rolling wheat fields rising gently towards the ridge, are two low clumps of stone buildings about a kilometre apart along the road leading west from the Caen–Falaise highway to St. André. On the map they are identified as Troteval Farm and Beauvoir Farm.

The two farms are the first objectives of the Fusiliers Mont-Royal, as two companies lead off, each with a 4th Field FOO, to walk across two kilometres of open country. Gordon Hunter (Baker Troop Commander) is with the company on the right that's to pass through Beauvoir Farm, and Brit Smith (Dog Troop Commander) is on foot with the company that's to clear Troteval Farm on the left about 450 metres west of the Caen–Falaise highway.

To confuse the snipers into thinking his rank doesn't deserve any special attention, Brit carries a rifle. And though it's a very hot day, his battledress collar is buttoned up to cover his tie, and his little camouflage veil is strung about his neck and wound around his epaulettes to hide the three captain's pips on each shoulder.

Adding to his sweaty discomfort, under his battledress he is wearing the body armour that was issued to all infantrymen and artillery carrier crews coming to Normandy: the fabric-covered, moulded pieces of dense plastic, designed to yield, but not break, on catching the impact of a bullet or shell fragment. Unlike the medieval variety, body armour in Normandy, 1944, is made up of separate pieces that dangle on shoulder straps, and is usually (but not always) worn underneath battledress pants and blouses. Your back is protected by one piece, an upside-down "T" across the kidneys and lungs, with the perpendicular part running up the spine between the shoulder-blades. Across the chest is a breast protector, and from it a belly-pad hangs down loosely, so that when you bend over, the two will fold. But when jumping down into a trench with knees bent, you can knock your wind out, since the lower piece is inclined to get jammed up and strike you across the belt line.

For this and other reasons – not the least of which is the very disturbing psychological effect of being constantly reminded of the vulnerability of your vital, life-sustaining, and life-giving organs – some men have quit wearing it after only a few days.* But for Brit Smith and thousands of others participating in the first infantry attack on the Verrières Ridge, those plastic pads are very reassuring when the hour comes to move out across some two thousand yards of open wheat fields, knowing there is no way to escape attracting

---

* While body armour largely disappeared from use by the end of the summer – as much left behind with the wounded and the dead as was discarded by survivors of Normandy – some men who came through it all unscathed or who actually knew they'd been saved from death by it were still wearing it in October along the Scheldt. And some looked like ghosts from the past as they wore it flapping outside their battledress – boldly, without apology, almost as if it were the mark of the long-service veteran. One soldier who wore it in this fashion was a Royals' stretcher-bearer – a man of proven, outstanding courage.

fire that can come at you with chilling suddenness: a burst of tracers out of nowhere accompanied by the distinctly nasty *bur-rup bur-rup* of a Schmeisser or MG 42 capable of 1,200 rounds a minute.

And very shortly Brit will learn that this body armour really works, that the long-fibred plastic, when hit, will stretch inwards forming a bulge that can bruise (and bruise painfully when it strikes where only a thin layer of flesh covers the bone), but absorbing and restraining otherwise lethal forces:

I'm going forward on foot with Major Mousseau [Fernand], an FMR company commander. My carrier is rolling along some distance behind, but walking with us is one of my signallers with a 38-set (a light sending and receiving radio set of limited range) with which we can send fire orders back to the signaller on the big 19-set in the carrier for relaying to the guns.

We've been told the clearing of the two farms on the way through is just an administrative move, that we are not likely to encounter any resistance simply because there's nobody there. According to a British report, the Germans have pulled back – a couple of their scout cars went through the area this morning and didn't see anybody.*

But, my God, the Germans have tanks hull-down in holes all over the place, and bags of infantry from a low-numbered division [1st SS Leibstandarte Adolf Hitler Panzer Division].

Almost immediately we encounter sniper fire. A lot of the wheat has been cut and stooked in the fields, and here and there

---

* At daybreak July 20, 4th Battalion County of London Yeomanry, an armoured regiment of the 22nd Armoured Brigade, having cleared Hubert-Folie east of the Caen–Falaise highway, was ordered to take the village of Verrières. By 10:00 A.M. a squadron had "mopped up" Beauvoir Farm, but opposition from Verrières was too strong, and it was withdrawn east of the highway. (Paragraph 195 Report 58 Historical Section Cdn Army H.Q., Dept. of National Defence)

in the stooks, are enemy snipers. So, very soon the FMRs start setting fire to the stooks up ahead, hitting them with phosphorous grenades. And when the snipers see the odd guy come screaming out of a grain stook, his uniform covered with burning phosphorus, they start popping up all over the place with their hands up.

Up to now we aren't being mortared or shelled (probably because we are passing among his snipers), and there's a lot of smoke from the flaming stooks. But when we send the prisoners running back to Ifs with their hands over their heads, shells begin to land around us.*

The foot-soldiers make it to the farm buildings [Troteval Farm] without too many casualties, but our tanks and anti-tank guns don't fare so well. Two Shermans brew up after being holed several times, and the others pull back. The anti-tank platoon of the FMRs is shot to hell. Fortunately the Germans don't waste their shots on a mere OP carrier. They let us go by, but when a T-16 carrier comes up towing an anti-tank gun, *wham!* he's gone. They knock out all the guns in that grain field from Ifs down to Troteval–Beauvoir road.

There are some stubborn SS in the farm buildings, and as they are being cleaned out, I take a Schmeisser burst along my chest that could have been very bad except for my body armour. Two 9-mm bullets leave indentations in my breastplate about an inch deep (deep enough that Quarter Stores will replace it without argument), but I'm only bruised. Once the buildings are clear, we pull out and dig in about a hundred yards away on three sides, reasoning that when he mounts his counter-attack, he'll focus his bombardment on the fixed target of the buildings.†

---

* The Fusiliers Mont-Royal took 149 prisoners, 49 of them only three hundred yards from their startline.
† Author interview.

However, the war diary of the Fusiliers Mont-Royal will record that they only start to consolidate about 5:00 P.M., when the newly captured positions are "for over an hour under extremely heavy mortar, shell, rocket and M.G. [machine gun] fire." This coincides with the arrival of a thunderstorm that had been threatening all afternoon, its cloud-bursting rain shutting down all air support, hampering radio communications, and bringing on early darkness to a confused and smoking battlefield. The scout platoon and one company, pushing south beyond the road between the two farms, are isolated from the rest of the battalion by shelling and mortaring, and by infiltrating enemy infantry and tanks. Then at 10:45 P.M. the company at Beauvoir Farm loses the vital support of their artillery FOO when Gordon Hunter, Baker Troop Commander, is wounded and evacuated.

Tankmen around Beauvoir Farm will later report: "The infantry cleared the top storeys of the farm buildings and reported the farm clear. One platoon was left in the Beauvoir Farm area and the advance continued towards Verrières. As soon as the advance was well-started, approximately one company of German infantry came out of the cellars of the houses and opened fire on the Fusiliers Mont-Royal from the rear."*

---

* "27 Cdn Armoured Regiment (Sherbrooke Fusiliers) Op 'Atlantic,' Overture to Breakthrough," p. 15, prepared by Directorate of History and held by Historical Section at Dept. of National Defence.

27

"IT'S BLOODY SUICIDE UP THERE!"

✳

BY THE TIME THE STORM BREAKS, THE CAMERONS HAVE GAINED part of St. André and the orchard north of St. Martin-de-Fontenay, and are holding onto the positions they have taken, though they are overlooked by the Germans on Hill 112 across the Orne, and are forced to endure merciless shelling.*

In the centre, however, the South Saskatchewan Regiment are driven to wriggling back over the ridge on their bellies through the wet grain and mud, seeking only to escape the savage machine-gunning and the crushing tracks of rampaging Panther and Tiger tanks. They hardly reach their objective (a field of peas beyond the crest, looking across at distant ridges and nearby enemy-held villages) before being hit by a hail of machine-gun fire, shells, and mortars and driven back from their exposed position into the wheat, the only available cover.

And even as they crawl through the three-feet-high wheat, the insensate steel monsters, with engines roaring horribly, follow them, trying to squash them or flush them out where their machine guns can get at them.

---

* German sources will reveal all the guns and mortars of 2nd SS Panzer Corps were directed on St. André and the orchard as though in retaliation for 2nd Canadian Corps' murder target on the village earlier in the day.

Mercifully, darkness comes early under the black rain-clouds. With their acting commanding officer, intelligence officer, and two company commanders dead, and all companies badly dispersed and riddled with casualties (66 dead, 116 wounded, and 26 taken prisoner), the remnants of the SSRs are finally able to make their way back through the Essex Scottish dug-in around Point 67, about halfway up from Ifs.

However, the sight of badly demoralized men making for the rear in disorder, many of them walking-wounded, does not help the morale of the Essex. Their spirits are already sinking from the realization they now are completely at the mercy of the German tanks, following the swift destruction of a troop of 17-pounder anti-tank guns of 2nd Anti-Tank Regiment which had rushed up the slope from Ifs to meet the expected German tank attack. In rapid succession, one after another as each came into view, they were knocked out by the German tanks: first their towing vehicles and then all four guns, killing twelve gunners and wounding eight more, even before trails could be dropped and their guns brought into action.

The memory of each grim hour of the next twenty-four on the ridge will remain forever vivid for Lance-Bombardier Kenneth Munro, a member of Capt. Grange's carrier crew in support of the Essex Scottish. They will be his last in action before being taken prisoner along with another member of the crew, Signaller Hans Nielson:

When Capt. Parker, of Easy Troop, is killed passing through Ifs with the Essex, and we take over, we move with the leading company up the long, gradual slope south of the village to take up a reserve position behind the SSRs [South Saskatchewan Regiment].

Artillery and mortar fire is heavy and it's very difficult for the infantry advancing without cover up the sloping ground. As we move closer to the enemy we can sense the confusion ahead. Then we start passing groups of the SSRs retreating from the front – very frightened men – a large number of them walking-wounded. Then we pass some of our anti-tank guns that have been knocked out and abandoned in a hurry, clear evidence our troops were pounced on quickly by enemy tanks and never got a chance to get into firing position. None of our tanks are moving with us. So it's our men against tanks – the best tanks in the war – at the same time facing heavy mortar and artillery fire.

We see no one surrendering, for we're still not quite in view of the enemy, but the sight of the SSRs retreating from the front in that frightened, unorganized way certainly has an effect on the Essex – especially when one SSR yells at us, "It's bloody suicide to go up there!"

Surely that's what every man is thinking. And those who were at Dieppe must be saying to themselves, "Here we go again . . ." I don't see any of the Essex turn and run, but talking to them next day, they mention that some did turn back as the battle grew more intense. Anyway, when we dig in, there are no infantrymen in front of us.*

Capt. Grange's OP is near the crest of the ridge, where it is intended the Essex will be in reserve, but it immediately becomes the front line. He will tell you later:

Throughout the night and next morning I bring down consider-able fire and am pretty useful in holding back the German infantry. It's here I learn the only certain way to protect yourself is to pull the guns right down on your own map reference [shell your own position]. After dark the German tanks move around

---

* This and the following quotations from Kenneth Munro are from an interview with the author.

the flanks, and when daylight comes and their attacks become more and more serious against the depleted ranks of the Essex, nothing resembling a front line is allowed to exist until the position is overrun in the afternoon.*

Meanwhile over on the left, some eight hundred yards away, driven from Beauvoir Farm and forced to give up trying to make it to Verrières, the FMRs have been able to maintain their foothold at Troteval Farm throughout the night and well into the next afternoon (July 21), only because of the intense fire from 4th Field guns.

Armed with rifles and Stens (the Bren is clogged with mud), the men of Brit Smith's crew supplement the small-arms fire from the now sparsely populated infantry trenches around them, killing many of the enemy when they work within twenty yards of their observation post. Smith repeatedly brings down all twenty-four guns in Mike target concentrations of thirty, fifty, and sixty rounds per gun:

They have about a dozen really big tanks (Panthers and Royal Tigers) as well as about fifty Mark IVs in the two or three miles I can observe from our slit trench. But you never see them all at once, and there's a confusing number of derelict tanks lying about, both his and ours, knocked out during Goodwood. For a while we are right between his tanks on the left and ours coming up on the right. One of his with an 88-mm gun (probably a Tiger) is dug-in over in a copse near the Caen–Falaise highway firing from a hull-down position. He's so bloody close – only about two hundred yards away – that each time he fires, the muzzle blast bangs our ears together and flattens the grain all around us as the shot screeches overhead and a shower of sparks

---

* This and the following quotations from Sammy Grange are from an interview with the author.

goes up from one of our tanks up on the hill, which he keeps hitting until it brews up.

The Typhoons aren't flying because of the rain. Anyway, the Tiger is too close. (We're much afraid of a Typhoon missing its target and hitting us.) So I put a battery of mediums on him and hammer him for about half an hour. (I may not have knocked him out, but I'll bet I loosened up the bowels of that crew.) It rains a lot during the night, and some FMRs decide to go back and find their rear echelon and get their greatcoats. They haven't eaten since the day before yesterday. They marched for hours getting up to the startline at Ifs after somebody cancelled their breakfast yesterday. And without any lunch, they were sent into the attack. Everybody is soaked to the skin and dripping with mud, for the slit trenches are now just sump holes and no one even has a ground sheet. In the morning Major Mousseau says, "Some of my men are missing." And at first light the Germans begin to attack in earnest. In considerable numbers they come crouched-over alongside the tanks and it's our guns that are driving them back.*

I don't know how many casualties we inflict because they fall flat in the wheat whether or not they are hit. At first their attacks are infantry only, and we are able to cope with them reasonably well with our artillery fire, but when they begin coming with tanks, we realize the jig is up. We have no anti-tank guns, no Piat ammunition, and the FMRs are very thin on the ground.

In some haste we have to abandon our OP in a forward trench and crawl back through the wheat to the farm buildings. Here we have to keep shifting our position to take on targets. For a while we are in a hole on the right side of the farm, engaging something – then we hear somebody calling, "They're coming in from the left!"

---

* Capt. Arthur Britton Smith was awarded the Military Cross for his gallant efforts.

By late afternoon [July 21] we've stood off at least three counter-attacks, but the company is getting low on ammunition and men, and the few left have had practically nothing to eat for two days. By now I'm the only link with battalion H.Q., and the only information they are getting about what's happening to the company is through me. I keep asking, Why don't they send up reinforcements — another battalion? My God, we're a mile and a quarter in front of Ifs. Where is the reserve battalion? The remnants of one company — no more than a platoon — is now holding this farm, and no one is making any attempt to reinforce it.

Major Mousseau is wounded and captured, and the last FMR officer I talk to arrives in my trench shot through the elbow. The bullet has not gone through the bone, but the muscle is badly torn, and when we bandage him up, we tell him, "We're going to try to get our carrier out of here, so if you want to join us, we'll take you out."

It's about 4:00 P.M. The last of the infantrymen have trundled off into the grain — grey suits are materializing and tanks are starting to wander around unmolested by anything. It's clear the only way we'll get out of here is under cover of some shell-fire. So I lay the guns on the position and tell them to "Fire until you're told to stop." I figure it'll take us five minutes to get away. But when we scramble into the carrier that's parked against a high stone wall at the rear of the barnyard next to the road, and help the infantry officer into a rear compartment, Bombardier May can't get it to start. The rain has done its work. By now tank engines are roaring all around the bloody house, but all May can produce is a pitiful *rurr-rurr-rurr* . . .

We've no choice but to climb out and help the wounded infantry officer out of the rear compartment so the side cover can be removed from the engine box to allow May to fiddle with the distributor cap and the ignition wires.

Everybody is sweating blood. The only uniforms now in sight are grey, and those big engines on the tanks are terrifying. They sound as though they're right beside us! We're against one of the stone walls alongside the road, and I keep thinking, Any moment now one of those monsters is going to drive right through that wall and it will be all over. Somehow Bombardier May is able to retain his wits as he works on the engine. Unquestionably the best OP ack God ever made ... always seems to know what you want before you ask ... continually reminding you of something you might otherwise neglect to do, but always the courteous gentleman with a great sense of humour – putting up with horrible handicaps and hardships without flinching or saying anything derogatory of the people who have put him in that position ...

At last the engine starts, and we all pile back in, all but the infantry officer, who has disappeared – captured I think. As we start moving out, our guns are still pouring hundreds of shells around the place, and Bill Murdoch [orderly officer and acting adjutant] comes on the blower to ask, "When are you going to stop? The paint is burning off the gun barrels." And I tell him, "Give me one more minute."

Pulling away we do our best to stay in the folds of the ground, but we attract bursts of machine-gun fire. All of a sudden I am being plastered with white stuff, and I think, "Oh God, now they're throwing phosphorous grenades at us!" But then other mysterious bits of sludge start flying around. So when we get back over a little dip in the ground, I get May to stop to find out what the hell has happened to us. The answer lies in a big tin of hardtack biscuits strapped on top of the engine and riddled with holes, punched by something very heavy, like half-inch machine-gun bullets, which blew the pulverized hardtack all over the carrier. The unsavoury bits of meat splattered about are from cans of bully beef, M & V, and other Compo rations we'd stored on the front of the carrier in a long wooden box – the kind Piats are shipped in. Box and contents have been smashed to hell by the heavy bullets from the tanks, but the carrier is undamaged. The paint is chipped off, but none of the bullets penetrated its walls.

Back at Battalion I inform them everybody has been pushed out of Troteval Farm, and I don't think many will succeed in making it back. They are either casualties, prisoners, or are scattered in the grain. Then I go back up with Major White's company to try to retake Beauvoir Farm that fell yesterday after Gord Hunter was wounded. But when we get just short of the farm, we see some Mark IV tanks up by Verrières.

Then a couple of Royal Tigers – probably the same ones which an hour ago cleaned out Troteval – roll in and around Beauvoir taking no precautions whatsoever, crunching around bold as brass. And nobody can do anything about it, for they've knocked out all our tanks and all the anti-tank guns as fast as they were brought up. They have the place to themselves, and White says, "There is no way we can go in there against those guys."*

Within the hour, the two companies of Essex Scottish (just west of there along the same road running past the farms to St. André) that were able to hold out against the German attacks overnight and through most of the morning of July 22 with the support of 4th Field guns, are also overrun. But before this happens, they are subjected to a demoralizing deluge of shells and mortars, combined with direct fire from German tanks – not just from their machine guns, but also from their 88s, used as sniper rifles at ground level.

So low do those shrieking shells pass over Lance-Bombardier Munro's head, "they feel as if they could almost suck you out of your trench." According to Munro:

---

* Author interview.

The Moaning Minnies are the most demoralizing – not only because of the tremendous impact of their explosions, but the effect of the terrifying sounds they make in flight. Some men cannot take the effects of this weapon. Occasionally fellows lose their nerve and jump up out of their trench – which is their only protection – and run, just run, not knowing where they are going, but yelling for their "Mum." It's always "Mum" – not God or anyone else – just "Mum." It's very tragic. You have to feel sorry for them.

Standing up is fatal. Jerry lets you have it if he sees any part of you. Mid-morning Col. Macdonald, the CO of the Essex, hollers at one of his men in a hole about sixty feet behind me to move out and get a count of the enemy tanks that can be seen. I hear the order and I advise the fellow to stay where he is, that I have a good view and can count what looks like thirteen tanks, though four or five may be only derelicts. Anyway the fellow accepts my count, but he stands up to relay the message back to his CO. At that instant, his back is ripped open by machine-gun fire. He moans for a few minutes, then silence.

Earlier I had talked to this chap from a distance. He said he had just arrived from Canada, after only a few days in England.

Munro's troop commander, Capt. Sammy Grange, will also have cause to remember those encircling tanks:

When dawn comes, they are behind us. And at one point I actually fire short of our position to try and get some of them. I'm already firing on our position when I order, "All North 100," to move the shells slightly to our rear. Not surprisingly, someone back at the guns questions this – don't we mean South 100? And I have to reassure him I really do mean to shell the area immediately north of here. Dicey, of course, but we're sheltering in trenches, and there's no alternative – the Germans are right there and we are just about surrounded.

As things are getting extremely hot and I am bringing the guns down almost constantly, the radio goes dead – we can't get through to anybody. So leaving Munro and Nielson to man the OP, I collect Pelletier [Gunner "Pooch" P.J.] and drive back to Bill Carr [Battery Commander] at Ifs to get fresh batteries or a replacement radio set, and report to him that things are in a very bad way up here.

Now, without the fire from 4th Field guns drenching the Germans with shells whenever they appear to be attempting to move in, it is clear to Munro that things are going from bad to worse:

From the moment Capt. Grange decides Nielson and I should stay behind "because it would not look good for all of us to leave, and perhaps they'll get a telephone line up here and you'll be able to get some badly needed fire," I have the feeling we'll never get out of this position.

The Essex have no tank or anti-tank support. Two of our tanks come over a ridge behind us about half a mile from the closest enemy tank. One is hit with the first enemy shot and burns, and the other does a 180-degree turn and flees. There is one 17-pounder anti-tank gun on the position, but someone has removed the firing pin [maybe during the SSRs retreat], and so it's useless. And because of the rain and clouds, there is no air support. There's a rumour the Camerons on our right, and the FMRs on our left, are pulling back, which would leave the Essex unprotected on both flanks.

To Nielson and me it's a hopeless mess – the Essex seem doomed. From my trench I have a very good view of the enemy directly opposite, across a depression and up on higher ground. As time passes, they increase their shelling and machine-gun fire, and around noon I tell Nielson I'm going to try to get back to Col. Macdonald (the CO of the Essex) and ask his permission to leave the position on our own. This seems to me better than sitting here like dopes waiting to be taken prisoner.

By now I have no hope — only a miracle can save us. After burying my map, field-glasses, and compass, I start crawling, and I make it, wriggling very close to the ground. My suggestion is turned down flat. But when, a moment later, a member of his [Macdonald's] crew is hit, two other men are allowed to try to get him back, while Nielson and I are obliged to stay. It doesn't make sense.

Now I can't get back to my previous position, because the enemy fire has become very intense — not only machine guns, but self-propelled guns firing armour-piercing solid-shot directly at us. I can't see as well here as I could before, but I can hear the tanks inching closer. And I'm sure there are some enemy tanks and infantry behind us also.

My hope is rekindled when Major Carr crawls up here alone, and has a few words with Col. Macdonald. But when I ask if I may go back with him, I am told to stay put.

About half an hour later, a couple of enemy infantrymen come into our position. I pick up a rifle that's handy, but they holler, "Me Polski!" For a moment, no one seems to know what to do. And before a minute passes, we are overrun with German infantry. The Regimental Sergeant-Major [Essex Scottish] puts up a white flag. It all happens so fast. Their tanks don't come right into our area, but three or four stand on the perimeter of the position. Thinking about it, the German infantry probably were closing in around us all day. Though from my first position, I hardly noticed any infantry.

The Germans are very noisy and loud, yelling at us to get our hands up and move. They wear the SS symbols, but what their outfit is, I don't know. Col. Macdonald isn't around. So I presume that when Major Carr came up to see him, arrangements were made to get him out.

By the time Capt. Grange gets back up to the Essex, they are overrun. Even crawling through the bushes, he can't get to where he left Munro and Nielson:

There are Germans – lots of them – wandering around the position. Obviously the whole thing is a disaster. While I see no wholesale surrender there are lots of Germans about, and I do a great deal of crawling though the mud on my way back. When I come across a dead German with a revolver in his hand, I become quite concerned, and pull out my own revolver to be ready for all eventualities. Fortunately I have no cause to use it, for the result could have been disastrous. When returning it to its holster, I find it's plugged with the mud through which I've been crawling.

Meanwhile, over on the extreme right flank, one 17-pounder gun of 2nd Anti-Tank Regiment is engaged in a deadly dual with a number of Panther tanks about to attack the Queen's Own Cameron Highlanders of Canada, now holding the orchard on the northern outskirts of St. Martin-de-Fontenay and St. André-sur-Orne, at this time under horrendous shell and mortar bombardment from masses of enemy weapons, many of them deployed west of the Orne and hidden by Hill 112.

"A striking example of what can be accomplished by courageous and determined well-trained gunners," is how this heroic engagement between one lonely 17-pounder on an exposed forward slope leading down into St. Martin and some distant, long-barrelled Panthers, will be described in the official history of the gunners of Canada.*

---

*   Col. G. W. L. Nicolson, CD, *The Gunners of Canada: The History of the Royal Regiment of Canadian Artillery, Volume II, 1919–1967* (Toronto: McClelland and Stewart, 1972), p. 299.

Having spotted a number of Panther tanks forming up in a hollow beyond the range of his 6-pounders, a troop of which is deployed in the orchard near St. André, Lt.-Col. H. E. Murray [commanding officer of 2nd Anti-Tank] brought up a 17-pounder to snipe at the enemy from a high point on the road north of the village. L/Sergeant I. L. Johnson of 20th Battery and his detachment manhandled the gun forward, putting it into action beside a knocked-out Sherman tank which was in full view of the enemy. As Murray had surmised, the Germans judged the 17-pounder rounds to be coming from the derelict Sherman, which their retaliatory shots quickly set ablaze.

Despite the enemy fire and the intense heat of the burning tank, the Canadian crew kept their weapon in action until a direct hit on the breech silenced it. By that time three of the detachment, including Sergeant Johnson, had become casualties, and Sergeant Ford had taken over firing the gun single-handedly until he too was wounded. But three of the Panthers had been put out of commission.

It was then that Bombardier G. A. Grassick of the 6-pounder troop came into the picture. When the gun he had been serving was destroyed by a German round, he crawled back from the orchard to the damaged 17-pounder, under fire all the way. Chipping away with an axe, he managed to break the semi-automatic gear and put the gun back into action. Then firing it himself he destroyed another Panther, bringing to four the number of enemy tanks knocked out by one 17-pounder.*

---

* Lt.-Col. Murray was subsequently awarded a DSO for his part in this effective action in scattering the German tanks. Sergeants Johnson and Ford were awarded Military Medals, and Bombardier Grassick was Mentioned in Despatches.

28

GUN BARRELS GLOW RED
LIKE CANDLES

_____ ✳ _____

FROM THE TIME THE GUNS OPENED UP ON BEHALF OF THE
Royals' attack on Louvigny two days ago (on July 18), opportunities
for sleep have been rare, and for the most part non-existent. On
that last afternoon at the position in the valley in front of
Carpiquet, all gunners had to be on duty for the Louvigny fire plan
and subsequent targets developing out of the attack. And as soon as
things started to cool down, the quads came up and all were kept
busy limbering up the guns and packing in for the move up to this
field between Louvigny and the Orne.

There'd been some chance for sleep in the quads while they
waited to move off, and during the long, slow move, but once here,
all hands were needed to put the guns in action and keep them serviced while the pits were dug. And it was well after dawn on July 19
before the gunners could turn to digging personal slit trenches into
which half of them might tumble for some sleep. Then the atmosphere was not conducive to sleep even for exhausted men. Every
man knew he had spent the night in no-man's-land, with German
burp guns (Schmeissers) behind them in the village firing tracers at
the Royals in the surrounding orchards, and with the dawn, no one
knew what to expect.

From mid-morning onwards all hands had to be on deck for a
series of fire plans: first, in support of the Maisonneuves clearing

the far bank of the Orne from up near Caen down to Fleury-sur-Orne; then on behalf of the Calgary Highlanders passing through them to attack Hill 67 late in the afternoon; and finally, in support of an attack by the Black Watch that took until midnight to clear the village of Ifs.

Shortly after midnight, the Army Service Corps arrived with those first 350 rounds per gun, making it imperative that every man remain on duty to keep the guns firing while ammo pits were being dug and shells and cartridge cases were stored below ground.

Now late this afternoon on July 20, in the middle of overlapping targets called for by FOOs around the shattered companies of the Fusiliers Mont-Royal, trying to hold Troteval and Beauvoir farms, and on behalf of the remnants of the South Saskatchewan Regiment, trying to crawl away from German tanks bent on machine-gunning them or squashing them like bugs in the wheat on the western end of Verrières Ridge, comes the torrential rain.

Hour after hour, all night long, it pours down in cloud-burst torrents, filling slit trenches and gun pits where men might have slept.

And then around 9:00 P.M., as though making certain no gun-crew member even gets the chance to rest huddled above ground under a ground sheet, Army Service arrives with the next instalment of ammo: 450 rounds per gun. A couple of hours later they come back again with another hundred rounds per gun, which they say is "a special order for 4th Field."

The field has now turned into a bog, and when the first truck sinks to its axles and has to be winched back onto the road, every case of shells and every case of cartridges has to be carried in from the road by the gunners.

With each passing hour the expression "human endurance" takes on new dimensions and meaning. Each steel case of four shells weighs 117 pounds – a weight of no great consequence to fresh, well-rested men under ideal conditions. But these gunners – already physically drained by the blistering heat and by the frequent, horrendous doses of shelling, aerial bombing, and strafing poured down on them for eight days in the previous position in front of Carpiquet – are now approaching total exhaustion from excavating tons of earth. To form a gun pit (18 feet in diameter and 3 feet deep) requires the excavation of some 28 tons, and to dig an ammo pit (12 feet wide, 18 feet long, and 3 feet deep) to receive the 250 cases of shells and 125 cases of propellant charges, representing 1,000 rounds per gun, calls for the excavation of another 24 tons of earth.

Each six-man gun crew, slogging back and forth through the mud and dark with 138 boxes of shells and 69 boxes of propellant charges, carries more than ten tons 300 yards.

By now, when weary gunners try to pick up a box of shells it feels as though it is anchored to the earth, and the very awkward twisting lifts required to lower them into the pits (and haul them out again later as they are needed) puts a wicked strain on back muscles aching for sleep.

Scarcely have the men wrestled and stacked those 18.5 tons of shells and cartridge cases down in their pits before they are hauling them up again and shovelling them into the guns at such furious rates of fire, the barrels glow red in the dark like candles, and buckets of muddy water must be poured down the muzzles to cool them off, producing spectacular geysers of steam and water.

And all the while the rain pelts down. Command post dugouts and their soil-covered roofs aren't designed to accommodate such a deluge, and technical work, demanding extreme accuracy, is carried out under miserable conditions.

Spoiled by two weeks of dry weather since arriving in Normandy, you and your staff have made no provision whatsoever for drainage, and your command post becomes a sump hole. By midnight, in spite of strenuous efforts to build a dike and dig a drainage canal across the mouth of the dugout to drain away the lake accumulating there, the muddy water, pouring steadily down the earthen steps, has risen almost up to your crotch.

At the same time the earth that was spread thickly, but loosely, over the sheets of corrugated iron brought along from the last position at Carpiquet to form the roof, is now completely saturated and dripping blobs of red mud down onto the artillery board as Bombardier Hossack tries to plot each new target. And before you can read off ranges and switches for the guns raging away outside, you must rest your battledress sleeve on the board and, with a scrubbing motion of your forearm, wipe away the mud.

Each time you expose the sparkling white expanse of waterproof talc that covers and seals in the gridded paper, you thank your lucky stars that events conspired to place you in action in 2nd Battery where you are a beneficiary of this truly marvellous invention by an ingenious ack — a veteran of the mud of Flanders in the First War. Long since posted because of his age to the reinforcement depot at Bordon, Hampshire, as an instructor. Sgt. Agner Emil Dalgas deserves to know how marvellously well his invention is working in action, and you vow to look him up one day and tell him.*

In between targets, careful not to move too quickly in the water that is now up to your buttocks, you and Hossack discuss Dalgas and this invention that curiously has not come into general use. It must have occurred to others on many occasions during training as they tried to plot their fragile white paper, huddling under the stingy little canvas cover of the board, vainly fighting to keep out the lashing rain, that artillery board gridded-paper might be covered with a sheet of translucent talc, through which the grid

---

* This was not to be. Captain Dalgas, of 1st Canadian Field Educational Section, on his way to visit 4th Field up in Germany, was killed on April 9, 1945, at the age of fifty-eight. An Engineers officer in World War One, he enlisted on September 11, 1939, with the 111th Canadian Field Battery in British Columbia with the rank of major he'd earned during peacetime service with a reserve battery. On learning he would not be allowed to proceed overseas as an officer because of his age, he resigned his commission (January 1940) and travelled to Ottawa to join the 2nd (Ottawa) Battery as a gunner. In August 1940 he came overseas with 4th Field to England, but his age again caught up with him and he was sent to #1 CARU as an instructor.

would show and on which an ack could write with an ordinary pencil. That it all could be sealed in against wet and dirt by an edging of adhesive tape and beeswax must surely also have occurred to other inventive minds. But then they must have abandoned the idea, stumped by the problem of the talc losing its waterproofing qualities by being endlessly punctured by thumb tacks securing the "arc" across the "zero line," and the pins of the metal pivot for the range-measuring arm positioned over the dot representing the "pivot gun" of the troop.

That the destructive pins on the pivot could be filed off and that renewable adhesive tape could be used to secure the pivot and the arc obviously did not occur to them. But it did to Dalgas.

Incredibly, no other battery in the Regiment adopted the Dalgas modifications, let alone other batteries of the Canadian Army. How they are managing to keep their paper dry and useable under conditions like these, you can't imagine.

Hossack locates his greatcoat from the bowels of GA (the armoured scout car) and pulls it on. It's a warm night, but the water sloshing around the thighs is cold. Signaller Harry Thorpe, a cheerful redheaded lad, who's been escaping the water by sitting cross-legged up on one end of the earthen shelf at which you and Hossack are working, sees you shuddering, and insists you wear his greatcoat. Being only a slight lad, his coat is bindingly small for you, and the sleeves only come two-thirds down your arm, but still you are very grateful for the comfort it offers.

As the night wears on, however, the air and water seem to grow colder. Your voice begins quavering when you speak, and Hossack's hands start shaking. Thorpe notices and asks if a shot of cognac would be permissible, if he were to supply a bottle?

When you both look at him with interest, he says he knows who has a bottle and he'll just "borrow" it without disturbing him. He assures you he can readily replace it in the morning, there's bound to be lots of bottles in those wrecked houses. You speed him on his way, and in a moment he's back with the bottle, performing an acrobatic feat in getting from the top of the stairs back onto his dry perch without falling in the water. And though scientists may claim that alcohol will lower the body temperature, not raise it, the shuddering ceases, life becomes tolerable again, and the irritability developing among those sloshing about this water-filled hole vanishes.

Dawn comes. Thorpe is relieved by another signaller, and off he goes on his scrounging mission with Gunner Oliver Ament, from whom he may have borrowed last night's blessed bottle. Over the past two days, enemy mortaring of Louvigny has been sporadic, but enough have crashed in there that you are no longer conscious of them landing. And so you'll never know exactly when it happened, but you're still wearing Thorpe's little greatcoat when they come to tell you that he and Ament have been killed by a mortar bomb in the village.

All morning the rain continues to pelt down, and the water rises so high in the gun pits that the breeches of the steaming guns begin to take on a rusty hue from splashing in and out of the muddy water on recoil. While this in itself isn't serious, gun platforms begin to lose their stability in the sludge at the bottom of the pits, now under almost two feet of water, and guns begin to slide so far back, their trails are jamming into the back walls of the pits. Gun crews take turns going out of action to try to stabilize, with fenceposts and railway ties, the heavy, round, steel platforms that form an integral part of the gun carriages.

Resembling a big, steel-spoked wheel, the platform is hooked up under the trail of the gun when travelling. On arrival at a new site, it is dropped to the ground so the wheels of the gun can be pulled up onto it, extending and locking in position two folding arms affixed to its hub and running up to the trail of the gun. Thus the gun is provided with not only a smooth surface for fast-traversing in action, but also a firm ground-anchor that makes it unnecessary for the trail to do what gun trails are traditionally meant to do, dig into the earth when the gun recoils. With the claws of the lower side of the platform pressed into the earth by 3,600 pounds of gun, it is usually a most stable and reliable device, giving the 25-pounder a clear advantage over every other field gun in the matter of rapid, unimpeded 360-degree traversing.

But today the rain-saturated, soupy sub-soil of the Orne flood-plain near Louvigny defeats the platform and all the wood the gunners can find to shove underneath it. After spending all morning vainly trying to stabilize the bottom of what are now pools of red sludge, the gun sergeants ask permission to pull the guns out of the pits and fire them above ground without any protection against the enemy shells and mortars that every so often slam into the position.

You have no choice but to grant them permission. It seems the Germans are now on the brink of breaking through and over-running everything all the way back to Ifs. And your firing has risen to insane crescendoes, beating off SS counter-attacks supported by tanks that are decimating the forward battalions and opening holes in the line that must be plugged by your shell-fire until fresh counter-attacks can be mounted to restore it. Targets coming in from the FOOs are overlapping: "35 rounds gunfire . . . 45 rounds gunfire . . . 50 rounds gunfire . . . fire until you're told to stop!"

By early afternoon on the twenty-first, most of the 1,000 rounds per gun, built up over the past twenty-four hours, are expended. Another 350 rounds per gun have to be rushed up by regimental ammunition trucks, some from the abandoned pits in the old valley positions, and the rest from an ammo dump north of Carpiquet.*

---

* John Drewry, Battery Captain (second-in-command of 14th Battery), was given credit for organizing the trucks and ammunition details that located these emergency supplies and got them up in time to head off a disastrous situation, which could have seen the guns forced to cease firing at the very time the whole front was collapsing and when shell-fire alone was preventing the enemy breaking through to Ifs.

Before the new supplies arrive, GPOs are becoming frantic, and you are actually in the act of reporting "only 12 rounds per gun left" to Battery Command Post when they tell you to send your gun crews out to the road to carry in the shells from ammo trucks that have just arrived!

The gunners' endurance is beyond belief. Though they've not slept at all for more than forty-eight hours, and must be on the point of collapsing from fatigue, they go on loading and firing their guns without a whimper. Target descriptions – brief as they are – still leave no doubt in anyone's mind as to where their shells are going: "SS ... Hitler Youth ... fanatics ... enemy counter-attacking with tanks ... scale 60 ... repeat ... repeat ..."

Sit reps (situation reports) are non-existent, and the messages and queries being passed back and forth are so sparse it is impossible to get a coherent picture of what is happening. However, it's clear the whole front is in danger of being overwhelmed. Only the Camerons seem to be holding their tenuous position at St. André.

The Fusiliers Mont-Royal, seemingly overrun by tanks and infantry, are being driven from both Troteval and Beauvoir farms. And the Essex Scottish, left exposed when the South Saskatchewan Regiment were driven back from off the crest yesterday, now in their turn are being overrun and routed, and at least one company has disappeared completely.

Fully occupied with the urgency of the overlapping targets, that clearly are dropping curtains of fire across the gaps left in the line by the routed battalions, you forget about Thorpe and Ament until word comes in that the advance party that left last night to recce new gun positions near Ifs has been shot up, and that lieutenants Bill Knapp and Howard Dawson are dead – clean-cut, pink-cheeked Knapp, who won the 2nd Corps' long-distance run at Waldershare Park last month; and Dawson, with whom you'd shared officers' training, who loved his wife so very much.

When you lay on the next target, you climb out of your candle-lit dugout. Blinking like an owl, even though the sky is deeply over-cast and a drizzle is still falling, you head across the wet field towards the nearest gun, sitting in shocking vulnerability, flat up on the turf beside its abandoned, watery pit. Serviced by its entire crew, it blasts away at unseen targets on the ridge across the river.

Stripped to the waist, the gunners haul and carry shells – remov-ing safety caps, adjusting charges, loading and firing them like robots – not even looking up when a big, hostile shell lands directly in front of the troop with a horrendous roar, sending up a great, black spout of steamy mud and smoke.

The gun-layer, hunched over on his seat, his wet back glistening with the falling rain, a soggy cigarette hanging from the corner of his mouth, never takes his eye far from the rubber eyepiece on the dial-sight, as he maintains a constant rhythm, his deft hands con-stantly touching gear wheels, ensuring the lay remains on his aiming point, and pulling the firing lever each time he hears the breech-block close.

You tap him on the back, and when he looks around, you make motions for him to get up and let you climb up in his place.

Then for a long time you fire the gun in raging vengeance – almost enjoying the vicious pitch and slamming recoil of this death machine throwing its deadly missiles at the ridge over the river.

29

FOOTNOTE TO GOODWOOD
AND ATLANTIC

✳

DURING THE THREE DAYS OF GOODWOOD, BECAUSE OF THE depth of the German gun lines and the awesome superiority of their tanks, dug in on high ground with an unlimited field of fire for their long-barrelled 88s, the British lose 400 tanks, a third of their tanks in Normandy.

Late on July 19, recognizing that the German gun lines are still intact and further assaults by his tanks would be suicidal (out-gunned as most of them are by the German tanks), Gen. Dempsey of 2nd British Army informs his 8th Corps he is arranging for the two infantry divisions of 2nd Canadian Corps to take over as soon as possible. At 10:00 A.M. on July 20, he issues a directive that 8th Corps is to discontinue the advance, that 11th Armoured will go into reserve when relieved by 3rd Canadian Infantry Division, 7th Armoured will complete the capture of Bourguébus, and the Guards Armoured Division will take up a defensive position on the east flank.

And when cloudburst rain descends late in the afternoon, turning the fields into a sea of mud and shutting down all support by the fighter-bombers, General Montgomery recognizes Goodwood is over and henceforth all further attacks on Verrières Ridge will be undertaken by the infantry of 2nd Canadian Corps – most particularly 2nd Division.

Students of strategy will argue for decades the meaning and intent of Montgomery's orders for Operation Goodwood–Atlantic: whether the operation was an attempted break-out, or merely a feint to hold the Germans around Caen. Monty will maintain he intended the latter, and admirers will give him the benefit of the doubt, believing that he was trying to draw the maximum amount of German armour on the Caen front to allow for his planned break-out by the Americans on their thinly held front at the western end of the bridgehead. His critics, on the other hand, will claim the weight of the British attack was so massive, it had to be an attempted break-out, and that the words of his directive – "exploiting in the direction of the Seine basin and Paris"– is a dead giveaway.

Whatever Montgomery meant, German commanders could only view the ferocious attack as complete validation of their long-held opinion that the Caen sector posed the greatest threat, and that they must continue to maintain most of their armour opposite the Canadians and British, at the expense of the western end of the bridgehead. That this conviction ultimately proved disastrous for them is irrefutable.

There is a suggestion that by the middle of July the highest military and political leaders were becoming worried that the Normandy campaign was in danger of bogging down into a stalemate – a battle of attrition such as developed after the first few weeks of fluid battles in 1914.

Certainly, to the clean-shaven, pressed-down-lapels world of Red Tabs – following the progress of the war with coloured pins on map boards and statistical summaries of expenditures of men and materials, not to mention the *Times* at breakfast – the succession of attacks initiated in June and July by both the British and the Germans along the Odon west of Verson, each ending in a bloodbath without significant territorial gain, could well have suggested a stalemate was developing.

The latest attacks by two British corps on Hill 112 southwest of Caen begun three nights before Goodwood (July 15), while achieving their tactical purpose of pinning down German panzer divisions so that Goodwood and Atlantic might develop east of the Orne, have been unable to gain significant territory. Operations Greenline and Pomegranate, by XII and XXX corps, constituting the third major attempt by the British to expand the Odon bridgehead, achieved only slight gains at terrible cost – again, reminiscent of the blood-letting battles of attrition for minuscule gains in World War One.

But all the disturbing conclusions that should have been drawn from the outcome of these and all the other attacks along the Odon and against Hill 112 – that Allied tanks simply are no match for German Panthers and Tigers – seem to have been ignored by the senior officers at SHAEF (Supreme Headquarters, Allied Expeditionary Force). And on top of this, the total failure of the thousands of RAF and USAF bombers to subdue the German gun lines and dug-in tanks along Verrières Ridge and beyond is incomprehensible to anyone watching, let alone anyone still clinging to the belief held after Dunkirk by the Air Marshal Sir Charles Portal, Chief of Air Staff, that the war would be won in the air, not on land, and the Army would return to the continent as an army-of-occupation only, the enemy's will to resist having been crushed by bombing – a belief still earnestly held as late as January 1944 by the Commander-in-Chief of Bomber Command, Air Marshal Sir Arthur Harris.*

General Eisenhower – needled by his deputy commander-in-

---

* On August 12, 1943, Harris wrote Portal: "I am certain that given average weather and concentration on the main job, we can push Germany over this year." And in January 1944 he was still optimistic that by April 1, Germany would be driven by bombing to "a state of devastation in which surrender is inevitable." (Max Hastings, *Overlord*, [London: Pan Books, 1985], p. 48.)

chief, Air Chief Marshal Tedder, calling for Montgomery's head – and some prominent war correspondents and instant-history writers are shocked into a state of petulance by the inability of Montgomery's forces to break out south of Caen.

Postwar historians, both British and American, finding this querulous style contagious, will use it again and again to express their impatience with the slowness shown by Canadians forces on the road to Falaise.

However, no such thoughts enter the heads of those occupying the slit trenches and gun pits around Caen. Not knowing what any attack is supposed to accomplish, apart from enlarging the bridge-head, there is no sense of failure, only bewilderment that so much high explosive, so liberally distributed, could not blow a path through the Germans. There is no loss of confidence in the leadership or in the ability of the Allied forces to ultimately overwhelm the enemy. It is now crystal clear, however, that it is going to take a lot longer than anyone expected, that the Germans are prepared to fight to the death for every foot of Normandy, and that German tanks are vastly superior to Allied tanks.

The Sherman, the most abundant tank among the Allies, may be fast and mechanically reliable, with a gun-turret traversing-speed much faster than the German tanks' (allowing gun-layers to get off opening rounds faster), but it is grossly inferior in crucial matters of gun muzzle-velocity and protective armour. Only 33 tons – compared to the 50-ton Panther, the 54-ton Tiger, and the 68-ton Royal Tiger – the Sherman is extremely vulnerable. It has shown such a tendency to flash into flame when hit that it has been given the grim nickname "Ronson" after the famous cigarette lighter.

A Tiger, armed with a long-barrel 88-mm, can sit back in hull-down position and knock out Shermans at ranges of up to two and a half kilometres, while the Sherman's gun can't penetrate the 80 mm of frontal armour of a Panther at any range, let alone the 102 mm on a Tiger I and the 150 mm on the slanted front of a Royal

Tiger. Even if a Sherman manages to close to 500 yards, the solid-shot from its 75-mm gun (capable of penetrating only 68 mm of steel) will just ricochet off a Tiger's 80-mm sides.

The 88-mm is a superior weapon mainly because of its multiple role as anti-aircraft, anti-tank, and mobile-assault gun. As a field gun it is distinctly inferior to the 25-pounder, because of its crest-clearance problems arising from its high muzzle-velocity and flat trajectory, which force many of its shells to be fired as erratic air-bursts. Clearly, it is as an anti-tank gun that it has earned its deadly reputation in Normandy.

Only the few "Fireflies" (Shermans converted by the British to take their superior 17-pounder anti-tank gun, allotted to Canadian tank units on the basis of one per troop of regular Shermans) are capable of knocking out the heavier German tanks. With a muzzle-velocity comparable to the high-velocity long-barrelled 88-mm, the 17-pounder, when armed with special tungsten-carbide Sabot ammunition, has superior striking power.*

Approved for issue in 1941, the gun was not mounted in a tank by the British until August 1943, and then not in a British tank, but a Sherman. Clearly the Churchill, a 152-mm frontal armour, would have been a formidable tank had its turret been redesigned to take a 17-pounder.

---

* The British 17-pounder armed with Sabot ammunition is capable of penetrating 231 mm of steel inclined at 30 degrees at 1,000 yards, compared to 164 mm for the long-barrelled 88-mm on the Royal Tiger. With Armour Piercing Discarding Sabot (APDS), the size and weight of the diamond-hard tungsten-carbide core projectile is reduced by more than half, but its velocity is greatly increased through the "choke principle." A split dumb-bell of soft alloy, taped around the projectile, shatters on point of firing, plugging the barrel and forcing an extra build-up of gases behind the slim shot before it is expelled. This rise in velocity, combined with the irresistible hardness of the slender tungsten shot, results in a remarkable increase in penetration. See Appendix C.

30

LIKE REMNANTS OF

A FALLEN CIVILIZATION

❋

AT 2:00 A.M. ON JULY 22, ORDERS COME TO MOVE FROM THE field between Louvigny and the Orne to a field directly across the Orne, just south of the smashed railway bridge in a bend in the river near Fleury-sur-Orne. As the crow flies, it's no more than three hundred yards away from where the guns now sit, but five miles by a tortuous route bulldozed through the dark ruins of Caen, crossing over the Orne on a newly erected Bailey bridge, through the industrial suburb of Faubourg de Vaucelles, and south along the high ground above the river.

To ensure at least one battery is available to respond to calls for fire at all times, 2nd Battery is to cross over first and get its eight guns on line before the rest are pulled out of action. As it turns out, it takes three hours and twenty minutes to complete the move. Passage through the appalling devastation that once was a city is very slow, and the convoy is frequently stopped for long periods in narrow defiles bulldozed through the rubble as traffic jams up in both directions.

More than guns and tanks must move over the Orne at night. Heavy trucks moving up, loaded with ammo, petrol, rations, and reinforcements, meet ambulances and long flatbeds carrying disabled tanks coming back, and compete for bridges, roads, and tracks leading to and from the open country south of the city, which in a few short hours will lie exposed to enemy observation and fire.

You had wondered why the recce parties had chosen not to return to Louvigny on discovering that the new positions near Ifs were on the fringe of territory still in dispute and exposed to point-blank fire from enemy tanks. (This much you'd gathered from targets called for by FOOs when enemy attacks threatened to roll back the front to Ifs.) Now, in this stop-and-go traffic, you understand.

As time passes, you find it harder and harder to keep your eyes open. With good reason: you haven't been allowed to lie down to sleep since the morning of the 19th, almost three days ago. And you've had no sleep whatsoever since 8:00 P.M. the day before yesterday (July 20), when advance parties were called and Hutch took off to recce the next position, leaving you, like every other subaltern in charge of the guns, without a second officer to spell you off.

As if that weren't enough, just before leaving the old position, Gunner "Hank" Wilkins, your troop gun artificer, lumbered over to you with a bottle under his arm and a slender liqueur glass filled with an unidentifiable liquid, remarking, "You sure look as if you could use a drink, sir." You tossed back the breathtaking, throat-paralysing substance, which, from the taste, could have been a shot of overproof alcohol laced with hydrochloric acid. It almost sent you to your knees, struggling for air. Wilkins, roaring with laughter, said it was Calvados.*

---

*   Raw Calvados, the kind most frequently found in '44, was atrociously under-aged and criminally overproof in its original state of 70 degrees alcohol, not yet cut to the legal commercial level of 45 degrees, the alcoholic level of Scotch or rye. Normandy farmers with apple orchards are the sole producers of the alcohol, which is distilled from hard apple cider fermented in huge oak barrels in their barns. It is aged for at least five to seven years, turning from white to amber and becoming as smooth as the finest cognac. Canadian soldiers, however, will remember only a throat-clutching drink, since just the unaged stuff was left above ground, unhidden from the Germans, still at its original eye-watering strength and rawness.

You try studying the map on your knees, but map-reading through Caen is impossible with its streets and intersections obliterated by the bombs. You're glad that for once Able Troop is not leading the battery, even though there's no chance of taking a wrong turn with only a single bulldozed track to follow through the city.

Stuck halfway back in the convoy, with no responsibility for its forward progress, you fight a losing battle against sleep and start dozing off for longer and longer periods. Just how long these lapses extend, you can't actually tell, as it's difficult to distinguish between dream and reality. Eerily outlined by the light of a half-moon that comes and goes behind drifting clouds left over from the rainy weather yesterday, the grotesque mountains of rubble swim in and out of your consciousness – sometimes appearing as a tumble of children's building blocks, and then as surrealistic piles of giant sugar cubes or as snowdrifts. And once, when you awake beside broken columns and arches arising from the rubble, it seems you are among the sad and ghostly ruins of a fallen civilization.

At last you surrender to total oblivion, sinking into the deepest possible sleep, from which you are rudely awakened some time later by the unbridled roar of a diesel engine spouting right beside your ear.

It's already dawn. The giant bulldozer is struggling with some rubble no more than three feet from the open window on your side of the truck.

Now fully awake and feeling quite refreshed, you pity Kirby, your driver, who has been forced to stay awake all night. But he's in remarkably good spirits and assures you he's fine and will catch some sack time later today. This is so typical of drivers, who can somehow draw on a reserve of energy denied their passengers, remaining fully alert, whether engaged in stop-and-start driving through a bombed city or hurtling over Welsh mountains with only pinholes of light from their blacked-out headlights to penetrate the fog and the rain.

And Kirby actually seems to feel sorry for you because you missed seeing Churchill – not once but twice – complete with cigar and his famous V-for-victory sign of two splayed fingers held up to the 4th Field vehicles passing him and Montgomery at some ragged intersection.

Drivers also have an uncanny knack for memorizing the routes they have been following, and with his help you orient yourself quickly. You are now across the Orne and moving south, close to and parallel with the river, but high above it on the plain.

Very shortly the convoy seems to break free of all restraints, and for a while it rolls at a good clip through a sparsely built area, broken and tumbled about from heavy bombardments. But as you close on the village of Fleury-sur-Orne, the leading vehicles slow down to a crawl as the road tips steeply down along the face of the cliff beside the river.

Over on the left, set back a short distance from the road, is the infamous mushroom-shaped concrete water-tower that seemed so menacing when studied through field-glasses from the much-tormented gun position back over there in the valley in front of Carpiquet. Now full of holes and forlorn, it has lost all its menace, and you wonder if it ever did harbour an enemy OP.

As you grind down the narrow track in bull-low, you pass the mouth of a huge cave in the cliff face, in which are assembled a crowd of men, women, and children, staring at the passing guns with discouraged, tired eyes, though some manage to nod and smile.

At the bottom of the hill you are met by a very weary, unshaven Hutch, who directs you to pass under the railway track at this end of the broken bridge, into a nice green area created by a big looping curve in the Orne.

This fresh-looking oasis, outlined by poplars marching along the riverbank, is the first relatively untouched bit of green you've seen since leaving the concentration area at Sommervieu, north of Bayeux. The vegetation has suffered very little from bombardment and has escaped the usual coat of red dust you've come to associate with Normandy battlefields, which manages to give even undamaged walls and surrounding vegetation a dried-out, worn-out, used-up, bleak, dead look. These green acres are divided into fields by drainage ditches, now dry and largely clogged with brambles, vines, and raspberry canes. Troop positions of 2nd Battery have been laid out with their backs against one of these bramble-filled ditches, and Battery Command Post is to the right of Able Troop next to the river.

At first sight this position looks too good to be true, but then you spot the 14th Battery gun markers behind you, even closer than they were to your guns in the valley in front of Carpiquet, less than fifty yards behind the ditch that runs behind your Able Troop Command Post. Obviously you will again have to get used to sleeping (if you ever get the chance again) with your head bouncing up and down on its improvised pillow each time the guns fire behind you and their muzzle-blasts pass over your trench.

When you inquire of Hutch how Dawson and Knapp got it at Ifs, you get a proper earful of old-fashioned, Prairie cussing – as lurid as it is earnest – making it abundantly clear that he holds in utter contempt those clots of senior rank who seem determined to deploy the field guns of 2nd Division, and 4th Field in particular, either up with the infantry or in full view of the enemy. However, you get no picture of what went on down there on the left, some two kilometres closer to the enemy (at positions that won't be occupied by 4th Field for another sixteen days), until you get to see Sgt. Hunt's diary at 26 Battery Command Post, now established in an underpass cut through a railway embankment nearby:

21 July 44: With first light we again set out for the new position. Arrival showed this to be a wheat field . . . A heavy rain was falling, which, with the lack of sleep, absence of breakfast, and futility of a single spade, wasn't the best preparation for the heavy shelling that followed. We took shelter in a haystack and awaited

events. Mr. Dawson left our shelter to join Mr. Knapp and Sgt.-Maj. Carlton in the latter's Jeep. It was an ill-fated move as shortly afterwards both officers were killed. Sgt.-Maj. Carlton lost a hand and received other shrapnel wounds. It was obvious the position was not tenable; accordingly were forced to withdraw [to this position].

By 5:20 A.M. 2nd Battery is in action and the other batteries can start moving. While this new position lies tantalizingly close to the old one, just over the narrow stream, it will be 9:15 A.M. before 14th and 26th are in position.

When gunners get a chance to visit the cave up the hill, they learn it's filled with refugees from Caen left homeless by the bombing. The gunners are so touched by their plight, especially by the little children, they start sneaking some of their Compo rations up to them – a practice officially frowned upon by the brass, but which, you are certain, will continue surreptitiously until the Regiment moves on, in spite of the cave eventually being declared out of bounds.

And from one of the cave-dwellers comes a possible explanation why so many German tanks, self-propelled guns, and mortars survived the saturation bombing preceding Goodwood. You are told the cave was already full of refugees from Caen, escaping the spasmodic Allied shelling by field guns and warships. But just before the heavy bombing of Caen started, German soldiers came and ordered them out of the cave, threatening to throw in grenades to speed up the process.

The refugees were forced to trek back into Caen and shelter wherever they could during the bombing. The lucky ones gained shelter in the Cathedral, which was untouched by bombs. Later many of them returned to the cave here.

This cave, and others like it around here – huge vaulted affairs capable of sheltering hundreds of people – were created centuries ago by stonecutters quarrying the granite blocks that built not only the cathedrals of Normandy, but also the Norman cathedrals in England.

One of the gunners swims over the river to collect his mess tins, which he left hanging on a fencepost, and on his return he reports that a British medium regiment has taken over the old positions and that Rear Division and Army Service Corps have established their headquarters at the Château.*

---

* A rather vivid description of Louvigny and environs as 4th Field left them is provided by the 2nd Canadian Division Army Service Corps historian:

> The Château had been a sore spot with the Germans . . . To relieve their injured feelings, the enemy had kept the Château under observation and fire since their hurried departure to the higher ground south of Fleury-sur-Orne. From this vantage point they could discern any movement on the floor of the Orne's watercourse and Rear Div and Service Corps HQ were in for the hottest time they were to experience during the Western European campaign. The nearby village of Louvigny had ceased to exist . . . decimated by our own and enemy fire. The Château was a grisly, eerie spot when Rear Div moved into it that afternoon. Long lines of varnished wooden crosses had been erected over the graves of scores of German defenders. Shells had smashed the buildings and stone walls, and the surrounding fields were filled with the bodies of cattle decaying in the hot sun. From three sides the Germans were in a position to bring fire on the Château, still having troops around Eterville, Maltot, and along the Orne south of Fleury.

From an unpublished document held by the National Archives of Canada, RG 24, Vol. 10906, *History of RCASC 2nd (Cdn Inf) Div., June 1944–Dec 1944.*

31

FEAR AND HATRED RUN
UNIMAGINABLY DEEP

✳

THESE NEW GUN POSITIONS OF 4TH FIELD SEEM TO BE LOCATED in some sort of charmed oasis, enjoying an unusual freedom from enemy shells and mortars, while all around, on both sides of the Orne, others continue to receive their grim rations.

Judging by the almost continuous round of muffled *crumps* over on the left beyond the railway embankment, where the whole area all the way back to Caen is under observation by the enemy on distant high ground, other gun positions and rear headquarters and echelons, including 4th Field wagon lines, are being shelled in rotation. While out front the Moaning Minnies regularly wind up their frenzied howling, and six overlapping, thunderous explosions lambaste the western hump of Verrières Ridge, plainly visible to the guns.

However, the only lethal metal flying about 4th Field gun positions today comes from a tank battle that develops across the river near Eterville during a late afternoon attack on Maltot by the British. While it's not possible to make out the progress of the battle, some Cromwell tanks are briefly visible – a momentary helter-skelter assembly behind a steep slope – before taking off with furious, raspy roarings that don't reach you until they've disappeared up and over the crest in the direction of Hill 112. Shortly there are some sharp *cracks* of tank guns. Then suddenly the air is filled with a weird, threatening sound of something headed this way, wobbling and swishing like nothing on earth. And tumbling end-over-end across the gun position, coming to rest in one of the gun pits under the trail of the gun, is a ricocheting solid-shot, still so hot it burns the fingers of the gunner who tries to pick it up.* And two more follow, one barely missing Gunner J. M. Millroy of Easy Troop as it digs itself in under D Sub's gun.

But the chief concern around the gun position today has been the menace of honey bees, buzzing about everybody's head in unusual numbers, suggesting their hives in some nearby apiary have recently been blown to smithereens. They show a disconcerting tendency to land on any accessible food, even when it's on the way to your mouth, thus encouraging the adoption of new eating techniques consisting mainly of waving a free hand over loaded fork or spoon until it's entirely in your mouth behind closed lips.

Fortunately the bees are good-natured little creatures without a vindictive streak, and they treat these competitions for the food as a game to be won or lost, without resorting to vengeful tactics, even though they are frequently rudely whacked by a hand frantically brushing the air space over, for instance, a hardtack cracker loaded with orange marmalade (to which they are most partial, and on which they will ride right into your mouth if allowed).

However, as the number of bees on standing patrols dwindles with the setting sun, the gunners become aware of other, more sinister buzzings, reminiscent of the bullets from out of the wheat fields across that sunken road at the Carpiquet position. The consensus is that these are coming from a stubby church tower, poking up through the trees some distance south along the river on the right.

Gunner F. C. Edwards, your ack-ack Bren gunner, asks permission to accompany Bombardier W. W. Scott over there on a patrol to try to winkle out the sniper or snipers. It could be a couple of Germans cut off by the Maisonneuve attack that went in through

---

* Solid-shot is a steel slug rather than a shell filled with high explosive.

there to take Etavaux, a kilometre beyond. On the map the next village is Bassé, but it doesn't show a church.

The little patrol is gone less than an hour when you hear excited shouting, quickly rising to a raucous chorus that spreads throughout the whole battery position as you climb out of your command post dugout to see what it is all about. Immediately the cause is evident: marching up from the south along the riverbank, in single file with their hands behind their heads, is a column of men in blue-grey uniforms escorted by Scott and Edwards, obviously on their way to the battery command post. You count them. Nine! Nine prisoners of war! Incredible!

The tremendous excitement generated at the gun positions is at first amusing. But as you watch men dashing about, grabbing up their rifles and Sten guns before running towards the battery command post to meet the marching column of prisoners, it suddenly is most unamusing. As you follow the stampede, for that is what it turns into, you can feel around you the frightening stimulation of the mob at work. It only needs someone to shout "Kill the bastards!"...

You understand their feelings. Dead Germans have long ceased to be a curiosity, but these are live ones, the first seen at close quarters, and every man present feels a fierce contempt for all men in uniforms like these, an opinion formed long before the war from newsreel images of arrogant, goose-stepping bullies harassing Jews and invading peaceful neighbouring countries. It was those images that induced them to volunteer to fight the Nazis in the first place. And all these years of forced separation from home and loved ones have deepened the hatred of an enemy that seems to enjoy imposing misery on helpless people. This hatred has been aroused to white heat in recent days through the agonies of terror imposed by the Germans' shelling, mortaring, and bombing, and the ultimate shock of seeing comrades die.

As you hurry to the side of Lieut. Gordon Lennox, standing outside Battery Command Post, you can see by the expressions on the Germans' faces that they understand what is developing and are terrified. Their eyes dart here and there at the encircling mob of gunners brandishing their weapons and growling curses at them.

Lennox is obviously as worried as you. He wears that grin he reserves for impossible situations as he whispers, "Where the hell are we supposed to send them?"

You don't know, but he should get them away from here as quickly as possible – to RHQ perhaps?

Right! He grabs onto the idea, ordering Scott and Edwards to march them double-quick over to RHQ for questioning, emphasizing in a loud voice the need to get all possible intelligence out of them.

With great relief you watch the men of 4th Field stand aside to let the Germans be marched away. But it will be a long time before that terrible look of hate in the eyes of your comrades fades from memory. You find you are shaking as you walk among them back to the guns.

Over beyond the briar-filled ditch and bushes, where the prisoners are passing other gun positions, you can hear men hooting derisively and hurling insults. But here all are silent and subdued as they make their way back to the gun pits and command posts. And for the first time you notice that almost all are wearing their steel helmets! Even in their rush to meet the German prisoners they had gone to the trouble of buckling on their tin hats, which had not been in common use throughout this unusually quiet day. A strange yet completely spontaneous, precautionary act, triggered by the prospect of finally coming face to face with the supermen, still fearfully menacing even when disarmed and clasping their hands behind their heads. Could this be anything less than the result of living so long with the nightmare of invincible hordes in blue-grey uniforms and jackboots, sweeping across Europe and North Africa before the tide turned – a product of fear and hatred of unimaginable depths?

32

A NEW LIFESTYLE HAS EVOLVED

✳

MOST SERVICEMEN WOULD AGREE THAT LOSS OF PRIVACY IS the prime sacrifice everyone makes on joining the forces. Regardless of rank, economic class, cultural background, experience, educational level, or intelligence, all undergo in their first days in the service a traumatic experience in loss of privacy. But with the passage of time it ceases to be a matter of any real concern, as all ranks are forced to accommodate, with a show of exaggerated nonchalance, situations no one can change or rearrange.

From the earliest days of training in Britain, every man, even those of high rank and seniority, learned to abandon when necessary all dignity in accommodating normal body functions on training schemes or out on the firing ranges – dropping his pants and baring his rump to the breezes in preference to facing worse consequences. On ten-minute halts of regimental convoys, every hour on the hour, during long hauls through densely populated southern England – its 155 vehicles and 24 guns and trailers extending seven miles or more along the road – some vehicles inevitably came to a halt on the main streets of villages. This always seemed to happen at the first stop immediately following morning or afternoon tea-break (provided by Curt Embleton's Auxiliary Service YMCA mobile canteen), guaranteeing a full turnout of all ranks at roadside, including those from the most unfortunately positioned vehicles. They, gritting their teeth, had to unbutton their flies and relieve themselves against stone walls and hedges (if lucky), or into flowerbeds or onto the open village green (if they were not), in full view of all villagers, male or female, who happened to be strolling by or gazing out of their windows.

Thus the unadorned, unprotected toilet now in use by all of Able Troop on the gun position at Fleury-sur-Orne is in no way remarkable, and you probably will squat over hundreds of similar latrine holes, on overturned Compo boxes with one of the bottom panels knocked out, without retaining a lasting memory of any of them. However, this one particular throne, halfway between the troop command post and Number One gun, set well back against the bramble-filled ditch, will for you be unforgettable simply because, as you sat there today, you were handed a copy of the new Northwest Europe edition of the *Maple Leaf*, which some unsung heroes, with commendable initiative, have begun printing among the ruins of Caen.

As usual, you are alert and listening for the warning whisper of a mortar or whine of a shell that will allow you but a split second to drop flat or dive into a hole – though as you sit you wonder whether to save your life, you could actually bring yourself to take shelter in that putrid mess in the hole below you. While this is a question of some substance, familiar to every soldier of every army in every war since cannons were invented, the scene hardly qualifies as unforgettable until you come across a strikingly relevant cartoon in the little tabloid. A soldier stands in a trench, with his head and shoulders emerging from what is obviously a Compo box toilet seat, shaking his fist at a circling Air OP Auster aircraft, which, as every gunner has come to know only too well, makes a whispering sound uncannily like an incoming mortar bomb whenever it glides in low over the gun position with its motor shut down. You can't help bursting out laughing. It's so easy to identify with that poor bugger, arising, suitably adorned, from that Compo box. And evidently so can everybody else, for suddenly there are explosive guffaws arising from all the gun pits where copies of the *Maple Leaf* have been distributed and are being devoured.

Taking stock of things, it is clear that a new lifestyle has been evolving in the bridgehead. All the way back to Caen, the yellowing fields are dotted with slit trenches, guns tanks, and vehicles. Long since you've learned to live in holes in the ground, seldom getting out when in the front line, and when in the rear areas never moving far from a hole and always keeping one ear cocked for the whisper or whine of mortar or shell. You drink water that's always warm, always heavily chlorinated and smelling like bleach, drawn from the Orne, where every hour of the day a body of a man or a cow floats by. If your stomach is strong, you still spoon into your steak-and-kidney pudding or M & V straight from the can, often warmed by the sun. If your stomach heaves when you dig through the doughy mass, you might pry open a tin of sardines, or spread some marmalade on hardtack or a slice of sultana pudding. And you suck boiled sweets endlessly, smoke, and wonder who the hell is getting those Compo boxes with the canned peaches and rice puddings. You develop a love-hate relationship with boiled Compo tea, learning to drink it before it grows cold and a leathery scum forms on the top, which you wrap around a stirring finger and fling away.

And all day long the guns rumble, and the "Tiffies" dive down through the frantic black puffs of flak, releasing their swooshing rockets on targets south of Verrières and St. Martin-de-Fontenay.

Sometimes your guns are required to fire red smoke shells to mark a target identified by one of the FOOs or the counter-battery people. Targets can be anything, but most often they are tanks, and it's against these that the four Canadian squadrons of Hawker Typhoons are proving terribly effective, judging from the terse reports coming back from the FOOs.*

The planes come in at full throttle without warning, four hundred miles an hour, and sometimes you miss seeing the first one dive. But the moment he releases his rockets, everybody across the entire front is aware that the Tiffies are operating. It must make the Germans' blood run cold, for even back here at the guns, three miles from the targets being attacked, the monstrous *swoosh* of the rockets ripping the air on their way down to the ground from the straining, diving planes can cause anxiety. Even after days of hearing them, the skin on the back of your neck tenses up whenever you hear the awesome *scu-roo-ching* of the rockets descending. You never fail to watch, for each pilot puts on a truly magnificent display of courage that is silently applauded by thousands of other watching Allied soldiers.

They come weaving in from the west, one after another, with short intervals between, diving down straight at their target through a rising fury of snapping, black puffs of flak saturating the sky above Verrières Ridge – each pilot holding the nose of his plane steady on the target for some seconds until he reaches a precise distance that guarantees his eight 60-pound rocket-bombs will have lethal effect. Only then does he release them, to leave smoky trails wavering in their wake above earth-shaking explosions that can be felt all the way back here at the guns.

It's incredible any of those planes survive those dives through skies polluted with the flak of more than six dozen 88-mm ack-ack guns covering the ridge. Sometimes a plane does disintegrate in a

---

*   While reports from FOOs received at the guns constantly dwelt on the success of Typhoon rockets on tanks, a 2nd Division report issued on September 22, 1944, analysing air support, declared "our own infantry say the enemy comes screaming out of trenches which are attacked by Typhoons."

ball of flames, leaving only a wisp of smoke when it's hit before its pilot can release his bombs. Now and then some poor guy, whose name you'll never know, simply doesn't reappear from his dive below the ridge, and you feel the earth shudder with the impact of his plane, and you watch for the funereal pillar of black smoke to rise above the crest.

33

THE RAVELLED SLEAVE

———————————— ✳ ————————————

IF YOU WEREN'T BENUMBED BY EXHAUSTION FROM LACK OF sleep, the supernatural intensity hanging over the bridgehead day and night would be intolerable. It's as though the grinding conflict of the immense opposing forces, exercising their colossal fire-power night and day without pause, is generating a static charge in the air about you, influencing everything you think, say, and do, stimulating and perhaps sustaining the will to carry on beyond normal endurance.

In a very real sense, Normandy has become a battle against fatigue as much as a battle for the domination of smashed and smoking villages. There are only five hours of real darkness (10:45 P.M. to 3:45 A.M. British Double Daylight Time) to inhibit matters of aggression. The interminably long days of attacks and counter-attacks and the tension and strain induced by the relentless sense of menace hanging in the dusty, foul-smelling air, combine to ensure a chronic lack of sleep and to produce this awful fatigue that afflicts all ranks. Men have learned to carry on by grabbing sleep whenever the opportunity arises, even during enemy shelling, as you did the day you came back to the guns from Eterville and bedded down in a shallow, open trench in the blazing sunlight of the treeless valley in front of Carpiquet, snoring away the whole afternoon, totally oblivious to the worst bombardment Able Troop has yet endured, according to your command post crew. Infantrymen describe falling asleep while continuing to walk robot-fashion up a road. And you know from experience a man can fall asleep standing up, having done so on more than one occasion recently while leaning over the artillery board.

For the past six days you've been largely confined to this candle-lit, primitively roofed dugout that is Able Troop Command Post, without a second officer to spell you off – Hutch having been posted to Battery Command Post immediately after being absent on that two-day advance party for the move over here. And all the while the guns have been firing constantly with only brief pauses between targets, seldom of sufficient duration (at least fifteen minutes) to allow you to grab a catnap sitting upright on a little folding canvas camp-stool, with your ankles wrapped around the wiggly, scissor-like legs to stabilize them.

Late yesterday, on the way to the latrine in a drowsy stupor, you walked under the muzzle of one of your own 25-pounders just as it fired, rendering you totally deaf so that you had to communicate entirely in writing until your hearing returned this afternoon.

Tonight you give fire orders in your sleep so convincingly you fool a new ack, Gunner William Hiltz, who just arrived today (July 23) and is on his first tour of duty. Sometime around midnight you provide the line, range, and angle of sight for a target fabricated in dreamland, only waking up after the guns begin firing. And incredibly it isn't the sound of the guns that wakens you, but your stern, subconscious reaction to hearing Hiltz break the strict code of fire discipline. In your sleep, or that mysterious state of stupefaction that passes for sleep these days, you listen without objection to Hiltz calling out over the Tannoy the fire orders to the guns as you dictate them. But when you hear him say "Fire!" – an order normally following the ordering of the range but which you withheld this time – you come up wide awake, demanding to know who the hell gave him the order to fire? Instantly realizing you are struggling out of a dream, but mystified by the reality of the guns thumping away, you ask Hiltz where he got the target. When he replies, "From you, sir," your heart almost stops.

My God! Where are those shells landing? Snatching the Tannoy mike from him, you yell at the top of your lungs, "Stop! Stop! Stop!"

You hardly dare breathe as you lean over the artillery board to swing the arm along the arc, plotting the line and range you'd uttered and Hiltz had methodically logged on his message pad. And your relief is beyond description when your pencil point dots the talc well beyond the FDL (forward defended line). Subconsciously you had fabricated a target from a mental store of ranges and switches from zero-line for the scores of harassing-fire targets you'd ordered over the past two days and nights. But the thought of what might have happened leaves you shaking.

You ask your embarrassed young ack where on earth he thinks you could get a target while sleeping over there in the dark? He explains that from time to time throughout the night they've been coming over from Battery Command Post with fire tasks, handing the slips of paper down to you through the folds of the tarpaulin that serves as a black-out curtain over the dugout stairwell. And when you started to give clear, decisive fire orders, he assumed another target had been handed in to you. Entirely logical. But please, you say, never, ever again make assumptions! Only in emergencies do acks fire the guns.

Even as you lecture him you find yourself again dozing off. To stir yourself to a modicum of alertness, you lay on the next timed target and climb out to visit the guns. To your dismay you find only one gunner serving each gun. The others lie like dead men on the floors of pits, their heads only inches away from the crashing, recoiling breeches.

Your first inclination is to rouse them indignantly. But then you check yourself. There is really no rush to get off harassing fire that is actually designed to be sporadic and unpredictable to the enemy. And these men have been digging gun and ammunition pits and shifting tons of shells around the clock for days on end. In just one twenty-four-hour period back at Louvigny, the Regiment fired 24,000 rounds. And the second-in-command visiting the guns last night reported that in the last four days 4th Field guns have consumed 40,000 shells – five hundred tons of H.E. (high explosive).

You watch the lone gunner lift out a hundred-pound case of shells, kick off the hasps, lift out a shell, place it in the breech, ram it home with the wooden rammer, slide a brass cartridge case in behind it, close the breech, mount the gun seat, check his lay through the dial-sight, and pull the firing lever. Methodically, without wasted motion, he repeats this routine over and over until he's fired the required number of rounds. Then, pitching the spent cartridge cases out of the pit, he sits down on the trail and wordlessly offers you a cigarette.

Over in the hole that is Battery Command Post, no one speaks either. They look up and stare at you a moment with red-rimmed eyes and then go back to work. For days, in incredibly dirty and cramped conditions, they've been working out targets and fire plans demanding extreme accuracy, calculating all the complicated data required to navigate shells to precise spots on the landscape, allowing for winds of various strengths and directions, and air temperatures and pressures at various strata above the earth through which the shells will loop on their way to the target – leaving only last-minute adjustments for the varying temperature of the propellant charges to the GPOs whenever extreme accuracy is called for.

They work with pencils sharpened to fine points, on talc-covered artillery boards, which they must struggle continually to keep clean of sifting dust, their noses almost touching the surface of the boards as they strain to see what they are plotting by the yellow glow of fading lamps–electric.

You hear heavy trucks milling around your gun position, and you return to find seventeen Army Service Corps three-tonners cluttering up the field among your four guns. When you inquire of the sergeant in charge if he's lost, fully believing it is a convoy that has lost its way, he asks, "Is this not Able Troop, Second Battery, 4th Field?"

When you admit it is, the softspoken man tells you he is here to drop off 640 rounds for each of your four guns. And his men could use the help of your gunners to off-load it. They spent yesterday off-loading ships and still have to make another trip back to the beaches tonight. They'd sure like to get off the road before dawn. On their way up planes dropped flares over them.

Using the Tannoy at your command post, you have the gunners, who are awake, rouse their sergeants so you can explain what must be done. As you pass the gun pits on your way back to the trucks, you hear the soles of hobnailed boots being kicked and mumbled explanations given.

What torture it must be for those men to force themselves to reject sleep for which their bodies are aching – let alone to start shifting 160 hundred-pound cases of shells and eighty boxes of cartridge cases per gun. But in the pits, where dark figures are staggering to their feet and yawning prodigiously, there's no word of complaint.

You tell the RCASC sergeant the gunners are exhausted from an awesome amount of firing during the past few days with very little sleep. He assures you he is well aware of the voracious appetite of the guns, having participated in shell dumpings the like of which, they are told, have never been attempted before: 86,400 rounds for 2nd Division alone in the past three days. Now tonight 46,000 rounds more, and before noon tomorrow another 26,000. In less than five days, 158,000 rounds for the division: 2,200 rounds per gun! Oh yes, he knows! Still, he wishes they'd move a little faster, he'd like to get that second trip wrapped up before dawn. It can get a bit uncomfortable riding in a truck with three tons of high explosive when Jerry starts bombing.

And you are reminded there is more to fighting a war than firing guns. Long after the trucks have pulled out and the first faint grey light is creeping in over the now-silent gun position, you ponder the lot of drivers who must toil night and day, moving up supplies of all kinds for the fighting troops, carrying on in obscurity, without the attention of war correspondents forever preoccupied with infantry and tank units with proud names and regional associations. Churchill said it so well before the turn of the century in his book *The River War*: "Victory is the bright-coloured flower. Transport is the stem without which it could never have blossomed."*

Denied even catnaps on your camp stool the rest of the night, you are still in a dangerously dull-witted state when you decide to leave Hiltz, slumped over the artillery board, snoring away, and go out and whip up the first brew of the day yourself. This turns out to be harder than you thought. Overnight there's been a heavy dew, and it is quite impossible to get flames to sustain among the straw and bramble twigs currently in popular use in place of petrol-drenched sand fires that characteristically produce tea tainted with oily smoke. Still, you know what to do, having seen gunners feed recalcitrant fires with spaghetti-like strands of cordite from discarded bags of Charge III propellant. Locating a blue bag from a pile thrown in an empty ammo box at one of the guns, you start adding a strand at a time to the smouldering sticks under a water-filled, square, green tin (the bottom half of a bulk container for hardtack) which rests on four stones in a cavelike firepit excavated in the side of the ditch.

---

*   Expanding on this thought, Churchill wrote: "The eye is fixed on the fighting brigades as they move amid the smoke; on the swarming figures of the enemy. . . . The long, trailing line of communications is unnoticed. The fierce glory that plays on red, triumphant bayonets dazzles the observer; nor does he care to look behind to where along a thousand miles of rail, road and river, the convoys are crawling to the front in unnoticed succession." *The River War* (London: Longmans, Green, 1899).

For a while nothing happens. And by the time this fact registers in your sleepy mind, a fair amount of cordite has accumulated under the pot. As you hunker down to see why it isn't flaring up in that sparkling brilliance others manage to produce under their boiling pots, there's an ugly, hollow roar and you are blown over backwards into a full sitting position by a violent puff of flame and soot — scorched clean, you'll soon discover, of not only your eyebrows and eyelashes, but several days' growth of shaggy beard. Fortunately fatigue doesn't dull the reaction-time of eyelids, and while you're left very red-faced (in reality as well as figuratively), sufficiently seared to require gobs of sunburn salve, your eyes are unharmed.

By the afternoon, you are so stupefied by lack of sleep that the only thing you'll recall of the entire day is passing into oblivion, with a desperate sense of relief, in the partially roofed slit trench your batman, Gunner Alexander Whitehawk, dug for you days ago in the ditch at the rear of the position.

That you had earlier in the day acted without a modicum of social grace in receiving your new troop leader (assistant GPO), you'll have to learn when Lieut. Bob Grout and you later become friends and he feels free to tell you it was with some trepidation he began his tour of duty with what was clearly a thoughtless boor. On arrival he'd asked someone to locate the GPO. And in due course a dishevelled, sandy scarecrow appeared at the mouth of the dugout growling, "Well, what the hell do you want?"

On being told, the scarecrow had simply said, "Okay, get the hell down in here and take over — I'm going to bed."

Fortunately, during the next twenty-four hours Grout is able to put your conduct in better perspective, while watching you become a source of amusement for all who come to peer in at you in your partially covered trench as you sleep the clock around, oblivious to an unending rain of dirt falling on your face from the dried-out earthen roof dislodged by the 14th Battery guns firing from only a few yards behind — each tormenting muzzle-blast, entrapped and swirling around in the roofed-over, closed end of your trench in the ditch, lifting your head and dropping it without causing any change whatsoever in the rhythmic breathing of your deep sleep. At least that is what he and others tell you when finally you come to life sometime on the twenty-fourth. And you are inclined to believe them, for you are never able to sleep in that pulsating trench again. Henceforth, when off duty, you sleep in the front of GA, the armoured scout car, curled up around the stubby nest of gear shifts, your bottom on one of the bucket seats and your head and shoulders on the other.

PART FOUR: JULY 24–AUGUST 2

Canadian Units Ensure American Break-Out Succeeds

34

A FOOTNOTE TO "MAIN BATTLE AREA OF CAEN"

✳

ON JULY 25 TWO MAJOR ALLIED OPERATIONS ARE TO BE UNDER-taken in the bridgehead, by the Americans on the right at St. Lô, and by the Canadians thirty-five miles east of there at Verrières – with totally different, unrelated objectives if viewed separately (the way the Germans must view them), but fully interdependent operations when viewed from Montgomery's perspective.

Each is vital to the achievement of a common goal: no less than the long-awaited "break-out from the bridgehead," leading, it is hoped, to the disintegration of German resistance on the perimeter, forcing them to retire to the Seine, where, with no bridges to cross, they'll have to surrender or be annihilated by the bombers.

"Operation Spring," the push south of Caen against Verrières Ridge and beyond by 2nd Canadian Corps (with two British armoured divisions available for exploitation), has limited territorial objectives. But to the attackers, as well as the attacked, it will have all the earmarks of a major offensive with a break-out as its ultimate aim. This is precisely how it is intended to appear; a threat so serious the Germans will continue to hold the bulk of their forces – particularly their armour – on the Canadian front, thus favouring "Operation Cobra," the American offensive Monty is counting on to break through the thinly held western rim of the bridgehead.

All of which is consistent with German thinking that the expected American attack through the obstacle-filled *bocage* countryside can be contained with minimum forces, while a renewal of the Canadian–British offensive in the rolling country south of Caen could succeed, spelling disaster for all German forces in Normandy unless opposed by maximum forces and fire-power.

Throughout July, most of the fresh German units arriving in Normandy have been directed to the British–Canadian front. Six of eight infantry divisions and all four new Panzer divisions, including two additional battalions of Tiger tanks, have appeared in the Caen sector.

And von Kluge continues to concentrate three brigades of Nebelwerfers (Moaning Minnies) – his entire Normandy complement of these dreadful, multi-barrelled mortars – on what he perceives to be "the main battle area of Caen."* Furthermore, most of the mortars and guns that halted operations Goodwood and Atlantic (more than 1,600 barrels) are still in position to drench Verrières Ridge with fire from both sides of the Orne.

The day before the assaults begin, Field Marshal von Kluge, Commander-in-Chief of German Forces West, responding to the dual threats, reinforces the American front with a mere battle group of 2nd SS, while transferring from Caumont the full 2nd Panzer Division to a position astride the Caen–Falaise highway. At Caumont it might have made a crucial difference in shutting down the American offensive; but moved east of the Orne south of Caen to meet the Canadian threat, 2nd Panzer Division merely thickens defences already ten miles deep holding a front of less than seven miles.

The end result is that on the eve of "Spring" and "Cobra," fourteen Canadian and British divisions are pinning down fourteen

---

* From the "Tempelhof Papers" (an appreciation by Hauser for von Kluge, July 19, 1944) as quoted in Chester Wilmot's *Struggle for Europe* (London: Collins, 1952), p. 389.

German divisions, including elite SS divisions such as the 1st SS (Leibstandarte Adolf Hitler) Panzer Division, armed with the best equipment the German high command can supply. At the same time nineteen American divisions (Bradley's fifteen and Patton's four) are opposed by a grab-bag of German battle groups and formations totalling only nine divisions.

And because the German tanks are so vastly superior in firepower to all American and British tanks, except a few "Fireflies" (Shermans equipped with a British 17-pounder gun), the six hundred Panthers and Tigers drawn to the Canadian and British fronts – leaving only 110 tanks and no Tigers at all opposing the Americans – will be the most telling factor in the outcome of these two operations: a decisive break-out on the American front (allowing Patton's army to drive almost unopposed in an eastern arc towards Paris) while the Canadians engage in a crushing, stalemated battle on Verrières Ridge.*

---

* The following details, showing the lopsided distribution of German tank forces between the American and Canadian–British sectors on the eve of "Cobra" and "Spring," are from page 364 of Chester Wilmot's *Struggle for Europe* (London: Collins, 1952):

On British Second Army Front (with 2nd Canadian Corps): Four Heavy Tank battalions and seven Panzer Divisions – of which five and a half are east of the Orne facing the Canadians.

On American First Army Front: Two Panzer Divisions, one Panzer Grenadier Division (with one battalion of assault guns only), and no battalions of heavy tanks.

35

"THE ENTIRE AREA LOOKS LIKE A CHARNEL-HOUSE"

※

MERCIFULLY, THE PRECISE DETAILS OF THE FORCES AMASSED opposite them are unknown to the bleary-eyed, tormented Canadian soldiers huddled in their sandy holes south of the village of Ifs, awaiting orders to go forward.*

Still, a man would have to be deaf, blind, and incredibly stupid not to be aware that the enemy is "thick on the ground" out there, that he can whistle up swarms of tanks, including his invincible Tigers, whenever required to crush an attack, and that "a helluva lot" of 88s and Moaning Minnies have registered every square metre of ground on the way to Tilly-la-Campagne, up those wide-open slopes to Verrières, as well as the orchards and fields around St. Martin-de-Fontenay and St. André-sur-Orne.

To the North Nova Scotia Highlanders of 3rd Division, who are to shield the left flank by taking Tilly-la-Campagne, and the nine infantry battalions of 2nd Division, who'll attack Verrières Ridge and beyond, it is clear that the swollen numbers of men, tanks,

---

* Survivors of these "holding attacks" – who one day would share in Montgomery's pride and satisfaction at the success of "his feints" in drawing the bulk of the German fire-power east of the Orne, allowing the Americans to break out – were, at the time, unaware that the purpose of their attacks was simply to maintain the bloody status quo.

guns, and mortars, committed by the Germans to the defence of their dominant positions, will deal as severely with the attacking forces as they did during "Goodwood" and "Atlantic," when in a single afternoon they stopped three tank divisions cold and cut to ribbons whole battalions of Canadian infantry.

The plan for "Spring" calls for 6th Brigade to clear the startline, which will be the road running from the Troteval and Beauvoir farms, on the left, to St. Martin and St. André on the right: the Fusiliers Mont-Royal retaking the infamous farms, and the Queen's Own Cameron Highlanders clearing all of St. Martin by midnight, July 24. The first phase of the attack will go in at 3:30 A.M. on the twenty-fifth, with the Calgary Highlanders leading the 5th Brigade assault from St. Martin to May-sur-Orne, and the Royal Hamilton Light Infantry leading off 4th Brigade, attacking Verrières. At the same hour the North Nova Scotia Highlanders are to attempt to "seize" from the fanatical 1st SS Panzer Division the fortified village of Tilly-la-Campagne, which lies on the tactically important high ground to the left of the Caen–Falaise highway, some 1,500 metres east of Verrières.

In the second phase of "Spring," the Black Watch will pass through the Calgary Highlanders to capture Fontenay-le-Marmion, while the Royal Regiment passes about 1,300 metres beyond Verrières to take Rocquancourt. And when all objectives are taken, 7th British Armoured Division will push south to the height of land along the Caen–Falaise highway known as "Point 122."

Since the attack is to go before dawn, some illumination of the landscape for the troops moving into position will be provided by searchlights playing off low-hanging clouds to produce "artificial moonlight" first used in that attack by the British ten days ago west of Carpiquet, with mixed reviews by participating troops.

In the opening phase, an extensive artillery fire plan will be carried out on German positions and gun lines by nine Canadian and British field artillery regiments, and three AGRAs (2nd Canadian, 2nd British, and 8th British Army Groups Royal

Artillery) containing nine medium regiments of 5.5-inch guns and two heavy regiments of 7.2-inch guns, as well as one heavy ack-ack, four anti-tank, and five light ack-ack regiments.

At 1:15 A.M. enemy bombers come over, and while no bombs land on 4th Field positions, they create havoc among other field and medium regiments spread across the densely populated fields reaching back to Caen. Many fires are left burning among vehicles and ammunition dumps. Nevertheless, throughout the night all three divisional artilleries continue desultory harassing fire, until 2:30 A.M., when, along with the mediums, they take part in a twenty-minute counter-battery program. At 3:28 A.M., just two minutes before H-hour for the attack to go in, the CO reports Phase 1 has been postponed thirty minutes. (Startlines have not been cleared at either the farms or at St. Martin.) By 4:00 A.M. FOOs are reporting it very foggy, as the three divisional artilleries open on a series of timed concentrations, which 2nd Division guns will con-tinue until 6:00 A.M., consuming 360 rounds per gun.

Any delay in opening an attack can cause confusion, as the timing of the units moving up is thrown off. And when the startline is still being fought over as the postponed attack goes in, the problem is compounded to a point where chaos threatens. So it is with the Calgary Highlanders and the Rileys when they have to subdue enemy on their startlines before they can launch their attacks and are unable to take advantage of the timed artillery program. And confusion extends to the battalions following behind, who must be in position to push on when the leading units have attained inter-mediate objectives.

With the guns raising a flashing, thunderous confusion across the whole front among the roiling mists lit eerily from behind by the low beams of searchlights, and plastered by enemy defensive fire, including salvo after salvo of Moaning Minnies crashing on the axis of advance, the Royals are forced to dig several sets of shallow slit trenches for shelter in the many hours it takes them to make it across a couple of thousand metres of grain fields – first following in behind the Rileys, and then surging forth in the van over the crest of the ridge to the left of Verrières.

"One horrendous foul-up in the dark, starting about 0300!" That is how Royals' Platoon Commander Bob Suckling will remember it.

In the infantry nobody tells you anything, which results in the birth of what are known as "shit-house rumours" – wildly exaggerated, panic-warped pieces of intelligence spread by word-of-mouth and growing with each retelling, until they are only slightly more reliable than army news despatches. And this night the rumours are particularly melodramatic. Eventually we learn the snafu is caused by somebody's failure to secure the startline. But in the meantime, we spend what seems hours in open ground in the dark, surrounded by horrific flashes and the grinding sound of tanks we're supposed to be following; not knowing why we are held up, but knowing we shouldn't be this close to the tanks.

If there is one infantry adage that should always be scrupulously observed, it is: Never follow a tank – in fact, never get close to one! The buggers draw enemy fire, and sometimes they run over you. A few of our men are lost this way after falling asleep on the ground.*

It's just starting to get light when the carrier in which Brit Smith and his 4th Field crew are moving forward with the FMRs back towards Troteval Farm, runs over a mine:

Four days before, when we were forced to bail out quickly from an OP near Troteval Farm in the pouring rain, I buried in the bottom of a trench my big 12-power binoculars and my new

---

* Author interview.

Burberry mackintosh I'd recently bought at Simpsons in London for twenty-five pounds.*

Damned if I was going to crawl through the mud in my expensive coat, with those big, awkward field-glasses dangling around my neck. So I had taken them off, and after wrapping them in my Burberry, covered them over with earth in the bottom of the trench – carefully noting its location for future reference.

Now on our way up to Troteval, I remember that slit trench is only a couple of hundred yards off the route we are taking, and decide to go over there and recover my binoculars and my rain-coat. It's still quite dark, barely light enough to see where we are going, but we catch sight of an FMR jumping up and down, waving his arms wildly and yelling something. It being impossible to communicate by voice over the roar of our barrage, I reach over in front of Bombardier May with a clenched fist, the recognized signal for a driver to stop.

Just as the carrier rocks to a stop, and I'm standing up to turn around to ask our French-speaking crew member [T. Robitaille] if he can make out what the guy is yelling, a mine blows under the track on the driver's side.

May is killed instantly. And one of my legs is shattered as I'm blown out in a cloud of sand from the layer of sandbags with which all our carriers are floored to absorb the force of just such an explosion. I go up very high, looping over before coming down in the uncut grain with an awful thump, thinking, "My God! I'm still alive!"

Immediately at least four machine guns covering the mine field open up, focusing on where they saw the flash of the mine. Bullets wham into the sides of the upturned carrier, and I, along with the two signallers (saved from serious harm by the steel

---

* About 116 Canadian dollars, equivalent to about 1,160 dollars in 1990.

bulkhead between them and the front compartment), start crawling away like mad through the grain, bullets snicking all around us. Broken leg and all, I crawl like hell for about fifty yards.

When we get far enough away to stop, I remember that Jack Thompson [the other 14th Battery troop commander] is on the move nearby with another company and should be approaching Beauvoir Farm by now. I send one of the signallers to find him and tell him we're out of action so he can pass the word back to Battery to get up a replacement crew.

While he's away, the other signaller gives me a shot of morphine, using one of my own self-contained (and incredibly blunt) hypodermic needles issued to all officers before we left England for just such a purpose. Then as he starts to rig up a splint for my leg using a rifle, I ask him if he's sure it's broken.

"Oh, it's broken all right," he assures me. "Between the ankle and knee, shards of bone are sticking through the skin."

My battledress trousers are almost non-existent, shredded by the blast and the sand, a lot of which has been driven into the skin of my legs. There's considerable bleeding, which he stops with several field dressings, including one on my neck, where a bullet, picked up as I was crawling back, is imbedded in the muscle.

After about twenty minutes, Thompson arrives showing great concern, and, before he leaves, locates stretcher-bearers to carry me out to an ambulance Jeep that can't come in from the road because of the mines.

It's only a few hundred yards, but that trip is hell. Every time a bunch of shells come in, they drop the stretcher and flop down. While I can't blame them a damned bit, it's quite an experience being dropped every hundred yards or so, and I am dropped at least five or six times. The actual wounding wasn't really that bad, but being suddenly dropped to earth from almost three feet up is pure hell.

I am also worried about the rifle they are using as a splint —
whether or not they ejected the last round from the firing
chamber before they strapped the butt to my ankle and stuck the
muzzle up under my armpit. At least three times on the way out,
I have somebody unstrap the rifle and open the bolt to check the
chamber to make bloody sure that nothing is in there.

When finally they get me to the ambulance Jeep, they put me
up on the top row, over the driver, which makes for an interesting trip as we start back along the highway towards Caen. We
have to drive right under the guns of a long column of tanks
forced to keep to the road after what happened to my carrier and
others among the mines. Their guns are depressed flat, pointing
across the fields at about a forty-five-degree angle, shooting at
God-knows-what. There is no more than a foot clearance
between their muzzles and our stretchers passing under them,
but they don't give a damn — when they decide to fire, they fire.
And it seems that every one of those damned tanks manages to
get off a round just as we are passing under its gun. Good thing
the stretchers are tied down! The muzzle-blast is incredible,
lifting and rocking the whole Jeep.*

At 4:40 A.M. the guns receive word that the North Novas are on
their objective, Tilly-la-Campagne. But as time goes on this report
appears premature. There are no reports on the progress of the
Calgary Highlanders and the Black Watch. The FMRs, aided by
tanks of the Sherbrooke Fusiliers (27th Armoured Regiment), have
retaken Troteval Farm with great dash and verve according to a
running commentary given by a tank commander and picked up
on the radio at Brigade. But Beauvoir Farm is still not cleared at
H-hour.

---

*   Author interview.

At 5:40 A.M. 4th Brigade is reported to have Verrières, but judging from the calls for fire from FOOs, this is questionable. Since first light, enemy tanks have been attacking, and clearly Stu Laurie, who with his crew went in with the Rileys, has been driven out of an OP.

As Laurie will remember it, the Rileys don't experience too much trouble gaining their objective. It's afterwards their troubles begin.

As we are approaching Verrières, going up a hill in support of the RHLI, we stop at a stone barn near the village where I can over-look the whole ridge. Immediately I see Germans running out there, and tanks coming up behind them. But when I call for the guns, I'm told, "The Major has them." This happens to me twice! And while I am waiting, in comes Colonel Rockingham, CO of the RHLI.* He has a bloody scratch right across his nose where a passing bullet has nicked it, which he ignores as he peers out the open barn door. After a moment he says, "Look, come along, we're going right into the village!"

And we do, we go right up the main street – the only street – until I find a place at the far end where I can see out across the front. The Jerry tanks don't shoot at us going in, but there's one terrifying moment when, just as we are passing under the gun of one of our own tanks, it fires at something up ahead. The muzzle-blast is awful!

Leaving the carrier back in the sunken road, I go forward about fifty yards, accompanied by MacAleer [Gunner J. R.], who as he goes unreels the remote control cable that will link us to the big radio set in the carrier behind us. We take shelter behind a stone wall where one of our anti-tank guns has just been knocked out, and the crew is lying dead around it.

---

* Lt.-Col. J. M. Rockingham had replaced Lt.-Col. W. D. "Denny" Whitaker, who was wounded at Verson on July 14.

Peering over the top of the wall, I see a great big Tiger tank just down the slope in front, with several officers standing around it directing its fire. Just then one of our tanks comes up and shows itself in the fringe of a little woods only about one hundred feet from where we are. The shot from the Tiger peels a silver groove right across its turret. And though it doesn't catch fire or anything, the metallic rip is god-awful – even at one hundred feet! What it must have sounded like to those guys inside the tank! Anyway, they get the hell out of there in a hurry.

That Tiger has control over the whole ridge where we are, and when I stick my head up to try to pin down a map reference, he starts shooting at me with 88-mm solid-shot – not at the centre of the wall, but chopping away at both ends. First he hits this end and then the other, knocking off a bit more of the wall with each shot. And he keeps this up until the wall, which was about fifteen feet long to start with, is down to about six feet. In the meantime Major Wren and the Colonel are still keeping the guns engaged elsewhere, and all I can get to use is a section [two guns] or some-times a troop [four guns].

Oh, I get some shells down, but nothing of consequence, nothing you would call real fire, before we have to leave. MacAleer and I are now alone – the few Rileys, who'd been out in the field with us, having disappeared when the tank started shooting. With our wall disappearing, our only hope is to make it back to the carrier in the sunken road.

As we get set to make the dash, I see MacAleer preparing to reel up the remote control cable, and I have to yell at him, "Forget your damned remote control and get the hell out of here fast!" And running like the devil we make it back the fifty yards or so to the sunken road where there is some protection. There we pile into the carrier and pull out with the remote control bouncing behind us.

Back at Riley headquarters the confusion is terrible. Everybody seems to be pulling back, and for a while no one seems to know what they should do – including the battery commander [Major James Wilson Dodds]. But then Rockingham takes charge. He's a wonderful guy – no question about that! When we tell him we couldn't possibly stay where we were, his advice is simple: "Go and find some place where you can stay."

And that's what we do. We take over an abandoned position along the front of a little woods to one side of the village. And whoever was here must have just pulled out, for the food they left is still hot.*

At the guns it's difficult to picture what is going on up there. Situation reports are either totally confusing, or, as in the case of the Calgary Highlanders and the Black Watch, non-existent. But all the guns on all sides seem to be firing – some plastering Tilly-la-Campagne, apparently to help extricate the North Novas from what seems to have become a disastrous situation. The guns are firing almost steadily on Mike and Uncle targets around Verrières, and at one point, to guide the Typhoons, Capt. Bill Waddell (the new commander of Baker Troop, replacing Gord Hunter) calls for red smoke to mark a clutch of enemy tanks. But the tanks are so close one of the red-smoke canisters, expelled from a descending shell, lands near RHLI tac headquarters and causes Major Dodds to complain: "Smoke fell short – our fine-feathered friends took us for the target – acted accordingly – fortunately no casualties."

By 10:30 A.M. it is clear that even though the Rileys still are heavily engaged holding off enemy attacks at Verrières, two 4th Field FOOs – Waddell and Sammy Grange (the latter in place of Laurie, who is fully occupied with the Rileys) – are going forward

---

* Author interview.

with the Royals in the follow-through attack that is supposed
to carry them over the crest of the ridge to the left of Verrières,
down the slope to Rocquancourt.

Waddell and his crew are going forward in their normal carrier
with a rifle company, but Grange and two of his crew are in a
Sherman tank provided by C Squadron, 6th Armoured Regiment
(First Hussars) that has been assigned to give close support to the
Royals.

Having been delayed several hours by the late clearing of the
startline at Beauvoir, the attackers are going in without the advantage of the timed artillery concentrations, which by now have all
been shot. Henceforth all support from the guns must derive from
the initiative of the FOOs who drench the landscape with shells,
driving the German foot-soldiers to ground whenever enemy
activity is spotted, and marking with red smoke, for rocket-firing
Typhoons and bomb-carrying Spitfires, all visible tanks and every
distant lump or scar emitting the slightest sandy puff suggesting it
might be a self-propelled gun or dug-in tank.

As the Shermans approach the crest, they become embroiled in a
raging battle with enemy tanks, and soon the field is obscured by
black smoke, drifting from burning German and Canadian tanks.
No match in a face-to-face shootout with Panthers or Tigers, let
alone Royal Tigers of sixty-eight tons, only three Shermans
survive. Most of the others are left flaming, with terrible consequences to their crews.

One Sherman, right up on the crest, is hit and bursts into flames
just as Bob Suckling and his platoon are approaching it:

Instantly the hatch flies open, emitting a cloud of black smoke as
survivors tumble out and leap to the ground. One man, in
flinging himself out backwards, catches his knees on the rim of
the hatch, and I watch in unbelieving horror as he hangs there,
blazing like a torch, before dropping to the ground on his head,
setting fire to the wheat. Stretcher-bearers have to dash forward

to extinguish the flames enveloping his body, as other Royals beat out the flaming grain. And before long tanks and carriers are burning throughout the whole area.*

Lieut. Tom Wilcox of the Royals' mortar platoon, positioned in an exposed chalk pit near the Caen–Falaise highway, will later recall that when the few surviving Shermans disperse, carriers pulling the anti-tank guns become prime targets for the German tanks, and after that, anything that moves, until "the entire area looks like a charnel-house, with dead bodies and blazing vehicles everywhere."†

In one small hedge-surrounded field, nine Tigers knock out eight of the Hussars' tanks, including the squadron commander's and the one assigned to his artillery FOO. Grange isn't in it when it's hit, having gone reconnoitring on foot with the squadron commander. And though it doesn't "brew up," he finds it well-holed by armour-piercing solid-shot when he returns, and it is with some trepidation that he climbs up to peer down into it to discover the fate of his crew.

To his relief the turret is empty except for a leg with a boot on it. Cleanly severed by one of the solid armour-piercing shots passing through, it had been left by one of the Hussars manning the tank, not by Grange's ack, Bombardier Gilmour Addie, as he first thought on learning Addie had been wounded and evacuated.

Bill Waddell will forever remember his "initiation as a FOO on a hill to the left of the village of Verrières," where he is able to observe

---

*   Author interview.
†   C Squadron's First Hussars, commanded by Major D'Arcy Marks, brother of Major R. Marks of the Royals, lost fifteen of the eighteen tanks with which they began the attack, having lost two others to bombs dropped by the Luftwaffe on their assembly area before coming up.

the whole scene, including Grange's tank being shot up: "All hell breaks loose as Tiger tanks start shooting up the 6th Armoured tanks. Codes and formalities in wireless procedures are completely ignored as we go on the air and scream for fire on the attacking tanks."*

Seven Royals' officers are lost in the attack, and their historian will record: "Once over the ridge, the assaulting companies are struck immediately by a hurricane of fire."† In the dead ground beyond the ridge, the Germans have tanks and self-propelled 88s dug-in, invulnerable to anything but a direct hit by a big shell or a Typhoon rocket. And when the weary men of C Company, under Capt. G. K. Singleton, their ranks already seriously depleted by casualties, continue to press down the forward slope, they suddenly are surrounded by German infantry rising up and firing out of the grain on all sides. Those who aren't immediately killed or wounded are taken prisoner. Only eighteen Other Ranks of C company survive this day's fighting.‡

At this time Waddell is sheltering behind a dip in the road, peering through the wheat: "Suddenly the lad next to me gets it right between the eyes, and in that instant – for the first time I think – I fully realize the reality of war. After dark we pull back and take cover in a ditch for the night. And at one point tanks pass between us and the crest of the hill, close enough we not only can hear them but can identify them as German even in the dark."

---

*   Author interview.
†   Major D. J. Goodspeed, *Battle Royal* (Toronto: Royal Regiment of Canada Association, 1962), p. 429.
‡   In ten days, from July 18 to 28, the Royals were to lose twenty-one officers. Casualties among Other Ranks were equally severe. By August 3, they had received 616 reinforcements: 80 on July 20, 254 on July 28, and 282 on August 3.

36

"DOUBLE INTENSE"

✳

NO INFORMATION WHATSOEVER HAS BEEN GETTING BACK
from 5th Brigade since early morning, when the Calgary Highlanders were to take May-sur-Orne and the Black Watch were to
pass through to take Fontenay-le-Marmion.* When a gunner,
coming back from sneaking rations up to the civilians in the cave
at Fleury-sur-Orne, reports seeing the fresh grave of Col. S.S.T.
Cantlie of the Black Watch, who, he was told, died of wounds
suffered before dawn at St. Martin-de-Fontenay, the day-long
silence of 5th Brigade becomes ominous. Then at 7:00 P.M., when
the guns engage in still another fire plan in front of St. Martin on
behalf of the Maisonneuves attacking the same predawn 5th
Brigade objective of May-sur-Orne, it's clear the earlier attacks
were crushed.

It will be some time before it is generally known that the
Calgary Highlanders and the Maisonneuves were severely mauled
and the Black Watch virtually wiped out. The Germans were
cunningly deployed to take advantage of a network of mine
tunnels and air shafts under the whole area from St. André to

---

* As late as 7:40 P.M. on July 25, the RCA log at 2nd Canadian Corps
recorded a message from Brig. Keefler's HQ: "No news on progress of 5th
Cdn Inf Brigade attack against May-sur-Orne."

Rocquancourt, allowing them to return unobserved to positions previously cleared or reported empty by patrols, popping up in the wheat when it suited them to put advancing troops under fire from all sides. (Six days later, on July 31, Army Intelligence will produce, for the FMRs taking over in St. Martin, a map trace showing the exact positions of the mine's main tunnels and air shafts.)

The few members of the Black Watch who manage to escape the murderous fire from machine guns, mortars, and tank guns sweeping the fields from all sides, up the slope to May-sur-Orne and beyond, and who make it back to St. Martin (only fifteen out of three hundred) can provide only tiny segments of the picture. The full story of how sixty men actually made it to the crest before most of them died on coming almost face-to-face with tanks camouflaged as haystacks, will have to wait until some of those taken prisoner are freed and the ground is retaken two weeks later, allowing conclusions to be drawn from the grim evidence revealed by the number and location of the bodies, including that of the gallant acting battalion commander, Major E. F. Griffin, lying among his men, all facing the enemy.

While there is no serious fighting during the night of July 25–26, it is clear back at the guns that the front remains in a state of high alert, with FOOs and battery commanders reacting to the slightest stirring of enemy activity. And this is captured by the last terse note entered for July 25 in 4th Field's war diary: "Attack petered out, but the guns firing steadily all night on Mike Targets, Uncle Targets, and counter-mortar targets."

But on the twenty-sixth the diary recognizes both an intensification of enemy activity and the crucial role the guns are playing in the desperate struggle to maintain a tenuous hold on Verrières Ridge: "Continuous firing all day breaking up counter-attacks. All counter-attacks were successfully broken up – almost entirely due to artillery support. At 1600 hours had fired over 16,000 rounds since 1600 hours 24th."

Forward observers with the Royals east of Verrières can hear and sometimes see the enemy digging in, and 4th Field guns are frequently asked to shell the ground beyond the ridge. On one occasion Waddell fires red smoke around some enemy tanks and self-propelled guns forming up for an attack, successfully guiding the Typhoons to them.

And when the Royals, frustrated by not being able to bring their weapons to bear effectively on the enemy, decide late in the day that D Company, commanded by Capt. A. MacMillan, should move forward some four hundred yards to gain a more dominant position on the crest, the heavy concentration of shells from 4th Field guns fired in advance of the move catch a large number of the enemy forming up for their own attack. Many are wounded and at least twenty are killed, all identifiable as belonging to the elite 1st SS (Liebstandarte Adolf Hitler) Division.

Thus the Royals gain their new, advanced position without reaping additional heavy casualties. For a while after the guns finish firing, it is strangely quiet – so quiet that while Platoon Commander Suckling is establishing his men in existing trenches along a hedgerow "which apparently the Heinies have been occupying at night," he finds himself trying to identify "curious, whispering sounds of irregular pattern" passing close to his head.

For a moment I remain standing there out of sight behind the hedge, mystified, until it suddenly dawns on me I'm standing up in the beating zone of some Toronto Scottish medium machine-guns firing from some distance behind.

Then just at last light, to our astonishment a German officer and NCO come walking leisurely towards us through the wheat field, with their hands in their pockets, chatting to each other as though out for an evening stroll.

Our men are warned to remain still and let them come in so they can be taken prisoner. But only the NCO is taken alive. When the SS officer realizes what's up, he dives for the nearest trench and is shot by its occupant, a Bren gunner named Steele.

Subsequently, in the pitch blackness, their "Hitlerjugend" pals encroach within a few yards of us, and one of them with a machine gun manages somehow to get around behind us. Among the pleasantries they shout at us is: "Surrender, Canadian cocksuckers!"

Twice they counter-attack, screaming obscenities in English. And twice they are driven back. But so determined are they to retake the position that some SS actually try to dig in within ten yards of our trenches, and have to be driven off, leaving their dead behind them.*

And there the dead will lie with dozens of other bodies, theirs and ours, growing more repulsive each passing day, bloating and turning black and giving off sickening odours. No one would dream of forming burial parties on this ridge, where men in the most exposed, advanced positions are forced during the daylight hours to use the bottom of their own trenches as latrines, covering their excrement with dirt clawed from the walls of their abodes, in preference to risking a burst of machine-gun bullets above ground.

There is a conception – first inspired by the opinions expressed by the veteran Desert Rats back in the valley in front of Carpiquet – that the fighting between the densely massed forces in the confined battlefields of Normandy exceeds in intensity all other theatres. Now there is the growing belief that of all the Allied formations along the rim of the bridgehead, the Canadians are taking the worst punishment from Hitler's most fanatically loyal divisions

---

*   Author interview.

pledged to fight to the death for their Führer in holding a front that must be held at all costs. And the awful casualties in recent days would seem to bear this out.*

---

* To rationalize the "butcher bills" mounting at unprecedented rates in Normandy, British War Office tables known as "Evett's Rates," used by staff officers to forecast casualties and replacement needs, had to be amended. Until Normandy, the tables set out three levels of action: Intense, Normal, and Quiet. A new scale was introduced to cover the fighting in the Normandy bridgehead: Double Intense. And among the Allied forces, the Canadians suffered the worst casualty rate: 21.79 per cent of a force of 92,616 – twice the U.S. rate of 10.31 per cent of 1,220,000; and 2.6 times the British rate of 8.6 per cent of 737,384.

37

"GOD! HOW MUCH LONGER CAN THIS GO ON?"

———————— ✳ ————————

THE PAIN AND SUFFERING ASSOCIATED WITH EACH AND EVERY casualty – including the acute anguish of those who suspect they may die – is something historians tend to forget or purposely overlook.

Casualty statistics, even when shockingly high, are still only impersonal, sanitized, orderly columns of figures – so many dead, so many wounded, so many missing. All very neat and tidy: as when the South Saskatchewan Regiment was overrun by tanks on the afternoon of July 20, and listed 66 killed, 116 wounded, and 26 missing; or when next day the Essex Scottish experienced the same fate on the very same hill, suffering 298 dead, wounded, and missing. It only takes a couple of lines of type to record that four days later, the North Novas "lost" 61 killed and 78 wounded trying to take Tilly-la-Campagne; the Rileys counted 45 killed and 154 wounded taking Verrières; and on the slope just south of St. Martin-de-Fontenay, the Black Watch suffered 332 casualties, of which 123 were fatal.

Thus presented, casualty statistics suggest quite manageable situations with everything well under control, with all the blood and filth and stench of death and disablement left for stretcher-bearers, orderlies, nursing sisters, and surgeons to take care of – hidden away out of sight, as in the tents of No. 8 Field Surgical Unit, set up just northwest of Caen in July 1944.

When the wounded can be collected by stretcher-bearers, and their unit MO has done what he can for them at the regimental aid post, they are taken by ambulance Jeeps back to a field ambulance station, the first stop on a journey that can see them flown to hospital in England within hours. From Field Ambulance they are taken by regular, enclosed ambulances with big red crosses on their sides to a casualty clearing station, such as the one to which No. 8 Field Surgical is attached. There, from the endless stream of casualties, the surgeon selects for immediate surgery those so severely wounded they cannot survive further travel. Inevitably the most seriously wounded from 4th Field and the infantry battalions you support were patients at the eleven-man Field Surgical Unit, led by Winnipeg surgeon Major John Burwell Hillsman, who followed the Canadians as they moved to Carpiquet. Almost certainly his compassionate eyes were the last seen on this earth by those of your comrades who made it back that far, but no farther.

In his postwar book *Eleven Men and a Scalpel*, written as a tribute to "hundreds of patient and uncomplaining soldiers," the profound compassion Hillsman felt for each and every one of his patients comes through.* Even brief excerpts read as background notes place in heartrending perspective the appalling Canadian casualties.

Surgery, difficult enough in a well-equipped, well-lit civilian hospital, was done in a canvas operating theatre in the middle of a bare field under the strictest blackout conditions, and on occasion within the range of enemy guns:

We operated in Secqueville (five miles north and west of Carpiquet) for ten days, and covered the attack that took Caen. During those days we became veterans. We saw the tragic sights from which we were never to be free for ten long months. Men

---

* Published 1960 by Columbia Press Ltd, Winnipeg. Excerpts are reprinted with permission.

with heads shattered, dirty brains oozing out. Youngsters with holes in their chests fighting for air. Soldiers with their guts churned into a bloody mess by high explosives. Legs that were dead and stinking – but still wore muddy boots. Operating floors that had to be scrubbed with Lysol to rid them of the stench of dead flesh. Boys who came to you with a smile and died on the operating table. Boys who lived long enough for you to learn their name and then were carried away in trucks piled high with the dead. We learned to work with heavy guns blasting the thin walls of our tent.

We learned to keep our tent ropes slack so that anti-aircraft fragments would rain down harmlessly and bounce off the canvas. We became the possessors of bitter knowledge no man has ever been able to describe. Only going through it do you possess it. Above all we learned about men – about the wounded and about ourselves. . . .

When [one particular soldier] was brought in it was just dark enough for the flashes of the anti-aircraft guns to light up the horizon. I had stepped outside the operating theatre to enjoy a smoke. The ambulance drew up to the admission tent and I could see the dim forms of the stretcher-bearers quietly moving the loaded stretchers. Soon one of my men came out and told me I was wanted in a hurry. I went in. In the dim light I went over to his stretcher. His eyes were closed, his face the colour of white wax. Already a transfusion was pouring into one arm. I felt his pulse. Very weak. "How do you feel, soldier?" His eyes opened. He smiled faintly, "Fine, Doc." The eyes closed again.

I pulled back the blanket. His uniform was muddy and blood soaked the blanket. The orderly cut away his clothes. There was a large hole in his right thigh. The muscle bulged out, torn and steaming. Nothing else in front. The orderly gently rolled him over. He woke, started to speak, then clenched his teeth.

There was another smaller hole in his right back. No signs of bleeding now from the outside. Slowly we lowered him. A faint sigh of relief and the eyes closed again. More examination. He was bleeding internally from a large vessel, deeply placed.

I walked to the other end of the tent with the resuscitation officer. Almost in whispers we planned how to save this boy. Pour the blood into him fast and then a quick attempt to stop the bleeding. I went back to the operating tent and called the men together. Thank heavens they were fresh after a good day's sleep. I explained, "A desperate case. Abdominal setup. A race with a serious hemorrhage. Be on your toes." Quietly they began to prepare.

I walked outside for one last smoke. The air raid was still on and the horizon to the west was bright with flames. Must have hit an ammunition dump. I thought of the boy and his family, and wondered what they would be doing. Probably going about their quiet ways, pathetically unaware of the desperate battle we were going to wage. I silently swore to them that we would do our best.

The resuscitation officer appeared. "Blood pressure fair. Can't get it any better. Advise going ahead with it."

I went in and began to scrub. The stretcher-bearers placed him gently on the operating table. The glare of the lights woke him. I walked over. "Going to have to do a little work on you, soldier." The same slow smile. "All right, Doc."

The anesthetist bent over him. I put on my gown. The painting and draping were quickly done. I looked at the anesthetist. He nodded. A quick incision . . . Furious hemorrhage . . . I can't see! He's bleeding too fast . . . Suction quick! . . . Still can't see . . . A pack! Press hard! . . . It's still flowing . . . Big forceps, quick! . . . I'll have to clamp blind . . . Oh, God, I hope I get it . . . It's no use. It won't work . . . To the main vessel quick . . . Another incision . . . Rapid dissection . . . the vessel is tied . . . Back again to the first incision. It's slowed, but not stopped . . . Suction! Pack! Sponge! Quick! . . . I straightened up . . . A sigh of relief. It's stopped. A quiet voice said, "I'm afraid he's gone."

I looked at the anesthetist. Then I walked over and sat down. A hell of a surgeon. You stopped it all right, after he was dead. I walked outside and lighted another cigarette. The infernal din was still going on. Stretcher-bearers passed me carrying the still form in a blanket. I felt like hell. "Sorry, I'm a lousy surgeon." A tap on the shoulder. "The resuscitation officer wants to see you, another belly...."

It was a tough night. I had earned a rest. As I walked wearily towards my tent, I saw a fresh mound of earth in the field and the Padre placing ropes around a blanket-draped form. I remembered the boy and felt miserable. I went over. The service began. Men slowly drifted around and took off their berets. I looked at their faces. This soldier was not alone. They didn't know his name, but he was a friend. I glanced at the road and saw some French peasants standing with their heads bowed. They crossed themselves. The boy was lowered gently and reverently into the grave. The service was ended. The soldiers shaped the mound of earth; they did it so carefully. It must look nice. Poor kid, all by yourself in the corner of a French field. Well, you'll soon have plenty of company.

As I started to walk away, I saw an old woman hobbling in through the gate. One hand clutched a cane, the other arm was full of flowers.

Painfully she knelt. Reverently she placed the flowers one by one on the grave. Several more women knelt beside her. All had flowers and soon the grave was covered. I walked over: "Merci, mesdames." I felt better.

Once, we never saw daylight for 16 days, unless you call daylight seeing the sun set as you get up and rise as you go to bed. We were working 12-hour sessions. I remember thinking one night as I walked from the operating table: God! How much longer can this go on? I sat down and took off my sunglasses. Funny, sunglasses at night. However, the barely imperceptible flicker in the lights was hard on the eyes. I listened half-consciously to the pounding of the generator. . . .

The corporal moved around setting up the table for the next case. I heard an argument going on. My assistant was hurling insults at the general duty orderly. The corporal went over and quieted them down. Then he came over and sat beside me. "The men are out on their feet, sir."

I knew. Two of them celebrated their 19th birthday here in Normandy. The things we saw were pretty tough on kids. I thought I'd seen every ghastly sight possible in civilian practice, but somehow this was different. You never got used to it. And they were tired. While I slept, these boys had to clean up and get ready for the next session. They didn't average six hours sleep out of 24. The argument broke out again. The corporal went over and they turned on him. The stretcher-bearers brought in my next case and laid him on the table. My staff stayed in a group. No breaking up into the efficient drill we'd practised.

I beckoned to the corporal. "Take over the sterilizers and send the boys to me." They came over slowly and stood awkwardly in a half circle. I got up. "Come with me." We passed through the blanket-draped passage into the resuscitation tent. I stopped and let them get a good look. The resuscitation officer and his two men were moving around taking blood pressures. From every stretcher rubber tubes went upwards to bottles of blood. I walked slowly down the double line of stretchers, then stopped before one boy. He was unconscious, thank God! He fought for air. His face was slate blue and a bloody froth ran out the corner of his mouth.

I moved on, then stopped again. Gas gangrene. The boy was awake and looked curiously at us. The gas had spread from his leg up over his abdomen. No use to do surgery here. Try the new drugs. I knew they wouldn't work though. I had tried them before.

And so the line of wax figures. Not a sound from a stretcher. All waited patiently until their turn came.

I walked back. My staff followed me into the operating theatre. They gathered round, but I didn't look at them. "Any man who thinks he is in worse shape than those boys can go to bed," I said, and sat down.

Quietly they dispersed to their jobs.

38

ALONG THE BLOOD–SOAKED
VERRIÈRES RIDGE

✳

BACK AT THE GUNS, MEN LIVE MOSTLY ABOVE GROUND AND GO underground only when necessary. But OP crews, holed up with the infantry along the Verrières Ridge, risk death every instant they appear above ground. Men at the guns have a variety of concerns, but up in the slit trenches along the crest of the ridge there's one overriding concern for all ranks: survival. And to stay alive, a man must remain in a hole every hour of the day and night, only getting out when it's absolutely essential.

Thus the impressions survivors are most likely to carry with them the rest of their lives will all have to do with the sandy holes in which they shelter. Gunner A. J. "Andy" Turner came in as a reinforcement to 2nd Battery just in time to ride an old Norton motorbike up in the dark to join Major Wren's crew as a Don R at the Royals' tac headquarters near Verrières.

Turner's first fear-blurred memories will be of digging with his bare hands, tearing away the earth in the bottom of his slit trench and throwing it over the side by the handful every time a shell or mortar bomb comes whistling in:

The Major's driver, "Chuck" McConnell, and I share a slit trench, roofed over with our shovels and whatever else we can lay our hands on, with earth piled up on it at least two feet thick.

And we dig it good and deep. But no matter how deep it is, it's never enough. Even half asleep during the night, I find myself digging deeper, and always with my bare hands, for it's the activity more than the additional depth we require. For a while we're in soft earth, and every time the Moaning Minnies come over, we dig like dogs, handfuls of soil. But after we get down to the shale, it's not so easy. And worse than that, down on the hardpan, you'd swear every time those big Minnies land they're landing right beside you. The concussion wave travelling through the solid earth really shakes you up.

One night the Royals get a bunch of reinforcements. They barely arrive when the Minnies start coming down, and these new, green guys are jumping around all over the place. I grab hold of one of them – a guy wearing a big black moustache – and pull him down into our hole. And when things settle down a bit, he asks me, "Is it always like this?"

I tell him, "Well, not always, but enough."

And he says, "Can you tell me how to survive up here?"

Well, I don't know too much myself, only having been here less than a week. But I've learned something, and I tell him, "Dig yourself one of these and get into it, and don't get out for anything."

For quite a while after that, whenever I spot him, he's digging. And every time he sees me, he tosses me a pack of cigarettes. Then he disappears – wounded or killed, I guess. I never did get to know his name.*

For Platoon Commander Bob Suckling of the Royals, memories of life on Verrières Ridge will always be "a blur of unbelievable exhaustion, lack of appetite, lice, dysentery, constant noise, dust, revolting odours, and paralysing fear – just surviving day and night bombardment by shells and mortar bombs. And everywhere the

---

* Author interview.

all-pervasive smell of decaying flesh and other disgusting things. Until Verrières I didn't know the bowels of animals and men move after rigor mortis sets in."*

But amidst the awful sights of death and destruction by high explosive, and the innumerable unburied bodies turning black in the sunbaked wheat, a single image stands out to haunt Suckling the rest of his life: the sight of his batman,

> standing upright in a half-dug slit trench on the reverse slope of the ridge with not a mark on his body – dead from concussion. . . .

> Sheer terror turns everyone's heart to stone. The traumatic shock of finding war at its worst, coming to believe that every day of war must be this bad, is enough to cause a number of self-inflicted wounds. And later, when conditions permit, military police interview me about a lance-corporal who shot himself in the foot right under my nose.

> And my own resolve is at rock bottom, believing the best that can happen to me is to be wounded, since becoming wounded or killed is a certainty. I find comfort in an honest belief that may be God-given, that no matter how bad things are, they can always get worse. This I firmly believe, and often repeat it to others. It seems to give me some strength. And I have developed faith in the beatitude "The meek shall inherit the earth." While this doesn't seem to apply in civilian life, many a meek man displays the fortitude and resolve to carry on here, while many a swashbuckler finds the first way out.

Sharing this grim existence are 4th Field FOOs and their crews occupying holes among the forward rifle companies on the ridge. For Sammy Grange, who, along with fellow FOO Jack Thompson,

---

* This quote and the next by Bob Suckling are from an interview with the author.

returns to the front on July 26 with the reconstituted Essex Scottish as they take over the left flank of 4th Brigade beside the Caen–Falaise highway,

this period will always seem the worst of my life – just getting there, just being there, constantly subjected to shelling and mortaring!

On my way up to establish an OP somewhere on the ridge, I report to Bill Carr (the battery commander) at battalion headquarters shortly after dawn. Jack Thompson is already there, having a cup of tea. So we have one as well.

When Jack finishes, he says, "Well, I guess I'll go ahead now." I tell him I'll be right along as soon as I finish my cup. And not more than five minutes later, when I go up, he's lying dead beside a derelict tank, half in and half out of a trench.

Just as I realize what has happened, another shell lands and something gets me in the back – a shell fragment or a stone. Whatever it was, it is clearly my own blood . . . and I get quite excited about this, and retreat in some haste to my carrier, about fifty yards back in a sunken road where I'd left it to go forward on foot to improve the view. And while the view is not as good as it would have been up there, I am quite content to stay here after what has happened.

But, oh God, it's here I see a little fellow with his arm blown off who actually seems to be happy about it. He's smiling and saying, "I'm out of it now!" as he holds up the stump with the blood streaming from it. And remarkably I have no difficulty understanding him.

By now I have become quite fatalistic, as every FOO must. Death seems so inevitable after exposure to Eterville, which is etched in my mind for all time – the smashed houses, the trenches in the orchard, masses of dead cows in the field, and the unburied bodies of men. Then there was that affair with the Essex on the slope in front of Ifs, and then the move up past Verrières.

As a FOO, I know I can't expect to survive unscathed, and all the time I'm hoping it will be a wound. That is the best I can expect. That is why the little fellow who lost an arm, and is holding it up for all to see, is truly happy – he's got what he wanted.

I remain here a couple of days, usefully firing the guns a number of times. Once, Bill Carr calls up and asks, "How are you up there?" When I reply, "Slightly wounded, but carrying on bravely," there is a long, pregnant pause, after which he rephrases his question, "How is the situation up there?" He couldn't care less about my personal state.

And when, after a couple of days, I finally get the chance to visit a hospital to have my wound attended to, with visions of being sent home with bands playing and a suitable decoration hanging around my neck, they put a form of Band-Aid on it and send me back up.

Now we all get dysentery, which in front-line service presents the real problem of having to get up out of your slit trench to go someplace else and being shot at in the process. Thus it is one of the happiest moments of my life when I find one morning that someone has dug a latrine right beside my slit trench. From it you can look down into your trench as you conduct your business, and the moment you hear Moaning Minnies coming, you can dive, with your pants still down, right into your trench! Oh yes, I shall remember that latrine always!

Conditions here have proven that some of the nicest guys are cowards. One young fellow left alone up at the OP while I am visiting company headquarters a short distance away, starts calling up and repeating, "I've got to see you – I've got to see you." When I get to him, he's absolutely shaking with fear. But for no obvious reason; no shells are landing. There have been, and there will be again, but none right now. I tell him to go back to the guns, for he is totally useless up here. I don't report it, and I'll always remember him as a nice fellow, a likeable fellow. But clearly the whole idea of being shot at is too much for him. Perhaps he has no overriding sense of duty to sustain him. Most of us hate being shot at, but we're not prepared to show our comrades how cowardly we are.*

At 5:00 P.M., July 28, the Essex Scottish conduct a well-organized attack to clean out an orchard between Verrières and Tilly-la-Campagne held by the SS. Crossing open fields to hit the orchard position just as 4th Field's concentration on the objective ends, the leading platoons bring off the attack with splendid effectiveness. Not only do they rout the Germans, but they capture a waterworks and reservoir that has been supplying nearby German-occupied villages. The great success of the attack goes a long way to restoring pride and confidence to the Essex.

The FOO is Capt. W. L. Stewart MacLeod, who, until a couple of days ago, was battery captain (2nd in command) of 26th Battery, with no obligation whatsoever to go forward in the high-risk occupation of FOO. It seems, when Reg Parker was killed, he insisted on taking over a carrier crew. And when Jack Thompson bought it so soon after Parker, Dawson, and Knapp, it affected him deeply, according to those who are close to him. As MacLeod goes forward on this attack, he openly vows to avenge their deaths.

Next day (July 29) he is fatally wounded by a burst of machine-gun fire that instantly kills his driver, Gunner Geoff Byatt, a popular member of Easy Troop.

Sgt. Hunt's diary will carry a striking tribute to the gallant captain:

Yesterday afternoon we learned that Capt. MacLeod had died of wounds. This was a shock, especially since we had been under the impression his injuries were comparatively light. He joined

---

*   Author interview.

us at Horsham and went about his routine job of battery captain in the manner of a professional soldier. It was not until we got into action that something of the buccaneer emerged from under the detail of "cartridges ordinary, shorts cellular," and that law of living, "Form 1098." Reports came back from the OP that the Captain displayed an enthusiasm for engagement equalled only by his enjoyment of its execution. Farewell, blithe spirit, the men in your party thought a lot of you.

You try to imagine the state of mind of the two surviving members of that OP crew (both of whom you remember well from your years with 26th Battery in England). Only nine days after seeing their Capt. Parker almost cut in half by an 88 solid-shot and having the sad task of removing the almost headless torso of their cherished buddy Gunner Geoff Byatt from their carrier, Signaller-Ack J. W. Schneider and Signaller-Driver Ted Ford (who was also wounded that same day, but remained on duty) witness the fatal wounding by machine-gun fire of another troop commander as he crosses through the wheat to contact the CO of the Essex.

On July 29, Capt. Bill Waddell is sent to St. Martin-de-Fontenay to support the Maisonneuves in an effort to drive out the Germans, who continue to infest the village, as they have since the Maisonneuves, along with remnants of the Black Watch, were driven back there on July 25.

Sit reps (situation reports) are sketchy, but it's clear attempts to take the village church end in failure. Later, on August 6, a detailed description of these grim hours will be given to an intelligence officer by Capt. Alex Angers of A Company:

By this time the company had approximately 45 men. . . . The attack was set for 2200 hours 29 July, supported by arty [artillery] and rocket-firing Typhoons which pounded the colliery to the south. . . . As we stepped out onto the St. Martin-de-Fontenay to

Verrières road, we were met with fire from an MG [machine gun] and rifles in the hedge to the east . . . and from two or three MGs sited around the church and firing through loopholes in the churchyard wall. . . . We reorganized just north of the church in the orchard where the wall gave us some protection.

By this time we had about 30 men and tried again. Lt. Mailas 9 Platoon managed to get across the road and started to crawl for the church. He came under MG fire from the stone wall and hedges as soon as he crossed the road into the open. He had to come back after losing quite a lot of men.

I decided to wait and try again at dawn. I asked for reinforcements and received from D Company eight men, one Bren and 20 mags. By that time Lt. Valerin 8 Platoon had his strength cut down to four. This was during a second assault when his platoon managed to get two sections through by running along the road. Jerry let two sections get in and cut off the entry of the third section and platoon HQ by heavy fire. The two sections that got through ran forward and assaulted the church to find nothing in it. Of the 14 men who went in the church, only two came back. We tried again at first light, about 0500 hrs July 30. . . . So few people were left (about 15 men out of the original 40 and the 8 reinforcements), that instead of company commander I became section leader with one of my lieutenants acting as Bren gunner. We got into the road and fired on their positions, and they fired so heavily on us . . . we gave up the attack and occupied the corner house directly across from the church.*

---

*   National Archives of Canada, File 145 2R6011 (D5) of Unit War Diaries covering July 1944.

39

A NOTE ON SHELL CONSUMPTION

---------------------------------- ❋ ----------------------------------

IN ELEVEN DAYS, ENDING JULY 26, THE FIELD GUNS OF 21ST Army Group fire 1,158,490 shells – 105,317 rounds on average a day (5,313 more a day than were fired daily during the famous ten-day battle of El Alamein in 1942).

On July 30, worried by the enormous shell consumption, the Major-General Royal Artillery of 21st Army Group issues a memorandum to 2nd British Army and 1st Canadian Army point-ing out that expenditures are "extremely heavy, considerably in excess of the figures for which we have asked the War Office for provision . . ." and "that production is not at the moment meeting expenditure."*

The War Office had projected 62 rounds per gun per day, based on consumption figures from other theatres, suitably inflated to take care of the extraordinary demands of an operation everyone knew must prove to be the ultimate clash of arms in the whole war in the west. That this projection is proving totally inadequate speaks volumes. These unforeseen across-the-board firing rates by the field guns of 21st Army Group – unequalled in any theatre in the war in terms of rounds expended per gun per day – provide not

---

* From National Archives of Canada records RG24, Vol. 10462, File 212C1.2009 (DIS).

only a truly authentic measure of the severity of the Normandy campaign as a whole, but a valid means of expressing the otherwise indescribable intensity of the clash of arms in which the Canadians have been thrust south of Caen.

And the field guns of 2nd Canadian Division, obliged to drop curtains of shell-fire, almost literally, along Verrières Ridge to stop the enemy from breaking through when battalions were overrun and driven asunder, have far exceeded the daily consumption by the field guns elsewhere in Normandy. While from July 20 to 27 21st Army Group guns were averaging 78 rounds per gun per day – the rate so worrisome to the high command – 2nd Division guns were having to draw an average of 385 rounds per gun per day. And the belief expressed by the Army Service sergeant at Fleury the night of July 22 that he was involved in an all-time record dumping of ammunition will be confirmed one day by facts recorded in a yellowing manuscript in the National Archives of Canada:

It turned out this dump (July 20) was the first of a series that would culminate in an all-time record for the dumping of artillery ammunition being established by the drivers of 2nd Div Army Service who supplied the ammunition and 2nd Div Arty who fired it.

In less than 30 hours (to 6 P.M. July 22) they had dumped 750 rounds of 25 pr [25-pounder ammunition] for each of 2nd Div's 72 guns. But the greatest job was still ahead of them – an all-time military record for the dumping and firing of ammunition was about to take place. . . . At 1830 hours July 22 the first of the record dump was initiated by HQ RCASC with the order that the formation would supply 120 vehicles for a 25-pounder draw that night from BAD [Base Ammunition Dump] at the beaches, and the lorries would make a double turn about drawing in excess of 44,800 rounds on the double haul. All night and far into the morning ammo poured into the gun sites as fast as the gunners could handle it.

And at a Quarter-Master General's conference July 28, Lt-Col Daziel reported: "Corps and Div Commanders are more than pleased. For the last show we dumped and shot off more 25-pounder ammunition than any other British division has ever done."*

Some perspective may be gained by comparing the average daily expenditure of 2nd Division guns during the last three weeks of July 1944 with expenditures per gun per day during the monster bombardments of World War One, such as the "artillery prepara-tion" for the 3rd Battle of Ypres (Passchendaele), which, according to the official *History of the Great War,* "established a record in the number of guns employed and amount of ammo expended."† In eighteen days, ending on August 2, 1917, 2,092 field guns fired a colossal 2,967,953 rounds. This, however, was a daily average of only 78.8 rounds per gun. Then there was Valenciennes, ten days before the Armistice. According to a 1933 pamphlet by Maj.-Gen. McNaughton, head of the National Research Council of Canada, 192 field guns, backed by 104 heavies, fired "the most intensive barrage in history ... in weight of gunfire approximating that used by both sides in the whole South African War, and exceeding in tons that fired at Jutland, the greatest naval battle of all time."‡ Still, the 192 field guns, consuming 56,200 rounds in two days ending noon November 2, 1918, averaged only 146 rounds per gun per day, which would not have been considered remarkable in 1944 by the gunners of 2nd Division in Normandy.

---

* National Archives of Canada, "History of RCASC 2nd Cdn Division, June–Dec 1944," RG 24, Vol 10906.

† *History of the Great War: Military Operations France & Belgium 1917, Vol II, 7th June–10th November, based on official documents by direction of the Historical Section of the Committee of Imperial Defence* (London: His Majesty's Stationery Office, 1948), p. 138.

‡ "The Capture of Valenciennes," Maj.-Gen. McNaughton, *Canadian Defence Quarterly*, Vol. x, No. 3, April 1933.

The twenty-four guns of 4th Field alone fired 93,000 rounds over a twenty-day period, ending August 1, averaging 195 rounds per gun per day. For three consecutive days they actually averaged 469 rounds per gun per day, and in one twenty-four-hour period, ending the afternoon of July 21, 1,000 rounds per gun were fired.*

---

* For comparison, 3rd Field in Italy, assaulting the Gustav and Hitler Lines in the Italian campaign, averaged 132 rounds per gun per day for eleven days. Col. G. W. L. Nicolson, CD, *The Gunners of Canada, Volume II, 1919–1967* (Toronto: McClelland and Stewart, 1972), p. 235.

40

"A DAY IN THE LIFE OF
A GUNNER"

❋

SOMEHOW THE CANADIAN ARMY FILM UNIT HAS BECOME AWARE of the record firing by the field guns and has decided it should record the business for posterity. One of their cameramen visited 4th Field a couple of days ago to arrange to spend a day here at the guns, shooting footage for a film with the working title "A Day in the Life of a Gunner."

He is scheduled to come back with his camera this morning, and you are looking forward to appearing in the film, however briefly, knowing how much your wife back in Canada would enjoy seeing you at an actual gun position in France. However, it is not to be. Just as you're coming off a midnight-to-dawn stint in the command post, preparing to hit the sack for a few hours, a signal comes from RHQ: you are to take over Able Troop OP crew and go up to relieve Bill Waddell at St. Martin-de-Fontenay, where the FMRs have taken over from the Maisies.

When the carrier arrives from the wagon lines, you are glad to see Ryckman, a most experienced driver, hunched down in the driver's seat. As you climb in beside him, you do your best not to let your nervousness show, but you don't relish having to make the trip up there. It would be bad enough going up after dark, but going up in daylight over a completely exposed ridge and down a long slope into the village seems simply to be courting disaster.

Every so often during the past eight days, alerted by the distant howling of Nebelwerfers, you've looked up to watch another six-bomb salvo of those violent rocket bombs plough the western hump of Verrières Ridge, some fifteen hundred metres south of here. Always they seem to land along the crest, near where the road south from Fleury-sur-Orne disappears over the ridge and (according to the map) heads down the slope straight as an arrow for St. Martin-de-Fontenay and St. André-sur-Orne, lying side by side in the valley.

Just after sunrise this morning (July 30), as you were brewing up the first "cuppa the day," that familiar, insane chorus wound up, and as you looked, black geysers of smoke and dirt billowed up from that same corner of the ridge, generating a deep roar that rolled back over the gun positions like thunder. As always you wondered what Jerry thought he was accomplishing, whacking away at that bald hill, which, as far as you know, is not occupied. Well, now you are going to get the chance to go up and find out. When you call in at RHQ to find out the safest route up there, Capt. G. M. "Tim" Welch, the adjutant, hasn't a clue. He suggests you "drop in" on the CO at Brigade on the way up.

Though it's a good three kilometres out of the way, you feel you have to get the advice of the CO. You find him in a particularly desolate corner of the parched and dusty landscape, standing in a ragged, gravelly hole that would hardly qualify as a trench, in the lee of a broken stone wall – a remnant of a shell-demolished farmhouse or barn just to the left of the Caen–Falaise highway. As far as he knows the whole Orne valley has been cleared all the way down to St. André. But he can't say how far the Brits have cleared the menacing high ground on the west bank. He doesn't suppose any route along the east bank of the Orne is very "healthy" in daylight.

Before you can ask why the hell 4th Field is keeping 5th and 6th Brigades supplied with FOOs, he draws your attention to a string of mortar bombs following a dust cloud rising in the distant fields behind a motorbike roaring this way from Verrières Ridge. Laughing, he throws up his glasses to his eyes to follow the despatch rider's wild and woolly progress, remarking "That will be Wren's Don R," as though that's explanation enough for anyone.

Not that it matters, for you have more important things on your mind. And as a black-haired, dusty Don R (Gunner Andy Turner) comes rolling up, grinning from ear to ear, you pull out towards Ifs.

Passing west beyond the village, you get a broad view of the lowlands down along the Orne. The sight is not reassuring. Derelict vehicles of all kinds – half-tracks, scout cars, carriers, Jeeps – lie burned out, dead, unmoving in the wheat fields.

You decide you'd better try making it by the road over the crest. Perhaps if you sneak up the slope as quietly as possible until you get to the top, then tear down the other side into the village, you'll make it before they wake up and get a bead on you.

When you tell Ryckman that once over the crest he'll be in full view of the enemy all the way down into the village, and that he'll have to "tramp on it" if he is to make it, he merely shrugs as if to say "what the hell," and starts grinding the carrier slowly up the slope at an angle meant to gain the greatest concealment before turning onto the road itself. The cool, deliberate, and remarkably quiet way he manoeuvres the sluggish machine up the slope is very reassuring. But when the carrier at last tips over the brow of the ridge and noses down, the breadth and depth of the sunlit panorama lying before you is even more startling than you imagined it would be. In the clear morning air, you can see for miles, far beyond St. Martin, now laid out below you two kilometres away.

And it's clear that if you have an unobstructed view, so must all the Germans' dug-in tanks and camouflaged 88s out there – each of them capable of destroying you with one shot from distances far beyond that first crest and the high ground they still hold over on the right, across the Orne. It's as though you're riding a shooting-gallery duck as the carrier dodders over the crest, almost stopping as Ryckman changes gears from the bull-low used to climb quietly up the steep route – for though he's highly skilled and moves smoothly and swiftly to change up to high gear, it still takes time to get a sluggish carrier rolling.

Even when he has it roaring down the slope with accelerator pressed to the floor, you know you're offering an easy target for guns that fire missiles faster than the speed of sound. The way is as straight as a Roman road all the way down to the village, without a house, a tree, or anything to obstruct their guns' view. And on all sides there is chilling evidence of their accuracy: the slope on the left is dotted with burned-out tanks; and down on the bottomland on the right, close to the Orne, is an appalling clutter of burned-out half-tracks, carriers – and even a smashed Jeep.

You find yourself holding your breath. Ryckman has the carrier roaring wide-open now, passing very close to the edge of a yawning cavity along the left side of the road, a quarry or gravel pit clearly marked on the map.

You're halfway there.... Then suddenly there's a heart-stopping, metallic *wham!* Ryckman involuntarily lets up a bit on the accelerator before realizing it's only one of the tracks taking a slap at the underside of the carrier body. Before he gets full power back on, to take up the slack in the tracks, both of them are slamming away at the undersides of the carrier, making a terrible racket. If the Jerries have been dozing, they surely are awake now, and hastening to man their guns.

But the village with its sheltering buildings is getting close. The stubby church tower over in the southeast corner, near the map reference you're headed for, is plainly visible.

Now you're passing a large orchard on the right. Only three or four hundred yards more and you'll be among the first buildings. They must be withholding their fire until you get so close that they'll be absolutely certain not to miss. You find yourself breathing, Oh please, not now ... now that we've almost made it!

Suddenly, from the orchard on the right, a soldier leaps out onto the road, directly in the path of the carrier, and waves his arms over his head, frantically signalling you to stop.

Even at a distance, the tall, rawboned man with a great shock of jet-black hair that no helmet could completely hide, is instantly recognizable as Gunner Lewis Milton Bryan, a member of Waddell's crew. As the braking carrier rolls up to him, barely halting in time, he's jabbing his left hand urgently towards a track leading off to your right. And when Ryckman skid-turns in that direction, Bryan hops up on the front of the carrier, depositing one hip on the fender in front of you, yelling urgently, "Get going! Back in there among the trees. Fast! You're under observation here – he still holds half the village."

Ryckman tramps the accelerator, rocking the carrier down the track towards the centre of what must have been a lush orchard extending west about 800 metres towards the Orne, but now leafless and forlorn. After ninety metres or so you see, parked deep among the scarred and blasted trees, to the left of the track, a carrier with the number 42 painted on it. Gesturing, Bryan directs Ryckman to park beside it. Jumping down, he yells, "Get out and find yourself a hole – quick!"

There are a couple of slits to the left of the carrier, and you and Ryckman promptly follow his advice. You're barely underground before you hear the banshee yowling of Moaning Minnies winding up just beyond the village, growing horribly louder and louder as they loop directly overhead and down into the orchard, crashing so close to where you are sheltering, the hot, hurricane blasts blow sand and bits of branches into your trench. After they land you start to get up, but a hand on your shoulder restrains you, and you hear Bryan's voice:

"Wait, he usually sends over a couple of lots."

And he's right. There is another salvo. Then, as you wait to be sure he's finished, Bryan, smiling quizzically, remarks, "I just happened to see you coming over the ridge, and went out to the road to make sure you found the track in here. But the way you were coming, you looked like you were going to drive right into the village!"

You tell him, you were – to join a company located near the church.

"They may be there, but Jerry still controls that street. Anyway, Capt. Waddell can tell you. He's at their battalion HQ, over there in that German bunker."*

Down in the bunker, which turns out to be remarkably deep, you find Waddell, who introduces himself and then the acting CO of the battalion – a Major Sauvé – and a couple of other officers you can barely make out in the gloom of the bunker, having come directly down out of the blazing sunlight. As your eyes adjust and you are able to take in the scene, you are struck by the uncanny resemblance to a stage-setting for the First War play *Journey's End*.

The Major, seated behind a little table with a map spread out before him, illuminated only by a guttering candle stuck in a black bottle, is the picture of outrageous fatigue. As he lights a fresh cigarette from a smouldering butt, he makes no effort to hide the fact he's fighting utter exhaustion if not despair. He has no idea what has happened to the company you've been ordered to join in the southeast corner of the village. In fact, he has been out of radio contact with all his companies since before dawn. And of course it is impossible for you to join a company whose status is unknown – and which may no longer exist.

Waddell tends to agree with him, suggesting you stop here at Battalion Headquarters. However, being new to the game and having received orders to go to a specific map reference, you feel obliged to try to get there.

---

*   Bryan, who unquestionably saved you and your crew from certain disaster, and who survived the war without a serious wound, was decapitated a few years later when he ran his snowmobile under a guy wire attached to a hydro pole one wintry night outside of Ottawa, where he was employed as a city police officer.

At this point, an officer you take to be the adjutant informs the CO that a runner has just come back from the lost company of FMRs in the village. On hearing this, the acting CO is highly indignant, demanding to know why he has not been told this before and ordering the runner to be brought before him at once!

While he waits, he confides in you that it is a very, very bad spot up here – the units they replaced suffered severe casualties, the Black Watch particularly. Actually, his own regiment is already dangerously under-strength in case of a major German counter-attack.

After a minute or two, an unassuming young soldier is ushered down the bunker stairs before the CO, who questions him intensely in French for several minutes. Satisfied the company in question is reasonably intact, the CO asks the soldier in English if he thinks he could "take this artillery officer up there?"

The boy shrugs, pursing his lips and rocking his head from side to side, as if to say, "I suppose so . . . if it must be done."

With that, the CO orders him to act as your guide. As you are leaving, he requests you give first priority on arrival up there to restoring radio contact with him, and has the adjutant provide you with the current wireless frequency on a piece of paper, suspecting there is some confusion in this regard.

You stop at your carrier long enough to don your sheepskin vest, in anticipation of the inevitable chill when darkness descends tonight, and to stuff your pockets with bully beef and hardtack, before slinging the walkie-talkie 38-set around your neck. Then, turning to your young guide, who has been waiting patiently, you follow him to the southeast corner of the orchard, imitating his bent-over, cautious approach as he sneaks along a stone wall covered with dried-up, dusty vines marking the southern boundary of the orchard, and hopefully hiding you from the enemy. He kneels down where the wall ends, just short of the road that you used coming down from the ridge and which constitutes the main street of St. Martin-de-Fontenay, leading south to the next village, May-sur-Orne, about a mile away across a shallow valley.

By the time you kneel down beside him, you are sweating profusely, and not just because the day is well on its way to becoming another muggy scorcher. The brooding terror that hangs in the sinister silence of this desecrated place is almost visible out there in the empty, sunbaked stillness of the rubble-cluttered street, leading off to the right between shattered buildings.

"I will go first," the FMR soldier whispers. "Wait until I am across ... then you follow. Run like hell ... we lose six men crossing here this morning."

With that he jumps up and squirts across the road like a scared rabbit. Sheltering behind a broken wall of a smashed house, he beckons to you to follow.

Taking a deep breath, you raise yourself up into the crouch of a sprinter, clutching your map board tightly under your left arm and pressing your right across the 38-set dangling from your neck to prevent it bouncing on your chest as you run. Then, with the soldier's words ringing in your ears – We lose six men crossing here this morning! – you run with every ounce of energy you can muster across that menacing gap.

Even before you reach him, he takes off, running a weird obstacle course through partially demolished stone buildings. Already drained by your lung-bursting dash across the street, you do your best to keep up, leaping here and there over the rubble and through broken walls, until you trip attempting to hurdle through a tall vacant window of a roofless house.

The spring having disappeared from weary leg muscles, the heel of one of your hobnailed boots has caught on the low sill, and you tumble head first down into a deep, rubble-cluttered cavity within a house that has largely collapsed into its own cellar, creating a most horrible racket as you roll into a tangle of rattling tin rubbish at the very bottom.

Lying perfectly still, face up in the blistering sunlight amidst what appears to have been furnace pipes, very conscious of your sticky underwear sopping with sweat, and fearing the consequences of having alerted every German within a mile, you struggle to get your breath. Then, worried you'll be left far behind, you disengage yourself from the rasping tin and crawl up out of the crater.

He's waiting. But as soon as he sees you, he takes off again, though now at a much slower pace. He picks his way cautiously and stealthily – at one point leading you in a crawl through one cellar window, down into a dank cellar and out another window on the other side of the house.

Arriving in a garden surrounded by a high stone wall, at the rear of a substantial stone house which appears to be more or less intact, you notice with relief that for the first time your guide walks confidently upright as he leads you to the back door. You've made it!

The enclosing wall gives you a wonderful feeling of security. Only a nearby church tower overlooks the garden. Abutting the kitchen door is a low, flat-roofed, concrete shelter (reminiscent of the blast-shelters placed before the doorways of London buildings), forming an entryway about ten feet long. Inside, you wait in the shade while your guide disappears in the house to find his company commander.

A soldier lies stretched out asleep in the shelter, face down in the dust on the bare concrete floor. Beside him is an 18-set radio, but there is no sound coming from the earphones hanging on its aerial. At first you assume the batteries are dead, but when you bend down to see the frequency at which it is set, you discover it's turned off! No wonder they couldn't be raised. And when you check the setting against the frequency they gave you back at Battalion, you find it's nowhere close.

The officer who arrives at the kitchen door seems awfully glad to see you. Georges Brégent – a pleasant, softspoken, earnest man – shows you such deference you find it difficult to believe he really is in command of the company. Catching you staring at his epaulettes, which carry only the two pips of a lieutenant, he readily volunteers he was a subaltern only five days ago, but with the heavy casualties he became an acting-captain, and now he's the company commander – an acting-major, he thinks.

You find his limited experience disconcerting, considering his company is hoping to survive in what, for all practical purposes, is no-man's-land, currently the worst battle-zone in all Normandy, where whole battalions have been shattered in vain attempts to drive out the SS. However, his frank and modest manner is so appealing, you like him instantly, and find yourself wanting to help in any way you can.

A minute ago, you were looking for reassurance yourself. Now you assume a pose you hope will reassure him, for you suspect from his manner he needs this more than anything else. It certainly wouldn't do him any good to know how limited your experience is.

He wants your opinion of a plan he has for when it gets dark, for "using the knives very quiet" to "destroy" the Germans in the house next door. He explains it must be done stealthily so as not to alert the Germans in the house next to them, who, in their turn, will have their throats slit quietly without arousing other Germans beyond them, and so on down the street. He wonders if you think it is a good plan.

You tell him it sounds like a wonderful plan, if he can find men with the nerve to carry it out. But even as you try to involve yourself in his problem, you can't take your eyes off the weary soldier in the dirty, rumpled battledress lying on the floor. A red hen has been killed and plucked, and the feathers are everywhere. In his restless sleep, the soldier has rolled in them and is covered with them. They even stick to his face. Somehow he typifies the utter exhaustion and endless misery which is the lot of the infantryman. Reduced to accepting the barest subsistence level, snatching food for his belly and rest for his aching legs whenever and wherever he can, he waits for the next orders to go forward.

Worried that you unwittingly may be encouraging Acting-Major Brégent into doing something really suicidal, you change the subject to the vital need to restore radio communication with his battalion tac HQ back in the orchard. You suggest he wake up his signaller and get him to net in his 18-set to the battalion frequency you've brought along with you.

He readily agrees, explaining, as he wakes the soldier, that he approved of the 18-set being turned off to save batteries only when they were unable to raise Battalion this morning.

Once the signaller is sufficiently awake and alert to what you're trying to tell him, it takes him only a couple of minutes to get in touch with Battalion using the new frequency. Then, using your 38-set and the call letters the signaller provides for the other companies, you search the dial until you locate each of them in turn, providing them with the new Battalion frequency. Thus, within minutes, full radio communication exists throughout the battalion, you're feeling awfully proud of yourself, and Company Commander Brégent is much impressed.

When you ask him where you can observe the zone, he leads you into the house and up two flights of stairs, through a tangle of broken lumber and plaster chunks, to the attic, now entirely open to the sky.

At first it seems like the perfect OP. While large sections of roof have collapsed in tangled waves of beams and refuse covering most of the third floor, the southeast corner must have been blown away completely for it is relatively free and open. You can walk right up to the chest-high, thick wall of dressed stone that remains intact around the perimeter of the whole house like a parapet.

Following the lead of the young Major, whose only concession to concealment is to drape his little camouflage net over his head and shoulders before rising almost fully upright, you take up position on his left and peer over the stone wall towards the rolling, sunbathed fields south of the village.

As at Eterville, you are struck by the deadness of no-man's-land – the complete absence of movement of any kind. You can see for miles, but no living creature moves anywhere out there, no smoke rises from any chimney, and roads and fields and barnyards are empty.

For the moment your companion is silent, and you have time to sweep the valley with your field-glasses, examining in minute detail the opposite slope leading up to May-sur-Orne, searching for the slightest tell-tale sign of movement. But you find none, and in that eerie deadness, you feel the sinister menace you've come to associate with the front line.

At last, your companion points south across the valley to haystacks on the side of the hill, which he suspects are camouflaged tanks. (If they are tanks, they're close enough to thread your needle, and, feeling the need to make yourself less conspicuous, you pull your head down into your shoulders like a turtle.)

Then he points to the factory-like minehead and hoisting tower just beyond the southern edge of the village, explaining it's connected with the network of mine tunnels and air shafts that are being used by the Germans to pop up in positions previously reported clear. (You lower your head a bit more.) Then he points to the church tower over on the left, so close you feel you could almost hit it with a rock, and tells you the Germans have at least one MG-42 machine gun in there. (You now stoop until only your eyes are peering over the rim of the parapet.)

Finally, he reaches out beyond the rim of the stone parapet and pointing directly down towards the ground, says, "And of course the house next door is full of them." Staggered, you drop down behind the wall. My lord, he really meant it when he referred to Germans in "the house next door"! Perhaps his plan "to use the knives very quiet" after dark isn't so crazy after all.

When he suggests you join him in some lunch downstairs you readily agree, pleased to have an excuse to get off this open deck for a while. There has been altogether too much arm-waving going on up here; it couldn't help but attract attention unless every damn German out there is sound asleep. Eventually they're going to loop over a basket of mortars. Why they haven't already done so is a mystery. And if there really is an MG-42 in that church tower over there – and your informant seems to know – why didn't they let fly a burst and cut you both down when they had the chance? Again it begs the question you kept asking yourself all the way down the hill in the carrier this morning: What are they waiting for?

Acting-Major Brégent volunteers a possible answer, suggested by the Maisonneuve company commander he relieved here this morning, whose company was reduced to only fifteen men by attacks yesterday and the day before on the church: "Jerry tends to keep his machine guns quiet, not giving away their position until you attack and then *pow!* He ambush you."*

Lunch turns out to be a can of Compo M & V (meat-and-vegetable stew) he'd left on the window sill to warm in the sun. Spooning out half the contents into a tin cup for you, he proceeds to eat his share out of the can, remarking with notable sincerity, "These Composite Rations are really very convenient, and *plutôt appêtis-santes*, do you not think?"

Appetizing? Of course you think he's joking. But then you see he really means it, and for a moment you have doubts about his sanity. It occurs to you that due to the general unreliability of messing for front-line infantry – deriving as much from their being perpetually in isolated and exposed positions, as from the capricious and inconvenient timing of their attacks and enemy counter-attacks – he simply hasn't had the chance to consume enough Compo rations to grow tired of them.

Now and then the methodical hammering of a Bren in short bursts can be heard from upstairs. Brégent explains it is merely his

---

* The Maisonneuve company commander, Capt. Alex Angers, in an intelligence report dated August 2, mentioned this phenomenon: "We noticed during these engagements that Jerry is willing to keep his automatic weapons silent for days if necessary in order that, when finally launching a big attack, we will be surprised by fire from unexpected sources." From File 145 2R6011 (D5) of Unit War Diaries covering July 1944, National Archives of Canada.

men ensuring the area is dominated by our fire. Having seen only a handful of men upstairs, you inquire where the rest of his company is located. He says that most of them are concentrated in the house. But he has a couple of outposts over on the left, along a hedge lined with dead Maisonneuves, killed yesterday in attempting to take the church.

During the afternoon, alone at the parapet in the open attic, you poke around enemy territory with one of your 25-pounders – first punching some holes in the church tower with H.E., then the minehead building, then some suspicious chalky scars that could be trench-work on the distant slope. And just as you are about to start bracketing one of the haystacks that could be a camouflaged tank, you get the message to return to the guns.

Greatly relieved that you will be able to get a night's sleep tonight, but not relishing the thought of having to retrace that harrowing route taken by your guide this morning on the way up, you bid farewell to Brégent and start back.

Hating every step of the way, fearful you may miss a landmark, you hesitatingly pick your way, trying not to break the menacing silence. Each time you dislodge a bit of rubble, you cringe in anticipation of something coming your way.

With mixed feelings you locate the cellar window out of which you crawled this morning; most grateful you recognized the damn thing, but feeling foolish as you worm your way back in and drop down into the dank gloom, merely to cross over and clamber out a window on the other side. Somehow you recognize other landmarks, including the open pit into which you'd tumbled among the furnace pipes, and at last you make the final dash across the road into the orchard where your carrier sits next to tac headquarters.

There you inquire of the 6th Field FOO who is replacing you what route he used coming up from the guns. He says straight across the fields along the river from Bassé that lies just south of Fleury. And though derelict vehicles dot the field in ominous stillness on all sides, Ryckman brings the rocking carrier back to the guns without incident, arriving just before the sun goes down.

The motion picture cameraman, a cheerful fellow named McGaughey, is just packing up to leave, very disappointed by the small amount of firing the guns have been called upon to deliver this day.

Bob Grout explains that the only target of any urgency was the one at about 9:00 A.M. when some fast but abbreviated fire was required on those "robot tanks in front of Verrières."

Robot tanks?

"Well, whatever you call them. You saw them of course?"

Saw them? Until now you hadn't even heard of them.

"Oh? Well, the attack must have occurred while you were in transit."

The description sent back to the guns was that the things resembled Bren carriers – tracked, but slightly narrower than a carrier. Within eight hundred yards of our lines they were abandoned by the drivers, and when their motors stopped, the things exploded with terrific blasts. But as the blasts were mostly upwards, and all out in the open, there was very little lethal fragmentation.

The machines were sent under cover of 88-mm air bursts and mortar fire. Our guns shelled them, but since the things were meant to self-destruct, it was impossible to tell if any of them were destroyed by our shells.

This new secret weapon appears to be rather a joke in its total ineffectiveness, but of course it was no joke to anyone up there this morning, including 4th Field carrier crews, when those strange things were crawling towards their holes.*

The fact that all of this took place beyond Verrières Ridge, out of

---

* For his courageous work on Verrières Ridge during this novel German attack, Lance-Bombardier J. W. Schneider, with Easy Troop carrier crew, was later awarded a Commander-in-Chief's Certificate. With the infantry calling for SOS fire, and the remote cable leading to the

sight of the lens of cameraman McGaughey, has added to his general frustration. With no major attacks to support, or large counter-attacks to cool down, the guns were reduced to a leisurely harassing-fire program and brief, periodic bursts, called for by FOOs inspired as much by suspicion as by any actual observation of enemy activity – shooting up scars on a distant hill that might be enemy trenches, a minehead useful to the Germans, and a ragged church tower harbouring a machine gun and possibly an artillery observer.

The disappointed man recalls that when he was assigned to shoot this film, he was told your guns were engaged in record-breaking firing, that during a four-day period ending July 22, your regiment averaged ten thousand rounds a day. And a couple of days ago, when he came up to make arrangements with you to film your guns, there were enormous piles of spent cartridges beside each of your gun pits. He recalls watching in fascination as a gunner cleared them from the floor of one of the pits, creating a veritable stream of ringing brass as he pitched one after the other onto a growing mountain outside the pit. And when some of them began to tumble back down into the pit, the gunner climbed out and attacked the slithering pile with tremendous vigour, driving an upraised, hob-nailed boot against it and pushing mightily until it shifted enough that the peak tipped over and an avalanche cascaded down away from the gun pit. What a shot that would have made for his film!

Now, even those mountains of brass, which could have provided mute testimony to the record-breaking firing, have been packed away in boxes and neatly stacked up.

He's very concerned that what he has captured on film is so very unrepresentative of life at the guns of Normandy as to be utterly

---

radio in the carrier cut by a mortar bomb, he left the shelter of the OP trench, in the midst of airbursting 88-mm shells and crashing mortar bombs, to carry target information from his FOO back to the carrier parked some distance away for transmittal to the guns.

silly: a man (Sgt. Nick Ostapyck) diving off the nearby newly built Bailey bridge into the murky Orne; another (Gunner E. G. Kent) paddling a patched-up canoe in the river unusually clear of human and animal bodies, which he had heard were always floating by here; a GPO (Lieut. Walter James Faber of Baker Troop) calling fire orders into a Tannoy mike; a gun getting off a round or two; a fleeting shot of a despatch rider (Gunner Turner) passing by on his motorbike; and finally, some men eating out of mess tins and drinking tea from enamelled mugs. Hardly the makings of a dramatic film – and certainly not representative in any way of what the gunners have been going through up here.

As he's pulling out, you inquire if this means that the film will never be released, that relatives back in Canada will never get the chance to identify their long-absent loved ones on the movie screen?

Oh no, not at all. Knowing the way the brass love to hide the dark side of the war and show only smiling faces to the folks at home, he expects it'll be released as a short for the theatres in Canada.*

But what makes for a dull movie, makes for a pleasant existence here at the guns. Overnight, life has become remarkably relaxed, even though harassing-fire programs can extend for hours – as today, when the guns sporadically shelled selected areas between May-sur-Orne and Rocquancourt.

Though Jerry continues to drop thousands of shells and mortars across the whole front, and nightly his bombers visit much of the rear areas reaching back to Caen, including 4RCA wagon lines and the guns of other regiments, causing damage and casualties, he continues to spare this small oasis in the bend of the Orne as though balancing things out after those wretched days in the valley in front of Carpiquet. Today, they tell you, there were only a few airbursts,

---

*   *A Day in the Life of a Gunner* was never edited for release.

the most disturbing being a premature from a Baker Troop gun, bursting with a terrible crack just after leaving the muzzle. Fortunately it caused no harm.

And with less demand on gunners and command post crews, and more opportunities for sleep and relaxation, everyone seems to be "coming up for air."

They've even adopted a mascot over at Baker Troop: a scrawny, long-legged, freckled pullet picked up back in the rubble of Louvigny by Lance-Bombardier Ralph Hughes and Gunner W. J. Brewster. The original idea was to keep it just long enough to fatten it up for a feast. But now that it has been given the name Hardtack, in recognition of its principal diet, it's clear no one would dare suggest a chicken pot pie – certainly not in the presence of any of its guardians, who now number most, if not all, of Baker Troop.

As you are dropping off to sleep in the gathering dusk, curled up on the bucket seats of good old armoured scout car GA, you ponder how different all this is from life up in St. Martin-de-Fontenay. This brief interlude of comparative ease for the gunners ends shortly after midnight, just after you are awakened by Bob Grout to take over "the graveyard shift" in the troop command post. By 6:00 A.M. 4th Field guns will have consumed 390 rounds per gun, while taking part in bombardments by the field guns of 2nd Division and 4th Armoured Division, and by the mediums of 2nd Cdn AGRA (Army Group Royal Artillery).

At 1:00 A.M. the guns provide support for a company of the Lincoln and Welland Regiment (10th Brigade, 4th Division), conducting a feint against the tiny hamlet of Tilly-la-Campagne from the northeast, while the Calgary Highlanders form up in the northwest along the Caen–Falaise highway to attack at 2:30 A.M. Supported by a squadron of tanks of the Royal Scots Greys (4th British Armoured Brigade), the Calgarys attempt to take that desolate confusion of rubble and broken walls, still firmly held by swarms of SS and still covered by as many machine guns,

Nebelwerfers, self-propelled 88-mm guns and dug-in tanks as were required to maul the North Novas so severely a week ago.

Early reports have the Calgary Highlanders in Tilly. However, as time passes, it becomes clear they have been driven back, when well after daylight the guns are called upon to support a second attack on Tilly by the Calgarys accompanied by the Scots Greys' tanks.

As in the first attack, there is a report they have gained the village. But again it becomes evident the violent fire from the German guns and mortars has forced them to relinquish their tenuous hold of the village, when at 2:00 P.M. the guns are called upon to fire another bombardment in support of a third attack by the survivors. This time there is no report of early success. Nor is there when the Lincoln and Welland Regiment attacks Tilly from Bourguébus just before midnight.

Sit reps are equally silent when a final attack by the Lincoln and Welland, supported by the guns, is undertaken at 2:45 A.M. August 2.

Tilly-la-Campagne, which could have provided the Canadians with an improved launching position for the next big push while denying the Germans their superior overview of Allied territory all the way back to Caen, is still in enemy hands. And the war diaries of 6th Brigade, the Calgary Highlanders, and the Lincoln and Welland Regiment will provide the reason as they document the devastating effect of the awesome fire-power 1st SS (Liebstandarte Adolf Hitler) Division was able to bring to bear in repelling five determined attacks on this one ragged hamlet in just slightly more than twenty-four hours.

Against the Calgarys' first attack, "the enemy gave battle with anticipated violence, laying down intense defensive fire with guns and mortars."* And while they failed to prevent some elements from gaining a foothold in the village, their fire, "mistaken by the

---

* Calgary Highlanders War Diary, August 1, 1944, Unit War Diaries Section, National Archives of Canada.

distracted riflemen for that of our own artillery, was so accurate, our troops were forced to retire and dig in along the railway."

When the Scots Greys tanks were ordered to go forward in daylight with the Calgarys on their second try, "elements again fought their way into the village, but severe losses of both infantry and tanks again compelled a withdrawal. At about 1000 hours, the straggling remnants of the Calgary Highlanders fell back under heavy fire, through a company of the Royal Regiment which was ordered to dig in along the main road [Caen–Falaise] to meet an expected counter-attack."

When incredibly the Calgarys mounted a third attack they were stopped only a few hundred yards beyond the startline. "Depleted, exhausted, and unable to move in the face of the concentrated fire of machine-guns, mortars and tanks, the Highlanders dug in, and supported by a squadron of the Fort Garry Horse and a company of the Royal Regiment, held their ground."

When the Lincoln and Welland Regiment, in their first attack in Normandy, moved out in a "silent attack" through the gloom from the direction of Bourguébus, at fifteen minutes to midnight, "their advance across 700 yards of open ground towards the village was broken up by heavy fire from machine-guns and mortars." And the same fate awaited them in the fifth and final assault on Tilly-la-Campagne: ". . . a second attempt was again defeated, and at dawn the project had to be abandoned."*

By now the brass mountains of expended cartridge-cases piled up at each gun pit have grown by another 100 rounds, to 490 per gun. But, of course, there is no photographer in sight.

During the day you learn the FMRs, taking advantage of the heavy diversionary fire distributed by the guns around St. Martin-

---

* Page 2, Report No. 65, Historical Section (G.S.) Army Headquarters, Dept. of National Defence, Dec. 23, 1953.

de-Fontenay during the first attack by the Calgarys on Tilly, conducted a totally successful assault on the church in St. Martin. You find yourself wondering if Acting-Major Brégent had any role in the assault. Did he and his men get the chance to use their knives and slit the throats of the Germans in the house next door?

With that infamous church and tower finally clear of Germans and firmly occupied by the assaulting company, led by Major Dextraze, the battalion's exhausted acting CO, Major Sauvé, should now manage to get some sleep.*

When you learn that the 6th Field FOO (Capt. D. E. McRae), who replaced you in time to take part in the assault on the church, was killed, you are swept by conflicting emotions: regret that such an obviously nice guy should have bought it, but humbly thankful it wasn't you.

During the eight-day period beginning July 25 and ending at 6:00 A.M. August 1, the guns of 4th Field alone fired more than 41,000 shells, averaging 5,210 a day, and consumption rose to 9,360 rounds the first day and the last day. Then for six days after the Tilly-la-Campagne affair, demands on the guns and the gunners cool down remarkably.

However, the lull in offensive operations – providing a much-needed period of rest for the gunners and maintenance of their weapons – does not improve, to any appreciable degree, the grim existence of front-line riflemen and the artillery FOOs and their crews huddled in sandy holes among them. And this fact, easily overlooked by history touching only on the highlights of a campaign, is recorded by the war diarist at 6th Brigade, who, in an inspired burst of descriptive prose, captures with supreme accuracy

---

* Major J. M. Paul Sauvé survived the war and, following the death of Maurice Duplessis, became Premier of Quebec until his own death one hundred days later. Major J. A. Dextraze remained in the army after the war, fought in Korea, and eventually became Chief of the General Staff.

the never-ending anxieties and risks of men in forward battle
lines:

> The noise of the conflict echoes across the fields from dawn to
> dusk, only to be taken up in new and uneasy tones as darkness
> closes in. And while losses never reach the proportions of the
> 25th of July (1,500 killed, wounded and missing), the static battle
> costs the Canadian Corps 100 casualties a day.*

---

*   6th Brigade War Diary, in Unit War Diaries section, National Archives
of Canada.

41

A SEPTEMBER '39 ORIGINAL
RETURNS AS CO

✳

IF ANY WORD TRICKLED DOWN FROM RHQ THAT LT.-COL. DRURY left the Regiment July 28 to become G1 (general staff officer, grade 1) at Headquarters 2nd Div, it never registered in your sleep-starved brain. And so when Bombardier Hossack shakes you awake around 4:00 P.M. this afternoon, on August 2, and you disentangle yourself from your camp-stool just in time to see a long-legged lieutenant-colonel slithering down the steep earthen steps of your troop command post, you are more than a little puzzled. And when he introduces himself as McGregor Young, your new CO, you really start to worry.

Commanding officers hardly ever visit gun positions. Even the fussiest of fuss-pots back in England left harassment of gun positions, if there was any, to his second-in-command. What the hell could he be looking for? Had he seen you sleeping? Should you explain that you are still trying to catch up on sleep lost over a period of several days when you were without a second officer to spell you off, and have survived with catnaps sitting on that crazy camp-stool?

But before you can start in, to your relief he makes it clear he only stopped by to get directions to RHQ. Your gun position was simply the first he encountered after coming down off the steep hill from Fleury. And after you tell him the best way to get there, and he does a cursory inspection of the layout of your cramped dugout, he turns to climb out. It is then you notice the extra ribbon on his chest – a DSO (distinguished service order), no less – and are much impressed.

But then he pauses at the foot of the dugout steps and inquires why you haven't left an opening in your dugout wall – the part above grade – through which you could keep your guns under observation for purposes of fire discipline?

Oh gawd, you think, not one of those guys!

As politely as you can, you explain that you took an instant aversion to open ports in command-post walls back at your very first position in the valley in front of Carpiquet, when you'd had a man wounded by a bullet from a strafing plane that ricocheted off the ground and in through a port you'd left open in the front of your dugout so you could see the guns. He was the only man wounded by that strafing plane. You go on at some length to point out that at night you can't see the guns anyway, and in the daytime you can always move up the steps and watch them better from there than through a restricted port.

By now, another type of senior officer (several of whom you have known), would have told you to shut up and get on with the reconstruction of the whole damned command post. But your speech leaves this man pursing his lips, raising his eyebrows as though in recognition of a novel concept, and rocking his head back and forth in a way, you think, shows he appreciates your plea for common sense. Then smiling broadly at you, he turns and climbs out of the dugout without further comment. As you follow him up and watch his long legs striding off to the waiting Jeep, you decide you like the new CO very much.

However, early impressions of another CO having proven wrong once before, you are curious as to what Bombardier Hossack thinks the reaction of the men will be towards his appointment as CO?

Good, he thinks. As far as he knows, everybody was sorry to see

"Mac" leave the Regiment when he was promoted second-in-command of some 3rd Division outfit in 1943. This, of course, means he's been in Normandy since D-Day, which would account for that DSO ribbon.*

Hossack is surprised you didn't recognize him – after all he was one of the 1939 originals of the Toronto 53rd Battery. You can only conclude that though you joined the Regiment in 1942, a year before he left for 3rd Division, you never met simply because until the tent camp in the backyard of Arundel Castle in the summer of 1943, 4th Field was never together as a regiment except during schemes or training camps.

---

* Over the months ahead you would witness firsthand the cool courage of this unassuming man. And from time to time you would hear fragmentary references to his heroism on D-Day and on other desperate days right after the landing, when the charged-up "Hitler Youth" of 12th SS Panzer Division were determined to follow their Führer's direct command to drive the Canadians back into the sea. And one day you would get an eyewitness account of one of his exploits among the assaulting forces from a new CO of the Royals (Lt.-Col. Lendrum), who was with the Canadian Scottish during those first days ashore. When a leading company was cut off, communications non-existent, and the enemy about to overrun the infantry battalion headquarters, "Mac" took charge of one of his regiment's 105-mm self-propelled guns. Directing it to push ahead with gun blazing, he opened a corridor through the SS to the desperate company, from whence he was able to call down such concentrations of fire from his other twenty-three guns on the surrounding enemy, the Germans were forced to withdraw.

PART FIVE: AUGUST 3-11

1st Canadian Army Ordered to Break Through to Falaise

42

A FOOTNOTE TO THE BREAKING
OF THE HINGE

---------------------- ✳ ----------------------

SUPREME ALLIED COMMANDER GENERAL EISENHOWER, IN AN attempt to place in perspective the extraordinary strength of German forces facing the Canadians relative to those facing the Americans, will one day say, "ten feet gained on the Caen sector was equivalent to a mile elsewhere."*

And as the Canadians have gone on holding Panzer Group West in close and deadly combat around Verrières Ridge, the American Operation Cobra, bursting through the thinly held western rim of the bridgehead, is, by August 1, a full-fledged break-out exploited by the newly arrived mobile army of General George Patton, south and west towards the ports of Brittany.

By August 3 the Brittany peninsula (apart from some key cross-roads and garrisoned ports) is said to be controlled by the French Maquis: some fifty thousand men distributed among numerous guerrilla groups, some led by British and French paratroopers of the Special Air Service, and most of them equipped with arms dropped by the RAF.

With no coherent front opposing Patton, Gen. Bradley, Commander of 12th U.S. Army Group, directs him to thrust south

---

* *Canadians at War 1939–45, Vol. Two* (Montreal: Reader's Digest, 1969), p. 481.

and east to Le Mans in the "wide sweep" envisaged by Montgomery in his original plan.

As Patton turns east on August 4, Montgomery issues a directive reinforcing the purpose and intent of his strategy: "Once a gap appears in the enemy front, we must press into it and through it and beyond it into the enemy's rear areas. Everyone must go all out all day, and every day. The broad strategy of the Allied Armies is to swing the right flank towards Paris and to force the enemy back to the Seine."

Montgomery counts on the Germans doing the militarily sensible thing: pulling back to a major water barrier to establish a line. The American break-out will deny them a retreat to the Loire, forcing them back to the Seine. There, encircled and pocketed against that wide river, without a single bridge standing and no adequate alternative means of getting themselves and their equipment to safety, the Germans must surrender or be annihilated by the Allied air forces.

However, on Hitler's orders the main German forces still press insanely north and west, as Patton's army races unhindered far to the south of them towards Paris, covering seventy-five miles in three days, almost reaching Le Mans by August 7.

Now the "Caen hinge," which the Germans have continued to defend with fanatical tenacity, and which they have been encouraged to shore up and buttress at the expense of other parts of the front, has to be broken to allow the northern, British–Canadian wing of this great encirclement to start east to the Seine.

To this purpose, on August 3, Montgomery orders Crerar's 1st Canadian Army to "break through the enemy positions to the south and south-east of Caen."

"Operation Totalize" will involve: (1) the improvisation of new equipment; (2) the unconventional application of regular equipment; (3) specialized training for the assault troops, tankmen, and drivers of the improvised armoured troop-carriers never before used in action; and (4) the unprecedented use of tanks and heavy bombers in support of an attack in the black hours of the night.

But in spite of all the special difficulties – not the least of which is persuading RAF Bomber Command to cooperate in bombing in close support troops on the ground, where an error by Pathfinder planes could be disastrous – this most demanding and complicated operation will be launched by 1st Canadian Army at 11:30 P.M. on August 7, a mere four days after receipt of the warning order.

This is possible only because General Crerar anticipated as early as July 29 that the Canadians would be called upon to smash out towards Falaise, and wisely turned over the planning of the attack to one of the ablest of Allied field commanders, with perhaps the most creative, original military mind of any general on either side in this war: Lt.-Gen. Guy Simonds, Commander of 2nd Canadian Corps.*

Anything less than Simonds' imagination and boldness of spirit applied to the problem of devising a way to break out of the suicidal deadlock in front of Verrières Ridge, and "Totalize" must certainly become a disaster surpassing Dieppe. A conventional frontal assault in daylight along the lines of British operations Epsom and Goodwood, or the U.S. Operation Cobra, against the fire-power

---

*   Chester Wilmot, on page 410 of his postwar book *The Struggle for Europe* (London: Collins, 1952), recognized as the definitive work on Allied operations in northwest Europe in 1944–45, judges ex-gunner officer Lt.-Gen. Guy Simonds to have been "a most able, forceful and original soldier." Conceding that he was "ambitious, reserved and ruthless" and "not an easy man to serve, for he was intolerant of minds less capable than his own," in Wilmot's judgement, "he certainly commanded confidence and respect. Like Montgomery, his approach to problems of battle was that of a scientist. Both were perfectionists, but whereas Montgomery was primarily the expert implementer, Simonds was a radical innovator forever seeking new solutions. Simonds' originality was strikingly evident in the plan he devised for this operation which was given the code name Totalize."

arrayed in such depth at this narrow front at Verrières, must end in failure, producing casualties far in excess of even the July rate for the Canadians on this front, already the highest rate for all of the Allied armies. And if, under pressure from on high (inevitably ferocious with the whole course of the war in the west at stake), a conventional assault were pursued for many days, 1st Canadian Army would cease to exist as a fighting force.

By July 31, Simonds and his staff have assessed the problem and worked out possible solutions. It isn't sufficient to break through the German line running from the southern outskirts of St. André-sur-Orne and St. Martin-de-Fontenay on the right to Tilly-la-Campagne on the left. There is another line five miles farther south – running from Bretteville-sur-Laize on the right to St. Sylvain east of the Caen–Falaise highway – that will have to be breached and rendered ineffective if a true breakthrough is to be accomplished. All attacks against the first line towards May-sur-Orne and Rocquancourt have been bloodily repulsed up until now, and Simonds recognizes that even if it is possible to break through those first defences, the Germans will just regroup at the second line unless it too is overrun.

Assuming there will be available air and ground bombardment equal to that which opened Goodwood, Simonds has to find a way to get his tanks – this time closely supported by infantry – through the first line of defence and crushing into the second line before the initial stupefying shock of the bombardment wears off. Then, unlike Goodwood, he must maintain a constant flow of air and artillery support to the spearheads exploiting the breakthrough. In Goodwood, the British armoured divisions left their infantry far behind, outran their artillery before they got to Verrières Ridge, and although the German gun lines remained intact covering the ridge no provision was made for continuation of the aerial bombing into the second day.

However, surprise – a fundamental condition for any successful military operation – can hardly be attained here, after all the intense and purposely threatening attacks Montgomery has had the Canadians make in this sector over the past three weeks to scare the enemy into moving a maximum number of men, tanks, and guns onto this front.

And the awesome losses during these attacks have pointed up the ultimate problem of getting tanks and infantry across open country that affords the enemy outstanding observation of Allied fields and roads all the way back to Caen and provides him with tremendous, unobstructed fields of fire for his guns, heavy mortars, and machine guns. Even if the assault troops are transported in armoured personnel carriers to reduce casualties from machine guns and mortars, the enemy's long-barrelled 88s – deadly accurate and lethal to Allied tanks at more than two thousand yards – can destroy the relatively thin-skinned armoured personnel carriers as fast as they are driven into view.

But what if they were not driven like shooting-gallery targets up and over the ridge in daylight, but were moved forward under cover of darkness, immersed in a column of tanks plunging forward behind a rolling barrage – taking advantage of the utter confusion left by a colossal bombing of front-line targets and bypassing all village strongholds still able to offer resistance? Might they not have a chance of driving miles into no-man's-land and establishing a series of firm bases before daylight, from whence full exploitation could be carried out by armoured divisions following in behind through the ruptured lines?

Simonds believes it possible, and surprisingly he is able to gain the confidence of tank commanders, who traditionally believe that tanks, being blind and ineffective in the dark, should be left hidden away from the battle in laagers at night. And perhaps even more surprisingly, he is also able to win the cooperation of RAF Bomber Command, which has never before attempted to bomb front-line targets at night in close support of an armoured breakthrough. While RAF strategic bombers are accustomed to flying in the dark to targets marked by Pathfinders, the need for accuracy has never been so critical. To ensure RAF Pathfinders do not make a mistake, the artillery is given the job of firing flare shells onto targets just before the Pathfinders are timed to arrive. And just to be sure it will work, the RAF insists on testing the effectiveness of the artillery-placed flares up near Ouistreham, on the coast north of Caen, the night before the bombing is to take place.

Once these key elements – Bomber Command and tank divisions – are sold on the idea of the novel attack, the principal problem is getting enough armoured carriers to transport the infantry. The White scout cars of a 4th Division motorized regiment are available, and many can be borrowed from the artillery regiments of 2nd Division, but to fill much of the need, Simonds has to come up with an improvised vehicle, and one of astonishing effectiveness is brought into being almost overnight.

He gets permission from the Americans to remove the 105-mm guns from the seventy-two Priests (the self-propelled guns on tank chassis borrowed by 3rd Division for the D-Day assault), and modify each open steel chassis to carry twelve infantrymen and their weapons. Four officers and 250 tradesmen, from twelve different units, are brought together for the job. The first carrier, immediately dubbed a "Kangaroo," is finished at 7:00 P.M. on August 3.

Modifications call for the removal of the gun, mantlet, seats, and ammunition bins, and for the welding of armour-plate over the opening at the front. When all available armour-plate is used up, pieces of lesser steel, scrounged from a variety of sources (some say even from landing craft stranded on the beach waiting for the return of high tide), are welded in layers two inches apart, and the space between is filled with sand. Working round the clock, they "defrock" the last Priest by 10:00 A.M. on August 6, allowing just enough time for the infantry to learn how to board and disembark at the ready, and for drivers to practise manoeuvring them in the fields behind Louvigny. Thirty-six Kangaroos are allotted to the Royals, while an equal number of armoured half-tracks are loaned the other two battalions (RHLI and Essex Scottish) by the engineers, recce, and artillery units. The other thirty-six Kangaroos are allotted to the British assaulting brigade.

Most of the drivers of the Kangaroos are the 3rd Division men who drove them as self-propelled guns. But twenty-eight drivers and four NCOs from Army Service volunteer to take over the twenty-eight new armoured half-tracks sent over from England to increase the pot of thick-skinned vehicles divided between Canadians and Brits.

The assault forces opening "Totalize" are the 51st Highland Division to the east of the Caen–Falaise highway, and 2nd Canadian Division to the right of the highway, supported by the 2nd Canadian Armoured Brigade which consists of 6th Armoured (1st Hussars), 10th Armoured (Fort Garry Horse), and the 27th Armoured (Sherbrooke Fusiliers).

The Canadian assault battalions will go forward from Troteval and Beauvoir farms over Verrières Ridge in four tightly lined-up columns: the Essex Scottish on the right, the RHLI in the centre, and the Royal Regiment on the left, with 8th Recce on their left. Leading each column will be a "gapping force," made up of flails (tanks with rotating drums out in front to which are attached heavy, logging chains slapping the earth as they move) exploding any mines lurking in the path of the advancing column. Then the tanks and AVREs (Churchill tanks of the Royal Engineers fitted with short-range heavy mortars known as Petards, and various devices for bridging), which this night will be marking corridors with white tape. And each column will have two troops of M-10s, self-propelled guns supplied by 56th and 33rd batteries.

43

ARMOURED BULLDOZERS DIG
GUN PITS

✳

FOR OPERATION TOTALIZE, THE GUNS MUST BE MOVED FORWARD
to gain as much range as possible for support of the assault columns
expected to gain the high ground seven kilometres farther along
the Caen–Falaise highway. For 4th Field, to gain two thousand
yards in range means a move of about four kilometres east and two
south, to a field just in front of Ifs.

On the afternoon of August 3, Major Gordon Savage, the second-
in-command, leads the three battery CPOs (Les Hutcheon, "Stevie"
Stevenson, and Ted Dack) up there to recce positions. Included in
the party are the regimental surveyors under Survey Officer Len
Harvey, who, from data supplied by 2nd Corps Survey Regiment,
must establish pivot gun markers to the accuracy of "theatre grid" –
a most unusual state of readiness for guns that won't even start
moving up until 10:00 P.M. the day after tomorrow.

After dark all three batteries and RHQ send up digging parties to
prepare gun and ammunition pits and command post dugouts, with
the help of an armoured bulldozer supplied by the Engineers. The
CRA 2nd Division (Brig. Keefler) deems this necessary because the
new positions between thirty-metre and forty-metre contours are
still under observation from the ragged pile of broken walls that is
Tilly-la-Campagne, just three kilometres distant on a seventy-
metre contour. So it is with some uneasiness your troop leader, Bob

Grout, accepts responsibility for the eighty-man regimental detail going up to dig the pits. And it does his peace of mind no good to discover, close to where Able Troop will deploy, the lonely crosses marking the place Dawson and Knapp died.*

After dark it's really weird – gun-fire lighting the horizon in front and behind, and shells whining overhead in both directions. And now and then there's a sound that I can't immediately identify, like the crack of a whip. After establishing where the pits for 2nd Battery are to go, and leaving a sergeant in charge of a digging party, I'm leading the other two sergeants to the locations selected that afternoon, when a plane flying low overhead drops parachute flares. We flop down flat on the ground. However, they drop nothing near us until just as the flares are dying out, when with a strange howling a large metal container about the size of a coffin, complete with lid [a disposable carrier for anti-personnel bombs], lands a few feet from us.

The plane is still above us, so I suggest we make a dash for some slit trenches I spotted in the afternoon on the other end of the field. But before we get to them, there are more flares. The sergeants make it to a couple of trenches with roofs. But the one convenient to me is open to the sky. This time the plane dives and makes a pass right over us, dropping a string of anti-personnel bombs. There's a close bracket across my trench, and for a moment I think they contain gas because the fumes are choking. Again he comes back – this time strafing with machine guns, and I thank my lucky stars I spotted these trenches before dark.

Later, when the planes have departed and the bulldozer comes up to the third position to start digging, the operator suddenly jumps down and runs for cover in a ditch. When I get to him to ask what's wrong, he says bullets are ricocheting off his dozer.

---

* They had been buried by Black Watch padre Honorary Capt. E. C. Royle, who "came across the bodies still seated in their shattered Jeep."

Then I hear more of those whip-cracks. Suddenly I remember
where I heard that sound before: working the targets in the rifle
butts at Petawawa. Bullets coming close, from only a couple of
hundred yards away, sound like that. There is a clump of trees out
in front just about that far away that could be sheltering a patrol.
After a while they appear to pull back, probably believing they
have come up against a tank from the sound of the bulldozer
engine. Anyway, the work on the pits is allowed to continue.
When at dawn I report all this to RHQ, they're surprised I wasn't
told to be on the look-out for a Heinie patrol in the vicinity of
Ifs last night.*

During the night regimental ammunition trucks move up the
first instalment of ammo: 3,242 rounds from Fleury (143 rounds per
gun).

Back at the guns things are exceedingly quiet – the quietest since
coming into action. Still, with Grout up at Ifs, you are stuck on
duty in the command post all night. To pass the time you decide to
get down, on the nice clean piece of musical-staff paper Hiltz
scrounged for you in the village, the words and music of a new song
you composed to send your wife for your third wedding anniversary, coming up on August 30. It will be the third you have missed
sharing with her:

From your pictures you're adorable, my dear.
From reports you are the lady of the year.
From those in the know these days I've heard,
You're beautiful to see –
You twinkle like the candles on an anniversary!
From informants you would seem to be immortal –
They have booked the hall of fame and burst its portal –

---

* Author interview.

From "enchanting" to "alluring"; from "endearing" to "enduring,"
But from memory, you're just swell my dear!

For a non-musician, self-taught composer, arranging harmony without a piano by imagining the keyboard is devilishly hard, and having to work by candlelight, scribing musical notes of varying value, whose precise position in relationship to the staff lines is critical, using a "straight" pen dipped in India ink, calls for the patience of Job. But around about dawn it's finally finished – every last dot, stroke, and wiggle has been inked in. Right then and there you should have returned the cork to the ink bottle sitting on the artillery board next to the finished manuscript, so that if and when a target came in, it wouldn't get knocked over. But you didn't, and in the scramble to clear the deck, it happens: one whole page is blotted beyond repair.

It takes well into the afternoon to construct a new page, and then locate the glue to paste it in place ready for mailing home. *C'est la guerre!*

At 9:30 P.M. on August 4, half an hour before 26 Battery is to lead off the move to the new positions over at Ifs, 5th Field reports heavy shelling of the area, and the CRA stops the move. Then at 10:00 P.M. the move is on again, and 26th Battery manages to get into position just after midnight, 2nd Battery at 2:30 A.M., and 14th Battery at 4:00 A.M.

When daylight comes, all ranks expect the Regiment to be hammered as it was back in the amphitheatre positions in front of the Carpiquet escarpment, but nothing of consequence occurs. In fact there's very little shelling activity in either direction all day. Some large calibre duds thud into the position, which would have caused damage to men and guns if they had gone off. One, landing on Baker Troop, drills a hole so deep that the bottom can't be reached with a fifteen-foot pole.

Still being able to see high ground occupied by the enemy makes everyone uneasy, and the gunners have plenty to do on their gun pits and ammunition pits before they have them to their satisfaction. While grateful for the excavations scooped out by the bulldozer before they arrived, the gunners find the holes are pretty ragged, and much pick-and-shovel work is required before the ammo pits are ready for the first instalment of the 857 additional rounds per gun that will be brought up during the next two nights by Army Service Corps.*

---

* In thirty-six hours 2nd Corps Army Service moved up 205,000 shells, 152,000 gallons of petrol, and 130,000 rations for Operation Totalize. By then a troop of ninety tank-transporters, modified to carry ammunition, could lift 2,700 tons of shells, as much as could be carried by ten transport companies using three-tonners. (Reported in Arnold Warren, *Wait for the Waggons* (Toronto: McClelland and Stewart, 1961).

44

IS 4TH BRIGADE TO BE
SACRIFICED?

※

APART FROM THE USUAL LIGHT HARASSING–FIRE PROGRAM CALLED for each night, there is very little demand on the guns during the first two days up here, just north of Ifs. And on August 7 the guns are again quiet throughout most of the day.

Just after 6:00 P.M. great swarms of Kangaroos and other armoured personnel carriers, transporting the three assault battalions of 4th Brigade, which for the past two days have been involved in manoeuvres in the fields west of Louvigny, suddenly appear on the sloping ground south and west of the gun positions. So suddenly do they "sprout" in the fields in front, some at least must have used the old Roman ford at Athis to cross the Orne instead of the new Bailey bridge at Fleury.

By dusk it is obvious that tremendous forces are about to be unleashed. Not only are the nearby slopes on both sides of the highway leading to Falaise covered with tanks, flails, Kangaroos, and other armoured carriers taking up position, but out of sight behind Ifs and down in the low ground in front of Fleury-sur-Orne there's been the creaking and clanking of tracked vehicles assembling all evening.

The tanks of 2nd Canadian Armoured Brigade will be with 4th Brigade, and east of the Caen–Falaise highway the British 33rd Armoured Brigade will lead another three columns of armoured personnel carriers with a brigade of the 51st Highland Division aboard.

Well aware of what 2nd Canadian Division infantry has been through in taking and holding the ground lying out there just ahead of the muzzles of your guns – the two kilometres from Ifs to the Beauvoir and Troteval farms and the last blood-soaked kilometre from there to Verrières – you can't help wondering if two brigades of infantry and two brigades of tanks could possibly accomplish anything significant in the way of a breakthrough beyond the ridge that forms the southern horizon.

In a message to the troops, it is clear Lt.-Gen. Crerar believes so. He obviously expects remarkable gains from a successful plunge by 1st Canadian Army through the German defences: "We have reached what very much appears to be the potentially decisive period of this five-year World War. I have no doubt we shall make August 8, 1944, an even blacker day for the German army than that same date 26 years ago."* A First War veteran, the General is referring to General Ludendorff's statement that August 8, 1918 – the day the British offensive began east of Amiens – was "the blackest day of the German army in the history of the war."

All the guns having been moved as far forward as possible to increase their range and extend maximum support for the attack, both during the barrage and afterwards, and the infantry having been pulled back from their most forward positions for safety reasons before the bombing begins, great masses of troops and vehicles have been compressed into a relatively small area. Brig. Keefler, CRA of 2nd Division, has decided, under the circumstances, to issue route maps and mark these routes on the ground with white tape so the masses of transport following the assaulting columns, and the two armoured divisions that will follow along still later, will not literally overrun the gun pits of the six artillery regiments in the

---

* Chester Wilmot, *The Struggle for Europe* (London: Collins, 1952), p. 411.

immediate vicinity of Ifs. Thus the forming-up areas for the leading tanks, flails, and armoured troop carriers end up very close to the guns. And in the gathering dusk, command post personnel, having completed all the preparatory paperwork on the barrage, amuse themselves trying to spot their own armoured scout car among the other armoured cars loaned by the Regiment and the other field regiments of the Division to provide additional thick-skinned vehicles to carry infantrymen forward.

Yesterday afternoon, as your car, GA, was being completely emptied out, and a great clutter of equipment and personal kit was being dumped onto the ground in a pitiful-looking mess, a rising tide of irritation among your command post gang was suppressed only when you reminded them that the big, five-ton, armour-plated touring car – eighteen feet long and six and a half feet wide – would be providing protection against small-arms fire and shell splinters for at least ten infantrymen tonight as they go forward behind the barrage blasting a gap through the German lines.

While the armour-plate encasing them is not thick, as in the Kangaroos, it still is of hardened steel ranging from six to twelve millimetres thick, and will certainly deflect 9-mm Schmeisser bullets and shell and mortar splinters.

All who normally ride in GA fervently hope she survives, for she has many proven virtues as a command post vehicle. In addition to being roomy, she's much less vulnerable than a conventional sheet-metal truck sitting on a gun position. And though equipped with four-wheel drive to pull through rough country and heavy mud, she's capable of reaching fifty-five miles an hour on good roads, if given a chance to get rolling.

For an hour or so there is an unnatural atmosphere abroad – quiet, but full of tension. Surely all of this activity this evening, at least some of it under observation, will have alerted the enemy that something very big is about to burst on them.

While it's impossible not to be impressed by the vast herd of armoured vehicles, forming up nose to tail on all sides, you'll wait and see what happens to them before becoming excited about the prospect of an early break-out. After all, these initial assault forces don't come anywhere near the size and fire-power of the British–Canadian forces involved in the integrated operations Goodwood and Atlantic, when the three best British tank divisions were brought to a flaming halt before this ridge only eighteen days ago, and 2nd Canadian Division infantry was left to take the ridge and withstand the enemy's counter-attacks, suffering the highest rate of casualties of all Allied divisions in the bridgehead.

You realize you've become more than a little sceptical of the promises held out for big attacks around here. And as you visit the men in the gun pits – now removing safety caps and stacking hundreds of shells in readiness for the long barrage – you realize this feeling is general here at the guns, so vastly different from the way it was at the beginning of Goodwood–Atlantic, when everyone truly believed that no resistance would exist after all that bombing and shelling.

With the obvious purpose of raising morale, Major Gordon Savage, the second-in-command, visited the gun position late this afternoon. After explaining to the troops that the Canadians have had to keep up the pressure on this front to hold the main German forces here on the eastern end of the bridgehead while the Americans broke out on the far western end, Savage explained what tonight's big show is supposed to accomplish.

While everybody earnestly hopes it will succeed, no one really believes that a single blow, regardless of how heavily it is delivered, can accomplish a significant break-out on this front; too many attacks have ended in bloody disarray along the Verrières Ridge for anyone to be optimistic about another. So the question naturally arises, "Is this really meant to be a break-out or is 4th Brigade merely going to be put through the grinder again to hold the

German tanks and guns here while the Americans continue to expand their break-out?"

And tonight, you feel the concern throughout the Regiment is legitimate, for over there, waiting, lined up in those columns on those dusty slopes, are a lot of friends: six FOOs and their crews in Universal Carriers, along with three battery commanders and their crews in White Armoured Scout Cars.

Some of the gunners have picked up a rumour that 4th Brigade is to be "a sacrifice brigade"; and they are comparing tonight's charge through the enemy gun lines to the Charge of the Light Brigade.

As in all predicted fire, after all the measurements of the line and range to each lift of the barrage are made for each troop on the artillery boards in the battery command post, and angles of sight are calculated for differences in the height of the guns and the height of the terrain over which the barrage will flow, there still remains the matter of the "correction of the moment." As close as possible to the time of the firing of the barrage, adjustments must be applied to all ranges and switches to compensate not only for the temperature of the propellant charges, but also for variations in air temperatures, air pressures, and the speed and direction of the wind at various levels through which the shells must loop on their way to target. These last figures are based on meteorological data in the "meteor telegram" produced by the Survey Regiment and received at the guns at frequent intervals throughout each twenty-four-hour period. These corrections are now applied to the gun programs just before they are handed out to each gun sergeant.

Then comes the call to the phone for synchronization of watches for H-hour, which for the guns is 11:30 P.M. – thirty minutes after the bombing begins and fifteen minutes before it ends at 11:45 P.M. At 11:00 P.M. coloured-flare shells, fired by some regiment nearby, start glowing on the horizon – red on the left and green on the right of the Caen–Falaise highway – designed to mark the target areas for RAF Pathfinder aircraft leading the 1,020 Lancaster and

Halifax bombers from England, which even now can be heard approaching from the coast. And as the wavering glow builds from more flares dropped by the aircraft, the roaring mass of bombers can be heard coming up from behind Caen.

Though the infantry has been pulled back outside the danger zone of two thousand yards, they've been issued wads of cotton wool for their ears, from bales flown from England earlier in the day. Presently, the first wave of bombers is passing low overhead, and the first of the 3,500 tons of bombs start to land with rumbling, thunderous flashes and earth-shaking *crumps*, seemingly just beyond the crest, though you know they are being dropped no closer than May-sur-Orne and Bretteville-sur-Laize.

Then at 11:30 P.M., the roar of eight hundred engines, in tanks and flails and armoured carriers, revving-up for their move to start-lines, adds to the enveloping din. You begin to worry the gun sergeants may not be able to hear the order to fire when it comes time to start the barrage fifteen minutes from now. (Corps calculates it will take that long for the mobile columns to move up and get in position on their startlines.)

But you need not have worried. The overpowering crash of guns on all sides in response to yells of fire from GPOs is beyond anything you've experienced before in Normandy. Not only are there 720 guns of all kinds supporting Totalize, but so concentrated are they that their thunderous roar makes voice communication impossible. Even shouting directly into another man's ear is ineffective, and the only sure way to communicate anything important, even down in the command post dugouts, is to write it out.

And so it is for the next hour as the stupendous bombardment straddling the Caen–Falaise highway ploughs a swath four thousand yards wide and six thousand yards deep. Every two minutes the guns lift two hundred yards. And the mediums are superimposed four hundred yards in depth.

Some 312 guns, including the heavies, will fire a twenty-minute intense bombardment on "known hostile batteries" an hour and forty minutes after H-hour, and then repeat this seven hours after H-hour.

Once the guns have completed the fire plan, they become available to respond to "concentrations on call," predetermined, code-named targets of possible trouble-spots along the ground over which the spearheads will pass on their way to their objectives.

When at last the barrage ends, and the noise drops to some distant rattles, pops, and burps here and there in the direction of glowing fires silhouetting Verrières Ridge, and the high-pitched whine of straining tank motors grows fainter and fainter, the whole front (at least from the perspective of the gunners) assumes an unreal calm unlike anything experienced before in Normandy. For the first time you actually feel the front receding into the distance.

Whether the German guns have been destroyed by the bombs, or are confused by the breakthrough and are scrambling to pull back, or are simply overwhelmed by the number of targets presented by the assaulting columns, they are inactive as far as the gun lines around here are concerned.

For the present there is nothing to do, which offers a glorious opportunity to catch up on sack time. But no one wants to sleep; all are too keyed up, their nervous systems still pulsing and agitated by the hammering roar of the colossal air and ground bombardment just ended. Everyone is hungry for some word as to what is happening up forward, but there are no sit reps coming back from the FOOs. Radio silence has been imposed on them until they are on their objectives, or until dawn, whichever comes first, so as to reduce radio interference with the radio directional beams guiding the columns.

Still, the gunners gather in little groups around the troop command posts to talk and speculate on what may be happening to 4th Brigade and their friends from 4th Field moving with them.

While the fantastic fury of the bombing and the gun barrage, which lit the sky for miles, all the way back to Caen, encouraged optimism that a break-out might occur this time, few are really confident that this won't be just another bloodletting for modest gains.

"Monty's Moonlight" is working well – at least here at the guns. The steady beams of the searchlights, disappearing far away in the smoke and dust on the horizon, light the gun positions brightly enough to read by. To prove it, someone from the command post produces the list of code names for the attack that uses the names of seventy-seven film stars, to cover the startline (Crawford), boundaries (Barrymore and Flynn), report lines (MacDonald, Laughton, Dressler, Valentino, Henie, and Lombard), and all the woods, high points, towns, and villages all the way to Falaise. And for a while those gathered at the command post amuse themselves discovering what Hollywood personalities have been attached to what: Verrières (Marx), Rocquancourt (Pluto), May-sur-Orne (Allen), Bretteville-sur-Laize (Faye), Falaise (Donald Duck).

And all night the red, jewel-like tracers on the 40-mm Bofors ack-ack shells – fired in groups of six every four minutes – sail gracefully in silent arcs across the sky overhead, resembling fantasy necklaces, following the curvature of the earth to oblivion.

Shortly after sunrise, concentrations are called for on behalf of the walking battalions attempting to clear the villages bypassed by the mobile columns immediately beyond the Verrières Ridge. For a while the fighting up at May-sur-Orne and on the left at Tilly-la-Campagne is so sustained you wonder if anything of consequence was accomplished by all that effort last night. When several open-topped half-tracks come back this way, packed with prisoners for deposit in a barbed-wire compound just behind Ifs – the first time anything like this has been seen in this sector of Normandy – you are encouraged to conclude the attack was truly a success.

However, what went on during the night in those undulating fields along the Caen–Falaise highway in the direction of Point 122 and Gaumesnil will remain a mystery until there are reunions with carrier and battery commander crews.

45

PATTING A PANTHER IN THE DARK

*

--- ✳ ---

ACTUALLY, NO ONE SEES VERY MUCH DURING THAT WILD DRIVE — wild not because it is fast, for much of the night most of the columns seem to be sitting still or barely crawling along, but wild as a hurricane or an inferno is wild, with dust and flame and flashing, thundering bombs and shells penetrating over the roar of hundreds of straining engines in tanks and troop carriers massed on all sides as they move forward.

Dense dust clouds are raised by the bombing and the rolling gun barrage, blasting the earth just in advance of the "flails" beating the same trembling earth, followed by the churning tracks of hundreds of tanks, troop carriers, FOO carriers and half-tracks tearing up the dirt as they play follow-the-leader over tinder-dry wheat fields. These impenetrable clouds, combined with smoke shells fired by the enemy to thicken up the ground mists already forming in the valleys, completely frustrate the efforts of searchlights to illuminate the battlefield in a useful way, at least in the early stages of the assault.

Navigators and drivers are so blinded and bewildered by the dust and smoke that each is reduced to trying to follow the dim taillight on the vehicle ahead. Though as time goes on the arrows of ack-ack tracers are a help in pulling them back into the right general direction, the armoured columns frequently shift to the right and left, and in the process disintegrate and reform, and not always with the same battalion column.

Diversions begin in earnest once the surviving German gunners recover enough to start brewing up the odd leading tank or vehicle. Using the flaming wreck as a reference point, they spray the area with mortars and small-arms fire, and hole, with 88-mm solid-shot, any other vehicle that shows up in silhouette as it tries to move past.

And the progress of the British columns east of the Caen–Falaise highway is equally slow, involving many collisions. Some vehicles straying from their course attract the fire of their friends, while others run into strong points they are meant to avoid. Within the first mile, three navigating tanks are ditched in bomb craters, and in trying to avoid these the advancing column loses direction and cohesion.

The commander of a British column will later report: "... chaos indescribable ... the blind leading the blind." A semblance of order is restored when officers dismount and lead small groups of tanks on foot, while the CO fires Very lights to show the way.*

Under such conditions, all sense of dash disappears from the attack, but they all go forward in the right direction. As do the Canadian columns over on the right of the highway, where similar conditions prevail and one column is temporarily halted and others forced into wide detours.

The RHLI columns, instead of passing to the right of Rocquan-court, as they are supposed to, are diverted by an active 88-mm that starts knocking out tanks and half-tracks in the Essex Scottish column on their right flank, first by random fire into clouds of dust and then by the light of the burning vehicles. This forces the Essex column to split up in confusion, and to escape a similar fate, the Rileys edge to the left and find themselves eventually in close-packed columns among the cobbled streets and lanes of

---

* Quoted in Chester Wilmot, *The Struggle for Europe* (London: Collins, 1952), p. 412.

Rocquancourt, pulling along with them B Company of the Royal Regiment, at that moment straying from their own battalion axis left of the village.

At this point in the strange affairs of the night, 4th Field FOO Capt. Len Harvey finds he is out of contact with the Royals' B Company, which his carrier has been following, and that now, he and his crew are quite alone, passing in their carrier along the blackness of a narrow village street. Suddenly Harvey sees a wall looming up on his left – so close, the side of the carrier is about to scrape it. He yells at Ryckman, his driver, "Keep right! Keep right!" When Ryckman protests that the carrier can't be scraping the wall on the left as it is already scraping the wall on the right, Harvey puts out his hand to be sure, and feels not cold rough stone, but warm smooth metal, vibrating under his hand! As he passes his hand over the metal and peers intently through the gloom to try to distinguish what it is, a brief flicker of light from an airburst or a wavering beam of artificial moonlight momentarily penetrates the dust cloud. His heart almost stops! He is patting a German hash-mark cross on the side of a tank! Fortunately, the occupants of the Panther, which is just sitting there with its engine running, are as confused as every-body else as to who is friend and who is foe, and Ryckman is able to guide the carrier past without scraping and slink off undetected into the swirling dust and smoke of the flashing, roaring night.

The confusion of the Germans is matched by that in the Essex Scottish columns as most of their armoured personnel carriers become separated from their leading company and the tanks they are following. For a time the ensuing chaos is horrendous, as official historians will later describe:

Some of their half-tracks and tanks were hit and burst into flames. Other vehicles turned, or backed, or collided with those behind, throwing the column into disorder, which increased as vehicles straying from other columns tried to join company. A platoon sent to deal with an 88-mm gun was driven off by machine-gun fire. By this time their commanding officer was missing, and Major Burgess, 2nd-in-Command, ordered the infantry to get out of their vehicles, deploy and dig in while the column was reformed. This was reported to Brigade at 0357 hrs.*

Attached to the Essex Scottish this night is another 4th Field FOO, Sammy Grange, of Fox Troop. He is riding, not in his carrier like Harvey, but in a tank supplied by 2nd Armoured Brigade at the rear of their column of tanks, immediately ahead of the infantry in their armoured personnel carriers. His tank is a dummy, designed not to fight, but to carry an artillery observer. Apart from its fake gun, however, it is a regular Sherman, indistinguishable from the other tanks in the squadron leading it. This will have significant bearing on the course of events for A Company of the Essex and for Capt. Grange during a bewildering, agonizing night, when it appears to him that he has led an entire infantry battalion astray.

By the time we are told about "Totalize," I am pretty jaded about war. I am convinced that death is inevitable – that it is only a matter of time. So on hearing about this great attack we are to make, I say to MacGregor Young, "Do you think there's any chance of success?"

He is shocked that I feel so gloomy about it. But that is the way I feel. Every time anyone has tried to go through here they got a bloody nose. Why should this be any different?

And that is what I am thinking as we take off – again in a tank – at the end of a column of tanks leading the armoured infantry carriers. We trundle over Verrières Ridge and down towards Rocquancourt, which we are to bypass on the right and carry on, following our tanks guided by white tapes the engineers are

---

* Page 25, Report No. 65, Historical Section (G.S.) Canadian Army Headquarters, Dept. of National Defence, Dec, 23, 1953.

laying down up ahead. But in the dust, the other tanks get away out of sight, and I am lost.

Of course I carry on, but go the wrong way. And then to my horror I find all the infantry Kangaroos and armoured carriers following me. We all end up in Rocquancourt. Fortunately the village is in the process of being abandoned (or at least that is how it seems to me), with them going out the back way as we are coming in the front, probably believing they are surrounded from the great numbers of people passing by them. Anyway, where I am, there is really no fuss. In fact I am surprised at how little opposition there is. Some shots are fired, but none from my tank I can tell you. And after it's all over, I find my tank is the only one there – all the others have gone to the right place. On top of everything, my tank is just a dummy – its gun couldn't fire anything! Then, when dawn comes, I discover huge quantities of infantry have followed me instead of the right people.*

So when later I get a call to go and see Bill Carr, my battery commander, I think, This is it! I'm going to be court-martialled and I deserve it. There is absolutely no defence I can offer. I just wasn't paying attention when I got lost. But when I get to see him, he says, "I just want to tell you, the infantry have asked me to commend you. You were the only tank that stayed with them – the rest buggered off!"

Vastly relieved, I don't tell him the truth that I led them astray. Nor do I reveal to the Essex that my tank, whose imposing presence had given them such comfort, had only a rubber gun.†

All those going forward in the bodies of Kangaroos – surrounded by a wall of steel, clouds of dust, and stunning noise –

---

* Some of the "huge quantities of infantry" may have been members of the South Saskatchewan Regiment, which suffered fifty casualties clearing the village that morning.
† Author interview.

are completely dependent on the drivers getting them where they are supposed to go, for they can see nothing but the flashing shells of the stormy barrage they follow for six kilometres. Gunner Turner, Major Wren's Don R, who on the Major's orders has tied his motorbike on the front of the scout car and climbed inside, sees even less, for he is forced to lie prone on top of equipment piled up under the canvas roof. While the position offers little protection, it still is preferable to riding his old Norton in the choking dust amidst the crush of tanks and vehicles pressing forward in roaring confusion.

Moving with one of the three companies of Royals that have been able to follow the leader and arrive in good order at their dispersal point before all other battalions in the attack, is Baker Troop FOO Bill Waddell. Just before first light, the Royals' column is halted to allow the company commanders to confer.

By now the effects of the spine-stiffening, pre-attack rum ration, and the excitement that helped sustain everybody during the initial charge through the enemy's forward lines, have faded – replaced by a growing sense of vulnerability as they peer about in the sinister, dark silence and reflect on how deep they are in enemy territory. They have no idea where the Jerries are or what may happen when dawn arrives.

Still, the Royals and their arty reps know where they are on the map, and so far have the advantage of surprise over the enemy. Since it will soon be light, Col. Anderson decides that A Company should move as fast as possible onto its given objective, D will take the objective formerly allotted to B (the missing company), and C will move up in reserve. And in spite of some enemy shelling and small-arms fire, the intrepid drivers of the Kangaroos take the three companies right up onto their objective on Hill 122, where they pile out and move into tactical positions best suited to defend this dominating feature.

By 6:00 A.M. the other battalions are still not on their objectives, and there is no sign yet of the 51st Highland Division, though there is now considerable evidence of unsubdued enemy troops in the area.

The first enemy attack develops at 8:30 A.M., when two Panther and two Tiger tanks move up the Caen–Falaise highway, and another group of them on the far side of Cramesnil opens fire. Firing heavily, several actually penetrate to within a few yards of the Royals' tac headquarters, which is on the east side of the road.

On the west side is the Royals' mortar platoon, along with some carriers and medium machine guns of the Toronto Scottish. All are still digging in when, suddenly, screeching, armour-piercing shots begin hitting the Toronto Scottish carriers. Then one after another the Royals' mortar platoon carriers are hit. As the carriers take fire, mortar bombs begin to blow up and the Germans spray the area with machine guns. The Tor Scots lose all their carriers and medium machine guns, and all seven of the Royals' carriers, along with all their mortars and ammunition, are destroyed.

In the midst of this threatening uproar, which grows more dangerous by the minute, Bill Waddell, the 4th Field FOO with the leading company, pinpoints the location of the German tanks and goes back on foot to lead up a troop of Sherbrooke Fusiliers tanks into position where they can get clear shots at them. And when he gets them close enough to be effective he directs their fire, knocking out at least four.*

Major Ralph Young, second-in-command of the Royals, an eyewitness to Waddell's heroism, will have difficulty later (even forty years later) finding words to describe it: "This guy is standing out in the open, all by his bloody self, pointing out a German tank here, another there, yelling at our tanks, 'Hit the goddam thing!' or words to that effect. Those are his fire orders. Oh yes . . . incredible! With him pointing and the tanks shooting, they knock out three, maybe

---

* Capt. William James Waddell was subsequently awarded the Military Cross.

four, of them – one or two self-propelled guns, and a couple of tanks. Oh, I remember Waddell! He doesn't last long after that, as I recall."*

By noon the RHLI are dug in close to their objective on the right, the Essex Scottish are in the process of occupying Caillouet, and east of the highway elements of British 154th Brigade have come up. At 2:00 P.M. the Royals push on another 1,700 yards to Gaumesnil, where they find Sherbrooke tanks awaiting them. They now are seven kilometres south of their startline at Verrières, at the head of what clearly is a massive breakthrough, and their casualties have been extremely light; only four killed and thirty-four wounded, clear vindication of Simonds' innovative attack, particularly his improvised armoured troop-carriers.†

------

* Author interview.
† German Field Marshal von Kluge reported "a breakthrough has occurred south of Caen the like of which we have never seen." And after the war the commanding general of 12th SS Division, Kurt Meyer, described how he, in the early hours of August 8, stopped the rout of his troops down the road to Falaise before the thundering barrage and the growling tank columns – the first German troops he had ever seen running away in panic. Placing himself in the middle of the road and lighting a cigar, he inquired of the sheepish men if they were going to leave him there alone to fight the enemy – even as his own legs were shaking and he was bathed in cold sweat. In the morning he sent a tank force up the road from Falaise to wipe out the spearhead before it could consolidate. There they met up with 4th Field's Waddell and the squadron of Sherbrooke Fusiliers tanks commanded by Major S. V. "Woppy" Radley-Walters. Among the dead left about Hill 122 was a Captain Michael Wittman, Germany's foremost tank commander, celebrated on the Russian front as the most successful panzer ace of the war, with a record of 117 tanks before he was posted to Normandy to continue his cavalier ways. At Villers Bocage (west of Hill 112) on June 13, using a Tiger, he destroyed five Cromwells, two Fireflies, and the half-tracks of an entire motorized rifle company of the 4th County of London Yeomanry. British writers attribute the demise of Wittman's last Tiger to Shermans of the Northhamptonshire Yeomanry.

46

WHEN THE DUST SETTLES
THEY ARE WAITING

❋

TO NO ONE'S SURPRISE, RESISTANCE TO THE WALKING TROOPS exists in every village bypassed by the mobile columns, but most particularly in Tilly-la-Campagne and May-sur-Orne, and throughout the morning the guns take part in divisional fire tasks. (During one of these, Sgt. "Lefty" Phillips asks Troop Leader Grout to time his gun crew with a stopwatch. They succeed in getting off an astounding seventeen rounds in one minute.)

The dust confronting the walking troops of 5th and 6th Brigades, who were withdrawn one thousand yards for safety at the outset of the RAF bombing, is horrendous as they move up to their startlines. Sent roiling by the bombs hundreds of feet in the air over the dark battlefield, and fed by the creeping barrage and the churning tracks of vast herds of vehicles, the dust is impenetrable. And so it remains for what "seems like hours" to Capt. J. E. "Elmo" Thibault, of the FMRs, leading his men up to a startline in the south end of St. Martin-de-Fontenay, near the church and the house. From here Thibault's D company and Acting-Major Brégent's B Company will go forth to clear May-sur-Orne.

Waiting for the dust to clear enough to see where they are going, the FMRs are very conscious they are about to cross fields where the Calgarys were shattered, the Black Watch virtually wiped out, and the Maisies severely mauled two weeks ago. Capt. Thibault mulls

over a question that will haunt him the rest of his life: In the preparations for Totalize, why weren't the mine tunnels taken care of? By
now all know of the network of tunnels under the field (some
1,200 feet deep, offering incomparable shelter from shells and
bombs) and are aware that the air shafts allow the Germans to reoccupy positions from which they were driven. Why haven't suitable
measures been taken to eliminate them?

When the dust settles, the Germans are ready and waiting (just as
they were for the Black Watch and the Maisies), having arisen
unscathed from their underground labyrinth and reoccupied their
old positions, including the minehead building from whence the
shot comes that kills Acting-Major Georges Brégent whose
company is passing that way.

Not until after daylight – when the Crocodiles (flame-throwing
Churchill tanks) dragging immense supplies of fuel in trailers
behind them, are brought up to disgorge, with horrible, roaring
blasts, huge balls of liquid fire across that dilapidated minehead
structure and many other known and suspected enemy positions –
do the FMRs make headway. Then it becomes "a walk-in."

At 1:00 P.M., an hour before 4th Canadian Armoured Division and
the Polish Armoured Division are to take off on follow-through
attacks exploiting the break-out, the first of five hundred heavy
bombers of U.S.A. 8th Airforce begin to drop 1,500 tons of bombs
beyond the now distant spearheads on potential trouble spots,
including Bretteville-sur-Laize.

After last night's spectacular RAF show by twice as many
bombers (1,020), dropping more than double the weight (3,500
tons), right out in front, no one shows much interest. Until suddenly bombs start tumbling down from a low-flying Liberator
back near Caen. Everyone stares in disbelief as, one after another,
twenty-four U.S. Liberators and Flying Fortresses, the sun glinting off their silver bodies, drop bombs on the mediums deployed
around Colombelles, at least 1,500 metres back of here, and on

Faubourg-de-Vaucelles, where 3rd Division is also concentrating for their move up.

It's all over in a matter of minutes, but an immense dust cloud is left drifting, and among the rising pillars of black smoke there are sporadic, muffled explosions and the faint, hoarse cries of desperate men.

What a terribly demoralizing experience for divisions preparing to enter battle, the two armoured divisions for the first time! Sgt. Howard Hill asks the question that is on everybody's mind: How in God's name could that have happened? Only last night in the pitch dark, the RAF bombed so close they had to issue our infantry earplugs, but not one bomb fell short. Now, in broad daylight, the Yanks drop their loads ten miles behind where they are supposed to!

Just how many casualties were suffered back there no one can learn, for all ranks are confined to their own areas, and the brass are not anxious to spread bad news and evoke despair. But rumours of awful carnage begin to circulate – even the 3rd Division commander, they say.*

---

* North Shore Regiment alone lost one hundred officers and men to the bombs. Many at 3rd Division Headquarters were wounded, including the division commander, Maj.-Gen. Keller. Of the 65 killed and 250 wounded among the Canadians and the Poles, a very high percentage were artillerymen – 44 killed and 137 wounded. Fourth Medium, waiting on wheels to move, had 12 killed and 28 wounded, as eight guns and five tractors were destroyed; 7th Medium, firing on a target at the time the American bombs tumbled down on them, destroying three guns, had 11 gunners killed and 18 wounded; 2nd Counter-Battery had three killed; 2nd Survey Regiment, 13 killed and 20 wounded; 8th Light Ack-Ack, four killed and 49 wounded; 3rd Light Ack-Ack, three killed; and 3rd Division Artillery HQ, four killed and two wounded, and all their vehicles destroyed. From Col. G. W. L. Nicolson, CD, *The Gunners of Canada, Volume II, 1919-1967* (Toronto: McClelland and Stewart, 1972), p. 318.

47

VERRIÈRES

---------------- ❋ ----------------

WAITING FOR THE GUNS TO COME UP TO THE NEW POSITION JUST to the left of the smashed village of Verrières, you wander alone among slit trenches of the recently vacated infantry position. Here and there in the wheat and sandy holes lie crumpled sacks of battle-dress which a few days ago were men. You pause beside the body of a captain, lying face down, half out of a slit trench, his head resting on one arm as though asleep. Curious as to whether he was RHLI, Essex Scottish, or Royal Regiment, you bend down and read his shoulder flash: 4 RCA. With a shock you realize you have stumbled onto the spot where quiet, gentle Jack Thompson died. He was one of the very few chosen for long-service leave just before D-Day, and you recall how eagerly you questioned him when he got back to England. What was it like for a man to return to his wife after many years of separation? "Incredibly beautiful," he said reverently, and his eyes glowed with the memory. But then he frowned and added, "But I don't know whether these leaves are good or not — you see, I left my wife pregnant."

As you turn away from the sad remains of this kind man, you wonder if your eyes are wet for Jack's baby, who will never see her father, or for your own little girl, whom you've never seen.

On your way back to where you planted the four banderoles to show where your four guns are to be placed — in the lee of a row of scrubby trees, not much more than bushes, running across the front of your position – half a dozen Sherman tanks come roaring back over the crest, down through a gap in your bushes, passing between the markers for Number One and Number Two guns, and continuing on back towards Ifs, following a track across the wheat fields.

Their passage worries you. Obviously this is a favourite tank route – the depth of the single tank track already worn across the parched field plainly tells you that. You have laid out a gun position directly across an "elephant walk." The image of a herd of clanking monsters, half-blinded by dust, ploughing through your position flashes through your mind. The risk is only too real. Still, you hate to move your markers. If you shift them enough to get rid of the problem, two of the guns will be out beyond the hedgerow and in view of a distant ridge, the occupancy of which you are uncertain. While you are still pondering the problem, another group of tanks (having replenished their fuel and ammunition) come roaring up from Ifs, following their preferred route.

Desperate for advice on how you might divert tanks from using this route between your guns, you try waving one down. To your surprise the first one stops. By yelling strenuously you're able to communicate your problem to the tank commander, who's standing in the open hatch.

The solution, he tells you, is quite simple. Erect any kind of barricade, regardless how flimsy, around your position and the tanks will respect it. Once the new diversion is marked by a few tanks, the barricade will no longer be necessary. Tanks meticulously follow a well-established track because of their fear of mines. Show him where you want them to go and he'll start the new track.

You lead him around the right end of the bushes, and the others follow him as he cuts back onto the track leading up and over the crest.

From then until the guns arrive just after dark, you tug and pull bits and pieces of old farm machinery into place along the back and front of the position – shafts off a broken cart, a relatively whole high-wheeled hayrake, a couple of barrels on which poles can be laid – anything you can find around the nearby farm that can be moved by one man. When finished, your barricade doesn't look like much, but it proves effective when a convoy of half-tracks come back over the ridge. Without hesitation they swing west, around the end of your position, and curl back behind you to take up the track again to Ifs, like the tanks that pioneered the bypass.

The first couple of half-tracks pass without incident, but then *pow* – a mine explodes under the right front wheel of one, just as it is passing around the end of your position. A soldier tumbles out onto the ground beside the smashed wheel, collapses face down, and doesn't move again. The drivers of the two half-tracks following stop and are examining him as you come up. Their verdict: Dead. Quietly they return to their vehicles and continue on to Ifs, leaving their dead comrade lying beside his disabled half-track.

Though it is dark when the guns arrive, Monty's Moonlight is again in vogue, and it helps facilitate deployment. But after the quads have wheeled about in their normal fashion, dropping guns and trailers, and have left for their wagon lines, a string of Hawkins anti-personnel mines, of the kind used by infantry to secure their positions, is discovered lying in the grass right across where guns and quads have just passed and repassed. Bdr. Don Finnie spotted what he thought was a signal wire, and when he tried to shift it so it wouldn't get sliced by a jabbing spade, up popped the mines, bobbing at intervals along the wire's length and recognizable as khaki-painted Johnson Wax tins, loaded with explosive, carrying TNT detonators in saddles soldered on the front of each tin.

How all those wheels and feet thrashing about here just now were able to miss all those mines is inexplicable, and provides fodder for discussion as the digging of gun pits and ammo pits begins.

It's a good thing the guns are not required to fire anything of consequence during the night, for the reserve regiments of 4th

Armoured Division move up past the position raising dust clouds so dense that gunlayers cannot see lighted aiming posts beyond ten yards. Even in the command post – constructed by turning a huge, round, cast-iron watering trough upside down over a normal command post trench – the dust is so bad you can hardly see the artillery board. How many tanks and vehicles pass, you do not know, but for more than an hour tanks, carriers, and armoured cars play follow-the-leader around your bypass before the dust is allowed to settle.*

Then, just as you are breathing a sigh of relief, as well as some dust-free air, and visiting the half-finished gun pits the men have been digging as the dust clouds rolled over them, your attention is drawn to two exceedingly bright lights – as bright as a pair of prewar American car headlights, coming from the direction of Ifs. At first you think they belong to some sort of heavy-equipment mover, for, though you can hear its diesel straining for power, it is moving at a snail's pace. But when finally it arrives, the vehicle turns out to be just an armoured bulldozer engaged in removing the soft topsoil from the track worn by the tanks, preparing a road to be used as a supply route from Caen to God-knows-where.

The problem is, the dozer operator is following orders given him by one who clearly is imbued with the Roman road-building principle of proceeding in a straight line come hell, high water, or 25-pounders. Nothing short of shooting him dead will divert him, and while this is tempting, it probably wouldn't be seen as justifiable by a court of inquiry. So gunners with poles hold Tannoy wires high overhead as he passes under them, and you stand waving a lamp-electric on the parapet of Number Two gun pit to ensure he doesn't fill it with earth.

At dawn, fighting the nausea you've come to associate with

---

* Some eighty tanks of the Governor General Footguards and eighty-four amoured carriers and half-tracks of the Lincoln and Welland Regiment, as well as dozens of support vehicles.

extreme fatigue (more pronounced than usual from eating dust all night) you can't face a breakfast of M & V. And when Hiltz suggests there may be something interesting to be found among the victuals left behind in the disabled half-track abandoned so summarily yesterday, you jump at the idea. But before you get to look inside the vehicle, you and he come upon what is left of the body of the poor man you saw fall dead here yesterday. It lies directly across what became during the night the path of hundreds of 4th Armoured Division tanks and vehicles. You and Hiltz return to the troop command post, empty-handed and retching.

48

FOOTSLOGGERS OFFER A
HUMBLING TRIBUTE

❋

FROM THE MORNING OF AUGUST 9, UNTIL THE REGIMENT LEAVES for a new position, the guns are silent. The calm produces a strange feeling after all that has gone on here on Verrières Ridge since it first became a concern of the guns way back at Louvigny at dawn on July 19, at the start of three grim weeks of bloody battles of attrition.

Still, the gunners will leave here with a sense of satisfaction, knowing all German attacks (and there were so many that brigades lost count) were shattered largely by concentrations laid down by the guns. Of this all ranks were aware, even as the struggles ebbed and flowed, simply by following the pattern and intensity of the fire requested. And the gunners recognize (though Intelligence won't confirm it for some time) that even the most fanatical German soldiers are showing a reluctance to attack in daylight when they know each attempt will be met with an instantaneous deluge of high explosive produced by Mike, Uncle, and Victor targets. Any remaining enthusiasm of the elite SS for launching attacks must surely have died during the last days of July on the slopes about here under gunfire of an intensity exceeding anything they had experienced before, according to statements volunteered by prisoners.*

---

* A July report by 2nd SS Panzer Division opposite the Canadians east of the Orne confirms this: "The incredibly heavy artillery and mortar

The ability of field artillery reps attached to the infantry (even the FOOs at the company level) to concentrate on a single target all the guns of a regiment, a division, or a corps, or even all the guns of the entire army, within a few minutes, has led to widespread belief among the German rank and file that 25-pounders are hopper-fed.

Prisoners, taken in the first hours of the breakthrough and brought back to the prisoners-of-war compound at Ifs, asked to see "your supergun – the automatic 25-pounder." These included two prisoners who were being used to raise buckets of water by windlass from an exceedingly deep well, at a house near your guns, to fill an endless line of water cans for their fellow prisoners behind the barbed wire. When they were told that 25-pounders must be loaded one round at a time, they merely smirked in disbelief, nodding their heads in a knowing fashion, as though to say of course we know you have to lie for security reasons.

This is understandable. Never having encountered on the Russian front anything like the ad lib concentrations of Mike, Uncle, and Victor targets, whose fury can erupt about them without warning, like spontaneous combustion, they have to have

---

fire of the enemy is something new for the seasoned veterans as much as for new arrivals from the reinforcement units. The assembly of troops is spotted immediately by enemy reconnaissance aircraft and smashed by bombs and artillery directed from the air; and if nevertheless the attacking troops go forward, they become involved in such dense artillery and mortar fire that heavy casualties ensue and the attack peters out within the first few hundred metres. Losses by the infantry are then so heavy that the impetus necessary to renew the attack is spent. Our troops enter battle in low spirits at the thought of the enemy's enormous superiority of *matériel*. The feeling of helplessness against enemy aircraft operating without hindrance has a paralysing effect; and during the barrage the effect on the inexperienced men is literally soul-shattering. The best results have been obtained by platoon and section commanders leaping forward uttering a good old-fashioned yell. We've also revived the practice of bugle calls." (WO219/1908 British Imperial War Museum.)

some explanation. And since their own artillery has never seen fit
to develop a system capable of rapid concentration of great
numbers of guns on a single target, they suspect a super weapon,
not a superior system of fire control providing the effect of a giant
machine gun beating a zone.

The idea of a supergun comes easily to a people nurtured in the
Krupp tradition.* It's hard for them to entertain the possibility that
the superiority of British and Commonwealth field artillery is
traceable to the speed and accuracy of their surveys – linking every
troop of every artillery regiment with every troop in every other
field regiment in the theatre of operations in total accuracy – so
that a FOO can call down instantly on a target of his choosing one
troop or all of them, as required.†

Unquestionably the Germans were prevented from breaking
through to Ifs, and perhaps beyond to Caen, by the awesome concentrations fired by both field and medium regiments, but most
particularly by the 25-pounders of 2nd Division, responding with
extraordinary scales of fire that sometimes overlapped on Mike and
Uncle targets, occasionally combining with the guns of 3rd and 4th

---

* Krupp's superior steel and design (first rifled guns and breechloaders)
were directly responsible for Germany's fragmented states becoming a
united country that defeated France in 1870. Henceforth Krupp's guns
were considered the key to victory.

† Non-gunner Lt.-Gen. Sir Brian Horrocks, in a postwar book *Corps
Commander*, wrote: "The core of the Royal Artillery was the fantastic
accuracy of their Survey Units. . . . Neither the Germans nor the
Russians, nor the French, who were always supposed to be the masters of
artillery fire systems, could approach the accuracy or the weight of concentrated fire power which . . . I had at my disposal. If a target was
sufficiently important to warrant all or most of Corps artillery to be fired
. . . in a matter of minutes, about 400 guns could be brought into action
where I wanted them . . . made possible by good surveying, good communications and a high degree of flexibility at the guns." Sir Brian Horrocks,
Eversley Belfield, and Maj.-Gen. H. Essame, *Corps Commander* (Toronto:
Griffin House), p. 177.

divisions on Victor targets. And at the most desperate moments, FOOs even pulled down fire from their own guns on their OP positions to flush out Germans swarming over the infantry they were supporting.

No senior officer or instructor during the years of training in England, including the walking-encyclopedias of gunnery, the Instructors in Gunnery of Larkhill and Senneybridge, ever once gave the slightest indication they knew, or even suspected, the terribly persuasive fire-power placed in the hands of FOOs by the invention of Mike, Uncle, and Victor targets.

In an OP in normal circumstances, when the rumble of neighbouring artillery or local enemy activity is not interfering with your hearing, there's a familiar sequence of sounds through which you follow your shells onto target. First comes a distant, faint thumping somewhere back behind you, then nothing for a few seconds. Suddenly overhead there's a sinister sizzling and crackling, followed by an abrupt, split-second silence, then a fury of cataclasmic flashes erupting in the target area amidst violent black puffs of smoke and dirt. This rapidly builds without pause into a hellish cauldron that gives off the reverberating roar of the wicked, overlapping thunderclaps that only 25-pounder shells pelting a Mike target can create.

Horrifying enough when viewed from a distance of three or four hundred yards, but until you have lived through the terrible screams of 25-pounder shells arriving on target, and experienced the distinctive, jolting whacks of their explosions around you, it is impossible to conceive of the full horror of a Mike Target to which attacking Germans are subjected again and again on a regular basis.

In the sweltering, dispiriting, dusty heat of the late afternoon of August 10, the Regiment is ordered to move south from Verrières about eight miles as the crow flies, to a new position a mile and three-quarters northwest of Bretteville-sur-Laize. Following the now well-established procedure designed to provide continuous support for the infantry, 2nd Battery leads off at 6:00 P.M., with the other two batteries following at one-hour intervals.

And you leave not an hour too soon, for the neighbourhood is changing rapidly, and not for the better. When ex-gunner Lt.-Gen. Simonds' 2nd Corps Headquarters settled in close by, 14th Battery was told to move its noisy guns a few hundred yards to the left rear. While unflattering opinions of the delicate sensitivity of high-level ears were expressed abundantly in tones loud and clear by gunners and officers alike, they promptly complied with the request. (In sharp contrast, you would later learn, to the reaction of a platoon of the FMRs when asked by an advance man of 2nd Corps to give up the only reasonably intact large house in May-sur-Orne, which they'd chosen as their bivouac after the war moved on from that godforsaken village. That they were in the midst of their first civilized meal since coming to Normandy – combining freshly fried chicken and champagne from the cool cellar – may have had something to do with their total lack of cooperation. When Lieut. Noel Meilleur inquired of the staff major if he was carrying a weapon, and the haughty man replied, "Of course!" he was quietly advised: "Well, you'd better be prepared to use it, for the only way you're going to take over this house is to fight for it the same as we did.")

As your 2nd Battery convoy crosses along the ridge to move down the Caen–Falaise highway past burned-out and derelict Allied tanks and vehicles, through what was no-man's-land for more than eighteen days, you are struck by the number of unburied German dead strewn across the shell-blasted fields, their upturned faces blackened by the sun and bloated by the torrid heat – many of them, unquestionably, the victims of the guns now rolling along behind you.

And for the first time you see disabled German tanks in numbers, some with their turrets blown right off and lying upside down on the ground, providing mute testimony to the accuracy and blasting power of Typhoon rockets. How often during the past three weeks you watched them go into a vertical dive straight down through the black puffing flak, releasing their rockets with terrible, hair-raising *scrootch*es, before disappearing below this ridge. The earth-shaking explosions that followed produced the derelicts lying here.

Surely the Typhoon is proving to be the most effective weapon of all in combatting the superiority of the enemy's armour, particularly his irresistible Tigers. Without the Typhoons, the Allies might never have subdued his armoured divisions to the point where a break-out became possible. They must seriously inhibit, if not entirely prevent, all movement of his armour in daylight.

After you turn right, off the main road and onto less-travelled tracks, with fewer derelict vehicles around which to detour, you come upon more infantrymen trudging forward in single file along the side of the road. It's very hot and exceedingly dusty along these powdery tracks, and your heart goes out to those weary footsloggers.

Even moving slowly, your vehicles, guns, and limbers raise swirling clouds of dust that sift up into the cabs of the vehicles and drift over the sweating infantrymen plodding along right next to them. At one point you slow the convoy to a crawl as you pass a company of men who have been broken off to rest at the side of the road. Since they are sitting and lying along the top of the bank of the sunken roadway, they are almost eyeball-to-eyeball with the men riding in the trucks. What with the wretched dust raised by your trucks roiling up around them, and the fact that you are riding while they, the indisputable *crème de la crème* of all who wear the King's uniform, are forced to walk, loaded with packs and weapons and ammunition, makes you very self-conscious. You half-expect them to call out some derisive remark, as they used to in England when they saw the artillery riding by, and are totally unprepared for what one of them calls out: "Keep it up, fellows. You're doing fine!"

Then another voice pipes up, "Good show, Arty! Keep it up!"

And then one of them stands up and starts to clap, and the first thing you know, a lot of them are standing up and clapping too.

It's so entirely unexpected, you feel tears welling up in your eyes. You want to call back to them, Bless your dear generous hearts, we should be clapping you! But you don't, of course. You sit there embarrassed until you pass out of sight of all of them. Only then does your driver, Gunner Art Harder, show any sign he heard or saw anything unusual. He turns and, in a low voice, husky with emotion, says, "My God, did you see that? They were clapping us! The infantry – clapping us!"

And you know every man in every truck in the battery is feeling that way, for they have come to look with awe upon the infantryman, fully aware of the appalling casualties all battalions of 2nd Division have suffered in the past month and the extraordinary depth of courage a man has to muster to keep going forward, when the best he can expect is a clean flesh wound to get him out of it.

Harder, who was slumping with fatigue and the effects of dysentery, which now afflicts a large proportion of the troop, is sitting bolt upright, with shoulders back and head held high, as he drives on at a lively clip now there are no marching troops along the road ahead.

49

EXCAVATING GUN PITS IN
SOLID CHALK

———————— ✳ ————————

THE NEW POSITION NORTHWEST OF BRETTEVILLE–SUR–LAIZE IS ON
high land just off a road running along the left bank of the river.
But to get there you have to pass through what remains of that poor
village, which died under tons of bombs two days ago, on the first
day of Totalize. After seeing Caen and village after village smashed
to ruins, you should be getting used to it, but the desolation is so
complete here, you experience fresh feelings of shock and regret.
The huge bomb craters and the clutter of broken stone and rubble
– requiring extensive shifting and filling by the engineers' bulldozer crews, struggling to provide some kind of base for a vehicle
route through the town – have obstructed the natural course of the
river. The diverted water runs whichever way it can, forming great
muddy pools and turning the newly formed road into a sludgy
causeway.

As your vehicle bumps slowly through this melancholy place,
you feel for the poor people who called it home, and who must
soon return here to begin life again. Reddish muddy water flows
through the tumbled stones and broken walls, and a sickly smell of
charred wood fills the air. With relief, you leave it behind and start
up a winding road with a sparkling, fast-flowing shallow stream
on your left and lush greenery cascading down steep slopes on
your right. And soon you are directed to turn right, up a chalky

road to a gently sloping plateau, where the air is remarkably cool and fresh.

At first sight the stubble field high above the river promises to be by far the most pleasant gun position in France so far. Here is a beautiful landscape, untouched by war and free of that eternal layer of dust that coats everything in Normandy. The only hint of the furies existing elsewhere is some tangled webs of silver-backed, skinny strips of paper lying here and there on the field and drooping like Christmas decorations on nearby bushes and trees. These are the remains of a blizzard of foil (known as "window") dropped by Pathfinder planes to confuse enemy radar the other night when bombers were operating over Bretteville.

To the right, a ravine full of bushes runs down the steep hill to the Laize river babbling softly over rocks and sandbars. And over the river and up a slope, a wide sweep of forest extends right and left, all the way to the horizon. It's so remarkably quiet and peaceful. But the position loses all its charm once digging begins.

Little more than a foot below the surface is solid chalk. Every shovelful has to be picked loose, and the pick shows a nasty tendency to stick with a frustrating *thunk* in the damp chalk, resisting all but the most strenuous efforts to pull it out.

Dysentery is now rampant, and its debilitating effect doesn't help the pace of the digging, which becomes maddeningly slow as the hours pass. You were one of the first to be afflicted back at Fleury, and are pretty well over it, but it still saps your energy.

When, dripping with perspiration and ready to drop from fatigue, you notice that everything on the position has suddenly become visible in the misty, grey light that precedes the dawn, now appearing as the faintest glow on the eastern horizon, you declare the command post finished. It still isn't deep enough to provide proper headroom for a standing man when it's roofed over, but if everybody else feels as utterly done in as you, it will damn well have to do.

When you visit the gun detachments, half expecting to find they have given up long since, to your amazement you find they have picked and shovelled gun pits of respectable depth. Some are still working, surrounded by great, greyish-white rings of chalk chips, but they move as men completely worn out by their effort. No one wants to engage in any chit-chat this morning.

Shortly after sunrise, you take a phone call from RHQ requesting volunteers to go on a patrol over the river to winkle out a sniper, or a nest of snipers, periodically producing menacing *phut-phut* sounds across the gun positions.

In spite of everyone having been up all night and aching with fatigue from digging, there is no problem getting volunteers. But you accept only four, making sure to include the troop ack-ack Bren gunner, Fred Edwards, who with Bombardier Scott brought in those prisoners back at Fleury. You figure the smaller the group the better. If it's only one sniper, a few men stalking him as unobtrusively as possible would seem preferable. If it turns out to be a pocket of enemy with no intention of giving up, then no matter how large your patrol, it'll be in deep trouble. Gunners are not trained or mentally tuned to infantry work, and you've had a minimum of training in infantry tactics, consisting mainly of a little common-to-all-arms training while at Brockville Officers' Training Centre. According to the map, that forest over there, Forêt de Cinglais, stretches two miles along the river and runs southwest about four miles. Directly across the valley from the guns there's a cul-de-sac in the forest, about three hundred yards wide at the river, extending about seven hundred yards up the slope into the trees. The consensus at RHQ is that the sniper is up the hill in the trees, at the far end of the cul-de-sac.

Crossing the shallow stream on sandbanks and rocks, and leaving Edwards at the riverbank to provide covering fire with his Bren if required, you and one man go up through the fringe of the woods on the right-hand side of the open field, while the other two winkle up through the trees on the left.

Halfway up the hill you realize that the woods could be full of snipers and you'd never find one. Only a sniper who wanted to give up would give away his position to a patrol wandering around looking for him. And when you stop and listen in the utter stillness, it occurs to you that if there were anything more than a single sniper up here, they would by now have let fly at you, for your progress through the woods has hardly been silent. Convinced you'll find no Germans on your objective, you move along at a good clip for the last hundred yards, and fortunately, your hunch turns out to be correct.

But they were here very recently, in large numbers, well dug in and camouflaged. Just within the treeline there is a long string of trenches, each shored-up with logs.

How different it would have been if you'd tried coming up here yesterday. It's not something you care to think about. For a hundred yards or more along the edge of the forest there are slit trenches and log-covered dugouts strewn with bits and pieces of equipment, including gourd-shaped aluminum water-bottles covered with moulded and varnished wood veneer, and a splendid black leather case that could have held a valuable instrument of some kind.

These trenches have not long been abandoned – probably only last night. Everywhere there are items of partially eaten food that insects, birds, and animals have not yet got around to cleaning up. And the way the open tins and eating utensils lie about suggests the occupants of these trenches left in a great hurry in the middle of a meal. There are loaves of black rye bread, as heavy as lead, some partially consumed and some whole, showing no sign of mould, still fresh enough to eat. There's a jar of ersatz coffee, and in another trench you find a package of highly aromatic tobacco and a blue pack of French cigarettes with some still in it – precious items to any soldier, not likely to be left behind except when pulling out in an awful hurry.

Though your patrol returns without a sniper, it doesn't come back empty-handed. Everybody seems truly pleased you got back at all, and are very interested in the German things. Those who try the black bread with marge and marmalade declare it quite good, if a bit rubbery. But there's no enthusiasm whatsoever for the cigarettes and ersatz coffee.

There's been no call on the guns to fire today, and the exhausted gun crews have been able to get some sleep. And now that the sniper scare has been settled (at least to the satisfaction of 2nd Battery), many go down to the river to bathe themselves and do some washing.

Your priority is sleep. But before you can climb into GA and curl up around the gear shift (now your favourite place to sleep), your attention is drawn to a low-flying Typhoon coming back from a sortie over enemy territory with a faltering engine that roars for a moment then flutters out, roars up again and then cuts out, sinking lower all the time. Suddenly he fires a raucous, chattering burst of his cannons and machine guns, and for a moment you wonder what he's shooting at. But when he turns his plane over and he falls out, just as he's passing over the guns, you realize he was warning everybody below his plane must soon crash. A wisp of white cloth streams up from his falling body, and you hold your breath, waiting for his chute to open. It doesn't. He lands with a sickening thud just behind the position. His plane crashes with a roar just a bit farther on, sending a black pillar of smoke billowing skyward like a funeral pyre.

Everyone is filled with that mixture of horror and inner rage that prevails each time you are witness to a particularly outrageous aspect of the brutality of war. That poor young man, whose broken body lies out there in the field, was a complete stranger, but you feel you knew him, for he took the time to warn you that he had to abandon his plane. In that instant he established himself as a caring person and sealed a bond of human fellowship with everybody watching on the ground below.

It all seems so damnably unfair! The poor guy, struggling to bring his plane home, had made it to friendly territory only to have his chute fail to open because of the low altitude. If he had not wasted time and altitude by firing that warning burst, perhaps . . .

At 6:00 P.M., the Regiment begins a move of some nine kilometres southeast, to take over positions from 23rd Field of 4th Armoured Division in a great stone quarry near the village of Hautmesnil, just to the right of the Caen–Falaise highway. To ensure continuous support of the guns, the batteries are moved forward one at a time, at one-hour intervals, 26th Battery leading. The new positions are well-forward among the reserve infantry battalions of 4th Division. And just before you enter the new gun position, there's an ominous sign:

THIS ROAD IS UNDER OBSERVATION FROM 88S

When 2nd Battery – the last one to move up – arrives about 8:30 P.M., the self-propelled guns of the battery that you are supposed to be relieving are firing furiously, and you have to sit and wait.

In contrast to the last position – which seemed so remote from the conflict, with its river of clear water babbling through its verdant valley untouched by war – here, in this vast, barren, dusty quarry, amid these strange guns hammering away, there is again the smell of urgency. And you feel rising within you all those familiar tensions with which you've had to cope since coming to Normandy.

When the SPs finish firing, they don't move out as expected, but continue to sit in position. On inquiring, you learn that the order "Prepare for tanks" is now in effect, enemy tanks having been spotted roaming around out there beyond the railway embankment that lies just along the southwest fringe of the position.

It seems 8th Brigade, attempting to get the drive moving again today, has been bloodily repulsed by self-propelled 88s and tanks infesting Quesnay Wood, a large forest of irregular shape (according to the map) about two kilometres wide and the same deep, lying astride, but mostly east of, the Caen–Falaise highway. While nothing develops locally, a tank battle does seem to be taking place on the distant height of land forward of the position, for a few high-velocity solid-shot scream overhead and thud nearby.

When the 23rd RCA gang finally does pull out, they leave behind two vehicles with wireless sets netted to two of their FOOs out ahead there somewhere with 10th Brigade, so that 4th Field guns may respond to any calls from them for fire, until their own guns are deployed in their new positions. This is most unusual, but seems to you an eminently sensible arrangement. Their FOOs, however, don't take advantage of it. Very soon one of them comes in, and the other remains out of communication until the two signal vehicles leave to catch up with their unit.

At last light you are told to make sure your guards are on the alert tonight. There's a possibility that, with all the reshuffling presently going on among divisions and units preparing for the next big push towards Falaise, virtually no friendly infantry or tanks are directly out in front of the guns here.

And this may well be so, since the infantry have not shifted over to the east in accordance with the move the guns have made. All three battalions of 4th Brigade and all 4th Field battery commanders and carrier crews are still way back in the area of Bretteville-sur-Laize, six kilometres to the west and two kilometres to the rear of the guns.

Unconcerned that their artillery is unprotected, the infantry are preparing to lead off an attack tonight by 2nd Division, supported by 2nd Canadian Armoured Brigade, in a sweep southwest from Bretteville-sur-Laize designed to clean out a large pocket of Germans assembled in that area. This information, arriving at command posts and guns deployed in and around the quarry, is more than a little worrisome, particularly when only recently German tanks were seen roaming around over there beyond that railway embankment a few hundred yards up ahead. And so suitable preparations are made for all eventualities.

On orders from RHQ, you establish an OP on the railway embankment immediately in front of the guns, and settle down out there, staring into the gloom and listening all night. However, apart from some desultory mortaring and a few airbursts, the night passes without enemy interference with the Regiment's harassing-fire program. Still, with most of the targets requested of the guns off to the west – up to 90 degrees from the zero-line and almost 180 degrees from the targets the SPs were engaging over to the east before they pulled out – some are wondering just who the hell is in a pocket – the Germans or us?

Rumours are rampant, left behind, you suspect, by the SP signallers, that the follow-through attack, expected to carry the armour all the way to Falaise, is in real trouble – that yesterday the British Columbia Tank Regiment was ambushed and virtually wiped out, along with two companies of the Algonquins, riding on the backs of their tanks.*

Clearly, German armour can still be overwhelming when concentrated to hold or retake a locality deemed vital by their commanders.

---

* On August 10 the B.C. Regiment, lost and cut-off, had forty-seven tanks knocked out, and suffered 104 casualties, sixteen of them officers. Of the forty who died, seven were officers, including the commanding officer, Lt.-Col. D. G. Worthington. Sharing in the tragedy were the two rifle companies of the Algonquin Regiment that had gone forward on the backs of the tanks. They were able to muster only seventy-nine men "fit for duty" after the battle, which took place on a hill (MR 143490) east of the village of Estrées, about two kilometres east of the Caen–Falaise highway, and twelve kilometres north of Falaise. (Report No. 65, Historical Section [G.S.] Canadian Army Headquarters, Dept. of National Defence, Dec. 23, 1953, pp. 33-38.)

And with each passing hour it becomes ever more clear that Bill Waddell's initiative on Hill 122 – directing, with incredible bravery, the Sherbrooke's Firefly to victory over 12th SS's self-propelled guns and tanks – saved the Royal Regiment from a disaster equalling, if not surpassing, that suffered by the B.C. Regiment.

PART SIX: AUGUST 12-13

2nd Division Outflanks Enemy Positions

50

A FOOTNOTE TO CLOSING THE
FALAISE GAP

✳

AT THE OUTSET OF OPERATION TOTALIZE, THE PURPOSE OF THE
Canadian drive, as seen by General Montgomery, Commander-in-
Chief of all Allied Ground Forces in Normandy, was simply to
break the Caen "hinge" on the left or east side of the German door,
which he expected would swing open by the force of the American
break-out gathering momentum from the west flank.

And an August 6 directive issued by Lt.-Gen. Crerar to 2nd
Canadian Corps and 1st British Corps, attached to 1st Canadian
Army, made it clear that British 2nd Army, driving from the west,
was expected to take Falaise, after which 1st Canadian Army would
"then swing to the east" and pursue the Germans fighting a rearguard action to the Seine.

But when Hitler not only refused to let his commanders pull
back to reform their line at the Seine as Montgomery expected, but
committed all possible German forces on the offensive towards
Mortain (even as an American spearhead was wheeling south and
east towards Paris against no organized resistance), the Canadian
push, only then nicely started from Verrières Ridge, took on
tremendous new significance.

On August 8, as the American spearhead neared Le Mans,
seventy miles south of Falaise, Supreme Allied Commander

Eisenhower recognized that Hitler was presenting the Allies with an incredible opportunity to entrap the German armies in Normandy in a more confined and deadly pocket of destruction than Montgomery had envisaged, if Allied forces could cut across their rear before they began their inevitable retreat to the Seine. Telephoning Monty from headquarters of Lt.-Gen. Bradley, commander of American 12th Army Group, Eisenhower suggested Patton be ordered to peel off a force from his drive for Paris and send it north towards Argentan to meet the Canadians now on the move towards Falaise. Monty agreed, as long as this diversion of forces did not hinder Patton's drive to the Seine, which he still saw as being of greater consequence at this point.*

Thus, overnight, the Canadian offensive turned from "hinge-breaking" to closing off the mouth of a pocket entrapping armies, the most vital action in the pivotal battle of the Falaise Gap, which in retrospect will be seen by Sir Brian Horrocks, commander of British 30th Corps, as "unquestionably the turning point in the whole war in the West."

By August 10, with the Germans in full retreat from the western extremities of the pocket before the main British and American forces hammering at them, it was clear that time was of the essence. All roads east out of the pocket had to be shut off as quickly as possible.

But then General Bradley decided to halt the American spearhead thrusting north at Argentan, fifteen miles south of Falaise, concluding that the forces available to Maj.-Gen. Haislip's XV U.S. Corps of Patton's Third Army weren't strong enough to close off the German escape route and keep it closed. Thus the whole responsibility for closing the gap devolved on 1st Canadian Army, still eight miles north of Falaise.

---

* Facts and quotations, vital to the development of this chapter, are derived largely from Report No. 65, Historical Section (G.S.) Canadian Army Headquarters, Dept. of National Defence, Dec. 23, 1953.

In his postwar book *A Soldier's Story*, General Bradley would provide a reasonable explanation for his decision, which was approved without criticism by both Field Marshal Montgomery and General Eisenhower:

> Although Patton might have spun a line across that narrow neck, I doubted his ability to hold it. Nineteen German divisions were now stampeding to escape the trap. Meanwhile with four divisions, George [Patton] was already blocking three principal escape routes. . . . Had he stretched that line to include Falaise, he would have extended his roadblock a distance of 40 miles. The enemy could not only have broken through, but he might have trampled Patton's position in the onrush. I much preferred a solid shoulder at Argentan to the possibility of a broken neck at Falaise.*

In effect, the commanding officer of all American forces in Normandy said, It's more than we can handle – the honour is all yours, Canada. And Montgomery, chief of all Allied ground forces in Normandy, recognizing the realities, issued a directive on August 11 to 1st Canadian Army that, after wresting Falaise from the Germans, it should complete their encirclement by driving east and south towards Argentan: "Canadian Army will capture FALAISE. This is first priority and it is vital. It should be done quickly. The army will then operate with strong armoured and mobile forces to secure ARGENTAN. A secure front must be held between Falaise and the sea facing eastwards."

Thus, for the second time in the course of a week, the priorities changed for the Canadian Army's push towards Falaise.

And now, with the Americans restrained at Argentan, the Canadians must not only fight miles beyond Falaise to link up with

---

* Gen. Omar Bradley, *A Soldier's Story* (New York: Holt, 1951), pp. 376–77.

them, but must make it without the benefit of an equal pressure on the Germans from the south by the Americans.

Coinciding with this rising need for a sustained drive by the Canadians, however, is clear evidence that their spearheads, so spectacularly driven through the German lines by Totalize, have now been contained, and that a new operation must be mounted to regain the momentum.

General Eisenhower, reflecting on the state of his armies on the night of August 13, in his memoirs, *Crusade in Europe*, will recognize what the Canadians have been going through and what still faces them: "The Germans were still fighting desperately just south of Caen where by this time they had established the strongest defences encountered throughout the entire campaign. The Canadians threw in fierce and sustained attacks, but it wasn't until August 16 that Falaise was captured."[*]

Directly facing 2nd Canadian Corps are parts of four infantry divisions, supported by elements of 12th SS "Hitlerjugend" Division. Along a line through Quesnay Wood and a string of hamlets about a thousand yards north of the Laison river, Divisional Commander Kurt Meyer has assembled fifty or more 88-mm guns and 110 tanks, including twenty Tigers. To build up his depleted forces, other regiments on his west flank, not so badly depleted, are "cannibalized, and the motley crews so acquired . . . injected with small numbers of SS men for stiffness."[†]

The new Canadian operation, which must destroy these newly formed lines, is given the code name Tractable. Scheduled for August 14, it will use much the same tactics as employed in Totalize, leading off with the bombing of close-in targets by a huge air armada of 811 heavy and medium bombers. Two main assault

---

[*]   Dwight D. Eisenhower, *Crusade in Europe* (New York: Perma Books, 1952), p. 313.
[†]   Report No 65, Historical Section (G.S.) Canadian Army Headquarters, Dept. of National Defence, Dec. 23, 1953, p. 62.

columns, with one brigade of infantry in each, mounted in Kangaroos, will follow spearheads of tanks and flails in tight columns behind an artillery barrage. And following on foot will be the two other brigades, cleaning up any resistance left in villages, farms, and woods.

There is one principal difference from Totalize: the attack will go forth in the daytime. In place of darkness, which hid the attackers so successfully from the enemy gunners, a giant smoke screen will be laid down by the artillery and sustained for at least the time needed for the armoured columns to plunge through the enemy gun lines.

All of these factors, combined with the recognition of the tremendous consequences of the operation, will ensure its place in history. But few students of musty archival files will ever note the significant contribution to its success produced by the preparatory attack and the fierce fighting involving 2nd Canadian Division on August 12 and 13.

51

A MAN OF SIXTEEN ON
THE ROAD TO FALAISE

❊

THE BUSINESS OF WIPING OUT POCKETS OF RESISTANCE AND conducting diversionary attacks, often far away from the main thrust, will always be dealt with in cursory fashion, or ignored completely, by the historian. And when the operation is not even given a name, but called a "reconnaissance in force," it would seem destined for oblivion.

Such is the attack by 2nd Division that goes in on August 12. But during the next two days, this nameless operation will move the right flank of the Canadian front so far forward on the west side of the Caen–Falaise highway – outflanking the Germans by three miles – that it will guarantee the success of Operation Tractable, lining up east of the road.

Without the benefit of heavy bombing preparations, and supported only by the tanks of 2nd Canadian Armoured Brigade, its own division artillery, and two AGRAs, 2nd Division will drive a wedge six miles deep down to Clair Tizon, almost three miles south of the German stronghold in Quesnay Wood, the first major obstacle Tractable will have to overcome.

The attack is on a single thrust line, with 4th Brigade leading and the RHLI in the van. After a night of manoeuvring for the startline under mortar and shell-fire, the Rileys move out at 7:30 A.M., accompanied by a troop of tanks. At first they experience no difficulty as they pass among the farms and woods towards Barbery, a tiny hamlet five miles southwest of Bretteville-sur-Laize, halfway to the ultimate objective of Clair Tizon.

Barbery, a mere collection of deserted houses and barns where nothing stirs, is bypassed and left for the 8th Recce to occupy. The Rileys continue south, with Major Joe Pigott's company wading through unharvested wheat on the left of the road, and Major "Huck" Welch's company proceeding on the right.

For a while all is peaceful for the sweating men ploughing through the dense, yellowing grain and the rumbling Shermans following them. The still fields and woods offer no hint of what is in store for them, and for the Royal Regiment, who with their accompanying FOOs will pass through the wounded, dead, and dying Rileys among burning tanks and carriers on their way to capturing the next village of Moulines.

The Germans are waiting for the Rileys about one thousand yards beyond the seemingly deserted village of Barbery, at a point where the woods close in on both sides of the road. And as Pigott's company draws near, it comes under a burst of fire from the copse on the left.

At once all companies are "enveloped in a storm of bullets and shrapnel" which their intelligence officer, Lyle Doering, will record as "the most intense mortaring and shelling the unit ever witnessed." And the German Panzer grenadiers are so aggressive, Pigott will remember them as "fanatical devils" who engaged his troops in hand-to-hand fighting as they came "running out of their slits, firing rifles and grenades."*

Forced to consolidate well short of their objective, the Rileys are digging-in when a private in Welch's company, pausing in his labour for a moment to peer at the woods, calls to his company commander:

---

* Quotations from Doering and Pigott are from *Semper Paratus*, the history of the RHLI, published by the RHLI Historical Association, 1977.

"Sir, are those our tanks over there?"

"Of course they are," says Welch, not bothering to look up.

"Jesus, they don't look like it to me!" says the private.

When Welch straightens up, trundling towards him is a Tiger tank.

The Shermans are no match for the massive Tiger that concentrates on knocking them out while accompanying Panthers spray the position with machine-gun fire. Though the German tanks stay back, well out of effective Piat range (which for tanks is about a hundred yards), the Rileys are pinned down by continuous fire, and by late afternoon are in bad shape. Then a shell scores a direct hit on their tac headquarters, wounding five, including their Col. MacLachlan and 4th Field's Major James Wilson Dodds, leaving them without an arty rep at the battalion level until Battery Captain Jack Drewry can make it up from 14th Battery wagon lines.

When the Royals, and their supporting troop of tanks, try to pass through the Rileys on their way south to the next village of Moulines, they find the going equally sticky. Their route takes them through the same open grain fields without cover from the fire of the defenders, and after only about eight hundred yards, they run into heavy machine-gun fire from a barn and copse on the left that drives them to ground. Still, A Company, supported by concentrations fired by 4th Field guns, is able to work its way up to some woods near a crossroads.

But here, plastered by mortar and shell-fire, they suffer many casualties. While there are some holes available, most have to find what cover they can in mere folds in the ground, for, with the intense and accurate sniping, it's impossible to dig in.

Sherman tanks come up and try to knock out the 88-mm firing from the right flank, but the leading tank is hit as it advances along a sunken road, and when it brews up, the others withdraw.

For a time Capt. Bill Waddell's carrier, moving with the forward company, is pinned down by the same terrifying, point-blank fire from the German gun. And for a sixteen-year-old signaller on his crew, there is a heart-stopping moment when an armour-piercing

88-mm slug rips in one side of the carrier and out the other, with a bloodcurdling, metal-tearing screech, unique to solid-shot drilling a hole through armour-plate at three thousand feet per second.*

It's Gunner Bill Knox's first tour of duty in a FOO's carrier crew moving with the infantry, and each terrifying minute will be remembered in infinite detail:

We're going through this slightly wooded area in a sunken road. Everybody along the road is wounded, and as we come up, one of the infantry guys jumps out in front of the carrier and yells, "Get the hell off this road! Everybody here is wounded or dead! The German artillery has got the road taped!"

So we pull off the road and get in behind some bushes in a field. That's where the 88 hits us, and everybody piles out as fast as they can into a nearby depression – everybody except me. I am on the left side of the carrier, the side exposed to the hill where the 88 is, and for a moment I bend down over the 19-set to collect my wits before climbing out. I still have my earphones on, and I hear "Blackie" Bryan, our driver, over in the depression, telling them back at the guns that I am dead. He is using the microphone with the long extension cord that Wally Driemel [the other signaller] took with him when he bailed out over the right side of the carrier. He's reporting we've been hit, that there is a hole in the carrier and one man is dead – meaning me.

---

* Gunner William J. Knox was born March 16, 1928. In the fall of 1942, he hitchhiked from Toronto to Montreal to join the army. Turned down, he hitched a ride to Ottawa, where he again lied about his age and was signed on by the artillery in the old Regal Building. He was fourteen years and nine months old. After training as an ack-ack gunner on the East Coast, he was shipped to England in the fall of 1943. There he was trained as a signaller in time to go to Normandy with a unit formed especially to man a relay station passing signals from shore to warships lying off the coast. When the need for this disappeared, Knox was posted to 4th Field, where he volunteered for duty on a carrier crew.

I yell, "I'm okay," and jumping out make it to the depression.

Capt. Waddell says we should run the remote up to that ridge ahead of us. So he and I go up there and fire Mike targets down into a town [Moulines] that we later take and where Major Wren is killed next day.*

While 4th Field carrier crews come through the day unscathed, the Royals suffer sixty-seven casualties, ten of them fatal, trying to cross open grain fields under fire from tanks, mortars, and machine guns. And the RHLI suffer even more grievously: twenty dead and one hundred wounded.

The last assault against their riddled companies comes late in the afternoon, the enemy's tanks moving in for what appears to the Rileys – now out of Piat ammunition – to be the *coup de grâce*.

Watching them come, Major Welch is astonished at the cool arrogance of the German tank commanders, standing up "exposed in their turrets, looking for targets through their binoculars, their guns traversing all the time." Suddenly they stop, make one last sweep with their machine guns, then turn about and disappear from the field of smoking hulks and dead and wounded men. The only possible explanation is that they are out of ammunition.

Back at the guns, apart from the odd airburst whacking overhead now and then, there's been no enemy activity to endure. Still, those spine-jolting, ear-splitting reports arriving unannounced, followed a split-second later by the shrieking rip of their coming, have been keeping everyone on edge; particularly after Gunner Don Kirby, on duty at the radio in GA, is wounded in the face with a bit of shell fragment and is evacuated.

It's been a long tiring day in the sultry air in the quarry. There is no protection from the dazzling sun reflecting off the vast acreage of stone shelving, and the great barren basin unmercifully amplifies

---

* Author interview.

each reverberating roar of the guns getting off an unending parade of Mike targets called for by the FOOs and battery commanders, trying to quell enemy shelling and mortaring pinning down the infantry.

This quarry at Hautmesnil will be remembered long after most gun positions are forgotten, but few will recall it with the pleasure of Sgt. Bruce Hunt in his diary: "Moved command post from house at cross-roads to a cave – a shrine of German ingenuity! Here we work in comfortable security while concentrations from the artillery massed around us blast away."

Bombardier Hossack's bleak note in his log is probably closer to the experience of the majority: "A built-up railroad obscures the enemy's view of us, but he finds our line and range with mortars and shells during the night."

Around 3:30 P.M., 4th Field receives two divisional fire plans: one to support 4th Brigade, and the other to support 5th Brigade, indicating the Colonel and CRA are taking a hand in affairs. Heavy concentrations by all seventy-two guns on Moulines and vicinity in advance of the 4th Brigade attack seem to work wonders. At 5:30 P.M., when the Royals try again to move into the village, they find most of the enemy have pulled out.

52

NO MEDICINE LEFT FOR
ENTERIC DISORDERS

————————— ✳ —————————

WHILE OVERNIGHT 4TH FIELD GUNS WERE TAKING PART IN AN
intensely noisy divisional harassing-fire program designed to keep
the enemy awake and anxious, an order came down warning that
advance parties would move off shortly after dawn. The new positions are two and a half miles farther south, near St. Germain-le-
Vasson, reconnoitred yesterday by Major Savage and Regimental
Survey Officer Lieut. Jim Nesbitt under rather "dicey" conditions.
Though no harm came to them, the situation offered some interesting possibilities, since the nearest infantrymen (5th Brigade)
were near Mesnil-Touffrey, a good mile and a half to the rear and to
the west of the new gun area.

Even at dawn today, with 5th Brigade two and a half miles
farther south, the axis of advance of 2nd Division remains one and
a quarter miles west of the new gun positions. In between is terrain
extensive enough and rugged enough to hide a whole division, as
the Calgary Highlanders discover at dawn, when the overnight
deluge of high explosive by 2nd Division guns on enemy territory
is replaced by a barrage of propaganda leaflets expelled from gently
popping 25-pounder smoke shells that have had their smoke canisters removed. A veritable flood of Germans, with hands high in the
air, present themselves to the astonished forward companies,
induced to surrender by the promise contained in the "Guarantee

of Safe Conduct Certificates," fluttering down on woods and gullies by the thousands. Every Jerry coming forward to surrender clutches a certificate in one of his upraised hands.

At the guns, encouraging rumours are circulating of large numbers of Jerries surrendering to the infantry – the first from the "pocket." And one wild rumour will later be corroborated by a vivid description of the event in the Calgary Highlanders' war diary: "Prisoners simply poured into our cage and looked like a queue going up to the ticket office at a theatre, with the Intelligence Officer acting as doorman. Each and every prisoner had an Allied 'Safe Conduct' leaflet assuring him of good treatment if taken prisoner."*

As you go forward with 4RCA advance parties at 5:30 A.M., you are inclined to take seriously the warning "The area may not be entirely free of Germans." However, all is peaceful and deserted as you and Bombardier Hossack wander about getting the lay of the land, now bathed by a brilliant sun that, even at 6:00 A.M., is beginning to bake the stubble of a vast field dotted with stooks of grain marching hither and yon.

To the left rear of this rolling, golden plateau, there is a very broad, shallow valley, beyond which you can make out the Hautmesnil quarry, where the guns can be seen puffing away at some target far ahead in another valley, creating a delayed rolling rumble reminiscent of distant thunder announcing the coming of a summer storm.

Out of sight beyond a hedge and a thick orchard, which will become the wagon lines of 6th Field deploying on your right, is a village that could be either Le Bout Roussin or St. Germain-le-Vasson, depending on how you interpret the placement of their names on the map. The second-in-command of 6th Field confirms the area still harbours at least one German, after the gas tank of his

---

* Calgary Highlanders' War Diary, Unit War Diary Files, National Archives of Canada.

Jeep collects a bullet hole on the way in here. It's likely a lone sniper, however, for there is evidence the Germans pulled out of this area in a great hurry. In the orchard just over the hedge, they left behind a troop of their precious Moaning Minnies – completely armed with rocket bombs, ready to fire.

There's always the possibility, of course, that once they discover they were startled into retreating by a mere artillery recce party (if that is what happened), they'll decide to come back to rescue their weapons. At any rate, 6th Field – uneasy that all 2nd Division infantry units are still far off on the right, and moving not this way, but south towards Clair Tizon – decides to establish an OP in the nearby church tower poking up among the trees on the right.

While this is probably a very sensible move, you wonder how they can spare the manpower. You and Hossack are fully occupied. The gun position allotted Able Troop is a broad, open field with no ditches, and there is no problem with crest clearance with the ground falling sharply away out in front, so it takes no time at all to plant gun markers, choose a distant aiming-point on which Hossack can orient his director, and get down to what you have come to believe is the real purpose of advance parties: the digging of the troop command post.

Ever since Fleury-sur-Orne, six gun positions ago, you and Bob Grout and your GPO acks have taken turns going on advance parties so that the digging might be more fairly shared. Continuous artillery support being a must these days, when the front is in such a state of flux, batteries move forward one at a time. In this case they are going to allow half an hour between each move, and with 2nd Battery not moving until 10:00 A.M., your guns won't arrive until at least 10:30. This means you and Hossack have more than three hours – plenty of time to produce a respectable command post ready for roofing, a pleasant surprise for the rest of the command-post gang when they come up.

Command posts for Able Troop have become of fixed design: two slit trenches, each about six feet long and two feet wide, dug parallel to, and about two and a half feet from, each other. While these trenches are dug below grade only about four feet, the excavated soil, dumped around the perimeter, builds up about three feet above grade, allowing headroom when the whole thing is roofed over with corrugated-iron sheets (your old friends from Carpiquet) carrying a couple of feet of earth. On one side of the earthen column or ledge left standing between the two trenches, the GPO is able to stand with Tannoy mike in hand overseeing his GPO ack at the artillery board. In the opposite trench the signallers carry on their duties, which, in inclement weather, include brewing tea and heating Compo rations.

Hossack starts on one trench, you on the other. It has suddenly become oppressively hot. The first foot or so of topsoil is easy to work, but then you hit chalk, solid chalk – not a chalky conglomerate of chips and stones, but solid, damp chalk that allows the head of your pick-axe to bury itself up to the handle with an encouraging, substantial *thunk*, but then refuses to allow you to withdraw it, regardless of how hard you tug, until you have wiggled and rocked it a discouraging number of times. And when it does come free, you find it has produced less than a cupful of loose chalk.

You soon abandon the idea of completing two trenches, and both of you concentrate on the one on which you've been working. By now the sun is high in the sky and broiling you as you sink in the pick and wiggle it, pry it, wiggle it, and wrestle it until you can pull it out, just so you can sink it in again. Hossack takes a turn on the pick, and for a while it seems he is managing a bit better, but the procedure soon exhausts his patience, which normally is considerable.

The effect on the depth of the trench after your combined labours are applied for more than an hour is almost imperceptible. You can't remember ever having been so discouraged about anything.

You and Hossack had looked forward to finishing the digging and retiring to the shade of a green grove of trees surrounding a farmhouse to the left rear of the position – perhaps even finding a barrel of cool cider. But after another hour of intensive effort, the trench is considerably less than two feet deep, and you are considering giving up and waiting for the others to come up and take over.

While you are over your dysentery, it has left you somewhat less than vigorous, and in this heat, the picking and scraping-out of each shovelful of chips is not just wretchedly frustrating, but physically draining.

It must be plain torture for poor Hossack, enfeebled by the debilitating malady now at its worst stage for him, as it seems to be for most of the afflicted members of the troop. And when he shows signs of the disorientation you are starting to experience, you call it quits and lead him over to a spot of shade under a tree along the hedge. Lying there, the war seems to fade away. Though the guns go on rumbling in the distance, there is only the hum of a bumblebee to disturb the silence here. And this is where Bob Grout and the rest of the troop command-post gang find you both, stretched out sound asleep, when the guns arrive.

While they don't dare say too much about the insignificant scar the GPO and senior GPO ack have gouged out of the chalk after all those hours up here, they manage to make it clear they are not impressed. But when they take over, with a great show of vigour and enthusiasm, they soon discover that this is the worst digging yet, and only a basin of mortar bombs dropping nearby – impressing on all the continuing need for a good deep trench – keeps them going at all. And then it is one man, and one man alone, who really sees the job is done. Whitehawk puts everyone else to shame with his grinding determination to see the job through.

Long after the others have begun to find excuses to avoid their turn on a pick or a shovel, Whitehawk continues his measured pace, seldom stopping to take a breather. His endurance is incredible. But just how incredible you fully appreciate only after he has finished and taken you aside to request, almost apologetically, that he be evacuated as a dysentery casualty: "Sir, I feel awful sick. Can you send me back to the MO so I can get some medicine?"

Your heart sinks. Oh, God, you think, if ever there was a man in this whole army more deserving than Whitehawk of getting the last drop of medicine for this cursed plague, you don't know who he might be. But you have to tell him that the MO has used up all the medicine he's been able to get his hands on, and has issued instructions that no more cases are to be sent back to the regimental aid post.

With deep hurt showing in his eyes, your friend points to his lips, grotesquely swollen and cracking, and pleads, "Please – I really feel rotten – I'm really sick – the doc must have something that would help."

You go to the phone and get the MO on the line. You know Doctor Dunham to be a most kindly, concerned, understanding man in normal circumstances. But this dysentery (he prefers to call it "enteritis") epidemic obviously has got him down.

When you plead with him to make a special case of Whitehawk, he turns severe, and you end up shouting into the phone something to the effect that it's about time he and the other sawbones got off their collective asses and demanded they fly over from England whatever the hell is necessary to treat this epidemic before the whole damned army comes to a full stop. When he hangs up on you it makes you even madder. And while all this does nothing to help Whitehawk, at least he knows you tried, and you are able to send him back to the wagon lines, where it should be a little quieter.

Then much grimmer news snaps you back to the realities of the bitter fighting, which is still going on over there, among the wooded hills and valleys, for little, insignificant villages, the names of which will not likely be remembered by any of those men who from minute to minute are risking death to secure them: Bill Waddell has been wounded and captured.

Then comes a report from the CO at Brigade that Major Gordon Wren has been fatally wounded.

No details are immediately available, because (as you later learn) the radio in his scout car was knocked out during the shelling of the Royals' tac headquarters in Moulines. But Lieut. "Hank" Caldwell, the battalion anti-tank officer, will one day tell of seeing "Major Wren standing in that Moulines farmhouse courtyard beside his command vehicle when the shell landed." It is an image he will carry in regret the rest of his life, for Major Wren made a very deep impression on him during that "ghastly learning experience at Eterville."

Back in those early days under almost continuous bombardment, we all were trying to act like soldiers should under fire, with our helmets pulled down over our ears, but inwardly despairing: If this is war, how on earth are we going to put up with it? Then one day Major Wren went back to his regiment overnight, and when I saw him next day, in one glance he changed my capacity to endure what was going on. He was wearing a beret! He said that after seeing the battle maps, etc., back at his headquarters he felt like a different person. And I caught the spirit from him. Bless him! Does that sound crazy? Well, it was a tremendous lift for me, and I hope I was able to help those under me to feel a little better about our plight.*

Turner, the Major's despatch rider, the last to speak with him, will remark on the fact that even as the Major was dying he was concerned with the welfare of his crew, that they should return to the guns. Turner will never forget that on the night of the big break-out from Verrières, Wren had him dump his motorbike on the bumper of the scout car and ride inside.

---

*   Author interview.

53

HOW DO MEN SUSTAIN THE
WILL TO CARRY ON?

❋

FROM THE POUNDING TAKEN BY 4TH BRIGADE YESTERDAY, August 12, it's clear that resistance has stiffened, that the Germans have no intention of allowing the Canadians to cut off their avenue of retreat and engineer the destruction of their armies in Normandy.

And while the Rileys were able to move through the Royals at Moulines during the night and take some high ground a mile southeast of there, the Essex have been unable to make any headway in taking Point 184 two miles farther on.

So in the early hours today, when the Royals are ordered to take over the offensive, with Bob Suckling's D Company leading, accompanied by a troop of tanks and 4th Field's Bill Waddell and his crew to ensure artillery support, all know it won't be any more "a piece of cake" than the day before.

Like the men of all battalions aiming at Falaise, relentlessly urged forward these past five days – particularly those units that were chewed and decimated along Verrières Ridge before Totalize even began – Suckling and company are carrying on in a state of utter exhaustion, both mental and physical.

The long marches, weighed down with personal equipment, shovels, weapons, and extra ammunition for the Brens and Piats; the frantic digging-in at each stop to get below ground as fast as possible to gain shelter from shelling and resist the inevitable counter-attack; and the never-ending tension that comes from living, minute to minute, alert and ready to react to every rustle of air, knowing that the worst could happen at any moment – all combine to guarantee that those who do survive attack after attack after attack exist at the outer limits of their endurance, in a state of fatigue that defies description.

In the six nights since assembling on the evening of August 7 near the village of Ifs for the beginning of Totalize, there's been only one night when Suckling's men have had a chance for what might be called restful sleep – as restful as sleep can ever be for a man fully dressed in his filthy clothes, complete with boots laced up on swollen feet, huddled over or hunched up in a gravelike, sandy hole that shudders and sifts sand on him every time a mortar bomb or a shell lands nearby.

Of course there was no sleep whatsoever on the first night of the opening attack, during the nerve-wracking, thunderous drive through enemy lines, enveloped by the fury of the bombs and the great gun barrage preceding them.

And shortly after dawn on August 8, the enemy counter-attacked the isolated spearheads, keeping everyone busy all day. That night, with the front still fluid and with little known of the enemy's whereabouts or strength, all units had to remain alert throughout the hours of darkness.

On the night of the ninth, the Royals finally got a chance to rest in reserve position. But the next night they were surrounded by Allied guns firing until dawn: 25-pounders, 5.5-inch mediums, and a battery of the big American 155-mm "Long Toms" fresh from the Cherbourg siege, required to fire fifty rounds per gun on Falaise during the night.

After dark on the eleventh, the Royals resumed the routine of no sleep at all when, after marching more than three miles southwest over to Bretteville-sur-Laize, they were sent trudging on another two miles south under intermittent shell and mortar fire to deploy astride the axis of advance near the village of Favrolle, north of Barbery.

From there they started out on an all-day attack stretching into the night of August 12 – marching and running and crawling and digging in – as they penetrated another two miles in the direction of Falaise and cleared the village of Moulines, at a cost of ten men killed and fifty-seven wounded. And today two more Royals will die and another forty-two will be wounded, taking an obscure hill about half a mile south of Moulines, known only by its elevation above sea level, "151." And in the process their artillery representative at battalion will be killed and the FOO with the leading company will be wounded and captured.

Suckling will always identify this day as

... the time one of my lance-corporals in the midst of a mortaring bombardment, with tears streaming down his face, gets up out of his hole and, like a hunted animal, darting this way and that, disappears from my world forever.

On top of everything else, dysentery is rampant, with everybody suffering to some degree from stomach cramps and nausea associated with loose bowels. For some it is dreadful: one of my platoon commanders has diarrhoea so bad it shoots five feet out of his rectum when he bends over.

Everybody is now having to scratch continuously, for we all are crawling with lice picked up from the slit trenches and those splendid dugouts abandoned by the Krauts. And as if all this weren't enough, I am tormented with the burning itch of watery blisters on my face from impetigo [a highly contagious skin infection] I've managed to pick up somewhere along the way.*

---

* Author interview.

The first attempt by Suckling's company to reach Point 184 comes to an abrupt halt even as they are moving up from a reserve position. An 88-mm knocks out the leading Sherman, causing the others to pull back, leaving the Royals scurrying for whatever cover they can find in ditches and folds in the ground as mortars and machine guns search for them. The enemy fire is so sustained, and from such close quarters, that Lt.-Col. Jack Anderson decides to pull the leading companies back four hundred yards to allow 4th Field guns to "stonk" the German positions and cool down their withering fire.*

But before this can be arranged, Anderson's tac headquarters in Moulines suffers the direct hit that fatally wounds his arty rep, Major Wren, and disables his command post vehicle.

Only the barest details get back to the guns, and as the awesome events of the next twenty-four hours unfold, dominating all thought, it will be some time before you hear the story (from Col. McGregor Young himself), of how Gunner Turner, the battery commander's despatch rider, keeps communications open between the Royals and 4th Brigade until Capt. Laurie is able to get forward to take over. The crucial situation reports Gunner Turner gets back to Brigade allows the CO to lay down fire from 4th Field guns so effectively the Royals take an intermediate hill, from which the enemy fire has been originating, and capture sixty Germans, thereby shutting down the fire of twelve machine guns, and opening the way for the Essex to take Point 184.†

And this encouraging success is built on by 5th Brigade, when

---

* A "stonk" involves the guns being laid in such a way as to ensure their shells land in a straight line along a selected map grid-bearing representing an elongated target such as the outer fringe of an orchard or hedgerow. The twenty-four guns of one field regiment could effectively stonk a target 840 yards long.

† The citation, signed by Lt.-Col. Young and Maj.-Gen. Bruce Matthews, that resulted in the Croix de Guerre with Bronze Star being awarded Gunner John Andrew Turner some months later, stated in part:

the Calgary Highlanders pass through to gain a small bridgehead over the Laize River at Clair Tizon, three miles west and half a mile south of Potigny, visible to the left rear on the Caen–Falaise highway.

For this attack across the river, there's an elaborate set of artillery tasks, involving not only 4th, 5th, and 6th Field, but also heavy bombardments by the mediums and heavies of 2nd and 9th AGRAs. The attack succeeds, and the guns earn a nice commendation from 5th Brigade: "We got exactly the fire we wanted, when we wanted it."*

When the Maisonneuves attempt to expand the bridgehead at last light, and are bloodily repulsed by very strong forces, it is clear the Germans are reacting to the threat 2nd Division poses to Falaise. Thus on the eve of Operation Tractable to entrap the German armies, 2nd Division has accomplished the full diversionary purposes of the so-called "reconnaissance in force," outflanking the German-filled Quesnay Woods by about two and half miles, and virtually guaranteeing the success of the final drive to Falaise and beyond.

However, 2nd Division battalions are left riddled with casualties and on the point of collapsing from exhaustion. By now you've come to feel sorry for all infantrymen you see, whether you are merely passing them on the road or moving with them. How they sustain the will to carry on day after day, risking death or crippling wounds, is a mystery.

"On one occasion south of Bretteville-sur-Laize, when enemy shelling was particularly heavy and his Battery Commander became a casualty, this gunner took charge of the remainder of the party and continued the necessary artillery support . . . the disregard of personal danger and the devotion to duty was an inspiration to all that worked with him. . . . his conduct under fire had a direct bearing on the successful outcome of the battle."
* Col. G. W .L. Nicolson, CD, *The Gunners of Canada, Volume II, 1919-1967* (Toronto: McClelland and Stewart, 1972), p.320.

Long after, reflecting on what he considered "the greatest problem, the constant fear and anxiety which dulls the mind and is absolutely unshakeable," Major Suckling will declare:

For me the fear of what was behind was greater than the fear of what was in front. Over the years I had been well indoctrinated with army discipline, and I'm sure this kept many other people going too. I've always admired the resolution of men who carry on solely because of their commitment to a cause of righteousness. In my own case, it was simply that I was more scared of what was behind me than what lay ahead of me – which is the best reason I know in favour of discipline. Weeks would pass before I got over the shell shock or anxiety neurosis, and it was much later before my mind settled down somewhat. While my body, even at the age of twenty-six, became increasingly weary to the point of exhaustion.*

And in *Battle Royal*, the story of the Royal Regiment, historian Major D. J. Goodspeed, marvelling at the capacity of men to carry on in spite of agonizing fear and grinding fatigue, will produce this vivid image of infantrymen and their supporting arms on the road to Falaise:

For brief or intermittent periods we may with justification speak of the "bright face of danger," but prolonged exposure to mortal peril brings not uplifting of the spirit, but rather a dull and almost despairing fatalism. . . . Some men broke under the strain and none can blame them. . . . The overwhelming majority plodded on, doing their duty, finding (incredibly) that extra spurt of energy when it was required and when the Regiment needed it. . . . Before the fighting, most men would not have believed that they could have been so tired and still survived. Night after

---

* Author interview.

night passed without sleep and day after day was spent with no more rest than was afforded by the odd cat-nap. Men fell asleep as they drove carriers along a road, as they plodded in single file with their sections, or as they huddled in slit-trenches under bombardment. Weariness built up until it laid its hand upon the very spirit. Men went for days on end in a sort of dazed mental stupor, in which they could not remember the events of an hour before, and in which they were utterly incapable of speculating upon the future.*

* Major D. J. Goodspeed, *Battle Royal* (Toronto: Royal Regiment of Canada Association, 1962), p. 460.

54

THE QUALITY OF MERCY

---------------------- ✳ ----------------------

ARTILLERY FOOS, BY THE VERY NATURE OF THEIR OCCUPATION
and the awkward conditions under which they must practise their
trade, are bound to accumulate strange experiences, but none could
be stranger than that of Capt. Bill Waddell today.

Certainly it will always seem out of place among the dismal
stories of death and destruction to which every hour in Normandy
is dedicated, for it is a heartening tale of mercy – a rare commodity
in these hellish days, almost incredible in the face of the enemy's
well-established reputation for brutal viciousness, now accepted as
normal in the Normandy fighting, including the shooting of
unarmed Canadian prisoners by Hitlerjugend of 12th SS Panzer
Division.

Waddell will recall that at an orders group called by Col. Anderson
at 6:00 A.M. he is assigned to go along with Suckling's D Company
of the Royal Regiment and its supporting squadron of tanks:

The RHLI having passed through during the night, we are supposed to be in a reserve position, but as it turns out, when the
leading company of the Royals move up along the front edge of
some woods, they find Jerries, not Rileys, on the startline.

Of this I am not immediately aware, for when I get back from
the O Group to my crew, they are just making something to eat,

so I decide to take a minute to have some too before joining the Royals – knowing we can easily catch up, since we'll be riding and they'll be walking. And when eventually we take off down the road, we are not warned by anyone at all as to what we are getting into.*

What Waddell and his crew are getting into is an unplanned reconnaissance well in advance of the infantry, since the Rileys are nowhere to be seen and none of D Company of the Royals are visible either, having been forced to take cover only five hundred yards down the road when they came under intense machine-gun and mortar fire and the tanks were fired on.

Only the abandoned Sherman – holed by an 88 and still in the process of brewing up, its exploding ammunition puffing smoke rings from its turret – is to be seen along the road. Once past that, Waddell and his crew are driving in no-man's-land, right into German territory. And this he begins to suspect when he notes the complete absence of tank tracks in the sand.

I halt my crew and go forward on foot to reconnoitre. Not seeing any fresh tank tracks, I am worried. Then I spot one or two Jerries in the wheat field, and I turn and take off, running for my carrier. That is when I am wounded. My crew is being attacked too, and have no chance of getting to me, so they turn back to the Canadian lines.

The bullet went through my right cheek and jaw. Fortunately it came out in front of my left ear and through my helmet. Two Jerries pick me up and I am taken into the hedgerow, where I lie for some time, during which we are shelled by a few rounds from our own 25-pounders. (I later learn that when my crew got back

---

* The quotations from Bill Waddell in this chapter are from an interview with the author.

and told Col. Anderson where I'd been captured, he had Major Wren fire some rounds up there to prove to the RHLI they'd given a wrong map reference for their position.)

After this I am led away blindfolded to a small village, which I believe is called Clair Tizon, or some such name. There, in a house, they sit me in a chair. Beside me is a Jerry, shot through the stomach. He can speak some English, and we both think that war is a rough deal. The doctor bandages my head. He tells me the bullet removed five teeth and part of the jawbone. He asks if I want a painkiller? I say no, because I don't know what is in it. Eventually he comes around again, and asks if I wish to go back to Canada. Naturally I say yes.

So they put the blindfold on again, give me a white flag, and lead me out to the point where I was hit. There they take the blindfold off. A German lieutenant comes out and a soldier as well. The latter takes off my Rolex watch as I am talking with the lieutenant, who is reluctant to let me go. I strongly tell him that the "Captain" told me I could go back to the Canadian lines. Eventually he lets me go, and I take off. But not before warning them not to shoot me in the back.

It is a long, slow walk, not knowing if they will shoot me in the back or not. Eventually a Jeep, flying a Red Cross flag, appears and I jump in. Turning on a dime, it takes me back to Royals battalion headquarters where Col. Anderson informs me: "You've been AWL for a few hours!" Then I am advised the battery commander Major Wren has been killed. And later I find out that my replacement lasts only long enough to go back with me from an advanced casualty clearing centre.

Royals' Lieut. "Hank" Caldwell, will never forget Waddell arriving at Royals' tac headquarters with "holes in both cheeks. I watch fascinated as he asks for a cigarette and tries to take a puff, but draws only air through his cheeks with gurgling noises. He obviously is much distressed because he can draw no smoke – a brave guy with guts to match."[*]

Waddell will remember leaving the Royal Regiment, sitting up in a Jeep, holding a cup of hot, sweet tea.

> From now on I am on some sort of painkiller. I pass through the casualty clearing station and am admitted to Bayeux Hospital, where I'm X-rayed during the night. Apparently they find that an operation is not immediately required, so I am sent back to England about 6:30 A.M. The DC-3 (Dakota) carries twenty-one stretcher cases and three walking-wounded. It is wonderful to see England again.[†]

When the details of Waddell's story finally filter back to the guns this evening, everyone experiences a lift. It's such a satisfying, dramatic story – and very, very welcome at this juncture, providing everyone with something to dwell on besides the heat, the damned sand fleas, and the accursed dysentery, which continues to devastate the troop.

Waddell was with the Regiment and Baker Troop just twenty-

---

[*] Author interview.

[†] Lt.-Col. Anderson of the Royals joined Waddell within a day in the same hospital at Basingstoke, England, after being shot accidentally in the knee by his own German P-38 automatic pistol when it fell out of his battledress blouse onto the slate floor of a farmhouse. He was able to report that after Waddell left he sent a German prisoner back to those same enemy lines to tell the Germans they were surrounded, but that if they would come in with their hands up they would be treated fairly. About 110 took advantage of the offer and marched in, following his POW emissary, and Waddell would always assume there was a direct connection between the humane treatment given the German and the subsequent surrender of so many.

four days, and during that time only a handful of people in the Regiment ever saw him, for almost continuously 4th Brigade was heavily engaged, and FOOs are obliged to spend their time with the infantry when they're in the line. But, though he's unlikely ever to become aware of it, he's already well on the way to becoming a legendary figure in 4th Field – as the story of his being shot through the jaw, captured, treated by the Germans, and then released back to our lines is told and retold.

It is almost irresistible to combine the image of him walking back through no-man's-land from the enemy lines, head swathed in bandages, with another image of him standing out in the open, directing the fire of our tanks on enemy tanks, and brewing them up one after another on Hill 122 – for, though that tank engagement took place five days ago on the first morning of the breakout, it is only during the last day or two that eyewitness accounts of his heroism that morning have begun to make the rounds.

55

THE NEBELWERFER BOOBY TRAP

--- ✳ ---

IN THE COOLING TWILIGHT JUST AFTER THE SUN GOES DOWN, AS you are enjoying a gentle, fresh breeze, after a wearing day of heat and digging and firing, the air is suddenly filled with a blast of blood-chilling sound: the wailing and screeching of a whole herd of Moaning Minnies, as though the sky is full of those horrible missiles, descending directly onto the gun position.

Everyone dives for cover, pressing face and body tight to the earth. But as the banshee wailing continues, growing fainter and fainter until it ends in a distant, thumping salvo, you gradually realize what has happened. Those captured Nebelwerfers, which were left in the orchard just over the fence all loaded up and ready to fire, have been turned around and unloaded on enemy territory by 6th Field gunners.

But even as most of the troop are still climbing out of holes and scrambling to their feet, grinning and bantering back and forth in relief as they speculate on the possible effects on Jerry of this curious event, the sound of another herd of Moaning Minnies can be heard winding up. This time, however, the volume is rising, not falling. By the time everybody realizes they are coming this way, there's barely time to hit the ground before the ungodly howling ends with earth-shaking blasts very close: just over the hedge in the orchard where the abandoned Nebelwerfers stand, where inevitably a crowd of curious 6th Field gunners will have gathered to examine the strange weapons and exchange views on the spectacular event of their firing.

In their bloody fashion the Germans have shown why, when forced to abandon their weapons for lack of transport, they left them intact and ready to fire. They knew the invitation would prove irresistible and that a great crowd would collect to watch the firing. All they had to do was lay other Nebelwerfers on the precise map reference where they'd abandoned them and wait.

Almost immediately there is a call on the phone from RHQ ordering you to collect half of all the shell dressings in your troop and take them to the wagon lines of 6th Field. They assure you the MO will replace them before the night is out. (Every soldier, regardless of rank, carries a shell dressing buttoned into a big pocket on his left front thigh, and another on the left lip of his steel helmet underneath a camouflage netting.)

As soon as the announcement is made over the Tannoy, a flood of shell dressings begins to arrive at the command post, and Troop Sgt.-Maj. Mann, who has just come up with rations and mail, is seconded to drive you and armfuls of dressings over to 6th Field by a tortuous route behind the positions. It is dark by the time you find the stone barn where the casualties are being treated. Inside is discouraging, dismal gloom, hardly penetrated by one hissing, smoking gasoline lantern and some hand-held lamps-electric moving about, briefly casting a vague yellow glow on white faces and red-stained uniforms.

The doctor (identifiable only because the gas lantern is being held in position for his benefit) and a couple of stretcher-bearers bend over the wounded, doing what they can to stem the flow of blood, dust sulpha on wounds, and now and then administer hypos to what seems to be a disastrous number of dark forms lying on blankets down on the ground, stretching into the darkness along both walls of the barn.

You are struck by the silence. Though the barn floor is covered with wounded men all crowded together, there is seldom a sound other than the odd cough or clearing of a throat. The doctor and his assistants hardly exchange a word, and when they do, they speak in very low voices. There is an air of deadly seriousness here that is totally unnerving. It is clear that you are witnessing a race with death, as the MO tries to assess the nature of the wounds and the chances of survival, and issues instructions to his helpers.

You can't possibly interrupt them, but as a folding table is being set up as an operating table, you get the chance to ask a stretcher-bearer where he wants you to put the dressings you have brought them. He gets another stretcher-bearer to help him pack them in a hamper he locates somewhere. And while they are filling it from the Jeep, you ask them how many of their guys were casualties. They say that at least eight are dead and about double that wounded. A sickening feeling of utter helplessness you have been fighting to control sweeps over you, and you find yourself cursing out loud at the terrible waste of men's lives.

Then realizing you aren't helping in any way, and could even be hindering, you return to your command post, thankful beyond words that your troop didn't find those Nebelwerfers. If the Germans had booby-trapped them they couldn't have been more devastating. And in one sense they actually had turned them into booby traps.

Long after you're back in the comforting familiarity of your dugout, surrounded by friendly, unwounded, whole men, you continue to live with that horrific scene in that gloomy barn among the dead and dying gunners.

PART SEVEN: AUGUST 14-23

Renewing Attack to Entrap the German Army

56

UGLY SOUNDS OF
HORRIBLE MEANING

✳

MOST SHELLS AND MORTARS SOUND A WARNING BEFORE THEY
arrive, and throughout every waking hour, you, like everyone in
the forward areas of the Normandy bridgehead, regardless of what
you are doing, go about with ears cocked continually for the sound
of something coming. Early on, you learned how to distinguish
from the sound which of them were going to land close by, which
were going to land well beyond you, and which were completely
off line and would land harmlessly some distance away to your right
or left. This saves a lot of needless diving into holes and flopping
down in the dirt.

Moaning Minnies are in a class by themselves in providing
warning with unearthly animal sounds, sometimes suggestive of
the agonized bellowing of a herd of cows hurtling through the sky
with butcher knives buried in their rumps, and at other times
sounding like the very hounds of hell itself might sound, baying
and howling with growing intensity as they descend around you.

Designed to alert the whole front, and keep everybody in dreadful suspense as to where the salvo of six big bombs of tremendous
blasting force is going to land, they daily and nightly accomplish
their purpose.

In contrast, the enemy's conventional mortar bombs, the more frequent visitors, signal their coming with very abbreviated swishing

or buzzing sounds, of varying intensity and pitch, depending on their size and velocity. Spinning shells moan, hum, whine, wail, shriek, or emit only an air-rustling whisper before landing. The most dangerous, those dead on line, provide the least warning: only a faint, vicious hum, screech, or crackle, then *wham!* And, of course, you don't actually hear the explosion of the one that lands really close to you. You feel it, but the shocking intensity of a shell or bomb exploding close by is so entirely overpowering, your eardrums, stretched to the point of bursting by the compression, can't register it. You feel the concussion, you feel the ground shake, and you see the flash even through closed eyelids, but you don't hear it.

Among the weapons sending projectiles this way, two are in contention for the title Most Demoralizing, but for entirely different reasons: the Moaning Minnie, because of the length and intensity of its bloodcurdling warning, and the 88-mm gun because of the total absence of warning, with the final vote probably going in favour of the 88.

The 88-mm shell, being faster than sound, flashes a paralysing explosion before you hear it coming. Suddenly, with no warning, there's a wicked *wham* from a black airburst puff over a crossroads or above the gun position, followed instantaneously by a metallic screech, a chilling, banshee *yee-ow!* that could only be duplicated by a giant ripping asunder a piece of boilerplate. And so, in rapid succession, it's *Wham! – Yee-ow!* . . . *Wham! – Yee-ow!* . . . *Wham! – Yee-ow!*, until Jerry decides he's thrown over enough for the moment.

The shocking crash of an 88-mm shell landing without warning beside a slit trench may be the cause of heart failure of those men who now and then are found dead in trenches with no mark on them and whose deaths are usually attributed to "concussion."

Even an armour-piercing, 88-mm solid-shot, passing just over your head in the open, is a deadly sound. But when one drills through

BRETTEVILLE-SUR-LAIZE TO FALAISE
("OPERATION TRACTABLE")

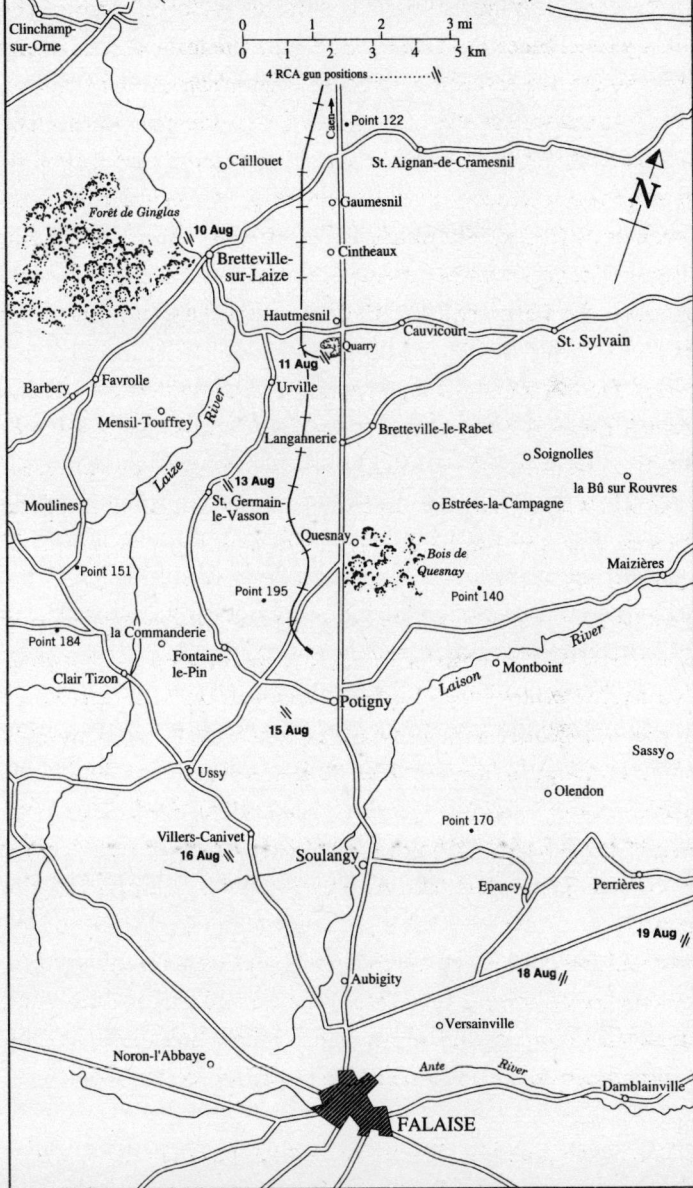

0   1   2   3 mi
0 1 2 3 4 5 km

4 RCA gun positions ....\\\

Clinchamp-
sur-Orne

• Point 122

○ Caillouet

St. Aignan-de-Cramesnil

Forêt de Ginglas

○ Gaumesnil

10 Aug \\\

Bretteville-
sur-Laize

○ Cintheaux

Hautmesnil

Quarry

Cauvicourt

St. Sylvain

11 Aug \\\

Urville

Barbery   ○ Favrolle

○ Mensil-Touffrey

Langannerie

Bretteville-le-Rabet

○ Soignolles

la Bû sur Rouvres ○

13 Aug \\\

St. Germain-
le-Vasson

Moulines

Estrées-la-Campagne •

Quesnay

Bois de
Quesnay

Maizières

• Point 151

Point 195 •

Point 140 •

• Point 184

la Commanderie

River

Fontaine-
le-Pin

Clair Tizon

Laison

○ Montboint

Potigny

15 Aug \\\

○ Ussy

Sassy ○

○ Olendon

Villers-Canivet

Point 170 •

16 Aug \\\

Soulangy

Epancy

Perrières

19 Aug ///

18 Aug //

○ Aubigity

Versainville ○

Ante   River

Noron-l'Abbaye ○

Damblainville

FALAISE

the stone walls of a house in which you are standing – in one side
and out the other, in a deafening split-second *rip* – it produces still
another heart-stopping effect. And this morning Jerry, by design or
accident, provides this experience while you are visiting a little
stone barn currently serving as regimental headquarters at the left
rear of the guns, down a rather steep slope exposed to distant ridges
still held by the enemy.

At dawn, just after you've climbed into your sack in your trench
along the hedgerow, and are luxuriating in those delicious final
moments of consciousness before drifting off, you get a message
from RHQ. You are to go back several miles to 2nd Division
Headquarters to pick up a fire plan and overprinted maps related to
the support expected of the guns during the opening of the final
drive through to Falaise.

Since your involvement in the aftermath of 6th Field's disastrous
Nebelwerfer affair kept you awake until you went on duty at midnight, you had a totally sleepless night, and your humour is foul as
you drive back many miles to a map reference not far from your
second-last gun position, on the high ground along the river northwest of Bretteville-sur Laize.

Still, as you drive west on the quiet road, in the open Jeep with
the rising sun behind you, you can't help recognizing a truly beautiful morning. While it will probably develop into another hot,
muggy day, the early morning air is a tonic – cool and fresh,
smelling sweetly of the dewy vegetation along the slopes of the
Laize valley, which still manages to retain its charming green
untouched-by-war look, in spite of an obvious increase in the
traffic through here.

You find the Division HQ trucks and caravans sitting in a peaceful, leafy orchard dappled with early-morning sunlight. Pinned
to a board on an easel is an impressive large-scale map showing
the developing Falaise pocket, which, if closed, will trap the
whole German army. A couple of clean, well-pressed, beautifully

turned-out officers are examining it with obvious excitement verging on gaiety. Conscious of your sandy, rumpled battledress, you get away from them before they can notice you and go looking for the major you are supposed to see. You find him, stripped to the waist, shaving from a folding, green canvas sink before a real mirror hanging from a tree. You study his clean, pink back and wonder what your own back looks like, as you haven't had your clothes off for more than six weeks, and have been scratching a great deal lately, having missed the delousing parade, when all ranks had had an anti-flea powder blown inside their tunics and pants through a tube inserted at their collars and waistbands.

You catch sight of a dirty, unshaven face in the mirror. With shock and guilt you realize it's your own, and involuntarily hide your filthy hands behind your back as the Major turns around, drying himself with a sparkling white towel. He's in high spirits as he pulls on a clean shirt. And as he leads you over to his caravan for the maps and plans, he tries to engage you in conversation as to "how things are going with you chaps up there. You know, if you can speed it up, we could end the war right here." But you snatch the roll of papers from him, and get away as quickly as possible before you run into the General.

It's while you are delivering the plans at regimental headquarters that a stray armour-piercing tank shell tears through the back wall and out through the front, with a hell of a *rip*, leaving a hole just above the sleeping adjutant's head. And strangely this makes you happy as the devil as you go back up to your guns.

Overnight there were massive movements of troops and tanks, as formations repositioned themselves for the attack, principally 3rd Canadian Division, 2nd Canadian Armoured Brigade, 4th Canadian Armoured Division, the Polish Armoured Division, and the 79th Armoured Division, that special British division equipped with various "funnies," including the tanks carrying fascines (enormous bundles of densely packed tree branches) meant to be dropped into the Laison river at shallow spots to provide causeways for tanks and recce cars.

And though a heavy harassing-fire program was conducted by the guns to cover the sound of whining motors and squealing tracks, the noise aroused a great deal of attention from German guns and mortars. So when the Polish Armoured Division became neighbours of 26th Battery in the early hours, attracting Moaning Minnies and 88s, the newcomers were not entirely welcome.

Still, few expressed their antagonism to the extent of one Gunner G. C. Henry, who, on awakening to the sound of encircling armour and crashing shells, had a dark figure drop in his trench uttering words sounding most Germanic to untrained ears. Hardly surprising that Henry (as Sgt. Bruce Hunt duly recorded) "laid violent hands on the importunate Pole, who, doubtless having heard of the more uncultured pursuits of his new comrades-in-arms, took off in haste, 88s notwithstanding, shrieking, 'Me Polish! Me Polish! See my hat!'"

Far over to the northeast, just short of the horizon, tanks of the 2nd Armoured Brigade are lined up in what an army historian will call "parade-ground order." Behind them are the armoured cars of 7th Recce, and then the 9th Canadian Infantry Brigade in Kangaroos. Behind them is 7th Brigade, and still farther east in the valley south of Cauvicourt, are the columns of 4th Armoured Division. In front are the flails of the 1st Lothians of the British 79th Armoured Division, who will pound a way through mine fields, leading the 21st and 22nd Canadian Armoured Regiments of 4th Armoured Brigade (each formed up almost track to track in four lines), with the 28th (British Columbia) Regiment and the Lake Superior (Motor) Regiment arranged in equally solid formations at the rear.

At 11:25 A.M. all the guns for miles around open up in a crashing roar, some firing red smoke to mark targets for the first wave of bombers. No one at the guns will be able to follow the course of the confusing operation, made even more confusing by bomber errors as the day progresses. But Canadian Army historians will later reconstruct an unusually vivid picture of the opening phase:

... the din grew to unbelievable proportions as noon approached on this glittering August day – the guns adding to the thunder of exploding bombs as the artillery opened up with its concentrations.

The resultant smoke and dust was soon obscured by greywhite billows of smoke pouring from the bursting canisters of 25-pounder smoke shells and filling the valley south of Estréesla-Campagne [five kilometres east of the guns, beyond the Caen–Falaise highway and Quesnay Woods] with a misty, impenetrable blanket.

At 1140 hours the suspense engendered by wireless-silence was broken with the words "Move now!" and the armoured brigades came on towards the startline to begin their daring and spectacular advance. Punctually at noon, under the canopy of bombers, our columns crossed their line between Soignolles (on the left) and Estrées-la-Campagne and, at 12 miles per hour, began their long crawl to the Laison River.

And as they moved south they gradually disappeared behind the continuous screen into which the white puffs of smoke (roiling from the 25-pounder smoke canisters) had merged. Almost at once drivers found it impossible to keep direction; they could merely press on into the sun with accelerator pedals pushed to the floor. Running blind behind their clumsy fascines, the Churchills began to stray stupidly among a welter of Shermans, carriers, Crocodiles, and Flails – each trying desperately to get back onto the required direction, with the heavier monsters trying to keep the head of the column.

Units lost formation and in less than an hour the almost ceremonial array of the forenoon had degenerated into a heterogeneous mass pouring down into the smoke-filled valley against a current of prisoners streaming to the rear.

In spite of the dust which obliterated land marks and made visibility extremely poor, obstacles were surmounted, mine-fields marked and by-passed, and after each brief halt to check direction the lumbering vehicles lurched forth again to disap-pear with a roar into the mist-like smoke, acrid with the stink of engines. . . .

Blinded by the smoke and dust, the enemy gunners frantically "searched" their defensive fire zones, but with comparatively little success. Many enemy infantry, deafened by the blast and bewildered by smoke, realized the utter uselessness of trying to resist the weight of steel bearing on them from every direction. . . . As the attack gained momentum, prisoners became so numerous that they were merely sent back along the centre line unescorted.*

That the assaulting columns succeed in all their objectives, cross-ing the Laison after sorting out massive confusion along its near bank as units pushed this way and that for fording places, is not something to which people in the rear areas give much thought as the afternoon progresses and the thunder of bombs being delivered miles behind the lines mounts to an awesome crescendo. Even Corps Commander Simonds, for a while at least, can't help being preoccupied with matters other than what is going on up front, as his armoured car is rocked violently to and fro by the concussions of errant 500-pound bombs landing around and about the quarry at Hautmesnil, where he has chosen to view proceedings.

---

* From pp. 66-67 Report No. 65, Historical Section (G.S.) Canadian Army Headquarters, Dec. 23, 1953, subtitled "Tractable: The First Phase (14 Aug)," based on unit was diaries.

57

RAF TAKES A TURN AT BOMBING
THE CANADIAN ARMY

✳

IT'S A BRIGHT SUNNY DAY, WITH ONLY WISPS OF CLOUD IN THE SKY, and they're bombing the Germans again just over the hill in front to get Operation Tractable, the final drive, moving towards Falaise.

The new offensive, involving 3rd Division infantry this time, got underway at noon, covered by the giant smokescreen fired by four field regiments across a front of more than three miles, moving forward in lifts like a creeping barrage to a depth of about two and a half miles, staying abreast of the advancing columns of tanks and armoured personnel carriers full of infantry.* The column on the right is led by 2nd Armoured Brigade with two brigades of 3rd Division following, the 9th in Kangaroos and armoured half-tracks and the 7th following on foot; while on the left, 4th Armoured Brigade conducts the 8th Infantry Brigade of 3rd Division in carriers, with 10th Brigade following on foot.

Fifteen minutes before H-hour (a little more than two hours earlier) guns of 23rd Field marked targets with red smoke shells for seventy-five medium Mitchell and Boston bombers, attacking gun and mortar positions along the wooded Laison river valley, while

---

* After observing from six hundred feet up in an Auster OP plane, Lt.-Col. Frank Lace, GSO 1 to Brig. Brownfield, BRA Canadian Army, reported he was very satisfied with the quality of the smoke screen.

Tiffies and bomb-carrying Spitfires attacked whatever they could find. Now eight hundred Halifax and Lancaster heavy RAF bombers, including those of No. 6 Royal Canadian Air Force Bomber Group, have begun to drop 3,723 tons of bombs, on targets bypassed by the assaulting columns, around Potigny, two and a half miles south of here, and Quesnay Wood, just a mile and a quarter east of your guns. Though dropping considerably less than the 5,200 tons dropped on German positions south of Verrières a week ago to start off Totalize, today's bombers will still unload 1,300 tons more than were dropped on Hamburg on the night of July 27–28, 1943, in what has become known as the "deadliest RAF raid of the war" because of the awful fire storm created.

Your guns are now silent, having participated in the timed concentrations on targets selected for ten minutes of drenching fire by four divisional artilleries and two AGRAs five minutes before H-hour. And now, having no part in the big smokescreen, all here at the guns have become spectators of the vast, roaring air armada swarming in from the coast, wave after wave of great black planes with bomb bays open, moving relentlessly, without any apparent enemy interference, towards the two dust clouds forming out front.

The concussions are monstrous. The ground shudders and blast-waves shatter and wrinkle the lacy clouds overhead, as stones might if tossed into a pond of milk.

As a towering black dust-cloud billows hundreds of feet in the air, you experience a creeping sense of horror at the depths of hell being sounded in that valley in front, where the targets are not war plants or concrete forts, but men sheltering in shallow holes.

Then suddenly they start bombing several hundred yards behind, and before the dust blackens out the scene, you see men running frantically as black bombs tumble down on them. Some bombers still stagger out of the dust cloud behind and pass over towards the dust cloud ahead, the menacing bombs clearly visible through their open bomb bays. Someone remarks that our carrier crews with their infantry battalions are back there somewhere, for only this morning 4th Brigade was pulled out of the line and marched back there for a few hours' rest.

Units of the Polish Division, some of which are parked alongside 26th Battery, are down there where the bombs are dropping, and you assume the men you see standing on tanks dotted about the valley floor, frantically waving swatches of yellow celanese cloth to identify themselves as friendly troops, are Polish troopers. Some have lit yellow smoke-generating canisters, and the smoke is drifting in gaudy streaks across the sunlit valley.

You wonder how many other units, including artillery outfits amassed to provide maximum support for this big push, are now being plastered in that dust-cloud.

A terrible disaster is taking place, and you are powerless to intervene. You think you're going to be sick to your stomach if you don't start doing something, even if it's only walking around in circles. There's a farmhouse almost hidden by trees to the right rear of the guns, a couple of hundred yards away. Maybe there's a barrel of cold cider there.

As you walk across the stubble field, between the stooks of yellow grain, you feel the earth tremble and shudder beneath your feet from the thunderous *crump, crump, crump* of the bombs landing on the slopes near the Hautmesnil quarry about a mile away and down on the valley floor covered with tanks and vehicles only four or five hundred yards away. Inexplicably some bombers still resist the temptation to add their bombs to the inferno in the valley below, and continue to lumber out of the dust and smoke with their bomb bays still loaded with big black bombs, passing overhead towards the towering dust cloud in the valley in front of the guns.

Then you see a little Auster aircraft, the kind used by artillery air OP officers, flying right up towards the bellies and the open bomb bays of the huge bombers, firing off red Very lights at them.

You, along with thousands and thousands of others watching from the ground, earnestly wish that brave man luck. If one of those bombs raining down round him strikes his little plane, there'll be just a split-second atomizing flash, and he'll be no more. And he obviously knows it.

Still he flies his tiny, fragile craft round and about, right up underneath the open bomb bays, waggling his wings and looping smoky red baubles from his Very pistol across the flight path of the great roaring bombers.

Seldom, if ever, have so many been witness to such a splendid display of courage by an individual as is now being displayed by that man in that fragile little plane up there.*

---

* Eversley Belfield, of the Royal Artillery, serving as a flying OP officer with the Canadian Army, recorded in his diary something of the extraordinary action he took on this afternoon of horror: "The weather was perfect as the first wave of heavy bombers plastered Quesnay Wood which had been holding us up for so long. Everybody felt very elated and excited and we were all congratulating ourselves on their accuracy, but the second wave arrived.... Suddenly to the east of where we were sitting on the open ground watching this attack, there was a vast billow of black smoke and the earth rocked as more and more Lancasters dropped their bombs there. Then some began to come over us at 3,000 feet, their bomb doors open and the bombs plainly visible. We dashed for some nearby German slit trenches, fearing the worst, but all the bombs seemed to land the other [east] side of the road. There was a lull and then I saw a third wave of bombers approaching. I leapt into a Jeep with one of the mechanics and made for one of the Austers (which were parked nearby). As he started it up, he offered to go up with me, but I refused, as his extra weight would have reduced the climbing performance. I climbed at full throttle; and with great difficulty (for I had forgotten how it worked), I fired off a red Very cartridge at about 2,000 feet and another at 4,000 feet. At about 6,000 feet, I was just below a large formation and twisted and turned to get their attention. I am certain that none of the third wave bombed our own forces, as I was in the midst of the stream of planes and noted, when one formation passed just above me, that I could plainly see the large bombs in the open bay. I was very fearful of bombs falling on me, as I was over the area that they had been bombing earlier." Quoted by Sir Brian Horrocks, Eversley Belfield, and Maj.-Gen. Essame, *Corps Commander* (Toronto: Griffin House,), pp. 44–45.

You find the farmhouse occupied by a command-post crew of another artillery outfit. Astonishingly, they are so absorbed with the progress of a fire plan, they're oblivious to the fact that bombs are falling short behind them. Feeling like an intruder, you retreat to the yard. In the shade cast by some trees are two kitchen chairs. On one sits a portable wind-up gramophone. Sitting down on the other, you pick up from the ground two recordings, one labelled *Blanche-Neige et les Sept Nains*, and the other, *J'Attendrai*.

Blowing the dust off *J'Attendrai*, you put it on the turntable and, for the next hour or more, play it over and over – only half-listening as you reset the needle and wind up the machine when it runs down – on and on like an automaton, so preoccupied are you with the bombing. Surely they'll discover their error before they start filling in the gap still remaining between the two gigantic dust clouds. Still, if they can bomb miles behind their actual strike zone, they have to believe it's enemy ground between that dust cloud back there and the one in front. Mechanically, you pursue your ritual of keeping the machine wound up and the record playing as you stare skyward, over the house and trees, at the undersides of passing bombers, clusters of bombs hanging in their bomb bays like monstrous black grapes.

Just how long you sit there, playing *J'Attendrai* over and over, you'll never be able to say, but finally you become aware that the thunder of bombs has ceased and only the fading drone of planes remains as the last of the bombers head for the Channel and their bases in England. As you abandon your gramophone, you wonder if any of those bomber crews know yet what they've done. When they're back in their messes in England tonight, having a Scotch-and-soda before dinner, will they become fully conscious of the disaster in which they participated, and get totally sloshed before going to bed and attempting to sleep?*

---

* General Guy Simonds, in a postwar lecture attended by the author, explained that the ground forces had been told yellow celanese or smoke

Unquestionably many have died back there, and you despair for friends in the 4th Field carrier crews and battery commander crews attached to 4th Brigade infantry who had only hours ago been pulled out of the line and sent back there for a rest.

Stu Laurie, who is attached to battalion headquarters as their arty rep since Major Wren was killed yesterday, barely arrives back with the Royals in their rest area near Hautmesnil when it becomes the epicentre of a torrent of bombs. Days later, it will still be an ordeal for him to recall the horror of having a bright, sunny d ay suddenly turn inky-black amidst a string of stupendous explosions.

Surrounded by a god-awful cacophony of four-engined planes roaring overhead and bombs screaming down to earth-quaking blasts, sweeping him with concussion winds of hurricane force loaded with sand and pebbles and larger hunks of debris, Laurie crawls about on his hands and knees in total blackness, convinced he has been blinded. Determined not to return home blind, he pulls his pistol from its holster, but before he can use it the dust cloud opens briefly, allowing a flicker of light to show him it isn't his eyes that are the problem, but the density of the dust.

I'm out in the open in a field when the bombing starts. We are all just standing around, watching the bombing out front. Then they start bombing to the rear. And for a while we watch everybody else taking it. They plaster the Poles – they're running in all

would be recognized by the airforce as the mark of friendly troops, and should be displayed whenever they were fearful they might be mistaken for the enemy by strafing aircraft. The airforce were told that yellow celanese or yellow smoke would mark the front line. Thus, when nervous units, bombed by the U.S.A. Airforce back at Caen a few days before, displayed yellow celanese miles behind the lines, it appeared to mark the front line to some airmen, who should have been, but were not, timing their run from the coast to their designated targets.

directions. I don't know what to think of this. But then they start to drop what seems like thousands of bombs down on us.

I crawl around on my hands and knees in the dark for what seems like all afternoon. You can't see anything. Finally I find a hole to crawl into. It turns out to be a hole in a mound – a great big ruddy mound – full of men.*

Earlier in the day Major Ralph Young, acting CO of the Royals, on arrival at Hautmesnil "for a few hours' rest before going forward to fill a gap between 3rd Div and 51st Highland Division later in the day," had discovered this huge German bunker and designated it his "alternative battalion headquarters."

The regiment is distributed among the houses of the village with battalion headquarters in a substantial farmhouse. Behind us is this sunken road, and beyond the road is this hell-of-a-great bunker, a really big thing which you enter from the road.

The support company is deployed around the perimeter of this field – carriers, mortars, anti-tank guns and vehicles, all of them parked in the shadow of the hedgerows.

It is a beautiful warm day, and the guys have taken off their equipment and most of their clothing, and are lying about relaxing in the sunshine, or down the hill at a mobile bath that's been set up nearby, when this thing starts north of Hautmesnil and progresses south until eventually the bombs are landing right on our position.

I am at an O Group at Brigade with my intelligence officer, David Henry, when I get an S.O.S.: "Bring back yellow smoke – we're being bombed three hundred yards north of us." Somebody produces a box of yellow smoke, and we take off. But when we get there, A Echelon has just arrived and is strung out

---

* Author interview.

along the road, blocking it all the way up the hill. Henry goes one way with an armful of smoke bombs and I go another. When I get to battalion headquarters there is a great hole outside the farmhouse and two pioneers lying dead on the rim of the crater. So I go to my alternative headquarters in the bunker. Half the battalion seems to have collected there – most of support company anyway – at least fifty people. It's a big room, maybe twenty feet by fifteen.

All of a sudden, bang . . . bang . . . bang – a string of huge explosions! Everything goes dark and pandemonium almost breaks out. I am more or less at the entrance to the bunker, and I, along with everybody else, think a bomb has buried the entrance, entombing us. This sets up quite a feeling of panic. It is starting, it is coming, but I am able to stop it by making them aware of a second exit, a ventilation opening at the other end I discovered when I was checking out the bunker as a possible HQ. As it turns out when the dust clears, the entrance is clear.*

Bob Suckling, commander of D Company, will also carry frightful memories of what it is like to be under the worst concentration of bombs ever dropped on troops by Bomber Command, for the Royals were at the very centre of that high-explosive hurricane today – a day that began so pleasantly for him:

We have just marched back some miles from a forward position to a little village [Hautmesnil] on the Caen–Falaise highway. I am now a company commander. In a matter of five weeks, I've been elevated from lieutenant to acting-captain to acting-major! Unable to locate within the battalion any "crowns" [embroidered shoulder-insignia identifying a major], I seek them at Brigade HQ, finally getting a pair from Jim Knox, the brigade

---

* The quotations from Ralph Young are from an interview with the author.

major, who fired me as liaison officer in England. He is surprised, and I am glad!

But then in the afternoon we are bombed intermittently for an hour and a half by Lancasters and Halifaxes of the RCAF and RAF at low level. For sheer terror, this is an afternoon of a lifetime.

I'm waiting in the south end of the village to meet our blanket truck and other soft-skinned vehicles to show them to the company area, when the bombing starts. The men mostly flee the village into the surrounding wheat fields – though it's impossible to know which way to run.

At one point I am in a partly dug slit trench, just deep enough that when I double up, the top of my head is at ground level – which is not very reassuring. A little later, having moved between bomber waves, I find myself in a bomb crater with Padre Harry Appleyard.

At the south end of the village there is an open space of about two hundred yards between us and a very large stone quarry. There I see some Royal Canadian Engineers, each holding a corner of an enormous piece of yellow chiffon [celanese] so the bombers can see it. They do. Their bomb bays are open approaching from the north. The bombs are released. They come down screaming over our bomb crater and land absolutely squarely on the yellow chiffon. The earth and stones blasted in the air make it seem like midnight on a bright sunny afternoon. And when all the crap settles back to earth, there is not a single vestige of yellow celanese or the four engineers to be seen.

By now the whole battalion area is ablaze, though most of the stone houses in the village are still surviving to some degree.

At one point I find my way to tac headquarters in the basement of a stone house, where I see a Toronto Scottish sergeant – his face pock-marked by sand and gravel – coming down the stairs with tears streaming down his face.

My company area is an apple orchard full of mature trees. Our company carrier was left parked alongside a stone fence. When I get back, there is not a tree standing – the whole orchard is under a foot or more of fresh earth. There isn't a sign of the carrier, though the nearest bomb crater is thirty or more yards away. Finally I find part of a bogey wheel about fifty yards away, but that is all. I keep thinking, all that armour-plate couldn't just disappear. But it has.

Support company vehicles are all on fire, and mortar ammunition and pioneer platoon supplies carried in them explode for hours.

My company [when collected] is practically naked, and only a few of them have weapons, simply because most of them were stripped down when the bombing started, and ran into the fields in their underwear.

Located in the big stone quarry just south of the village, in the turret of an armoured car with our corps commander, Guy Granville Simonds, watching his planes carry out their great bombing attack, was Air Marshal Sir Arthur Coningham, Commander-in-Chief RAF Tactical Forces. Even he couldn't do anything to stop them. I'd like to know what he was thinking as he bounced around inside that armoured car during that hour and a half!*

When the bombing finally ends and Major Ralph Young comes outside the bunker, he sees no one:

The battalion has disappeared. My adjutant and I walk around the area and meet no one. All our carriers, mortars, and anti-tank guns are destroyed. The field where they were parked is a total shambles. A smashed carrier is upside down in a hedgerow. Then we discover Jack Stothers's company in a cellar under a house.

---

*   Author interview.

Gradually others begin drifting in from the fields and up the hill from the mobile bath. And after a while to our relief we find we have lost only fifty-six – a grim enough toll, but nothing to what it might have been had they not scattered into the countryside.

But the Royals have lost most of their clothing, personal equipment, blankets, ammunition, and weapons, including six anti-tank guns, fifteen mortars, seventeen machine guns, twenty-nine wireless sets, and twenty-four vehicles of various kinds.

And in the aftermath, 4th Field FOOs and their crews, who shared this dreadful afternoon with the Royals, will be left with indelible images: of half-naked, stunned men, some in bare feet, straggling back to the village and wandering aimlessly across freshly turned earth of neighbouring fields, searching in vain for any sign of the vanished equipment or clothing; of stretcher-bearers wending their way around giant craters searching for the wounded; of the endless parade of ambulance Jeeps assembled from other units, flying Red Cross flags and loaded with blanket-wrapped soldiers, threading their way back along the traffic-choked roads to casualty clearing stations in the rear; and of the silhouette against the setting sun of a burial party, with the padre carrying out the sad duty all padres must perform as the battle dies away and the furies recede.

After so many nerve-wracking days of plodding forward – fighting to secure another rise, only to be ordered on again to fight for yet another, indistinguishable from the last – for this to happen now is almost too much for men to bear. Morale is about as low as it can go, before a rum ration is scrounged and a supper of sorts is put together for the haggard men.

By midnight the Royals' quartermaster, Capt. Dan Wilkie, manages somehow to procure replacements for much of the lost weapons and vehicles, and has outfitted the men with enough clothing to allow the battalion to move out in the morning to fulfil its obligation to the left flank of the final drive south towards Falaise. But seriously under-strength, the battalion is a very ragged-looking outfit, with most of them still lacking battledress blouses. The troops that Stu Laurie (now acting-commander of 2nd Battery) accompanies down the Falaise road in the morning are armed only with shovels.

No unit within or close to the perimeter of the maelstrom will establish a list of casualties for at least twenty-four hours, for when the bombs began to tumble down, scores of men, including men from the 4th Field wagon lines, ran from fields that appeared next in line for the carpet bombing then moving south. Some ran in terror until they dropped from exhaustion, and won't reappear until after they are listed as missing.

An accurate casualty count will never be possible because of the difficulty in separating casualties of the bombing from other casualties on August 14. Next day's estimate of four hundred casualties – 150 dead and 250 wounded – must serve as a final count, but to those who were within sight and sound of it all, those figures will always seem to understate the facts. To anyone watching, it will always seem a miracle that anyone emerged alive from that horrendous rain of bombs.

Coming only six days after the Americans bombed behind you south of Caen, causing 380 Canadian and Polish casualties – many among the same units as were bombed today – this tragic error is, for many, unendurable. In the opinion of "Hank" Caldwell, the Royals' anti-tank officer (shortly to become a company commander), "the wounded of the bombing consisted almost entirely of men who were left nervous wrecks. Afterwards I saw General Guy Simonds standing by the roadside as truckloads of such casualties went by."[*]

Clearly the official casualty toll, grim as it is, will never tell the true story, for no count will ever be made of the untold numbers of

---

[*]   Author interview.

men, who, though they came through the day with no visible wounds, discover their nervous systems are so shattered they will never recover the emotional resilience necessary to survive shelling and mortaring without losing their grip and breaking down.*

---

* Months later in the Rhineland, the author saw Royals, recently returned from hospital after recovering from "battle exhaustion" induced by the Hautmesnil bombing, break down again under heavy shelling.

58

GUNNERS LYING ABOUT AS
THOUGH DEAD

※

THERE ARE ALMOST AS MANY THEORIES AS TO THE CAUSE OF dysentery afflicting the Canadians on the highway from Caen to Falaise as there are cases. Perhaps most suspected as the culprit is polluted drinking water, which from mid-July until now has been drawn from the Orne River, where bodies of dead men and animals lie in stagnant backwaters or drift slowly downstream and out to sea.

Certainly, all those in 4th Field who watched the parade of water wagons at Fleury-sur-Orne, backing up to the river near the collapsed railway bridge right behind the gun position, to fill their tanks with the turgid liquid, could easily believe that water is the cause.

Gunner Saunders is not likely to soon forget a 4th Field water wagon with its suction tube inserted in the river only a few feet away from the upturned, glistening bottom of a German body, caught in a weedy backwater. At first he thought the shiny, blueish-black object was a bladder out of a football – until he poked it with a stick.

But when you raised the matter of water quality with Gunner Tommy Dodds, the 2nd Battery water-wagon man (trained to add the contents of this bottle and that bottle to his tank, and conduct tests on the water until he deems it safe to drink), he assured you,

"That water is so loaded with chlorine, you could sell it as bleach back in Caen. No germ could ever live in it."

And from the smell and taste of the water in your water-bottle, you are inclined to accept his verdict. Furthermore, though dysentery made its appearance at Fleury, it wasn't really widespread until after Ifs, where the Regiment feasted on the clear, cold water from a deep well behind the guns on the outskirts of the village. This, of course, has inspired the theory the Germans dropped something in the well.

Another theory attracting a great deal of support is that the dysentery is caused by flies fresh from feasting on the abundant decaying flesh of men and animals, alighting with polluted feet and proboscises on food even as it is being carried on a spoon from mess-tin to mouth.

Certainly there are millions of flies. The first morning at Ifs, you were conned by Bombardier Hossack and Gunner Hiltz into walking some distance over to a farmyard to examine a shiny, black-enamelled two-wheel cart – after they had drawn you into speculating as to what it possibly could be used for, it being the only well-painted cart so far seen in all Normandy.

They, of course, had already been over to it, and watched with amusement as you went over and discovered it wasn't painted, but was completely covered with shiny black flies – every detail, from the shafts to the box, including the spokes of the wheels, the rims, and the hubs, every visible square centimetre, hidden under a seething mass of flies.

Oh yes, there are lots of flies here. And it's easy to accept the theory that with the abundance of decaying bodies lying around unburied throughout all of July – not to mention the tons of human excrement in thousands of uncovered latrines throughout the bridgehead – very little in the way of food is consumed that has not been touched by a fly that has just flown in from some foul spot.

Still, there are others who believe that because some men have not succumbed at all, or have been only lightly afflicted, the illness may have its origins in a lowered resistance caused by extreme fatigue or anxiety. But if this were so, then on this unusually quiet day today at the 4th Field guns, you might have expected that there would be some improvement in the dysentery problem, since today has been given over to maintenance and rest here at Able Troop, as 3rd and 4th divisions carry the attack east of the Caen–Falaise highway, with obvious success following yesterday's bombing of enemy positions by those planes that did manage to land their bombs properly on target. However, the perverse affliction seems to flourish in relaxed bodies – at least the debilitating effects seem to become more pronounced when men are relaxing and catching up on sleep. This you discover in dramatic and disturbing fashion early in the evening.

Late in the afternoon recce parties are called to go forward to line up new gun positions about five miles farther on towards Falaise – a few hundred yards to the right and just beyond the town of Potigny. And at about 8:00 P.M., the order comes from RHQ to limber up and form up in regimental convoy out on the road behind the position, ready to move off. This you pass on to the guns in routine fashion over the Tannoy speakers just as the gun quads are rolling onto the position to park in attendance at their respective pits to receive limbers and guns.

But when the command post has been dismantled, and everything is packed into GA and TL (including the two long strips of corrugated iron from Carpiquet aerodrome used to support the earthen roof), and you look around the position expecting to see the guns hooked up to the quads waiting patiently the order to pull out, you can hardly believe your eyes.

The quads sit there devoid of limbers and guns. Absolutely nothing is going on. The guns still rest in the pits. And near them you see men lying on the ground, unmoving as though dead.

The scene is unnerving! You start conjecturing wildly: your first thought is that you have a mutiny on your hands. . . . All that digging they've had to do recently, three gun pits and three ammunition pits in three days, all of them in solid chalk! But why on earth would they want to do this now, when they've had practically nothing to do but sleep all day? That they're drunk is a more likely possibility. . . . Somebody must have discovered a cache of Calvados somewhere, and in their weakened state that overproof stuff has knocked them out. As you hasten towards the nearest gun past a quad, you notice the driver is leaning forward over his steering wheel, head down, as though sleeping. Oh no, not the drivers, too! You recognize him: Ross Wilcox, a most dependable man. You stop and call up to him, "Wilcox . . . what the hell is going on?"

Raising his head he stares at you a moment before replying laconically, "Just suffering the shits, sir – like everybody else."

Is it possible? Has the dysentery that has plagued the troop for days, and for which the MO has no medicines, culminated in this?

Confirmation comes from Sgt. Carl Mayhew when you lean down to question him as he lies on his back beside his gun pit, his arms folded over his eyes. No odour of alcohol rises from his puffy, feverish lips as he uncovers his eyes and laboriously rolls over until he's kneeling before you. For a moment he looks at you blinking, as though trying to comprehend what you are asking, then, in a weak, husky voice, says, "Sir, we're all too sick."

This of course is unacceptable. And you can tell by the way he says it (not in defiance, but as a plea for mercy) that deep within him he knows it, too. It is clear what must be done, but how to accomplish it is another matter. Barking out orders and threatening to put men on charge will not work here – not with men such as these, who for interminable periods during the past month have carried on beyond human endurance without a growl or complaint. But if those guns are to move tonight, they must somehow be persuaded to get up on their feet.

Convincing men, who are so sick they don't know what's going on around them, into getting up and limbering up guns is something beyond all your training and experience. But you count on the character of these men, whom you've come to admire so much, reasserting itself with a little encouragement.

You start with Mayhew, talking encouragingly as you grasp his hands and pull him to his feet, reminding him of the one thing no gunner could ever refuse, a call for help from the infantry. They are depending on these guns for support, and unless they are moved forward, they'll be out of range and unable to bring down fire to break up counter-attacks. Surely he doesn't want to let those poor bastards down now — now they're so near to closing off the pocket and capturing a whole German army, and maybe ending the war right here.

And when Mayhew's up on his feet, you go to each of the other three sergeants and do the same, saying whatever comes into your head that might encourage them into making what, for them, must be a superhuman effort to get their guns winched out of the pits and hooked up to limbers and quads, reminding them over and over how much the infantry is depending on them. And then you watch as the astonishing leadership of the gun sergeants begins to work its magic. Soon every man is on his feet and moving, albeit slowly.

You will never admire men more. While their conscience leaves them no choice, you know what they are going through, for you were one of the first to suffer the convulsive cramps and cold-shuddering fever associated with this damnable scourge just before the break-out from Verrières.

They move, but they move like men who are dying on their feet – so slowly the Regiment (with surprising good grace) accepts your report of the situation and leaves you and your troop behind, to find your own way later to a map reference about a mile southwest of Potigny.

And when finally the four guns are limbered up, and you are moving off in the dark into a thickening fog, you think what an indescribable nightmare it must be for infantry suffering dysentery even to drag themselves over hill and dale for miles laden down with weapons, ammunition, trenching tools, and the like, let alone dash here and there for cover on the way, dig in on their objective, and then brace themselves with what little will and strength they have left to resist the inevitable counter-attack. How do men summon up the necessary physical and moral courage to continue doing this, day in and day out, when the best they can expect is a flesh wound that will release them from the obligation of going forward against the enemy?

The fog becomes a real pea-souper just about the time you enter a corridor that's been cleared through a very deep mine field.

A cursory reconnaissance on foot, after you spot a sign warning of mines nailed to an old German "ACHTUNG MINEN" sign, reveals a corridor some twenty-five yards or more wide, marked by wisps of white tape tied on the tops of steel posts planted every fifty yards or so along each side.

But the night is so black and the fog so dense, you can never see more than one festooned guidepost at a time, and for long intervals you lose sight of both the post behind and the one ahead as you crawl forward, staying as close as you dare to the right side of the corridor. Fearing your scout car may drift out of the corridor, leading the troop to disaster among the mines, you get out and walk ahead of it, now and then stopping the column until you locate the next post on the right.

After much stewing and sweating, you and the guns make it across without mishap. Near the new gun position, you are met by Bob Grout, who warns that the whole area is dotted with huge, yawning bomb craters, and that the gun sergeants will have to lead the quads in on foot. Baker Troop has had to winch one quad, limber, and gun out of one.

Your guns make it without mishap. But now it starts pouring rain. Tempers are short, and one of the gunners on an ammunition truck takes umbrage at something said (or the way it was said) by the bombardier in charge of the detail, and hangs one on him. Of course he is put on charge, and eventually he'll face a court martial.

This is damned unfortunate, for both are men of high character who have been doing a hard job for days on end, moving untold tons of ammunition forward from position to position each time the guns move – five new positions in seven days, three of them requiring digging gun pits in that chalk. Clearly the incident is the result of fatigue bordering on outright exhaustion, and you vow to make this clear at the court martial.*

Your command post is in a little stone farmhouse – the first time it has been set up in a building of any kind since coming to Normandy – and it's nice and dry. But the outlook for your dysentery-ridden gun crews, too weak to dig gun pits, is bleak, until you decide to break with the normal drill and keep the quads on the position to provide them with shelter from the pelting rain. This turns out to be a good move, for there are no calls for fire of any kind all night.

---

* With his GPO appearing as a character witness to describe the extenuating circumstances, and defended by Adjutant Sammy Grange, who one day would become a judge of the Supreme Court of Ontario, Gunner William Wright escaped without a conviction to mar his war record.

59

WAR BECOMES A BLUR FOR MEN
BEFUDDLED BY FATIGUE

※

SO OFTEN DO THE GUNS MOVE (SEVEN TIMES IN NINE DAYS, ending August 19, and usually at night), and so often are you forced to remain awake all day, either with recce parties or covering off the command post while your troop leader takes his turn going forward with advance parties, that fatigue becomes chronic, and in your befuddled state you will remember almost nothing of the two days just before Falaise is taken, and will always be dependent on a hodgepodge of images provided by others.

Among these is the startling picture of a group of women, carrying great bouquets of flowers, marching in from no-man's-land to greet the advance guard of the Polish Armoured held up by the Germans at Potigny. The village is a unique community made up of people of Polish origin, families who long ago had migrated here to run the iron mine. When some women of the village overheard Allied prisoners speaking Polish as they were being marched down the road by their German captors, they rushed over to them and engaged them in excited conversation. And on learning there was a whole Polish division of many thousands of men coming this way with the Canadian Army, the women returned home, filled their arms with flowers, and in spite of dire warnings from the Germans, marched up the Caen–Falaise highway to welcome their liberators.

And there's the strange sight of Poles in British battledress giving cigarettes in welcome to Poles in German field-grey uniforms right after they've been taken prisoner and before they change into Canadian battledress and join in the drive to close the Falaise Gap. The alacrity with which men can change sides, and how swiftly others are able to extend forgiveness to their fellow countrymen – at least on the battlefield – brings forth expressions of dismay in Sgt. Hunt's diary.

Unaware that captured Poles must become a source of badly needed reinforcements for the Polish Division, Hunt wrote bitterly on August 15: "The Poles take some prisoners, snipers from the nearby woods. For this we are grateful, but when the Poles give the snipers cigarettes we give the Poles . . . well, I mean to say, what? It seems the prisoners are, by birth, Poles. Even so, one wonders how many Canadians fell before these mercenaries surrendered to smoke Canadian cigarettes."

Then there is the unforgettable image of a Hitler Youth of the 12th SS refusing to surrender, though his covered hole is overrun. He has to be dug out and shot like a groundhog.

The company of Royals with whom Len Harvey and his carrier crew are moving saw him disappear in a covered dogleg trench as they came up, but when they call to him to come out with his hands up, he yells back, "Come in and get me, Canadian bastards!"

Twice they toss grenades into the open end of the trench, but he is able to duck around the corner of the dogleg and escape the blasts, leaving him unscathed and snarling defiant obscenities. Finally the Royals unlimber their shovels and remove enough of the roof to shoot him dead, leaving him there like the animal he'd become – rather than the boy he might have been.

Then there's the bizarre duel between a sniper in a tree and a company commander of the FMRs on the ground, conducted with both bullets and grenades.

Though 2nd Division has been in action only a month, casualties have been so high, infantry companies now look like platoons when on the move, and the FMRs are no exception.*

Because of the need to maintain a roster of experienced officers to help boost sagging morale, wounded officers sometimes feel obliged to spend the later days of their convalescence with their units in the line. Capt. Noel Meilleur of the FMRs is one of these. Hit by shell fragments on July 20 at Beauvoir Farm and evacuated to a British hospital in Bayeux, he discharged himself after two weeks and hitched a ride back to his unit at St. Martin-de-Fontenay, where, still limping, he took part in the big push on August 8.

Now, on August 15, Meilleur's company has been chosen to take the principal strong point along the axis of advance on Falaise, a large house known as "*la Commanderie,*" eight hundred yards north of Clair Tizon, simply because his company, with a complement of forty other ranks, is currently the strongest in the battalion.

Officers being prime targets for snipers, Meilleur has removed his epaulettes with their tell-tale officer's pips, carries a rifle, and is draped with khaki-cotton bandoliers of bullets criss-crossing his breast and overlaying the two Bren-gun magazine pouches fixed to his webbing and bulging with tins of bully beef, hardtack, a change of socks, and smokes. He thus presents an authentic image of an Other Rank.

As he sends a section this way and another that way, Meilleur gives unobtrusive hand signals, but still he attracts the attention of a sniper, hidden up in a big, leafy tree in the backyard of the house. The sniper gets him in the leg with a bullet before he can make it into an abandoned trench. Then, peppered by grenades dropped from above, he escapes from two successive slit trenches as grenades

---

* By August 17, Canadian infantry casualties having reached 76 per cent and reinforcements being insufficient, the nine battalions of 2nd Division – the hardest hit of all Allied formations – were almost 2,000 under fighting strength of 5,040 (9 × 560).

roll into them and explode. But when he rises up to see where a third grenade has gone, the explosion gets him full in the chest, wiping away not only the bandoliers of small-arms ammunition and bully-beef-packed Bren pouches, but also his battledress breast pockets, filled with letters and snapshots from home, wads of Compo toilet paper, and other precious possessions.

Though he suffers blast injuries to his face that will cause him the loss of one eye, he is saved from death by the body armour which remains intact under his shredded clothing. But left with "the granddaddy of all headaches," he is so enraged he throws caution to the wind and, hopping about on his good leg, goes searching for his grenade-tossing tormentor. Moving around the bottom of the tree, he spots him up among the thick foliage, and shoots him dead.

And there are Bombardier Hossack's diary notes for these days:

> The troop moves up to a German-vacated wheat field overlooking the burning city of Falaise. The roads are rough and dusty, and lead through villages of destroyed and burning houses where the smell of death is very evident. Cows have been left unattended at a farmhouse adjacent to the guns and our farmers-turned-soldiers milk them for us daily. . . . Enemy planes put on a very fine daylight show of aerobatics, but their continual weaving and turning to avoid ack-ack fire disrupts their aim and their bombs and machine-gun bullets land mostly in unoccupied fields. The BBC news tells us that the Americans are in Paris. Our joy is greatly overshadowed by that of the natives when we tell them, "Les Americans dans Paris."

Finally, a striking little image supplied by Sgt. McEwan's diary: "As we advance through a village completely destroyed by our bombers, beside a house that is merely a shell is a small garden a few feet square. In it, not touched one iota by the blast, are three beautiful spurs of gladiolas and a few dahlias, forming an odd contrast to the destruction around them."

60

FALAISE IN FLAMES

———————— ✳ ————————

THE MORNING OF AUGUST 16 ARRIVES CLEAR AND FRESH, AND there's an early move away from the moon landscape of giant bomb-craters to a sun-bathed position among stooks of grain in a stubble field enclosed by green hedgerows untouched by war. There, the new battery commander – a Major Don Cornett, who seems a decent sort – drops by for a chat on his way up to the Royals to take over from Stu Laurie, who has been acting as their arty rep since Major Wren was killed.

You hear that Bombardier Jim Fraser and Lance-Bombardier Russell Green of 26th Battery, reported missing a couple of days ago when they failed to return from a scrounging expedition on a motorbike somewhat beyond the established FDLs, have been found dead. Sad news indeed. They were good guys. To you, Fraser always seemed to suggest the spirit of Huckleberry Finn, and he'd occupied a special place in your heart since that cold, wet day a couple of years ago when he offered you a steaming piece of chicken from a pot he had boiling on a Primus stove in the back of a moving truck in the middle of a regimental convoy.

You were on a motorbike, "riding herd" on the regimental convoy headed for Wales, when you picked up the delicious odour of cooking chicken as you roared up past the moving line of guns and vehicles to get to the head of the column to direct traffic at the next crossroads. Tracing the tempting smell to its origin, you found yourself riding behind one of your own troop's 15-hundredweight trucks, face to face with Fraser, who was looking out from under the canvas hood right next to the tailgate.

For a moment he attempted to look dumb and brazen it out, but then deciding bribery was his best move, he broke into a wide grin. Leaning down, he speared a chunk of chicken from a pot and brought it up where he could examine it with a critical eye, while beckoning you to move in close to the tailgate. Fully aware there was no way he could have acquired a chicken without "borrowing" it from a henhouse along the line of march, and that winking at this wanton act, while countenancing the use of a lighted Primus stove in one of his majesty's trucks in a moving convoy, made you equally if not more culpable, the smell of the chicken suppressed all considerations of good order and discipline. Nudging your sputtering Norton forward, you were just able to grasp the tender morsel from Fraser's precariously extended fork.

Fraser loved life, and he loved good grub, and he and Green may well have been looking for a chicken or two when they bought it.

Still it was madness for them to go junketing through countryside not totally clear of the Germans. In the fluid conditions existing before Falaise, with no clearly defined front line, there is no telling where you may bump into pockets of enemy troops, or from what quarter you may be fired on. To this, Stu Laurie can attest when he returns to resume his duties as battery captain:

Somewhere south of Potigny I was walking with Ralph Young [acting CO of the Royals] when we saw an 88, no more than ten feet away, sitting in a field just inside a gate through a hedge. Of course we all went over to look at it. It appeared undamaged except it had been stripped of its gears. And right beside it sat a Tiger tank, also undamaged as far as could be seen, and which only recently had been abandoned, for when we went around it examining it and feeling it, it was still nice and warm.

Someone should have poured petrol over it and thrown a grenade at it to set it on fire, but we just moved on and left it. And this turned out to be a mistake. Next day we couldn't settle down anywhere but a bloody 88 was shooting at us. And we never could tell where the fire was coming from: first it was from behind us, then from the side, then from the other side. But it was that Tiger tank all right, for when I was on the way back to the guns, I looked in on that field and it wasn't there!*

That Falaise is still occupied by determined enemy troops, Fox Troop Commander Sammy Grange is able to report when he goes well beyond the FDLs to establish an OP in the town's northwestern outskirts. And while recognizing that the real liberators of Falaise are 6th Brigade units that attack the town next day, wiping out many of the last of the 12th SS Hitlerjugend fanatics (up to one hundred of them dying in the flames of a walled monastery or school that burned over them as they fought to the death), Sammy will always lay solemn claim to having been "first in and first out of the birthplace of William the Conqueror." "In on the 15th, out on the 16th," is the way he puts it when he gets the chance to tell you of it:

I think it was Bill Carr's idea to send me up accompanied by a dozen or so Essex Scottish to provide protection. I never really understood the purpose of my expedition. All he said was, "I'm going to send you into Falaise. . . . We don't know what's in there. . . . No one has been in there yet. . . . I'll get a section of the Essex to go along with you to protect you." About a dozen Other Ranks came along, and while it was nice having someone there concerned with my protection, I would have preferred to be there alone, for all they did was draw fire.

---

* Author interview.

We were right in the outskirts of Falaise, in some farm build-ings looking down from a hill. The view was excellent – I could see the whole town. While I couldn't see any Germans, there were snipers all around. And of course my infantry guards started to draw fire when three or four of them exposed themselves (in the military sense), chasing a hen round and about with the object of killing and plucking it for the pot. At least two of them were hit, one serious enough I had to go out and bring him in. So much for their concern for my safety!

Normally I would have brought down neutralizing fire, but we were then beyond the range of our guns. They were sup-posed to be moving up closer (at least Carr had given that impression), but they didn't. It was then I realized there was nothing more useless than this patrol. It turned out to be my last tour of duty as a FOO before becoming battery captain and turning over Fox Troop to Jack Cameron, the CPO."*

Next day 6th Brigade attacks Falaise, and the following day (August 18), when 4th Field advance parties pass through, the town is still burning, new fires having been started the previous night by Luftwaffe bombers.

The flames are so fierce in places, the searing heat raises blisters in the paint on the side of the 2nd Battery command post scout car as it is guided gingerly through the rubble-cluttered streets by Driver George Bracken, with all its armour-plate shutters in place over windshield and side windows because of snipers. Incredibly, the Provost Corps has already erected signs: LOOTING: PENALTY DEATH.

Positions south of Falaise are laid out and surveyed, but never occupied. The guns are redirected to a wooded plateau, high in a

---

*   Capt. S. G. M. Grange's thirty-eight days as a FOO during the worst fighting Normandy could offer from Caen to Falaise was recognized when he was later awarded the *Croix de Guerre avec Étoile de Vermeil*.

range of hills (Les Monts d'Erain) southeast of Falaise, overlooking what the BBC is calling the Falaise gap – that narrowing corridor, still open to the retreating Germans, between the Americans in the south and 1st Canadian army pushing towards Trun and Chambois. Up here in a stump-filled clearing, it is impossible to dig in, but there are plenty of logs to build up protective bulwarks to form command posts, gun "pits" and "slits."

Waiting for the guns to come up in the evening, you watch a battle raging on another hill one thousand yards away that gives every appearance of being the main thrust by the Germans in their attempt to keep the pocket open. There's a feeling that this may become a hot place, but, with Jerry guns and planes preoccupied elsewhere, the night passes quietly, if uncomfortably. For those off-duty and able to bed down, there is not a square yard of level ground devoid of roots, stumps, and stones.

Around midnight there are some tense moments when low-flying planes throb overhead and start dropping parachute flares – more and more until the sky is filled with orange, white, red, and yellow flares, lighting up the landscape in all directions in noonday brilliance. When they buzz off without dropping anything else, it is assumed they are Allied planes lighting up the gap, especially the Polish position on another hill now cut off and needing to be supplied from the air.

Before dawn you are aroused from a lumpy bower and sent forward to establish an OP and listening post down over the brow of the hill, only a few hundred yards in front of the guns. There has been a report of Germans heading up this way. But nothing happens, and when dawn comes, though it is a grey morning with scattered showers, you bring up your NCOs to see what they can see. This must be a very disappointing experience for them, for while it is possible to see at least fifteen miles from up here – a complete overview of the pocket – there is absolutely nothing to be seen moving down there. The only things at all suggestive of the destruction and carnage the BBC broadcasts now claim is being visited on the Germans in the pocket are some Tiffies and Spitfires flying past almost at eye-level and diving on unseen targets, adding muffled *crump*s and rumbles to the faint thundering roar of shells landing far off, and a vast pall of smoke drifting across the landscape from numerous fires including those in Falaise.

An evening move on August 19 takes the guns to Perrières, near Vicques, which Hossack's diary calls "a heap of rubble that once was a village." Enemy air activity is impressive:

Darkness brings planes and flares. It is the enemy this time and his bombs and bullets put us to earth. In response to ack-ack fire, an enemy plane's machine guns can be seen to flash back at the gun sites. The downward streak of enemy fire presents a dramatic picture against all the tracers racing upward, and the plane's position above the flares is momentarily revealed. In a fanatical effort to knock out one nearby ack-ack gun a plane roars very low overhead – the noise is deafening and we hug Mother Earth as we seldom hugged her before. The flares twinkle out and the rain starts.

Everyone not on duty is sleeping under canvas [tarpaulins], although little protection is gained for all the tarpaulins were pretty well shrapnel-ventilated back at Carpiquet. Blankets and clothing are soaked. Morning reveals last night's enemy planes made an effort to drop supplies to their hard-pressed comrades in the Falaise Gap, but their map reading was poor – the food supplies fell to the nearby Polish Division and the petrol rations landed on 26th Battery's position.

61

A SMOKY HAZE HANGS OVER
FALAISE POCKET

❋

SENT UP TO THE FRONT, NOT TO REPLACE A FOO, BUT TO ADD
another pair of eyes watching for any sign of Jerry attempting to
break through here, you find it difficult to establish an OP and be
sure you are observing hostile territory – or are even looking in the
right direction. It is impossible to obtain a clear picture at any given
hour of the perimeter of the ever-shrinking pocket as the Yanks
press against the southern shoulder, the British push in from the
west, and the Canadians, with elements of the Polish Armoured
Division now in the van, drive south.

And while much of the Polish fighting strength is immobile,
cut-off and surrounded on a nearby hill, there's a report that some
have been able to link up with the Americans at Chambois, southeast of Falaise.*

---

* Two Polish regiments did get through on August 19 to join up with an
American division at Chambois, where they found the enemy in terrible
shape: among piles of their dead from air attacks and artillery bombardments. Still, the Germans continued to prevent reliable communication
between American and Canadian armies until the Canadian 4th Division
tanks linked up with the Poles at Coudehard on August 21. At the same
time, two thousand Poles and seventy tanks, cut off from all ground-
delivered supplies of food and ammunition from the 19th, until rescued

However, the pocket is still open, and with the Tiffies and Spits handicapped by low-lying clouds and the smoky haze hanging over the pocket from the fires smouldering in the misty rain, the guns are now expected to play a major role in shutting down the escape routes.

Eventually you find a place where you are reasonably certain you are overlooking, if not enemy territory, no-man's-land. Your ack, Gunner John Elder, who was with you in your first OP in that hellish orchard back at Eterville in July, is twenty today, August 19.

Of the terrible drama unfolding in the pocket, nothing can be seen here, and your most satisfactory target of the day is found, not way out in the hazy panorama, but in the immediate vicinity of the Royals, who are now securing some bridges over the Dives river against use by the Germans. A Lieut. Ross, recently made responsible for the Royals' reconstituted scout platoon (which through casualties had ceased to exist), turns out to be an old friend from collegiate days. Colin, or "Hefty" as he was known to most everybody in those far-off times, was one of the first to enlist with the Cameron Highlanders in Ottawa on that sunny Sunday that Britain declared war. The Monday sports pages had made much of the fact that a perennial stalwart of the Ottawa Roughriders would be lost to them just as the season was about to start. You'd lost track of him until 1943 in England, when he again briefly donned football togs to help a hastily assembled Canadian Army team beat the American

---

by the Canadian Grenadier Guards on the 21st, held "Maczuga" ("the mace"), as they dubbed their dominant Hill 262, overlooking the main escape route to Vimoutiers, driving back attack after attack by Germans trying to push east out of the pocket, while resisting attacks from the east by a newly arrived 2nd Panzer Division brought down from Abbeville–Amiens area to help keep open the corridor (not to be confused with 2nd SS Panzer Division caught in the pocket). In the drive for Falaise and the closing of the gap the Polish Division suffered 1,450 casualties, 450 of them killed.

Army football team in an exhibition game in Wembley Stadium, London.*

Today, when you come across him, he and his scouts are just back from five days of improvised training for their precarious occupation, and are moving up through your position to take on their first assignment: ensuring a house out in no-man's-land is clear of snipers. While you are glad to see him, you can't help feeling sorry for him, for no infantry subaltern lasts long here – and scout officers least of all.

Since there is a total lack of cover leading up to the house they are supposed to clear, he and his men are delighted when you suggest your guns have a go at it before they risk trying to get across that open ground. And to the obvious relief of all, a few rounds of high explosive poured into the house from a single gun of Able Troop, blowing holes in roof and walls, produces fast results: a white sheet at a window. And when you stop your shelling, half a dozen Jerries march out with their hands up.

However, in your search for troops attempting to escape the pocket, only once do you see anything moving: a distant line of men and horse-drawn wagons, barely visible in the misty rain that falls most of the day. A lack of identifiable landmarks out there makes accurate map-reading difficult, and corrections are needed to bring the shells onto target. By then they have scattered, but you think you discern remnants of wagons and horses among the debris left behind.

Even though it remains cloudy and drizzly throughout the day, Spits and Typhoons continue to fly low-level sorties, strafing, bombing, and rocketing, without having to face any enemy ack-ack as far as you can see. Unquestionably, desperate engagements are taking place, for the sounds of battle can be heard in the southeast and southwest, but along here, there is only a smouldering, ominous stillness. You shell some likely places on the assumption that even

---

*   Other stars of the "Big Four" on the team were: Major George Hees, Toronto Argonauts half-back; Lt.-Col. Denny Whitaker, Hamilton Tigers quarterback; and Major "Huck" Welch, a famous punter.

random shelling at this stage can hardly miss causing havoc, with every road and track in use by some vehicles and desperate foot-soldiers seeking cover in every bush and gully as the British snap at their heels from the west and hourly the pocket shrinks.

After dark you can see fires burning, and all around the horizon guns continue to flash and rumble. By now there are at least three thousand guns within range and firing from three sides into the pocket, and the BBC continues to tell of the awesome slaughter taking place.

It will be weeks, however, before you get any real concept of the extent of the carnage – not until you receive a firsthand account from an officer you'd known at the Brockville Officers' Training Centre, who after the battle is put in charge of a party collecting bodies for burial, combing the gullies and the thickets. He will tell of fields and woods littered with dead, hundreds in field-grey uni-forms, sprawled in black pools of dried blood carpeting the ground, filling in some ditches and lying in layers in gullies. Horrible, bloated things expelling a stench so powerful Air OP pilots retched as they flew low overhead.*

---

* That he did not exaggerate will be born out by General Eisenhower: "Roads, highways and fields were so choked with destroyed equipment and with dead men and animals that passage through the area was extremely difficult. Forty-eight hours after the closing of the gap, I was conducted through it on foot to encounter scenes that could be described only by Danté. It literally was possible to walk for hundreds of yards at a time, stepping on nothing but dead and decaying flesh." (Dwight D. Eisenhower, *Crusade in Europe*, New York: Perma Books, 1952, p. 314). Besides the destruction wrought by shelling, 2nd (British) Tactical Airforce destroyed 210 tanks and 3,000 motorized and horse-drawn trans-port, 115 tanks and 1,500 other vehicles on August 19 alone. Between August 10 and 25, 25,000 Germans died in the pocket and 40,000 were taken prisoner. In Normandy, the Germans lost 400,000 men, of whom 200,000 were taken prisoner, 135,000 between July 25 and August 31.

62

COMRADESHIP

--- ✳ ---

COMRADESHIP – THAT SPECIAL RELATIONSHIP BETWEEN PEOPLE who share awful conditions and whose lives depend on mutual support – will always be a source of fascination. You used to think that it was just another word for friendship, but you know now that the most caring, sharing, selfless comrades can be men you've never met before and who will remain forever nameless, unless you meet them again under more civilized conditions someday, when in all likelihood, you'll not recognize them after the war, for their eyes will be cold and impersonal, not filled with the compassion and understanding you see in them here.

Phrases like "tightly knit unit" and "*esprit de corps*," which you once thought meant something significant, seem to have lost all validity, at least among the infantry. Battalions have been so riddled with casualties that officers, NCOs, and Other Ranks are largely strangers to each other. It can hardly be otherwise when a battalion has to replace 100 per cent of its fighting strength over a period of only a couple of weeks as the Royals have done, absorbing 80 reinforcements (six officers and seventy-four other ranks) on July 20, another 254 on July 28, and a further 282 (two officers and 280 other ranks) on August 3.*

---

* D. J. Goodspeed, *Battle Royal* (Toronto: Royal Regiment of Canada Association, 1962), pp. 425, 432, 435.

And more often than not, these reinforcements are brought up in the middle of the night, introduced to holes already dug for them (two to each slit trench) by officers or NCOs whose faces they can't see, and told to stay in those isolated, separated holes regardless of what happens. Some will be wounded and shipped back down to hospital never having had a chance to make an impression on anyone in the whole battalion, let alone nurture friendships. And some will die right there in their first trench, and later be buried by a padre who never had an opportunity to look upon their living faces.

When the Royals were on Verrières Ridge, nine reinforcements were brought up one night after dark to Jack Stothers' platoon and placed in previously prepared trenches. By dawn all were lying dead in the wheat. Stothers blamed this tragedy on the reinforcements' lack of training and discipline; choosing not to follow his orders to stay in those holes until dawn, regardless of what happened. When the Germans infiltrated between their positions and spewed tracers around, giving the impression the platoon was overrun, they left their holes to escape and were promptly cut down by other Royals following orders to shoot anything moving above ground.

While the sense of comradeship in the front line is very real, particularly during the more hellish periods, it tends to be on a spiritual level of mutual support, rather than social, for there is little opportunity, and even less inclination, for socializing. Just having to remain constantly alert while on duty, forever preoccupied with matters of survival, in an inexplicable way absorbs all the time left between those brief periods of intense activity that periodically arise. And off duty, sleep takes priority over everything else. All normal interests tend to be held in suspension by these overpowering preoccupations. And so men occupying slit trenches only thirty feet apart for days on end can remain total strangers, even as they remain committed to dying for each other if necessary.

During the long period of training in England, there was so little contact between artillery and infantry, it could hardly be said that they had any relationship, good or bad. Even on big training schemes, like Spartan, involving all the various branches of service, gunners were never really concerned whether the infantry was theoretically successful or defeated in their "attacks." And when on rare occasions they did come in contact with the infantry marching along the verges of a road, the footsloggers, jealous of the gunners riding by in their gun tractors and trucks, would hoot at them in derision.

But since coming into action, a very special relationship has developed between gunners and infantry. The gunners, totally involved and following every minute of the terrible battles that involve the infantry and tanks they're supporting, have come to hold front-line soldiers in awe. At the same time the gunners have won the profound gratitude and respect of surviving veteran infantrymen, who have seen how effective the guns can be in breaking up counter-attacks and softening up the enemy before they attack.

And this special relationship is sometimes expressed in a most touching way:

A company of the Royals has broken off to bivouac in a barn for a couple of hours, to sleep inside out of the rain before moving forward again. The 4th Field FOO and crew attached to the company, having had to make a detour for rations and petrol back along the line of march, arrive at the barn after everybody has settled down, and every inch of floor space is covered by prone infantrymen, their packs, and their weapons. The artillerymen stand hesitatingly at the door as they swing the weak beam of a lamp-electric over the clutter of sleeping forms and their equipment.

Always now, regardless of circumstances, gunners tend to show tremendous respect for the infantry, and they are especially con-scious of not wanting to disturb their rest this night, knowing how far they have walked and how desperately tired they must be. But as they turn to go out, they are spotted by a hoarse-voiced sergeant, who calls out from the darkness: "The FOO and his boys need some room to rest, too, lads."

That's all he says. It's not an order. It's only an appeal to decency and generosity, but it works wonders. There's a general shifting of the whole floor of bodies. Many are already asleep, but their neighbours nudge them awake, explaining, "The arty guys need some room." There's no grumbling, no discussion, only a low murmur now and then. And, miraculously, enough room appears on the floor beside the door that four members of a 4th Field carrier crew can lie down and stretch out in dry comfort, while the rain lashes the barn roof.

At dawn, as the company is preparing to move on, the French farmer appears with a pail of steaming ersatz coffee and a mug to portion it out to the yawning men. A truly good-natured man, it would seem, for last evening (according to Company Commander Capt. Jack Stothers), while you were back picking up rations, these same Royals uncovered and consumed the man's entire stock of *prime vieux* Calvados, which he'd been able to keep hidden from the Germans throughout the occupation, dug-in in the barnyard, a bottle here and a bottle there, their corks just below the surface of the earth. When Stothers had broken off the weary men to bed down in the barn, and they were dragging their feet across the yard, one of them stumbled over something in the ground. Curious, the man had bent down to see what had tripped him, and poking around discovered it was the neck of a bottle. Of course when a full bottle was pulled out and brushed off, everyone began to examine the ground and dig around. And in minutes a dozen bottles were raised and being consumed when the farmer appeared. Taking in the scene, he grabbed his head, exclaiming in awe: "*Mon Dieu! Les Boches sont ici depuis quatre ans et ils n'ont jamais trouvé mon Calvados. Les Canadiens arrivent et dix minutes plus tard, ils ont trouvé toutes mes bouteilles!*" (My God! The Germans were here for four years, and they never found my Calvados. The Canadians are here ten minutes and they have every bottle!)

Now the smiling man is serving coffee to the hung-over looters – albeit ersatz, and so awful-tasting it may be a form of revenge.

Back at the guns Bombardier Hossack's diary will record:

Ordered to move on the morning of August 20, we drive along vehicle-littered roads in teeming rain to a large apple orchard. . . . Few targets are called for. The nearest town, Grand Mesnil, is almost totally destroyed. Refugees walk the roads, and a small shelter nearby houses 24 French people. They have no sanitation and human excrement is all around. "No lights" [meaning not even the faintest glow from the tiny holes in blacked-out head-lights] is again the order as we move on the night of August 20–21. The objective is Vimoutiers. The drivers do a remarkable job of nursing their vehicles along in the "pea soup" fog. The roads are busy with two-way traffic and the convoy is split up several times as lead vehicles speed up, make wrong turns and fail to see dimly lighted route signs.

For some reason Hossack chooses not to record a fog-related incident involving Sgt. Ernie Offord, about which everyone is still talking when you return from the infantry. It seems that when the guns were coming in here last night in the rain and dark, the sergeants were unaware that scattered about the fog-enshrouded field were unburied cows that had been dead for some time – their legs held up in the air by bellies hugely distended to the point of almost bursting. And when Offord, intending to guide his gun to its marker, jumped down from the high door of his quad, he landed squarely on one of those cow bellies, bursting it and almost disappearing inside the gruesome cavity.

Enveloped by its horrible contents and gagging on its revolting gases, the poor man struggled free and, screaming, started off on a crazed run into the fog and dark. As soon as his comrades were able to grasp what had happened, they piled out of the quad and set out in pursuit, fearing he might kill himself running blindly into a tree or some other obstacle. When, after a bizarre chase through the foggy night, they were able to locate and capture him, they conducted him to the farmyard pump, where they washed him clean and settled him down.

For such a thing to happen to anyone would have been shocking, but for it to happen to Offord – the epitome of good grooming and personal hygiene, always the best turned-out soldier in the battery if not the whole Regiment – seems particularly horrifying. Your heart aches for him when you seek him out to see how he is getting on. Obviously he's very depressed. But in the bright light of morning, nothing is ever so bad as the night before, and he manages a wry grin. And you honestly feel that what is now bothering him most is that he looks as crummy and unkempt as everybody else, in his newly washed-and-dried battledress, a bit shrunken and a mass of wrinkles.

63

BOULEVARD OF BROKEN DREAMS

---------------- ✳ ----------------

OFFICIALLY THE FALAISE POCKET WAS CLOSED TWO DAYS AGO, on August 19, when units of the Canadian Army reputedly linked up with the Americans at Chambois. However, groups of determined Germans, riding on tanks or in half-tracks, or moving with a single self-propelled gun, are still roaming just outside the pocket – either escapees from the trap or holdovers from 15th Army units rushed down here from the Calais area to help keep escape routes open. Whoever they are, they may be encountered in varying numbers on any road leading east. To inhibit their escape to the Seine, 2nd Division units are sent wheeling east on August 21, crossing behind the last bitter struggle by 4th Division and the Polish Division to seal off the pocket about Chambois, Trun, and St. Lambert.*

That night 4th Field recce parties, laying out gun positions within a mile of Vimoutiers to support the infantry engaged in shutting off the Trun–Vimoutiers–Orbec road, the main German

---

* It's at St. Lambert-sur-Dives, during three days (August 19–21) of fierce fighting to contain Germans desperate to escape the Falaise pocket, that Major David Currie, South Alberta Regiment, an armoured recce regiment of 4th Armoured Division, won the V.C.

escape route, begin to have serious doubts as to who is in possession of what. Sporadic bursts of Schmeisser fire near the lonely positions keep them alert and standing-to most of the night, until the guns move up.

And when the Regiment moves again at midday the next day, it is along a sunken road that only a short time before was plugged solid with smashed German vehicles, dead horses, and dead men. Bulldozers have been used very recently to push everything helter-skelter up onto the banks on both sides of the road, and some wagons and motor vehicles still smoke and smoulder and flame up as you pass through mile after mile of awesome refuse. All along there are dead horses, torn and bloody, still harnessed to wagons with broken wheels, for the long column of transport, caught in this deeply sunken road and unable to scatter from the fighter-bombers, was largely horsedrawn.

Still amongst the horses are broken half-tracks, self-propelled guns, towed guns, staff cars, civilian cars, lorries, and at least two Red Cross ambulances overturned at the roadside. Bodies of men are everywhere, some spilling out of vehicles, and some half-covered with refuse as though tossed onto a garbage dump. And over all is the stench of death.

Passage along the road, which, as you proceed, looks increasingly like a refuse-strewn trench, is very slow, with drivers having to thread their way between derelict vehicles. And so you are able to take in every detail of a scene the like of which you never expected to encounter and never expect to see again, except in a nightmare: a pageant of destruction beyond anything imagined by the most extravagant film director looking for a way to make still another statement against war. There is something reminiscent of the imagery of Napoleon's retreat from Moscow here, the same suggestion of retribution you always sensed in paintings and films depicting the slow death of *la Grande Armée* on its way home. When someone suggests the name Boulevard of Broken Dreams for this corridor of death, it seems entirely suitable – the words "of world conquest" being implied, of course.*

---

*   Among the troops shredded in the pocket were remnants of the 12th SS "Hitlerjugend" Panzer Division, marked men from the day after D-Day, when they rolled into battle so arrogantly and then began killing unarmed 3rd Canadian Division prisoners in their frustration at not being able to drive the Canadians back into the sea, even conducting a mass murder in a walled garden of the Abbaye d'Ardenne, where SS Standartenführer Kurt Meyer had his brigade headquarters. After Falaise, 12th SS could muster only ten tanks, no guns, and only three hundred of the twenty thousand young fanatics with which it had begun the Normandy campaign. Likewise 2nd SS "Das Reich" Panzer Division had earned its destruction without mercy by its action on June 10 on the way up from southern France at Oradour-sur-Glane, fourteen miles north-west of Limoges, where it shot all the men of the village after herding them into six barns, and murdered four hundred women and children in the church, in reprisal for the disappearance of the colonel of the 4th SS Grenadier Regiment. After Falaise they counted only 450 men and fifteen tanks.

State of Panzer Divisions as Reported by Army Group B, August 22–23.
2nd Panzer: 1 infantry battalion, no tanks
21st Panzer: 4 weak infantry battalions, 10 tanks
116 Panzer: 1 infantry battalion, 12 tanks, 2 batteries guns
1st SS Panzer: weak infantry elements, no tanks, no artillery
2nd SS Panzer: 450 men, 15 tanks, 6 guns
9th SS Panzer: 460 men, 25 tanks, no guns
10th SS Panzer: 4 weak infantry battalions, no tanks, no artillery
12th SS Panzer: 300 men, 10 tanks, no artillery
(Panzer Lehr and 9th Panzer were wiped out by American Operation Cobra and in German attacks at Mortain.)

[The foregoing statistics are from page 101 of Report No. 65, Historical Section (G.S.) Canadian Army Headquarters, Dept. of National Defence, Dec. 23, 1953, p. 101.]

64

4TH FIELD SUFFERS WORST
ONE–DAY CASUALTIES

* * *

※

* * *

NEXT DAY, ON AUGUST 23, THE THRUST FOR 2ND DIVISION IS north towards Thiberville, at the junction of the Lisieux–Rouen highway and the road leading up from Vimoutiers, both main escape routes for the Germans. This, of course, means the infantry and supporting artillery units start cutting across other less distinguished but equally useful German escape routes leading northeast to Elbeuf and the Seine. Thus, even as FOOs with 4th Division and the Polish Division – left to contain the Germans in the pocket – are firing concentrations south and west on desperate groups of Germans trying even in daylight to probe the perimeter for weak spots, FOOs with 2nd and 3rd Divisions, moving away from the pocket, are firing north and east on Germans heading for the Seine.

Three or four German half-tracks or tanks can roar across a road right in front of an Allied convoy without a shot being fired. Or they can cut through the middle of an infantry column with their machine guns spewing fire, leaving artillery FOOs and anti-tank gunners (their anti-tank guns rolling along limbered up) mentally pawing the air in frustration.

They can join the end of a convoy at night by mistake, or on purpose as a means of camouflage to get them as far as possible towards the Seine before being discovered, and leave again without firing a shot, as though they are out of ammunition. Or they can use up the last of their ammunition shooting up the rear vehicles in the column as they wheel about and disappear up a side road.

The Royals experience all these variations in the frantic but determined withdrawal tactics of parties of Germans during two or three confusing days and nights when they themselves are almost continually on the move, first east towards Orbec and then north towards Lisieux. In fact during this one day, August 23, they have three or four variations in separate encounters, including one with remnants of 1st SS.*

The most serious encounter occurs in the black of night during a heavy rain when the battalion intelligence officer (Lieut. R. E. C. McCaul) and three ORs are killed by fire from two half-tracks mounting ack-ack guns that come up against the rear of the regimental column, just when the Royals are in the process of debussing from troop carriers. When the German half-tracks are taken on in a shootout by a platoon of Toronto Scottish machine gunners riding at the rear of the column, they turn their headlights full on, wheel around, and go tearing back and up a side road.

This grim incident of flashing and rattling confusion occurs just after four German tanks suddenly burst through the column and roar across the road at full speed with guns blazing, causing at least four casualties, and just before four more tanks appear at the rear of the column, but leave without firing a shot – out of ammunition.

Earlier, while still daylight, at a crossroads in a wooded area,

---

* General Kurt Meyer, who escapes the pocket by forcing a French civilian to guide him, joins what is left of 1st SS Panzer Corps on August 20, and is saddened by the state of his beloved Liebstandarte: "I couldn't help the tears from running down my face. Thousands of my comrades lay dead in the Norman earth.... Our expulsion proves that west of Seine there remains no stable front." (Tony Foster, *Meeting of Generals* [Agincourt: Methuen, 1986], pp. 397–98.) Meeting up with Field Marshal Model at Rouen he is put in charge of an improvised fighting group to delay the Allies at Elbeuf and in the Forêt de la Londe.

where Battalion tac headquarters' vehicles halted briefly to allow a reconnaissance to be carried out along the forest tracks, three German tanks came up a side road so casually they appeared to believe they were joining friends. And they might have driven right through the men and vehicles clustered around a house at the cross-roads, without anyone realizing they were German, if one of them, standing up in the turret of his tank, hadn't shouted out in German a warning to the other two when he discovered they had joined an Allied column.

Gunner Knox, the sixteen-year-old Baker Troop signaller, was standing out in the road in front of the house, "chewing the fat" with buddies Purvis Vickers (the driver) and Lorne Garrow (the other wireless operator) when the three tanks pulled up next him, and he heard a voice yell, "*Engländer! Engländer!*"

When we all look up and see the cross on the side of that tank, we get the hell out of there, but fast. I make it to the other side of the building, but Garrow and Vickers dive under the carrier.

As the German tanks roar off up the road, the last one opens up with his machine gun. Vickers is killed and Garrow is wounded in the head.

Next day we're in a field supporting the infantry, and there are four of our tanks about us. Suddenly they start getting picked off, one after another. As each tank is hit, the crew bails out and runs for cover. But when one takes fire it produces the most shocking sight I've seen so far. A man in the turret is on fire, and when he rolls out over the top of the turret and falls on the ground, both his feet are gone.

This really has an effect on me – makes me ask myself: Why am I here? I could go home; I only have to go to someone and confess I am still three years under the legal age. But then there is no way I could do that. I have a duty. . . . I have to see this thing out. And when I hear Smitty, a Royals' stretcher-bearer, giving the trooper first aid while waiting for an ambulance to come to take him out, assuring him he will make it all right because the burning cauterized the stumps of his legs preventing bleeding, I feel somewhat better. Smitty is a wonderful guy. They say it isn't beyond him to go ahead and talk to the Germans to see if they have any wounded they want taken care of.*

Meanwhile the guns, pointed at Orbec and deployed at the village of Friardel near its substantial church, come under the worst shelling since Carpiquet. Last night 6th Field guns on the left flank were shelled and fifteen were wounded. And now, at 2:00 P.M., shells begin to arrive on 4th Field gun positions and wagon lines, and before it's over, the Regiment suffers twenty-two serious casualties, two of them fatal.

Dead are Gunners Patrick J. K. Harty and Charles Kolesar. Among the wounded are Lieut. John Gerby and Easy Troop Sgt.-Maj. Jim Hart.

The shelling is so accurate everyone is convinced they are under observation. But from where, no one can guess. The only spot an observer could get an overview of fields obscured by hedgerows and woods is in the church now in the possession of 26th Battery, with their battery command post in the house of the *curé*. Still the accuracy is unnerving – three vehicles, including the petrol truck, are immediately set ablaze, sending up pillars of black smoke and attracting even more shells. And before the other vehicles can be moved, thirty-two tires are slashed by shell fragments.

Memories of such hours must always be scanty, limited to what eyes can see when blurred by anxiety bordering on terror, particularly when your face is only a few inches above the earth, buried in a thick bed of marigolds alongside some hollyhocks at the front door of a little farmhouse. For the rest of your life, you know that every time you catch a whiff of the pungent odour of marigolds, a confusing blur of what was August 23, 1944, will return: those first

---

* Author interview.

whacking airbursts leaving black puffs over the trees you had thought were hiding your guns; the ripping geysers of earth spouting among the tombstones of the churchyard; the burning vehicles sending up pillars of smoke and attracting even heavier shelling; the uncanny accuracy with which the enemy's shells follow the guns and wagon lines as you move in haste to new positions; and, when finally it grows quiet, the urgent needs of the wounded and dying.

PART EIGHT: AUGUST 24-SEPTEMBER 5

Being Welcomed
as Liberators

65

YOUR ADVANCE PARTY
LIBERATES BOISNEY

※

AS 2ND DIVISION TURNS NORTH TOWARDS LISIEUX, THEN EAST towards Rouen, there is clearly no line of defence. Groups of enemy, some of them small and others large and strongly supported by guns and tanks – either troops brought down from Calais to hold open the gap, or units that escaped before the gap was closed off – are competing for all roads leading to the Seine.

Today you liberate the crossroads village of Boisney, on the main highway from Lisieux to Rouen, some five miles in advance of all Allied troops. This happens when you are given an incorrect map reference for the rendezvous of recce parties and run out of radio range before they get around to sending out a correction. The fifteen-mile stretch of highway from Lisieux to Boisney is a white stretch of concrete as straight as an arrow, inviting you to find out just how fast a five-ton armoured scout car can go. Never before have you had such an opportunity, and you tell Bracken, your driver, to push it to the limit. It takes miles to get the sluggish vehicle up to a shuddering sixty miles an hour. By then you have to start slowing Bracken down, for there is the crossroads rushing at you.

Parking directly opposite the side door of the crossroads café, you wait. Not a soul is in sight. Peculiar, you think. But then your party had made a special effort to pack up and leave in a hurry so as to be first at the rendezvous. Just to make sure you didn't made a mistake, you check your decoding of the map reference. It is correct, and this crossroads is unmistakable. You ask the signaller to get RHQ on the blower, but he is unable to raise them or anybody else.

This being the first intact, operating café you've come across in Normandy, Dunsmore thinks a cool beer would go down well. But when he tries the door, it is locked. He bangs on it, but there is no response. Convinced that the publican, a Monsieur Morin according to the sign, is within, he continues to bang on the door. Finally you see the lace curtain move slightly, and immediately a bolt is pulled, the door opens, and a hearty, middleaged man flings himself out the door at Dunsmore, embracing him and yelling, "*Bienvenue, Tommy! Bienvenue, Tommy!*"

"Non-non! Canadien, dammit!" protests Dunsmore.

"*Canadiens! Canadiens!*" Monsieur Morin repeats in rapturous joy, as he hugs each of you and kisses you on both cheeks as one by one you pile out of the scout car. Then he calls to his son, who has just appeared, to go into the backyard and dig up the special bottle of Calvados hidden from the Germans for this day.

Once the bottle is uncorked, the son runs off up the street to ring the church bell and his father starts pouring out little glasses of the amber liquor. Toasts are drunk to France, to Canada, to Britain, to the United States, to *soldats Canadiens*, to Tommies, to Yankees, to sailors, to airmen, to de Gaulle, to Churchill, to Roosevelt, to Stalin. By now the church bell is ringing madly, and people are swarming into the street.

Someone reports that the Germans are up in trees down the road, but no one takes this seriously. You are getting worried, though, that no one else from 4th Field has shown up. Then, far back down the road along which you came half an hour ago, you spot a recce car creeping this way, the head of its commander, who has field-glasses to his eyes, barely visible above the turret. Leaving the crowd now growing in front of the café, you walk out to the centre of the crossroads and beckon him on. As he comes rolling in, now standing erect in the turret, he can hardly wait to ask what the hell you are doing miles in front of everybody, and whether there are any Germans around here. You tell him that a Frenchman claims they are just down the road a bit. Has he seen any vehicles with unit sign "42" on them back there along the road anywhere? He says about five miles back there is a "42" arrow pointing north along a side road.

When you get back to the guns, deployed in a field off a road parallel to the main highway, but several miles north of it, the battery is in a ferment of excitement. One gunner from each troop has been chosen to accept an incredible invitation from a farmer living in a house some distance across the fields. According to your troop leader, Bob Grout, the ecstatic farmer, his eyes shining with emotion, had come across the fields carrying ten gallons of fresh milk, apologizing for such *"une expression chetif"* of his family's profound gratitude to their liberators. Though the fresh milk was tremendously welcome, and his pails were speedily emptied into the gunners' cups, the farmer continued to apologize, and just before leaving – obviously convinced his gesture had been entirely inadequate – asked Sgt.-Maj. Mann to select "two worthy soldiers to honour his home by sleeping with his two daughters."

Grout assures you the chosen ones' sergeants have accepted responsibility for seeing they are aboard their quads if the battery has to make a sudden move during the night.

Now surrounded by most of the troop as he shaves, washes, and combs, Able Troop's selectee is besieged with offers of aftershave lotion and ribald advice.

Believing there may be a gross misunderstanding of the farmer's intent due to language difficulties, you quietly warn Able Troop's ambassador, as he leaves, to proceed with caution.

Days later, when he chooses to give you a report, he will tell you that there was no mistake – though at first he thought there had been, when, after dinner, the family sat around chatting. But when bedtime came, he and his pal were escorted upstairs with their respective girls and shown to their bedrooms by the mother, carrying lamps.

While this form of gratitude, expressed with the blessing of all members of a family, must certainly be rare, if not totally unique, the Regiment becomes aware over the next few days of a remarkable change in the reception people along the way are giving the passing troops. Now that you are outside the areas of severe destruction, where people, if seen at all, were grim refigees totally concerned with survival, the residents of untouched villages and unscarred farms of green fields and live cattle, are exuberant in their welcome as the guns roll by.

When one day you try to set down a record of these days, there's a kaleidoscope of images: "madly cheering French civilians lining the streets of villages gay with tricolours as at Thiberville . . . the refreshing green, rich farmland and apple orchards . . . the barrels of apple cider . . . tomatoes, apples, and masses of flowers pressed on the vehicles . . . weak, ersatz coffee, sometimes laced with all-powerful Calvados and cognac . . . urchins begging, '*cigarette pour papa — chocolate pour mama*' . . . the freedom-fighting Maquis with red, white, and blue arm bands and the inevitable Mauser rifles slung over their shoulders . . . laughing women yelling '*Merci Canadiens*' . . . and church bells ringing . . ."

These are exciting days. The Germans seldom are seen in strength, and the infantry are moving as fast as possible, using whatever transport available, forcing the guns to make up to four moves in a twenty-four-hour period. The result is that small groups of Germans are left in buildings and woods, and it is no longer unusual to see a gunner marching three or four bedraggled Germans, hands clasped behind their heads, out of a field being laid out for a gun position by an advance party.

So briefly are the guns in position in most spots, that digging is being restricted to personal slit trenches, and very infrequently are these needed. And it's a good thing, for you no longer carry the slabs of corrugated iron taken from the hangars at Carpiquet aerodrome for the roofs of command posts. Before setting out on this "chase" to the Seine, the Regiment was ordered on August 19 to get rid of all excess baggage, and reluctantly those old, rusty, mud-caked friends, which had held roofs of protective earth over some eleven successive dugouts, were abandoned.

66

SHOWERS OF STEEL SHARDS
IN FOREST

✳

FORÊT DE LA LONDE, TEN KILOMETRES LONG AND FOUR WIDE AT
its widest part, lies next to the west bank of the Seine, which snakes
its way with countless horseshoe bends past Rouen on its way to the
sea, and provides dense cover from the air for Germans assembled in
there waiting to be rafted over the river after dark. From the fierce
fire the RHLI and the Essex attract at railway underpasses in the
forest, it is clear that the Germans intend to retain command of
forest and hills (some with sides of clifflike steepness) until they get
all they can over the river.*

Not only have they placed guns and mortars and machine guns at
strategic points, covering railway underpasses and forest openings,

---

* According to German generals quoted by Chester Wilmot in *The
Struggle for Europe* (London: Collins, 1952), in terms of equipment lost or
abandoned, the rearguard action from Falaise to the Seine was a disaster
for them almost as bad as the Falaise pocket was in terms of casualties.
Field Marshal Model, German Commander in Chief West, reporting to
Hitler on August 29, when the last of his troops were crossing the Seine,
the average strength of panzer divisions was "five to ten tanks each." Of
the twenty-three divisions in Normandy, seven by then had been wiped
out completely; and of the other sixteen, only enough to man four divisions got back over the Seine, "for the most part equipped with nothing
more than small arms."

but any attempt to take command of the high hills – as the Royals do at one point – is made costly by guns firing from across the Seine. These could be silenced by 2nd Division guns, deployed since early morning on August 27 halfway between Bourg-theroulde and Elbeuf (4th Field near St. Ouen du Tilleuil), but firing across the Seine is banned. The reason: it might conflict with crossings by 3rd Division upstream. (When the leading Royals were approaching the forest via Elbeuf at 3:00 A.M., they met up with an American officer in a recce car, and later the marching troops were met by a company of Winnipeg Rifles under Capt. Cliff Chadderton.)

Still, the guns make things wretched for the Germans in the forest, with 4th Field alone firing seven thousand rounds during the two days and nights the Germans hold out. When there is no observed fire being called for by FOOs buried deep in the forest without any field of observation, either the major at Battalion or the colonel at Brigade lays on fire on likely spots. And each night the seventy-two field guns of the division fire a slow but long harassing-fire plan to make things miserable for the Germans moving through the forest to the riverbank.*

Just how miserable, the Canadian infantry and their supporting artillery carrier crews can now readily testify. All have come to dread the arrival of German shells and mortar bombs anywhere near them in the forest, for they detonate in the trees overhead with horrible, resounding airbursts that shower the forest floor with branches and steel shards that can maim and kill.

---

* According to Gen. Blumentritt, Model's chief of staff, of the 2,300 tanks and self-propelled guns committed to Normandy "only 100 to 120 were brought back across the Seine." While they fought a courageous rearguard action and maintained some sixty ferries for varying periods between Elbeuf and the sea, many were merely rafts of cider barrels lashed together or logs cut from trees in the forest. And while they got men across, nearly all their guns, tanks, and half-tracks had to be left behind.

And while the combination of air attacks and shelling account for a great many German vehicles along the riverbank, reminiscent of the Falaise gap, and allow the enemy no peace as the infantry persists in trying to clear the forest, the German rearguards hold out until they decide no more men and equipment can cross the river. Their last effort is to threaten a counter-attack before fading away. Where to, no one quite knows or cares; the relief that the battle is over is universal.

The three armoured divisions of the British 30th Corps are now over the Seine at Vernon, twenty-five miles further upstream towards Paris, and about to drive to the Somme, and then on to Brussels and Antwerp, with the same dash as has been displayed by Patton's armour when unopposed. Canadian 3rd Division is firmly over the Seine and beginning to occupy Rouen abandoned by the Germans. And now beckoning is Dieppe, suggested as a suitable objective for 2nd Division by Montgomery.

Only three members of 4th Field carrier crews were casualties in the forest (including Gunner C. S. "Sid" Williams, a handsome young man of joyous temperament, who will lose a leg at the thigh). But the infantry has taken a bloody nose, which, after the severe casualties on the road to Falaise, none of the battalions of 2nd Division could afford – the Royals least of all.

By the night of August 29, when they march back to a concentration area where they can get a good night's rest after their exhausting experience of the previous few days, they have lost twelve officers and 137 men – thirty of them killed.

Not since the Dieppe Raid has the fighting strength of the Royals been so low. With the loss of so many of their experienced officers, including three company commanders and all their second-in-command captains, the battalion is in serious condition. The senior officers hold a meeting to decide whether four skeleton companies should be maintained and reinforced, or one strong company formed of what is left until reinforcements become available to build up new companies. It is decided to retain the four-company structure, although none can muster a full platoon. Major Ralph Young, the acting commanding officer, later explains the reasoning behind the decision: "In the end it is up to me. I have to decide if we are to cut the battalion down to one or two companies. If we do this, I believe we'll be withdrawn from the line and never go back in again – we'll be written off. So we retain four companies, though we have only eighteen men in one of them and none have the personnel to form a platoon."*

The Royals are now twelve officers and 280 other ranks short of their fighting establishment, and these shortages are mostly in the rifle companies. Officers, who only weeks ago were untested lieutenants, now command companies. And there is a serious shortage of NCOs. After the Dieppe disaster, the battalion had nearly two years to rebuild a unit. Now it must be rebuilt on the march, between attacks. And the Royals have much in common with other Canadian battalions that have been closing on the Seine.†

---

* Author interview.
† Of 20,178 Canadian casualties in Normandy (5,401 fatal), including 1,603 officers (461 fatal), suffered by the three Canadian divisions and the armoured brigade, between June 6 and August 31, the two infantry divisions (2nd and 3rd) accounted for 78 per cent: 7,869 dead, wounded, or missing per division, the highest casualty rate in all fifteen divisions in 21st Army Group. Of the 7,869 casualties per division, 5,980 or 76 per cent were infantry. The magnitude of this reduction in the fighting power of each division can only be fully understood when it is recognized that the 5,980 infantry casualties per division occurred among a fighting establishment of only 4,590 per division. And among Canadian officers, the casualty rate was even worse: 1,603 (461 fatal), the two infantry divisions averaging 625 officer casualties per division, 475 of them among the fighting establishment of only 270 infantry officers per division (30 × 9 battalions), producing a casualty rate in only two and a half months of 176 per cent. (Casualty records, National Archives of Canada, RG24 Vol. 18,502, File 133.009 (D1); and tables in *Memoirs of Montgomery of Alamein* (Cleveland: World Publishing, 1958), pp. 268-69.)

67

NOW THEY'LL NEVER HAVE
THEIR HONEYMOON

---- ❋ ----

IT IS LATE AT NIGHT WHEN LEN HARVEY SEEKS YOU OUT IN A
large, cavelike storage bunker the Germans had dug into the side of
a hill, protected from the weather by a piece of tarpaulin hanging as
a blackout curtain across its mouth, to tell you Jack Cameron is
dead.

Knowing the news will hit you as hard as it hit him, Len shoves a
partially consumed crock of cognac into your hands. And for a
long, long time you and he hold a kind of a wake for your old
buddy of 26th Battery. He says Jack was killed three days ago, on
August 26, while fooing with the Essex Scottish as they were
moving up to start clearing the Forêt de la Londe. A mortar bomb
set fire to the gas tank of a vehicle under which he'd sought shelter.

The image of it rocks you rotten. Big, smiling Jack was the first
officer of 4th Field you met on arrival at the Regiment back in
1942. And all that fall and throughout the winter of 1943, when
you weren't out on training schemes, you, he, and Harvey shared an
unheated bedroom on the ground floor of a house used as the 26th
Battery officers' mess, halfway between Barnham Junction and the
Labour in Vain pub at the next crossroads.

Obviously all your secret reservations about never allowing
yourself to become emotionally connected with any comrade,
because his death might be too hard to take, never worked in his

case – couldn't possibly work with such a loveable guy, always smiling, always glad to see you, ever the patient, tolerant, helpful friend.

Every day, without fail, he wrote to his wife, with whom he shared only one day of married life before leaving Canada three years ago. And like you and every other married man over here, he'd promised himself a glorious honeymoon of infinite length, when the war was over.

Your heart aches for that poor girl in Canada, who'll continue to get his letters long after she's received a telegram from Defence Headquarters – until the letters stop forever.

Each time you learn of the death of a fellow officer, sadness and regret sweep through you, and if you knew him well, there is a great sense of loss. But you know you must not dwell on it, that in fact it is unhealthy to dwell on it, so you put it out of your mind as soon as you can. And if you were to be totally honest, you would have to confess that this is not really difficult, for each time it happens, you are profoundly thankful it wasn't you. There are no such thoughts, however, on hearing the news of Jack.

It is more like the death of a family member – most probably because you are with Len, who shares so many memories involving the three of you. And it is Len, using the strange vernacular of the day, who best expresses what you are both feeling: "Son of a bitch! Of all the guys who should never have bought it. . . . This one really hurts."

To Sammy Grange, "It was a terrible blow. Within a month of taking over Fox Troop from me, he was dead. I found this very hard. Of all the fellows in the Regiment, I think he was the one I was most fond of. He was just a prince of a fellow – thoroughly nice."

And one of the finest tributes an officer could ever hope to earn will appear in Sgt. Hunt's diary: "The news has a depressing effect on all of us. Few men hold so even-handedly the respect and affection that were his. An officer and a gentleman in the best Canadian sense of the words, Capt. Cameron is a very real loss to the battery."

As you are going to sleep, you find yourself recalling a November 11 back in the early thirties that fell on a Sunday, allowing schoolchildren to attend the ceremony at the cenotaph. Watching the veterans march by, you hadn't been favourably impressed by their appearance. They looked not at all like the warriors you imagined – many of them looked truly seedy and down at heel. Of course most of the poor devils were unemployed. Tonight you solemnly vow that if you get back to Canada, you will never miss a Remembrance Day ceremony as long as you live.

Back at the guns in the morning, you find life "laughing onward." Elder's pals are still ragging him about the fix he was in a couple of days ago, just north of Brionne, when the battery command post "Y" vehicle, on an advance party, ran over a mine. The vehicle's big, heavy spare tire pitched up and came down over his shoulders, pinning his arms and immobilizing him in the back of the car while everybody else piled out in a rush to get away, expecting the punctured gas tank to catch fire and the whole thing to go up in flames. (Fortunately it didn't.)

Obviously Elder thinks it all very unfunny, remembering hearing his pals talking from a safe distance, as he waited for someone to come back and release him:

"We sure were lucky! Seems only Elder has bought it."

68

A LESSON IN CHARITY

✳

IT IS AUGUST 31, AND THE SUN IS ABOUT TO SET ON A REALLY remarkable day. You've just planted your gun markers to show where the guns will drop their platforms when they arrive, and have given the acks on the advance party permission to go over to a distant farmhouse to capture some Germans who, according to the farmer who visited Bombardier Morty Hughes on Baker Troop position, "want to give themselves up."

Now you look around for a place to relax. There isn't much choice. Between your gun flags and Baker Troop's is a huge, perfectly round crater, about thirty feet across and fifteen feet deep, excavated by a wayward buzz bomb that failed to make it even to the English Channel let alone its ultimate target of the London docks. You try sitting on the edge of the crater with your feet hanging down, contemplating the twisted remnants of its ram-jet engine rusting in the bottom of the conical hole. But there is nothing to lean against, and you want to catch forty winks before the guns arrive, so you move away to sit with your back against one of the stooks of grain that dot this very large stubble field.

As you lean back into the rustling dry sheaves, the dust you stir up has a homely, earthy, granary smell that is so comforting in its association with more peaceful days in other quiet fields glowing yellow from the dazzling rays of a setting sun. Even before the little scouting party of acks has disappeared up the lane leading to the farmhouse hidden in a clump of trees some five hundred yards away, you are dozing off.

You hope you were right in approving their enterprise, and that they took seriously your parting admonition to be careful and not get themselves shot up.

There's been a strange quality about this whole day, starting with the unusual early-morning stillness that lay over the whole front as the guns were being limbered up back on the south bank of the Seine at St. Ouen de Telleuil. This was in deep contrast to the previous three days of incessant, reverberating roars in the Forêt de la Londe aroused either by the enemy's mortars and guns or those of 2nd Division.

It seemed evident that the last of the enemy crossed the river during the night, when shortly after dawn recce parties were called and the order came to limber up and prepare to move to a new position across the Seine from Elbeuf, southeast of Rouen. But no sooner were the guns and limbers hooked up to the quads, ready to move off, than a target came down.

Quads wheeled the guns around back into the field, trails were dropped, and for the first time since coming to France, they were brought into action and put on line by the old "crash action" method, allowing them to respond quickly with "fire for effect." In fact the guns engaged two targets, called for by a FOO in rapid succession, each involving a respectable scale of forty-five rounds per gun, said to be required to break up a counter-attack. But it was clearly only a skirmish with a pocket of Germans still attempting to make it to the river, for no sooner had the Regiment fired off the second target, than orders came to cease fire and limber up.

By 6:30 A.M. all batteries were out on the road, moving briskly along in regimental convoy, rolling over the crest of a high hill so openly and boldly it felt as though you might take off into the blue morning sky, with the beautiful, sunlit valley of the Seine spread out below, its shining silver waters snaking and winding away to the left in search of the sea.

This was all in great contrast to the furtive tactics required of carrier crews with the infantry, tormented day and night by airbursts among the trees of Forêt de la Londe, and the cautious, pinched-up, frequently stalled movements of the guns since Falaise – to be associated forever by the gunners with the names Friardel, Orbec, Livarot, and Elbeuf. There was abroad this morning almost a holiday atmosphere, which persisted, and may even have been enhanced, when the pace was reduced to a crawl by a congestion of trucks, armoured cars, and tanks waiting their turn to drive over the chuckling planks of the gently rocking and dipping pontoon bridge that stretched its impressive length across the great, shimmering river.

And the feeling that it was a holiday commemorating some notable event became reality when, after a brief stop at a gun position southeast of Rouen, the Regiment rolled into the city to as tumultuous a welcome as ever was extended to a crowned head in those ancient streets. Totally unexpected, the enthusiastic expressions of gratitude, so warm and genuine, struck all ranks with shocking force. Suddenly there were thousands of cheering, flag-waving men, women, and children lining the streets, many of them crowding dangerously close to rotating wheels and clanking tracks as they handed up fruit and wine and flowers – such masses of beautiful blooms, the dusty old vehicles took on the appearance of colourful floats, and the regimental convoy, so tired and battle-shabby only moments before, was transformed into a victory parade.

Only for a fleeting moment did a dark echo of the detestable years of German occupation mar the glorious passage through Rouen. Having noted during one of the abbreviated halts several glum-looking women along the route, standing in doorways with towels draped around their heads like turbans, you inquired of a male bystander who had greeted you in perfect English why so many women had chosen to wash their hair this morning. He explained the towels were covering not wet heads, but bald heads, shaved bare by members of the French Resistance in punishment for having consorted too intimately with the hated enemy during the occupation. Why had they chosen to appear in public, wearing their badge of dishonour in full view of the liberating troops? He couldn't say, but perhaps they were ordered by the FFI to thus display their shame. Anyway, you were glad when the convoy moved on out onto the highway to Dieppe, and you could no longer see the sad eyes of those embarrassed women.

For hours after, at a gun position ten miles north of Rouen, in farming country untouched by war – so peaceful and quiet after that clamorous reception in Rouen – you could feel everyone glowing with satisfaction and pride, in themselves, the Regiment, and the army of which they are part. For weeks, everybody has been aware that the guns are a decisive factor in the taking of ground and holding it against enemy counter-attacks – often the most decisive factor, for, unlike air support, the guns are always available regardless of weather or cloud conditions in daylight or in darkness. And all ranks – from the CO down to the lowliest of the ORs – know that the gunners have done everything that could ever have been expected of them, and, on occasion, more than ever should have been expected of ordinary mortals. They don't need to have anyone tell them this. But still, it took the Rouen experience to place things in proper perspective, to bring significant meaning to that symbol of the Allied invasion: the crusader's sword and shield.

Those joyous crowds – sometimes applauding and sometimes cheering deliriously – showering symbols of their thankfulness on the Regiment as it passed along the streets within sight of the great Cathedral and other noble buildings (pock-marked by Allied fighter-planes strafing German headquarters during the occupation), could not fail to leave a remarkable impression on all who passed that way today. Witnessing the joy and gratitude of a people released from bondage, all were reminded of the primary purpose of the invasion – something easily forgotten during the sordid, strenuous weeks in the bridgehead before the break-out, when personal survival was the chief objective for days on end.

And now this evening, as you enjoy the pleasant feeling that you and your comrades have justified your manhood and those long years of training in England, you allow yourself to consider the intoxicating possibility that the end of the war may be near. Paris has fallen – the German garrison surrendering without serious fighting. Surely this means that German resistance is collapsing everywhere. Even if Hitler is able to persuade his generals to keep it going, postponing his own fate for a few weeks, the worst of the fighting must surely be over.

Suddenly, from the direction of the farmhouse, you hear the rattle of a machine gun. You jump up and make for the lane leading up to it, believing the worst has happened, that the acks have been led into an ambush. Almost completely untrained in infantry tactics, they can get themselves badly messed up. You hope and pray they'll pull back . . . But as you enter the tree-lined lane, you see marching towards you a platoon of soldiers in grey uniforms with their hands behind their heads. As you step to one side to let them pass down the lane, you count forty-five before you come across one grinning gunner with a Sten bringing up the rear.

"What was the shooting about?"

"Oh, one of the young guys fired by mistake. He'd never seen live Germans before up close, so when this mob started coming out of the orchard and the house, he got a little excited and fired off a burst."

"Did he hit any of them?"

"One of them in the neck. He's lying dead on the road up there."

When you reach the farmhouse and the dead German soldier lying in the dust of the roadway, you find that a bottle of cognac has been found in one of the several wagons in the large orchard to the right of the house and it is being passed around. Everybody is overly excited and ready to laugh at anything, as though trying to shake off the useless killing of a man trying to give himself up.

Gunner F. M. Westaway, a Baker Troop batman – normally not part of an advance party, but who must have volunteered to come along, ostensibly to help dig the command post, but in fact to get a chance to poke through derelict houses for booze or other loot – makes what he thinks is a hilarious gesture when he lights your cigarette with a flaming hundred-franc bill, and hands you a packet of fifty more crisp, brand-new banknotes, with the expansive remark: "Here, have five thousand on me, sir!"

· In the dust not far from the German's body is Westaway's source: a black leather bag, somewhat like a doctor's bag, its top spread open.

Examining it closely, you see it's jammed with packets of freshly printed notes. There must be hundreds of thousands of francs in there! How unfortunate they are worthless. (Before you left England they told you that all money in circulation on the continent would be worthless until new money was printed to replace what the Germans had debased. And to overcome this handicap you were issued specially printed Allied script to be used in place of regular money.) At that moment, Lieut. E. A. McCarey, a Signals Corps officer attached to 4RCA, arrives in his Jeep with a message that the guns will not be up until morning, but that the advance party is to remain here for the night. Spotting the black bag with the money, he bends down, snaps the lid closed, and throws it into the back of his Jeep. When you inquire what he hopes to do with it, he says, "Oh, the boys at the guns might like some as souvenirs."*

---

* Weeks later Gunner John Elder made the discovery that French banknotes were perfectly good when his bank in London accepted for deposit a tissue-paper-looking thousand-franc note that the younger Gunner Walkden had given him as a joke on his birthday. Then Lieut. McCarey revealed he had deposited the entire contents of that black bag in his bank account in London.

For a moment you wonder about his sudden altruism. But just then someone finds another bottle of booze in a wagon under the hay the Germans had mounded up in each to hide its contents and the "gold rush" is on. Everybody chooses a different wagon and starts feeling under its thick mattress of hay among ammunition, rifles, and other equipment; obviously this was a quarter stores that got cut off from the retreat by the rapid advance of 4th Brigade.

Choosing a wagon, you lean over its low tailgate, raise the hay, and stick your head and shoulders under it. In a clutter of webbing, water-bottles, and other equipment, you find a bottle of cognac. Placing this on a narrow ledge outside the tailgate, you dive under the hay again. But you find no more, and when you come out from under the dusty rustling mass, you discover your original find has vanished.

Swearing that if you find another bottle, you will sit down and consume it on the spot, you go to another wagon. After some searching you locate a long-necked, bulbous bottle that turns out to be a full litre of Benedictine. True to your oath, you climb up onto the hay and start sipping away at the strong liqueur. Not having had anything to eat since noon, you find the sweet liquid delicious. And this being the first time you've been without responsibility for a gun position or an OP since coming to France, the sense of relaxation is marvellous – and gets progressively more so with each passing hour.

When the sun goes down, a great orange harvest moon rises over the orchard, inspiring you to start singing "In the Evening by the Moonlight," beating time on the side of the wagon with the now-empty bottle. This seems to act as a beacon for a shadowy figure coming through the orchard. In due course he looms up beside the wagon to ask a most improbable question of the "officer and gentleman" reclining there: "Sir, you officers all carry shots of morphine, don't you?"

That each officer before leaving England was indeed issued two shots of morphine, to be carried in holes drilled in a little block of wood buttoned in the watch-pocket, on the right leg of your battledress, doesn't make the question any less astonishing. The voice, recognizable as that of the wandering batman, Westaway, continues:

"You know that German we all thought was dead? Well, he's still alive. The French people have got him up on a bed upstairs in the house, and he needs a shot of morphine real bad, sir."

The response of said Christian officer and gentleman is immediate, precise, and stern: this morphine is for Canadians, and you have only two precious shots.

Westaway refuses to be put off.

"But won't you just come and look at him, sir? He's in awful bad shape!"

Giving in to his plea, you get down off the wagon with some difficulty, for a litre of Benedictine on an empty stomach does wonders to relax legs, not to mention your cross-level bubble, and you weave your way through the orchard, managing not to miss a single low branch of an endless lineup of trees conspiring to block your path to the house.

In the gloom of the front hall, you are confronted by a most formidable staircase leading to the second floor, so awfully steep and long – almost disappearing into the darkness above – that for a moment you pause at the bottom step to gather your determination. What little light there is in the entrance hall is spilling from the parlour on the right, from candles on a table in the centre of the room, around which people with solemn faces are sitting, stiffly erect, on chairs. No one is talking. The atmosphere is clearly that of a death watch; the candles, the woman with bowed head holding her hands in an attitude of prayer, and the eyes of the man when he looks at you, all seem to say, A man is dying upstairs.

As you struggle up the stairs, largely on your hands and knees, you marvel at the attitude of these people. This morning that bugger up there in his grey uniform and jackboots was a hated enemy. Now they really seem to care what happens to him.

Westaway is waiting at the head of the stairs and leads you into the first bedroom on the right, lit by another candle, which sits wavering on the bureau against the wall at the foot of the bed. On top of the bed covers, fully clothed, just as the family had picked him up from the dust of their laneway, lies the German. He is on his back, unmoving, his eyes closed. Still alive, he breathes noisily through a gaping, blood-encrusted hole in his neck, just below his chin on the left side. But for how much longer, you wonder, for his face is the colour of gun-metal.

In spite of everything, there is something about the way he lies there that reminds you of your brother, and with this thought a wave of compassion sweeps through you; a man who could be your brother is dying alone among strangers, without medical aid. Suddenly you realize you are no longer struggling to function in a fuddling haze. Something in the shock of seeing a dying man, looking like your brother, has sobered you up – if not entirely, at least enough so that you now remember the drill for administering morphine laid on by the MO.

He is lying more on the left side of the bed, and as you move around there, you realize you'll need a knife or something sharp to slit his tunic sleeve so you can find a muscle in his arm in which to stick the needle. Westaway doesn't have a penknife either, but, seemingly now quite familiar with the contents of the room, he readily comes up with a pair of manicure scissors from the dresser. As you cut a wide slit in the man's sleeve, you review the procedure that sounded simple enough when the MO described it in England when they were issuing the stuff.

You remove the adhesive tape from the wood block and pull out one of the little vials. It resembles a miniature toothpaste tube with a disposable hypodermic needle attached. A wire pin, resting loosely in the top of the needle, underneath a tiny protective glass sheath, has only to be depressed to break a seal and make the needle operative. After discarding the pin, the needle is ready to be stuck into the arm or rear end of the wounded, but you must make sure that it goes only into a muscle – never a vein. After you've squeezed the collapsible tube to eject the morphine, you will have to mark his forehead with a black "M," so that those giving him treatment later will know that he's had a shot.

With his left upper arm bare, and one of the little needles ready for action, you grab hold of his arm and jab the needle hard into the muscle. You hope it's in far enough. But when you squeeze the soft little tube, the contents run down his arm and drip down onto the bedspread. You've blown your first attempt.

You're astonished at how resistant flesh can be to a needle – especially this very blunt needle. You have only one more chance. As you depress the pin to break the seal, remove it and discard it, and get the little tube firmly in your fingers, you find your hand is shaking. This man may not survive even with the morphine, but without it, he surely will die. You simply have to get it deep in the flesh this time.

Taking a deep breath, you jam the needle into his arm with all your strength. This time you know it's in far enough, for the stubby little needle is in up to its neck. Slowly you squeeze the tube, and with satisfaction note this time you don't lose a single drop. You remove the needle and rub the arm as you've seen nurses do.

In a matter of seconds, the German's colour begins to improve, and soon he opens his eyes. And although he makes no attempt to move even his lips, he calls out one word in a thick, but understandable accent: "*Dok-tor.*" He repeats it over and over, "*Dok-tor . . . Dok-tor,*" while his eyes follow you and beseech you to help him.

You send Westaway off to get a message back to Regiment to send up a stretcher-bearing Jeep to transport the German back to the MO. And then you try to reassure him that he's going to be all right, that you're going to get him back to a doctor as fast as you can. But he doesn't seem to understand, and continues to call "*Dok-tor, Dok-tor,*" with only a slight decrease in frequency as you pass the time waiting for the stretcher, trying to find something to mark "M" on his forehead.

A few days later, when you get a chance to talk to the MO, you ask him if he thinks the German you sent back, with a red "M" inscribed in lipstick on his forehead and a big hole in his neck, survived his trip back to a field surgical hospital. The MO is quite certain he did. Obviously no artery had been severed, and all bleeding had ceased long before he'd seen him. He believes that all he needed was a few pints of blood and that hole in his neck sewn up and he'd be okay.

You marvel at the sequence of events and mixture of motives that went into saving that man's life. Westaway, clearly, was poking around where he shouldn't or he never would have come across that German in that upstairs bedroom. What he was after, you don't want to know, but clearly it was connected in some way with self-interest, for he's not one to expend any more energy than is absolutely necessary on anything not of direct material benefit. For instance, he always chooses to eat his own meal first before delivering one to his officer. This has the obvious advantage of messing up only one set of mess tins and eating utensils. He cleans the mess tins of travelling dust meticulously before eating his own meal out of them, and so feels it necessary only to bang out the remnants of his meal and refill them for delivery to his officer. While the shared knife, fork, and spoon, swilled off in the remnants of his tea, are dried off in a most memorable fashion as he goes, sawing them under an armpit of his battledress right up until the moment he presents them to his officer with a flourish worthy of a waiter at the Savoy, cheerfully and solicitously announcing, "Your dinner, sir! Better eat it while it's hot."

On the other side of the coin, however, is the indisputable fact that a man was pulled back from the grave and given another chance to live out a normal life after the war, solely through the initiative of Westaway, who may not be quite "thou true and faithful servant," but who truly believes that, enemy or not, "a man's a man for a' that," and persuaded an "officer and gentleman," very much against his inclination, to follow his leadership in common decency and humanity.

69

THE MOST SIGNIFICANT
CANADIAN PARADE OF THE WAR

———————————— ✳ ————————————

ON THE FORTY-MILE RUN UP TO THE COAST FROM THE JOYOUS reception in Rouen, 2nd Division units cross the path of only a couple of small pockets of Germans (at Tôtes and Longueville). By dark on August 31, 8th Recce armoured cars are just short of Dieppe, and, at ten-thirty next morning, they enter the town, meeting no opposition. The Germans have gone.

They left in great haste, it seems, when they heard Canadians with dark-blue patches on their shoulders were headed this way. This is according to the owner of the Château d'Ambrumesnil, close to where 4th Field is directed to park the guns and vehicles for rest and maintenance. About eight miles as the crow flies southwest of Dieppe, the château was used by the Germans as an officers' mess of the Dieppe garrison near Offranville.

Fortunately the abandonment of the port was discovered by some Royal Marines who landed last night, and the RAF bombing raid that was scheduled to precede a ground attack by 2nd Division was called off in time. Marines, standing outside a café with glasses of beer in their hands, are among the first to welcome a 4th Field FOO with the troops arriving on the outskirts of town.

Anticipating a delirious welcome from the people of Dieppe for each and every man, and fearful things may get completely out of hand, Divisional Commander Foulkes decides the bulk of the division should bivouac outside town until a formal parade can be arranged after the troops have had a chance to rest for a couple of days and spruce up.

This is eminently sensible, as for many this is their first chance since arriving in France to peel off all their filthy, flea-infested clothing and bathe – this being the first time the guns of 2nd Division have been out of action and at rest since July 9, fifty-three days ago.

When you remove your two pairs of socks, worn one over the other, they stand up like rubber boots. And when you pull off your woollen undershirt, the appearance of your back causes a sensation among onlookers, causing one to ask, "What the hell happened to you?"

For weeks you've been scratching, particularly around your wrists and ankles and back – sometimes ferociously scrubbing your back up and down against a post or tree – but until they produce two polished-steel hand-mirrors and allow you a view, you have no conception of the vigour of your attack: a mass of dried and blackened blood covers your back from top to bottom. What caused that ferocious itching? A heat rash, you think.

Sgt. Dunsmore, who happens to be passing as you advance this possibility, lets out a yelping chortle: "Heat rash, my ass – you're just lousey, sir! Let me have your battledress blouse."

Protesting that you have checked the seams on more than one occasion without finding any cooties, since you first started itching back at Ifs after sleeping on a cot in an abandoned German dugout, and the next day on a bare mattress left by the Germans in a barn near Verrières, you nevertheless give him your blouse and follow his advice to "watch closely and be quick when I spread open a seam." And there, wiggling to get out of sight, is a yellow sand-flea – and another, and another, and another.

After some kind soul soaps and washes your back, the burning itch is intolerable. The MO finds it difficult to believe that such massive irritation could have been caused by fleas, and asks, "Has anything been bothering you?"

Turned speechless by the question, you can only listen as he goes on to say, "If this calamine lotion doesn't clear it up in a couple of days, I'll have to evacuate you."

To which you reply, "With the war about to end? Like hell you will."

It is to get your mind off the damned itch that you and Bob Grout head up the road that evening for a village café in search of some drinkable cognac, and end up visiting the Château d'Ambrumesnil on the advice of the publican, who has nothing but the rawest of raw Calvados in his little café.

Even when you are still some distance down the lane from the noble building, the "squire," as he will later refer to himself jokingly, calls out from the front door in perfect English, "Come on in, fellows, and have a cup of coffee."

It turns out he is a Dutchman by birth who in the twenties learned English in North Africa from an associate travelling-salesman for Wills Tobacco. He was in Canada seeing the Dionne quintuplets the day war broke out, and he refers to the unreliable German flying bombs that have crashed all over the landscape around here as "Tin Lizzies" after Model-T Fords. He's kept a scrapbook of both German propaganda and clippings from Allied publications he somehow managed to get his hands on. He tells how he inwardly wept and raged when the German officers held a boisterous party here in his house to celebrate the destruction of the Canadian raid on Dieppe. That night, taking pride in their athletic prowess, as always, on their way down to dinner they vaulted, one after another, over the banister, their hobnailed boots crashing on his fine parquet flooring. (He points to the desecrated hall floor.)

After dinner one of them, an Olympic champion discus or javelin thrower (he isn't sure which), "to amuse the peasants," pulled the pins on grenades and fired them high in the sky to explode like fireworks.

This spring they'd become very nervous, certain the invasion was coming, and he taunted them that Germany was losing the war and that the Canadians would soon come to settle an old score. While they pooh-poohed this, claiming Hitler's secret weapons would wipe London off the face of the globe and end the war, they gradually lost faith when they saw more V-Is crash in France than took off over the Channel. There were countless false alarms, when they all rushed off on bicycles, returning after a while looking sheepish. But yesterday, when they learned Canadians with dark-blue patches on their shoulders were on their way up from Rouen, they took off. And this time they didn't return.

They would always be a mystery to him. They treated him and his wife with the utmost courtesy, even apologizing for causing her some mental anguish when corporals brutally disciplined their own soldiers in full view of her kitchen window, promising that henceforth when soldiers were required to fall on their faces on the ground while standing rigidly at attention, it would be out of sight of her window.

After lunch the next day (September 3), as you watch the first of some fifteen thousand men – all of them astonishingly well turned-out considering what their uniforms have been through – go swinging six abreast down the long steep hill into town, to turn right into a street covered with flowers cascading down from above, you wonder how many of them are having to flex their shoulders to get the cloth of an undershirt massaging an itch, as now and then you must, to the obvious amusement of the men in the troop behind you.

But when the moment comes for the artillery regiments to move off down the road into Dieppe, you forget the itch and are swept up in the significance of this great march – as much a march to honour those who were lost at Dieppe as a victory parade.

"The most impressive and meaningful Canadian parade of the war," is how Canadian war correspondent Ross Munro sees it.

Munro, who broke the first eyewitness account of the Dieppe Raid to the world in 1942, appropriately was in one of the first 8th Recce cars entering Dieppe two days ago. And one day, in his book *Gauntlet to Overlord*, he will describe his "pilgrimage" to Blue Beach at Puys, just east of Dieppe, where in 1942, in a ship just off shore, he'd watched the Royals and a troop of 4th Field gunners spill out of their landing craft and charge up the beach for the sea wall in the face of murderous fire from the cliffs.

> I went through the lonely, gray-brown town, and down the gulch towards the beach. The mines on the road had not been lifted and I had to pick my way cautiously. When I reached the beach I wished I had not come alone. It was like walking in a tomb. I shuddered to look at the beach, at the 12-foot stone wall across its top, where so many of the Royal Regiment were cut down before my very eyes. I shuddered as I looked at the quaint houses still there on the cliff top from which fire had poured into our boats. Here one of the finest regiments in the Canadian Army had fought and died. . . .*

As you march into town, the reception is incredible. Though nine infantry battalions have already passed the reviewing stand before the gunners come up, blooms are still showering down from the outstretched arms of women at windows high above the street. And the densely packed crowds of men, women, and children lining both sides of the street are still cheering earnestly without pause, in a steady, uninterrupted way you never have heard before anywhere.

The surging, wailing gale of human voices, which reaches you at least a mile before you get down into town, and which never for a second lets up until the tail of the parade has moved through town

---

* Ross Munro, *Gauntlet to Overlord* (Edmonton: Hurtig, 1945), pp. 208–209.

and up the road for Puys, is so intense it is disorienting – drowning out the Essex Scottish pipers leading 4th Brigade and the brass band beside the reviewing stand, where Army Commander General Crerar is taking the salute, flanked (most appropriately you think) by two 4th Field 25-pounders.

When at last you're broken off near a cliff edge to stare down at the beaches where men came ashore in 1942, you can hardly believe your eyes. Down there rusting in the gravel of a narrow stretch of beach is a Churchill tank, its puny, pea-shooter, two-pounder gun pointing at the base of the cliff. Where on earth was it supposed to go?

And farther east along the coast at Puys, walking down the narrow defile to where Capt. George Browne, Capt. Tommy Archibald, Lieut. Tait "Moose" Saunders, and the 20 Other Ranks from 4th Field plunged ashore and the Royals were cut down by the dozen on the gravel as they headed for the high sea-wall covered with a tangle of barbed-wire coils, you wonder how any of them managed to get through here and reach the fields and bush at the top that day.* They would all have been under observation every step of the way from the fortified house at the left of the defile with a field of fire covering the entire beach and the full length of the narrow, steepsided valley through which they had to go in daylight. That George Browne, Col. D. A. Catto, and nineteen others made it to the top, cleared two houses, and held on until 4:30 P.M., is a miracle.

The gloomy silence of the dead houses along the cliff top, the

---

* Sgt. J. W. Dudley, Lance-Bombardier F. M. Lalonde, and Gunner Donald McClean of 4th Field were killed, and the others were captured. Capt. Browne escaped twice – once from the Germans and then from the Vichy French – got back to England with valuable intelligence, and returned to France on D-Day, with 3rd Division. Out of the 528 Royals on the raid, 487 were casualties – 227 died.

rusting derelict landing craft in the restless shallows on the beach, the endless coils of barbed wire, the ragged, faded cloth strips in the camouflage netting, fluttering forlornly at a deserted gun emplacement, and the threatening ACHTUNG MINEN sign with its skull-and-crossbones warning trespassers of the danger of anti-personnel mines, all combine to induce a state of melancholia, and no one wants to linger here.

There's a ceremony in a cemetery above Dieppe where the Canadian bodies were collected by the townspeople and buried under neat wooden crosses of their devising. All would wish to attend, but the cemetery is so confined that only a select number from each unit are allowed to attend, with priority being given to those very few who are returning to Dieppe for the second time.

All next day Dieppe is out-of-bounds to officers so that they will not be around to inhibit the enjoyment of the troops (from 2:00 to 11:30 P.M.) as the people of Dieppe take them to their hearts, entertaining them as lavishly as possible. That this is lavish indeed, at least in terms of liquid refreshment, 4th Field drivers can testify. At the request of the mayor, attending a 4th Field officers' reception held in a house near Offranville after the parade, the Regiment supplies several trucks to transport wine from distant points. And according to the drivers, Dieppe is not likely to run dry for some time to come. There is also the rumour that champagne will flow like water tomorrow night at the mayor's reception and dance for the officers, to be attended by the belles of the town.

However, the officers of 4th Field will never know whether the rumour is true, for just as they are about to pull out for the reception, there is a conference phone call for battery commanders, warning them to have all personnel packed up and standing by, ready to move on short notice. And though the Regiment doesn't move off until 4:15 A.M., towards another concentration south of Montreuil, no one gets to attend the officers' reception though it will be talked about for years after by the infantry officers who attended.

It seems the party provided them with a wonderful chance to get some things off their chests with brigade commanders and up. Mostly they'll recall taking turns asking Gen. Foulkes why he exposed five of his badly under-strength battalions to 577 needless casualties in the attempt to clear the Forêt de la Londe when it could have been bypassed and the Germans left to rot in it until ready to give up.

The disappointment among 4th Field officers at having to miss this great "bash" does not, however, run very deep – for two reasons. First, many are still recovering from a regional "pub crawl" last night – especially from the effects of a heavy intake of Benedictine at a certain café beyond a trout stream named Scie. To reach the café you used an obscure ford that you and Bob Grout had discovered the second night here when confronted with the fact that all bridges had been destroyed by the fleeing Germans. At this café (where a child displayed a hat badge acquired from a Royal Regiment of Canada soldier two years ago), the sweet liquor was a welcome alternative to the raw, throat-rasping, unaged Calvados served in every other village café for miles around. The result, however, was giant hangovers – not to mention the bruises and lacerations suffered by the occupants of a Jeep that failed to locate the right turning to the ford on the way home and twice drove off the end of a bridge that wasn't there. These painful injuries are most visible on the visages of Bill Murdoch, the driver of the wayward Jeep, and one of his passengers, "Stevie" Stevenson (now noticeably short a couple of teeth), who was dozing in the back when the intrepid Murdoch, not once, but twice, managed, within a few hundred yards, to drive off non-existent spans.

The second, and perhaps more meaningful reason for the lack of resentment at missing the mayor's party, stems from the fact that everyone is convinced the war is about to end, and it would be preferable to be among the spearheads converging on Berlin than languishing here at Dieppe. And British tanks (according to the

BBC) are rumbling through Belgium three hundred miles north of here on their way to *Der Vaterland*.

That the war will continue for another eight months, and that for much of the time you will be engaged in bloody battles in the most horrendous conditions of mud and water since Passchendaele in World War One, is of course beyond imagination. Even the most pessimistic soul could never conceive of a course of events that will see eleven thousand more Canadian casualties as the Canadian Army clears the Scheldt Estuary to open the port of Antwerp and next spring clears the lower Rhineland. If anyone were to suggest that five months hence your guns will participate in the biggest barrage and attendant bombardment of the entire war, involving 2,645 guns in support of a 400,000-strong Canadian Army pushing through the Siegfried Line, and that the fire-power of 3,411 guns for the Rhine-crossing next March will exceed the fire-power for the Normandy landings, you would write him off as a lunatic.

APPENDIX A

ONE OF FOUR ALLIED ARMIES IN NORMANDY

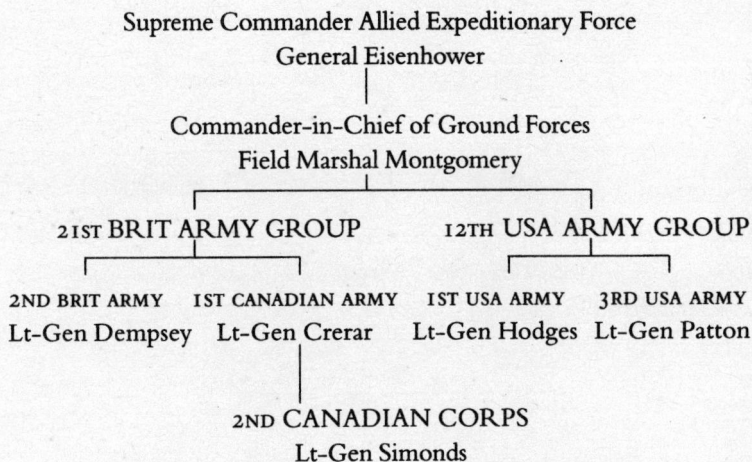

Supreme Commander Allied Expeditionary Force
General Eisenhower

Commander-in-Chief of Ground Forces
Field Marshal Montgomery

21ST BRIT ARMY GROUP   12TH USA ARMY GROUP

2ND BRIT ARMY	1ST CANADIAN ARMY	1ST USA ARMY	3RD USA ARMY
Lt-Gen Dempsey	Lt-Gen Crerar	Lt-Gen Hodges	Lt-Gen Patton

2ND CANADIAN CORPS
Lt-Gen Simonds

2nd Cdn Infantry Division

4th Brigade
The Royal Regiment of Canada
The Royal Hamilton Light Infantry
The Essex Scottish Regiment

5th Brigade
The Black Watch (Royal Highland
  Regiment of Canada)
Le Régiment de Maisonneuve
The Calgary Highlanders

6th Brigade
Les Fusiliers Mont-Royal
The Queen's Own Cameron Highlanders of Canada
The South Saskatchewan Regiment

Divisional Troops

8th Reconnaissance Regiment
  (14th Canadian Hussars)
2nd Cdn Divisional Engineers
2nd Cdn Divisional Signals

4th Field, 5th Field, 6th Field,
  2nd Anti-Tank and 3rd Light
  Anti-Aircraft Regiments RCA
The Toronto Scottish Regiment
  (Machine Gun)

3rd Cdn Infantry Division

7th Brigade
The Royal Winnipeg Rifles
The Regina Rifle Regiment
The Canadian Scottish Regiment

8th Brigade
The Queen's Own Rifles of Canada
Le Régiment de la Chaudière
The North Shore (New Brunswick)
Regiment

9th Brigade
The Highland Light Infantry of Canada
The Stormont, Dundas and Glengarry Highlanders
The North Nova Scotia Highlanders

Divisional Troops

7th Reconnaissance Regiment
(17th Duke of York's Royal
Cdn Hussars)
3rd Cdn Divisional Engineers
3rd Cdn Divisional Signals

12th Field, 13th Field, 14th Field,
3rd Anti-Tank, 4th Light Anti-
Aircraft Regiments RCA
The Cameron Highlanders of
Ottawa (Machine Gun)

4th Cdn Armoured Division

4th Armoured Brigade
21st Armoured Regiment
(Governor General's Foot Guards)
22nd Armoured Regiment
(Canadian Grenadier Guards)
28th Armoured Regiment
(British Columbia Regiment)
Lake Superior Regiment (Motorized)

10th Infantry Brigade
The Lincoln and Welland Regiment
The Algonquin Regiment
The Argyll and Sutherland
Highlanders of Canada

Divisional Troops

29th Reconnaissance Regiment
(The South Alberta Regiment)
4th Armoured Divisional Engineers
4th Armoured Divisional Signals

15th and 23rd Field Regiments RCA
5th Anti-Tank Regiment
8th Light Anti-Aircraft Regiment

1st Polish Armoured Division

10th Polish Armoured Brigade
1st Polish Armoured Regiment
2nd Polish Armoured Regiment
24th Polish Armoured (Lancer)
   Regiment
10th Polish Motor Battalion

3rd Polish Infantry Brigade
1st Polish (Highland) Battalion
8th Polish Battalion
9th Polish Battalion

Divisional Troops

10th Polish Mounted Rifle Regiment
1st Polish Divisional Engineers
1st Polish Divisional Signals

1st and 2nd Polish Field Regiments
1st Polish Anti-Tank Regiment
1st Polish Anti-Aircraft Regiment

2nd Canadian Armoured Brigade
(independant brigade from D-Day landings)

6th Armoured Regiment (The 1st Hussars)
10th Armoured Regiment (The Fort Garry Horse)
27th Armoured Regiment (The Sherbrooke Fusiliers)

1st Canadian Parachute Battalion
(of 6th Brit Airborne Division)

Other Army and Corps Troops

2nd Cdn Army Group Royal Artillery
   (3rd, 4th and 7th Medium Regiments)
2nd Cdn Heavy Anti-Aircraft Regiment
19th Cdn Field Regiment
6th Anti-Tank Regiment RCA
6th Light Anti-Aircraft Regiment RCA
2nd Survey Regiment RCA
1st Armoured Personnel Carrier Regiment
25th Cdn Armoured Delivery Regiment
   (The Elgin Regiment)
1st Royal Cdn Army Group
   Engineers

2nd Corps Engineers
1st, 2nd, and 3rd Battalions,
   Royal Canadian Engineers
1st Cdn Army HQ Signals
2nd Corps Signals
Army HQ Defence Battalion
   (Royal Montreal Regiment)
18th Armoured Car Regiment
   (12th Manitoba Dragoons)
Number 1 Cdn Railway
   Operating Group

In addition to the units listed above, are the Royal Cdn Army Service Corps, the Royal Cdn Ordnance Corps, and the Royal Cdn Medical Corps, providing crucial services without which the army could not function. A large number of Ordnance personnel (detached sections of the Royal Electrical and Mechanical Engineers), and of the Medical Corps (one medical officer and one dental officer per regiment), serve at the fighting-unit level.

The war establishment of a Canadian or British armoured division is about 18,800 men, of which 2,500 are in three infantry battalions of its one infantry brigade. An infantry division calls for 19,300, of which 7,500 serve in three infantry brigades (of three battalions each), and 3,400 in five artillery regiments: three field regiments, an anti-tank regiment and a light anti-aircraft regiment.

APPENDIX B

RECORD RATES OF SHELL CONSUMPTION

RCASC DUMPS OF 25-POUNDER AMMUNITION
OVER 7-DAY PERIOD ENDING JULY 27, 1944

	At 2nd Div Guns (72 guns)	At 4th Field (24 guns)	RPG
July 20 (0030 hrs–0900 hrs)	25,200	8,400	350
(1645 hrs–2100 hrs)	33,400	11,334	464
(2100 hrs–2300 hrs)	2,400	2,400	100
21 (early afternoon)		8,400 *	350
22 (0240 hrs–1230 hrs)	12,000	4,000	167
(1230 hrs–1830 hrs)	12,000	4,000	167
22–23 (2000 hrs–0730 hrs)	46,800	15,600	650
23 (0730 hrs–1200 hrs)	25,200	8,400	350
26 (2000 hrs–0600 hrs)	36,000	12,000	500
	193,000	74,534	
Total rounds per gun:	2,680	3,105	
Rounds per gun per day:	383	444	

* An emergency dump by 4RCA trucks and ammunition numbers who brought up unexpended rounds from previous gun position and from an RCASC dump beyond Carpiquet, when the guns threatened to run out of ammunition.

ROUNDS FIRED PER GUN PER DAY BY 4TH FIELD

(As recorded in gun log D Sub, Easy Troop, 26 Battery, which can be taken as representative of all guns of 4RCA, since all targets during the period were Mike or higher, involving all guns in the Regiment)

24 hours ending 2030 hours July 19	518
20	505
21	384
22	230
23	30
24	80
25	390
Total fired per gun during 7-day period:	2,137
Average fired per gun per day:	305

APPENDIX C

A COMPARISON OF TANKS AND THEIR PERFORMANCE

Tank	Armour		Armament	Muzzle Velocity	Penetration
	Front	Side		in feet per second	at 30 degrees
Churchill VII	152 mm		6-pounder	2,700	63 mm
Tiger MK I	100 mm	80 mm	88-mm KwK 36 (barrel 16.2 ft)	2,484	102 mm
Tiger MK II	150 mm	100 mm	88-mm KwK 43 (barrel 21.5 ft)	3,186	164 mm
Panther	100 mm	45 mm	75-mm KwK 42 (barrel 17.2 ft)	3,070	110 mm
Firefly	75 mm	51 mm	17-pounder (plain shot) (Sabot shot)	2,900 3,950	113 mm 231 mm
Sherman	75 mm	51 mm	75-mm	1,950	68 mm

Data in the above table for the two 88-mm guns, provided by the Militargeschichtliches Forschungsamt, are recorded in *Taschenbuch der Panzer 1943–1954* by von Senger and Etterlin, Munich, 1954. Slightly lower muzzle-velocities (2,463 and 3,156) are recorded by Fritz Hahn in *Waffen und Geheimwaffen des deutschen Heeres, 1933–45*. Data on 17-pounder provided by the Imperial War Museum.

INDEX

The Guns of Victory

A Soldier's Eye View,
Belgium, Holland and Germany 1944-5

ON THE ROAD
TO VICTORY
1944 - 1945

To all the loved ones of all who didn't make it back – especially those who know their fathers only through fading photographs

CONTENTS

PART TWO – NOVEMBER 9–FEBRUARY 15
THE NIJMEGEN SALIENT

PART THREE – FEBRUARY 8–MARCH 10
THE THIRTY-DAY BATTLE FOR THE RHINELAND

MAPS

INTRODUCTION

✳

In the final eleven months of the six-year struggle to gain unconditional surrender from Hitler's Nazis, Canadians made a contribution out of all proportion to their numbers, on land and sea and in the air, but particularly on land, starting on D-Day (June 6, 1944) when 3rd Canadian Division and tanks of the 2nd Armoured Brigade penetrated farther inland than either of the two British divisions or three American divisions in the assault.[*]

In three subsequent major operations – each of them crucial to an Allied victory in Western Europe – 1st Canadian Army played a pivotal or leading role. First, there was the formation and the sealing off of the Falaise pocket, dooming to destruction the German armies in Normandy. Then in October there was the clearing of the Scheldt estuary and the opening of the port of Antwerp, the only port big enough to supply all Allied armies with the mountains of essential supplies required for the final showdown battles with an enemy defending his homeland. Finally, in early spring, 1945, there was the last great battle on the Western Front – a

---

[*] Tanks of 6th Canadian Armoured Regiment reached the Bayeux–Caen road three kilometres ahead of their assaulting column, but turned back to the main Canadian line, ten kilometres inland. By evening 75,000 British and Canadians were ashore, compared to 57,500 Americans.

massive assault through the Siegfried Line to clear the lower Rhineland and allow: crossings of the great river to be made by irresistible forces; Holland to be severed from Germany; and Allied spearheads to plunge with lethal force into the heart of the Reich.

In *The Guns of Normandy* an earnest attempt was made to allow readers to live day-by-day, hour-by-hour (and occasionally minute-by-minute) through the titanic struggle for Normandy in the summer of 1944, which peaked in intensity in late July for the Canadians along Verrières Ridge, when record-breaking shell consumption by field guns reached "insane levels," laying down "curtains of fire" to plug gaps in the line torn by the 1st Panzer (Leibstandarte Adolf Hitler) SS Division with swarms of Panther and Tiger tanks.

The Guns of Victory, prepared with similar intent, carries on the story through the last eight months of the war on the Western Front. Some of the fighting was conducted in the drifting snows of the worst winter in fifty years in Holland, but mostly in appalling conditions of mud and flood-water that have been compared, by veterans of both great wars, to the legendary miseries of the mud and water of Passchendaele – both in the fall of 1944 along the Scheldt and in the spring of 1945 along the Rhine, causing the men of 3rd Canadian Division, who fought through the worst-flooded landscape in the Rhineland, to assume the title "Water Rats."

As in *The Guns of Normandy*, the view of the war is usually from the gunpits or forward observation posts of 4th Field Regiment (one of three field artillery regiments supporting 2nd Infantry Division) with particular responsibility for bringing down "Mike targets" (fire from all its twenty-four guns) in support of the three battalions of 4th Infantry Brigade. But being constantly linked by radio and accurately oriented, by precise land-survey, with all the other Canadian and British field guns in the theatre of operations, 4th Field guns regularly participated in impromptu shoots on "Uncle targets" (involving all seventy-two guns of the division); and, occasionally, on "Victor targets" (involving all 216 field guns of 2nd Canadian Corps) called down by a FOO (forward observation officer) to crush counter-attacks threatening to roll up the whole front.

Though intended to be the story of the guns, this is as much the story of the infantry and the tanks, for without some picture of what the troops at the cutting edge faced in gaining objectives and maintaining tenuous holds on shell-tortured ridges, burned out farms, and smashed villages, the periodic demands on the guns for outrageous concentrations of shells would make no more sense than those endless scenes in war films of guns puffing mindlessly away at dear-knows-what, creating the impression that gunnery is simply a matter of pointing the guns in the direction of the enemy, tipping their muzzles up enough to ensure the shells won't land on their own troops, and periodically (at the whim of some senior officer somewhere) lobbing some rounds into enemy territory.

Without some appreciation of the objective of the troops and the severity of the resistance confronting the weary, hollow-eyed, mud-encrusted infantrymen, no one could possibly understand the constant calls for fire by FOOs at the mouth of South Beveland Peninsula and in the Breskens pocket in the autumn of 1944; let alone comprehend what impelled the gunners, in the struggle for the Rhineland the next spring, to carry on without complaint to the point of total exhaustion – day after day – manhandling their guns through the mud into each new position (when their towing quads bogged down and had to winch themselves back out to the road); shovelling tons of shells into guns glowing red; and endlessly slogging back and forth through the mud, carrying 115-pound cases of shells and 62-pound boxes of cartridges to their ravenous tubes from trucks stopped an indecent distance away, on roads barely distinguishable from the surrounding rutted and shell-gouged landscape of glistening mud and water.

The Guns of Normandy ended with Hitler's armies shredded in the Falaise pocket – the shattered remnants of his elite SS divisions largely devoid of tanks, guns, and transport after escaping across the bridgeless Seine by improvised rafts not capable of supporting heavy equipment – disorganized and mostly leaderless, scurrying to keep ahead of the Allied spearheads driving for the Fatherland, as behind them the sounds of wild cheering rose up from crowds delirious at the sight of Allied recce cars, tanks, and guns rolling into Paris, Rouen, Dieppe, Brussels, and Antwerp.

That the war was won and would soon be over seemed very clear – not so much from anything reported by official military sources, but from the excitement that sometimes crept into the delivery of the BBC news picked up on little 38-sets. The normally studiously impersonal newscasters seemed to be gloating as they read their bulletins – even showing a touch of nationalistic bias, by way of a sneering tone, as they revealed that Herr Goebbels, Hitler's Minister of Propaganda, was appealing to the population to engage in "a people's war in defence of the sacred soil of the Reich . . . to fight in every street and every lane to save the Fatherland from the final humiliation of invasion by Allied armies."

The hopelessness of Goebbels' appeal seemed to be underlined by two other BBC bulletins: as many as ten thousand Germans a day were being taken prisoner, and the Reich was mobilizing fourteen-year-old school children in regions adjacent to their borders.

The Guns of Victory is the third volume of a trilogy about World War II from the perspective of one regiment of 25-pounders – the second volume being *The Guns of Normandy*, published in 1995.

The first volume, with the working title *Where On Earth Are the Guns?* (as much in deference to the fact the Regiment waited two years for its guns, as to the number of times they were lost during training in that maze of unsigned roads that was wartime Britain) will be published only if enough interest is aroused in readers curious to know how war came to a generation of young Canadians one sunny September weekend in 1939; and how a grab-bag of volunteers from all walks of life – many of them mavericks and misfits from a depression-ravaged land, more inclined to creating situations suitable to comic opera than to the conduct of His Majesty's business – gradually assumed the character of a proud regiment, which in 1942 was declared "the best field regiment in Britain," at a fire-and-movement competition on Salisbury Plain.

PART ONE: SEPTEMBER 6– NOVEMBER 8

Clearing the Channel Ports and the Battle for the Scheldt

I

BACK TO WAR IN
FLOODED COASTAL LOWLANDS

❋

"REVEILLE 0230, BREAKFAST 0300, MOVE OFF AT 0415."

These predawn orders sound more like instructions for a training scheme in England than a return to the stern business of war, after four euphoric days at Dieppe with the guns out of action for the first time in almost two months. Still, as 4th Field Regiment pulls out in the early-morning gloom, onto a road heading northeast to a 2nd Canadian Division concentration area near Montreuil, fifty miles away, there is a disturbing sense of returning to reality, and you have to work hard to suppress the ugly thought you may still buy it before Germany packs it in.

Your ultimate destination is a mystery. All you know is that Canadian Army is to clear the coastal areas of France and Belgium, and in the process to achieve two objectives of tremendous consequence: the elimination of the V-1 launching sites, bringing to an end the flying-bomb attacks on Britain, and the capture of ports required for landing the mountains of supplies still being trucked up from the Normandy beaches.

While 2nd Division was relaxing at Dieppe, British XXX Corps' tanks and recce cars were racing north through Amiens, Arras, and Douai – plunging deep into Belgium to occupy Brussels on September 2 and Antwerp on September 4, with even more dash, in terms of speed and distance, than the Yanks achieved on their highly acclaimed drive for Paris after their break-out from the Normandy bridgehead. The American spearheads, confronted by no organized resistance of consequence, in three days almost reached Le Mans on August 6, a truly exciting advance that captured the imagination of all the war correspondents after the long weeks of bloody containment – particularly when the general commanding this dashing force packed a pearl-handled pistol on his hip in traditional cowboy style.

However, General Patton's seventy-five-mile thrust in three days pales in comparison with Lt.-Gen. Brian Horrocks's XXX Corps' thrust north through France into Belgium after crossing the Seine – 230 miles in six days, the Guards Armour covering the final seventy miles from Douai to Brussels in a single day. In fact, so swift was the initial British hundred-mile run to the Somme that General Eberbach, Commander of Fifth Panzer Army, was captured in his pyjamas at Amiens.*

During today's long move – according to the diary assiduously kept by Bombardier Ken Hossack, your senior GPO Ack† since arrival on the continent on July 7 – there are only two events worth mentioning: the Regiment passing over the Somme river without anyone remarking on it; and your Number Four gun breaking its axle. Since broken axles on guns are unheard of, it is something of a miracle when Gun Artificer "Hank" Wilkins locates a replacement so promptly the gun is able to join the troop in time for another all-night move to Hazebrouck, twenty miles south of Dunkirk – to the disgust of Sgt. "Lefty" Phillips and his

---

* By comparison it took the swaggering Patton thirteen days (from August 6 to August 19), including three days clearing Chartres, to get from Le Mans to the Seine at Mantes, a distance of only about 140 miles.
† GPO stands for "gun position officer"; and Ack for "A," a carryover from the old British phonetic alphabet, stands for "assistant."

crew, who'd settled in a nearby café for an indefinite period of relaxation.

The night is inky black with driving rain, and there is only one map per troop. So when Troop Commander Len Harvey's universal carrier misses a turn and ends up in a water-filled ditch – submerging him and the map – GA, your armoured scout car, takes over the lead, and you make your way, according to Hossack, "By guess and by God." On safe arrival, though, his diary gives you full credit: "GPO guesses well."

Another all-night move (this time by moonlight) to Gistel, in Belgium, with you reading a map from a four-day-old London newspaper when the convoy leaves GA behind nosed over on its side beside a muddy stream.

Finally, on September 9, the guns deploy for action near Ostend, while the Rileys (Royal Hamilton Light Infantry) occupy the port seized yesterday by 18th Armoured Car Regiment (12th Manitoba Dragoons) feeling out the countryside in advance of 4th Division. Next day, with the Essex Scottish moving left towards Nieuwpoort, and the Royal Regiment of Canada moving right, along the coast towards Zeebrugge, the Regiment has to split up. Second Battery moves northeast behind the Royals, while the other two batteries (14th and 26th) go southwest to mark concrete coastal gun emplacements with red smoke for the rocket-firing Typhoon dive-bombers, affectionately known as "Tiffies."

Tootling about as a FOO (forward observation officer) at this time can be frustrating, as you discover when sent up to the Royals near Blankenberge. The daily allotment of shells is a mere twenty-five rounds per gun, and when these are used up, that's it. So later, when you are on reconnaissance along the west bank of the Bruges–Zeebrugge canal with Major Hank Caldwell, looking for a possible crossing point, and you spot Germans sunbathing on the far bank, you are unable to treat them to a single shell, which leaves Caldwell pawing the air.

Meanwhile, ammunition restrictions notwithstanding, the guns have to move often to stay within range, and Lieut. Bob Grout, your troop leader (as the assistant GPO is known), conducts the troop on a couple of dicey moves through flooded lowlands, where long stretches of roads are inundated. It's easy to drive off the road and submerge, as the Battery Command Post scout car did, soaking clothing, equipment, and stocks of cigarettes.

On September 11, 2nd and 14th batteries deploy just west of Bruges, a city of some fifty thousand with a large German garrison, including, according to local Resistance blokes, several thousand convalescent German soldiers wounded in Normandy. The Royals and the Royal Hamilton Light Infantry, after moving into the suburb of St. André to relieve units of 4th Division (the Royals taking over from the Lake Superior Regiment) that have had the city under mild siege for four days, are ordered "to make a show of strength," while 4th Division does a flanking move five kilometres southeast of the city from a bridgehead they have secured over the canal at Moerbrugge.

At noon on September 12, the guns move up into the outskirts of Bruges, Regimental Headquarters setting up shop in a notable building where King Leopold of Belgium capitulated to the Germans on May 28, 1940.

Soon reports of a city gone wild with joy reach the guns via "lost" truck drivers. Gunner Andy Turner, the Major's Don R (despatch rider), claims he was the first Canadian to enter Bruges – at least the first in that section of the city into which he blundered, to be overwhelmed by a mob of laughing, cheering people treating him to food and drink.

Later you hear Royals Capt. Tom Wilcox and his driver are being recognized as liberators of Bruges. Sent into the city on reconnaissance by his new CO, Lt.-Col. R. M. Lendrum, to discover the truth about reports that the enemy had flown, Wilcox was on his way back, after exchanging shots with some retreating Germans, when he was stopped by masses of cheering people pouring into the streets. Lendrum, hearing church bells ringing and cheering in the city, ordered the battalion to move in.*

The Rileys must have moved at about the same time, and no one will ever persuade Major Joe Pigott that *his* company was not the first to enter Bruges and be swallowed up in the surging mass of joyful humanity, which grabbed his soldiers, one after another, and hauled them off to parties, until he and his sergeant-major found they were leading no one.

However, officers and men of 4th Canadian Armoured Division will always claim they were the real liberators of Bruges, for it was they who first laid siege and who eventually negotiated, through a priest acting as the mayor's emissary, abandonment of the city by the Germans.

Most appropriately, when Brig. Robert Moncel, CO of 4th Armoured Brigade, enters the city – closely followed by Maj.-Gen. Harry Foster, OC of 4th Armoured Division – they are conducted by cheering crowds to the city hall to be made honorary citizens of Bruges.

Still, danger continues to lurk just north of the city, where FOO Len Harvey and his veteran carrier driver, Gunner George Ryckman, are wounded, seriously enough to be evacuated, by a booby trap attached to a German corpse.

By evening the sounds of revelry are everywhere, and men, women, and children crowd onto the gun position as though it's a freak show at a fair, paying their way with bottles of cognac, champagne, beer, and milk, and handfuls of eggs, apples, tomatoes, and onions.

At first it all seems harmless and amusing. But as the tippling goes on and the carnival atmosphere grows more and more pervasive, it becomes threatening and worrisome. You are not at all sorry when

---

* Wilcox was invited back on the first anniversary of Bruges' liberation to receive an engraved bronze medallion from the *Bürgermeister*.

the Germans intervene to the extent of attracting the attention of a
FOO somewhere on the north side of the city, resulting in a target
coming down and the gunners taking post. Just what these naïve
people crowding round the guns expected when they saw them
being loaded only they could say, but with the first deafening
smashes of muzzle blast, exaggerated by the surrounding buildings,
they turn into a panic-stricken mob, scattering in all directions as
though the devil himself is after them, dragging squealing children
by the hand and snatching up tiny tots who cannot keep up with
their headlong dash for homes and cellars.

At any rate, the guns are no longer treated as a sideshow, and
while the effects of gifts in bottles linger well into the night, no dis-
ciplinary problems are brought to your attention. And if some
gunners take advantage of the libertine spirits now abroad both
here and up at Middelkerke next day, when the Regiment returns
to the coast before the move back into France to lay siege to
Dunkirk, they do it with discretion.

Only one name makes it into Hossack's diary: "Bombardier Earl
Killeen celebrates his return to us by almost missing the early-
morning move."

2

BESIEGING DUNKIRK

--- ✳ ---

AT 4:00 A.M. ON SEPTEMBER 13, 4TH FIELD MOVES OFF ON
its return to France, carrying all 4th Brigade infantry not conveyed
by their own limited transport, many of them riding outside the
vehicles – some even perched precariously on guns and ammunition limbers. Hossack's diary records this as "a first," and reports
with obvious satisfaction that "the infantrymen speak well of our
support, and we take turns buying drinks at a café that opens early
as the convoy halts."

Within sight of Bergues, a hilltop German-held town six kilometres south of Dunkirk, the Royals are dropped off to make their
way on foot to the village of Warhem, while the guns deploy.

A couple of days ago, at the same time the normally staid BBC
was reporting, with undisguised pleasure, the end of five years of
nightly blackouts in Britain, they announced an end to further
training of the Home Guard, which had been frantically organized
in 1940 in the grim days of Dunkirk, when Hitler's legions were
expected to follow up their swift victory on the continent with a
cross-Channel invasion. Now, with some relish, you recognize that
your guns, laid on a zero line pointing at the Germans in Dunkirk,
are deployed in the very fields from whence the Germans besieged
the British rearguard. The British 25-pounders had gallantly held
on until they had to be blown up to keep them from falling into
enemy hands – while behind them on the beaches, thousands

cowered among the sand dunes, exposed to shells, bombs, and strafing hour after hour, awaiting their turn to wade out to the little rescue boats shuttling back and forth from England.

Still, the cold reality is that you are again in action against determined forces: as many as ten thousand in Dunkirk, and a three-hundred-man garrison of grenadiers led by SS officers (according to the French Maquis) holding Bergues' medieval-walled heights, looking awfully formidable on that solitary hill humped up on the pancake-flat landscape. The full realization that you are again truly at war strikes with uncomfortable force as you are informing Troop Sgt.-Major Tommy Mann that your recommendation for his long-service leave to Canada has been accepted and that in a few days he'll be leaving for home. The sight of tears welling up in his eyes at the prospect of seeing his wife and son after more than four years does you in.

Like everyone else, you have been expecting to hear that an Allied armoured column has thrust deep into Germany and the war is over. The rapid moves following 4th Brigade hither and yon the past few days reinforced the idea the German war machine is disintegrating and the end is near. But as you joke with Mann that you'll not be far behind — may in fact pass him at the transit depot in Aldershot — you are plagued with the thought you may buy it from a sniper bullet or a mine, even as the Reich collapses. It is not a healthy thought, and when you learn you have been promoted captain, and as Able Troop Commander must now take up fooing full-time, you do your best to suppress it.

Late in the afternoon you are sent up to take over a Baker Troop carrier crew left leaderless and stranded beside an isolated barn out in the barren flatland that is no-man's-land. They are about a mile west of Warhem, and about the same distance east of the enemy-infested Bergues, glowering down on you from the left flank.

That there are snipers within range, your predecessor, Capt. John Bagley, a newcomer to 4th Field and the fooing business, discovered when he tried sneaking forward among the drainage ditches towards a canal some seven hundred yards in front, on an inexplicable mission of his own devising that left his veteran crewmen mystified and remarkably unsympathetic to the fact he absorbed a bullet in his nether end. When you express concern, they startle you with the vehemence and the extremely colourful language (even for gunners) they use to convince you he has only a minor wound and will crawl back after dark to the battalion aid post in Warhem.

You don't pursue the matter, for at this point you realize you have inherited a crew in various stages of inebriation, the most advanced being Gunner W. J. Jordan, generally known as "Biff," a likeable character, settled in at the radio set among a clutter of empty beer bottles in the left-rear compartment of the carrier. Red-faced and beaming, he provides a lasting impression of a signaller so well-trained in his discipline he could function perfectly well even when loaded to the gills. You might not have even noticed his condition had he not felt the need to explain, each time you came near him, "I'm entirely a victim of circumstances, sir."

According to another member of the crew, Signaller "Wally" Driemel, the "circumstances" were simply that for some considerable time this morning they'd been left to their own devices near a brewery. Naturally they'd filled the carrier with cases of the stuff (and a couple of bottles of Advocat) before coming over here, and when it seemed they had been abandoned for an indefinite period, they'd gotten their snoots into the brew again. Admittedly, old Biff is a little the worse for wear, but he is a good man, and they've all been through a lot together. He hopes you'll make allowances. And you are preparing to do just that (aware you haven't many options) when the third member of the crew, a very young signaller, staggers on the scene with faulty step and glazed eyes, determined to impress you with his superior wisdom and maturity, even if it means asserting his opinions in a loud and belligerent voice.

Establishing his name is Knox, you send him packing to the barn's hayloft to sleep it off, determined to pursue the matter with some severity when he sobers up. And you probably would have but for Driemel, who undertakes to plead the case for leniency: Bill is really a good lad, and he's been through a lot. He usually isn't like that at all – just had more to drink than he's used to. And are you aware he is only a kid – barely sixteen – having lied his way into the army when he was only fourteen?

Coming from almost any other gunner, such intercession would be intolerable, but back in England you had come to think highly of Driemel's judgement upon learning he shared your taste in music, at least to the extent of being an enthusiastic fan of a song you composed for your wife, after that swinging piano-player Signaller Ralph "Coop" Cooper and his regimental dance-band added it to their repertoire for Saturday night dances. Driemel's pleas have their effect, and as you cool down you try to imagine the extent of the lie a kid of sixteen has to live – emotionally and every other way – just to survive among his peers and not be spotted and sent home for being three years under the legal age for active service. You end up packing all of them off to bed in the barn and take over the radio-watch yourself for the next four hours.

At last light, two companies of Royals (Major Hank Caldwell's and Major Bob Suckling's) pass through on their way up to the canal in front, which they will cross using a rubber raft towed back and forth with ropes. Before dawn they must establish a firm base on the northern bank, in the eastern end of the only narrow strip of land still above water.

From your first view of this watery landscape, you have despaired of troops managing a successful assault on Dunkirk. That one road to Dunkirk – a skinny seven-kilometres-long causeway stretching through the water to infinity from that spit of land forming the far bank of the canal, under observation every foot of the way – must surely become a road to suicide.

Suckling and Caldwell are more than a little disappointed when they learn you won't be crossing with them. And, for a moment, you feel so uncomfortable you almost change your mind. But you know that here is a real test of the credo of your old friend Don Wilson, passed on to you by Stu Laurie back in Normandy. Wilson, your 1942 troop commander and a D-Day 3rd Division battery commander, visiting 4th Field briefly in July, had criticized the high casualty rate among FOOs. He'd derided the practice of artillery carriers crawling along with the infantry at walking pace, instead of moving at high speed by leaps and bounds to places of cover, as the infantry gained or passed such cover. He'd stressed the point that FOOs should take every precaution not to get pinned down with the infantry in the attack, declaring: "You're no damned good to them with your face down in the dirt beside theirs."

And as you explain this to Caldwell and Suckling, you seriously expect that enemy fire will shortly be erupting about them at the canal. Instead, before crossing, Caldwell's company accepts the surrender of five Germans who swim over the canal to him; and both companies of Royals cross without any opposition.

This, you reason later, could only have been due to the attention of the enemy being diverted from the canal and the Royals' crossings by the very heavy concentrations fired by 4th Field on Bergues and the furtive activities of the RHLI over on the left as they prepared the ground for an attack on the walled town at 4:30 A.M. The Riley plan called for their scout platoon to cut a gap through a wire barrier, with the Pioneers lifting mines as necessary, after which a platoon of Royal Canadian Engineers would blow a hole through the twenty-foot-high town wall to allow two companies to enter. However, the Riley attack was aborted even before it got going, for reasons later explained by your friend "Stevie" Stevenson, of 14th Battery, who went forward as a FOO with the assaulting force:

As the company I was supporting had to approach the wall over a wide flat area, I was on foot with a radio set on my back. The sappers were there with scaling ladders, but the wily Hun was prepared for us. He'd located drums of oil around the perimeter of the wall, and as we came up he applied a lighted torch until all were ablaze. Immediately our approach was light as day, and their enfiladed fire raked the front. Casualties were heavy, and only by crawling on one's gut did most of us manage to withdraw.

3

RELISHING REVENGE

AS GUNS SMASH ATTACK

❋

WHILE THE NAMES OF THOSE WHO SERVE AS SECOND-IN-command of infantry battalions may never appear among the postwar lists of commanding officers, some are chalking up more time in command of their battalions than many who will be so honoured in unit histories. Such a one is Major Ralph Young of the Royals, who recently acted as CO of the battalion for almost a month, from the day Lt.-Col. Jack Anderson was wounded until Lt.-Col. R. M. Lendrum arrived five days ago from the Canadian Scottish Regiment to take over.

Exuding a steely determination, which you sense could border on the ruthless if such were required to see the unit through a sticky go, he always manages to wear a big smile even in the most wretched circumstances. It is incomprehensible, unless you take his smile to be a kind of sardonic comment, a smile of contempt by one taking a cosmic view of the ongoing human condition. But what-ever is behind that smile, you usually find it reassuring – except when he arrives unexpectedly at a company you are supporting, for his sudden appearance can mean a crisis is brewing or an attack is being planned.

So shortly after dawn today, September 15, your anxiety level rises sharply when, with uncanny clairvoyance, Young appears beside you in your hayloft overlooking the canal and the road leading up to Dunkirk just as a swarm of Germans mount a blazing

counter-attack against two companies of Royals beyond the canal.
He had spotted them streaming out of a house at the left end of the
spit of land as he drove up to your barn in his Jeep, and scrambled
up the ladder to your loft to alert you before the last of them spilled
from the house into view.

Through holes you punched yesterday through the tiles in the
barn roof, you can see them running crouched over, now and then
dropping down, only to rise almost immediately with Schmeissers
blazing in the direction of the Royals dug-in among some trees at
the right end of the "island." With the canal house as a reference
point, it is easy to give the guns a precise map reference, and you go
right into "fire for effect" without ranging: "Scale 10" (ten rounds
per gun), using one battery of eight guns only, for there isn't room
between the attackers and the Royals to safely use all twenty-four.
The target area you choose is slightly ahead of the advancing
Germans, anticipating they'll arrive just in time to walk under your
deluge of eighty shells. And so it happens.

Steadying your glasses on a rafter pole to counter the rocking
sponginess of the hay under your feet, you focus on the hunched-
over, running, blue-grey forms from whom streams of glittering
white tracers periodically spurt into the trees ahead of them. You
see their faces clearly as your shells sizzle overhead, and then violent
black-and-orange puffs flash and spout among them. Only for a
moment can you follow them – some go down immediately, others
try to run, then crumple over and go down – then smoke from the
torrent of explosions blots out everything. Satisfied with the way
your shells are falling, you order "Scale 20 – Repeat" (twenty
rounds per gun at the same line and range).

As your shells rip and tear that narrow strip of land where you
saw them go to ground, you feel you are finally taking revenge.
After all the times you and your comrades have cringed, paralyzed
with fear, under *their* shelling, *their* mortaring, *their* strafing, and
their bombing – without ever once being able to get them in your
sights – you finally have them. And you find yourself mumbling:
"That's for always-smiling Jack Cameron (who every night wrote

his wife, whom he married only two days before being sent over-seas) ... and that's for quiet Jack Thompson (who left his wife preg-nant on his last leave) ... and that's for my Grace's gentle uncle George Marsh, the Birmingham air-raid warden (who died on duty) ... and that's for Dawson and Knapp and Parker and Thorpe and Ament ..."

The Royals' historian will record: "Three times the enemy massed for counter-attacks on A Company's position, but each time they were dispersed by accurate artillery and mortar fire, and the direct fire of a 40-mm Bofors ack-ack gun." But you will recall only ordering and reordering, "Scale 20 – Repeat" until the sur-vivors rise up with hands stretched high over their heads and walk into the Royals' position – thirty-six only, including two officers, of the 186 who marched down here from Dunkirk last night, accord-ing to the haggard prisoners.

For once you are able to give command posts and the men on the guns a graphic description of the results of their shooting. However, before they have time to take satisfaction from their morning's work, at about 11:00 A.M. they are on the receiving end of unusually heavy and accurate shelling from German guns around Dunkirk – something everybody had been expecting since 4th Field moved forward yesterday into full view of what the gunners call "Burg-on-the-hill."

Sgt. Bruce Hunt's diary will report: "Command posts, troops and kitchen – each in turn receives a well-directed, vicious effort." But while tires and gas tanks are punctured and kit of all sorts is blown to oblivion, 2nd and 26th batteries miraculously suffer no casual-ties. Less fortunate is 14th Battery; they suffer six casualties. As the guns are being limbered up to try to escape the shelling by moving back to the former gun position, Gunner John S. Sherwood is killed. And Sergeant Nicholas Ostapyck and gunners Edward J. Cuff, F. H. A. Nicholson, Michael McLeod, and John Rutherford are wounded.

And 14th Battery FOO "Stevie" Stevenson tells you later of another rough go for him with the RHLI. Shelled out of a church tower – his carrier damaged, his radio knocked out, and his signaller badly wounded – he's desperate as he wades back through a water-filled ditch to the Rileys' company headquarters.

They are in the process of withdrawing over the fields, but I can't join them because I don't want to leave my wounded signaller behind. I get through to Battalion on their radio and ask Jack Drewry, my battery commander, for smoke to cover the route I'll take.

Back at the church we load the wounded signaller into the carrier and lay on our route with the driver, who'll be driving blind through smoke. When it arrives, we move off with our heads down. All the way back, the sides of the carrier are pitted with small-arms fire, but we make it to Battalion HQ. Everybody seems rather surprised to see us.

The effectiveness of the German counter-battery fire creates an urgent demand for precise information on the location of the offending guns, and you are sent to spend the night flash-spotting the guns of Dunkirk from a towering church steeple in Hondschoote, right of Warhem.

As you settle down on an open stone balcony, far above the world, you wonder why in 1940 the British allowed this tower to survive overlooking their entire rearguard forces holding off the Germans. Never, in your wildest conjectures, while reading to your training troop in Petawawa from "Return Via Dunkirk," by a gunner officer using the pseudonym "Gunbuster" – the story of a British field regiment supporting the gallant rearguard – did you imagine that one day you'd be here at Dunkirk with the roles reversed. From up here you can readily identify that part of the "naked plain," some eight kilometres away near Rosendael on the eastern outskirts of Dunkirk, where those immortal 25-pounders were deployed in their final stand that last night before being blown up by their battery commanders at virtually the eleventh hour, while behind them burning Dunkirk "glowed red like a cinder."

ɪnen, as now, much of the countryside was covered with water, flooded by the French opening sluice gates to discommode the Germans who had to cross that same canal glistening down there before you that the Royals crossed last night. And farther on, a mile from Dunkirk, though you can't identify it, is another canal into which the British gunners dumped all their shells "considered surplus" to their last-hour needs – an incredible move. Why they didn't fire them off at the enemy before spiking their guns is something that has always bothered you; and you wonder if those shells are still lying there on the bottom of that canal.

How remarkably different this whole business of seeking out targets and dropping shells on them has become since those days. The equipment you carry to do all required of a FOO – field-glasses, compass, Chinagraph pencil and map (frequently removed from its protective talc-covered case and stuffed in the front of your blouse) – would have seemed incredibly primitive to "Gunbuster" when the shooting war began for him, somewhere west of Brussels in May 1940. As that earnest gunner officer settled down in his tower to carry out the prescribed procedures of 1914–18 vintage – first to draw a panorama pencil sketch of the zone, then to carry out "silent registration" of potential targets – he had with him a survey instrument known as a No. 7 Artillery Director, a range finder, and an artillery board holding gridded paper and an "arm" and an "arc" to measure ranges and switches to targets. How he and his poor ack ever made it up a tower, lugging all that stuff, you can't imagine.

As it is, even without all that baggage, the number of steps and ladder rungs you have to climb to reach this eyrie leaves you breathless and heaving. And for your hungover, repentant crew, it is a penitential climb of intimidating proportions each time they have to ascend from ground level: first with cables and phone, and then down and up, down and up, to relieve the pangs of hunger, thirst, and other bodily functions, which seem to be functioning more than usual this evening. There has been no "hair of the dog" for them today, of that you have made certain, and as the night tips over into the early hours of September 16, and the telephone goes dead, they pay the price for their excessive indulgence yesterday, as, sweating and panting, they take turns climbing up and down the darkened interior of this great tower trying to get the thing to work.

The recalcitrant instrument went dead just when you collected a clean bearing on a gun firing from Dunkirk – a really big flash you suspect was from the muzzle of the coastal gun they have turned around and are using to harass major Allied supply roads many miles inland. Radio silence having been imposed tonight for some reason, it is essential to get the damned telephone to work.

Finally assuming there's a break in the line snaking back to Regiment, you wait for the Signal Section to fix it. But when the first misty predawn light appears and the line is still dead, you decide to pack everybody into the carrier and go back along the road to locate the break. Your weary men are soon patiently taking turns stumbling along the ditch, running the signal wire through their hands, when they meet the signal truck coming up, its crew industriously winding in the cable on a big spool!

Incredulous, you listen to Signal-Sgt. Ryder informing you that the Regiment pulled out an hour ago for Belgium, on their way to Antwerp. Hadn't anyone told you?

Surely he's joking, especially that ridiculous Antwerp bit.

He assures you the guns left at 0430 for a staging area ten miles east of here.

When finally you catch up with the Regiment at Hoogstade, you learn that 4th Brigade is being rushed to Antwerp to prevent the Germans returning to destroy the port facilities. It seems the nervous garrison had been more concerned with being cut off from *das Vaterland* by the tanks of British 11th Armoured Division than with blowing up the port facilities, and they have been left virtually intact in the control of the Belgian Resistance after the city was overrun by the British tanks and the garrison commander captured by the accompanying infantry. Now, realizing their error, the Germans are trying to return.

And Dunkirk? It will be screened off and left to rot.*

At 0915 on September 16, the Regiment, again carrying the infantry packed in and on the quads, trucks, and gun limbers, pulls out for Antwerp, following a route through the heart of "Flanders Fields." All morning you see road signs associated with legendary battles of the First War. Ten miles into the journey, there's the road leading to Poperinghe. Then comes Ypres with its Menin Gate, a great stone arch carrying the names of sixty thousand British and British Commonwealth soldiers of the First War for whom there were no known graves, and where each evening at sundown three members of the Ypres Fire Brigade assemble to raise their bugles and blow the Last Post in grateful memory of their sacrifice.

Six kilometres northeast of Ypres, and six west of Passchendaele, you pass the towering thirty-five-foot granite pillar supporting the famous "brooding soldier" – a giant bust of a soldier bowed over his folded hands which rest on the butt of his rifle standing muzzle-down at "arms reversed" – marking the entrance to a cemetery near St. Julien of two thousand graves of Canadians who fell during the Second Battle of Ypres in 1915.

The great helmeted head, bowed forever in reverent sorrow, is so striking and its message so powerful that for a while you are over-come with murderous hatred for a people who wildly cheered their leader as step by step he led them into vile aggressions that would plunge the world into another round of slaughter, within a mere twenty-one years of the end of the one commemorated here.

However, as emotional exhaustion adds its weight to the stupefying

---

* The Allied High Command sensibly decided it was not worth the price it would cost to pursue the attack across that flooded landscape. Dunkirk was left contained by a screen of armoured cars of the Czech Brigade for the rest of the war.

effects of some thirty hours with only catnaps, you slump down in the rocking carrier and drift off in a sleep so deep you don't wake until its tracks are clattering along a cobblestone street lined with substantial buildings whose façades of rich and intricate design suggest an ancient city of some consequence. Your driver, Gunner Bill Walkden, reveals you are passing through Ghent, seemingly unharmed by whatever the 7th Armoured Division (Desert Rats) had to do to capture it a couple of days ago.

Hazy memories of Browning's poem " 'How They Brought the Good News from Ghent to Aix' " are stirred: "I sprang to the stirrup, and Joris, and he;/ I galloped, Dirck galloped, we galloped all three...." And though no "cocks crow" at Lokeren, and at Boom no "great yellow star" appears, you follow the very route Browning's imaginary horsemen galloped towards Aix until you reach Boom and 4th Field turns north to Antwerp. But unlike the over-stressed horses that began dropping dead as their awesome gallop reached a climax, not a single quad or other 4th Field vehicle breaks down on this long and strenuous drive.

The way the Regiment's vehicles are standing up on these long hauls through northern France and Belgium is a measure of their excellent maintenance by conscientious drivers and the support of dedicated battery motor-mechanics, who daily labour beyond the call of duty.

The reliability of the big trucks, travelling back and forth from supply dumps, bringing up tons of shells, petrol, and rations, is taken for granted by all except the "motor-mechs." Seldom have vehicles failed to keep their place in convoy on these all-night runs, and when on rare occasion vehicles have broken down, motor-mechs usually have them moving again in short order.

Major repairs are supposed to be by LAD (Light Aid Detachment), a section of REME (Royal Electrical and Mechanical Engineers) detached and travelling with the Regiment. If LAD can't handle the job, it is sent back to REME Base Work Shops set up in buildings suitable for machine shops and sophisticated repairs. But many major repairs are made at the side of the road, or in open fields, by 4th Field mechanics. Officially, batteries are limited in the stores they can carry with them, but battery motor-mechs never miss an opportunity to add to their stocks of spare parts, pirating fuel pumps, carburettors, water pumps, and the like from disabled vehicles along the way.

Whether the nature of the trade attracts a certain type of man, or whether it's because they are daily involved in pursuits of a con-structive nature, while all about them others are sharpening their skills for destruction, motor-mechs invariably appear as men of greater maturity with strong leadership qualities. Without excep-tion they are accorded high respect by all ranks. Some, like 2nd Battery Bombardier G. J. Vosdingh, are looked upon as supermen. Affectionately known as "Sledge," for sledgehammer, he is believed capable of fixing anything with "a bit of wire and a pair of pliers." And over the years you have heard this, or something similar, said of at least one mechanic in every battery.

Recently this legendary ingenuity was taxed to the limit when "Sledge" and 2nd Battery's Sgt. Keith McConnell replaced a clutch in the middle of the night in a truck bringing up a load of petrol to the Regiment. Obviously this was a job for a well-lit, well-equipped workshop, which in normal circumstances would have been turned over to LAD or towed back to REME.

However, in McConnell's judgement there wasn't time. Without that load of petrol, the Regiment could be immobilized, a very serious matter for the rapidly advancing infantry who have come to count on the continuous support of the guns of 4th Field, night and day, in fair weather and foul. Fortunately, they were carrying in Battery Stores a spare clutch for a 30-hundredweight truck, which they had the foresight to scrounge somewhere back in Normandy. Working under a tarpaulin draped over the vehicle to prevent light from their lantern attracting a marauding German bomber to this load of petrol, they removed the defective clutch and replaced it well before dawn, and were able to catch up with the Regiment before any gas tanks ran dry.

Motor-mechanics will never be awarded medals for keeping vehicles in operation, for the same reason signallers are not decorated for keeping wireless sets operating. Their work is now so taken for granted it is unlikely that any mention of them will ever appear in the Regimental war diary, let alone in despatches from war correspondents, who, quite naturally, overlook the dull, winding columns of trucks coming up behind, in favour of the flashing guns and the roaring tanks and armoured cars in the spearheads thrusting into enemy country.

Still, anyone choosing to reflect on the matter will agree that dependable transport, like constant communications, is crucial for the guns to be there whenever the infantry and tanks need them to support attacks and subdue counter-attacks. And the extent to which this is not always true of the German artillery may account for the ultimate success of our infantry against Hitler's élite divisions.

4

THE SOUND OF
REVELRY BY NIGHT

✳

AFTER TEN HOURS, THE CONVOY ARRIVES IN ANTWERP JUST as the sun is going down on a beautiful evening, the guns rolling down the Grand Boulevard between dense, cheering crowds and beneath a succession of giant elongated Belgian flags, hanging down from cables stretched across the street, their red, orange, and black stripes wavering gently like flames in the sunset as the quads brush under them on their way across town to the docks in the north end.

This great reception is totally unexpected. After all, twelve days have passed since four British tanks nosed their way tentatively into Antwerp, making it Allied territory. But tonight, with the Germans in the northeastern suburb of Merxem, threatening to reoccupy the city and perhaps carry out reprisals, people have turned out to express their gratitude to the first large contingent of Allied troops that has come this way with a comforting number of guns. Men, women, and children, many on their fathers' shoulders, line both curbs of the great boulevard's right roadway, cheering the passing parade.

Now and then someone darts from the curb to pass up fruit, cigars, wine, or beer to a gun sergeant leaning down from the roof-hatch of a passing quad or to a soldier reaching out from his perch on a gun or limber. A big bunch of grapes and a handful of fine cigars land *plop* in your lap just as your carrier is passing what you'll later learn is the opera house, a noble structure at an intersection with a main business artery that leads right, to the Rex movie theatre, sidewalk cafés, the railway station, and the Century Hotel.

The convoy pauses a moment later to drop off the infantry, and your carrier peels away to follow the marching Royals down narrow back streets to an area of factories and warehouses along the Albert Canal, which separates Antwerp from the Germans in Merxem. The guns proceed north to deploy on and about the docks, with muzzles pointing across the empty ships' basins towards Merxem. The luck of the draw places 2nd Battery in pre-prepared gun positions with excellent German-built dugouts just north of the docks at Noordkasteel. The cooks set up shop in splendour in an aquatic clubhouse complete with swimming pool.

As the guns are put on line, the infantry take up positions along the canal and at other strategic points, such as the installations known as "sluice gates," which, you are told, the Germans must seize if they are seriously to disable the harbour. Until now, these all-important gates controlling water levels at the port, eighty kilometres up the Scheldt river from the North Sea, have been held somewhat precariously through the gallant fighting and astute manoeuvring of Belgian Resistance fighters, now known as the White Brigade because of the white butchers' coats they assumed as their uniform on moving their operations "above ground."

You spend the entire first night finding your way from the Royals Tac HQ, in a school a few blocks from the canal, to 4th Brigade HQ, in a mansion on the other side of town, to pick up maps; and it's mid-morning before you finally settle in your OP, the attic of an empty multi-storey factory building down on the canal.

Almost encircling the gloomy vastness under the rafters on the top floor, is a substantial rubber conveyor-belt nearly five feet wide, resting, unmoving, on a bed of rollers on a waist-high steel frame. Placed a few feet from the windows, it provides a convenient springy-but-firm extended platform from which to view the zone through small dormer windows high up in the steeply slanting mansard roof. However, as an OP, to be occupied over a long period, it is seriously flawed. The slanting part of the roof is only the thickness of asphalt shingles laid over one-inch boards, offering little or no protection against anything but a spent bullet. Shells and mortar bombs could rip through it like paper. For the first time, you decide you must take advantage of a privilege extended by custom to artillery forward observers by the infantry, and ask them to provide you with "protection," which can be interpreted in many ways – in this case a "pillbox" built of sandbags on the conveyor-belt.

Company Commander Suckling is somewhat taken aback when you make your request as you are bedding down that night on one of the cots sitting on duck-boards in the partially flooded basement where he's established his headquarters. But sympathetic to your position, he arranges for a squad to haul the necessary number of sandbags up the several flights of stairs and stack them in a semi-circle on the belt, leaving a viewing-slot in front and roofing it over with more sandbags. When the nest is "floored" with chesterfield cushions, you're absolutely delighted, even though it immediately draws undisguised scorn from an observer crew for the Toronto Scottish's 4.2-inch mortars, the officer and his signaller lounging like oriental potentates in deeply upholstered chairs on the conveyor-belt in front of neighbouring windows.

Unquestionably the war is serious business for the infantrymen along the canal and the gunners among the docks, but the drawing power of a city untouched by war – full of cafés, restaurants, hotels, and pretty women – is irresistible, and the powers-that-be know it. So the second night, five-hour leaves uptown are started for a portion of the gunners at a time.

When Sgt.-Maj. Tommy Mann, who leaves tomorrow for Canada, picks you up at the OP to drive you uptown, he brings along Sgt. "Lefty" Phillips, the man who'll succeed him as troop sergeant-major. After locating what seems to be the heart of the city and parking the Jeep by removing the rotor from the distributor, there's still the puzzle of how to proceed. Uncertain where to go in the blackout, you stop and listen. The sounds of music and laughter lead you through a blackout curtain and upstairs to a beautifully appointed restaurant and dance floor jammed with people in evening dress. All over the room, smiling people beckon you and your companions to join them at their tables, and waiters follow you with chairs and a tray of drinks. But as you squeeze in between an immaculately dressed man and woman, you become conscious of your bulky sidearm, your dirty hands, and your stained and rumpled battledress.

Although they pooh-pooh your concerns, you get a waiter to lead you to a washroom. It turns out to be one that serves both women and men at the same time, and for the first time, you have the peculiar experience of being attended in such a place by a woman. She hands you a tiny sliver of soap and a towel; and when, after washing, you go into a cubicle and get comfortably seated, reflecting how much better this is than a Compo box with its top panel punched in, she knocks at the door and hands you in two sheets of toilet paper.

When you rejoin your companions, you find they've decided they can't stand such affluence and want to try somewhere else. Every other place is jammed, for it appears Antwerp has decided spontaneously to celebrate this day as their Liberation Day, something they had delayed doing until the few British tanks and infantry and their gallant resistance fighters were reinforced by the Canadian battalions and the 4th Field guns.

For a while it looks like a dry night, but suddenly you find a quiet side street full of small luxurious bars with nobody in them. It isn't until you have had a drink in four or five different establishments, and become bored with the utter stillness of the perfumed luxury of each of them in turn, that one of your companions asks the lady proprietor why they have so few customers. The Madam explains the facts of life as she knows them on this street, and offers him one of her "girls," a woman old enough to be his mother.

You go back to following the sound of revelry in the blackout, and are led to a small restaurant in a converted house. Inside, a pianist at an upright piano with a vase of roses on it accompanies an attractive lady singing "Roses of Picardy." Looking around the room, it dawns on you that these people, listening so intently with a far-away look in their eyes, are old enough to have gathered around a piano and sung this song at the height of its popularity in 1916. Having driven all the previous day along poplar-lined roads that "Colinette with the sea-blue eyes" would have recognized, you feel extraordinarily close to these people and their thoughts, and suddenly you realize the 1914–18 war, which always seemed so long ago, was really only yesterday.

Days later, when you visit the guns, you will find your GPO Bob Grout and new Troop Leader Lieut. Bernie Ackerman imbued with similar thoughts, having been led into the subject by Gunner John Elder's father. Brig. Herbert Elder, Deputy-Director Canadian Army Medical Services, and senior medical officer in this theatre of operations, had paid a surprise visit to the guns to see his son, who, until then, had kept the matter of his father's high rank hidden from his comrades. The Brigadier, a courtly gentleman six-foot-three-and-a-half-inches tall, had served as a bugler at his father's field hospital in Flanders in 1914 when he was only sixteen.

Bombardier Hossack's diary, however, presents a less sentimental view of Antwerp:

Collaborators are being rounded up daily, and the women who "informed" on the resistance forces, or were otherwise unpatriotic, are publicly shamed. Made to stand all day in a main-street window giving the Nazi salute, they are removed to the street at 5:00 P.M., where a barber clips them bald. A woman shorn of her locks loses much of her beauty. There follows the public march, or rather the chase, to the cages of the nearby zoo, with all civilian bystanders vying for a chance to slap or spit on the unfortunate ones. A particularly angry mob has torn the clothes from one young lady and she covers the route to the zoo in record time.

The cost of high-living is telling on the boys. Our extra smokes, soap, and chocolate disappear for francs, but we're still poor. In the end everything from Jeeps to dirty underwear claims its price. Enemy shells seldom land near us, but his mortars are active against other units. One shell does land on our cookhouse just ten minutes after we (including cooks) had dispersed.

For sixteen days, 4th Brigade and its supporting guns (along with the rest of 2nd Division from September 19) remain here, preventing the Germans from spoiling what the High Command considers a plum, while all priority of supply on the Western Front is given over to Montgomery's "Market-Garden" operation, which is meant to leap over the Rhine, utilizing huge British and American paratroop and glider forces to secure the vast Grave bridge over the Maas (Meuse) river, the Nijmegen bridge over the southern branch of the Rhine, and the Arnhem bridge over the Neder Rhine, while XXX Corps drives a corridor north towards them along the ground.

Most things still come all the way up from the Normandy beaches, and ammunition, while sufficient for emergencies and some harassing fire, is strictly rationed, which means you restrict your firing to targets you can clearly identify among the streets you overlook in Merxem. An exception to this is the great bulging roof of the ice-hockey arena, into which you drop a shell now and then to discourage its use by the enemy for storage or billetting.*

Your most intriguing target involves a dead-end street leading away from the canal directly opposite you. Each noon German soldiers trickle out in ones and twos from between two houses down

---

* Weeks later, on a balmy early winter day, as Belgian workmen strove to repair holes in the great arena's roof and stem the inward flow of warm air, 4th Field's regimental hockey team (managed by the FOO who'd punched all those holes) participated in a game (the only one they got to play on the continent) in fog so dense that, from behind the players' bench, only centre-ice faceoffs could be seen before the action disappeared into the white void; and only the sudden cessation of clicking and clacking of sticks and a return to visibility at centre ice of players and referee for another faceoff revealed the fact that a goal had been scored.

near the canal on the left side of the street and take off in a mad gallop to the far end, where they cross over and disappear. At first they'd strolled casually, one even walking a bicycle, obviously believing they were unobserved. But now, knowing the street is "registered," they run for their lives when they enter "Green Street," the name you've given it because of the carpet of grass growing up between the cobblestones through the absence of all vehicular traffic. Why they don't use a hidden route to their cook-house for their noon meal is beyond comprehension, but day after day without fail they maintain their routine, and each day your guns are loaded and waiting to ambush them. This greatly amuses Bob Suckling and neighbouring company commanders Caldwell and Stothers when he invites them over to inspect the "pillbox" his men built for you, and they time their visit to coincide with your noon-day show.

However, for the men on the guns who can't see the interesting effects of the fall of their shot, it's a matter of vast irritation that every noon, just as the cooks have doled out their hot meal, your order comes down to take post. And after loading and laying their guns on the target, they wait interminably for the order to fire, while their grub grows cold and greasy in their mess tins, and leathery membranes form in their mugs on the surface of their "Compo tea" – that unforgettable concoction obtained by boiling tea leaves, powdered milk, and sugar together.

When enemy mortars become active for short intervals from somewhere in the grounds of a castle-like structure among the trees over the canal, counter-measures are arranged for rocket-firing Typhoons, with your guns marking the suspected target area with red smoke. Then the night of September 20, the Essex Scottish, on the left, are attacked in such strength, one company is forced off its position; and the Germans are driven off only after 2,400 rounds are expended by the Regiment in a flurry of firing.* However, such

_____

* L/Sgt. Joseph Harold Lewis (Troop Signals NCO of 26th Battery) was

activity is unusual here. Apart from the loony Jerries in Green Street each noon, you seldom spot anything to hammer, and the hours from dawn to dusk pass very slowly – particularly in the cramped positions you must assume to fit into your sandbag nest, for while it is a masterpiece of strength and security, it is not spacious. Still, you sustain the belief that one of these days the Germans will have to conclude the observer for the guns harassing them each noon is up in a window high in this building directly opposite Green Street, and when they do, your caution will be vindicated.

At noon today it happens. As always you are curled up in your "cocoon," as your mildly insulting Tor Scots neighbours refer to it as they recline in their easy chairs to your left. As usual you've laid the guns on Green Street to await the stubbornly methodical Germans who, despite the fact you have shelled them every day for a week, will appear as usual to run their awful gauntlet. You wait impatiently, for you are scheduled to go uptown for a few hours this afternoon. But right on time the first appear, galloping up the street. You yell "Fire!" into the phone and immediately the guns start thumping behind. In seconds, sinister whispers pass overhead – a split-second silence – and then roaring vicious flashes, black smoke, and dust fill the street.

As you wait for the dust to settle, there is a nasty fluttering sound overhead and a mortar bomb crashes through the roof – then another and another and another in rapid succession, blacking out everything with choking attic dust. In the dark stillness that follows, there is the sound of groaning and then cries of "Stretcher!" from the mortar crew. Yelling to them that you are going for help, you feel your way over to the stairs, and skitter down to locate stretcher-bearers.

---

subsequently awarded a Military Medal for re-establishing communications between OP and guns by land line, "following a route that was under shellfire continually, and, at a critical stage, under direct fire from enemy automatic weapons." (Quoted from citation.)

This accomplished, you make your way out through the back alley, crouching over to keep out of sight. After a block or two you are able to straighten up, and wait for a free ride uptown on one of the little yellow streetcars that dare come down this far. When one arrives, it stops just long enough for a brisk and friendly motorman to swing the trolley arm around and change his control-crank from front to back, and it rattles and scrapes back the way it came, taking you to scenes of civilian life going on totally oblivious to the rumble of guns in the distance.

The streets are full of shoppers, including women with toddlers and baby carriages. Sidewalk cafés are crowded with civilians and soldiers watching the girls go by. The spacious lounge of the Century Hotel is filled with immaculately groomed people conversing over the gentle strains of a vintage salon orchestra, and dawdling over their glasses of Advocaat served by discreet waiters in dinner jackets. While up the block, the ice-cream parlour is doing a land-office business soothing throats that haven't tasted anything cold for months – let alone ice-cream – some customers starting at the top of a menu on the wall and successively ordering every sundae listed.

When your five-hour leave is up, you catch a streetcar back to the canal where you take up the business of war again. Tonight you fire diversionary shelling, to draw their attention away from friend Lieut. "Hefty" Ross, the now-legendary Royals' scout officer, who, in anticipation of the attack that everyone knows must soon be made over there, swims the canal and crawls around on his belly in the cinders of a dark Merxem parking lot, locating German positions by following the smell of cigarette smoke and the faint, desultory conversation between sentries meeting at the boundaries of their allotted rounds. Around 3:00 A.M., he returns via Suckling's company. Soaking wet and shuddering, black-faced with shoe polish, and with a balaclava pulled over his head, he pores over a map with Bob, identifying the enemy positions he's pinpointed.

5

CLEARING THE CHANNEL PORTS

❋

FATE MUST SURELY HAVE BEEN MINDFUL OF THE TERRIBLE sacrifices made by 2nd Division on the beaches of Dieppe in 1942 to have arranged events in such a way as to spare its units from fighting for a Channel port.

Remarkably, the only two Channel ports of consequence taken without a struggle were those assigned to 2nd Division for clearing: Dieppe and Ostend, which, according to Intelligence, were the only ports Hitler didn't place on his list to be held at all costs. Then on the eve of what surely would have been another blood-letting in the flooded land in front of Dunkirk, 2nd Division was suddenly withdrawn and rushed to Antwerp to occupy static positions in relative comfort, periodically enduring breathtaking brushes with civilian luxury on pass uptown.

Meanwhile, other divisions of First Canadian Army, including attached British divisions, have been forced to fight for every metre of ground in the vicinity of every one of their designated ports.

The first, Le Havre, earmarked for American use, required a heavy assault by two British divisions, the 49th West Riding and 51st Highland, supported by massive fire-power from land, sea, and air – most particularly the air from which 4,000 tons of bombs were dropped during the siege and 5,500 more during the attack itself, which began September 10. From the sea the 15-inch guns of HMS *Erebus* and *Warspite* shelled the coastal gun emplacements. And

BATTLE OF THE SCHELDT

OCTOBER – NOVEMBER 1944

N

4 RCA gun position

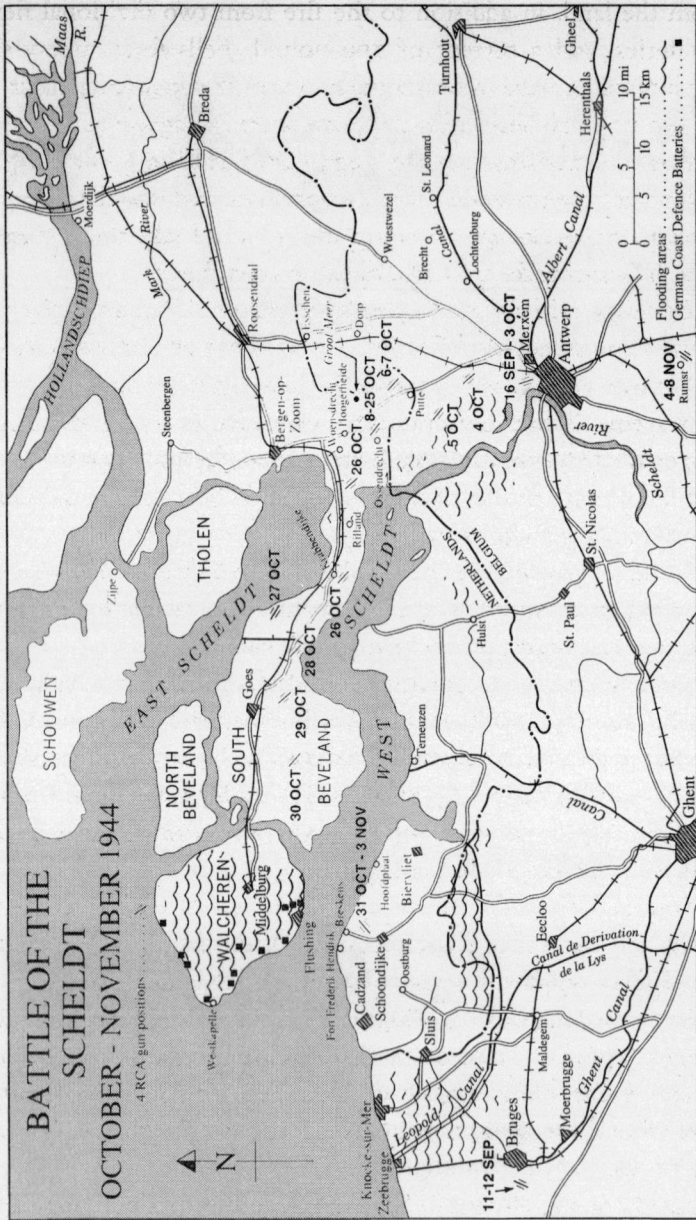

Flooding areas
German Coast Defence Batteries

0   5   10 mi
0 5 10 15 km

Maas R.

HOLLANDSCHDIEP

Moerdijk

Breda

Riet

Mark River

Roosendaal

Steenbergen

SCHOUWEN

Zijpe

THOLEN

EAST SCHELDT

NORTH BEVELAND

SOUTH BEVELAND

27 OCT

28 OCT

29 OCT

30 OCT

31 OCT - 3 NOV

WALCHEREN

Middelburg

Flushing

Westkapelle

Fort Frederik Hendrik

Breskens

Cadzand

Schoondijke

Oostburg

Sluis

Biervliet

Hoofdplaat

WEST SCHELDT

26 OCT

26 OCT

Rilland

Ossendrecht

Kreekrak

Woensdrecht

Hoogerheide

8-25 OCT

Putte

Bergen-op-Zoom

Wouwsche

Groot Meer

Deep

6-7 OCT

5 OCT

4 OCT

16 SEP - 3 OCT

Merxem

Antwerp

4-8 NOV

Rumst

Scheldt River

St. Nicolas

St. Paul

Hulst

NETHERLANDS

BELGIUM

Terneuzen

Ghent

Canal

Eecloo

Canal de Derivation
de la Lys

Maldegem

Moerbrugge

Bruges

11-12 SEP

Leopold Canal

Ghent Canal

Knocke-sur-Mer

Zeebrugge

Brecht

Westwezel

Loenhout

St. Leonard

Turnhout

Herenthals

Gheel

Albert Canal

Canal

from the land, in addition to the fire from two divisional field artilleries, and a torrent of 100-pound shells from ninety-six medium guns, were the awesome *crumps* of 200-pound shells from sixteen 7.2-inch heavies blasting away at the strongpoints.

Hardly surprising that the siege ended after only forty-eight hours with the surrender of 9,500 survivors, and that the demolition of the docks was so complete, it would take more than a month to restore the port installations to usefulness.

Boulogne is in no better shape when captured. The assault by 3rd Division on its garrison of 10,000 and its ninety guns of various calibres up to great coastal guns, all well-protected by thick concrete emplacements, had to wait until Le Havre fell and the guns of 51st Highland Division and 9th British AGRA (Army Group Royal Artillery) could be moved north to join 2nd Cdn AGRA and double up the land-based fire-power.

In the meantime, German positions, marked by red smoke by the field guns, were subjected to twenty-nine attacks by medium bombers and swarms of rocketing Typhoons.

On September 16, opening day of the assault, the Typhoons carried out twenty additional strikes, but these were dwarfed by the 8,541 bombs (3,310 tons) dropped by 752 Lancaster and Halifax heavy bombers and 40 Mosquitoes on five target areas. And while the bombs were still falling, 328 guns opened up on a series of timed concentrations on strongpoints.

Brig. Stanley Todd, CRA of 3rd Division (ex-CO of 4th Field), had under his control five field regiments, five medium regiments, three heavy regiments, and one heavy ack-ack regiment. And considering the long hauls for ammunition, the scale accumulated was astounding: 38,400 rounds for ninety-six 25-pounders, 14,000 20-pound shells for forty-eight heavy ack-ack guns, 12,000 100-pound shells for eighty mediums, and 800 200-pound shells for eight 7.2-inch guns.

In addition to all this, to keep the big coastal guns of Boulogne preoccupied during the assault, Brig. H. O. N. Brownfield, the BRA (Brigadier Royal Artillery), the highest ranking gunner officer of

First Canadian Army, arranged for supporting cross-Channel fire from two 14-inch Dover guns, coyly known as "Winnie" and "Pooh," and two 15-inch monsters of 540th Coast Regiment at Wanston on St. Margaret's Bay, directed on targets by an Air OP officer, the CO of 660 Squadron, flying a little Auster aircraft above the Channel, augmented by observations by ground observers brought over from Dover.

The Wanston guns scored a direct hit on a 16-inch enemy gun at Sangatte before their 1,920-pound shells began to land in the sea – their worn barrels (the fourth replacements in three years) no longer capable of producing the muzzle velocity necessary to send their huge missiles to the continent. However, "Winnie" and "Pooh" fired again on the 19th and 20th, damaging three of the four 28-cm (11-inch) guns in the German coastal battery in the Cap Gris Nez area.

After six days of fighting for a seemingly endless number of strongpoints, the last of the Boulogne fortifications fell and 9,517 survivors of the 10,000-man garrison surrendered on September 22.

Canadian losses numbered 634 killed, wounded, and missing.

For the next two days long convoys of guns, Canadian and British, moved north for the attack on Calais, which opened on September 25 with another massive bombardment from sky and land. Five days before, 633 planes of Bomber Command had dropped 3,000 tons of bombs on Calais defences, reputedly with good results. But on the morning of the assault a thundering armada of 900 heavy bombers came over from England to plaster strong-points. Unfortunately, bad weather prevented many from completing their sorties, and much of the 1,300 tons of bombs dropped were off-target, leaving intact many pillboxes and gun emplacements.

Half an hour after the aerial bombing began, the positions of twenty-one known enemy batteries were bombarded for forty minutes by three heavy regiments, eight medium regiments, and two heavy ack-ack regiments – 224 guns in all. Then thirty minutes before H-Hour these same medium and heavy guns joined 144

25-pounders of six field regiments in several earth-shuddering concentrations on the objectives of the assaulting troops.

On the left of Calais, 8th Brigade, with only the guns of 13th Field providing close support, captured the garrison at Cap Blanc Nez, and next morning, September 26, the battery of giant 406-mm (16-inch) guns in the nearby hills surrendered.

During the day, close to seven hundred RAF planes dropped 3,600 tons of bombs on Calais and Cap Gris Nez. Still the big guns on this headland escaped damage and would not surrender.

Fortunately, not all strongpoints were defended with such tenacity. For instance, old Fort Nieulay — five miles in from the sea and dominating the plain before Calais — could have been a wretched business. Upgraded by the addition of machine-gun pits along the top of embanked walls, and 88-mm guns in corner emplacements, the ancient fort presented a formidable obstacle in the path of 7th Brigade, in particular the Royal Winnipeg Rifles, following a road east towards Calais, passing by the principal gate into the fort. However, when their Carrier Platoon, commanded by Sgt. Joe Roshick, went forward to recce the outskirts of Calais, and one of the three flame-throwers suddenly did a smart left turn and let fly a roiling ball of flame up against the wooden front door of the fort, setting it on fire, a white flag appeared.

Capt. Cliff Chadderton, whose "Charley" Company was following close behind and was first to enter the fort, met an astonishing scene:

> The Commandant, a very fat officer, stood at the centre of the open courtyard holding a white flag. Clearly prepared for a ceremonious surrender, he stood beside a table covered with a white cloth on which were arranged glasses and a bottle of champagne. As he and several other officers were being disarmed, he was told to bring all his troops into this central square, including those on the parapet manning the 88-mm guns who were glaring down quizzically as though not sure what they should do. To the relief of the handful of Winnipegs in the fort, outnumbered at least ten

to one, when the Commandant waved at them to come down, they came. All in all the garrison numbered about 200.

When, with the Commandant in tow, we entered the command post of the fort, a telephone was ringing. We ordered him to answer it, but he refused. So we picked up the phone and said, "We have your fort." A surprised voice answered in German and we turned for help to a Winnipeg soldier who could speak German. In the ensuing conversation the officer in Calais, obviously of superior rank, insisted we put the Commandant on. When the agitated man took the phone and confirmed the situation, he was given a severe dressing-down and promised a court martial.

Now the parapets, which seemed to rise forty or fifty feet above the square on all sides, were seized by Winnipegs running up the zigzagging stone steps to a succession of galleries that looked for all the world like those in that unforgettable fort in the old film *Beau Geste*. This accomplished we signalled the Canadian Scottish on our left and the Regina Rifles on our right that Fort Nieulay was no longer a threat to their advance.[*]

Next morning, September 27, 342 Lancasters cascaded 1,700 more tons of heavy explosive on the inner defences of the port. Then leading up to and during an attack by 9th Brigade with some tanks in support, against the Cap Gris Nez batteries (fifteen miles southwest along the coast from Calais), the huge guns were subjected to an eighty-minute non-stop bombardment by 14th Field, four regiments of mediums, a regiment of heavies, and a regiment of heavy ack-ack. The awesome bombardment produced results: all three batteries, which periodically had been turned inland on targets, were silenced, though not until they were overrun – one gun crew getting off a final round even as the infantrymen arrived on their gun platform.[†]

---

[*]   Author interview
[†]   Derived from G. W. L. Nicholson's *Gunners of Canada, Vol. II,*

On September 28, the commandant of Calais garrison was granted a forty-eight-hour truce by the Commander of 3rd Division (Maj.-Gen. Dan Spry) to allow for the evacuation of 20,000 civilians. This seemed to be in preparation for a final bitter showdown, but when the attack was resumed at noon on the 30th, German resistance was noticeably thin.

At 7:00 P.M. the German commandant surrendered the city, for which the bleary-eyed, unshaven, staggering-tired infantrymen of 3rd Division were profoundly grateful. They had suffered almost three hundred casualties subduing the outpost forts and gunsites, bringing their losses in dead, wounded, and missing in the taking of Boulogne and Calais to nearly one thousand.*

McClelland and Stewart, 1972, which also provided the statistics on shelling and bombing of objectives described in this chapter.

* From D-Day in Normandy, June 6, to October 1 when the clearing of the Scheldt began, 2nd and 3rd Canadian divisions suffered more casualties than any other divisions in 21st Army Group:

FORMATION	CASUALTIES	FORMATION	CASUALTIES
1. 3rd Cdn Div	9,263	9. 59 Inf Div	4,911
2. 2nd Cdn Div	8,211	10. 51 Inf Div	4,799
3. 43 Inf Div	7,605	11. 11 Armd Div	3,825
4. 15 Inf Div	7,601	12. Guards Armd Div	3,385
5. 3 Brit Div	7,342	13. 4 Cdn Armd Div	3,135
6. 50 Inf Div	6,701	14. 7 Armd Div	2,801
7. 49 Inf Div	5,894	15. Polish Armd Div	1,861
8. 53 Inf Div	4,984		

6

ONLY THE PORT OF
ANTWERP IS BIG ENOUGH

✳

ON OCTOBER 2, 4TH BRIGADE AND 4TH FIELD REGIMENT
are required to abandon "Shangri-La" and with the rest of 2nd
Division finally undertake a full role in opening a port – the greatest of them all – capable of handling 40,000 tons a day, when both
shores of the Scheldt Estuary are cleared of Germans and ships are
able to sail in from the sea.

By now it is clear the war is not about to come to a swift end.
The ebullient view of only a few days ago – that Montgomery's
drive, September 17–25, to the Rhine, outflanking the Siegfried
Line at Nijmegen in Holland, was the start of a drive to Berlin –
shrivelled when General Brian Horrocks's XXX Corps failed to
reach the British 1st Airborne Division, which was holding the last
crucial bridge over the northern branch of the Rhine at Arnhem.

If this failure proved anything, it was that for the final drive into
Germany all Allied armies would have to be properly supplied,
with all necessary petrol and ammunition, not by shifting priorities
among formations, but by building up forward dumps and shorten-
ing supply lines. Currently the largest port in operation is Dieppe,
capable of handling only 7,000 tons a day. Obviously Antwerp, with
its unrivalled capacity to land all that is necessary for all Allied
armies on the Western Front, will have to be made usable. The job
is given to First Canadian Army. And, with General Harry Crerar
ill in hospital, Lt.-Gen. Guy Simonds is totally in charge.

With the fall of Calais, 3rd Division turns north to deal with the German 64th Division, confined by 4th and Polish Armoured divisions in what is known as the Breskens pocket – a sodden, dike-laced corner of Holland peculiarly placed southwest of the Scheldt, bounded on the west by the North Sea, on the south by the Leopold Canal, and on the east by Braakman Inlet jutting down from the Scheldt, twenty-eight miles west of Antwerp.

The 3rd Division will clear the south bank of the Scheldt to the sea, crushing the determined forces that were left behind to hold the Breskens shore when German Fifteenth Army (the Pas de Calais force) evacuated eastwards – by way of Antwerp until the British arrived, and since then across the Scheldt to Walcheren Island. The 2nd Division will clear the north shore as constituted by South Beveland Peninsula snaking west to Walcheren. Only when both banks of the broad estuary are clear of Germans, can the big coastal guns, denying Allied shipping the mouth of the river, be dealt with by sea-borne landings of British units under command of First Canadian Army.

Once again, as in the closing of the Falaise pocket, Canadians are to play the pivotal role in an operation crucial to the ultimate success of all Allied forces in Western Europe, and so recognized by Supreme Allied Commander Eisenhower in a signal to Field Marshal Montgomery on October 9: "Unless we have Antwerp producing by the middle of November, entire operations will come to a standstill. I emphasize, that of all our operations on the entire front from Switzerland to the Channel, I consider Antwerp of first importance."

Before 2nd Division, its right flank secured by 4th Armoured and Polish Armoured divisions pushing towards Bergen-op-Zoom and Breda, can begin clearing South Beveland, it first must take Merxem and push north 23 kilometres (14.4 miles) and secure the villages strung across the mouth of the peninsula.

Preparatory to joining in the divisional drive north (once 4th Brigade has cleared Merxem), 5th and 6th brigades, deployed on the right along the Albert Canal east of the city, must get over this obstacle and wheel west to gain still another barrier, the Antwerp–Turnhout Canal curling northeast from the Albert Canal near Merxem.

On the night of September 27, seven kilometres east of the docks, a Calgary Highlanders' patrol, crawling across a partially wrecked footbridge – for much of the way hanging by their hands over the dark water as they swing from one rusty remnant to another – manage to subdue all opposition long enough for the battalion to cross and establish a bridgehead firm enough to resist two strong counter-attacks, and to allow a bridge to be built. (The leader of this courageous patrol, Sgt. G. R. Crockett, was subsequently awarded the Distinguished Conduct Medal.)

Gaining a foothold on the far bank of the Turnhout Canal is more difficult. An assault by the Fusiliers Mont-Royal and the South Saskatchewan Regiment twelve kilometres northeast of Antwerp (September 24) is roughly treated by a strong force of infantry and tanks. The FMRs, after suffering 130 casualties, 27 of them among the Belgian White Brigade serving with them, pull back over the canal. The SSRs soon follow.

On September 28 another attack is tried further east. With the SSRs mounting a diversionary attack across the canal, Le Régiment de Maisonneuve gains a bridgehead, from whence the Black Watch takes St. Lenaarts and another town, Brecht, two or three kilometres further west. During the fighting many Germans are killed and 200 taken prisoner, but the Black Watch over the period of just three days lose 119 wounded and killed. The troops confronting the Canadians have received the following from General von Zangen, Commander of Fifteenth Army: "The German people are watching us. In this hour the fortifications along the Scheldt occupy a role which is decisive for the future of our people. Each additional day that you deny to the enemy the port of Antwerp, and all its resources, will be vital."

7

CANAL WATERS REFLECT
A FLAME-LIT SKY

※

FOR SOME TIME, PERHAPS FROM THAT FIRST HOUR SIXTEEN days ago, when you occupied that OP in the attic of that abandoned furniture factory and peered across the canal for the first time into Merxem, you knew that one day you would have to accompany an infantry attack to clear it of the enemy. Still, as the moment approaches, you are filled with dread.

All day October 2, two companies of the Royals have been over there among the burning buildings and fearsome noises of battle. Shortly after midnight last night, Major "Paddy" Ryall's C Company crossed in assault boats, with two companies of the Belgian White Brigade.* Then just before first light today, Bob Suckling's D Company, accompanied by 4th Field FOO Lieut. Bill Dunning and a signaller, crossed over, penetrating deeper into Merxem.

A couple of hours ago (2130 hours) you got a signal to report to Royals' battalion headquarters in Antwerp with Major Hank

_____

* The brigade was commanded by a former sea captain, Eugene "Harry" Colson, leader of 600 of the 3,500-strong Antwerp underground army – recruited by a regular Belgian army officer, Lieut. Urbain Remier – that early in September took control of the sluice gates, crucial to the maintenance of water level in Antwerp harbour, and prevented the retreating Germans from destroying them.

Caldwell when his company was ordered back from the detached vigil they had been sharing with fifty members of the White Brigade, guarding several miles of the Antwerp–Turnhout Canal that runs up from the Albert Canal past the village of Schoten northeast of the city.

As you approach the dark and deserted Sports Platz stadium where Caldwell's company has been ordered to assemble for the crossing, the guns in the docklands, northwest of the city, are pouring shells into Merxem, where several fires are burning fiercely, their ugly glow in the smoky sky reflecting disturbingly in the waters of the canal, turning it blood-red.

Nor is the news reassuring when you and Caldwell arrive back at Battalion Headquarters, in the principal's office of a school in Antwerp, for briefing by Col. Lendrum and your battery commander, Major Don Cornett. Interrogation by Intelligence Officers of the first prisoners taken – 25 Belgian SS and 44 Germans from the 1018th Grenadier Regiment, diverted from its intended role on the Russian front, for the purpose of regaining control of the Antwerp docks – suggests you are up against aggressive troops.

Passage over the Albert Canal by Ryall's company and the White Brigade contingent this morning was heavily contested, and casualties among the Belgians were severe. You'll be crossing where they did, passing through Ryall's company now consolidated among streets adjacent to the canal. However, beyond there progress may be "sticky," for Suckling's company, deeper in Merxem, is now cut off and in danger of being overwhelmed. At dusk the Germans infiltrated between the two companies, and are now attacking Suckling's position from the rear.

All day communications have been poor – wireless transmission by portable 18-sets inhibited by the densely built areas on both sides of the canal. Now the lack of sit reps is taking its toll of the normally calm and self-assured Lendrum sitting behind the principal's desk opposite Cornett. The decisive, firm manner you have come to expect is noticeably absent. His comments on what Caldwell may encounter over there are clearly speculative, and the long pauses between comments, during which he rearranges pads and pencils and desk accessories, are disconcerting. Like Cornett, hunched over his map, he is obviously more concerned with the immediate plight of D Company.

Suddenly the civilian phone on the desk starts ringing. Lendrum reaches over and picks it up, a reflex action only, for the civilian phone system has not been working. To his astonishment, Suckling is on the line explaining that two White Brigade men – phone technicians – have just connected the phone in the Tramways Office in Merxem to a line they have maintained with Antwerp comrades throughout the siege. As the conversation continues, Suckling's voice sinks lower and lower, and you and the other onlookers surrounding the desk are alerted to this fact when Lendrum asks: "Bob, why are you whispering?"

His answer, inaudible to the eavesdroppers, sends Lendrum into gales of laughter. Looking up and covering the phone mouthpiece, he reports: "Bob says, 'The frigging Germans are just outside the door!'"

A moment later Lendrum hands the phone to Cornett, explaining the Germans have been advancing down the street with a light gun, periodically shelling selected buildings, and are being held at bay by one platoon showering grenades down on them from an upstairs window of a house. But if they are to hold on, they must have some arty support. Suckling is turning over the phone to a White Brigade operator on the ground floor of the building who will transmit fire orders shouted down to him by FOO Bill Dunning observing from an upper storey. Even as he grabs the phone, Cornett is calling to his signaller: "Mike target! Mike target! Mike target!" And it seems the signaller hardly finishes transmitting the map reference and "Scale 5 . . . Fire" before the guns are thumping, sending 120 shells crashing where needed. A couple of "repeats" and the counter-attack is snuffed out.

You have no inkling that from this hour resistance in Merxem will begin to crumble, and as you walk back with Hank to his company, waiting in the gloomy infield of the big stadium, you can't shake the image of a company cut off and fighting for its life. So when a platoon commander, who has been down at the canal checking on the assault boats deposited there earlier, returns to report to Caldwell that all but two have been sunk by mortar fire, and that the two survivors are half full of water, you really start to "get the wind up."

On your way to your carrier to fill your pockets with hardtack and bully beef, and to advise Gnr. Bob Stevenson, who'll be going over with you carrying the 18-set radio, to do the same since there's no telling how long it will be before you'll see the carrier again, an unfamiliar voice calls out your name and hands you a letter. Curious, since mail normally only comes up with the rations, and no rations came up tonight, you seek out an empty dressing room under the grandstand where you can show a light. The little blue airmail envelope is from your father who seldom writes to you. As usual he has little to say, his excuse being "your mother will have given you all the news." But few as they are, his casual offhand comments have a remarkably soothing effect. You find yourself recalling one dark fall evening when you were a little squirt. He'd asked you to go to the barn, locate a lantern hanging (unlit of course) on a nail in the dark cow stable, and bring it back. Seeing you hesitate, he'd smiled and said, "You're not afraid of the dark, are you?" And though you were terrified of the sinister creaking sounds in the dark barn, and the strange crunching and snuffling noises animals make when eating, you simply had to go and fetch that lantern to prove you were not. Afterwards you glowed with joy at his pride in you. Now holding the little airmail in your hand, you can almost hear his voice again asking, "You're not afraid of the dark, are you?"

Suddenly you realize that all the painful anxiety and tension afflicting you only a moment ago have disappeared, and when you and Stevenson go down to the boats with Hank, you paddle across a canal that is as silent as a country night, the only sound the swirl and gurgle of paddles dipping and pulling at the water. Even the fires, which earlier seemed to be consuming Merxem, have calmed down; and shells no longer explode anywhere in the town.

On the roadway along the canal bank near where you land is a veritable mountain of parkas and sheepskin coats, obviously abandoned by the German brigade, which was diverted to Belgium (currently enjoying balmy fall weather) after being equipped for the Russian winter. As you go forward with Caldwell to find Ryall, you leave Stevenson, resting with the Royals on the pile of parkas, using his 18-set to alert his buddies back in the Sports Platz so that when 4th Field passes this way, they pick up some of the coats.

Ryall's company headquarters turns out to be in a tiny, cramped cellar of a nearby house, and you are left alone down there sitting on a trunk while the two company commanders go off to decide where Caldwell should locate his company. The cellar is dimly lit by a candle on a table in the corner, and in the shadowy light you could swear that just there on the floor ahead of you a pile of sheepskin coats, similar to those you just passed on the dock, is moving gently up and down as though breathing. For a moment you think you're going batty, but when you bend over and lift one of the fluffy skins, the tousled head of a beautiful teenage girl appears, and as you continue to hold up the coat, staring in disbelief, two stunning, if sleepy, eyes open wide on yours, and a husky voice says, "Eh-low."

Yawning and rubbing her eyes, she gets up, and sitting down on the trunk beside you asks if she may have a cigarette. Then for the next half hour you are enthralled with the proximity of this lovely young creature and everything she has to say.

No, she is not a refugee; she and that other girl, still asleep under that other pile of sheepskin on the floor, came over as "nurses" with the White Brigade soldiers accompanying the Royals. Of course they aren't really nurses, you understand. Actually, she is a student who has been working as a volunteer at the headquarters of the White Brigade in Antwerp. When she learned they needed people to go along on the attack to help with the wounded – like stretcher-bearers, you know – she and her friend, having had first-aid courses at school, volunteered. Oh, it was awful! The White Brigade men had no training or experience for fighting like this. Major Ryall said they should have spread out, but they were all bunched up on the canal bank, and when the mortar bombs started coming down on them, it was terrible . . . so many wounded . . .

Their supply of bandages, a mere handful, and a bottle of iodine, so pitifully inadequate in the face of so many terrible wounds . . . It was so horrible that she and her friend wanted to cry. If she lives to be a hundred, she will never be able to forget.

Abruptly, as though to get her mind off the events of this day, she starts discussing her favourite American hit tunes, which she has been able to keep up with using the radio her family had hidden away to listen to the BBC news.

Now that the war is almost over, she can start thinking of things like going to a ball. This has been her dream for a long time – that one day she would get a long, backless evening gown and go to a beautiful ball. That was the way she had come to visualize what it would be like when freedom finally came, for, of course, she was too young to remember much about what it was like before the war.

You could have gone on listening to her all night, but Paddy Ryall returns and tells you Hank and his company have started off up a side street. And so you are wrenched back to the reality of the war in the sinister darkness outside.

Though at one point a German patrol clumps noisily across an intersection just up ahead, causing the company to freeze in the shadows of a building abutting the sidewalk, the company doesn't fire a shot this night. After walking silently for a time towards the eastern outskirts of the suburb, Hank distributes his platoons, establishing company headquarters in an empty house to which he gains entrance by sending a man up over the back kitchen to break in an upstairs window.

Next morning, October 3, you are wounded, but not by the enemy, who appear to have pulled out overnight.

In preparation for a move north from Merxem, you and Hank had gone up to the end of the street to gain a view of the land beyond, on the way traversing endless backyards, which, though this is Tuesday, are filled with fluttering lines of laundry – the war having interfered with the Merxem ladies' traditional washday yesterday. It's on your way back, having decided to chance the open streets, that you and Hank meet a Royals' patrol – a sergeant and a private with a Sten gun slung over his shoulder. Fortunately the gun, cradled in his right arm facing you, is pointed down at the pavement, for suddenly – *bang!* – it goes off and you feel a thump on the calf of your left leg. Instantly a torrent of expletives from Hank draws attention to the fact his knees have taken the brunt of the concrete bits dislodged by the bullet ricocheting off he sidewalk. Cursing, he rolls up his pant-legs and starts picking cinder-like bits out of his kneecaps.

"That's the third time it's done that this morning," says the soldier in wonderment as he pulls back the cocking-lever of the Sten, now pointing directly at your stomach, and doesn't turn the knob into its safety notch.

Pushing the muzzle away from you, you tell him, "For God's sake, man, put it on safety!"

In obvious bewilderment, he asks, "What's that?"

Hank, hearing this, bobs up from attending to his smarting knees, demanding, "Where the hell did you get your weapons training, soldier?"

"I never had any weapons training, sir," says he apologetically, "I was a cook with Army Service until I was sent up to the Royals."

Now as you rub the numbness from your leg, you realize it's wet. And when you pull up your pant-leg, you see two little holes where the bullet passed in and out of the calf, barely beneath the skin – the absolutely perfect flesh wound that everybody hopes to get! But it is too perfect. By the time you get the opportunity to visit the Royals' MO (Dr. Ken Mickleborough, a fellow ex-Glebe Collegiate type) the bleeding has stopped. Daubing it with antiseptic, he applies a kind of oversized, homemade Band-Aid, and wishes you better luck next time as you return to duty. So much for old collegiate connections!

However, on balance it is a good day. Passing through Schoten at noon you learn from a White Brigade man over a bottle of Belgian beer, partaken in the street, that your shells on the church tower yesterday wiped out an enemy artillery observation crew in residence there.

Your new friend is much impressed when you manage to get through to him by way of atrocious French and pointing at the tower and then at yourself that it was you who shelled it. And he proceeds to attract a crowd when, in stentorian tones, he announces to passersby that it was you who destroyed the Boche in the tower. Flattered by the smiles and the admiration shining in eyes on all sides, you share with them the interesting fact that the gun you'd used had actually faced you from the other side of Antwerp – showing them on the map the unusual positioning of the target between you and your gun, supporting your explanation with pantomime to show how your shells snarled directly at your face before landing. However, you choose not to describe the blind ranging you conducted on that damned tower, when each ranging round aroused in you an uncontrollable urge to flatten out on the floor below the window sill of the upstairs bedroom you were using for an OP.

Somehow you feel it might leave the wrong impression of the calibre of their liberators, if you tried to explain to this excited, chattering crowd the meaning of "cellarosis" (timidity unbecoming a soldier developed from spending too much time in cellars or other relatively safe havens). And of course it is impossible to describe in any language the incredible difference between the casual sound of a 25-pound shell sizzling overhead on its way out into no-man's-land, and one coming in to burst in front of you.

8

SUDDENLY TRAFFIC
IS NOTICEABLY SPARSE

✳

NEXT MORNING, OCTOBER 4, THE DRIVE NORTH BY 2ND Division towards the mouth of South Beveland begins in earnest – not with a massive attack preceded by heavy artillery preparations, but with silent infantrymen trudging single-file up the verges of narrow roads crowded with rumbling armoured cars, growling half-tracks, clinking carriers, and purring Jeeps. Some of the Jeeps with tall aerials wavering above them carry red-tabbed, frowning brigadiers exuding urgency and seemingly bent on giving the impression they are riding close herd on this business of clearing the Scheldt – suddenly top priority with First Canadian Army, 21st Army Group, and General Eisenhower's Supreme Headquarters.

By mid-morning, however, shelling of crossroads by lone German guns and periodic bursts of MG 42-fire from wooded flanks have given notice that troops passing this way must pay a toll, and soon traffic becomes noticeably sparse. In fact, as you approach a blown culvert over a narrow stream, following the Royals' leading company, and a German field gun starts dropping shells randomly to harass anyone trying to reconnoitre another way over this obstacle, your carrier is the only vehicle within sight or sound.

As you shrink well down below the rim of its steel walls, you have your driver, Gunner William Walkden, turn off the engine. Suddenly it's so quiet you can hear the water burbling along the swollen ditches and, more importantly, the *thunk* of the gun as it fires from somewhere in the bush beyond the field on the right. You count the seconds it takes the shell to arrive: six. It's a small-calibre field gun, and judging by its drawn-out whine, of low velocity. Using the muzzle velocity (MV) for Charge II of a 25-pounder and applying your rule of thumb of three seconds per 1,000 yards, the gun is only 2,000 yards away.*

But to get a compass bearing on the sound of the gun you'd have to get out and away from this steel box, exposing yourself to all the shell fragments whipping around out there. As you contemplate the prospect with distaste, and are about to conclude "not bloody likely, old boy," you see out of the corner of your eye, passing no more than twelve inches away, the head and shoulders of Col. Mac Young! Though he knows perfectly well he's passing your carrier, he doesn't even glance your way as he walks on. You, of course, pile out and follow him.

As you catch up, he asks, "Any theory as to where it may be?"

You tell him that judging by the time-of-flight of its missiles, it's only about 2,000 yards away, but you don't yet have a bearing.

He stops and holds out his hand: "Let me have your compass."

At that moment you hear the gun *thunk* over on the right, and this time the tone of its whine clearly indicates it's coming directly this way. The Colonel seems to realize this too, and as he receives the compass he leaps for the water-filled ditch. Instantly you follow. Too late, you realize he doesn't mean to jump into the ditch, but over it. You land floundering in icy-cold water up to your hips. Struggling to regain your feet, you look up just in time to see him unconcernedly kneeling, squinting into the compass, outlined against a flashing geyser of black mud and smoke spouting up with an awesome roar no more than fifty yards in front of his unflinching face.

He makes no comment as he stands up, leaps back over the ditch to the roadway, and leads you, dripping, back to your carrier. There,

---

* Charge I (MV 640 fps): 5 seconds for 1,065 yards; Charge II (970 fps): 3 seconds for 970 yards; Charge III (1,450 fps): 2 seconds for 966 yards.

after only a moment's study of your map, he puts his finger on a clearing in the bush and in his calm drawl says, "Try plastering around there."

With that he turns away and starts back down the road as casually as he'd come, ignoring the next round that comes whistling over the carrier to land just beyond the road. Feeling you have been bracketed, you rush to get some rounds down where he suggested – a Mike target of Scale 3. After it kicks up quite a fuss over there, you wait a while to see if the gun opens up again, before ordering a repeat. But no more shells are needed. Either it was hit, or the reign of terror from near-misses persuaded it to move somewhere else. At any rate, the result is totally satisfactory and the advance continues.

Opposition is uneven for all brigades at the outset. But on the next day, October 5, the Essex Scottish come up against the stiffest opposition since Merxem, when they are hit by a counter-attack in a long, skinny town called Putte straddling the Belgium–Holland border, and strung out a remarkable distance along the main road that runs through it from Antwerp to Bergen-op-Zoom. The leading platoons are driven back, leaving Fox Troop Commander Ted Adams stranded in a church tower.

Subjecting the town to heavy mortar and shell-fire, the Germans manage to close within 150 yards of Adams's OP, but the excellent overview of the town afforded by his tower allows him to catch many of them in the open street with all twenty-four guns of 4th Field concentrated on a Mike target. The effect is devastating, and the Essex not only are able to retake the ground they lost, but are able to seize possession of the whole town, thus establishing a bridgehead over a canal cutting the main road north. (The gunners will later learn the importance of their contribution when Capt. A. E. Adams is awarded a Military Cross and his ack, Bombardier Ernie Hodgkinson, is awarded a Military Medal.)

At the same time as the drama in Putte is being played out, over on the left, around the Belgian village of Berendrecht, about four kilometres west of the track the Royals are following north, there is a rattle of heavy machine guns, punctuated now and then by sharp cracks of high velocity guns. Later you'll learn that this flurry of firing is mainly by the weapons of a troop of 8th Recce Regiment armoured cars, pushing into the heart of Berendrecht with such intimidating agressiveness that a hundred Germans, grateful they survived the furious onslaught, surrender to the troop commander, Lieut. Colin Ridgway.*

Meanwhile, a couple of kilometres west of Putte, after crossing the canal by another bridge, the Royals push on about two miles in open country with Zandvhiet visible on their left, before taking up a defensive position for the night.

Here an enemy plane drops propaganda leaflets containing a clumsy attempt to arouse suspicions among the "Boys of the 2nd Canadian Division" that they are being sacrificed as at Dieppe "to fight and bleed for England" in the upcoming "God damn slaughter." That the German High Command would, in spite of diminishing resources that now must be strained to the limit, give priority to preparing and printing large quantities of a special message for the Canadians, and assign a precious plane and crew to dropping it over this spearhead of 4th Brigade approaching the mouth of South Beveland, means you are in for special attention of a more intimate nature very soon.†

---

* Lieut. Ridgway was subsequently awarded the Military Cross.
† This same night, October 5, Col.-Gen. Kurt Student, Commander of German First Parachute Army, ordered Lt.-Col. F. A. von der Heydte to break off holding up the Polish Armour, near Alphen, and move in haste his 6th Paratroop Regiment southwest to confront a Canadian force reported on its way to Ossendrecht with the obvious intention of capturing the mouth of South Beveland and cutting off all access to Walcheren garrison. Student's 30,000-strong First Parachute Army had been brought into being on Hitler's orders September 3, by recruitment from odd sources including convalescent Luftwaffe airmen and redundant Luftwaffe ground crew, but it was larded with well-trained and highly motivated survivors of paratroop regiments and the remnants of SS units that escaped the Falaise pocket. Von der Heydte's 4,000-strong 6th Paratroop Regiment, the élite of the élite, who'd been given top priority for equipment, began its counter-attack against the Royal Regiment the next afternoon, October 6.

9

A NOT-SO-COMIC

OPERA

*

BY FIVE O'CLOCK IN THE MORNING OF OCTOBER 6, THE Royals are on the move again, with you walking at the rear of the leading company with its commander, your eyes searching for indentations of sinister portent in the road or track over which must pass the tracks of your carrier clinking along behind you in bull-low. During the past two days casualties have been light, the battalion suffering only one officer and four Other Ranks killed, and one officer and seven ORs wounded, mostly from mines.

The drill is now well-established and will continue as long as enemy opposition remains light. Companies take turns passing through each other to take the next objective, which is normally a concession road crossing the line of advance at right angles. A FOO is expected to take off with each leading company as it passes through, and proceed with it to the next objective, where you again take up with the next company passing through. Normally there would be two FOOs, with the battalion taking turns going forward with leapfrogging companies, but Baker Troop is currently without a troop commander, acting troop commander Bill Dunning having been posted to 2nd Division Headquarters as a liaison officer.

By late afternoon, D company, the leading company, reaches an east–west lateral road – Middel Straat, Hageland – on high land overlooking open fields towards Hoogerheide village, which lies just beyond the immediate objective, Ossendrecht, mostly hidden down on the left, beyond where this lateral road turns north past a row of houses.

While there is still no sign of Germans, your imagination begins to work as you study some substantial buildings in the middle distance; brickworks, according to the map. In the deadly still fields and roads, they look sinister and forbidding, as lifeless buildings in no-man's-land always do. You find yourself exercising a degree of caution you haven't been concerned with all day when you instruct Walkden to drive the carrier farther west along Middel Straat and park it out of sight behind a farmhouse at the corner, where the road turns north down the hill past that row of houses. And when you peer around the corner of the first house, and you see a church steeple poking up malevolently out of Ossendrecht in the valley, you immediately seek out a six-pounder gun crew, commanded by Corporal Jack Williams, to put some rounds through its belfry.

In the meantime a second company of Royals, to whom you normally would attach yourself for the next move forward, arrives at Middel Straat, believing they have arrived at their objective. They claim D company did not identify an earlier farm track back yonder as their objective, and came on a concession too far. As maps are being studied and claims discussed, a third company arrives and pauses in confusion. Before things are properly sorted out, the fourth company arrives. By now things are sufficiently complicated that advice must be sought from Battalion Tac Headquarters following somewhere behind.

There is a great deal of milling about. Altogether too many men have assembled along a short section of road in an overlapping mess.

Suddenly a Jerry gun begins shelling beyond that row of houses – a high velocity gun that is out of sight but very close, for there is almost no lapse of time between the *wham* of its firing and the roar of its missile landing against those houses. Fortunately it is concentrating on something other than this clutter of troops here, but those stunning, reverberating roars, enveloping the whole area, cause great consternation among men with no trenches in which to shelter.

Then a clutch of 8th Recce armoured cars, of the towering, heavily armed Daimler variety (coaxially-mounted two-pounder cannon and Besa machine gun), which had just come up and were last seen moving cautiously down the road past the row of houses, roar back up the hill. As they skid around the corner and disappear along Middel Straat, causing some soldiers to scramble out of their way and others to exchange sober glances, you hear a voice call: "Tank!"

And you are not immune to the drawing power of those retreating recce cars. Common sense tells you, as it must all who witnessed their unseemly haste, that those courageous types, whose job it is to take tremendous risks as they scout uncleared hostile territory, would not be retiring so fast if they hadn't seen something coming this way that they with all their fire-power couldn't handle. For a few minutes the situation threatens to dissolve into utter panic, as the roar of the retreating Daimlers and the crashing shells drown out the shouting of four company commanders and several platoon commanders, competing for attention as they disentangle their companies and move them back along the road to form some kind of defensive position.

Since it is not at all clear which companies are to stay put and which are to move, and with everybody suddenly consumed by the urge to travel, it appears you may be left stranded if you don't watch out. Not relishing having your carrier trapped forward of all this, with a German tank crawling up the hill, you run to where it is parked in a confined, brick-paved entryway behind the house at the corner, and get your crew packing up everything for a hasty withdrawal. But just as you finish coiling up the last few feet of remote-control cable and are helping your ack, Gnr. William Hiltz, to heave the heavy spool into the carrier, making ready to follow the recce cars and infantry, Bob Suckling suddenly appears around the corner of the house yelling over the crash of the German gun:

"Come with me! I've located it. It's a self-propelled gun – not a tank. Come – I'll show you!"

Yelling at Stevenson, who is manning the radio in the carrier, to order the guns to "take post," you take Hiltz and Walkden with you, telling them to space themselves out as human relay-stations so they can get your fire orders back to Stevenson.

The German shells continue one at a time, horribly close, but still mystifyingly out of sight, as you and Suckling take turns pounding on locked front doors of the row of houses on the left side of the street, where an upstairs back window could provide observation of the field sloping down to Ossendrecht where Suckling says the gun is.

When at last a door opens, he unceremoniously brushes aside the bewildered woman standing there, and leads you thumping up the stairs two at a time to a back bedroom window.

"There!" he yells, pointing down a broad, grassy slope towards a tree-lined ditch or creek, "Right there!"

And there indeed it is, your attention drawn by the spurt of smoke that jets from its muzzle as it fires, its vicious *wham* coupling with the instantaneous smash of its shell on the back of a house just a few doors down to the right, creating intimidating reverberations.

Crash!

Panic threatens to blind you as you glance from map to gun and back again, trying to establish a map reference. It seems to be sitting on a culvert over a tree-enshrouded ditch or creek. You *must* be right – you may only get one chance! But speed is paramount! You scribble down a six-figure coordinate and dash across the hall into a bedroom at the front of the house. Throwing open a casement window, you yell the figures to Hiltz standing down in the street, coupling them with "Mike target – Mike target – Mike target! Scale 5 – Fire!"

As you listen to him call your orders up the road to Walkden at the corner, who will relay them to Stevenson in the carrier behind the house, who in turn will send them to the guns, the crash of shells from the SP measures its relentless march up the line of houses, coming ever closer, each unnerving roar causing everything to shake and rattle. Though you've never seen Jerry use such tactics before, and it's hard to think clearly, it appears the gun is systematically working over each house in turn, starting at the bottom of the street. And when he gets to the top, they'll attack.

As you rejoin Suckling in the back bedroom where he continues to maintain a vigil from well back in the shadows, you do your best to suppress your dread of the guns not getting enough shells up here in time to stop that gun before it puts a round in through this window.

The explosions are very close now. And when you throw up your field-glasses to study the SP, to your horror you seem to be looking right down its muzzle. How on earth can Suckling stand here so calmly watching that gun gradually ratcheting this way? Any minute now it will rip a shell in this window, and yet he remains standing here!

Crash!

Fully aware, even in your fuzzy-headed anxiety, that the success or failure of the German attack hinges on whether you are able to silence that demoralizing gun, you know you should remain here where you can observe the fall of your shells and make corrections until it is knocked out or driven off. But as the acrid fumes of those terrible explosions drift in through the open window, the only course that makes any sense to you is to run down the stairs and find a door to the cellar, if there is one, before it's too late. The problem is, you can't leave Suckling up here alone.

As you turn to face him, you wonder how you should put it. With all your heart and soul you want to say right out: "For God's sake, Bob, let's go downstairs to the back of the house where at least we'll have a chance. To stay up here is plain suicide." But something in the eyes of this resolute man as he looks at you makes you clam up. He seems confident you will silence the German gun. There is even a slight smile of amusement on his face as he waits to see you do it. My God, doesn't he realize how bad the odds have grown, and what is about to happen? But then in a calm voice he poses a question that makes it clear he's well aware that time is of the essence:

"How long should it normally take them to get something up here?"

You tell him, two ... three minutes ... four at most ... depending ...

Crash!

You retreat to the front bedroom overlooking the street, where you'll be able to hear Hiltz when he relays the message from the guns, "Shot Mike One" – the signaller's message that the shells are on their way. You start pacing back and forth and try to imagine current activities at the guns.

Crash!

By now the Tannoy loudspeakers in the gun pits are spewing out line, range, and angle of sight; gun-layers are twiddling their dials, whirling fine-tuning gears, and levelling their bubbles; shells are being rammed in the chamber, cartridge cases inserted behind them, breech-blocks closed with their distinctive metallic clunks ...

CRASH!

A particularly awesome concussion, followed by the sound of glass and debris cascading down out back, ends your imaginings. That's it. They've started on the house next door. You're next. God – what are they doing back there at the guns? Why aren't they getting something up here? Are they all asleep? But then you hear Walkden calling, and immediately there is Hiltz's welcome shout: "Shot Mike One!"

Even before you get settled in the back room with your glasses to your eyes, the first shells are sizzling overhead. Instantly, furious orange and black eruptions engulf the creek area and the SP in the gap in the trees, building and building into a continuous roaring inferno.

Just before you lose sight of the SP in the smoke and dirt, you think you see a round strike it, but you can't be sure, for many are striking trees around it.

Suckling is now tapping you on the back and shouting excitedly in your ear, "Look! Look! Don't you see them? There's your target! Can you move some of your shells down there?"

Since you are concentrating on a maelstrom that's blotting out everything in your vision, you have no idea what he's talking about.

Pulling your arm and your glasses down from your eyes, he says, "You don't need your glasses. Look – right down there in the field, lying on their bellies!"

For a moment you still don't see any Germans, for you are looking for distant figures. But then you look where he's jabbing his finger, down at the ground, at a point barely visible beyond the window sill which can only be seen by moving dangerously close to the window; and, there they are – a great many of them incredibly close – more than halfway up the slope – no more than a couple of hundred yards away!

Quickly you estimate the distance from the creek and the SP, and running back to the street bedroom window, yell down, "Southeast three hundred – Repeat!"

As you rejoin Suckling, you wonder how in the world all those Germans could have crawled that close without him spotting them. He explains that just seconds before your shelling began, a platoon of Germans appeared and started to move up the slope towards the houses in an open-V formation. The whine of your incoming shells had driven them to earth. Now he starts laughing and pointing: "Look at those silly buggers."

And while you fail to see the humour in the situation, you have to admit it's a unique sight. If you didn't know it's impossible to follow a 25-pounder shell in flight, you'd swear they were watching the shells sail over their heads and land behind them; all are looking skyward or back towards the creek.

In the brief lull, while the guns are applying new lines and ranges in response to your correction, a single German soldier stands up and runs back down the slope towards the trees – then another and another and another. Then groups of two or three jump up and tear off down the hill to disappear in the bushes. So by the time the new batch of shells start blotting out the field and the running figures in geysers of dirt and smoke, a lot of the prone figures have disappeared from the slope.

And when the shells cease coming and the smoke clears, only a few grey forms can be seen lying crumpled and unmoving in the grass. But in your profound relief and happiness at the way things have turned out, you are totally unconcerned that most of them managed to escape. It's enough that the guns turned them back and sent them running. And you glow with pride in the gunners of 4th Field when the veteran infantry officer at your side labels their performance "a really good show."

Scanning the bushes along the creek-bed with your glasses, half expecting the SP to have disappeared, you are delighted to find it sitting silent, obviously immobilized or it would have pulled back. But to make certain you send Hiltz off to find Royals Corporal Jack Williams and his anti-tank crew and ask them to bring up their six-pounder gun to puncture its vitals with some armour-piercing shot.

Never before have you knowingly disabled a tank or a self-propelled gun, let alone one about to blow apart your OP, and it is with feelings of satisfaction bordering on ecstasy that you focus your glasses and feast your eyes on the silent monster and its awesome gun jammed askew at a peculiar angle that most certainly would have blown you and Bob Suckling to eternity had your shells not arrived when they did. But then you remember that the principal role in frustrating the German attack was played by this calm, modest man – that Suckling alone was responsible for preventing them from taking this line of houses, which they clearly intended to do once the SP had finished its shelling of them.

Later that night, holed-up at D Company HQ in a house down the hill, Suckling makes it all sound like a comic opera as he regales Major Tim Beatty with the story of the aborted attack. According to him it was all terribly amusing, with the Jerries scuttling away one after another, abandoning their officer until he too, finding himself alone, jumped up and ran. This outrageously understated version is triggered when you try to make sure Beatty, who has just returned to take over D Company after recovering from a wound suffered at Louvigny in July, is fully aware of Bob's cool-headed action, and will view it as worthy of official recognition, perhaps a gong.

However, the very earnestness of your appeal backfires. Suckling's modesty, as much a part of him as his courage, compels him to turn your story into a joke, thus downplaying his role. Obviously if there was no serious attack, there was no serious role for him to play — completely ignoring the fact it had been a very close thing.* Even a minute or two more delay in the arrival of your shells and the Germans would have made it into these houses unopposed, and the Royals, instead of taking Ossendrecht against light opposition, would still be back there in the fields somewhere, having to mount another attack against an alert and reinforced enemy ready to contest every house and barn.

The extent of the enemy's disorganization in Ossendrecht, since their counter-attacking force was sent packing, is revealed by a leading platoon of Royals penetrating deep into the village after dark. After overrunning a German headquarters, they wait quietly in the dark and capture enemy patrols as they report in. A total of thirty prisoners are taken that night, and next morning another fifty while clearing the village.

But it could have been quite another story. Just how ferociously the Germans are prepared to fight to retain possession of these little villages strung out across the mouth of South Beveland and the bleak polders in the neck of the isthmus, quickly becomes evident when the Calgary Highlanders, the Maisonneuves, and the Black Watch combine to try to drive through Hoogerheide, only three kilometres north of here, on their way past Woensdrecht to Korteven.

---

* Suckling's jolly version ended up in *Battle Royal*, the history of the Royal Regiment. However, corroboration of the facts, as described herein, is found in the Artillery Operations Log — RCA 2nd Cdn Div for 6/7 Oct 44, Serial 2249: "Time 1755, from 4 Fd. OP 41 reports at 1730 SP gun at 633158 knocked out. Casualties seen; enemy dispersed. SP gun finished by high velocity friends. No fire coming from this sector now. Sub units moving to objective." — National Archives of Canada RG 24 Vol. 14325.

IO

TWO BRAVE MEN DIE
DEFENDING THE GUNS

❋

THE GUN POSITION, NO MATTER WHERE IT IS OR HOW BRIEFLY occupied, is home to all who serve in an artillery regiment, regardless of rank. In the speech and language of the gunner lies evidence of this. He is forever talking about "going up to the guns" or "going back to the guns," "moving with the guns," or "leaving the guns" to go somewhere. Always, the guns are his point of reference.

For carrier crews spending most of their time with the infantry, the gun position may exist only as a map reference that is forever changing. But in this transitory world, it's important to know it's there – that you have a place with which you can identify, in much the way people identify with a village or a town in Civvy Street. When on rare occasions you make it back to the guns, it truly feels like you are returning to your home town. Everything looks as familiar as Main Street. All the faces are friendly and you could put a name to most of them if you had to. Many call out greetings and inquire, "How you doin' – okay?" And when you tell them, Okay, and ask how things are with *them*, they tell you it could be a lot worse. And have you time for a cuppa – they've just whipped up a fresh brew?

You get the feeling you are visiting a very special place – one of the most welcoming places you will ever visit in your whole life – even though you are conscious that tomorrow, or before today is out, this field will be abandoned, never to be seen again by you or any of these fellows. How strange that something that has no permanence by way of form or location should become fixed in your mind as something of substance, something reliable to be counted on in this shaky, impermanent world, an island of stability and order in a churning ocean of disorder, an ultimate refuge to which you can withdraw if everything else disintegrates: home.

And just as you would on Civvy Street, you try to get back home whenever there's a death in the family. And there were two at the gun position late yesterday when Able Troop, fulfilling the tradition of gunners "to fight their guns to the muzzles" if need be, drove off an enemy fighting-patrol that attacked the guns as they were deploying in scrubby bush and sand-dune country, two kilometres south of Ossendrecht. The universally popular George "Lefty" Phillips, your Troop Sergeant-Major, died while directing one of the guns onto the Germans. And the earnest and brave Fred Edwards, the troop's ack-ack Bren gunner, who, with Bombardier Scott, brought in those first German prisoners back at Fleury-sur-Orne in Normandy, died with his Bren gun blazing from the hip.

The news reached you during the night of October 6 in Ossendrecht, and at dawn you have permission to go back for a brief visit with your troop, which you expect has been badly shaken by the experience.

You hitch a ride back and are let off at RHQ, just west of the main road from Putte, where you can get directions to 2nd Battery.

Regimental Sgt.-Maj. A. J. Addie meets you with tears in his eyes for the loss of his pal "Lefty," inquiring bitterly: "Why the hell is it that it's always the good guys who get killed?"

You try not to let the implications of his question bother you as you walk over to 2nd Battery, about a quarter of a mile east of there, up a bush track leading through some scrubby pine woods to an open area of sand dunes with patches of low bushes. As you come within sight of the position, the guns are firing due north over the sandy track you are following. Then suddenly, to your astonishment, all the guns in the battery swing around 180 degrees and start firing at a target directly south towards Putte! And by the time you make it to Able Troop Command Post, at the far end of the positions, the guns have completed the target to their rear and have swung back again onto their zero line pointing north.

You find your GPO Bob Grout and his troop leader, Lieut. Bernie Ackerman, swept up in wonderment at these extraordinary demands on the guns, but glowing with relief that they were able to handle such an unprecedented target. The arm and arc on the artillery board, set up to plot targets in the zone in front of the guns, were totally useless of course, and they were forced to improvise, working out the range and switch from zero line from the map.

The target? Obviously 5th or 6th Brigade coming up on the right hit a pocket of Germans just as the guns here did yesterday. Lurking in the bush some four hundred yards right and forward of the gun position, the Germans had not bothered anyone on the regimental advance party, and only began to spatter Able Troop guns with small-arms fire as they were being put on line by Ackerman.

At first no one was too concerned. All had heard similar sounds before without anything serious developing. But soon the fire became so intense, all were forced to take cover behind vehicles or guns.

Grout first became aware of the enemy small-arms fire when he mounted the lip of a saucerlike sand-dune in which GA had parked and where his crew were setting up the troop command post. He'd climbed up there to watch the guns being put on line by Ackerman, who had joined Bombardier Hossack at the director out in front of the guns:

At first I thought the loud buzzing I heard was the sound of a swarm of angry bees. I remembered seeing several beehives only thirty or forty yards away when I was choosing this spot for my command post, and I turned in that direction expecting to have to order some curious gunners away from the hives. Instead I saw a stream of tracers passing waist-high. Immediately hitting the dirt, I crawled down the protected side of the dune and dashed to the command post, where, with the help of the others, I tried to pin down where the fire was coming from. The consensus was it was coming from the ridge about four hundred yards out in front.

Edwards, our ack-ack gunner, was keen on going out to locate the source and taking it on with his Bren. Sgt.-Maj. Phillips volunteered to go with him. He was instructed to pinpoint the enemy and assess their strength, but not engage.

I put in a request to RHQ for permission to engage with open sights [gun laid directly on target using the anti-tank telescopic sight] as soon as a target was identified. Then Phillips returned, covered with blood, reporting he and Edwards had spotted the machine-gun and had been fired on — and that before he could stop him, Edwards had sprung up and charged the MG's position, and had been cut down almost immediately. He had crawled to him and tried to help him, but shell-dressings were insufficient to handle the series of wounds across Edwards's lower abdomen, and so he'd come back for help.

We decided our armoured scout car should go out to pick him up. But it took time to unload the command post equipment, essential if the guns were to be prepared to fire in support of the infantry, always our number-one priority. Edwards was dead when it got out to him.

Meanwhile, Ackerman and Hossack, in their exposed position out in front of the guns at the director, had managed to pass the zero line to only one gun before the bullets, buzzing around them, drove them back to the guns. There Ackerman was able to put the other three guns on line using the "dial-sight method," meaning that guns were brought parallel by one gun passing reverse bearings from its dial-sight to the dial-sights of the others. By this time, Grout had received permission to engage the machine-guns, and was about to go over and direct a gun onto them, when Phillips suggested he should go, since he knew exactly where the fire was coming from. Ackerman recalled the final moments of the sad story:

I decided to take over Sgt. Graham's gun and act as gun sergeant, with Graham acting as gun-layer, and his bombardier loading the gun. I called for a target at 600 yards using Charge II. It was then Sgt.-Maj. Phillips came running over to me to point out the exact location of the enemy fire. We fired three shells. He stood at my right shoulder, and pointed to my left: "Sir, look! Over there!" I started to swing the trail of the gun to fire the way he directed, when they opened up on us. Two shots penetrated the shield of our gun like it was cardboard and one bullet hit him in the temple, above his left eye. We all dropped flat, and I had the unpleasant task of pushing Lefty's brains back into his head and using my field dressing to bandage it. I escaped with only a nick in the end of my nose – either from a splinter from the shield or the same bullet that hit Lefty. Gunner John Rawlings was wounded in the shoulder.*

Later you learn there were other casualties that day: Sgt. Walter Brown and Gunners Roy Seabrook and Harold Wiens. Wiens, however, was wounded not by enemy action, but by a phosphorous grenade he had taken away from a Dutchman walking through the wagon lines. On his way to burying it, it went off in his hand, splattering burning, clinging phosphorus onto various parts of his body, producing frightful wounds.†

---

* Sgt.-Major George R. Phillips was posthumously awarded the Belgian Croix de Guerre avec Palme, and a Commander-in-Chief Certificate.
† So frightful were his burns that one year and ten days would pass before he would be discharged from his last hospital. Arriving at his first hospital in Brussels, stripped of his clothes, his bandages and his stretcher kept soaking wet to prevent his body from smoking, they scraped off the phosphorus, shot him with penicillin and painkiller, and shipped him on to a civilian hospital in Basingstoke, England. After skin grafting on his neck and arm, he was shipped to a hospital in Canada.

II

EPIC STRUGGLE
FOR HOOGERHEIDE

———————— ✳ ————————

BY OCTOBER 8, HOOGERHEIDE, THE FIRST OBJECTIVE OF the Calgary Highlanders and the Maisonneuves, is barely secure, after three days and nights of close, bitter fighting, during which individual houses change hands several times. The German paratroopers show a bold tenacity matched only by the SS back in Normandy. In fact, the Black Watch, who were to push on past Woensdrecht to Korteven, are forced to add their strength to the defence of Hoogerheide just to maintain the Brigade's hold there, as the paratroopers, supported by heavy mortar- and shell-fire of a strength not encountered since last July around Verrières Ridge, not only prevent the Calgarians and Maisonneuves from securing the startline for the Black Watch, but push them back and threaten to drive them out of Hoogerheide as well.

The Black Watch, attempting to gain an intermediate objective only 300 yards beyond their unsecured startline, suffer eighty-one casualties including three officers and nine soldiers killed. However, that evening the paratroopers, infiltrating Hoogerheide in large numbers, pay severely for their boldness when they attack D Company just as the battalion Scout Platoon, alert and ready, joins it.

The battalion war diarist will record with evident satisfaction: "They held their fire until the enemy was fifty or sixty yards away and then opened up with everything they had, killing more than fifty." Still the enemy persists: ". . . the attack develops throughout the sector. Very heavy fighting ensues and it is more than two hours before the enemy decides he has had enough. We lose no ground and account for many Germans."

Similar notes in the Calgary Highlanders' war diary of October 9 will further underline the stubborn aggressiveness of the paratroopers:

0400 hours: Able Company reports "Hun infiltration"...

0421: Dog Company busily engaged in breaking up Jerry infiltrating party . . . To discourage the bold Hun, arty [5th Field] dropped a few rounds . . . an extremely effective shoot!

0515: Able Company's situation not clear . . . fighting still going on in some of the houses around the company area, but in general there is a perceptible decline in the ferocity of the Hun attack . . .

0602: . . . Able Company again in the throes of another counter-attack.

0640: . . . infiltration definitely beaten off and prisoners taken . . . Fighting still continuing in Charley Company area . . . Tracked vehicles heard again in Able Company direction . . . arty called in to do a little dusting off . . . 10 more prisoners taken . . .

1615: Able Company again being counter-attacked . . . coming in from all three sides. Able and Dog under heavy mortars and terrific shelling.

1655: Word comes Able withdrawing . . . Dog Company was able to put up a determined stand and hold out against strong pressure. Tank and arty assistance required . . .

1705: Able Company is still trying to rally for a stand and will try to hold on until assistance comes. The battle increases in intensity . . . communications with Able Company cease . . . when contact is made the Company commander and another officer are casualties and a lieutenant is in charge.

0248: Acting Able Company Commander returning to his company (from reporting in at Battalion Tac Headquarters) finds his original position occupied by the enemy. Travelling about between Dog and Charley companies he locates survivors of his own company. Gets the arty [5th Field] to shell about 40 Huns (spotted during his travels) approaching from the west across a field. The shells fall directly on target with devastating effect . . . the enemy can be heard screaming. Apparently the German officers and NCOs kept driving the survivors forward.

The Black Watch war diarist is clearly impressed with the vigour of the enemy:

Identification of bodies and of live prisoners taken (24) show the troops we are meeting are definitely the cream of the crop. They . . . range in age from 20 to 26, and are fine physical specimens, keen, with excellent morale.

At 1600 they opened an artillery bombardment that lasted two hours. Then came in on a counter-attack. Once again the attack was general on the sector, but more heavily on Calgary Highlanders. For a while things were very sticky, but once again this attack was repulsed without loss of any ground. There has been close cooperation between the artillery [5th Field] and our forward companies, and our guns have been firing continually on targets . . .

The grim determination of the hard-nosed paratroop battalions, grouped under the intimidating name "Battle Group Chill," rushed here to hold open the mouth of South Beveland at any cost, is reminiscent of the fanatical resistance of the SS units along Verrières Ridge in Normandy last summer. However, as in Normandy, their stubborn reluctance to withdraw, inspired by fanatical loyalty to their Führer, is costing them dearly in numbers killed, wounded, and captured. And in the end, as in Normandy, the dogged, unforgiving pressure by ordinary Canadian footsloggers "in baggy pants covered with mud, their boots and socks always wet" (to quote a local Dutch woman) – carrying an unemotional, unspoken, but unquenchable desire to destroy anything in a field-grey uniform and "get this goddamn war over and done with" – prevails at Hoogerheide.

Battalion commanders may mutter under their breath that the Army is now "scraping the bottom of the barrel" to fill up the ranks of the infantry (even posting gunners to rifle companies instead of back to their own artillery units when they recover from wounds). And they may curse the politically-minded staff officers who send up reinforcements so seriously deficient in training they don't even know their personal weapons, as witness the still tender bullet-hole in the calf of your left leg. But let no one ever fault their courage. Though many of them, if not most, are experiencing full battle conditions for the first time, and fear, as on any battlefield, is the dominant emotion, they are showing bags of courage. No one writing of these days will ever do justice to the courage of those who refuse to be driven from Hoogerheide, or those who will go forward to take Woensdrecht, or those who must push out into the misty, forbidding polders in the neck of South Beveland to wrest long, dismal stretches of muddy dikes from stubborn defenders and drive off counter-attack after counter-attack by screaming para-troopers.*

---

* A German report of these days makes much of "the stubborn resis-tance of the Canadian troops" in repulsing the "vigorous attacks" of their "battle-seasoned" paratroopers to try to regain Hoogerheide: "In the two following days [October 9 and 10] attack and counter-attack alternated. Three times the vanguard unit, Combat Group von der Heydte [formed from two battalions of 6th Paratroop Regiment] succeeded in thrusting [from the north] through the southern edge of Hoogerheide. Every time, the position gained had to be given up again for lack of force against the enemy counter-attack." – British Imperial War Museum MS/B798.

12

OUT IN THE
MIST–ENSHROUDED POLDERS

———————————— ✳ ————————————

AT THE SAME TIME 5TH BRIGADE UNITS ARE FIGHTING FOR
Hoogerheide, the Royals move west into South Beveland.

All of the peninsula, stretching west some twenty-six miles to
Walcheren Island, is land reclaimed from the sea by the Dutch, who
for five hundred years have progressively diked off the sea into large
rectangular areas, pumping them dry and producing fertile fields –
perfectly flat and enclosed by dikes twelve feet or more high. These
fields are known as "polders." Here and there, tucked away in a
corner of a polder, partially hidden from its neighbour by looming
dikes, is a little farmhouse with its barn.

Major Beatty's D Company moves out on "a reconnaissance in
force" from Ossendrecht along a dike road between two flooded
polders, to polders not flooded on the way to a "sluice basin pumphouse" at the narrowest part of the isthmus, four and a half kilometres west of Woensdrecht.

Walking with Beatty, behind the long line of infantrymen
snaking through the mist, is 4th Field FOO Capt. Leslie "Hutch"
Hutcheon, while his carrier, with his crew (Gunners Wally
Driemel, Mel Squissato, and John Copeland) grinds along behind.
Following them are two sections of 3-inch mortars, two anti-tank
guns, a troop of 8th Recce armoured cars, a Toronto Scottish
platoon of machine-guns, a detachment of Engineers, and a
number of Dutch maquis.

Some polders, like the one D Company is approaching, are three kilometres long and half a kilometre wide. Here, the advantages are all with the defenders. Attackers can obtain no concealment from an enemy dug-in along the dikes; and vehicles, forced to travel on top of the dikes, provide easy targets for anti-tank guns located at intersections. Thus, without the heavy mists – to which the soggy polders are susceptible on cold days – the Royals could never make it out there, let alone overcome by surprise (as they do) a German outpost, and push on almost to the pumphouse and important sluice gates, using a series of platoon attacks with guns preceding each attack with a healthy "stonk."*

At dusk when Hank Caldwell's A Company moves out to reinforce Beatty's, they hold between them an area two miles wide, and while not close to cutting off the isthmus, they present a menace to the main road from Walcheren, passing north of Woensdrecht, to Bergen-op-Zoom.

Next day, October 9, the Germans engage in really dirty pool. After Hutch lays down some fire on "a threatening counter-attack," some fifty Germans indicate they wish to surrender. But when a platoon is sent out to escort them in, they open fire with machine-guns, and the Royals just manage to get back with the aid of smoke laid down by their own 3-inch mortars.

Today, October 10, you and your crew take part in an attempt by the Royals to move north from where the two companies are entrenched in the polders, to close off the isthmus by fire if not by occupation. In early afternoon, Tom Whitley's B Company and Paddy Ryall's C Company move out from Ossendrecht.

Fortunately, again today, there is a heavy ground mist screening you from the German artillery observers in Woensdrecht, barely visible on its ledge. Even so you feel naked as you walk along the dike, which is like a causeway, conscious that for eight hundred

---

* In a "stonk," guns are laid in such a way as to ensure their shells land in a line along the compass bearing of a linear target.

yards, the only available shelter from shelling and mortaring is the icy ten-foot-deep water lapping the verges of the road.

At first Whitley's company is in the lead, and it is with him you walk with your carrier grinding beside you. As always there is about him that intimidating aura of determination to see things through regardless, of which you first became conscious back in that terrible orchard at Eterville in Normandy. And it is just as reassuring now as it was then, when, exhausted from constant bombardment, and looking like a scarecrow, he snarled his defiance. How different he looks today, so beautifully turned out: his tie perfectly knotted, his web-belt with holster in place, and his boots clean enough to be going out on a battalion parade square, rather than on their way into battle in the muddy polders.

Some distance beyond the flooded polders, there is a rendezvous at a farm that is to become Battalion Tac HQ. There you leave your carrier to go forward with Signaller Stevenson, who is back-packing an 18-set radio, walking north with Ryall's company in extended line towards the pointed end of this narrow polder hidden in the deep mist a thousand yards ahead. Their ultimate objective is a farmhouse in the next polder, just beyond where the left-hand dike converges on the dike angling up diagonally on the right.

As you walk in the swirling mists through the short wet grass of a mowing meadow, with only the sound of many feet rustling and squishing, and the deep breathing of men on each side of you, there is a sense of unreality.

To achieve maximum surprise there will be no arty preparation or covering fire until you've walked the length of the polder. But then there will be concentrated fire for ten minutes by the 25-pounders, with the mediums joining in for the last five minutes, as you shelter on this side of that next dike somewhere up ahead in the fog.

The fire-plan is precisely timed, so everyone is urged to walk briskly to make sure all are there at the dike, ready to rush over the top and hit the farm as soon as the firing ends. What will happen if they are on the dike waiting for you when you appear out of the fog is too unpleasant to contemplate. But clearly it is on everyone's mind, for when the dike looms up out of the mist, and no Schmeissers *bur-rup bur-rup*, the body language of deep relief of all within view is unmistakable, as shoulders unhunch, necks lengthen, backs straighten, and firm, confident strides replace the irregular, stumbling footfalls induced by fear and foreboding.

Seconds after you and Stevenson – breathing heavily – flop down with the infantrymen against the wet, grassy slope of the dike, there is a distant booming of guns from behind Ossendrecht. Shortly the air sizzles overhead and a crashing storm of shells exploding just beyond the dike rises to a hellish din that shakes the ground. You time the firing so as to help the infantrymen to be ready to go over the top as soon as the last shell arrives. But when the firing ends, before you can say anything, a bull-moose voice close by yells: "Okay, let's go!"

As you look that way, a thick-set sergeant scrambles up the dike, and immediately men on all sides are scrambling up and over with him. Small-arms fire starts snapping and crackling, and you and Stevenson move to the top of the dike where you can observe what's going on. The shooting is over so quickly you wonder if the farm was really occupied. But then you see bodies lying on the ground in the barnyard.

You have Stevenson send a message back on his 18-set that the carrier can come up now, for you want the more reliable 19-set radio in the carrier available to bring down fire when the inevitable counter-attack comes in. As you move down and across the farmyard towards the house to check out its possibilities as an OP, you pass among the German casualties.

They lie sprawled here and there between the barn and the house. Your shells had caught them in the open as they were trying to get at you and the Royals crouching behind the crest of the dike waiting for the fire-plan to lift. Most of them lie as they fell, but some are squirming and dying in agony, ignored by the Royals' stretcher-bearers who are fully occupied attending their own wounded. You are overcome with inexpressible horror. Until now you have never had occasion to pause on the ground immediately afterwards, and walk among men dead and dying from the high explosives and flying steel you had called down on them. Over the past four months you'd fired tons of shells on suspected enemy positions, but if you saw any movement at all, it was as though you were watching a movie playing in your field-glasses of shells bursting among little distant figures running for cover.

There had been that time in front of Dunkirk when you'd caught eighty of them in the open attacking a company of the Royals trapped between a canal and flooded land. Many had fallen and disappeared in the flashing, black puffs of your shells, and you'd watched with satisfaction, mumbling your grim litany: "That's for big, smiling Jack Cameron . . . and that's for quiet Jack Thompson . . . and that's for Dawson and Knapp and Thorpe and Ament and . . ." through a long list of dead comrades.

But now, staring down at the young German whose boots have just stopped twitching, you feel confused as you fight a flood of compassion that threatens to overwhelm you. You tell yourself that had he got the chance to use the Schmeisser lying beside him, you might now be lying dead here instead of him. But logic doesn't work, and you know you'll never be quite the same again. Time and again in the months ahead you will shell them with hate in your heart, but never again with the simple, straightforward satisfaction and enthusiasm of that young Forward Observation Officer in front of Dunkirk.

As you gain control of your emotions, you notice the dead man's jack-boots are almost new, and you wish you had a pair like them so you could pull them off at night and dry your feet; and when a counter-attack came in, you could pull them on without having to lace them up.

As though reading your mind a rough voice behind you says: "Nice boots, eh? Why don't you take them?" Receiving no reply, and undoubtedly sensing your queasiness, the Sergeant reaches down, yanks off the boots, and hands them to you.

You mumble, "Uh . . . .thanks." And gingerly holding them by your fingertips, you dump them into your carrier that has just arrived, grateful to be rid of them, for the warmth of the dead man's feet still breathes up from within the leather.

(A couple of days later, when they are cold, you will cut them down into Wellingtons and wear them with great comfort.)

On checking out the second storey of the little brick house, with most of its roof missing, you decide you can observe the zone from the dike in front just as well and with a lot less risk.

Ryall, worried about his right flank, which produced a strong counter-attack against Tim Beatty's company yesterday, directs his right-hand platoon to spread out to the right along the dike carrying the road to Woensdrecht, to a point about two hundred yards beyond a junction with another dike running north towards a prominent road-and-rail junction, a reputed strongpoint, with (according to the Dutch Underground) deep, bricked-in trench-works. As it turns out, there are some Germans along the dike over on the right, manning a 75-mm anti-tank gun, which the Royals capture with remarkable ease after a brief skirmish.

Your only contribution is to drop neutralizing shell-fire around some farm buildings on the right flank, but it brings you to the attention of a sniper who almost ends your war, when you cross over the north-south dike skirting the right side of your little house, and walk with Paddy a short way out in the polder to try to make out what's going on. You have your field-glasses to your eyes, when there's a shocking smack in your left ear as painful as the slap of an open hand. From experience working the rifle butts, where bullets flying at paper targets just inches over your head make that smacking sound, you know its significance. Paddy's ear must have caught a similar smack, for he drops as quickly as you. Without comment, you both scramble back over the dike into the barnyard.

The Royals have their slits only half-finished when the German counter-attack comes in. But the dike offers excellent protection against small-arms fire, while providing almost rifle-range conditions, with an incomparable field of fire, for the riflemen and machine-gunners confronting the shadowy, grey-green, helmeted figures in flapping, mottled smocks materializing in the mists.

They come in a stumbling run across the muddy field, flopping down among the sugar beets, firing bursts of flickering tracers and then rising to run forward again.

As you call back over the remote control for a Mike target to land in front of their line of advance, Lee Enfields are cracking, Stens are sputtering, and Brens are hammering away methodically all along the dike. And by the time your shells start sending up geysers of mud and smoke in the field just beyond the dike, putting an end to the attack, many of the paratroopers already have ceased to rise and run forward.

Then in the brief lull before their mortars and airbursts begin, a veteran sergeant — festooned with two captured Mauser rifles, one hanging down from each shoulder on its sling — starts marching back and forth along the crest of the dike in full view of the enemy, haranguing his men who crouch down behind the dike, sheltering from the menacing buzzing sounds that follow him as he passes back and forth.

Your first thought is the poor guy has cracked up. But when he comes close to where you are lying against the leeward side of the dike, you detect the smell of rum on the evening breeze. It's obvious he's had a bit too much spine-stiffener on the way up here today. Yet as you listen, it becomes clear this is not just an alcohol-induced display of bravado. He has a serious message to get over to his boys, and he's running a big risk to make his point. He most certainly has their attention, as he tells them he didn't hear enough fire from their weapons when they were attacked just now (a common complaint of company commanders): "The more you fire at them, the less they'll fire at you. Here now! Keep your heads up! There aren't any Heinies within miles. If there were, would they let me walk around up here?"

At that moment he's tramping just above where you are lying back against the dike, and you notice there's now a nasty, intimate *snick-snick* to the bullets. And when a smirking rifleman, on his knees working on his trench below the crest nearby, catches your eye and winks knowingly, you decide it's time the sergeant came down before he's shot down, an eventuality that will benefit no one's morale.

It will probably take the persuasive authority of the company commander, Paddy Ryall, or his second-in-command, Len Gage. But before you go looking for them, you call and beckon him to come over where you might talk to him quietly. To your astonishment and relief he not only comes over, but slides down the side of the dike beside you, inquiring: "Yeh, Foo?"

Clearly it is a day of honour for the Royals. By 5:00 P.M. Whitley's company is on the near side of the embankment carrying the railway through the isthmus less than three hundred yards from the sea lapping its north shore, in position to dominate by fire all roads to and from Walcheren Island, denying their use, at least in daylight, and ultimately contributing something of consequence to the island's downfall. In taking their objectives the assaulting companies had destroyed many of the enemy and taken 104 prisoners at the relatively low cost of three dead and twenty wounded. And in all this, the guns played a significant role.

Buoyed by success, the Royals decide Hank Caldwell's A Company should go forth next day, October 11, to clean out that strongpoint 1,000 yards north of Ryall's company and about the same distance east of Whitley's where his railway embankment meets a dike.

Overnight the balmy fall weather, the one decent feature of life here, disappears. By morning the chill of approaching winter is descending from dark grey skies in the form of an icy drizzle that later turns to rain. Thus bomb-carrying Spits and Tiffies, which could have helped, are unavailable. Still, a heavy fire-plan is laid on by Col. Mac Young at Brigade, involving field and medium guns, along with Tor Scots' 4.2-inch mortars and the Royals' 3-inch mortars plastering the objective, while heavy ack-ack fills the air above it with airbursts.

The attack goes in about 3:30 P.M. over the dike directly in front of your OP. You have them in view all the way. Jerry lets them get almost to the railway embankment before he opens up. By then they are much too close to the enemy for you to safely shell the source of their torment. When Hank comes back to use Paddy's communication with Battalion HQ to request permission to withdraw, he is badly shaken. His leading platoon has been severely mauled, and the rest are pinned down under heavy mortar and machine-gun fire short of the crossroads. To aid them in getting back, you pop smoke shells along the railway up to the crossroads. Already misty, the polder is soon blanketed in dense, white fog from your fuming canisters. But you can't use H.E. Some wounded Royals may be lying close to the objective and unable to crawl away.

While they gained no territory and suffered thirty-three known casualties, Hank's men must have fought with intimidating aggressiveness, for they managed to bring back forty prisoners!

That night the Germans launch a strong counter-attack involving flame-throwers on both Paddy's company and Tom Whitley's over on the left. You are asleep in your bedroll on the floor of the little storage room attached to the kitchen at the rear of the house, the only room that can be blacked out, other than the tiny cellar beneath the kitchen in which company headquarters is set up.

Paddy wakes you and tells you the heaviest firing (judging by the amount of tracer bullets) is originating from the polder just over the dike in front, and from over on the right where they captured the German gun this afternoon. Still half in your bedroll, leaning on one arm and holding a dim lamp-electric over your map-board on the floor beside you, you are able to give Stevenson, manning the radio only a couple of feet away, a Mike target to send back to the guns. Having registered several spots in the polder just beyond that dike before dark, it's a simple matter to choose one near the source of trouble and identify it for the guns by its code name. After plastering it with a heavy scale of fire a few minutes, you move the shelling: "West 200 . . . Repeat!" Then: "East 400 . . . Repeat!" Back and forth you move the fire.

In each successive lull, as the guns are being "switched," the snap and chatter of small arms along the dikes is noticeably reduced, until it dies away completely. When it does, a weary Paddy Ryall, coming in the back door and passing through your storeroom into the kitchen on his way to his headquarters in the cellar, calls out, "Good shooting, old boy! Thank your gunners for us, will you?"

High praise from an infantry officer, for which they will be most grateful. Thank goodness he saw nothing incongruous in a FOO shooting from the map while still ensconced in his bedroll.

It takes a while to go back to sleep; you keep expecting the Krauts to try again. And while you wait for sleep to return, you amuse yourself watching the shadows cast on the wall behind the table by the signaller's candle as he tries to read the *Reader's Digest* your wife sent you in a recent parcel. Outside, a basin of Moaning Minnies end their howling flight with tremendous crashes, and suddenly you are conscious of the vulnerability of that wall to a shell or mortar – an outside wall of light construction facing Woensdrecht.* Not good. Not good at all. In the morning you must get the crew to erect an inner wall of sandbags. In addition to greatly improving the sheltering quality of the room, it will give them something constructive to do and perhaps get their minds off the rather awful vistas of death that surround them on all sides here. Morale is still quite good considering, but . . .

---

* Nebelwerfers (or Moaning Minnies to the troops) were rocket mortars, with six to ten barrels, of varying calibres and ranges.

CALIBRE	PROJECTILE	RANGE IN YARDS
150 mm	75 pounds	7,300
210 mm	248 pounds	8,600
300 mm	277 pounds	5,000

13

A FARM HAS BECOME
A PLACE OF DEATH

✳

BODIES OF MEN AND BEASTS LIE EVERYWHERE UNBURIED.
The initial shelling, preceding the move in here, killed the horses
and cows. Even the chickens lie dead in the yard.

One old driving-horse, which somehow survived the awful
torrent of shells and was still standing in the yard halfway between
the house and the barn when you arrived, became the special
concern of the boys on your crew for a while. Though he stood
rooted to the spot as though paralyzed by shock, his hide perforated
with shell fragments, there was no sign of serious bleeding, so they
were encouraged to hope he might survive if sheltered from further
wounding from the Jerry airbursts and mortar bombs, which began
to arrive with increasing frequency. But when they tried to lead
him to the barn, they couldn't budge him. Gradually, his head hung
lower and lower, and when for more than three days he didn't move
an inch from where he stood, and began to weave on his feet, they
decided he should be put out of his misery. A bullet through the
head from one of the captured Mauser rifles, stacked in the corner
of your room off the kitchen, and he crumpled down only a few
yards from the unburied Germans.

In the barn, three big work-horses died, convulsing in great
agony from shell splinters while tethered side by side in their stall.
They lie in a repulsive confusion of legs, heads, and bodies, so completely and so consistently covered with red brick-dust – from the

roof tiles pulverized by the shells, which had slowly settled on them over a period of days – that the effect is of a sculpture moulded of red clay designed to illustrate the madness of war. Bulging eyeballs, tongues hanging from agonized mouths, great hoofs and fetlocks that died pawing the air, lacerations and blood-matted manes and tails – all equally and evenly coated with red dust of one tone and one texture – on first sight arouse within you a new sense of horror, unlike anything you have experienced before on gazing upon the face of death.

And in the fields are dead cows and God knows how many dead men. Two German stretcher-bearers with red crosses on their smocks appear out there this morning, wandering around in the mist in front of the junction of roads and railway, stopping every so often and bending down – obviously checking bodies to make sure none are still alive. For half an hour they are left to go about their business unmolested – but then the Royals begin to get suspicious.

When their zig-zagging brings them close enough to the dike to pinpoint the Royals' trenches if that is their intention, a sergeant stands up and waves them in with a Bren. After a slight hesitation, they obey. But when they are paraded in front of a stern Major Ryall in the kitchen they vigorously protest, in highly accented English, being taken prisoner – boldly demanding their rights under the clause in the Geneva Convention covering the safe conduct of non-combatant stretcher-bearers. Paddy shouts them down, telling them they should count themselves lucky they were taken prisoner and not shot, as they shot one of his stretcher-bearers only a couple of days ago in broad daylight.

During a long lull in the German mortaring (probably due to their not knowing where their meandering stretcher-bearers are), the farmer, Sief Pijnen, who'd taken refuge at a neighbouring farm, comes up with a horse and cart to rescue any animals still alive.

All he can find are a few little pigs in a sheltered pen near the back door. As they are hastily loaded and driven off, you believe you are watching the last living creatures (other than soldiers) depart this place of death. However, this belief is shattered late in the day when an ungodly screech – unlike any sound ever uttered by anything of this world – draws your eyes to the attic crawl-space above the kitchen. Up there, barely visible in the gloom, stands a wild-eyed little dog.

How it's been able to resist coming forth to beg food before now is incomprehensible, until you try to reach for it to bring it down for some of the M & V stew giving off the odour that enticed it from its hiding place. As your hands touch its shivering body, the screech it emits is so horrific you topple backward off your precarious perch on an upturned Compo box. Clearly the poor mutt has been driven insane by the shells that blew off chunks of roof and ceiling from the bedroom in which it was seeking refuge from the terrifying explosions.

Reassembling your courage, you mount the box. This time, prepared for its awesome bellow, you grab the quivering bundle of stiffness and drop it to the floor, where it scuttles under the table. There it lurks, screeching at every pretext, even when food is pushed towards it, until the next day when you drive it out the back door, your nerves unable to cope with its insane shrieks each time your feet pass close by.*

During the afternoon you receive a signal from Col. Mac Young at Brigade to mark with red smoke that strongpoint on the next dike where it joins the railway embankment – now becoming infamous under the complete misnomer "Five Ways Crossroads" – and subsequently to observe and report the effectiveness of the 500-pound bombs the Spitfires will try to drop on it.

While it's easy enough to produce red smoke shells on target, judging the effectiveness of bombs is something else, even when observed from a superior vantage point among the ragged rafters of

---

* On visiting the farm twenty-five years later the author felt foolish at the depth of his relief on learning from Sief's brother Louis (who shared the farm, but was trapped north of Woensdrecht during the battle) that "Fanny," the little "hounde," recovered and lived to a ripe old age.

the upper storey of your house, creaking and rattling from the cold wind of almost-gale force that has been blowing all day. One after another, a few seconds apart, five Spits sweep in over the polders from the east, arousing a fury of black flak from around Woensdrecht. You follow each of them in turn with your glasses as they close in on the crossroads. Clearly you see each black bomb plunge earthward in a wobbly arc to a tremendous flashing gush of smoke and mud, feel the earth-quaking jar even before you hear the roar of the explosion that seems almost under the tail of the plane as it scurries away from the concussion wave.

It all looks mighty impressive, but what they accomplished is impossible to tell. And all you can report with certainty is that all five Spits delivered their bombs in the target area and got away from the flak unharmed. Later, when the CO unexpectedly drops in on you (for no reason that you can discern other than to make it clear he fully understands how sticky it is up here) he tells you the bombing of the crossroads is in preparation for a full battalion attack by the Black Watch through here tomorrow.

However, as it turns out, the first attack in the morning is against the Royals holding the Black Watch startline, of which their historian will one day write: "Action on the 13th opened at four o'clock in the morning with an enemy counter-attack, which began against B Company (Whitley's) and continued on down the battalion line. This was repulsed within twenty minutes with the aid of strong artillery support."

(No mention, of course, of the artillery FOO, aroused once more by his company commander, again shooting from the map while still in his bedroll propped up on one elbow.)

14

WHAT PRICE ANTWERP?

---------- ✳ ----------

SOMETIMES YOU FORGET THAT THE REAL PURPOSE OF ALL this costly fighting to choke off the neck of the isthmus of South Beveland and drive the Germans from the length and breadth of the peninsula, is to open up the back door to Walcheren Island and silence the big guns there, so Antwerp's port can be used. And when the sense of purpose disappears, the whole wretched business takes on the bleak and hopeless aspects of a blood-letting. If you can have these lapses, what must it be like for the weary riflemen of the Royals clinging to their miserable, rainsodden dikes out there; and for the men of the Black Watch, who, at 0615 this morning, tried to make it across that misty sugar-beet field behind artillery and 4.2-inch mortar concentrations, but got no more than 250 yards before being pinned down and driven back by a hurricane of airbursting shells, mortars, and machine-gun fire?

Now, just before last light, as they wait to be sent out there again to try to clear out that meeting of road and rail-line running along the top of the next dike less than a kilometre away, what are they thinking? Can they have anything else on their minds but survival?

They've been told, of course, that, since the battalion was driven back at 0830 this morning, a dozen Spitfires have dropped bombs and strafed a brickworks north of Woensdrecht, from whence offending mortars have been originating; and that twice, once at 2:30 P.M. and again at 3:00 P.M., "Angus," the code name for that fortified crossroads, was treated to attacks by rocket-firing Typhoons, led there by your red smoke shells. They'll have ten tanks in support, including heavy flame-throwers, and while they cannot move forward with them, they'll be firing from the flank. Also, belt-fed Vickers machine-guns, firing from the top of the dike over the heads of the advancing soldiers, will attempt to neutralize enemy fire from distant dikes, while 17-pounder anti-tank guns will fire over open sights at possible enemy OPs in Woensdrecht on its high ground only 1,500 yards away. And of course the artillery "preparation" and prearranged concentrations of field, medium, and heavy ack-ack will be heavier than this morning.

Still, you look with pity at the men sheltering behind the dike waiting for zero hour, saying little, having a last cigarette. Just above them, along the brow of the dike, vaguely silhouetted against the darkening sky, sit the Vickers, their silent muzzles pointing out over the flat, forbidding polder, completely devoid of cover of any kind.

Casualties are bound to be high, though you can hardly anticipate that by midnight all their company commanders will be killed or wounded, and ten men – all that can be mustered by one surviving officer in that churning cauldron – will be requesting permission to withdraw.*

As Spitfires hum in and drop more bombs, the guns over behind Ossendrecht open up and pour shells into the polder beyond your dike in a deafening roar. The Vickers are now chattering, and Jerry starts to respond, ploughing the dike with mortars. One flashes right beside a Vickers' crew, and the gunner falls over backward down the dike. Immediately another leaps up behind the gun, and it continues firing with barely a pause. You glance at young Gunner Hiltz, who has crept out beside you on the dike, and he wags his head in the odd way that men do when they marvel at the courage of other men.

---

* On this "Black Friday" the Black Watch lose 183 officers and men, 56 of them dead, bringing their total losses to 264 since they began fighting at Hoogerheide to close off South Beveland five days ago.

Most of the Black Watch are either cut down as they go over the dike, or are down and crawling before they get very far. Fewer than a dozen manage to get across the muddy beet-field anywhere close to those crossroads on the enemy-held dike. At least that's what one surviving officer (Major Bill Ewing) who comes back to the house about 11 o'clock seeking permission to withdraw, tells his CO on the phone connecting Paddy's cellar to a farm in the rear shared by tactical headquarters of both the Royals and the Black Watch: "We're at the railway dike, but still at least four hundred yards from the objective, and all we're able to muster is ten men."

By now the number of wounded coming back is so heavy, the walking-wounded have to be directed to the barn to await their turn on one of the ambulance Jeeps provided by many regiments, arriving and departing in a steady stream – one at least driven by a Dutch civilian lad from a neighbouring farm. An MO (you assume he's Black Watch) has set up in the gloomy kitchen in discouragingly poor light, which must be kept subdued since that room, unlike yours, cannot be blacked out. There, using the kitchen table as an operating table, he provides emergency treatment for some. But the majority of stretcher cases are patched with shell dressings and shot with morphine in your little storeroom by the stretcher-bearers who bring them in, and then are put aboard stretcher-carrying Jeeps bound for hospital as they become available.

For hours the Black Watch stretcher-bearers have been going out into the darkness of no-man's-land before Five Ways Crossroads, the only light the flashes of mortar bombs, carrying in the most severely wounded and propping them up around the walls of this room you've sandbagged and made as liveable as possible.

As they cut out arms and legs of battledresses and pack on shell dressings, you marvel at their cheerful demeanour. One of them in particular, a robust lad, pours forth a steady stream of reassuring nonsense at the stunned men with white faces, many of whom will never live to see the inside of the hospitals back in Antwerp, where the stretcher-bearing Jeeps are now taking them.

"Will I make it?" asks a boy with a row of holes across his chest.

"Of course you will – you lucky devil! You'll be home in Canada for Christmas!" And he lights a cigarette and shoves it between the boy's pale lips, before he goes on to the next man.

You're fascinated with the idea the Black Watch would have been issued with special blood-red underwear, until finally the truth dawns on you. Feeling yourself growing dizzy, you go out into the night and sit down in the darkness of the little outside toilet, putting your head down between your legs until the dizziness goes away. Back inside, you notice your crew look pale and drawn, and to break the spell of horror, you get them brewing up tea and handing it around to those who can drink it.

Now one of the stretcher-bearers – a mere boy – his humanity stretched beyond the limit, breaks down and starts to cry, repeating over and over between sobs: "Did you see those guys out there? It was plain murder. They never had a chance." For a while no one says anything. Then the robust, cheerful stretcher-bearer, still going about the business of bandaging a man's belly, yells at him ferociously: "Why don't you go home and suck your mother's teat? Talk about women – talk about anything else, but shut your goddam mouth!" A murmur of approval goes up around the room, and you know they're justified, for some will never see the dawn. But still you feel sorry for the poor, sensitive boy, who now slinks out into the darkness where his sobbing will be unobserved.

Insensitivity now dominates life. If it didn't, everyone surely would go mad. But when Ralph Young, second-in-command of the Royals, making a visit relates "a shocking incident" he witnessed shortly after dawn at 5th Brigade HQ (now sharing a farmhouse with Royals' Tac HQ), you agree there are unacceptable levels of insensitivity. "Hefty" Ross, intrepid leader of the Royals' Scout Platoon, was tongue-lashed unmercifully by the Brigadier of 5th Brigade for picking up, and bringing back in his Jeep for medical attention, two seriously battle-exhausted Black Watch lads he met staggering away from the front with unseeing eyes.

15

A TOWER SILHOUETTED
AGAINST THE SKY

✳

ON THE AFTERNOON OF THEIR SEVENTH DAY IN THE POLDERS, the Royals are relieved by the Calgary Highlanders and undertake a long route march of some thirteen kilometres, from the extreme left of the line in South Beveland to the bush area east of Ossendrecht near a lake called Groote Meer, where the topography is so strikingly different from the treeless, mud-and-water polder-lands in the isthmus as to seem of another country. A land of sand dunes and pine woods, all above sea level, it even has a hill of respectable height, thirty-one metres (more than one hundred feet) according to the map. And on its crest stands a fire-ranger's tower.

It's a long trek for the heavily laden, weary troops plodding back through Ossendrecht and east to the main highway from Putte to the mouth of a bush road that leads in to the lake; and, on the way there, there are several delays from enemy shelling. Then just after dark – word having been received that the South Saskatchewan Regiment, now attached to 4th Brigade, whose right flank the Royals are moving to strengthen against increasingly violent counter-attacks by infantry and tanks, is again under severe attack – the tired men are broken off for a hot meal in the grounds of a secluded, substantial building left of the highway. And while this is being served, an Orders Group is held in a brightly lit, sterile room the like of which you'd forgotten existed. Company commanders are briefed on their holding role and assigned areas in which to deploy around and about the northwestern end of the lake, about one and a half kilometres from here. You make sure Cornett attaches you to the company that will be closest to that hill with the wooden watch-tower. This turns out to be Hank Caldwell's A Company.

A great storm of shell-fire is now roaring over in the area where you are headed, but no one seems greatly concerned. As the companies form up in single file, by platoons, to continue their shuffling way up the highway to turn right into the bush road towards Groote Meer, you marvel at the degree to which everyone has become blasé about German counter-attacks that seem to hit selected spots in each sector at least once or twice a day or night. In a matter-of-fact way Cornett reports that all the shelling up ahead is by 6th Field on map reference 662184, directly northwest of Groote Meer. The fact that that is right next to where the Royals are headed, and that those shells are designed to help extricate a sub-unit of the South Saskatchewan Regiment that has been overrun, seems to concern no one, least of all your Battery Commander.

He tells you that last night Bill Carr, 26th Battery Commander, currently attached to the SSRs, reported firing on targets over in this same zone to gain relief for another company of SSRs "cut off," and that about 4:00 A.M. he'd reported the "sub-unit of friends in great difficulty." However, by mid-afternoon today the tide had turned, and Carr was reporting the SSRs had taken thirty prisoners and that "forty more were on their way back."

While the Major admits conditions up there currently appear a bit sticky, the situation will stabilize in due course – a conclusion, you believe, more readily arrived at by one who will be remaining here at Battalion Headquarters, than by one heading off at 9:00 P.M. in the pitch-black with Hank's company nosing up the narrow, bush-lined road for Groote Meer, just as an Uncle target is being shot by the 72 guns of 2nd Division on "four tanks and 100 infantry . . . at map reference 658181," only 800 yards from the lake.

Taking up positions in the dark in unknown territory must

always be fraught with nerve-wracking difficulties, but confusion can assume terrifying proportions when the occupation is attempted during an enemy counter-attack. For what seems like hours, bewildered and anxious, the column is stalled in the inky-black confinement of the narrow, bush road, while Schmeissers *bur-rup bur-rup* close by and high explosive is liberally dumped up ahead where the companies are to deploy.

However, fulfilling Cornett's optimism, things eventually get sorted out, and though shells from the direction of the enemy keep roaring and flashing in the woods nearby, the Royals continue to move forward.

Miraculously, all companies make it to their positions without bumping into hostile troops, though it takes them until well past midnight to dig in because of periodic sessions of some very heavy enemy shelling.

On the map, Groote Meer shows as a good-sized lake about one and a half kilometres long and about half that wide if measured across its western end, where is situated the only building for miles around. Hank heads for this. It turns out to be a sizeable lakeside residence with some out-buildings, and there he establishes his company headquarters in the basement, making full use of what appears to be a formidable water barrier out front in placing his platoons on the flanks.

Damage within the house on the side facing the lake suggests it has been the object of machine-gunning and mortaring. All the glass is missing from the windows and French doors.

With no room in the basement for you and crew a ground-floor room off the living room is made as safe as possible by blocking off a window in a side wall with an upturned mattress held in place by a bureau pushed against it, and by installing a blanket over the door as a blackout curtain to prevent light from spilling out into the living room every time someone goes in or out at night. Hardly a bomb shelter, but the wide lake out front provides a sense of security you haven't felt for a long while as you bed down for a couple of hours.

But when dawn comes and you go out into the shadowy living room to peer through the ragged windows over the lake, you can hardly believe your eyes. You rush down into the cellar and bring up Hank to have a look. He is aghast. The lake, on which he had based the defensive disposition of all his platoons, does not exist. From shore to shore, it is completely dry – its exposed clay bottom veined with wide cracks. An enemy patrol could have walked over here last night and entered this open lakefront door unmolested.*

However, the fire-ranger's tower on the crest of the hill, which starts to rise only a short distance from the circular drive at the rear of the house, is real enough. On your first trip up there you are pleasantly surprised to find one of Hank's platoons dug-in among the pine trees at the base of the wooden structure. This you didn't expect since the tower is so distant from company headquarters – at least half a mile by way of a torturous trail winding up through the bush. It seems you are not alone in looking upon this height of land as an asset that must not fall into enemy hands.

When you crawl up the ladderlike, open stairway to the top, you find it really is a very high structure, rising well above the mature pine trees of the forest in which it stands. Any higher and you might not have the stomach to climb it. And you anticipate that as time goes by, there will be periods of irrepressible anxiety springing from the thought that if you can see so far, this tower silhouetted against the sky must be visible to every German 88-mm on the whole front.

But for a while you are almost drunk with the view and the power it gives you as an arty FOO. Accustomed to looking out from

---

* When in 1973 the author visited the restored lakeside house, Groote Meer was still dry – a sorry, tangled mess of weeds. Local residents had concluded that earth-quaking tremors from bombs or a heavy artillery bombardment opened an underground fissure, allowing the lake to drain out into the low lands beyond Ossendrecht. Since the war the question of how the lake might be rehabilitated was raised again and again in political forums without results.

a hole at ground level, or through a narrow hole poked among the tiles of a roof of a house or barn, this is a dream OP. The only problem is communications, and this is solved the first day by the signallers running a line from your room in the house, where the 19-set radio from your carrier is manned twenty-four hours a day, to a field telephone installed up in the tower. And for the next six days you spend most of the daylight hours, and a great many hours of darkness, crouched behind the low, wooden barrier-wall around the platform at the top of the tower, peering out at the zone.

The yellow telephone line, snaking up an incline of varying steepness to the pine-covered rolling plateau where the tower stands, follows a trail of sorts through the underbrush – very rough and laced with fallen trees and other obstacles, including a dead German soldier lying face-up right across the path, which could trip the unwary. The trail is well enough defined to be followed easily in daylight. But at night it's necessary to run the signal line through your hand and exercise care if you're not to trip and go crashing headlong into the underbrush that always seems to be dripping wet from mist or rain.

The combined height of the hill and tower provides a view from the top of the platform for many miles in all directions, but, because of the continual misty weather, very little detail is identifiable beyond a couple of miles. In a way, this is just as well, for ammunition expenditure, except on DF (defensive fire) tasks, has been restricted to sixty rounds per gun in each twenty-four-hour period.

Apart from shelling one made-to-order target of enemy soldiers attempting to dig-in in broad daylight, and dropping some red smoke shells around a distant church tower to mark it for demolition by 500-pound bombs dropped by Spitfires at its base (after you'd spotted what looked like a long wireless antenna sticking out of the louvres of its belfry), your observed fire has consisted mainly of spattering a few shells from one troop of four guns on suspicious-looking scars of new earth that could be enemy trench-works.

To conserve shells while extending the harassing aspect of such shelling you use "troop fire," whereby each of the four guns of your troop fire in turn at prescribed intervals. Thus "three rounds troop fire at ten-second intervals" means the enemy will be harassed for almost two minutes instead of less than half a minute at the regular "gunfire" rate.

Three days after arriving here, you are called upon to provide a small fire-plan involving smoke mixed with H.E. in support of an attack by a strong fighting patrol sent out by D Company, with a troop of tanks, to clean out positions directly in front of them, from which the enemy has been making life difficult for the Royals by way of machine-gunning, shelling, and mortaring – the severity of which reached an intolerable level yesterday, October 16, with the Battalion reporting one bomb or shell arriving in company areas every twenty seconds.

From your tower you have a grandstand view of the attack as it moves out through fairly open country with the odd sandy bank showing among patches of gorse and clumps of scraggly pine so reminiscent of Petawawa. Right at the outset a Sherman runs over a mine and humps up in a cloud of dust and smoke. Though it doesn't catch fire, it is immobilized, and its crew, expecting it to brew up, pile out, and the other tanks, fearing the same fate, leave the infantry to go on alone.

About the time your bombardment is to end, you notice the odd shell is failing to clear the tops of some tall, widely spaced trees through which the troops are passing, bursting with a wicked flash and violent black puff right over their heads. While none appears to have been hurt by the shower of steel and branches, you later learn those airbursts were devastating to the nervous systems of some men who only recently returned from hospital after recovering from that RAF bombing back at Hautmesnil last August. Two at least are again being evacuated as casualties of battle exhaustion. Otherwise the attack proceeds so smoothly that by mid-morning all objectives are attained and you are left with the impression you have been watching a training manoeuvre.

Clearly not all the Germans fighting around here are taking

seriously Hitler's edict (revealed by prisoners) to fight to the death. You might reasonably suppose that the less aggressive are members of the "White Bread Brigade," men with stomach ulcers or other digestive-tract problems, requiring a special diet, who reputedly were posted to garrison this zone when it was still isolated and quiet.*

Knowing Signal-Sgt. Ryder is due to come up from the guns this morning with a box of Compo rations, and hoping he'll have some mail this time, maybe even a parcel of goodies from home, you go down the hill to the house for lunch.

Ryder's visits, which occur every three days when conditions allow, have become real highlights of the limited existence you pursue up here. Always a cheerful fellow, ready to share the latest bit of scuttlebutt and news about what's been going on back at the guns, he is like a breath of fresh air, and he never fails to leave you and your crew feeling better for hours after his visit.

Ever since he accidentally put a bullet hole in the wall just above your head as you lay resting on your bedroll on the floor of the little room off the kitchen at Paddy Ryall's headquarters at that farm out in the polders – missing your skull by no more than a couple of inches with a shot from a supposedly empty rifle he'd selected for examination from a pile of captured Mausers stacked in the corner – he has taken an outsized proprietary interest in your well-being. And in recent days, before coming up, he noticeably is taking the trouble to go beyond the Battery (to RHQ you suspect) to equip himself with information he thinks may be of interest to you.

---

* More of the "White Bread Brigade" might have surrendered had it not been for fear of their officers. Years after, Sief Pijnen, of the battered farm out in the polders, told you of spurning (out of fear of treachery) an offer of a Luger pistol from the German soldier in whose trench he was sheltering from your shells, prior to the Royals' attack. The German private urged him to take it and shoot his officer in the next trench so he and his buddies could surrender.

Thus you learn that Capt. Sammy Grange has become the Adjutant replacing Capt. "Tim" Welch, the Adjutant since way back at Horsham in England, who has taken a job back at Division.

You also learn that a Capt. Jack Cooper, an older brother of Major Don Cooper, who commanded 26th Battery when you were with it back in 1942–43, and who for a while was second-in-command of the Regiment late in 1943, has joined 4th Field and been posted as a troop commander to his brother's old battery.

16

WOENSDRECHT

✳

AFTER THE EXPERIENCE OF THE ROYALS AND THE BLACK Watch out in the polders under fire from guns and mortars controlled by observers in Woensdrecht, it is clear the village must be taken, and the RHLI are chosen to do the job.

Woensdrecht is only a short walk northwest of Hoogerheide, but conscious of what it cost 5th Brigade battalions to take and hold this smashed and forlorn place – in a battle that swayed back and forth over a few houses for three bloody days and nights – every Riley moving up to the startline, accompanied by tanks of the Fort Garry Horse, knows it could be the longest walk of his life.

When they set out in the black early hours of October 16, following a creeping barrage, they do their best to follow the spirit, if not the letter, of the advice given them "to lean into it and get there before Jerry has a chance to recover and get his head up." Shivering and sweating at the same time – half-intimidated and half-stimulated by the raging linear inferno of blinding flashes and hot concussions, seemingly erupting just before their faces – they plunge through the sour fumes and stumble over steaming gashes left by the violence that just passed, desperate to keep up, but at the same time dreading the moment when they will confront the enemy.

The enemy, however, anticipating the barrage, has pulled back, and the leading companies are allowed to move through Woensdrecht and out onto the low ridge beyond. Then about 10:00 A.M.,

A Company, still settling in on their exposed slope, is hit with such force by paratroopers, tanks, and self-propelled guns, they are routed in disarray, and within minutes paratroopers and tanks are dominating the northern part of the village – one tank stopping just outside the house 4th Field FOO "Stevie" Stevenson has chosen as an OP.

Clearly, the battalion is in a desperate way – its only hope for recovering and stabilizing the front resting on the shoulders of Major Joe Pigott's reserve company and what help they can draw from the demoralized remnants of A Company, turned around to face the enemy by Pigott and Lt.-Col.Whitaker brandishing pistols.* But first the enemy about Stevenson's OP and Pigott's company must be dealt with; and with the approval of that intrepid Riley officer, Stevenson pulls down on the position an Uncle target – all seventy-two guns of the division.

That this does all it's meant to is confirmed in a situation report to Div Headquarters RCA at 6:35 P.M.: "Now much quieter. Believe U 203 held position for RHLI. First [Uncle target] brought down deliberately on our forward troops. They were pleased. Killed many Jerries." And the gunners receive a message of gratitude from the Rileys' CO (that will one day find expression in the history of the gunners of Canada): "The fire caught the enemy in the open, whereas our men were deep in slit trenches having been warned. Our troops cheered; the slaughter was terrific."

But, when, in their turn, the Rileys counter-attack and regain their positions with the help of a company of Essex Scottish and more tanks, they are hit again and again with fierce counter-attacks by paratroopers and tanks, each attack preceded by fearful doses of shelling and mortaring, including endless heart-stopping airbursts of 88-mm shells arriving unheralded, and streams of blood-curdling banshee-wailing flights of Moaning Minnies,

---

* *Tug of War* by Lt.-Col. Denis W. and Shelagh Whitaker, Beaufort Books, New York and Toronto, 1984, p. 194.

looping in and crashing with monstrous reverberating booms among the ravaged buildings.

After Stevenson's house is struck by four shells or mortars, it collapses about him, forcing him to set up elsewhere. Casualties mount – ninety-one in the first few hours,[*] and the Rileys maintain their tenuous hold on the smashed and fire-gutted houses and barns only with the help of rocket-firing Typhoons attacking the German armour, and by the shattering concentrations of shells called down at crucial moments by Stevenson and another 4RCA FOO, Capt. Douglas McDonald, getting his first taste of battle, having just joined the Regiment from Canada.

Back at the guns, the action is reminiscent of Normandy: first, the thundering roar of the orderly fire-plan by the guns of 2nd Division and three medium regiments (7th Canadian, and 84th and 121st British) lighting up the black dome of cloudy predawn sky with ragged flashes; then the strange calm, when all the guns go silent, extending until daylight, when the expected report comes that the infantry have gained their objectives. Then comes the inevitable enemy counter-attack. At 7:35 A.M., over all earphones in the Regiment comes the urgent call: DF (SOS) 1029 – Scale 2 – enemy infantry concentrating for attack."

Then from a FOO: "Mike target – Mike target – Mike target . . . Enemy attacking in force with tanks." And for the rest of the day, the guns thump away, consuming 5,000 shells in response to calls for fire – the demand rising and falling with the intensity of the attacks.

Late in the day the Flying OP, in his little Auster plane, scudding back and forth behind the guns, low to the ground so as to not present a target for the Jerry 88s – only rising up a couple of hundred feet to observe the fall of his shot – helps direct 4th Field guns on "enemy guns now firing" and "enemy infantry."

After dark, the infantry's position about Woensdrecht remaining precarious, on urgent appeals from 14th Battery Commander

---

[*] RHLI casualties over five days totalled 167, including 21 dead.

Major Jack Drewry at RHLI Tac Headquarters permission is obtained by Col. Young from Brigadier H. Keefler, CRA, at 2nd Division Headquarters, to fire DF (defensive fire) tasks normally allowable only by brigadiers or up.*

At 11:16 "attempted enemy infiltration" is hammered by DF 112; and half an hour later DF 1019 and DF 1012 are shot for similar purposes. And in the next twelve hours four more DF tasks are fired, the last at 10:45 A.M. "to frustrate enemy forming up to attack."

When eventually there is a lull in demand for defensive fire by 4th Field, a thank-you message from the CO of the RHLI is passed on to the gunners. Without reservation Col. Whitaker gives the guns full credit for preventing a disaster.

The guns of 4th Field, helping to stabilize the front, are some five kilometres south of Woensdrecht, deployed in a muddy field just east of Ossendrecht, near the east–west road known as Middel Straat, Hageland, having moved here eight days ago on October 8.

All day long it is grey, cold, and miserable, with occasional showers, but the gunners, sweating from their exertions, have little time to notice. During lulls in the firing, as they take time to collect and pile up the latest crop of spent cartridges – some 200 per gun to add to the 675 per gun already in piles – they carefully stack the empty green shell and cartridge boxes in such a way as to suggest they have shelters in mind, and for very good reason. Though battery and troop command posts are set up in nearby buildings, the

---

* This is to prevent nervous front-line officers giving away the defensive fire-plan in response to enemy feints. Defensive fire targets (areas designated as vulnerable to enemy attack so that lines and ranges may be worked out by battery command posts in advance, allowing the guns to respond instantly without ranging in the event of a serious enemy attack) call for three minutes "intense" (five rounds per gun per minute for three minutes) for field guns (25-pounders); three minutes "rapid fire" (one and a half rounds per minute) for the mediums; and three minutes "rapid" (one round a minute) for the heavies when available.

men on the guns have been without any shelter since moving here, and the cold wind, with the smell of approaching winter in it, has begun to gust strongly.

Over the next four days, as the guns are called upon to break up a string of counter-attacks by some two thousand paratroopers clearly determined to regain all the ground they've lost, regardless of cost, 4th Field guns fire 13,104 more rounds, emptying 3,276 shell boxes and 1,638 cartridge boxes – thus providing each gun crew with 204 additional "building blocks."*

During the final twenty-nine hours of the paratroopers' attacks, ending at about 4:15 P.M. on October 20, 2nd Division Headquarters RCA will log no fewer than 32 Mike targets fired by 4th Field. And at one point this afternoon, Mike targets from FOOs are "queued up three deep waiting their turn," according to Sgt. Hunt's diary that carries a good description of life at the guns during the seventeen days they are here getting off 37,000 rounds:

Flood waters encroach on the area, and the wind sweeps across in terms of a gale, as meteor telegrams show. The gunners have few tarps under which to shelter from the rain. In the morning, those off duty rise warily from underneath their inadequate ground sheets, so as to not disturb the rivulets of water gathered in the creases. The signallers have their exchange in a pigsty inhabited at the same time by those for whom it was constructed. Here they sleep, eat, and work in great good humour. Battery Headquarters is more fortunate, with a dry barn, good straw, and a sufficiency of onions to make even bully beef palatable.

The mobile bath we patronized a few days ago was hit by a

---

* In Woensdrecht municipality, shells and mortars destroyed 427 homes – 72 by fire and 355 so ravaged by high explosive as to be not worth repairing. Another 235 were damaged but repairable. (Official figures of Woensdrecht Town Council)

flying bomb, resulting in 9 dead and 27 wounded, including two from the Regiment – L/Sgt. Howard Hill and Gunner Joseph Mikituk.

The YMCA (Curt Embleton and helper) set up their moving pictures in the barn. We hear that Jerry is planning a counter-attack in this area on a large scale. Orders are to dig in. Slit trenches fill with water and don't invite occupation. More rain and consequent discomfort for the gunners who have no shelter nor place for drying clothes.

Among the battle casualties are veteran carrier crew members Gunners P. J. "Pooch" Pelletier and Gordon Henry. Bombardier Ivan Cook is wounded while laying a signal line to an OP during the first day of the RHLI attack. And that same day, October 16, Gunner George Garrity dies of wounds. Two days later, Gunner James MacFarlane also succumbs to wounds.

The security blanket laid over the sister front southwest of the Scheldt ensures you will forever carry a confused and foggy picture of the bitter struggles under appalling conditions of mud and water in the Breskens pocket, though the rumours of the moment, and the tales told weeks later over beer-soaked tables in Belgian cafes, will one day be authenticated in published works.

The initial assault on October 6 had been across the Leopold Canal by 7th Brigade (Canadian Scottish, Regina Rifles, and the Royal Winnipeg Rifles), following a barrage of searing flames from an extended line of twenty-seven Wasps (flame-throwing Bren carriers with big fuel tanks to sustain the roiling blasts).

The crossing had been successful, but it took seven days to gain a thousand yards. Meanwhile 9th Brigade (The Highland Light Infantry, the Stormont, Dundas and Glengarry Highlanders, and The North Nova Scotia Highlanders), to relieve the pressure on 7th Brigade, crossed the Braakman inlet in Buffaloes (amphibious tracked vehicles able to carry thirty infantrymen) and gained a lodgement behind the enemy, menacing the strongpoint of Oostburg.

17

THANKSGIVING DINNER
ON GROOTE MEER

꙳

A FORWARD OBSERVATION OFFICER'S CREW IS NOW NORMALLY made up of a carrier driver, a signaller, and an ack, who may not be trained in both signals and OP work sufficiently to qualify in the technical sense as an "observation post assistant," since the supply of trained OP acks available for OP work has tended to dry up as the grand tour of the continent continues.

When the Regiment first entered battle, carrier crews were so completely trained that in a pinch anyone could substitute for anyone else with reasonable proficiency. However, from the earliest days of Normandy, demand has tended to put a strain on supply, since all who serve on carrier crews, other than the officers, must be volunteers.

Common sense demands this, for the casualty rate among FOOs and their crews is inclined to be high, not only because FOOs are always attached to the leading rifle companies, which suffer most of the infantry casualties, but because their tracked vehicle is very conspicuous in the attack; and unlike the foot-soldiers with whom it is travelling, it cannot go to ground and remain invisible in drainage ditches or among bushes and rocks – even lying doggo in unharvested grain – until the situation is sorted out. And if an 88 or a mortar fails to get it, it can always blow itself up on a mine, being, more often than not, the first Allied vehicle to traverse roads and fields in the attack or on the line of march.

Thus it would not be fair to fill vacancies in carrier crews with anything but volunteers. While as yet there is no shortage of men ready to serve on OP crews, you suspect that as time goes by it could become a problem. Already it is noticeable that vacancies are being filled more and more by newcomers to the Regiment – those least likely to know the score – leading you to suspect that they are being conned into taking on this "exciting work . . . up where the action is . . . where there's lots of loot and Luger pistols to be had," by troop sergeant-majors desperate to fill out replacement crews.

However, there are some who still look upon attachment to an OP crew as they did during training in England: a privilege reserved for the élite. So when you split up a brother act – sending the younger one (Walkden, B.) back to the guns so two boys from the same family won't be wiped out by a single 88-mm shell or an errant mortar bomb landing in the carrier – the older brother (Walkden, Wm.), your driver, could not have been more disgusted.

Now the morale of a carrier crew is a fragile thing, and his resentment, taking the form of silence – simply not communicating with you or anyone else – has begun to irritate everybody, with the result that all are beginning to act in an irritating fashion towards each other. If he wasn't such a good carrier driver, you'd send him back to the guns too. Of course, he'll get over his resentment in time, but meanwhile something has to be done to raise the morale of the others. Even before this problem arose, spirits had been wilting, as day after day, surrounded by dead and dying men and animals at that smashed farm out in the gloomy polders in the neck of the isthmus, they'd had nothing to look forward to but more of the same.

Then during the move over here to Groote Meer (October 14) their spirits had sunk to a new low when Capt. Len Gage, Major Ryall's second-in-command, was killed by a shell shortly after you left him along the line of march. You had just been walking with him, and unquestionably would have died with him, had not your carrier, bringing up the rear of the company, stalled and refused to start again without a tow from a tank, forcing you to leave the Royals and drive back to the gun position in a nearby field to get a fresh starter-battery. It was on the way back up, racing along the same road to catch up to the Royals, that they'd spotted Len lying dead beside the road, not a hundred yards beyond where you had said goodbye to him.

Though they had had little direct contact with Len during the five days they spent out at the bleak farm in the polders, they had become very conscious of the tall, quiet man holed up behind a table in the tiny cellar, looking up with sad eyes at visitors over a wavering candle and a water-glass never less than half full of rum. At first they'd been inclined to write him off with joking disdain, until you brought them up short – pointing out you met him first at a hellish place called Eterville near Caen, where some men came apart at the seams with nerves permanently shattered . . . that his platoon led the way into Louvigny where 112 fell in the first attack by the Royals in Normandy . . . and God knows what all else he'd lived through since then.

From then on he had ceased to be a curiosity, and their attitude changed first to one of respect, and then to real affection when one day the unsmiling, reserved man split his last precious package of cigarettes with them on learning their canned ration of Goldflakes (to have lasted them for three days) had come out of a Compo box covered with green mould.

His death hit them hard and the collective morale of the whole crew is suffering. Something is needed to take their minds off the lousy war, at least for a few hours. But what? If only you could send them off overnight to some place where they could remove their dirty clothes, have a bath, and sleep in a real bed. Even a civilized meal would help, a change from the eternal Compo – the everlasting sameness of homogeneous M & V stew and glutinous steak-and-kidney pudding. Suddenly it strikes you that this could be the answer: a special meal – one of those hens wandering out there behind the house – a real feast – a Thanksgiving dinner – it must be close to Thanksgiving Day in Canada; as you recall, it was always around this time in October.

The proposal is warmly received, at least by Stevenson and Hiltz.

They too are ignorant as to the date Canadians celebrate Thanksgiving, but recommend that this very day, October 21, be arbitrarily declared Thanksgiving Day so as to get one of those hens into the pot before the infantry get them all. Immediately they volunteer to contribute tasty homemade items for dessert from recent parcels — including some brownies and macaroons. All you can find in your private hoard in your ammunition box are some rather soggy salted peanuts and some greying chocolate-coated after-dinner mints.

Obviously it won't be the greatest Thanksgiving dinner menu of all time, but to the delight and surprise of all, Walkden begins to show an interest, pointing out you can't have a chicken potpie without vegetables, and he spotted vegetables unharvested out behind the shed — some carrots and onions for sure, and maybe some potatoes too. And so, during the day, while you are up at the OP in the tower, they put together a great chicken stew. You swear you can smell it even while you are still on the trail going down at last light, long before you arrive in the circular drive before the house, where you are surprised to find Stevenson and Hiltz waiting in the gathering gloom.

They explain that during the afternoon the same delicious aroma from their bubbling stew, wafting down into the cellar to A Company headquarters, had drawn Major Caldwell and his second-in-command, Capt. Ross Newman, upstairs to investigate. The subsequent drooling and groaning of those cunning gentlemen, as they leaned over the steaming pot, had been so pitiful, they had momentarily succumbed to Christian charity and invited them to return and share it when it was ready. They earnestly hope this is all right with you, for the aforementioned officers are even now back upstairs, waiting in the little room off the living room you have been using as living quarters.

When you hesitate, Stevenson, reading your mind, assures you there is more than enough for everybody, Walkden having rather overdone the quantity of vegetables he'd tossed in the pot with the dismembered hen, which had turned out to be a monster.

Naturally you approve; after all, they'd done all the work. And it turns out to be a truly memorable Thanksgiving dinner, even though those conscienceless foot-sloggers will forever after spread a scurrilous rumour that gunners can live in an atmosphere devoid of oxygen. (Some days later you'll actually overhear Major Caldwell asking one Major Ryall if he is aware that gunners prefer to breathe carbon dioxide, saturated blue with cigarette smoke and thickened with steamy cabbage and onion fumes, in an oxygen-free room sealed off by a mattress over the window and a blanket over a closed hallway door.)

However, they do contribute a nearly full bottle of Johnnie Walker and some real Canadian fruitcake for the table; and if you overlook their periodic melodramatic gasping and coughing spasms, they contribute much to the general conviviality of the evening. After dinner, Hank, an accomplished jazz piano player with a wicked right hand, accompanies you through a series of duets covering much of the music of the Thirties on the piano out in the dark living room near the glassless French windows, sending wild, syncopated cadenzas across the waterless lake, until complaints begin to come in by runners from nearby platoon commanders worried that "your goddam racket" is drawing unnecessary attention to this area.

Deflated, but not defeated, you push the piano into your lighted room, making it even more crowded than during dinner, and enhancing the title it already has been awarded by your uncharitable guests: "The Black Hole of Groote Meer."

The party might well have gone on the whole night, but for a signal from Sunray (the commanding officer) ordering you back up to your tower, to spend the night flash-spotting German guns and mortars presently doing a job on Woensdrecht.

Hiltz seems unnaturally anxious to accompany you, and while there is no more reason for him to go up with you tonight than on previous nights when you went up alone, you don't turn him down, for you really feel the need of company tonight.

18

THE STORY OF A STARRY NIGHT

❋

IT TAKES FIFTEEN MINUTES OR SO TO MAKE IT UP TO THE tower, running the telephone line through your hand as a guide – a spooky trip in the dark, becoming particularly tense about halfway up where you must use some form of animal radar to avoid stepping on the bloated body of the dead German lying directly across the path. Up near the top there is always the chance a nervous infantryman will let fly at you if you wander off the route you are expected to take through the trenches of the platoon position near the tower – a real possibility since you must navigate the last one hundred yards across the spongy floor of a rather open pine forest, without the guidance of the signal wire, it having taken off on a shortcut of its own through a thick tangle of undergrowth.

Slightly fuzzy from all the good spirits you shared tonight, it's comforting to hear Hiltz behind you, whistling softly his favourite tune – the theme from Tchaikovsky's Sixth Symphony – which, according to him, has been popularized back home under the charming title "This Is the Story of a Starry Night." His whistling suggests he had something more in mind than simply keeping you company when he volunteered to come with you. You've noticed his whistling is involuntary; whenever he's engrossed in repairing equipment or mulling over something, he whistles. And always it's that same appealing little melody.

Of course there's no conversation on the way up as you both

concentrate on not tripping and falling into the damp bushes, for while it's a frosty, clear, starlit night in the open, it is very dark in the forest. (Astonishingly once again, in the same mysterious way you have on previous nights, you both avoid stepping on the dead German.) But when finally you climb up the tall tower and settle down to your watch, under a sky filled with stars, Hiltz launches into his subject.

He wants your advice: he's fallen in love with a girl in Antwerp. You will recall he has spoken of her before – the one living with her parents in a penthouse on a tall building on the main street . . . the people with the grand piano he wanted you to meet. Well, that's still his wish. When you both next get leave, will you go with him to meet her and her parents, so you can assess the situation and help him decide what to do? He is so intensely earnest, you assure him you will, even as you wonder what on earth you're getting into.

And from then until the endless vault of star-drenched sky begins to decay with the first light of dawn, he talks of her.

In a hundred ways he describes all the things about her that make her so utterly charming, and how hospitable her nice parents have been, while posing innumerable rhetorical questions clearly indicating how worried he is about the ultimate effect on their relationship of all the apparent wealth and affluence surrounding her. How could he ever hope to support her in the manner to which she is accustomed? Is she not just mesmerized by the romantic circumstances of liberation and his appearance as a gallant liberator from across the seas?

The more he talks, the more impressed you are. While you liked his fresh, open countenance, and his relaxed, good-natured style from the first day he came up to the troop as an ack back at Fleury-sur-Orne in Normandy, you realize you are only getting to know him as he talks away the night. And what impresses most is the depth of his love for the girl, which is causing him to worry more about the risks to her happiness than to his own.

By dawn he's talked out, and you send him down to the house to get breakfast started. Stand-to passes without any problems from

Jerry, but just as you are preparing to climb down, "Hutch" Hutcheon comes thumping up the tower ladders, with the welcome news that he and his crew are relieving you so that you and your crew can go back for a couple of days' rest.

While you are putting him on the ground (pointing out prominent points in the wide panorama of enemy territory and relating them to the map), he undertakes a line of inquiry that makes it plain that he questions the advisability of using this tower as an OP. Why, the bloody thing sticks up like a sore thumb above the bush!

You frankly admit you have never been entirely comfortable up here in the daytime, but so far Jerry has restricted his shelling to the other Company positions around and about and has left the tower strictly alone.

But why on earth has he left it standing?

You can only suggest that the Germans can't believe any sensible person would risk occupying such an obvious OP.

How long do you usually stay up here at a stretch?

You feel a little silly as you explain that in daylight you remain only until you get the creepy feeling that somewhere out there the muzzle of an 88 is swinging around and lining up the tower in its sights. Then you scramble down to the ground as fast as you can.

To Hutch, a natural-born pragmatist, this must sound insane. As you prepare to take your leave, he remarks that since he had no breakfast, he might as well go down and have an early lunch before settling in up here for the afternoon.

Strolling down through the bush, comparing notes on your recent experiences in the polders – in complete agreement that fighting a war below sea level is totally without virtue – you're vaguely conscious of some loud banging up behind you, in the woods you just left. But since shells and mortar bombs are constantly dropping throughout the area, you don't consider it at all significant. However, reaching the foot of the hill, you find Hank Caldwell standing uncharacteristically at the door of the house waiting, and as you draw near, you notice he's staring at you strangely and wagging his head in disbelief.

"Wow – am I glad to see you guys! How the devil did you manage to get down from your tower without anybody seeing you?"

You and Hutch can only exchange quizzical looks.

"You don't know what happened, then?"

Receiving only stares of bewilderment, he proceeds to enlighten you: "I just got a call from my platoon up there – the Krauts shelled the hell out of your tower – cut it to pieces, apparently – left it a shambles! Surely you must have heard it going on when you were on your way down? I thought for sure you'd bought it when they said no one had seen you come down from the tower. I was just on my way to inform your crew when I spotted you walking out of the bush!"

"Jesus," Hutch is murmuring to himself, "if I hadn't decided to come down with you for lunch!"

You look his way, but you are not seeing him. You are remembering all those hours in that tower during the past five days, during which you'd suppressed your imagination, putting out of mind the image of the very thing that has just occurred. You begin to feel dizzy.

Hank notices and says heartily:

"I think a shot of rum all around would be in order just about now – a stirrup cup for the lucky buggers going out for a rest."

For a moment you'd forgotten. You're only too happy to supply the rum. When you go to the carrier to fetch a water-bottle full of it, you see the boys have everything packed and ready to move. And when you go in the house to collect them, you find them in a buoyant mood. Obviously yesterday's Thanksgiving dinner worked wonders. And after a hefty slug of the dark, over-proof issue liquor, all are in splendid spirits as you pull out to go first to the guns near Ossendrecht for rations and mail, and then another three miles to Putte, the first town along the road to Antwerp, straddling the Dutch–Belgium border.

Hiltz is vastly disappointed when you stop in Putte. It seems that from the moment he heard you all were going back for a rest, he nurtured the belief you would be going all the way back to Antwerp. To him the chance was heaven-sent. Regretfully, you have to point out that you have not been given leave, but a short rest behind the lines, subject to instant cancellation without warning. Even coming back as far as Putte might be thought by some to be stretching things.

Putte gives the impression of being a one-street town, albeit a very long one – lined on both sides with stores, cafés, churches, municipal buildings, etc., the southern half Belgian, the northern half Dutch. The first night you hole up on the Dutch side of the border in the municipal office building, which cannot be locked because of shell damage. However, Monday morning a Dutchman arrives while breakfast is being heated over your Primus stove on what may be his desk, and he makes it quite clear he doesn't care for this invasion of his bureaucratic domain, even by his country's liberators.

That afternoon and evening old friend Len Harvey, just back from hospital after recovering from an encounter with a booby-trapped German body back at Bruges September 12, joins you in a search for new digs. Influenced by his normal cavalier improvidence in such matters, this quickly turns into a search for cognac when he finds the cafés are offering nothing but sweet, insipid beer.

The logical place to locate cognac would seem to be in a liquor store on the main street in the Belgium sector, but the pleasant couple operating the little store explain they have no stock left for sale – that all the bottles on display are fakes. However, if you would care to join them in their living quarters at the rear of the store, they'd be glad to share some of their own personal supply with you. Their living room is exceedingly modest, but this being the first time you've been socially welcomed into any home anywhere on the continent, the sense of returning to civilization is even stronger than it was in the luxury of the Century Hotel in Antwerp.

When it comes time to bed down somewhere, rain is descending in torrents outside. On learning you have no accommodation, they offer a small but completely empty attic room over the kitchen, just big enough to accommodate five prostrate bodies and their kit, including your precious cartridge case containing the contents of the parcel from home you picked up at the gun position yesterday. This linoleum-floored oasis is reached by a steep set of board-ladder stairs, leading up to a trap door.

The trap door has to be left open for ventilation, and as you bed down right next to it, advice is exchanged on why one shouldn't go sleepwalking in the night. The room is lit by one light bulb hanging directly over the trap door, and when this is turned off, the room is as black as the inside of an ink bottle.

At dawn, you're awakened by *slap-slap, scrub-scrub* sounds coming from the kitchen down below; and when you open your eyes, you find yourself looking directly into the eyes of a tiny little girl who has climbed up the stairs to a level just high enough to allow her to peek over the edge at the strange Canadian soldiers snoring in the gloom. Suddenly you identify the sound coming from below as someone mopping the kitchen floor – and immediately you are overwhelmed with a terrible sense of remorse, as you remember what you did last night.

Sometime during the night, your kidneys had produced a desperate urge requiring immediate attention. Very hazy from the generous shots of cognac you'd taken on board earlier, you realize that even with a light, it would be difficult for you to manage that stairwell, and without a light impossible. Standing, teetering dangerously close to the yawning chasm, you stretch out an arm and try to catch hold of the light bulb you know is suspended there. But in vain you paw the inky darkness, while you struggle to keep your balance and resist gross incontinency.

Finally you lose the battle and do the only thing that seems logical to your feeble wits at the time. Now, in the cold, dim light of dawn, as you listen to the sounds of that poor woman down there mopping the floor, and stare into her little girl's big, round eyes that seem to be accusing you, you are paying the price!

You can't confess your crime and apologize. But you can make restitution in secret: you open your ammo case and start lifting out cans of salmon, Spam, corn niblets, candy, chocolate bars, and tobacco, and handing them to the little tyke. She takes them without uttering a peep, but her eyes grow bigger as her arms grow fuller.

At last her little arms can hold no more, and she starts her descent, going down backwards, one step at a time (the only safe way on such steep stairs), excitedly calling out to her mother, at each step, the Belgian equivalent of "Mummy, Mummy, look what I've got!" And the sensation caused by her arrival at the foot of the stairs with her loot does your heart good, and goes a long way towards assuaging your conscience.

Your open-handed gesture pretty well empties your ammo box of all the precious stuff you got in your last parcel, but satisfied you've made restitution without embarrassing yourself, you descend incognito with the others to a breakfast of delicious home-fried potatoes.

But you reckoned without the child. As soon as she spots you, she points you out to her mother, and while you don't understand her words you know very well what she's saying. And the smile the mother beams at you is not so much a smile of gratitude, as a smile of amusement, the smile of a charitable woman who knows perfectly well what prompted one man among these soldiers to be so generous this morning.

As you're leaving and saying goodbye to the family, you see Hiltz remove his beret, complete with brass gun-badge, and give it to the pretty little ten-year-old. Strictly against the rules, but you say nothing, for you remember how much he misses his kid brother back in Halifax.

On the way back up the line, you drop in at A Echelon in the bush south of Hoogerheide for a fresh box of Compo rations.

Just as you and your gang are pulling out to go up to rejoin the infantry as they turn west into South Beveland in the big 2nd Division push going in this morning (October 24), you are waved down by Harvey who has been ordered to take over your carrier and crew. You are to report to the Colonel at Brigade Headquarters. Someone will take you up.

You feel a rush of resentment and more than a little jealousy as you dig your bedroll and kit out of what has been "your" carrier for so long, and pile it into the back of the waiting Jeep. But as you pull away you manage to smile and wave at them, for they must be feeling a little uneasy too. And for a moment they stop stowing away Harvey's kit and smile and wave at you.

When you arrive at Brigade, the news is waiting. They've run over a mine – Hiltz and Stevenson are dead.

19

AN ARTY REP CONTROLS
AWESOME FIRE-POWER

✳

YOU KNOW YOU WILL ALWAYS MOURN THEM; YOU KNOW you will forever carry in your mind a picture of them smiling and waving goodbye a few minutes ago; that their faces will always be among those who "shall not grow old as we who are left grow old." You know that for the rest of your life every time you play that plaintive Tchaikovsky theme, or hear it played, you'll hear Hiltz whistling "This Is the Story of a Starry Night"...

But at this moment your sensibilities are totally unreliable, short-circuited by the all-enveloping grossness of war, and your mourning is shallow and transient as you head for the barn to report in to the Brigadier with mounting apprehension as to what may be expected of you up here at this level of command.

On the way here you hadn't worried, believing you were merely joining the Colonel to assist him in some minor way or other, perhaps providing liaison with the battery commanders at battalion headquarters some distance ahead. However, when his batman was breaking the news to you about your crew (even before you climbed out of the Jeep in the barnyard), he also informed you the Colonel had already left for the headquarters of one of the battalions in the attack, and that you are to cover off for him here at Brigade.

Inside the barn you stop to look around, dumbfounded by the scene that confronts you – totally strange to eyes accustomed to the primitive set-up at battalion tactical headquarters confined almost always to poorly lit basements, cow stables, abandoned German dug-outs, and even open trenches. This brightly lit scene of officers on folding benches, sitting at folding tables on which papers and maps are spread out, with remote-control units and field telephones at their elbows – while behind them others plot coloured dots and arrows on large map-boards standing on easels, electrically lit by little shaded bulbs hanging over them – provides an immediate impression of a well-ordered office.

The only incongruous feature is an oversized caravan-truck that has been backed in on the barn floor and rests just inside the big closed doors. You are received perfunctorily at the back door of this mobile command post by the Brigade Major (handsome, aloof Jim Knox) who assumes you know what you are here for, and merely points out Col. Young's spot at a central folding-table a few feet to the rear of the stubby little steps leading to the back door of the caravan.

Opposite you at the table lounge two British officers, a captain and a major. The captain, a tall, handsome, outgoing type, stands up and offers his hand as he explains they too are "arty reps" – the major representing a medium regiment, and he a regiment of heavy ack-ack guns (3.7-inch) now being used in a ground role.* Each in his own way assures you that on demand they can, as the Captain puts it, "add considerably to the general din when the need arises," and not to hesitate to call on their support.

The major is a reserved, reticent chap, and the amiable captain, a career officer with the regular British Army (1st Brigade Royal Marines you later learn) is obviously happy to have someone to talk

---

* Attached directly to 4th Field Regiment at this time were the heavy ack-ack guns of 1st Brigade Royal Marines and the 118th Heavy Ack-Ack Regiment. Attached to 2nd Division Headquarters were the British 115th Heavy Ack-Ack and two medium regiments, the 84th and the 121st.

to. With vast amusement he speaks of a Scottish Division (52nd Lowland) about to enter battle for the first time in the war – establishing a bridgehead on South Beveland ahead of our troops – fighting below sea level though all its training has been for mountain warfare involving packhorses and special 3.7-inch guns that can be dissassembled for easier transport.

Thoughtfully he makes you aware of the fact you also have at your disposal a squadron of Spitfire fighter-bombers and a squadron of Typhoons, which, he explains, you can "whistle up using that signaller sitting over there at that radio set."

Suddenly you realize they are taking for granted that you are assuming the role of coordinator in the planning and use of all this fire-power, since you are substituting for the colonel of a field regiment (normally the senior gunner officer at Brigade) – which means that if the need arises, they will expect you to act as the senior artillery advisor to the Brigadier, rank notwithstanding! Even the thought of playing such a role is subduing. All you can do, if by chance you are called upon to allot all that fire-power to an attack, is try to recall the scale and timing on behalf of other attacks of similar size in which your guns have participated.

But you earnestly hope the Colonel will get back before the need arises. How typical of the man to want to be forward with his battery commanders. He knows things are sticky up there, and maybe he can be of help, bringing into play more of the heavy stuff at his disposal, if he gets a better feel for the battle at a battalion headquarters.

Just as he had appeared out of nowhere beside your carrier under bombardment that first day when the push north from Antwerp was being held up, or the morning he arrived without warning at your OP in the polders at dawn after listening for much of the night to you calling for Mike targets on screaming paratroopers attacking the Royals with flame-throwers, you visualize him now suddenly appearing at the side of one of his battery commanders. Don Cornett would be your guess. He is now short a FOO with Harvey out of action, and Lendrum will be anxious. Of this morning,

October 24, British war correspondent R. W. Thompson will one day write in his book *The 85 Days*:

> Frankly one would have thought these Canadians would have had enough; too much . . . death had become personal, a daily and nightly lottery in which each man of the forward battalions held a ticket. . . . After Woensdrecht the Canadians had become welded together, kindred, a tight community. The truth is they wanted to feel alone — alone with the sustained and terrible experience which they began to clasp to themselves as something personal, and upon which no one had a right to intrude. I marvelled then, and I marvel now, at the spirit of the Canadian 4th Infantry Brigade of 2nd Division as they turned to force their way through the narrow neck of the isthmus. Some craters on the main road were gigantic — huge cavities defeating the bulldozers. One was seventy feet across, measured by an engineer.*
>
> Thin trees had been felled to add to the obstacles. Schumines, Teller mines, mines with names known only to engineers, mines in scores were sown carefully over all that way. Absurd to attempt to account in detail the water-logged progress. In individual minds it lives merely as discomfort, a blurred memory of men's feet blown off in a grey, futuristic landscape, something of Dali's. Waves of 20-mm fire held men tight against dike banks and made others thankful even of the water. Airbursts from 88s worked in with the hideous barrage of mortars with a sound like green seas on iron decks, a drenching sound, horribly threatening.

---

* An electrically wired buried torpedo (according to the Dutch) that blew up the Able Troop carrier, killing Hiltz and Stevenson. The awesome charge blew everything, including the engine, out of the steel box of the carrier that landed beyond the next dike. Miraculously, Capt. Harvey and Walkden, saved by a bulkhead, escaped with minor cuts and bruises.

20

ROUGH TREATMENT
FOR A TOUGH BROAD

———————————— ✳ ————————————

WHATEVER ROLE THE COLONEL HAS IN MIND FOR YOU WHEN
he gets back – liaison with Div or whatever – it would seem imperative that you gain some kind of overall picture of what's going on.
You study the big "I" map, and ask questions of your gunner con-
federates. They are, you find, surprisingly well-informed, and if
somewhat fuzzy as to what precisely is occurring at the moment,
they at least can construct a very detailed picture of what is supposed to be happening, both on the Brigade front and elsewhere –
something entirely new to your experience. Of course, on
reflection the extent of their knowledge is understandable, this
being one of the principal nerve centres for the conduct of the
battle, and they having little else to do but follow what's going on.

You learn the final clearing of the area immediately north of
Woensdrecht was completed yesterday, October 23, by the Calgary
Highlanders and the Queen's Own Cameron Highlanders of
Canada, supported by a great fire-plan, including two barrages.
Resistance undoubtedly was weakened by the drive by 4th
Armoured Division that began two days ago as a right hook from
the southeast eight miles north of Woensdrecht to the next sizeable
town with the intriguing name of Bergen-op-Zoom. Here in
South Beveland the plan calls for the Royal Regiment to open the
attack into the isthmus, overcome the forward line of defence,
reconnoitre in force the one major road and a minor road south of

the narrowest part of the isthmus, and seize this area as a base for further exploitation. The Royals started out shortly after midnight to ensure their startline is secure in a partially inundated salt marsh, bounded on the left by a dike and on the right by the main dike road. Both flanking dikes are separated from the marsh by ten-foot-wide drainage ditches. The enemy are dug-in the full length of both these east–west dikes, and where they meet a lateral dike that is the objective of the Royals, the Germans have built strongholds of bricked-in trench-works and concrete emplacements for anti-tank guns and machine-gun nests covering both the dikes leading up to the junctions and the surrounding marsh.

Covered approaches being non-existent, and any manoeuvring impossible because of deep drainage ditches criss-crossing the marsh, the attack is made by two companies of Royals moving up the two dikes behind a creeping barrage, with the northern flank covered by timed concentrations, and the heavy mortars of the Tor Scots bombarding the objective to shut down fire from there.

The guns had opened up at 4:00 A.M. and the soldiers following close behind had to almost feel their way forward in the flashing, roaring, confusing darkness, as they bumped into successive German posts along the dike and subdued them in what the Royals' historian would describe as "bitter hand-to-hand fighting."

By now (7:00 A.M.) all companies are on their objectives. There is a report that the Germans are shelling themselves, until it becomes known that the shells are being laid on them by the mediums and the heavies of 9th British AGRA firing from across the Scheldt.

Still, Germans do die from their own fire. Capt. Bob Suckling of D Company will not soon forget the grim business of witnessing the death of fifteen German prisoners collected from posts overrun by D Company moving along a dike. Told to lie down behind the twelve-foot-high embankment until they could be evacuated, they were all killed by one of the first salvoes of German mortars landing right on them.

The original plan called for exploitation of the Royals' success by two mixed columns of armour from 10th Armoured Regiment and the 8th Recce Regiment, with the Essex Scottish riding with them in Kangaroos as back in Normandy the night of the break-through at Verrières Ridge.

However, Brig. F. N. Cabeldu, on being informed by the Royals that the secondary road along the southern part of the isthmus was impassable due to cratering, mines, and mud, decided the second phase of the attack should be launched along the railway embankment nearer the northern rim of the isthmus.

And so the Essex Scottish and their armoured escort are ordered forward at 10:00 A.M.

The columns are to debouch through gaps bulldozed in the first dike and rumble up onto the main highway up the isthmus.

Privately you question the ability of tanks and armoured cars to operate anywhere out there. Many polders are flooded deeply and the others, criss-crossed by swollen drainage ditches, are too soggy to sustain heavy vehicles. Thus restricted to moving along roads on the tops of dikes, silhouetted against the sky, tanks and recce cars must be picked off like sitting ducks. And it comes as no surprise when the Essex Scottish attack bogs down shortly after take-off.

Before noon a signal comes in from Major Carr at Essex Scottish Tac Headquarters, somewhere near the leading edge of their attack on "Mary," the code name for a line running through a junction of dikes in the isthmus: "Fetch Sunray to the blower."

Properly interpreted by the signaller on the set, this means: "Bring the Commanding Officer to the radio and turn over the earphones and mike to him." So when you go on the air, Carr is taken aback. For a moment he hesitates, but only a moment, for the imperative demands of the battle in which the Essex are involved allow him no time to fritter away in merely satisfying curiosity. From the growling tension in his voice, it is obvious the Essex have suffered a bloody nose in their attack on the junction of dikes with that sweet and gentle code name "Mary." And this is underlined by the facetious style he uses in reporting: "Our Mary is turning out to be a very tough broad."

He needs a fire-plan – a heavy concentration of short duration directly on Mary in support of a renewed attack by the Essex. He asks for a stonk along the dike by the guns for at least ten minutes before H-hour, thickened up by whatever heavier stuff is available at the time, including help from "our fine-feathered friends." He assures you that for the bombing the Essex will be pulled back four hundred yards.

Somehow you manage to carry on in a manner you hope will appear to him and the others watching you as confident and self-possessed, while feeling entirely otherwise. As you assure him "Roger Wilco, Out" (message understood – will carry out orders – ceasing transmission), and turn from the radio, you are momentarily afflicted with a brain-numbing case of nerves. Never, in your wildest dreams, did you imagine being thrust into a situation like this. Realizing the eyes of your colleagues are on you, you fight down a rising sense of inadequacy and carry on as though you know exactly what you are doing. A battalion attack is being mounted, the success of which will depend largely on the effectiveness of your fire-plan. Many of the Essex will die if your plan is inadequate.

Though conscious of the current need to conserve ammunition which has to be trucked so far, you decide to use everything available to you. You will send in the Spits with 500-pound bombs for the intersection of the dikes thirty minutes before H-hour (which is 1330), and Typhoons at H minus-15 to rocket-bomb whatever they can see by way of trench-works or guns along the dikes on the flanks. The medium guns will lay a stonk along the dike at the objective, firing at their normal rate from H minus-10 to H-hour; the heavy ack-ack will airburst over the target area for the same period; and 4th Field will fire a stonk on the objective, using the intense rate of fire from H minus-5 to H plus-5; at which time they will move their fire to a point four hundred yards farther west along the same dike from H plus-10 to H plus-15.

When you are ready, you call your artillery colleagues together for an "O" group. They listen intently to your every word and scribble notes. Watches are synchronized. Then they go quickly about translating your orders into their own lingo and transmitting them back to their guns. Meanwhile you lay on the aircraft support and give 4th Field guns their part in the show. Finally you go on the air to tell Carr the fire-plan is ready to go and that he can expect the air support to begin at a time you transmit in code.

And that, seemingly, is all there is to it. Your job is done. Now others are responsible for seeing that the many tons of high explosive you ordered are moved and shifted and dumped on the enemy in and around the objective at the times you have ordered. How astonishingly easy it all is when you don't have to do any of the dirty, heavy work, or the critically accurate technical computations to get the job done, while responding to endless other problems connected with "man-management."

And still you feel pleased with yourself, as though you actually have done something worthwhile. Is this the way generals and high-ranking staff officers feel? Is this what men find fascinating in the conduct of war? You find yourself recalling an article in a London paper by American columnist Dorothy Thompson last winter, describing similar notions as she watched wooden blocks, representing squadrons of planes, being moved about like pawns on a giant chessboard at tactical headquarters of RAF Fighter Command during an air raid on Britain.

The fire-plan goes ahead without a hitch and Carr is able to report "Attack successful – Mary taken." But later, when you have the chance to get a first-hand account of the effectiveness of your fire-plan, you will learn that the attack was not as neat and tidy as Carr's terse report of the moment suggested. According to Ted Adams, the FOO with the leading company in the attack, it was "a very sticky go." And to illustrate, he tells the story of an infantry subaltern who collapsed in a dead faint when he learned he would have to lead his platoon through a gap in a dike covered by a German machine-gun, clearly perceiving he had been condemned to die: "When he came to, he alerted his platoon and they took off. He was the first man around the end of the dike. As he anticipated he was met by a burst of Spandau fire. He died instantly with a bullet in his forehead."

Concentrated neutralizing fire by the guns always helps, and in cases like "Mary" is essential, but if any objective is ever to be taken, the enemy must ultimately be subdued by the P.B.I. (the poor bloody infantry) who always pay the worst "butcher bills."

You learn that real progress has been made over on the 3rd Division front across the Scheldt. Breskens fell a couple of days ago (October 22) to the Stormont, Dundas and Glengarry Highlanders breaking out of the right flank of 9th Brigade's bridgehead across the Braakman inlet. After many days and nights of stiff fighting with German troops anxious to prove their loyalty to their Fuhrer's orders to fight to the death and save their families from retaliation back in Germany – first, just to stay ashore, when in one day they fought off (with the aid of 4th Division guns) six furious counter-attacks, and then during the taking and holding of the town of Hoofdplaat beyond the range of the guns – "the Glens" were able to take the highly fortified town of Breskens with comparable ease. Conducting a daring attack along a seawall, using buoyant kapok equipment to get over a twelve-foot-deep and twenty-foot-wide anti-tank ditch filled with water (something the enemy didn't think possible) they took the garrison by surprise and 150 surrendered.*

---

* The CO of the Glens, Lt.-Col. Roger Rowley, was subsequently awarded a bar to his DSO for his "brilliance," "courage," and "speed" in mounting the attack.

21

WORDS WILL NEVER DO
THE INFANTRY JUSTICE

❋

NEVER DRY, ALWAYS COVERED WITH MUD, NEVER STANDING completely upright, always hunched over well below the crest of the dike he is following, never able to relax in the dread of mortar and machine-gun fire that can arrive with little or no warning as he moves crablike along its sloping side, forcing him to throw himself against the steep incline, pressing his body into the spongy wet turf as tightly as he can until they stop, or until they stop him – perhaps forever . . .

That is how the FOOs and their signallers, weighed down by heavy 18-sets on their backs, will remember the infantry with whom they move day after day across the flat, sodden country, attacking still another junction of dikes to gain domination of another polder, as indistinguishable from the last polder as it is from the next – another and another and another – polders and dikes seemingly without end.

Words will never do justice to the courage of the infantryman – eternally cold, eternally wet, eternally bone-weary – who at any instant may be blown apart by a mortar or cut down by machine-gun fire even as he waits at the rear of the battalion stretched out along the dike – waits to take his turn in what he knows will be a lottery of death when his section takes over the lead for the platoon crawling up along the dike or wading through a flooded polder churned by mortar bombs and rippled with machine-gun bullets.

While tanks and armoured cars can briefly lace strongpoints with intimidating fire from afar, they are next to useless in taking ground in polder country. And while artillery FOOs can bring down prompt and accurate concentrations of shells on suspected mortar positions and on a section of dike from which tracers are originating, cooling down enemy fire and occasionally snuffing it out, the ground must be taken by flesh-and-blood men with haggard faces and mud-encrusted hands, doing their best to keep their weapons clean and functioning while they themselves grow filthier and more exhausted with each passing hour. And it is only by extraordinary and continuing acts of courage by ordinary soldiers of the rifle companies and their leaders – the subalterns, the sergeants, and the corporals – that any forward movement is possible.

At the outset, passing through the slender neck of the isthmus barely fifteen hundred yards wide, only one battalion at a time can be utilized, and it must leap-frog its companies, and companies leap-frog their platoons, edging their way up a single road.

And even beyond the neck, where South Beveland widens to four or more kilometres for the next ten miles to a major water barrier, a wide ship canal, only two battalions can be used at a time, following two dike routes roughly pointing up the axis of advance.

At the outset you despair that the peninsula can be taken in less than a month, and then only at terrible cost. From the beginning of the fighting out here among the polders almost three weeks ago, it seemed transparently obvious that in this flat land, ribbed with high dikes, the defenders holding the dikes with unobstructed fields of fire have almost insurmountable advantage over the attackers.

However, what quickly becomes evident, that was not evident during those first battles for the most heavily defended strongpoints in all the polders west of Woensdrecht, are the serious drawbacks to defensive positions located on well-defined, narrow dikes, particularly at well-defined junctions of two dikes. Every artillery rep, from the FOOs with forward companies, back through the majors at battalion headquarters to the colonels at brigades and the Brigadier CRA at Division, knows exactly where the enemy will be dug-in and where the neutralizing fire should be concentrated before any attack, in contrast to trying to pin down enemy positions in other terrain confused by hills, woodlands, gullies, orchards, tree-enshrouded farms and villages, where the Germans can be remarkably cunning at disguising their positions and holding their fire until it can be most effective in halting an attack.

Here, apart from the odd farmhouse, defenders must dig in on the dikes, for holes dug down in polders simply fill with water. Of course dike junctions – providing fields of fire up the roads in all directions and across the polders – inevitably are infested with machine-guns, and frequently anti-tank and ack-ack guns, making them prime targets for fire-plans designed to shoot the infantry onto their objective. And on top of this, contesting only dike positions seriously inhibits the flexibility of the German defensive tactics. Ordinarily their drill is to pull back from the opening artillery concentrations, allowing the attackers to get on their objective before counter-attacking to drive the intruders back in disorder. However, this initial pulling-back won't work when the only cover to which they can retire is the next dike several hundred yards to their rear.

The result is six hundred prisoners are taken by 4th Brigade in its three-day assault up the peninsula, before they turn over responsibility to 6th Brigade for finding a way over the Beveland canal twenty kilometres west of Woensdrecht and halfway to the causeway to Walcheren Island.

The next day, October 26, the guns of 4th Field finally move from their Ossendrecht positions out into South Beveland peninsula, and move again within hours to keep within range of the front which, according to 4th Field's war diary, appears to crack wide open.

Bombardier Hossack's personal log sets down his impressions of the miserable battlefields of Hoogerheide, Woensdrecht, and the polders – most particularly the infamous junction of dikes and railroad for which so many died in vain on Black Friday the 13th – as the guns roll out into South Beveland isthmus to deploy in the very polder where the Black Watch soldiers were cut down in front of your old OP at Pijnen farm:

Nearly all buildings show signs of the ravages of war as we advance to open fields near Woensdrecht. This is our first position on South Beveland peninsula and the battle against rain, mud, water, and the Germans is only beginning. There is no point digging trenches here – no sooner started than water rises in them.

A few hours here and we move on without firing a shot. We've lost interest in days and dates as we advance in bad weather over soggy terrain.... Numerous dead Jerries are sprawled over roadways and dikes – mute evidence of fierce fighting. All the fields are pock-marked with water-filled shell holes, and the litter of a battlefield is everywhere – mess tins, rifles, machine-guns, tin hats, greatcoats, boots, rations, etc., etc., spilled all over the place in disorder. Railway tracks running atop a dike are broken and curled up in the air [from the bombs dropped by the Spitfires on the red smoke canisters with which your guns marked that target]. Well-sighted enemy SP and anti-tank guns have knocked out all too many of our Recce cars, tanks, and carriers.

Rilland on our left is the target for many enemy shells. We do considerable firing ourselves.

Dutch youth sell crates of apples for ten Belgian francs or a few cigarettes – very good apples too. The rain continues steadily, and those of us who are not housed in the one large barn are soon drenched.

Hunt's diary will note that mines have become a greater hazard than usual and expresses gratitude for the thoughtfulness of Dutch civilians marking German mines embedded in the roads of a dark town:

At night, when all good folk are abed save those whom providence has condemned to duty, minimum recce parties are called

for 2300 hours. A considerable cavalcade, with the CRA [Briga-
dier R. H. Keefler] leading, sets off into the darkness. We pass
through a deserted town whose noble burgers had marked mine
emplacements with chairs and other pieces of furniture. That
this was a worthwhile precaution we realize later when an RHQ
vehicle strikes a mine (unmarked) and is wrecked with casualties.

Of this same night (October 26), the regimental war diary notes:
"Many vehicle casualties. RHQ [on arrival at new position] finds the
advance party has five German prisoners locked in the cellar."

At 4th Brigade HQ there is real relief that 6th Brigade is now
passing through (the FMRs on the left, heading for Hansweert, and
the Queen's Own Cameron Highlanders of Canada moving
through Yerkse), closing on the wide Beveland ship-canal cutting
across the peninsula. To head off a repeat of the bloody struggle that
ensued for so many days at the mouth of South Beveland, Army
Commander Simonds has arranged for the Germans holding the
canal to be outflanked by the British 52nd Lowland Division,
coming across the Scheldt estuary and landing beyond the canal in
waves of amphibious vehicles. This is another first for Simonds,
though the amphibious tracked vehicles (Buffaloes), amphibious
wheeled vehicles (DUWKs), and amphibious tanks (DDs) are all the
product of the fertile mind of British genius General Sir Percy
Hobart, who equipped 79th Division with its "funnies." Your
British friends tell you that many of the platoon commanders of
52nd Division are Canadians.*

---

* Known as "Canloan Officers," 673 (mostly lieutenants) volunteered in
1944-45 to serve with British units, who were short of trained subalterns.
All British divisions, and most battalions, had Canadian subalterns serving
in them throughout the campaign. Seventy-six per cent of them were
wounded or killed.

22

THE FIRST AMPHIBIOUS
ARMADA IN HISTORY

✳

THE TEN-KILOMETRE SHIP CANAL, RUNNING NORTH AND south across the start of the main bulging body of South Beveland, joining the Ooster Scheldt with the Wester Scheldt, is twenty-one feet deep and sixty-four yards from bank to bank at its narrowest point. With banks rising five feet above the water, and twenty-foot-wide drainage ditches flanking it, it constitutes a formidable obstacle to assaulting forces.

The map shows locks with roads at each end of the canal. A road and railway pass over it a mile and a half from its south end. At the north end the main road from Yerseke to Goes passes over a bridge a mile and a half from the canal mouth. Of course all crossing points are covered by enemy guns and all bridges are blown as soon as the first Canadians approach the canal. Troops must resort to assault boats.

To aid the Canadian crossing, by outflanking and menacing the German rear, at 4:45 A.M. October 26, about the time the Canadians are making their canal move, two brigades of the British 52nd (Lowland) Division (156th and 157th in two waves) carry out a seaborne operation the like of which has never been seen before.

Using an unprecedented number of amphibious tracked and wheeled vehicles – Buffaloes, Alligators, and Weasels – they cross the Scheldt Estuary from Terneuzen to points ten kilometres beyond the canal, with all their equipment, including a small bulldozer to pull vehicles through weeds and the silt and mud up to two feet deep over the sand at marshy landing places. More than 175 amphibious craft of limited seaworthiness manage to wallow through nine miles of choppy black water and deliver the first wave – the 6th Cameronians and the Royal Scots Fusiliers – reasonably intact on objectives, guided only by tracers from ack-ack guns sailing over-head through the blackness towards the jagged flashes on the distant shore, where thunderous shells, weighing 200, 240, and 360 pounds, end their moaning flight across the estuary from the heavy and superheavy guns of 9th AGRA, deployed in the Breskens pocket for the ultimate assault on Walcheren Island.

Only four DD (Duplex Drive) Tanks (British-converted Shermans made buoyant by a huge collapsible bucket of canvas affixed to and enclosing its body, turret, and gun), propelled through the water by two screws, which swivel to provide steering, manage to make it ashore. But firm lodgements are secured by infantrymen clawing their way through the water, weeds, and mud onto the solid land beyond the marshes along the southeast corner of Beveland's bulging body. Despite mines and bombardment of landing areas by guns and mortars, which grows more severe as Jerry reacts to what is happening on his right rear, the bridgeheads build up rapidly and are joined and expanded by following waves of men and supplies.*

Despite this, the Germans defending the canal against the Canadian assaults, unaware of the extent of the landings far to their right rear, continue to defend the crossings with vigour, and when patrols of 6th Brigade try to use the lock gates to gain the far bank, they are driven back by intense fire. However, by midnight October 26–27, the South Saskatchewan Regiment has established

---

* Night and day for three days the Buffaloes (each capable of carrying thirty men), Weasels, and the rest of the strange flotilla churned back and forth, bringing more than seven hundred loads of men and supplies to the beaches.

a bridgehead, near the remnants of the road bridge blown by the Germans, sufficiently firm that in the afternoon of October 28 the Engineers are able to put a bridge in place to allow the vehicles of 4th Brigade HQ to pass over.

As soon as the SSRs are firmly established, 4th Brigade, led by the Rileys, return to action, paddling across in assault boats and pushing west against light opposition towards Gravenpolder five miles away. It is now obvious that things have been made easier by the Scots expanding their bridgehead beyond Oudelande. When the Royals cross that afternoon to take over the westward thrust, they meet little opposition until Gravenpolder. There Jerry decides to make a stand, and Major Tim Beatty's D Company, not strong enough to drive them out, watches from a nearby farm as the unfortunate village is subjected to an awesome bombardment by those 9th AGRA guns from over the Scheldt.

The Royals take twenty-two prisoners on the 28th, along with four 75-mm howitzers, a number of heavy mortars, fourteen horses, and seventeen wagons loaded with ammunition. Most of this loot is captured by Beatty's D Company when they ambush two enemy reinforcement columns. After the first ambush, Beatty sends the horses and prisoners back to Battalion, but the second time he is told "Just send the men back – keep the horses and wagons." At this they turn the horses loose, and tip the wagons over and spill the ammunition into the water beside the road.

A 3rd Division liaison officer arriving at 4th Brigade makes it clear the fighting in the Breskens pocket is at least as bad, with water and mud forcing attacks along the dikes to be undertaken by single, "leap-frogging" companies. Before he left, a Chaudière company was wiped out on the way to Oostburg, and another was saved only by a company commander getting 13th Field FOO Capt. Jimmy Else (formerly of 4th Field) to plaster the enemy over-running his newly taken concrete trenchworks, the startline for the Queen's Own Rifles to take the town.*

---

* The company commander, Major Michel Gauvin, was awarded a DSO.

23

DRESS STANDARDS LAX, BUT
REALLY, OLD BOY!

*

FROM THE CANAL ONWARDS, FOR FOUR KILOMETRES, GRID lines are marked as objectives for leap-frogging battalions and assigned the names of literary giants, starting with Shakespeare at the canal and going on to Dryden, Browning, Chaucer, and Kipling. Somewhere just beyond Kipling in the direction of Gravenpolder contact is made with British 52nd Division. Capt. Tom Wilcox of the Royals' Carrier Platoon, on standing patrol on the left flank, comes across a Scottish lieutenant-colonel carrying a shepherd's crook in place of a swagger stick, so perfectly turned out in all respects that the bedraggled, mud-spattered Canadian will remember him forever as "the finest soldier I have ever seen in my life." Wilcox is so impressed and voluble on the subject, his description – involving a comparison with his own shoddy appearance that would fit most any Canadian officer in a forward position these days – will one day find its way into the official history of the Royals:

He had a small pack neatly adjusted on his back. (I had absolutely no idea where mine was and couldn't care less.) His gas-cape was neatly rolled above the pack. (I'd last seen mine about Eterville, last July.) He had his pistol in a neatly blancoed web holster. (I had mine in my hip pocket.) He had a neatly kept map case. (I had mine in my breast pocket.) His boots were nicely polished. (I was wearing turned-down rubber boots.) . . . He asked if I could direct him to Battalion Headquarters. I did better than that. I escorted him there. I was taking no chances of losing such a beautiful specimen of a soldier to the German Army.[*]

While standards of dress take a low priority with Canadians along the Scheldt, there are limits, and you realize you have gone a bit beyond the generous limits allowed around 4th Brigade Headquarters when you begin to notice the startled looks on faces as you pass by in your German parka – not mottled with the normal green, grey, and black camouflage, but striped with orange, yellow, and black configurations resembling an ostentatious tiger.

Selected as a curiosity by your carrier crew when they grabbed several from the great mountain of grey, green, and black parkas as they passed through Merxem several days ago, it was the only one left unclaimed in the carrier when suddenly it turned cold and you felt the need of warmer clothing.

You are normally unconcerned about your appearance, but your weird parka, obviously designed for a sniper lurking amidst the colourful foliage of fall, induces a self-consciousness which is unendurable, and you resolve to get rid of it as soon as you can get your hands on a replacement. Fortunately, before you get around to tossing the damned thing in an ashcan, you make the acquaintance of an American flyer and, amazingly, the jacket provides the key to the acquisition of a garment that allows you to dress in style. This comes about when 4th Brigade Headquarters' trucks are pulling into a barnyard, and a young fellow, dressed in ill-fitting farmer's garb, calls out to you: "Hi, Bud, got a deck of cigarettes to spare?"

On questioning by the Brigade Intelligence Officer, he reveals his glider-towing plane was shot down six weeks earlier on its way back from up near the Rhine (Groesbeek) where they had towed gliders and dropped parachutists to secure the bridges at Grave,

---

[*] Major D. J. Goodspeed, *Battle Royal* (Toronto: Royal Regiment of Canada Association, 1962), p.509.

Nijmegen, and Arnhem. To prove his story, he digs up from the garden behind the farmhouse a box containing his papers and his flyer's uniform, including a fur-collared, olive-green, nylon flying jacket, lined with silky brush wool, which is glistening new, having been issued to him just before he took off on his last flight.

Desperately hiding all signs of envy, you obliquely plant the idea of a possible trade for the priceless garment you are wearing, "an authentic German sniper's parka from the Russian front."

To your astonishment, he responds with enthusiasm. He reveals he is entitled to a complete new kit and a month's leave back in the States for managing to escape from enemy-held territory after being shot down, and would be delighted to return home with such an unusual war souvenir. In a twinkling you change from being unquestionably the weirdest dressed, if not the worst dressed, officer in Canadian Army, to one of the best.

And of profoundly greater importance, it is the most comfort-able cold-weather garment you have ever donned in your life. So light in weight you wouldn't know you had anything on, when its zephyr-smooth zipper is run up from its snug, knitted-wool belly-band to its soft furry neck, the wondrous garment is so roomy, warm, and comfortable (the designer even thought to place eyelets in the armpits for ventilation) you believe you could, if necessary, sleep in it without further cover.

The depth of ignorance in which fighting troops are kept as to what is going on on their flanks strikes you with particular force when provided with news on Operation "Suitcase," which, until now, had not been mentioned at 4th Brigade, although the security of 2nd Division's rear is totally dependent on it. It involves 4th Division's driving north to take Bergen-op-Zoom (October 27), and the Polish Armoured Division advancing to Breda (October 28) before pushing on, with the 49th British Division on their right and the American 104th Division (now under Simonds's com-mand) on their extreme right, to clear the lowlands to the mouth of the Maas river at Moerdijk.

24

LIKE THIRTEEN FOOTBALL
FIELDS LAID END TO END

✳

FOR A DAY AND A HALF, VILLAGES OF CENTRAL SOUTH BEVE-
land, with names like Nisse, Heinkenszand, and Veldzicht, fall one
after the other, the enemy offering only relatively light resistance
when they do choose to make a stand at a crossroads or a village
against 4th or 5th Brigade, pushing on towards the mouth of the
great causeway stretching almost three-quarters of a mile across the
sea to Walcheren Island.

Moving on parallel but separate axes, each brigade of 2nd
Division is driven by the need to be first to the causeway and thus
to escape having to take part in the assault across that pitiless plateau
of embanked rock and earth, which rises more than twenty feet
above the high-water mark, some 1,300 yards long and 45 yards
wide, like thirteen football fields laid end to end.

Now there is about Brig. Cabeldu and his Brigade Major a disquieting aura of anxiety and concern when they deign to consult
you as to the whereabouts of Col. MacGregor Young, who seems
to have disappeared (by design you suspect) among the battalions
churning their way forward. Before the Brigadier returns to his
caravan, he asks you to let your Colonel know he wishes to see him
as soon as possible. The Brigade Major explains the Brigadier is
uneasy at being out of touch with Col. Young at this time. It seems
the Acting Division Commander (Brig. R. H. Keefler) has made it
clear that the brigade that seizes the fortified positions at the near

end of the causeway will not have to participate in the assault across it, and Brig. Cabeldu is determined 4th Brigade will be the reserve brigade this time.

Although by now all the sodden, mud-encrusted troops of 2nd Division are nearing exhaustion from almost continuous forward movement with little sleep, under constant strain of knowing sudden death or frightful dismemberment is always just a step away from the next basin of mortars dumped along the road, or the next burst of Schmeisser fire from that farmhouse up ahead, 4th Brigade units plod on, and by the afternoon of October 30, the Royals are less than three kilometres from the causeway.

Here, however, real resistance is encountered, and when 8th Recce armoured cars and an Essex Scottish patrol cautiously feel their way forward, they are driven back by heavy fire from field guns and machine-guns set up in pillboxes, weapon pits, and emplacements, arranged in a semi-circle behind rolls of barbed wire, trip wires, and a minefield.

Thus the Royals are committed to a full battalion attack supported by a heavy fire-plan involving the guns of 4th and 5th Field, and all available mediums and heavy ack-ack, as well as the 4.2-inch mortars and medium machine-guns of the Toronto Scottish Regiment.

While the target area of the objective itself is relatively small, the timed artillery concentrations are designed to not only neutralize known forward enemy positions and prevent them from being reinforced by way of the causeway, but discourage, as far as possible, fire from their reserve positions on Walcheren Island, which, according to Dutch Resistance people, are concrete shelters and emplacements recently sunk along that far shore to which an estimated two thousand Germans have retired.

The fire-plan is designed in complete detail by the Colonel, still up with the infantry at Royals' tac headquarters. All that is required of you is to acquaint yourself and your two British arty reps with the plan; see that Brig. Cabeldu gets one of the two copies delivered to you by Don R; and get off the other by Don R to the

Brigadier CRA at Div Headquarters where the whole business can be coordinated, including alerting Army Service Corps to ensure ammunition needs are met at all gun positions well before H-hour, set for 2:00 A.M. October 31.

Lendrum's plan is for A Company, now commanded by Capt. Jack Stothers, to push north along the sea dike, while Major Tim Beatty's B Company pushes west along the dikes of the north shore towards the entrenched positions. The remaining two companies are to keep the enemy preoccupied meeting their pressure from the front.

One day Stothers will tell you it worked only because he was able to persuade Lendrum to allow him to attack along the muddy shoreline beyond the sea-dike, in behind the enemy trench-works, pillboxes, and gun emplacements, for, while they still had to contend with barbed wire, mines, and booby traps, they had the advantage of surprise when they hit the Germans from the rear. One strongpoint required the action of a flame-thrower, but before 3:00 A.M. Stothers's A Company, reinforced by platoons from C Company, reached the mouth of the causeway, and by dawn, with B and D companies closed in from the east, the Royals dominate it.*

Your only problem throughout the night has been your inability to respond to a demand from Brig. Cabeldu, passed on frequently and with increasing impatience by his Brigade Major, to produce your commanding officer. Throughout the length of South Beveland the Brigadier seemed perfectly content not to have his senior artillery adviser at his side, but from the moment his fire-plan for the Royals' attack arrived, the whereabouts of his trusted "Mac" seems to have become a matter of prime importance, and he is threatening to lose patience, if you can judge by the deepening frown of the Brigade Major each time he comes out the back

---

* Major John Stothers, Lieut. Morris Berry, and Lieut. A. C. Gillespie were awarded Military Crosses for "conspicuous gallantry and leadership."

door of the command vehicle to inquire if you have had any luck, and all you can tell him is what you've told him before: that Major Cornett says the Colonel is on his way back and should have been here long ago.

With each passing minute, you start worrying more. Something must have happened to this good and courageous man who need never have gone forward of this headquarters, but did so because he was concerned with the unusual need of gun support for the battalions of the brigade attempting to get to the causeway first so as not to have to attack across the damned thing. And if nothing serious has happened to him, then won't he be in trouble for not being around when the Brigade Commander needed him? When finally the Colonel's batman appears and whispers in your ear that Col. Young is back, the relief is great. But it is only temporary, and you become even more concerned when he whispers: "But he's flaked out on his cot in the HUP . . . a bit the worse for wear . . . had one over the eight, I think, sir. He already had his boots off and was flopping down on his cot when he got your message that the Brigadier wanted to see him. He just laughed, and curled up in a blanket and started to snore."

As you go rushing out to the HUP parked in the gloom of the barnyard, temporarily blind and stumbling from having just left the relatively bright light in the barn, you wonder how much force a captain can use in persuading his Colonel to wake up, get on his boots, and make his way to the Brigadier's command vehicle? Inside the HUP, you can see nothing until the batman produces a lamp-electric. In its dull glow you shake the Colonel. Surprisingly he comes awake without too much shaking, but on hearing your plea to get up and accompany you to the Brigadier, he tells you in a slow drawl: "Go away . . . tell the Brigadier, the war is over . . . the Royals have the mouth of the causeway . . . Tell him to go to bed . . . there's nothing more for him to do." And this he repeats, without losing his temper, each time you plead with him just to come with you.

Finally, more in exasperation at your stubbornness than compliance, he allows you to pull him to a sitting position on the side of the cot and push his feet into his boots. As you are lacing them up you ask why it took him so long to get back to Brigade. He tells you he got lost. Then, chuckling, he explains that after suffering the greatest fright of his life, he stopped in at the Rileys for a smash or two with Jack Drewry to settle his nerves. It seems that when he realized he was lost on a dark road in no-man's-land, and was turning around, he managed to get the bumper of his Jeep hooked into some fence-wire at the side of the road, and when he reversed the vehicle, up in front of him rose a German, first the unmistakable helmet, then the whole man, no more than six feet from his face. Dead of course. But in the brief moment it took to recognize this, it was an awesome experience.

On the way to the barn on your arm, he doesn't stagger, but when you leave him on his own to mount the few steps to the door of the caravan, he stumbles and plunges dramatically through the door. Your British friends purse their lips and wag their heads significantly as you return to the table. But soon a storm of laughter shakes the whole caravan. You suspect "Mac" has just reached the part of his story where the German cadaver rose up in front of his Jeep. Almost immediately the caravan door opens, and Brigadier and Colonel descend arm in arm, followed closely by a smiling Brigade Major. And all are laughing at something the Colonel is saying, as they disappear out the back door, clearly on their way to raising some toasts to the Brigade's success.

The war, which a moment ago seemed to be of such desperate importance, goes into a state of suspension, at least here at 4th Brigade. Telephones, which were ringing and buzzing urgently, go silent. Radios, though continuing to hiss and blabber, produce no messages for the sigs to rush to the caravan door. When a clerk goes about switching off the lights on the map-boards to save batteries, the friendlier of the two British officers suggests you and he might also relax a bit. He has a crock in his kit out in the cow stable, and if you can get that pesky acetylene lamp of yours working to provide light, there are a couple of feed barrels for chairs and a table of sorts at one end . . .

So when at 4:00 A.M., October 31, 4th and 6th Field are ordered to pull out of action and drive back through Antwerp to what had been the Breskens pocket, to join the mass of guns assembling to support two seaborne attacks on Walcheren Island scheduled for 0445 next day, November 1, the Colonel and you proceed "independently" after the Colonel manages a few hours' sleep.

This day, with a bridgehead over a north–south canal at Retrachment, on the western Dutch–Belgian border (gained by the Stormont, Dundas and Glengarry Highlanders and the Highland Light Infantry), the last and largest town in the Breskens pocket, Knocke-Heist, is threatened by the North Novas advancing during the night, taking outposts and prisoners. At 4:00 P.M., November 1, Major-Gen. Knut Eberding, commander of 64th Division, and his staff of one hundred, emerge from deep concrete bunkers with their hands up, ignoring the spirit and letter of his own order at the start of the campaign to fight to the death,[*] and now only concerned with the security of the cases of kit he will be taking with him onto captivity.[†]

---

[*] Eberding had warned that premature surrender would be considered desertion, and "in cases where the names of deserters are ascertained these will be made known to the civilian population at home and their next of kin will be looked upon as enemies of the German people."(Quoted in Wilmot, *Struggle for Europe* [London: Collins, 1952], p. 546.)

[†] "He [Eberding] told his servant Frank to pack his bags for a long captivity, and not to forget his chess-set and books. So Frank piled in the staff officer's trousers, the polished high boots, the suit of civvies, the fur-lined gloves, the extra stock of general's insignia, hats various, the underwear, and above all the General's chess library – some fifteen printed works and manuscript notebooks." (Intelligence Summary #52 HQ 3rd Inf. Division Appendix B, Public Archives)

25

HELL IS A CAUSEWAY
SWEPT BY ENEMY FIRE

❋

THE ROYALS' ATTACK TO CLEAR THE MOUTH OF THE CAUSE-way proceeded with such despatch that by dawn all companies were on their objectives and the enemy troops in the vicinity were so demoralized that they surrendered in droves. Two officers and 153 men came in with their hands up, abandoning three 75-mm guns, two anti-tank guns, many machine-guns, and quantities of essential quarter-master stores.

However, with the coming of daylight, though the enemy makes no attempt to recover their position, their guns and mortars on the far shore undertake to make life miserable for the Royals, bombarding them all day as they wait for the Black Watch to come up and take over after last light, preparatory to attacking across the long land-bridge.

Until now that bleak neck of rock and earth, stretching flat and featureless, except for rows of poplars bordering the railway and roadway it was built to carry across the water to Walcheren, has been known simply as "the causeway." Now with its mouth and western approaches under intense bombardment from enemy shells and mortars, it becomes that "goddamned causeway" or something equally suggestive of its accursed nature.

Under fire from noon until dark from machine-guns, an anti-tank gun ricocheting shots down the centre of the roadway, and field guns and mortars of various calibres dropping H.E. along the length of the causeway, most of the Black Watch are only halfway across, and a mere handful have made it to within twenty-five yards of the far end, when around 7:30 P.M. they are ordered to withdraw. Evacuation of the wounded is naturally slow, particularly those from the far end of the causeway, and many are still out there at 11:40 P.M. when an artillery concentration is brought down.

Before midnight the Calgary Highlanders are ordered to take a crack at getting across the causeway, but when their leading company loses most of its first platoon just getting halfway to the objective, they are withdrawn.

At dawn November 1, they are ordered to try again, and this time they manage to get across and overrun the roadblock at the far end, taking fifteen prisoners. By 9:33 A.M. they have established a shallow bridgehead, but enemy pressure mounts during the day, and before night falls strong enemy counter-attacks supported by intense mortaring and shelling drive them back onto the causeway, back to a giant crater about halfway along its length.

Next morning, November 2, at 4:00 A.M., with the support of a stormy barrage laid down by three field regiments, and the thunder of three medium regiments conducting counter-battery fire, the Maisonneuves are sent on the same mission. Their D Company, at least those who manage to survive the torrent of enemy fire they are exposed to all the way along the causeway, reach the Walcheren end and seize a bridgehead some four hundred yards wide, from which they expect to be relieved at 5:00 A.M. by the Glasgow Highlanders of British 52nd (Lowland) Division whose responsibility it will be to debouch from the bridgehead into Walcheren.

For nine hours the Maisonneuves courageously maintain their holding, saved on occasion by the guns of 5th Field and the timely intervention of rocketing Typhoons diving on marauding tanks, while reinforcing companies try to reach them. During the morning one platoon of the Glasgow Highlanders crosses the causeway and joins the remnants of D Company in the bridgehead, and the rest of the British battalion gradually makes its way up the causeway, replacing the Maisonneuves. But conditions on the fire-swept causeway are such that their battalion historian will record that it was like being "led into hell . . . to move a foot in daylight was nearly impossible; to advance at night was an adventurous success.*

At 2:45 in the afternoon the survivors of D Company, now numbering no more than twenty, and the one platoon of the Glasgow Highlanders that first came up and made it to the bridgehead, withdraw under a smokescreen laid down by 5th Field guns, directed by their FOO, Lieut. D. G. Innes, who, though wounded, remained with the Maisies throughout.†

There will be no more attacks along the causeway. That night 52nd Division, led by 6th Battalion of Cameronians, cross the Slooe Channel two kilometres south of the causeway, walking in single file along a narrow ford through treacherous mud and sand that two intrepid British sappers had reconnoitred and marked with white tape the previous night.

While the heroic effort by 5th Brigade – unsurpassed in the matter of courage anywhere along the Scheldt – will be deemed a failure, no one should ever refer to it as such in front of a Maisonneuve. Lieut. Guy deMerlis, who, with Lieut. Charles Forbes, the other surviving platoon commander of D Company, played leading roles in the affairs of the beleaguered company, will tell you: "We did exactly what we were asked; we crossed the damned causeway and established a bridgehead from which the British were to attack into Walcheren Island. They chose not to."‡

While all this was going on at the causeway, 8th Reconnaissance Regiment (14th Canadian Hussars) engages in a saltwater sea-crossing of its own to North Beveland, an island eleven kilometres long and five wide lying just one hundred metres off the northern shore of South Beveland, along which a squadron of recce cars under

---

* George Blake, *Mountain and Flood: The History of the 52nd (Lowland) Division* (Glasgow: Jackson, Son & Co., 1950).

† Lieut. D. G. Innes was subsequently awarded the Military Cross.

‡ Author interview.

Major Dick Porteous has been pushing for some days, protecting the right flank of 4th Brigade.

On learning from the Dutch Resistance that North Beveland was being used as a transfer point for enemy movement to and from Walcheren Island, Porteous, with the full support of his commanding officer, Lt.-Col. Mowbray Alway, commandeered a long barge and some fishing boats at a ferry station and crossed to North Beveland on the night of November 1, taking with them, besides their own vehicles, a company of heavy mortars (4.2-inch) and medium machine-guns (Vickers) of the Tor Scots, as well as about twenty-five armed members of the Dutch Resistance.

Their first success was the capture of a German hospital ship. Then, though the commandant of the German garrison in Kamperland, the principal town on the island, first scorned an 8th Recce ultimatum to capitulate – promising to fight to the death – 250 of his men and two officers promptly surrendered when the Tor Scots lobbed a few 4.2-inch mortar bombs at them, and a squadron of Typhoons swooped over them as though to attack them on their way to targets on Walcheren.

The final bag of prisoners taken in clearing the island totalled 367, and the invasion force did not suffer a single casualty.[*]

---

[*]   Details of North Beveland invasion by 8th Recce from Denis and Shelagh Whitaker, *Tug of War* (Toronto: Beaufort Books, 1984).

26

MASS OF GUNS IN
A SEA OF MUD

---　❋　---

AFTER AN ELEVEN-HOUR DRIVE VIA PUTTE, MERXEM,
Antwerp, the Ghent tunnel, and then northwest along the south
shore of the Scheldt Estuary through villages, completely smashed
and desolate, 4th Field arrives at the village of Schoondijcke in
what had been the Breskens pocket, to deploy amidst a vast array of
field guns, mediums, heavies, and superheavies, at about 3:00 P.M.,
October 31.

After weeks among the flooded fields, mud, mists, and rain of
South Beveland, you should be used to the bleak vistas of polder
country in these bitter wet days of fall, but the sight of the grim,
grey sea of mud into which the guns are ordered to deploy next to
the shattered village is appalling. This must surely be the ultimate in
miserable living conditions, which no human being should ever be
asked to endure.

However, as you slosh about on your way to locating shelter for
the night in a partially intact building near RHQ in the remnants of
the village, despairing for those poor devils at the guns who face the
descending night without shelter, you hear not one single word of
complaint. On the contrary, as you pass by your old Able Troop,
there are attempts at humour and good-natured joshing: "Great
weather for ducks, eh, sir? Tell me, have you looked between your
toes lately?" And when he receives no reply, "To see if any webbing
has sprouted yet?"

The gun sergeants, ready as always to strike an upbeat note, assure you they'll "make out all right." They've been told that to gain surprise for the seaborne commando attacks on Walcheren Island gun sites there will be no firing until H-hour just before dawn, which means the boys can take turns getting some rest in nearby buildings.

Fortunately, all battery and troop command posts find space they can black out among the derelict buildings. Able Troop's command post is in an abandoned tobacco kiln made remarkably cosy by the heat from a little Primus stove. As the night progresses, the temperature falls, and when ammunition thermometers at the troop positions are read for the purpose of working out the "corrections of the moment" to apply to the gun forms, adjusting ranges and switches to accommodate the latest meteorological conditions just before the big shoot begins, the mean temperature is a chilly 50 degrees Fahrenheit.

To gain maximum range for weapons of various calibres, Corps CRA Brig. Bruce Matthews has had to jam gun positions together in closer proximity than you've ever seen them deployed before.

Field gunners seldom pass a 7.2-inch gun position, and until now superheavies have entered your consciousness only as distant deep-throated booms. Here, at last light, the 7.2s and the 155-mm "Long Toms," along with their superbrethren of 8-inch and 240-mm calibres, are visible silhouettes on the horizon at the rear. There are, you are told, 314 guns assembled here. In addition to those heavies and superheavies (3rd Cdn and 9th AGRAs) capable of reaching the big guns at Westkapelle and delivering a weight of shell to do them damage, there are 240 25-pounders, 112 5.5-inch mediums, and 48 3.7-inch anti-aircraft guns to engage the area of Flushing, only three miles from this shore and about six miles from the field and medium guns. Also, for the first time ever on the Western Front, from the Allied side, a battery of rocket launchers, manned by Canadians, will fire three salvoes of 96 rockets per salvo onto ack-ack positions north of Flushing.

All these weapons crowded together do not escape the notice of the big guns on Walcheren. However, all the shells that moan over from the Island in late afternoon and evening land well out in front of 4th Field.

The extensive fire-plan for the early-morning shoot, received by Regimental Headquarters this evening, is considered "a work of art." This will be a very big show, second only, you are told, to Normandy in complexity, for the snout of Walcheren facing into the North Sea is more strongly defended than were any of the Normandy beaches.

A disaster equalling Dieppe might have occurred without Lt.-Gen. Guy Simonds's insistence on Bomber Command opening up four great gaps in the saucerlike outer rim of the Island (a dike thirty-two feet high and in places one hundred feet wide at its base), thereby letting in the sea and rip tides and forcing friend and foe to take refuge on scanty high ground or in upper storeys of buildings, reducing German mobility and cutting his supply lines. As it is, casualties are bound to be high for those in small naval craft moving just offshore and attracting enemy fire while commando boats surge through the gaps in the dikes to attack the guns from the rear.

It is raining at 4:30 A.M. when, with a thundering wave of sound and concussion, enveloping everything and everybody on the crowded gun positions and blowing tiles from the roofs of buildings still blessed with roofs in the village, the great shoot begins – 4th Field adding "just a small voice in the roar of cannons around us," to quote the war diary. For two and a half hours the guns continue to pump fire on designated targets, including the hostile guns that could be brought to bear on the commando forces and the assaulting brigade (155th) of 52nd Division constituting "Infatuate I," who'll be taking Flushing.

Four hours after "Infatuate I" goes in, the assault in the gap in the dike south of Westkapelle is to be carried out by the 4th Special Services Brigade with very heavy naval support. H-hour for this is

9:45 A.M. and another timed program for the mediums and the heavies begins seventy minutes before then – continuing in bursts of firing for varying periods up to 10:45 A.M. on the casemated guns west of Flushing and about Westkapelle.

The second seaborne attack of the day, "Infatuate II," involving a large flotilla from Ostend directed at Westkapelle on the nose of Walcheren Island, is engaged by the enemy shore batteries around 8:00 A.M. Later you will learn that while some German guns are knocked out by the naval ships escorting the flotilla, most of them are taken out by the commandos who get ashore while small naval ships purposely attract the attention of the gunners.

All elements of the assaulting forces from the sea are British, except for medical services, which are provided by the Royal Canadian Medical Corps going in with the commandos.*

---

* One day you will read a vivid account of what those gallant doctors and their helpers faced when they sailed in through the Westkapelle gap, in a book by the leader of Number 8 Canadian Field Surgical Unit, D.r Major John Hillsman, an American surgeon who gave up his citizenship to join the Canadian forces before the United States was drawn into the war by the Japanese attack on Pearl Harbor in December 1941. Hillsman landed on a shoulder of the Westkapelle gap before most of the assaulting commandos. Burbling ashore in a wallowing Buffalo from a landing craft laced with fire, he and his gallant band immediately became involved in collecting and treating casualties among burning vehicles and enemy fire. By the end of the day they'd treated 150 casualties. At noon next day, three Buffaloes, loaded with seven tons of ammunition, were hit by hostile shells and began to burn and explode, causing many casualties to both Brits and German prisoners. Hillsman and Captain Lou Ptak, of his transfusion unit, had to crawl around on their bellies with the exploding ammunition shooting at them from one side and the Germans from the other. "For the next half hour," Hillsman writes, "we lay on our faces in the sand, dressing wounds, stopping hemorrhages, and splinting fractures." That night a gale blew and he operated in a tent six feet by nine, so crowded (by five men) he had to crawl under the operating table when he

News is sketchy, but seemingly the assaulting forces are gaining one position after another of those still above water in the flooded basin. Early on November 2, the guns fire on the Flushing area. Otherwise they are quiet all day.

Again, early next morning, heavy fire is called for about Flushing. And in the afternoon some Victor (Corps) targets are engaged, even as a regimental recce party is sent sixteen kilometres south of Antwerp to a place called Rumst to find "billets" for a rest out of action once all the guns of Walcheren are silenced.

Today (November 4), as usual, the guns open up early on a strongpoint near Flushing, but this turns out to be the last shelling needed. During the morning all resistance on Walcheren appears to end, and the order "prepare to move" comes down at noon. At 3:00 P.M. 4th Field, with no regrets, pulls out of the churned mud and water, heading for the village of Rumst, chosen, you are told, because Antwerp has been under bombardment by V-1s and V-2s since early last month. However, just before the Regiment arrives, the chosen billet is flattened by a V-1, and new digs must be found in schools, cafés, and factories.*

Officers are billeted in private homes, and you draw a sweet-smelling house, redolent with odours of the fruit maturing on vines and trees flourishing in a glass-roofed conservatory opening on the dining room of your hosts, two charming middle-aged ladies.

———

"wanted to change sides." In two days he and his team performed fifty-two operations, using instruments sterilized in basins of fluid sitting on the floor, and on occasion operating by the light of an acetylene lamp when the generator packed it in. See John Hillsman M.D., *Eleven Men and a Scalpel* (Winnipeg: Columbia Press, 1948), p. 101.

* From October 7, 1944, until March 30, 1945, 3,709 V-weapons (2,448 flying bombs and 1,261 giant rockets) exploded in the Antwerp area. At least 1,214 landed in the city itself, killing 3,000 (including 131 dock workers) and wounding 15,000.

27

SEDATED IN MALINES –

REVIVED IN ANTWERP

--- ✳ ---

FOR FOUR DAYS THE REGIMENT PAYS ATTENTION TO ITS OWN needs with no outside obligations, apart from a Corps Commander's briefing for officers and warrant officers in a theatre in Malines.

Observed from your place far up in the balcony, deeply embedded in blessed anonymity, the solitary figure striding forth unannounced from the darkness of the vast empty stage has your sympathy. Dwarfed by the towering proscenium arch as he plants himself at the centre of the wide stage apron to face this audience of hardened veterans of two of the bitterest campaigns in the long story of war, he is not in an enviable position, you think.

However, Lt.-Gen. Guy Simonds is no ordinary mortal, and he proceeds with such self-confidence in every word, gesture, and posture, you find yourself marvelling at the bold arrogance of great generals that allows them to conduct themselves with such assurance in circumstances such as this – obviously the same arrogance that sustains them in making awesome decisions that send thousands to death and disablement, the unavoidable consequence of every major operation.

However, the content of his address, mainly a dry, pragmatic appreciation of accomplishments in Normandy, at the Channel ports, and along the Scheldt, coupled with an uninspiring view of a future that holds out months of tedious, uncomfortable times before the enemy is finally defeated, is less than impressive, particularly when, by implication, he suggests officers and NCOs are currently showing levels of leadership and discipline that must be improved remarkably if a lowering in morale throughout the Army is not to occur this winter in static positions up in the Nijmegen salient.

Having come to admire Simonds greatly from afar for his remarkable originality and imagination in devising unique operational plans never before attempted, and for utilizing equipment in novel ways to keep casualty rates as low as possible, his talk, that seems to go on for ever, is a great disappointment. Not only do you not learn anything of real consequence, but he succeeds in creating an atmosphere you thought safely buried in old diaries of training days, as he affects that cold, glowering, threatening style used universally in England by patronizing senior officers as they delivered pep talks on morale-building and the need for junior officers "to take over" – larded with endless platitudes that have become meaningless over here.

The result is a stupefied audience that files out of the theatre in silence, resisting comment until they are safely ensconced with trusted peers in neighbouring watering-holes. The consensus of your peers is that the Regiment, like every other outfit in Canadian Army, is tired and filthy, but all it needs is time for personal maintenance, equipment maintenance, rest, and recreation – with special emphasis on the latter – and it will immediately regain its resilience.

Divisional commanders appear to agree with this consensus, for twenty-four-hour leaves to Antwerp are immediately introduced, and every day for four memorable days, a quota of officers and Other Ranks, enough to fill three or four 60-hundredweight trucks, proceed into the city, replacing an equal number who have spent the previous night in this beautiful city – so alive, so pleasant, so civilized – revisiting familiar haunts and looking up civilian acquaintances made while the guns were in position in the dock area back in September.

Devoid of all official duties (the Colonel having no need for an assistant while 4th Brigade is out of action) you move into the Century Hotel to live in splendid luxury, represented especially by an incredibly soft bed with white sheets and pillows, a gleaming white bathtub with endless hot water at the twist of a tap, and something you had almost forgotten existed, a smooth, clean floor beneath your bare feet when you get out of bed and pad to the bathroom, and a warm toilet seat, properly formed to receive a human posterior comfortably.

As long as there are others from the Regiment on overnight leave in town, you know you can't be left behind by a sudden move of the Regiment called back into action without warning. But each noon your position feels mildly illicit and slightly precarious as you say goodbye to fellow officers dutifully returning to Rumst, leaving you alone in a relatively deserted hotel.

There are, of course, late each afternoon, a couple of anxious hours' waiting to see if new truckloads come in. But the very uncertainty – that this may be your last day in this marvellous place – revives a full appreciation of your privileged status, when, with dusk falling in the wet and windy streets outside and the warmth of the soothingly lit lobby of the Century assuming its most welcoming aspect, you at last spot a friendly face from the Regiment among the arriving guests, and know you will spend another enjoyable night in the new glittering cabaret they've established for officers in the ballroom of the Excelsior Hotel adjoining the Century Hotel.

Then, over and beyond partaking of the amenities of this luxury hotel and amiable city, there is always the chance you may meet up with a friend you haven't seen for years, for Antwerp is a strong magnet these days for anyone getting time off. Your current run of luck produces a wonderful reunion with old Pembroke friend Ramsay Garrow, now a captain with the Sherbrooke Fusiliers, who without warning drops down on a chair beside you at your table in the Excelsior Cabaret.

For hours, completely oblivious to the swirling dancers, the swinging big band, and the ebb and flow of the laughing gabble of voices trying to make themselves heard all around you, you shout and laugh, exchanging precious news of family and friends back home and showing each other your latest batch of snapshots of loved ones, in your case particularly those of your little girl now almost two years old.

Only this morning, while wandering up the main boulevard, eating ice cream cones purchased at the famous ice cream parlour, does the conversation get around to the war. But when it does, the grey morning turns even greyer and all the exuberance – the like of which you haven't felt in years – immediately disappears as he provides you with some truly horrifying insights into the life of tank-men. He has managed to survive all the way from the D-Day beaches with the Sherbrooke Fusiliers, but in the process has formed quite a low opinion of most Allied tanks – so low you find it astonishing that tankmen can go on accepting their inferior equipment with such equanimity.

In fact there's an upbeat quality to his description of ways the Sherbrookes have tried to make up for the inferior armour and armament of their "Ronsons," as Shermans are known for their proclivity for "brewing up" when punctured. Sqdn Commander Major "Woppy" Radley-Walters, DSO, MC, who has had three tanks and three armoured cars shot out from under him (not to mention nine other tanks holed but left serviceable), claims that if the armour-piercing shot from the 75-mm gun of a regular Sherman (incapable of penetrating the frontal armour of a German Panther) is ricocheted down off the bottom of the bulging mantelet of the Panther, the slug will drive through the thin surface armour. And to ensure incoming enemy slugs meet an uneven surface and are diverted ever so slightly from their normal, lethal course, the ingenious "Woppy" has started a trend of welding hunks of track from derelicts around the Shermans' bodies and turrets.*

---

* When an Ordnance pooh-bah decreed this "junk" must be removed, since the extra weight could reduce a tank's running life by five hundred miles, Radley-Walter's blunt answer was that without that "junk" those tanks might not make it even to the next hill.

28

OUR HEARTS LAID BARE
BY LYRIC WRITERS

✳

"WISH ME LUCK AS YOU WAVE ME GOODBYE . . ."

"I'll walk alone . . ."

"I'll be seeing you – in all the old familiar places . . ."

"We'll meet again – don't know where, don't know when – but I know we'll meet again some sunny day . . ."

"I haven't said thanks for that lovely weekend – those two days of heaven you helped me to spend – the thrill of your kiss as you stepped off the train – the smile in your eyes like the sun after rain . . . Then you had to go – the time was so short – we both had so much to say – your kit to be packed, the train to be caught – sorry I cried but I just felt that way. But now you have gone, Dear, this letter I pen, my heart travels with you, till we meet again. Keep smiling my Darling and someday we'll spend, a lifetime of peace as that lovely weekend."

Words like those in the lyrics of current songs, expressing so poignantly the thoughts and feelings of lovers wrenched apart today by the war, perhaps permanently, may appear to future generations of youth as embarrassingly sentimental, or just plain dreary, as lyrics of many of the First War songs appeared to you when you were growing up.

However, it should be clearly understood and recorded, while our memories of this war are with us, still living-fresh, that no collection of official documents now being filed away by the great political leaders and military commanders for their memoirs, no scrapbook of newspaper and magazine clippings, nothing now being placed in print and on film that historians one day will claim for posterity to be the true story of the War, will ever capture the spirit and soul of these days in the way popular song lyrics are doing.

Could any statesman's diary or news report ever come close to matching the childish bravado embraced by the British public during the "phoney war" – when nobody on the western front fired a shot either way – expressed in the lyrics: "We're gonna hang out our washing on the Siegfried Line ..." and "Run Rabbit Run."

And when the seemingly invincible German hordes overran Western Europe, forcing the British soldiers to abandon all their weapons and equipment in France and make it home as best they could, and when the need to fight despair was paramount, it was a song lyric that captured the spirit of the times and the feelings of the British and their friends all over the world: "There'll always be an England, and England shall be free, as long as England means to you, what England means to me."

For years now, most Englishmen would be too embarrassed to sing words like that. But let the world remember, there was a time after the fall of France – when the droning and stuttering noises of the battle for domination of the sky over Britain filled the air – when those words were sung loud and clear, not only by the British, but by people across the seas.

For you the picture is still fresh of several hundred men at a service club luncheon in the Château Laurier in Ottawa standing and singing those words with tears in their eyes, just after applauding the speaker of the day, British poet Sir Alfred Noyes (of "The Highwayman" fame) for calling author H. G. Wells "a liar" in alleging the soldiers at Dunkirk had been abandoned by their officers.

As inspiring as Churchill's stirring declarations of defiance were in 1940, when he hurled them at the Germans in the face of overpowering odds ("We shall fight on the beaches ...") the spirit abroad among the common people during that awful period of suspense, awaiting the expected invasion from the continent, was more accurately captured by the lyrics of a gentle little song expressing the longing for a return to normalcy, for the days when the children were at home: "There'll be blue birds over, the white cliffs of Dover – tomorrow just you wait and see . . . The shepherd will tend his sheep, the valley will bloom again, and Jimmy will go to sleep in his own little room again . . ."

Will these words someday be labelled sentimental twaddle? Perhaps, but let those who choose in the distant future to research this era take note that in the early 1940s, when thousands of children were being sent away from the danger of the Blitz to live apart from their parents, people found those words profoundly moving, expressing the very essence of the civilized values they believed worth fighting for.

Song lyrics have captured a wide spectrum of the strangeness of life for the new recruit: the great contrast between pampered life in Civvy Street and the coarse conditions of the training barracks ("This is the army, Mr. Jones, no private room or telephones . . ."); the tedium and drudgery of life for common soldiers buried in helpless anonymity in some drab depot or reinforcement unit ("You'll get used to it – you gotta get used to it . . ."); and the pervasive need of all those new to hard service discipline to put down those in authority who are making life miserable for all the lowly odds and sods of this world ("Don't forget to wake me in the morning and bring me in a nice, hot cup of tea – Kiss me goodnight Sergeant Major – Sergeant Major be a mother to me").

But no song exposes the secret yearnings of the soldier on his way up to the front as well as the German song about Lilli Marlene, said to have been "captured" by 8th Army Desert Rats in North Africa.

Nightly it is the piece most requested of the Belgian swing band playing at the dances in the Excelsior ballroom cabaret. These remarkable affairs, that only came into being this week when Antwerp was suddenly flooded with men and officers on twenty-four-hour leaves from exhausted Canadian Army divisions released from the mud along the Scheldt, and that will cease abruptly in a couple of days when First Canadian Army moves north to the Nijmegen salient, are providing those lucky enough to share in them memories that will last a lifetime.

Tonight, as always, every seat at every table is taken. Most wear holstered pistols and some have knives slung on web-belts around the shirred waists of their battledresses, still wrinkled and baggy from crouching in the rain in water-logged holes on the Scheldt — survivors of struggles in which hundreds of their buddies were struck down.*

There are dark circles under their eyes and their faces are weatherbeaten and lined with fatigue, and for some time after they arrive, they seem like old men unable to smile. They stare around the bright, noisy, merry room and at the lovely-gowned girls out on the dance floor in utter disbelief. Then after a couple of cognacs they spot some friend they haven't seen since OCTU or a boyhood chum they haven't met since school days, and join in the general hubbub, adding to the noise level rising to a din that threatens to drown out the orchestra playing the song hits of the Thirties: "Marie, You're Laughing At Me," "Sunrise Serenade," "Deep in a Dream of You," "Star Dust"...

Then, for at least the sixth time tonight, the Belgian musicians on the bandstand succumb to calls from the room and start whistling "Lilli Marlene," stomping their feet rhythmically as though marching — softly at first, then more loudly, and still more loudly as the room grows quiet and attentive. Now the musicians pick up their instruments and play as though a military band is passing by, their feet marching heavily. Gradually they drop the volume, until there is only the faintest sound of men marching away whistling "Lilli Marlene." Finally that too disappears, and for a long moment there is silence.

---

* First Canadian Army losses on the Scheldt totalled 12,873 killed, wounded, and missing. Of this total, 6,367 were Canadians.

PART TWO: NOVEMBER 9– FEBRUARY 15

The Nijmegen Salient

29

SETTLING IN THE
NIJMEGEN SALIENT

＊

THE REGIMENT ARRIVES IN THE NIJMEGEN SALIENT NEAR Groesbeek just before noon November 9 after a 110-mile overnight drive from Antwerp. It has travelled over roads laced by rain and hail and severely congested by other Canadian units moving up to take over from a mixture of American paratroopers and British artillery who have been holding this zone since September 21, when XXX British Corps, driving north from the Meuse–Escaut canal in Belgium, reached here in its ill-fated attempt to reach 1st British Airborne Division still holding Arnhem bridge over the Neder Rhine.

At a roadside briefing of officers, deep in a pine woods where the Regiment bivouacs waiting for the British 112th Field Regiment to vacate their gun positions next day, Col. Young makes it clear the troops must be encouraged to build substantial dug-outs – not only to withstand the rigours of winter, but to gain maximum protection from expected heavy counter-battery activity by the enemy. Senior officers of the American 82nd Airborne Division, briefing senior officers of 2nd Division this morning, gave the impression that this is a very sticky sector, absorbing an unholy amount of Jerry shells and mortars along the front line running through Groesbeek and among the gun positions spotted in clearings in the bushland behind the village. And since the unflappable Colonel is known to

THE RHINELAND
8 FEBRUARY - 10 MARCH 1945

Flooded areas . . . .
German defences . . . .
4 RCA gun positions . . . .

0   2   4   6   8 km
0   1   2   3   4   5 mi

RHINE RIVER
RHINE RIVER
RHINE RIVER
MAAS RIVER

Wesel
Rheinberg
Ginderich
Menzelen
Ossenberg
Alpen
Wimmelthal
Veen
Issum
Xanten
Lüttingen
Wardt
Hamb
Bönninghardt
Metzekath
Geldern
Labbeck
Sonsbeck
Kapellen
HOCHWALD
6 MAR
Kervenheim
Berendonk
Marienbaum
Kappelen
5 MAR
Udem
2 MAR
Mooshof
Eben
27 FEB
Holthuysen
Kevelaer
Wetten
Weeze
Wemb
Goch
Buchholt
Halvenboom
Schroarzenhof
Kranenbergshof
Wilmshof
Halvenboom
23 FEB
Louisendorf
Bedburg
Moyland
Hasselt
16 FEB
Warbeyen
Hau
Calcar
Hönnepol
Wissel
Grieth
Husberden
Rees
Haffen
Emmerich
Hurendeich
Kellen
18 MAR
Cleve
Materborn
Hau
Bresserberg
Nütterden
Esperance
Schottheide
REICHSWALD
11 MAR
Heikens
Asperden
Kessel
Zelderheide
Ottersum
Gennep
Afferden
Oostrum
Well
Wanssum
Langstraat
NETHERLANDS
GERMANY
Hekkens
Niers
Frasselt
Groesbeck
Galgensteeg
Kranenburg
Mook
St. Jansberg
Middelaar
Cuijk
Boxmeer
St. Antonis
Donsbruggen
Kartenbosch
Keeken
Duffelward
Warthausen
Niel
Mehr
Rindern
Beek
Kekerdom
Millingen
Nijmegen
Hoch Elten

26 DEC
28 DEC
7-10 JAN
11 JAN - 15 FEB
9 NOV - 25 DEC

N

be totally disinclined to dramatize conditions, this information is taken seriously by all ranks.

From the first days in action it has never been necessary to issue orders to the troops to dig in. Early experience with horrendous enemy bombardments of gun positions in front of Carpiquet sorted out that matter for all time. However, until now, the troops have never had the opportunity to do a real job on dug-outs and command posts. Now, with bags of time available, there develops a sense of competition to see who can build the most comfortable underground living-quarters, usually constructed by pairs of men or small syndicates – some even felling trees and building log cabins in holes to be covered with earth. Most, however, build shacks below grade, using, in place of plywood, doors from the ruined houses of Groesbeek village, inside doors as well as outside doors, to shore up earthen walls and provide sheathing for roofs to receive their thick covering of soil.

At the outset, they utilize shelters left by the British, while working hard and long with a sense of urgency, improving dug-outs and excavating new ones, bracing themselves for the expected bombardments.

However, either Jerry has suddenly decided to lay off shelling this sector, or those American paratroopers, never having been sub-jected to the weight of shelling endured by 4th Field in Normandy or along the Scheldt, are not equipped to judge what constitutes heavy shelling, for these gun positions behind Groesbeek turn out to be among the quietest ever occupied by the Regiment in action. Apart from some widely spaced shelling on the flanks, and the odd airburst over the gun positions, Jerry restricts his attention to the infantry. And even up front, though OP logs regularly record a bit of shelling by 75-mm or 105-mm guns, he seldom shows any real inclination to expend large numbers of shells or mortar bombs.

Periodically a basin of Moaning Minnies descends on Groesbeek, and now and then the desolate and deserted village is subjected to a leisurely bombardment by one gun of fairly large calibre – ten or fifteen wailing shells arriving one at a time, with long intervals between, their ground-shuddering concussions and roars reverberating among the confined streets and derelict buildings, creating the impression of something very large and terribly lethal.

Your OP is a ridiculously exposed and atrociously vulnerable tall windmill standing forth on the brow of a height of land to the right of Groesbeek village, looking across an enemy-dominated valley of misty, low-lying farmland stretching to the German frontier three kilometres away, easily distinguishable by the fact the map shows the border running along the foot of the distant formidable ridge, covered with a dark and dense evergreen state forest called the Reichswald.

The main part of the tower is quite substantial, with thick, brick walls capable of stopping small-arms fire and shell fragments, with a base virtually impregnable to any ordinary field piece or anti-tank gun, surrounded as it is by a deep, earthen berm of fortresslike proportions between eight and ten feet high. Moreover, there is a truly splendid means of access to what might be described as the basement of the mill. Cut deeply through the berm, fortuitously away from the enemy and completely hidden from their view, the entry doors are wide enough to allow your carrier to drive inside and be hidden from air reconnaissance. However, to observe the zone, you must use the cupola at the very top, with its fan-window opening almost down to floor level of the moveable dome, and hunch down, back in the shadows, next to the huge wooden gears and the thick shaft supporting the great windvanes now hanging sail-less outside the rear of the mill, facing back in the direction of the guns.

In normal times the cupola would be turned by the miller's pushing on a great brace, running from the back of the cupola down to the base of the mill, so the vanes face into the prevailing wind, but now, while the valley in front remains no-man's-land, the cupola will stay as is with its fan-window facing the Reichswald.

The mill is, at the same time, the best and the worst of OPs: the best for providing the widest panoramic view of no-man's-land and enemy-held territory, and the worst for its ridiculous vulnerability.

Its fan-window must appear to the enemy as an evil, menacing eye, complete with looping eyebrow, an open invitation to a burst of machine-gun fire or a shell from an 88. The thin wooden boards that form the roof and walls of the cupola wouldn't inhibit the passage of a bullet, let alone high explosive. A single shell of respectable calibre would blow this flimsy loft away in a shower of matchwood.

Nevertheless, until now the Germans have chosen not to attack the cupola with any kind of fire. Why they continue to leave it alone, you can only speculate. There is lots of evidence that the mill's dominant position in the village was seriously contested in the early hours of the American paratroop and the glider landings. A German soldier lies dead on one of the lower floors, and though the heavy brick structure shows few scars of battle, the surrounding turf is cratered and torn by shells that barely missed it.

It is, of course, idiotic to use the mill as an OP, for any tower that provides wide observation must be suspect. If it were in German-held territory, you wouldn't rest until it was chopped to ribbons by your shells, anti-tank solid-shot, and Typhoon rockets. But even as you realize the risk involved in using it to observe the zone, you continue to climb up to the cupola each morning simply because the broad panorama it provides from the top is irresistible to a FOO. It surely is the outstanding OP in the Nijmegen salient, and may well be without peer on the whole Western Front.

The fact the Germans have left it alone until now encourages you to believe they may continue to do so. Still, you never completely suppress the memory of that fire-ranger's tower you occupied for several days unmolested on that hill in the bush back at Groote Meer near Woensdrecht, and the way it was smashed by Heinie shells just moments after you vacated it for the last time.

For the first few days, you occupy the mill around the clock, observing the zone from the cupola during daylight hours, retiring to a lower floor during the hours of darkness.

However, there being no way to black-out completely any part of the tower, it isn't possible to expose a light strong enough for reading, which makes the longest nights of the year seem longer

still. Also, continuous exposure day and night to the chimney effect
of the tall tower, which induces unpleasant, icy draughts to sweep
up through the completely open stairwells from floor to floor has
given everybody on your crew a head cold.

Thus, when the weather turns particularly nasty one afternoon,
you agree that the crew should check out a farm they like the looks
of down on the right a couple of hundred yards, on the west side of
the road, labelled on the map Herwendaalsche Straat.

And though you are a bit uneasy about its unprotected location in
a sort of no-man's-land between the Royals and their neighbours,
with no evidence of men from either battalion nearby, as darkness
falls and a gusting wind sends snowflakes swirling in through your
fan-window, their enthusiastic reports of a pile of dry firewood in
the kitchen and a full bin of coal at the back of the farmhouse make
the idea of moving over there for the night irresistible.

However, the dream of spending your first evening in the cosy
luxury of a dry kitchen, warmed by a glowing range, is ruined by
the Germans early in the evening, when they open up with a
variety of guns and mortars all along the front. While they are not
disturbing your house, you get a signal to return to your OP in the
mill to flash-spot hostile guns and mortars until dawn.

This means sitting alone in the cold and gloom in utter
boredom, fighting sleep, watching the dark zone in front of you
until you catch sight of a flash of a gun or mortar. Then with your
prismatic compass, lit by a shielded lamp-electric, you read the
bearing, and report it to the Regiment for passage on to Div, along
with the precise time the flash was observed – being careful not to
report flashes of our own shells or mortars sent over by other units.
On receipt of two or more reports of flashes, recorded at the same
point in time, Counter Battery at Div, knowing the map location of
each OP reporting, can use the bearings to establish by triangulation
a map reference for the enemy gun, on which counter-battery
bombards can be arranged.

The accuracy of the map reference thus arrived at is of course
totally dependent on the accuracy of the compass bearings supplied,

and accurate readings are extremely difficult since the flashes are, more often than not, vague by virtue of coming from behind a crest, or diffused by fog and mist.

Usually the spotting FOO does not try to engage the flashing weapon, since it is next to impossible for him to establish the offending gun's position from a split-second, pinpoint flicker or a splash of light on the horizon. But during the first part of the night, the urgent need to cool down Jerry's heavy harassing fire on Groesbeek and vicinity, and in recognition of his habit of removing his Moaning Minnies and guns to other locations after firing a few rounds so as to frustrate flash-spotting efforts, you immediately engage any suspected area in the vicinity of the flashes with a few rounds' gunfire, in addition to reporting the bearings to Counter-Mortar.*

While the chances of hitting a hostile gun or mortar with this kind of random firing at flashes on the horizon are slight, the small expenditure of shells is, in your opinion, still very worthwhile as a morale-booster for the harassed men living out a wretched existence in filthy, cold, fearful conditions along the front here.

Many of those poor fellows are bound to be recent reinforcements, some of them experiencing their first tour of duty in the front line crouching on muddy straw or pine boughs strewn across the slightly congealed, half-frozen ooze on the bottom of their

---

* Where practical to instal and maintain the equipment, more-accurate readings on locations of hostile mortars and guns were obtained by the Sound Ranging Troops of 2nd Survey Regiment of 2nd Corps. Close-in mortars were monitered by microphones spaced out across the front, hooked up to jiggling four-pen recorders; and distant guns by six microphones placed in overturned pots in camouflaged holes in the ground, 1,500 metres apart across the front, hooked up to a recording device of running film-negative registering impulses from each microphone – from the "gun-firing wave," the "incoming-shell wave," and the "shell-bursting wave" – each showing up on the film as meaningful "blips" to the trained eyes of sound rangers.

partially covered slit trenches. To those men, cringing out there in the dark, praying their hole won't receive a direct hit – helpless, unable to fight back – the sound of some friendly guns thumping behind them, followed by the sizzle of shells passing overhead on their way to land with flashing roars on distant enemy territory, must surely be music to their ears.

On the 17th of November, 1st Canadian Calibration Troop arrives at the Regiment, and over three days all the guns are measured for wear and calibrated. All gun barrels absorb wear from each and every shell driven out their length with such tremendous force. As time goes by the stream of shells reams the bore larger and larger, until the gases, expelling the shells, start escaping past the copper drivingbands meant to provide a seal between shells and the rifling of the bore. This causes a lowering of the velocity of the shell and a drop-off in the distance it will travel at any given range setting.

Up to a certain point, the drop-off in muzzle velocity from wear can be compensated for by acute adjustments to the ranging sights by expert artificers, which in effect tip the gun muzzle slightly higher when each elevation is applied by the gun-layer. Though the FOOs have not discerned any fall-off in the range of 4th Field guns, it is only reasonable to assume that after the record-breaking firing they have engaged in, their barrels will prove to be badly worn when measurements are taken by the calibrators using photo-electric cell equipment.

However, the drop-off in muzzle velocity is astonishingly slight for 1940 tubes that, during the past four months, have fired an average of 10,128 rounds each, including occasions in Normandy when they glowed red-hot and, which, by all logic, should have caused severe wear. Typical of the calibration results were those for Sgt. McEwan's gun, as recorded in his gun log:

On November 17, 1944, the muzzle velocities of 25-pounder gun barrel L/24006, of "D" Sub of Easy Troop, 26 Battery, 4RCA, was measured at each of the four levels of propellant charges, and recorded against the original muzzle velocities in feet per second:

	Original MV	*17 Nov 1944*
Charge I	645 f.p.s.	635 f.p.s.
Charge II	987 "	971 "
Charge III	1463 "	1433 "
Super Charge	1742 "	1698 "

No one seems particularly impressed with the staying power of their superstars. Field gunners are inclined to take for granted the extraordinary flexibility of their weapons, which can be brought into action in less than a minute, ready to fulfil their role as howitzers or guns – capable of traversing 360 degrees on their own steel platforms – something no other field gun in the world can do. And so they also take for granted their remarkable durability, and on countless occasions have demanded of them more than should ever be expected of any gun, pounding away for outrageously long periods, at firing rates far in excess of the limits laid down by those who should know their capabilities. For the reliability of the 25-pounder to be fully appreciated, it must be compared to other formidable weapons earning honoured places in the history of this war – the 5.5-inch medium gun and the 40-mm Bofors ack-ack gun – whose barrels frequently must be replaced after intensive fire.*

---

* During August 1944 the replacement rate of 5.5-inch barrels in the Canadian Army was eight per day. Rated for 7,000 rounds of E.F.C. (equivalent full charge), 5.5-inch barrels generally accomplished only a third of that, ending life at 2,400 E.F.C. And Bofors barrels were inclined to bulge when furious firing rates were sustained, as during their use in a ground role during the opening of Operation "Veritable" in the Rhineland in February 1945. 38th battery reported eleven barrels bulged among twenty-four guns of two troops.

30

BIT OF AN OVERSIGHT,

EH WHAT?

✳

AFTER THE ENEMY WAS CLEARED FROM THE SCHELDT AND the big guns of Walcheren silenced, it took nearly one hundred British minesweepers three weeks to clear the eighty kilometres of winding estuary from Antwerp to the open North Sea, blowing up or neutralizing 267 German mines.

Those first ocean-going freighters, led by Canadian-built *Fort Cataraqui*, and manned by the Royal Navy, steaming up to Antwerp quays on November 28, near where 4th Field guns once stood, represent the culmination of a great operation by the Canadian Army – a victory of decisive importance to the prosecution of the war, and so recognized by both General Eisenhower and Field Marshal Montgomery.

The Supreme Allied Commander in Western Europe will say: "The end of Nazism was in clear view when the first ship moved unmolested up the Scheldt."

And the 21st Army Group commander will write: "The Canadians have proved themselves magnificent fighters, truly magnificent. Their job along the Channel Coast and clearing of the Scheldt was a great military achievement for which they deserve the fullest credit. It was a job that could have been done only by first-rate troops. Second-rate troops would have failed."

And surely no one is unmindful of the terrible cost in Canadian blood of this day of triumph – that in thirty-eight days of merciless struggle, in the most appalling conditions men could ever be asked to fight, 3rd Canadian Division suffered 2,672 casualties, and 2nd Division even more, 3,364 dead and wounded.

Thus it is entirely fitting that there be a ceremony to mark the port opening. And one is held, appropriately involving a salute by bands playing national anthems as the first ship of a nineteen-ship convoy is escorted into harbour by a boatload of dignitaries, including the *Bürgermeister* of Antwerp, Field Marshal Montgomery, and a number of naval and military chiefs of Belgium, Britain, and the United States. However, the Canadian anthem is *not* played. For reasons never explained, no Canadian – from Lt.-Gen. Simonds, who planned and led this huge and complex operation, down through all levels of Canadian officers and men who fought those awful battles – was invited to the ceremony.

And since Antwerp is out of bounds to all military personnel except those on official business, ever since a V-1 landed on the Rex movie theatre with awful results, few Canadians could have been in the city today.* Therefore, to be able, one day, to casually drop the fact you were in Antwerp on this historic occasion, being in possession of a pass for "official business," will surely sound impressive – particularly if you neglect to explain you weren't aware of any ceremony and your business was to purchase a supply of booze so that some officers, residing in the cold, misty Nijmegen salient, might get together for a drink in a remarkably large dug-out at 14th Battery gun position near Groesbeek.

This underground phenomenon, constituting the first, last, and only "officers' mess" ever established during action in Northwest Europe by any battery in the Regiment, completed the third week of November, is something of a triumph in design and decoration,

---

* On November 28 the ack-ack ringing Antwerp shot down 35 V-weapons, but one of the fifteen that got through landed with a roar at an intersection, killing eleven civilians just as the first ship was arriving at the docks.

being a room ten feet by fifteen feet with seven feet of headroom, entirely below grade, with an exotic decor that could best be described as a blend of Eastern Mediterranean and the South Seas.

The basic wall-covering is bamboo matting, plainly suggestive of palm trees and Dorothy Lamour. Draped over this are rich tapestries, and covering the earthen floor is a thick oriental rug. Finally, adding to the sense of glowing opulence is the subdued lighting supplied by wall lamps with sexy little brown shades, powered by current from 12-volt radio batteries fed through a 110-volt converter salvaged from a broken 19-set.

A velour curtain hangs across the doorway at the foot of the stairs to prevent the winter draughts, now swirling through the frozen bushland above, from leaking into the room. A Nederland version of the Quebec Heater, the venerable Canadian parlour stove, fed with coal filched from the tender of the nearby abandoned locomotive, keeps the place warm and cosy, and dries out the upholstered chairs, which, like the rug and tapestries, were "rescued" from sodden houses in Groesbeek. Distributed around the perimeter, between some rather splendid casual tables, the chairs are fairly dry – at least visitors no longer appear wraithed in steam when they arise from them and go above ground.

Never will you forget the first time you descended the slippery steps from the bleak, wintry landscape above, and passing through a stained and ragged piece of tarpaulin, hanging just outside the velour curtain at the doorway, burst into that beautifully appointed room. Just back from a two-week stretch in a dirty, cold OP your first thought was that the thing must surely be some kind of elaborate joke. And the 14th Battery batman, showing it to you – obviously harbouring mixed feelings about this masterpiece on which he'd been obliged to lavish so much ingenuity and labour – said it so well: "Ain't war hell, sir?"

Major Jack Drewry, the battery commander, whose enthusiasm alone brought it to fruition, naturally wants to show it off at a regimental officers' bash, to which he's invited the officers of the RHLI at whose tac headquarters he spends his time when they are in the line. Justification for the bash is contained in a pious title on the invitations: "Get-to-know-your-neighbour Cocktail Party" – meaning of course the "Rileys." However, the objective could apply equally well to 4th Field, for casualties and promotions during the last few months have produced a multitude of strange faces among the officers. It is because 14th Battery has so many new officers of limited experience that Drewry requested you be transferred to 14th "to thicken up their experience," at least until the spring offensive starts.

So the great party is scheduled for 5:00 P.M. tomorrow, November 29. But even as the invitations were being distributed yesterday, Drewry discovered the 14th Battery officers' booze cupboard (more precisely an ammo box in his possession designated to carry such goodies) was in a particularly barren state. While issue rum was considered quite a pukka base for a mess punch in England, and an extra gallon could have been scrounged for the purpose, rum, now being of daily issue, does not seem quite special enough. Someone must go to Antwerp on a buying expedition and Drewry, knowing you are about to be seconded to 14th Battery to take over D Troop, invites you to take on the job. Old friend Len Harvey decides to keep you company, being free of regimental duties as he awaits posting to a training course for pilots for a new Canadian Air OP Squadron being formed under Major Dave Ely, once your troop commander in Britain.

Thus you and Harvey are in Antwerp when the history-making opening of the harbour takes place. However, having no access to English papers or the BBC, you would have remained totally ignorant of the event except for a precocious little ten-year-old girl, enthroned on a high stool beside her mother behind the bar in a café in Rumst, when you are persuaded by Harvey to take the thirty-minute drive south of the city so he may revisit his favourite Flemish watering-hole and deliver some candy bars to the effervescent tyke, who captured his heart when the Regiment was billeted here just three weeks ago.

As you enter, she is filling the bar with her laughter in typical fashion. And what has set her off? Well, it seems the newspaper lying before her on the bar, showing pictures of the ceremony in Antwerp harbour, reports the first ship to dock was carrying salt. To her this is hilarious. In English, extraordinarily good for one who only began to pick it up three weeks ago, she declares:

"All that fighting you did to open up the port, and what do they bring us? Salt!!" (a gale of laughter) "With the sea full of saltwater, and saltwater flooding everywhere through the broken dikes, they bring us a ship loaded with salt!!"

She laughs so hard, she almost falls off her high stool. But suddenly she stops, and covers her mouth with her hand, as she spots the candy bars Len is holding out to her.

Back at the Century Hotel, you find the lobby absolutely empty of people – not one customer. Three weeks ago this long, high-ceilinged reception room was pulsing with life every afternoon and night. When you remark on this to the desk clerk booking you in, he sighs:

"Ah yes . . . no more . . . the joy has gone . . . the hotel is almost empty of guests . . . the v-bombs you see."

And the ballroom next door in the annex hotel – the Excelsior?

"The same . . . nothing. If you wish a drink, gentlemen, the bar in the basement is open."

You go down and look in. Except for the barman, it's deserted. Len decides to hit the sack. You hang on for a while with the object of taking advantage of the baby grand piano on the platform in the corner, which you recall is well-tuned, a rarity on the continent of Europe.

But before you move to it, two colonels with red-banded forage caps – one distinguished by a black patch over one eye, and the other by white hair – come in and sit down on the bar stools beside you. The white-haired colonel looks familiar, and when he introduces himself, the name Eric Harris rings a bell. You met him at Barnham Junction when he visited his old 26th Battery he'd brought to England in 1940.

He and his companion, Colonel Wardell, were over on Walcheren today examining gun sites hit by the rockets that were fired by weapons designed by Colonel Wardell. Perhaps you saw them in action in the Breskens area when your guns supported the attack on Walcheren? "No ... well, you will ... in all major operations in the future ... you most certainly will!"*

Before you can ask for more details, he inquires, "Where is this swinging Antwerp we've heard so much about? We were told Antwerp was the swinging capital of Europe."

You explain they should have been here a month ago, before the V-1s and V-2s started arriving.

He then asks how 4th Field made out in Normandy. But as you begin telling him how rough it was, you realize he's not listening. He starts to tell Wardell about leaves he had here in Belgium in the last war, and you don't think he even notices as you excuse yourself to leave for bed, thoroughly depressed by having been patronized and then ignored by an old soldier trying to recapture his youth.

---

* While rocket artillery was designed and developed through the initiative of a British Guards officer, Lt.-Col. Michael Wardell, full credit must go to Lt.-Col. Eric Harris that Canadian gunners introduced it on the Western Front for the first time in World War II, on November 1, 1944. Wardell had been the champion of rockets as ground artillery from when he'd improvised the defence of his position in North Africa in 1942 and dispersed the enemy using an anti-aircraft rocket projector. He lost an eye in the engagement, but he became a staff officer, and got the chance to promote his ideas. Though he successfully demonstrated his rockets in trials at Larkhill in the winter of 1944, the British brass decided it was too late in the war to refine the weapon and develop a supply of rockets. Among the spectators was Harris, former 26th Battery commander, who had set up the Canadian School of Artillery at Seaford. To him Wardell's "collection of pipes" was too good to be relegated to the scrap heap. He recommended Canadian Army should develop a rocket-firing battery. To the credit of Gen. Harry Crerar and the BRA Brig. H. O. N. Brownfield, senior gunner officer at Canadian Army Headquarters, approval came quickly.

31

FILET MIGNON FOR BREAKFAST

---------------------------------- ✳ ----------------------------------

FROM DAWN UNTIL DUSK EACH DAY, AND SOMETIMES AT
night when required to flash-spot active enemy guns and mortars,
FOOs keep enemy-held territory through to the Reichswald under
constant observation. The "O Pip," or "Oboe Peters" (as observation posts are now sometimes known, under the bastard phonetic
alphabet produced by an amalgam of British and American ver-
sions) from which all this surveillance is conducted in the
Nijmegen salient, are, topographically speaking, quite superior,
providing broad and deep overviews of the zone.

However, the quality of accommodation for bones and muscles,
which remain crouched, slouched, hunched, or otherwise cramped
in awkward postures for hours on end, varies greatly from one OP to
another. Sometimes you hunker down under the slanting rafter-
poles of a frigid farmhouse attic or a barn loft, with the wind
whistling through the cracks between the tiles, and scuttle about
crablike when you change position, as much to keep yourself from
fossilizing in some grotesque shape as to gain a different view of
no-man's-land.

All observation from buildings tends to be restricted, for it must
be conducted discreetly so as not to draw attention to a position
that will be continually occupied by FOOs for weeks. So viewing
of the zone always is from back in the shadows, away from openings such as the holes blown in the roof by unfriendly mortars, or

purposely opened by your unwiring some of the tiles from the rafter-poles and letting them skitter off down to the ground.

One of the strangest OPs on this whole front is with an isolated company of Royals in some battered buildings forming an island several hundred yards out in a broad lake of flood water, created by the Maas river overflowing its banks in the general area of Middelaar.

One chilly, black night in early December, you are sent up to meet the rowboat coming back for rations for "Paddy" Ryall's company, then occupying that island. This entails a nerve-wracking drive in a 15-hundredweight, at a snail's pace up a narrow road only barely above the level of the flood waters lapping the road on both sides.

One moment the water is glistening black right next to the left front wheel, and the next instant it is menacing the right wheel, as the veteran driver, Gunner Ed Crosier, struggles to track an imaginary centre line in total blackout. Breathing hard, he explains it isn't just the possibility of running off into the water that bothers him; the verges have not been cleared of mines, and if he fails to recognize the rendezvous point, he'll deliver you to the Jerries, whom he's been told are not far beyond here.

About the time you become convinced he has long since passed the crucial point and that you may expect a burst of Spandau fire through the windshield at any moment, you spot some white tape draped on stakes at a widening of the road. With nerves thoroughly frazzled, you leave the truck, collect your bedroll and your signaller with his 18-set from the back, and climb into the canvas rowboat to sit atop a load of Compo rations. Straddling a kitbag full of mail and parcels, as you are rowed through the blackness, you face the future with some trepidation, expecting to be delivered to a partially submerged, waterlogged hovel.

But when Paddy receives you with such obvious pleasure at his island-building – a sort of mill warehouse – "handing you out" with courtly grace onto what in normal times would be a loading dock for wagons, and leads you upstairs to a dry candlelit storeroom with mellow wooden floors and partitions exuding comfortable odours of corn or bran, you start thanking your lucky stars and relishing the prospect of spending the next two weeks here.*

Alas, next night you are hauled back to become Dog Troop commander and occupy OP 46 with the RHLI two kilometres southwest of Groesbeek.

Along this sector the distance between opposing forces varies tremendously, from just the width of a village street in a crossroads hamlet, such as Knapheide, to a thousand yards in the open, soggy fields, though the gap between the lines narrows considerably at night when both sides send out patrols and listening posts among the derelict American gliders strewn about the valley.

Artillery OPs are sometimes so close to the enemy the FOO must move in after dark, and then quietly, if he doesn't want to attract a shattering burst of Schmeisser fire of hair-raising intimacy. Such a place is OP 46. And going up after dark without a guide, trying to follow an ill-defined track across muddy fields intersected by deep drainage ditches filled to the brim with ice-water, can be treacherous. This you learn on a black and rainy December night when one of these water hazards claims you, up to your hips, when, attempting to jump over it, you misjudge the distance between its slippery banks.

It happens just after you abandon the dry snugness of the cab of a 15-hundredweight truck, following a disconcerting conversation with the driver, again Gunner Crosier, when the track he's been following begins to peter out in suspicious fashion, suggesting it no longer is a road but a farmer's lane. From long experience with drivers, who always seem to know the best route to a neighbouring unit or the safest way to an awkwardly placed OP, you took for

---

* This island position was not without its drawbacks. One was the unavoidable delay in evacuating casualties. Frank, the younger brother of 2nd Battery Don R Gunner Andy Turner, serving with Ryall's company and wounded here, was dead on arrival at hospital because of such a delay.

granted that Crosier would know the way up to the Riley company to which you've been assigned. He, on the other hand, never having been up here before, carried on in the belief you knew precisely where you were going and would make sure he didn't stray off the track. If you hadn't become worried, when the muddy road grew less and less distinct, and questioned the wisdom of driving on, he would have driven out into no-man's-land never realizing the blind was leading the blind. As it is, you land at Major Joe Pigott's company headquarters, set up in a partially wrecked, tiny brick farmhouse, a sodden mess, covered with mud and cursing after dragging your lower extremities dripping out of the ditch.

In the morning you learn that as a place for observing no-man's-land this sad little farmhouse, sitting in an open field halfway down a forward slope, isn't in it with most of the other OPs along this front, but as a position in close and continuing contact with the enemy it surely would top any list. Now and then a Spandau sprays bullets at the north and east windows of the house to discourage their use for observation purposes; and when, in a fruitless search for a better OP, you spend an educational day with a forward platoon, you experience one of their regular exchanges of rifle-grenades with the Germans in the houses on the opposite side of the *straat* that runs through the hamlet.

Later this becomes one of the most interesting targets you are required to engage at any time on this front, when Pigott, after experiencing firsthand one of these bizarre grenade exchanges during a visit to his forward troops, decides those German grenadiers should receive a sharp reprimand. On returning to his headquarters in the little farmhouse, he insists you shell them, even though no more than seventy or eighty feet separate the enemy houses from those on the near side of the street.

You warn him that even by using Charge 1, to ensure the highest possible trajectory for the shells looping onto the target, it is entirely possible that every one will strike the first row of houses going in – that is, those within which his troops will be sheltering.

He understands but is ready to take the chance. So with the

connivance of his troops, who are warned to take shelter as best they can, you drop a stonk along that street – a "stonk" being a target requiring all the guns to drop their shells in a line, for a specified distance, along a selected bearing running through a map reference. Dispensing with prior ranging so as to catch a maximum number of the enemy by surprise with the first salvo, all possible care is required at the guns to ensure extreme accuracy, including application of "corrections of the moment" for meteorological conditions, and the use of their Sands Graphs to adjust the range of each individual gun, to compensate for the way gun pits are intentionally staggered to present a less concentrated target for marauding planes.

While no one is able to say what proportion of the shells hit the intended target, since none of the forward troops can keep their heads up, and it is far too foggy for you to gauge their effectiveness with any accuracy, some undoubtedly land where they are supposed to, providing a terrifying experience for any Heinie caught on the upper floors of any of those houses. At any rate, for a time at least, they stop firing grenades across the road.

Every day, from dawn to dusk, misty rain and fog enshroud the whole front, often restricting visibility to less than two hundred yards, which encourages patrol activity in both directions and makes everybody a little jumpy. But apart from some light mortaring, and those random burp guns splattering the house now and then, there is no really serious enemy activity. As the days pass you become convinced that the greatest threat to your continued existence comes not from the enemy, but from a mechanical monster devised by an ingenious member of Pigott's headquarters gang: a stove – a roaring, house-shuddering stove, roughly based on the principle of a blow torch and occupying much of the free floorspace in the little kitchen.

The principle is childishly simple: A couple of inches of petrol, in the bottom of a jerrycan, is set to boil on a little gas-operated Primus stove. While the lid is tightly secured on the jerrycan, a nail hole has been drilled about two-thirds of the way up the side of the can. As the gasoline heats up, a white spume of fumes begins to shoot out the nail hole in a steady, horizontal stream for a distance of about four feet. And when a match is tossed into this spume, it flashes into bluish white roiling flames with a pulsing roar, resembling, to an uncanny degree, the sound of the German jets periodically scooting overhead trying for the Nijmegen Bridge.

To contain the flames and turn them into something useful, this flame-thrower is set up at the open end of a rectangular structure built of bricks from the rubble outside – about a foot and a half wide, four feet long, and about three feet high, open at the top, with a base of bricks laid on the kitchen floor. Utilizing the grills from the oven of the regular kitchen range, to span the open top and hold pots and pans, this energetic cooker is capable of bringing potatoes to the boil in two or three minutes.

Its invention is not just an exercise in ingenuity to pass the time. When company Sgt.-Maj. Stewart "Pinky" Moffatt and two other volunteers of commendable initiative lure a cow, grazing in the field across from the kitchen door, into a barn beyond the orchard, where it can be turned into meat for the table, the need arises for a large-capacity stove that won't give off tell-tale smoke when fired up in the daytime, as would the conventional kitchen range.

Though the battalion kitchen prepares two hot meals a day for delivery in insulated Hay Boxes to the forward companies – supper after dark, and breakfast before dawn – the basic grub is still Compo M & V and the like, the same boring stuff all have been eating for months. Once the idea of cutting into a real honest-to-goodness steak takes hold of the mind, it easily becomes an obsession, particularly since within this company headquarters group is a man who was a professional butcher in Civvy Street – one Danny Butler.

Thus, peering out into the drizzle from the door of the woodshed late one foggy afternoon, you fully understand the awful frustration of Moffatt and his fellow conspirators (one grasping the cow by the tail), when they fail to persuade the suspicious beast to saunter in orderly fashion to her doom in the barn. And when at last the Sergeant-Major, whose feet are only now and then touching the ground, lets go of her neck and falls head-over-heels down the muddy slope, cursing mightily (in preference to being carried by the bellowing animal into no-man's-land and on into Germany) you bleed for him, while at the same time struggling to suppress the idea there is anything funny about him calling out, just before he lets go, "Oh to hell with it, lads, let her go!" – unaware that he alone is trying to restrain the indignant animal, the other two having abandoned him to his fate at least a hundred yards back.

However, during the night additional cowboys are enlisted, and next morning there are great chunks of meat on the dining-room table, which, you are told by Private Butler, will provide the choicest of steaks, the rest of the carcass having been sent back to the battalion cooks.

When the group decides there should be filet mignon steaks for breakfast, and they light a little Primus stove and place its hissing, blue flame under a jerrycan quarter-filled with gasoline, you retreat out the back door, believing the odds are better in risking a sniper's bullet in the mist than remaining in that cluttered kitchen where they are boiling a substance with an explosive power equal to TNT. But after a few minutes, as you get used to the muffled roar, and the delicious smell of frying beef drifts out through the passageway into the woodshed, you assemble enough nerve to return inside.

In the crowded kitchen the resemblance of the Rube Goldberg stove to a jet engine is even more remarkable, as the roiling flames fill the brick cavity and overflow upwards, licking around the frying pan so that the cook must turn the steaks almost continually to keep them from burning. The gas is expelled at such pressure from the jerrycan that the flame doesn't start until it is eight or ten inches from the nail hole. And as you study it, you become aware that that remarkably durable can, designed to withstand the impact of a drop to earth from a low-flying aircraft, is bulging out on both sides from the extreme pressure. When you point this out to the designer of this set-up, he bends down quickly and turns down the Primus stove flame. Slowly the jerrycan subsides to a more normal shape. And from then on whenever the stove is operating you make it your business to stand by and protect the size and shape of the jerrycan, reducing the Primus stove flame when necessary.

At lunchtime, you, along with all the others in Company HQ, have your second steak of the day – a full sirloin. And for supper you have your third steak. And around about midnight, the fourth steak of the day is delivered to you as you lie in your bedroll on the floor at the foot of the stove. You don't ask for it, and don't particularly want it, when you awake to the sound of the stove roaring and the sight of flames darting out between the loosely laid bricks a few inches from your nose.

Sgt.-Maj. Moffatt, obviously feeling the need for a midnight snack after returning from delivering the rations, rum, and mail to the forward troops, is standing at the frying pan with spatula in hand. When he spots you pulling back from the licking flames, he leans down and hands you a knife and fork, and places a dinner plate with an enormous brown, steaming steak on it on the floor before you. And you, leaning on one elbow, proceed to eat it with relish.

Next day, you consume nothing but the odd cup of tea. You aren't ill. You simply do not feel the need for food.

32

'TWAS THE EVE OF
THE FEAST OF SAINT NICK

✳

BY NOW THE DUG-OUTS BACK AT THE GUN POSITIONS ARE extraordinarily comfortable. No one, taking a casual walk through the gorse patches and stubby pines close by the battery gun positions, would ever suspect the snug comfort of the dwellings lying beneath the columns of blue smoke issuing from stubby, ground-level chimneys, manufactured from 25-pounder brass cartridge cases or pieces of regular stovepipe, sticking up here and there through the frost-covered ground.

The men have ransacked shell-ravaged, deserted Groesbeek for every conceivable thing useable for building; especially doors, handy substitutes for plywood. By the last days of November, poor old Groesbeek was virtually doorless, inside and out.

To this you can testify, for right after you were posted to 14th Battery, 4th Brigade was pulled out of the line and you and Gnr. Alexander Whitehawk were forced to set up new housekeeping arrangements from scratch near your D Troop guns. As Johnnies-come-lately, you searched through the ghostly empty village for the better part of one afternoon without turning up one door still hanging on its hinges. Finally you'd been forced to knock apart a chicken coop and haul it back to your chosen allotment in the frosty bushland near the guns.

Without Whitehawk's awesome capacity to get things done –

springing as much from his placid optimism and quiet staying power as from his extraordinary energy and initiative – that discouraging pile of weathered old lumber full of rusty nails would have lain where it dropped until spring. However, to your amazement, a few hours after he'd politely suggested you occupy yourself somewhere else and leave him be, he'd converted that unprepossessing pile of splintered junk into the snuggest dug-out anyone could ever hope for; not big – not much more than six-feet square – but big enough to accommodate two built-in wooden bunks stacked one over the other, while leaving enough room for one man at a time to get up, dress, shave, wash, and sort out kit.

And all of this in warm comfort, for, while engineering this veritable miracle, his ingenuity brought into being, using an empty petrol tin and a piece of clay drain-pipe embedded upright in the earthen wall at the foot of the stairs, an incredibly efficient little stove capable of heating up the dug-out in minutes when fed but a few sticks of wood.

If you live to be a hundred, you'll never forget the sense of total luxury the first night you occupied it, lying cosy and warm on your top bunk listening to a "Mary of Arnhem" broadcast on the 38-set – putting up with periodic interruptions by that saccharine-voiced *Fräulein* inviting you to defect and spend Christmas on the other side of the Rhine – to hear Crosby croon "I'm Dreaming of a White Christmas" and a swatch of familiar ballads from the vintage years of pop music before the war. As you read and reread special letters from home and exchange reminiscences with the taciturn Whitehawk each time he arises from his lower bunk to brew up still another cuppa char, it all seemed too good to be true.

By now only those few free spirits, who scorn secondhand building materials and have harvested piles of logs to erect cabins underground, are still involved in construction. The outstanding example is Major Bill Carr, of 26th Battery, an energetic soul determined to create an underground log cabin of such staggering proportions it is fast earning the title "Carr's Folly."

Candles and petrol lanterns are principal sources of lighting, but many dug-outs are lit in the manner of Major Drewry's subterranean wonder using rechargeable 12-volt radio batteries hooked up to 110-volt converters "borrowed" from derelict 19-sets and fed into electric lamps scrounged in Groesbeek. And some 2nd Battery dug-outs along the railway cutting are hooked into the regular power line running close to their position, the electricity reputedly coming from a generating station which the Germans have agreed not to shell or bomb as long as the power is allowed to cross the Rhine for their use as well.

However, since plumbing and drains do not exist here, latrines manage to maintain the primitive aspects you've come to associate with them in spite of noble engineering efforts by troop and battery sergeant-majors – including Sgt.-Maj. Ed Blodgett – to enhance seating arrangements with boards and timbers and burlap screens. And as the weather has worsened and the snows have come, on mornings or nights when arctic winds billow and whip those protective burlap screens about like sails in a gale, it takes great courage, courage born of sheer desperation, to bare one's extremities and press them down on boards freshly cleared of snow. You so detest using these primitive obscenities that, when back at the guns, you plan your daily routine to include regular visits to the RHQ building to coincide with certain cycles of your metabolism with which you have become familiar, so as to take full advantage of a truly great luxury: a flush toilet with a warm seat!

However, all things considered, all at the guns seem quite happy with their living conditions, and so no one in Dog Troop is particularly enthusiastic when, on the afternoon of December 5, orders are received from RHQ to pull their guns out of action and tow them back a few miles to a village called Groot Linden for forty-eight hours' rest and maintenance. By contrast, you and your crew, called back from a frigid OP to share the experience with the troop, are quite enthusiastic – visualizing warm billets and maybe even real beds.

But by the time Sgt.-Maj. Hill has led you to the modest little house in the village where he's arranged for you to sleep, and you've dumped off your bedroll and personal "ammunition box" with its precious goodies you've been hoarding from Christmas parcels from home, your enthusiasm is beginning to fade. The space allotted you is a clammy, unheated, narrow, ground-floor room off the living room, devoid of all furnishings except a kitchen chair and a Singer sewing-machine.

From then on, though you force yourself to maintain a suitably cheerful front (trying not to overdo it and appear deranged in the eyes of the troop), you secretly sympathize with the point of view frequently expressed by the Other Ranks during a very boring evening. According to the schedule decreed by RHQ, the troop is supposed to enjoy relaxation and good-fellowship, aided by a keg of wishy-washy Belgian beer and a double ration of rum served in their own chipped and battered enamelled mugs on stained wooden trestle-tables in a dimly lit hall, while nibbling distractedly on Compo cheese and hardtack.

As time goes on the gunners express their dim view of all this loudly and distinctly (if obliquely) in a variety of colourful ways to each other – sometimes using revised song lyrics, one of the most popular being sung to the tune of "Auld Lang Syne" – "Sit down you bum, sit down you bum, sit down you bum, sit dow-w-n!" – whenever one of their peers assembles the nerve to stand up and tries to get their attention.

But when they want to make their point of view known to their Troop Commander, it is expressed in the form of a question, such as: Why the hell, sir, didn't they let us just pull the guns out of action and do our maintenance on them right there in our pits – and let us relax in our own dug-outs?

You, of course, must manufacture phoney reasons. You know that they know they are phoney. But this doesn't worry you, for most of them are veterans of many years' experience with the ways of the army, who know that officers always have to defend the orders of officers senior to them, even when (as on many occasions in England) orders appeared to all ranks to be plain, unadulterated crap. And you remind them that whatever they think of the arrangements, they were made with the best of intentions and the sole purpose of making life a little more pleasant.

Around 10:00 P.M. you excuse yourself and return to your billet, intending to write some letters. The house is black, except for the lamp in the kitchen, but the lady supplies you with a kerosene lamp and you use the sewing-machine as a desk. Very soon your hands are so cold you can't hold the pen. You decide to get warmed up before piling into your bedroll on the floor, and go out and rap on the kitchen door. When they invite you in, you sit at the end of the kitchen table, facing the big range glowing with heat, opposite the man of the house who is writing with pen and ink – slowly and meticulously drawing each letter of each word as though he is engraving. Resting just beyond his writing pad on the table is a homemade cardboard house obviously coloured with wax crayons.

Immediately it is clear what he is doing. Late in the afternoon, just as you were being shown to your billet by the Sergeant-Major, you had witnessed a fascinating tabloid: A tall man with long, white beard, dressed like a bishop in mitred hat and flowing robe of purple and gold, accompanied by a black-faced man in fancy maroon, oriental dress with a turban in matching colour, carrying a bishop's staff – surrounded by a swarm of very young children – made their way slowly down the village street. The Sergeant-Major, who'd been here since morning with the advance party, was able to explain. This, the fifth of December, is the Eve of the Feast of Saint Nicholas, the day that benevolent gentleman and his black servant traditionally bring gifts to the good children of Holland. This year, however, he was having to tell the children that with the war on, some gifts might not be possible.

Now, that must be what this father is doing – writing his children individual letters from St. Nicholas. You question him as best you can with the odd Dutch word, while pointing at the cardboard house and the writing pad. And while he replies only in Dutch, his meaning is clear when he adds some pantomime; the cardboard house is the one and only thing they have from St. Nicholas for their two little kids now asleep upstairs.

You jump to your feet and rush to your room, where your ammunition box with its goodies rests beside your bedroll on the floor.

A can of real Canadian red salmon, a bag of saltwater kisses, and a bag of gumdrops (from your mother's latest parcel), and two giant-sized milk chocolate bars and a full pound of salted peanuts (from your wife) make quite a respectable pile when you carry them in and dump them on the kitchen table before the astonished father.

The tearful, joyous reaction of the man and then his wife – who turns from stirring something on the stove, on hearing him cry out – is almost enough to make tears come to your eyes. You point to the things and say "St. Nicholas" and then point upstairs to where the kids are sleeping. Then you point to yourself and wag your head "no, no" – and repeat again "St. Nicholas" as you point at the candies and peanuts. When finally they understand that the kids must think the stuff came from St. Nick, they smile and nod vigorously, and wipe away their tears.

The lady insists on giving you a cup of tea, while the man, with great ceremony for your benefit, tears up the letters he had written to the children, and throws the bits into the stove, brushing his hands with obvious satisfaction. And after you've had your tea, they wring your hand, and escort you to your bedroll. And you go to sleep feeling absolutely wonderful.

33

NO MAIL FOR MORIN

❋

MAIL, SOME WRITTEN A MONTH AGO, COMES UP TO THE OP with the rum ration this morning, December 24. The real Christmas mail including parcels arrived days ago, so this was a grand surprise.

Reading letters from home is a reverent matter, one demanding as much privacy as conditions will allow, for it is the closest thing to sharing intimacy with your beloved you can have over here. You drink in each sentence, sometimes each word, savouring the meaning. Some letters are reread a dozen times, as you squeeze out every last drop of meaning where you sense more meaning was intended than mere words can convey, or that she has dared express on paper.

But even so you ration yourself – one reading now and another reading later tonight, or maybe two tonight, if you are in a dry place where you can show a light. You are starved for love, but still you must be careful not to suffer from overexposure to its afterglow. This peculiarly subtle, self-imposed dehumanization process, for which you were entirely unprepared when you first arrived overseas, involves the forced forgetting of your beloved wife, the repression of your most tender and loving memories of her so as to retain your sanity. Through long practice this has become an almost automatic process, so different from those first few weeks of separation – when memories of those last days and hours before you parted were still fresh and vivid, and "forgetting" required an act of will almost as painful as the searing heartache and desire from which you were trying to escape.

There's a widely held belief that the Army Postal Corps each year holds up delivery of mail on this side of the Atlantic during the first part of December, letting it accumulate so as to make sure that everybody gets at least one letter just before Christmas. This may be a myth, since letters from home tend to bunch up at any time because of the peculiarities of the system, and frequently you've received on the same day four or five letters from your wife mailed days apart from Canada.

However, if they don't play games with the mail at this time of the year, they should. Mail matters a great deal at any time, but at this season it matters very, very much; particularly to those who have been away from home for years. This will be the fifth Christmas overseas for most of the Regiment. And for Lieut. Jack Bigg of Baker Troop, who arrived in Britain with 1st Division before Christmas 1939 as a gunner with the RCHA, it will be his sixth Christmas away from his beloved wife, Gladys, and his little daughter, Phyllis.

It was nice that everybody on your crew got mail for Christmas, and, as you press her little blue air letter to your nose to smell her Evening in Paris perfume before opening it, you find yourself hoping everybody back at the guns did too. But as your mind is forming the wish, you also know there is at least one who will receive nothing from his family: Gunner Morin (Joseph Jean Conrad Paul Henri), a batman in 2nd Battery. A friendly, outgoing, cheerful man, always whistling happily – strong, robust, blessed with seemingly boundless vigour – he never appears tired or out of sorts. And most of all he is a man sincerely concerned about the welfare of others.

It was he and he alone, who, when the Regiment was brought together last winter to live in Nissen huts at Monks Common near Horsham, Sussex, became aware that a new man, Gunner White-hawk, was suffering racial harassment. While this apparently was no more than mild slurs on his Indian heritage couched in barrack-room humour, no worse than other slurs being tossed about daily at other racial groups and individuals (frequently by members of minority groups themselves), it was nonetheless hurtful. And in bringing it to your attention, Morin suggested his competent friend would appreciate being invited to become your batman – a move that proved mutually beneficial.

How damnably unfair that this admirable, warm-hearted man, of all men, should not be getting mail from home; and not just at Christmas, but at any time, all because he'd volunteered for service in the Canadian Forces against the wishes of his stepfather. He came from a small place in Quebec, and when he'd enlisted on November 1, 1939, it seems his stepfather had sworn never to forgive him for volunteering to fight the war for *les anglais*, and even had forbidden his mother and other members of the family to write to him or send him parcels.

Typically, he'd never complained to you or anyone. One day when you'd offered him a cigarette, he'd told you he'd quit smoking; and when you'd asked if he'd done so for health reasons, he'd volunteered the story. Unlike everybody else, he never received smokes from home, and since he couldn't afford to keep himself supplied with English cigarettes, he'd been forced to bum from his pals. This of course had been much too embarrassing, so he'd quit.

Back at the guns a few days ago, on a cold, grey day preparing to snow, he went out of his way to come over to the 14th Battery position to look you up just after coming back from hospital. You recognized his friendly, vibrant, tenor voice, calling your name across a wide expanse of frost-whitened gorse before you recognized him, for he was wearing dark glasses. His greeting, always warm, was especially so. At first you ascribed it to the fact you hadn't bumped into each other for some time, but his effusive manner as he wrung your hand made it clear that for him at least this was in the nature of a reunion. Not aware that he'd been wounded and had been away for some time, you were forced to do some fancy footwork to cover up your ignorance when you asked him why he was wearing dark sunglasses on such a dark day, and he told you that he'd been blind for some time in hospital in England.

"You knew, of course, Captain, I'd been wounded?"

"Oh yes . . . yes, of course!"

"It was back in Normandy in August – just after Falaise."

"Ah yes . . . How stupid of me to have forgotten!"

"But of course there were many wounded that day."

"Yes, a great many."

"Twenty-six, I'm told – and four of the boys died . . ."

Of course – the smell of marigolds! Friardel on the way to Orbec: the heavy shelling of the churchyard – those damp and pungent flowers as you pressed your face down into that flowerbed beside the little stone house. The wagon lines (where Morin would have been) were particularly hard hit.

"But did I hear you correctly, Morin, that you actually were blind for a while?"

"Oh yes, Captain, the doctors at the hospital in England said I'd never be able to see again. And when the nurse told me they were going to ship me back to Canada, she said they had applied for a seeing-eye dog for me. But one morning I think I see a little bit of light – and I call the nurse and tell her, 'I think I see a little bit of light.' She says that is most unlikely – that perhaps I am mistaken, and not to get my hopes up. But she goes and gets the doctor, and when he removes the bandages and shines a bright light into my eyes, I tell him, 'The light is so bright it hurts.' And he says he thinks I am right – that my eyesight is coming back. They move me into a dark room, and every day they let in a little more light. Finally I get that I can see everything, and then they give me these dark glasses to wear and move me out into the ward with everybody else. But when I ask them when can I go back to my regiment, they tell me, never. They say it is a miracle that my sight has come back at all, that my eyes are so delicate they must never again be exposed to bright light, and I will have to wear dark glasses during daylight for the rest of my life. And because the risk of losing my dark glasses, or having them broken in action, is so great, I am being sent home to Canada."

"But Morin," you protest, "you're still here?"

"Next day I get the nurse to bring me my clothes, and to allow me to get up and walk around a bit – in preparation, I say, for leaving for Canada. That night I climb out through the window of the hospital and start hitchhiking back to the Regiment."

"But why," you ask, "when you know you are running such a great risk? You were safely out of it – why didn't you go home? You could have gone back to Canada with honour – you'd done your share."

For a moment he looks at you in bewilderment that you, of all people, should have to ask: "But, Captain, all my friends are here in the Regiment."

Down in your little dug-out, sharing a piece of Christmas cake and a couple of drams of Scotch with him and his pal Whitehawk, listening to them compare notes and bring each other up to date, you come to realize the full significance of his declaration.

You know this modest, self-effacing man would explode into uproarious laughter if anyone were to suggest he is a hero for just being here, carrying on like thousands of others. But for you, he is and always will be one of the truly admirable, courageous men of this war.

Comparing your situation with his at the time of enlistment, you come off rather badly. Within your family and the society in which you were raised, it would have been very difficult, if not impossible, to remain a civilian. While no one ever said anything, the pressure to enlist had been there from the hour war broke out. But Morin knew as he volunteered to go and fight for his country that he not only faced the possibility of disablement or death, he risked being ostracized by his own family. And now, when he could have gone home, he hitchhiked back to the Regiment, wearing dark glasses!

34

THE TOXIC BREW THAT
SICKENS THE MIND

✻

ANTICIPATING THEY WOULD BE IN THE LINE FOR CHRISTMAS, all three infantry battalions of 4th Brigade held their Christmas dinners a few days early – the Royals four days ago, not as a battalion affair, since no accommodation of suitable size was available, but as company dinners.

Their special Christmas rations, which you assume the gunners will also enjoy when they attend dinners in two shifts, half at noon today and half at noon tomorrow, Christmas day, included canned turkey and cranberry sauce, fruitcake and Christmas pudding, oranges, apples, and an issue of canned beer.

This you know only because you happened to visit Bob Suckling for a mug of seasonal cheer just as his D Company was preparing to hold their dinner in a convent billets. It was only December 20, but as you stood with Bob, just inside their kitchen door out of the way of the nuns and soldier cooks, sipping your whisky from a delicate glass – now and then enshrouded in clouds of steam full of the most delicious odours of things you'd almost forgotten existed – it was suddenly, truly Christmas morning as you remembered the special atmosphere of such mornings in other times.

It may have been the way the nuns bustled about with supplies of civilized cutlery and plates, fine tablecloths and candles, reminding you of the bustling about of other ladies on other Christmas mornings, that gave substance to the illusion.

In every possible way they were trying their best to ensure the occasion would be memorable for the soldiers – something the Mother Superior guaranteed for you and Bob at least, when, in her hesitant English, she remarked, "How nice to hear the boys singing their songs of Christmas!" as she passed the cooks of D Company attending their burners in the snowy courtyard and singing lustily: "Roll me over in the clover – roll me over, lay me down, and do it again!"

Bob had pressed you to stay and share dinner with them, and you'd been sorely tempted, but knowing that the turkey was rationed at four ounces per man, it would have been criminal to accept. But the illusion that it was Christmas day persisted, and undoubtedly accounted for a rare bout of homesickness that night, which took the miserable form of feeling trapped, shut off from everyone you hold dear.

Normally you are not inclined to chafe under the confining rules of military dictatorship, though they are real enough, with most of your choices of movement, action, dress, words, and manners (even facial expressions) restrained by the whims, orders, and decrees of others, fully authorized by rules and regulations ascribed to the Monarch himself, and carrying the full force of law. These matters have been the very fabric of life as you have known it far too long to cause you any concern. After all, it was of your own free will, and for the very best of reasons, you voluntarily exchanged your wide-ranging civilian freedom for the peculiar imprisonment of a service uniform in wartime. From the first hour of enlistment you have been conscious that until your service ends, you are restricted to whatever part of the globe the army cares to post you, that your comings and goings must be accounted for every hour of the day and night, that you cannot travel any distance from your unit without an authorized pass, and that you must not expect to recross the Atlantic and see your home again until this war ends.

All of this has long since been accepted by you and everyone else over here, and arouses no unmanageable feelings of resentment throughout most of the year. However, at Christmas, the traditional time for families to gather to share in the seasonal joy, the rigid constraints of the cold-hearted military, shutting you away from home and loved ones in Canada even to the extent of prohibiting you the use of the trans-Atlantic telephone for the duration, can suddenly become a suffocating burden of cruel bondage.

Fortunately homesickness is an infrequent visitor, for it is absolute torture when the insidious forces of sweet, poignant memories, and the desire to hug and be hugged in love once more in the bosom of your family, combine – as they did four nights ago – to form the toxic brew that sickens the mind, body, and soul; that cannot be willed away, but must pass in slow agony through diminishing levels of melancholia, leaving you hung-over in an aching void for hours or even days.

You and Whitehawk had settled down in your bunks for the night in your cosy dug-out at the guns, rereading letters from home and listening to Christmas carols broadcast by the sugar-voiced "Mary of Arnhem" spilling from the big earphones of the little 38-set hanging on a nail at the head of the bunks. Somewhere between "Hark! The Herald-Angels Sing," "Joy to the World!" and "O Little Town of Bethlehem," you succumbed to a flood of warm, glowing memories, memories going back through her shining eyes on Christmas Eve 1939, when you gave her your engagement ring beside the blazing hearth at your family home.

Once unlocked, memories swirled out of the treasury of the years in heart-smothering vividness – memories of old love-filled houses, always overheated on Christmas Eve for the sake of little, bare feet creeping down the dark stairs before dawn to see what Santa had left at the tree.

As during other pre-Christmas bouts with homesickness, you've done your best to suppress the effects of memories too vividly recalled, by telling yourself how lucky you are compared to Russians facing their fourth winter battling the Germans in the cruel snows of the Eastern Front, or those poor guys captured at Dieppe in 1942, including twenty-two from the Regiment, spending their third Christmas in a Heinie prison camp. And, dammit, you are still alive and whole, in mind and body, which, in the face of the awful casualties in Normandy and along the Scheldt, is something you should be grateful for.*

Still, such efforts to divert your thoughts from Christmases past are only partially successful, for deep within you there smoulders a craving to live again those shining memories, even if it means being left with an aching heart and damp eyes. Nor does the prospect of spending Christmas in an OP help, and as you climb up inside the frigid windmill tower this morning, you simply can't resist feeling sorry for yourself. Thus, when, soon after settling down on the frost-laden cushions in the cupola, you get a message to report back to the Colonel at Brigade Headquarters, prepared to spend Christmas eve and Christmas day at their imposing Swiss-style chalet hidden deep in the bush west of Groesbeek, you respond with undisguised enthusiasm.

---

* By December 31, 1944, the Canadians in Northwest Europe had suffered 30,719 casualties. The severity of 2nd Division casualties from July 11 to December 31 – 11,875 in five and a half months – is brought into focus when placed against 3rd Division's 11,575 with a month more service, and the 10,586 suffered in eighteen months by 1st Division, involved in some of the harshest fighting of the war in Sicily and Italy. By war's end, though in action only ten months, 2nd Division's 15,493 casualties exceeded all other Canadian divisions. Of course the bulk of these were infantry casualties: 13,051 in ten months, compared to 3rd Division's 12,315 in eleven months, and 1st Division's 11,262 in nineteen months (allowing for a month's travel time from the Italian front to Holland in the spring of 1945). Armoured units suffered fewer casualties: 4th Armoured Division, 4,592; and 2nd Armoured Brigade, 1,077.

35

JERRY CAROLS, THEN
SHELLS TANNENBAUMS

✳

THERE WILL BE SOME IN THE NIJMEGEN SALIENT WHO WILL
remember Christmas 1944 as a day when a truce of sorts existed
along their part of the line. During the morning, 4th Brigade
Headquarters receives reports from the Royals that some forward
positions hear Germans in nearby trenches singing carols. And
over on 3rd Division front, Lieut. Donald Pierce, with a platoon
of the North Nova Scotia Highlanders, on a dike half a mile from
the misty Rhine, will record in his journal that will one day
become a book:

Not a sound anywhere, not a shot. I have a strong sense of being
able to see silence. The river, which is clearly visible beyond the
icy fields, bearing a few floating branches, and the snowflakes
that are rather idly falling, are the only things with any motion. A
few minutes ago I was sure I could hear the snowflakes dropping
onto my battle jacket. A shout would carry for miles. I have
never seen such stillness. I wonder if it's the same along the entire
front? Up here both sides seem to have decided to call everything
off, as though this day were beyond the war.*

---

* From *Journal of a War* (Toronto: Macmillan Co. of Canada, 1965).

However, others only a few miles away will remember this day as one of violence with little seasonal charity being shown by either side. Sgt. Hunt, in 26th Battery Command Post at the harassing-fire position among the snowy *tannenbaums*, will report in his diary: "Air full of such exchanges as are in order between us and friend Hun. We appear to be giving more than getting, and the extent of our seasonal rejoicing is limited to the difference. Even so, Jerry lays down a heavy concentration on Easy Troop, which despite its density results in only one casualty."

Logging the same incident, Sgt. McEwan, of Easy Troop, implies a generous amount of good cheer of some potency has been passed around among 4th Field drivers Christmas morning: "Jerry threw over a few 88s, and Sgt. Morley Stokes was wounded in the leg. After a hectic ride back to the MO, during which the wounded man threatened to drive the vehicle himself, he was removed to the Casualty Clearing Station on his way to hospital."

Then back at the wagon lines, just before noon, Jerry sends over more 88s, seriously wounding Gunner Leon Batke and "drawing blood" from Gunner Ken Brock. Brock is just about to climb aboard his gun tractor to drive a load of fellow drivers over to RHQ for Christmas dinner when the first 88 arrives and he is struck by a fragment.

Being wounded is never a laughing matter, but Brock succeeds in breaking up those who come to his aid, when, as he is being carted off for medical treatment, growls: "The dirty bastards have done me out of my Christmas dinner!"

And when you hear the story, you know exactly how Brock feels, and you fully appreciate his sentiments, because those same "bastards," indirectly, but just as effectively, are in the process of cheating you out of what was to be a legendary feast at 4th Brigade, an event to which you have been looking forward with a degree of anticipation that only a man who has not seen a Christmas dinner since 1941 can develop.

When, the night before last, December 23, 4th Brigade moved back into the line, and you had to go up to occupy an OP, it looked

like you might miss Christmas dinner for the third year in a row —
thus setting some sort of record in view of the importance the
powers-that-be, both military and political, attach to the matter of
seeing "the boys" have at least one good meal a year.

The first Yuletide dinner you missed was back in 1942 at
Barnham Junction. Just as your 26th Battery was about to sit down
to a festive board in the village hall, you were sent off in a Jeep to
collect some British ack-ack blokes on isolated gun sites around
Tangmere and Ford airfields, and deliver them to a dinner at regimental headquarters. So well-camouflaged were their gun sites,
hidden behind high thorny hedges in far-off corners of fields, that
by the time you delivered them, and got back to your own meal at
Barnham, there wasn't even a spoonful of gravy left. So it had been
fried bully beef hash in the deserted kitchen of the officers' mess.

Christmas Day 1943 topped even that sad tale, when, designated
duty officer for the day, you were stuck alone and forgotten in the
deserted regimental office, waiting in vain for someone to bring
you dinner. Regimental Clerk Sgt. George Lloyd had been with
you, but you'd sent him off to have his dinner, from which he did
not return.

Bemused by the merrymaking sounds of a roaring party in the
sergeants' mess that could be heard now and then through the walls
of the Nissen hut, you'd gone on waiting for someone to relieve
you, or at least to bring you some food. However, not until mid-
afternoon did a good Samaritan, in the guise of longtime buddy
Lieut. W. G. "Sink" Sinclair, arrive with a deck of cards, a cribbage
board, two glasses, and a bottle of gin — but no food, of course.

So, when yesterday morning the co called you back to take over
for him at Brigade so he might participate in a regimental carol and
communion service at midnight, and be present at the two Christmas
dinners scheduled for Rusthuis — half the unit on Christmas Eve and
half today — it seemed the gastronomic gods were at last about to
smile on you. Before taking leave of you, the co made it clear you
were in for a real treat, explaining that Brig. Cabeldu decided a
month ago that Christmas dinner 1944 at 4th Brigade Headquarters

would be, for those lucky enough to partake of it, their most memorable meal since leaving home. He had even sent his Belgian liaison officer, who was an Antwerp wine-exporter in peacetime, to the south of France to select and bring back an exotic range of the finest vintage wines his educated palate could locate.

Thus the staggering impact of the news at noon today, just as you join others assembling for a predinner drink: the meal is off – not postponed, but *off*! It is unbelievable, until it is explained that 3rd Division has been ordered to take over this front, so that 2nd Division can become a mobile force to deal with an imminent airborne attack related to the Battle of the Bulge on the American front in the south. According to Dutch Underground sources, a German airborne division is poised to strike a blow in front of Von Rundstedt's spearheads, driving with astonishing speed through the Americans towards the Meuse (as the Maas is known in Belgium) – their ultimate objective Antwerp, cutting off the British and Canadian armies in Holland.

Though 3rd Division units will not move in until dark, it will take all afternoon to load the Brigade vehicles because of the tedious procedure laid down to prevent enemy air reconnaissance from discovering the chalet is an important headquarters. Only one vehicle at a time will be brought to the front steps for loading, and it must follow the track through the snow made by its predecessor.

While this preserves a single set of innocent-looking tracks in the snow, the pale winter sun is going down before all Brigade Headquarters vehicles are loaded and parked with motors shut off under the trees along the road in front of the chalet.

Now, as long, dark shadows form in the snow-filled woods, you receive a message from the Brigade Major, Jim Knox, to join him and Brig. Cabeldu in his command caravan up ahead, prepared to arrange diversionary fire, as it may be required during the turnover of battalions. As you head up past the line of vehicles towards the rear door of the big caravan, the first of the 3rd Division vehicles begin to arrive at the chalet.

From the raucous shouting back and forth among their drivers, as they crowd their vehicles helter-skelter into the area in front of the chalet creating a minor traffic jam, it's pretty obvious they haven't allowed their move over here to interfere with having their full share of Christmas cheer – in whatever form it may have been presented.

Big flakes of snow are beginning to drift down as you mount the steps to the door of the van. Inside an officer shifts over on one of the padded benches that line both sides, so you can sit down facing the Brigadier. There are no lights on in the van at the moment, for the blackout curtains on the windows are still open, but it's nice and warm, and very quiet and very civilized. Even the normal radio garbage that continually spews out of the earphones of the signallers, two of whom can be seen sitting behind a glass partition at the front end of the van, is very subdued.

No one is talking. Everybody seems fascinated with what is going on out there among the newcomers. And what they can observe leaves them speechless. With none of the ebullient 3rd Division crowd showing the slightest concern, the pristine single set of tracks leading to the door – so tediously preserved by 4th Brigade at the sacrifice of their gourmet dinner with wines of matchless vintage – has already disappeared under an intricate maze of tell-tale tracks from the clutter of vehicles filling the whole of the snow-covered circular space in front of the chalet.

The Brigadier stands up to look, but immediately, as though he can't stand to watch it, he waves his hands together to have the blackout curtains closed. This allows for a gas lantern to be lit and hung from the ceiling, and the van turns into quite a cosy little room. You wish a conversation would start, but the initiative is clearly up to the Brigadier, and he chooses to remain silent, staring down at the floor, concerned, you suppose, with what could happen to his battalions on their way out of the line.

As you study his face as he sits frowning down at his feet, you try to imagine the cumulative effect of the awful strain on the minds and souls of men of high command whose orders continually place the lives of hundreds at risk, and who, more than anyone else, must be eternally conscious of the awesome numbers of their brigade, or division, or corps, who didn't make it through to Christmas.

You become conscious of the muffled voice of a signaller on the other side of the glass panel talking into his mike, repeating weird code names as he writes down a message. Sliding open the glass, he hands the paper out to the Brigade Major. Decoded, it means two companies of the Royals are safely out of the line.

As more and more reports come through of an orderly turnover without incident, the atmosphere in the caravan noticeably relaxes. Behind the glass the signallers start to sing in harmony:

"Si-lent night – Ho-ly night – all is calm – all is bright . . ."

The Brigadier looks up frowning quizzically. Then, as though suddenly remembering what day it is, in a wondering voice he exclaims:

"My God, gentlemen, it's Christmas night."

No one says anything; everyone is too deeply immersed in his own thoughts. Even the Brigade Major, who always seems capable of coming up with a suitable comment of a reassuring nature when the Brigadier expresses himself, is now totally possessed by his own reveries.

Soon the changeover of brigades is reported complete and you are released to return to your own vehicle to get ready to move out.

As you walk back past pine trees laden with snow, now falling steadily and mercifully to cover the messy lacework of vehicle tracks around the front yard of the chalet, you recall with a pang snowy winter nights like this in Canada shared with your beloved, such as a memorable sleigh-ride to Teskey's dance hall at Hog's Back outside Ottawa. You can almost smell the hot chocolate and hear the joyful bantering over the booming jukebox. Colin Ross, the Royals' Scout Platoon officer, was on that sleigh ride. You must remember to ask him some time if he remembers.

Oh, God, how you envy Major Bill Carr, who was notified yesterday he is to return immediately to Canada for a staff job in Ottawa!

36

MORE FUN THAN
A BARREL OF OYSTERS

❋

THE DAY AFTER CHRISTMAS 4TH FIELD IS ORDERED TO SAY goodbye to the cosy dug-outs on which so much effort has been lavished, and move north three kilometres to new positions in the frozen land, where empty boxcars – draughty, frigid, and smelly – sitting in the drifting snow of a railway siding, are considered prime billets, coveted by all but the few who gain their barren possession. Two days later, with snow lying thick on the ground, the guns are deployed in battle positions two kilometres southeast of there.

And then on December 30, with the sun going down on what feels like the frostiest evening of the winter, the Regiment moves off in convoy to travel some fifty miles south to Boxtel, halfway between Eindhoven and 's-Hertogenbosch, where the German paratroopers are expected to drop in aid of their armoured spearheads driving through the Yanks towards Antwerp, which already have created on Allied maps an ominous bulge.

All night you follow a truck with white smoke pouring out of a stovepipe protruding out the back between the canvas flaps. Riding in your open steel bucket, your envy of the occupants of that truck, warmed by a coal-burning stove hidden within, rises with each passing hour. The trip, over ice-glazed roads, takes seven hours, and at one halt, when you try to climb out to relieve yourself and have a smoke, you find you are too stiff to make it over the side without help from your driver, Gunner "Palm" Knight. Only with the greatest difficulty are you able to undo the necessary buttons, and without his help you cannot secure a cigarette and light it. Though he too rides in the open front cockpit, separated from the hot engine box against which the signallers keep warm, his blood is kept moving by his driving exertions.

When at last the Regiment arrives at Boxtel and disembarks at a school, which is a medical college when in use, marvellously over-heated with steam coils, the like of which you haven't encountered since leaving Petawawa, it is as though you have arrived in heaven. Your body drinks in the heat, and when told you must sleep in your clothes (the Regiment being on four hours' notice and FOO crews on one-hour notice) you go to sleep with a complete sense of luxury.

As the first day of 1945 dawns frigid and misty, 4th Field, along with 4th Brigade and the rest of 2nd Division, is held out of action, but in a high state of readiness. Recce parties are out at dawn plotting the defence of Tilburg and a nearby airdrome. The rest have no duties.

While some brave souls take the opportunity to borrow skates from Dutch residents skating merrily on the frozen moat of a nearby castle, you and most others are quite content, after that marrow-freezing ride last night, to drowse away the day inside the warm school.

However, this delicious prospect is nipped in the bud by orders from above that troop route-marches are to be held "to enliven the spirit and bring tone to the muscles" of all below the rank of major. (Why majors and up don't require enlivening of the spirit and muscle toning is not explained.) Thus it happens that at 9:00 A.M. almost every worthwhile member of 4th Field is outdoors moving in various directions among the narrow streets of Boxtel to witness, at least in part, the swan song of the Luftwaffe.

The streets are glazed with a thick coating of ice, guaranteeing there is more slipping and sliding than marching. Remaining upright while making discernible forward progress demands not only acute mental alertness but more than a little acrobatic ability. Thus no one shows much interest in the succession of fighter planes scudding in from the east over the rooftops and disappearing in the early morning mists. All are too busy trying to maintain their footing on the glassy cobblestones of a confined street that echoes and re-echoes with the clattering and scraping of hobnailed boots finding it impossible to keep in step. Then one plane, circling leisurely over the village, attracts attention when it banks very low, just above the street.

For a split-second you find yourself looking right into the eyes of the pilot. Then, just as your unbelieving eyes spot the German cross on the side of the plane, somebody yells: "It's a Jerry!"

And you shout: "Take cover! Take cover!"

This is easier said than done. Even when, slipping and sliding, all manage to make it up over the curb, the only cover available is in the shallow doorways of the old stone buildings that line the street cheek by jowl, forming a solid wall tight against the narrow sidewalk abutting the vehicular road. Mighty poor cover if Jerry returns and strafes the street. Fortunately he doesn't. And you are left wondering whether the swarm of planes you hear in the distance, periodically whining and stuttering, are German. And what are the implications?

In the afternoon you hear that the Allied tactical air forces based in Western Europe have been put out of action by German fighters simultaneously attacking all the mist-shrouded airfields in Holland, Belgium, and France this morning. Flying down on the deck, to avoid radar detection, they caught squadrons totally unprepared.

Weather conditions being so poor, few standing patrols were up over any of the airfields at the time; and hangovers from New Year's Eve partying had not enhanced the speed of response to the raids.

Those enemy fighter planes curling leisurely over Boxtel this morning were obviously getting their bearings before going into a slashing attack on the airdrome near Eindhoven. The attack lasted only twenty-two minutes but created chaos resulting in many deaths and in the destruction of dozens of Spits and Typhoons still sitting on the ground.*

Eindhoven, you recall, is the base of a Spitfire pilot posted for a couple of days over Christmas to 4th Brigade Headquarters to learn firsthand what war on the ground is like for the troops he is supporting. A most pleasant chap, he'd told you he cherished a dream of leading a crusade for seatbelts in automobiles in Canada after the war, convinced seatbelts in Spitfires saved his life twice when his planes pranged and were complete write-offs. While his idea sounds like a pipe dream, he was so very earnest in his desire to see car seatbelts brought into universal use, you hope he made it through those grim attacks this morning.

At the New Year's "at home" thrown by the officers of 4th Field in an improvised mess here at 4:00 P.M., with all the senior officers of 4th Brigade, including their Brig. Fred Cabeldu, in attendance, the devastating German fighter attack is a topic of lively discussion, second only to the sensational trays of oysters on the half-shell passing to and fro among the astonished guests.

All of this, of course, is entirely hearsay since you – along with several other officers of commendable initiative but no experience in and even less talent for opening oysters – are closeted in the scullery, chopping notches in oyster shells and prying open an endless number of the gnarled darlings from a seemingly bottomless

---

* Ten Luftwaffe fighter groups, consisting of nearly one thousand aircraft from more than thirty-eight German airdromes, some of them two hundred miles from their targets, converged on sixteen forward Allied airfields in Holland, Belgium, and France at precisely 0920 hours New Year's morning, 1945, and with cannon and rocket fire attempted to destroy parked aircraft and vital ground installations. Total Allied losses were 46 airmen killed and 241 aircraft put out of action, 130 of them totally destroyed. But in gaining this victory the Luftwaffe suffered irreparable losses: more than 300 planes and 253 of their most experienced pilots.

barrel in a losing struggle to maintain supply in some semblance of balance with demand.

Junior officers, who go forth to pass around the trays of the bivalve mollusks, report a smash hit, that this "at home" will go down in history as the most remarkable of all time. Which is all very nice if you can open the obstinate critters.

Secretly you curse the unique initiative of Lieut. Jack Bigg (Baker Troop Leader) and Capt. Ted Adams (Fox Troop), who, appalled at the prospect of corned beef sandwiches being served at a 4th Field reception, took off at dawn this morning to South Beveland to rake the oyster beds shown on the map. And then on their way back added further lustre to their glittering reputations as master scroungers, when they "borrowed" a barrel of rum that somehow tipped off a loading dock of a British supply depot into their passing Jeep.

Strange carryings-on for two ex-RCMP constables, you might say. But then anyone who knows their story is aware that Adams and Bigg, buddies ever since they conspired to get themselves kicked out of the RCMP in the fall of 1939 so they might join "C" Battery 1st Field RCHA in Winnipeg as gunners in time to sail for England before Christmas, are not men to stand on ceremony. Denied by their superiors the right to enlist in anything but the Provost Corps when Canada went to war, they simply revealed they were both married men, which in the eyes of the RCMP constituted an unforgivable misdemeanour before a constable completed at least five years with the force.*

---

* The RCMP did not forgive Captain John Bigg for marrying without permission. At war's end, on returning to the force, he was treated as a rookie, assigned to opening doors on Parliament Hill and posing in his scarlet tunic, breeches, riding boots, spurs, and all, for pictures with American tourists. Later, with some satisfaction, he returned to Parliament Hill, as the Member for Athabaska, to serve seventeen years with the Diefenbaker government and after.

But, damn their eyes, you wish today they'd scrounged some chickens or a suckling pig – something not requiring shelling. Just about the time you decide that before you go mad you must have a change of pace, and are preparing to go out among the guests to pass your own tray – a great, round affair you have just finished loading with a mass of glistening oysters on half-shells on a thick bed of ice garnished with seaweed – into the kitchen comes one of the newer subalterns, Lieut. J. L. McLean, begging you to allow him to take the tray and serve the Colonel and the 2 IC who are at that moment talking to Brig. Cabeldu.

While his weird reasoning that the moment is propitious for him to become a waiter – that serving oysters with élan to the Brigadier and the Colonel will somehow get him out of the doghouse in which he is presently residing – makes no sense whatsoever, his begging is so pitiful and your present mood so sour, it strikes you this pioneering experiment in "sucking-up" might provide some fresh insight into human relations.

From the half-open swinging door, you watch as he staggers towards the little group of distinguished officers in the centre of the room, carrying high over his head your carefully arranged great tray of oysters, seaweed, and ice. Just as he reaches them he seems to fumble the tray as he is lowering it to a presentable level, and dumps the entire mess on the head and down the front of the Brigadier.

Feeling a twinge of conscience, you make for the unfortunate subaltern as fast as you can. As you are passing the 2 IC, he snarls:

"Get him out of here, and place him under close arrest!"

When you come up behind him, he is engaged in picking seaweed off the chest of the Brigadier – pawing away with all the delicacy of a nearsighted bear. For a moment, as you take hold of his arms to turn him around, you really feel sorry for him, for it seems he's crying in boyish anguish, horrified at what he's done. But then you realize those strange moaning sounds he is making are unsuccessful attempts to suppress laughter! And as he turns to come away with you, he breaks into such a fit of laughing, it stops the last remnants of polite, covering conversation still being attempted.

"Oh, my gawd," says he in a hoarse, gurgling whisper that can be clearly heard in the farthest corner of the now attentive room, as you steer him to the hallway door, "Did you see the seaweed in his hair?"

In other days of other COs and CRAs, such conduct would have been enough to write finis to a potentially illustrious military career. But current senior officers must have a sense of humour. Not only does Lieut. McLean survive, he's posted as a liaison officer to Brig. Frank Lace's staff at Division.*

For five days the Regiment marks time with lectures and troop deployments, while the senior officers work on operation orders to cover every possible emergency deriving from enemy parachute landings. Then on January 6 a regimental parade is held to watch Brig. Lace present four brave men with Commander-in-Chief Certificates: Gunner Art Harder, Bombardier M. E. Jeffery, Lance-Bombardier J. W. Schneider, and Signals Corps Lance-Cpl. Priest, attached to RHQ.

Next day, the threat of an enemy parachute landing having faded, the Regiment returns to the Nijmegen salient, with everybody looking forward to getting back into their snug old dug-outs. But before this happens, the guns are deployed elsewhere in the snowy bush, and the gunners have to make the best of what they can find. Some get billets in houses, but most have to make do in nearby boxcars or in the poor-excuses-for-dug-outs left by 12th Field.

---

* Still, a unique penalty for overindulgence was devised by Brigadier Lace to rein in the ebullient McLean. At war's end 2nd Division Headquarters was in a beautifully preserved stone castle (Godens Schloss, near Oldenburg) complete with portcullis, drawbridge, and moat. When McLean had you up for dinner, he sorrowfully told you he'd been "put on the wagon" and warned that if he fell off, he'd have to mount the battlements in his best serge, complete with Sam Brown, and dive into the moat among the lilypads and frogs. Of course the inevitable happened, and he took the plunge in full view of the CRA and staff.

The day the Regiment moves back into the old positions behind Groesbeek, January 11, your D Troop is ordered northwest of Nijmegen over many miles of ice-glazed dike roads to deploy two and a half miles southeast of the villages of Leeuwen and Druten near the Rhine, to support the rescue by motorized assault boats of a number of walking-wounded from the far shore who have been in hiding over there since the parachute drop at Arnhem failed last September. The operation is called "Heaps" after Capt. Leo Heaps, a survivor of the parachute landing, who persuaded the High Command that many wounded parachutists, including a "high-ranking officer" (Brig. John Hackett), left behind during the fast evacuation, could be brought back if his plan were followed.

During the day you remain out of sight at the HQ of Major D. G. Mackenzie's D Squadron, 7th Recce Regiment, in what normally would be the principal's office of a regular school that has been converted to a convent school by nuns whose convent was burned over their heads when the Polish armour took this area many weeks ago. At night you go down to where the assault boats are hidden in a brickyard near the water's edge, to watch for the signal that the refugees have arrived at the far bank (the flare of a Very light looping briefly in the black sky), at which time you are to start your diversionary shelling a mile to the left of where the assault boats are to land. Night after night you wait with Heaps and his boatmen in the cold windy darkness, but no signal comes, and after eight days your troop is ordered to rejoin the unit.*

---

* How Hackett and others, aided by the Dutch, eventually made it back over the Rhine is told in Leo Heaps's *The Grey Goose of Arnhem*, Paper-Jacks, Markham, Ontario, 1977.

37

A HELMET LEFT HANGING

ON A SNOWY CROSS

❋

IN A LAND THAT IS FROZEN SOLID MOST OF DECEMBER and January, and where a succession of blustery storms do their best to fill in all uncovered trenches with drifting snow, some OPs are just open holes dug into the forward slope of a hill and floored with straw or pine boughs to cover the muddy sludge that continually forms in the bottom from the body heat of their occupants. And when you rejoin the Regiment and the Rileys return to the line for two weeks, your OP is such a trench, almost lost among the deep undisturbed white drifts billowing across the brow of a sparsely wooded ridge rising 250 feet above the nearby Maas river's flood plain.

With no Rileys within sight or sound, it is a remarkably lonely spot, in distinct contrast to Battalion Headquarters down in the valley behind you, where each morning, as you pass on your way to the trail up the steep slope to your OP, a boisterous group, including their CO, Lt.-Col. Denny Whitaker, and your Battery Commander, Jack Drewry, make something of a Spartan ritual out of shaving and washing in the snowbanks among the pines – bare to the waist and steaming like walruses in the frosty, predawn grey light, some even engaging in roaring snowball fights as you go by.

But once beyond the range of their cheerful bantering, you hear no other human voice until you come back down this way again at dusk.

Sometimes when you climb up through the deep snow, threading your way between the young pines, about the size of Christmas
trees, and reach the crest of the hill, your trench has been so well
camouflaged by snowdrifts you are able to identify it only by the
Canadian steel helmet hanging by its web strap on a melancholy
wooden cross poking up in the snow. The solitary grave lies right
on the floor of the dog-leg entrance to a deep, well-constructed
trench constituting the OP, and you spend hours trying to imagine
how he was killed, starting with a jumping anti-personnel "S"-
mine (Schützenmine), in wide use around here.*

Or perhaps it was a mortar bomb? Or maybe a Jerry crept up and
heaved a grenade into the trench? But after days of considering the
matter, you are inclined towards the likelihood it was a sniper –
who right now could be lining up your head in his telescopic sights.

Because the weather is so cold and miserable, and you don't
really need a signaller up here with the telephone line laid right up
to the OP, you come up alone each morning. But with no one to
talk to, it does make for a long day, even with the few hours of daylight. Almost nothing is ever seen moving in the valley below you,
though it is reputed to be infested with German outposts.

On particularly cold days, when something piping hot at midday
would go down well, you recall that miraculous self-heating can of
oxtail soup they issued you on the ship coming to Normandy, and
wonder whatever became of the supply. If ever issued, it has been
creamed off by the rear echelons. Never once has your carrier crew,
or any infantry unit with whom you've served, received one can,
however much it would mean by way of nourishment for the body

---

* The much hated and feared "S" mine consisted of a canister of 350
ball-bearings packed with explosive, dug in the ground with only a
stubby neck, ringed with little prongs, showing. Brushed by a boot, a
broken prong triggered the canister to jump up about three feet above the
ground, exploding the charge and ball bearings.

and comfort for the soul to men shivering in the sodden, flooded polders of the Scheldt last fall, and now huddled in open trenches among the drifting snowbanks of Groesbeek and Mook.

Sitting for hours without moving, snuggled down in your flying jacket, worn under your windproof Don R coat, the cold air makes you intolerably drowsy. Now and then you go to sleep, which disturbs you greatly, for you have been around long enough to realize fully how vulnerable you are up here even when you are awake and alert – completely isolated, alone, and devoid of all infantry protection. But no matter how you lecture yourself, chainsmoke and eat boiled sweets to stay awake, you frequently doze off.

Once it is quite dark when you wake up, and for a brief moment you have to fight down panic when you try to stand up and remove yourself in haste from what has become a cold, dark tomb and find it impossible to walk, let alone walk quickly. With all your instincts tuned to flight, your muscles and joints are too stiff with cold to function. Mentally coaching yourself, you thresh your arms back and forth across your chest as strenuously as possible, while stomping your feet with all the vigour you can muster. At first the efforts of your arms and legs are so feeble, it's as though you are still dreaming. But shortly you become mobile enough to stumble, trip, and slide down the dark snowy trail to light and warmth and human companionship – not to mention scalding hot tea laced with rum.

Apart from being mildly curious, no member of your crew shows any sign of having been worried about you not appearing at last light. They'd just gone ahead and eaten supper, and for this you are entirely grateful, for on the way down, you'd been unable to invent a credible substitute for the truth. But when the current ongoing argument, as to whether any malt whisky could ever match a fine blended Scotch, peters out, and before the next argument begins, it occurs to your driver, Gunner "Palm" Knight, to ask what held you up.

Preparing to shade the truth, you take a deep breath, but before you can begin, Gunner Eugene Bowers – who handles the duties of

OP ack and likes to pose as the "elder statesman" on the crew to the continuing irritation of Knight – offers to bet any reasonable sum with anyone that you merely had fallen asleep.

This is an irresistible challenge to Knight, who, when back at the guns, allegedly runs an illegal "crown and anchor" casino, though this is yet to be proven, for, his unique round shack is built entirely of Groesbeek doors standing upright, and with all the door-handles still in place and only one door actually operating, a surprise raid is almost impossible when the snow is tamped down equally all the way around the structure. Before you can intervene, Knight has taken an even-money bet of 200 Belgian francs that you didn't fall asleep.

When finally they turn their attention to you, you can't help bursting into a fit of uncontrollable laughter. Your esteemed driver scowls, curses, and pays Bowers.

Each night you and your crew pass the hours of darkness in this small cave excavated by some previous crew in the side of the hill at a particularly steep part, not far from Battalion Headquarters. It is so snug and safe that each afternoon you normally have difficulty waiting until the light fades before trekking down the quarter of a mile or so through the snowy woods to the hot meal you know will be waiting for you.

The one and only serious drawback to life in this cave, whose structural stability is dependent on frost, is its proclivity to rain down drops of dirty water over everybody and everything whenever the combined heat of bodies, the Primus stove, and the gasoline lantern warms the air sufficiently to melt the frozen earth overhead. Whenever this occurs, the lantern has to be doused and the canvas door slung open until it cools down enough to solidify the ceiling again.

38

WINTER INTERLUDE

❋

WHILE NO FORWARD OBSERVATION POST COULD EVER qualify as entirely pleasant or comfortable, particularly in the swirling, bitter winds of what is rumoured to be the worst winter Holland has seen in the last fifty years, you are truly thankful when you again occupy the top floor of this tall black windmill in Groesbeek, where you lie on cushions on the floor and observe the zone through the open fan-window in the cupola.

They told you on the way up this time that enemy mortaring and shelling have cooled off considerably on the Groesbeek sector in recent weeks, and hopefully there won't be the same need for flash-spotting as last time. You sincerely hope they're right, for the air feels as though it's from the Arctic today as you climb up the old, steep, wooden stairs from floor to floor, up to the cupola housing the great wooden gears on the end of the windmill shaft.

It is so cold today, January 20, that when you try ranging on a house with a smoking chimney in no-man's-land, your first rounds fall noticeably short, something that has become a factor since the really cold weather arrived, with ranges increasing as the guns warm up. Recently, right after the guns were calibrated, a testing shoot on all guns, carried out by Ted Adams, Easy Troop commander, showed they fired on average fifty yards short when cold. However, that test must have been done on one of the less cold days, for you've witnessed drop-offs much more than that.

A deep silence lies over the whole front, broken only now and then by a creaking in the ancient wooden shaft of the mill as a gust of frigid wind tries to move the giant, skeleton vanes hanging motionless outside. Your signaller tries to write a letter, but he seems to spend more time blowing on his fingers to keep them from freezing.

Below the window on the snow-covered fields, sloping down into the valley and the German border, lie dozens of broken gliders. In front of the gaping mouth of one is an abandoned Jeep, and in another can be seen the bowed, helmeted heads of American soldiers machine-gunned as the glider landed four months ago.

Four out of every five days mist and fog reduce visibility to a couple of hundred yards. Today is a rare day – sunny and bright, and even colder than usual. They report from the guns that the ammunition thermometers register minus 14 degrees Celsius (4 degrees Fahrenheit).

Across the silent white valley, dotted here and there with lifeless farmhouses, the dark evergreen mass of the Reichswald frowns down from its ridge, mysterious and formidable – so dense and easily fortified it forms the lower bastion of the Siegfried Line.

Although battalions of Germans lie in wait out there, and you are certain that every farmhouse cellar shelters some of them, days go by without spotting a sign of life, though you sweep the valley with your field-glasses from dawn to dusk.

In all the weeks you've taken your turn in the observation posts along the Rhine and this ridge, the only movements you've seen have been some wisps of smoke from a couple of chimneys, a German Shepherd dog trotting between a house and a barn, and one distant German soldier running at full tilt a crazy pattern through the snow-covered open fields in the valley, disappearing and reappearing for more than half an hour, never once approaching one of the farm buildings or giving a clue to his mad venture.

Like the Germans, our infantry lie concealed all day in cramped, straw-floored slit trenches or, if they're lucky, in dug-outs or farmhouses, waiting patiently for hot food and drink to be brought up after dark.

But in spite of the discomforts and long periods of boredom, interspersed with brief periods of fear, morale generally remains at a reasonably high level, and there seems to be no limit to the ingenuity of men trying to make the most of what is available.*

Where conditions allow, such as back at the guns, dug-outs have been made unbelievably comfortable, with improvised stoves, bunks, and, in the case of 2nd Battery (thanks to the experience of pre-war Hydro lineman Signaller Jack Snowell and the advice of ex-Hydro foreman Sgt.-Maj. Ed Blodgett), electric light tied into a local power line.

Soldiers will work on a project for days, even if it's only trying to lure the sole surviving cow from a forward slope into a barn where it can be safely butchered. Others spend hours modifying their dress to conform to current fads.

For instance, it is currently fashionable among the gunners to cut the arms out of greatcoats and sew them into the armholes of leather jerkins, ever since the German camouflaged parkas, picked up back at Antwerp, were taken away from them, along with German vehicles and Schmeissers they'd acquired along the way. (The reason given by the brass was that you couldn't tell a Canadian

---

* Half a century later, Maisonneuve company commander Jacques Ostiguy would still be marvelling at the parachute-silk walls of the dugout his men secretly constructed as a surprise Christmas gift for him at the front near Groesbeek. Led after dark on Christmas Eve to his new two-room HQ (albeit two tiny six-by-six-foot rooms), Ostiguy was "overwhelmed" by the effect of the white silken walls, shimmering in the candle-light. Affection for his generous men – some of whom had been with him throughout Normandy and the Scheldt – shone through even as he tried to strike a critical note: "Those crazy guys! Imagine . . . risking their lives out in no-man's-land to secure parachutes discarded by American glider troops . . . for my dugout!"

from a German without a program, particularly at night when they both were using burp guns.)

After dark, the front comes to life. Rum rations and hot meals are brought up to the troops in the trenches in canisters, carried in wheelbarrows, baby carriages, or on children's sleighs – depending on the weather. Jerry, knowing this, starts dropping mortar bombs along the suspected supply routes.

Our guns open up periodically with harassing fire or diversionary fire to cover infantry patrols making their nightly, agonizing forays into the enemy lines to try to bring back prisoners and satisfy the curiosity of intelligence officers as to whether or not new German units are thickening up this sector in anticipation of our big spring offensive.

Patrol work by the infantry – when a few men, led by an NCO or a lieutenant, creep out into no-man's-land after dark seeking information on enemy locations and numbers, taking prisoners where possible, and now and then engaging in a shoot-out with an enemy outpost – is being carried out constantly all along this front.

Division and Corps seem to have an insatiable need to interrogate fresh prisoners. But prisoners are difficult to come by at any time through patrolling; to surprise an armed man in the dark of night and persuade him to surrender so he can be brought back alive will always remain a difficult feat. And along this front the enemy seems to have developed a high degree of alertness, reinforced by trip wires and trained guard dogs, making it next to impossible to surprise an outpost. With the continuing dearth of prisoners the pressure on all battalions to bring some in has grown.

Even when the big guns are silent, and there are no sputtering bursts of small-arms fire at suspected movement, Very lights rise and fall here and there over no-man's-land throughout the night.

Mail from home comes up with the rations to the forward troops at night, and parcels can be opened and contents enjoyed in the dark. But letters must wait for dawn, and sometimes they are never read when they are buttoned into the breast pocket of a battledress that goes out on patrol and doesn't make it back.

39

SOMETHING BIG AFOOT

--- ✳ ---

SOME TIME AFTER THE FACT YOU WILL LEARN FIELD MARSHAL
Montgomery, on January 21, 1945, issued a directive calling for converging attacks to clear the west bank of the Rhine between
Nijmegen and Düsseldorf, preparatory to crossing that great water
barrier and engaging the enemy in mobile war north of the Ruhr.
While no one at your lowly level will be privy to such precise information for some days yet, on the very afternoon of this directive,
you learn something very big is afoot from a brief, but extraordinarily intimate, contact with two famous corps commanders.

From early morning, cold drifting mists have blotted out most of
the valley. A heavy hoar-frost covers everything along the road
coming up the hill to the Groesbeek windmill: the trees, the bushes,
the stiff weeds sticking up through the snow at the side of the
pockmarked road. Even the broken power lines, drooping down to
the roadway from their shattered poles, are coated with a greyish-
white fuzz. On this frigid day the Generals choose to call, you are
up in the cupola of the mill, lying on mouldering chesterfield cushions rescued from a house in the village that has gradually been
chopped to pieces by the shells and mortar bombs dropping sporadically on this desolate place since shortly after the American paratroopers and gliders landed last September.

You recline beside the huge, wooden gears on the end of the windmill shaft, well back from the fan-light window, and the telescopic

sights of snipers or the field-glasses of artillery observers. Not that you have to worry about them today, for the whole valley is shrouded in a cold fog, which the pale winter sun has yet to burn away.

With your field-glasses you try to spot the Americans still sitting with heads bowed in one of the gliders, killed by a German machine-gun that raked their glider as they landed four months ago in the field, only a couple of hundred yards from the mill.

You doze off, but are awakened by the sound of boots thumping up the wooden ladders. When you open your eyes, you are staring at a familiar face under a black beret, barely above floor level, but rising as its owner ascends the last rungs.

With a gut-clutching shock you realize that face belongs to one Lt.-Gen. Guy Simonds, Commander of 2nd Canadian Corps. As you scramble up to salute as best you can in the confined circumstances, another head appears wearing a red-banded forage cap bearing the same rank badges as Simonds. For the moment you are unable to place this thin-faced, grey-haired officer who smiles at you so pleasantly as he scrambles up the last rungs of the ladder and immediately goes down on his knees beside Simonds on your cushions.

You hope the stern-looking Simonds didn't see you sleeping, for your excuse for slumbering, the fog, has now lifted. If he did, he gives no sign, as he requests to be "put on the ground," which consists mainly of your pointing out Kranenburg, Cleve, and the "saddle" along the left end of the Reichswald ridge, and relating each of these distinctive features to the map. The saddle area seems to excite the British Corps Commander for some reason, and in his discussions with Simonds refers to a prominent lump to the left of it as the "Nutterden Feature," as though its placement is of some consequence, and its speedy attainment of prime importance in future operations.

Suddenly you realize this pleasant Englishman, with whom you are literally rubbing shoulders as he waves his expressive hands about and gives expression to his thoughts with such erudition as to seem almost voluble beside the taciturn Simonds, has to be Lt.-Gen. Brian Horrocks, Commander of British XXX Corps, which from Normandy onwards seems always to have been on Canadian Army's right flank, when it wasn't driving for Brussels or the bridge that proved to be too far at Arnhem last Fall.

With growing fascination you watch as the two great field commanders, down on their knees on your dank and scruffy chesterfield cushions, sweep the palms of their hands over the maps and mention army corps and divisions – such and such a division here and another there – obviously planning a very big show.

In their desire to get a still wider view of the front they keep edging closer and closer to the fan-window, until finally you are obliged to warn them not to get too close, reminding them that you have to go on living here after they have gone.

Immediately they draw back, and Horrocks apologizes, remarking that it is most curious that the mill has been left alone by Fritz until now – at least it doesn't show any signs of having been hit by enemy fire. Have you any theories why?

You can only offer your old line: that the Germans must believe that no one in his right mind would occupy such an obvious observation post. But the suggestion amuses Horrocks, who with a roar of laughter slaps his leg and says, "You know, you are probably right!" Soon after that, they leave.

In the days that follow, the mill sees a steady stream of British brigadiers, colonels, majors, captains, and subalterns thumping up the stairs and ladders to the cupola to be "put on the ground."

This, of course, nourishes an old and continuing fear you have always harboured about the mill: that the enemy must come to notice any unusual amount of coming and going. This concern is apparently shared by the brass, for much care is taken by the visitors, and rigorous control is imposed on any movement in the area occupied by 2nd Canadian Division.

A Reconnaissance Report Centre is established at Grave, where all wanting to view the battlefield have to report. The number entering any particular area is controlled by a system of passes allowing them access to an OP for a definite period. And because English battledress is a lighter-coloured khaki, all British officers, before going forward where they might be under enemy observation, are outfitted with darker Canadian battledress. Adherence is ensured by sentries posted at intervals on access routes where passes must be shown.

Of course it has been clear to all at the guns for some time that a major push is being planned for this, the extreme northern end of the Western Front. The heavy ammunition-dumping program that began the second week of January – even as the daily allotment of shells for current firing continued to be strictly limited – would alone be enough to convince the gunners that something big is in the wind.

By January 16, 23,000 rounds were on 4th Field gun positions – a very respectable 958 rounds per gun. Now the complement of H.E. per regiment has been raised to 33,600 rounds, a figure unheard of even during the record-breaking firing back in Normandy about the Verrières Ridge – a staggering 1,400 rounds per gun, over and above first-line standing complement of 144 H.E., 16 smoke, and 12 armour-piercing solid-shot per gun.

This you learn from Col. Mac Young when he comes up to your windmill to study the zone in a remarkably detailed way, his curiosity spiked by sitreps (situation reports) from OPs in recent days that have been providing evidence Germans are being spotted more frequently than usual. Either they have become more careless or there are more of them out there to be spotted.

He asks you to point out every last spot you've seen enemy activity or detected signs of his presence, such as smoke rising from a chimney in daylight, which you noted a few days ago; where you've seen tracks through the snow between house and barn; and where you saw Spandau tracers coming out of nowhere one foggy morning, down the slope out in front near one of the derelict gliders.

And you have to establish for him the area where you heard the hollow *thunk* of a mortar firing, somewhere down behind houses along the road passing the distant graveyard, where a woman's coffin still rests above ground beside an open grave, just as it was abandoned by her mourners last September when the American gliders and paratroopers landed out there and the cemetery became part of no-man's-land.

As is his custom, the CO speaks very little, only when he seeks assistance in establishing a map reference of some spot of interest. But the way he stares for long periods through his field-glasses, it is as though he is charging to memory the complete layout of the valley and the ridge beyond for future reference.

If he knows the details of the upcoming operation, he chooses not to reveal them when you ask, but points out it would have to be a remarkable show to make use of the 33,600 shells now accumulating at every field artillery regiment position in the Nijmegen salient – including eighteen additional positions staked out for British regiments, which won't be occupied until a day or two before the big attack. Canadian arty units presently in position in the salient, including 4th Field, are having to unload and stash away the Brits' allotment as well as their own. When 4th Field gunners have finished digging in their 33,600 rounds, they'll be required to manhandle another 33,600 rounds onto a vacant position next to them staked out by an advance party of Brits.*

After the CO leaves, you amuse yourself calculating that each six-man 25-pounder gun crew will have moved more than eighty tons of earth and steel by the time they have completed manhandling 2,800 rounds (their own and the Brits') and dug a hole eighteen feet long, fifteen wide, and three feet deep to get their own 1,400 shells and cartridge cases below grade. Each ammunition pit will require

---

* Gen. Crerar provided the following illustration of the immensity of the stocks of shells of all calibres dumped in the salient: "If the ammunition allotment for the operation, which consists of 350 types, were stacked side by side, five feet high, it would line a road for thirty miles. Total ammunition tonnage provided from D-Day [February 8] to D-plus-three [February 11] would be equivalent in weight to the bomb drop of 25,000 medium bombers."

excavation by pick and shovel of thirty tons – thirty cubic yards at a ton per cubic yard of earth – while manhandling 2,800 shells and 2,800 cartridge cases (their own and their neighbours'), amounting to another 51.1 tons.

At a briefing today (February 6) you learn that the day after tomorrow First Canadian Army, with British XXX Corps under command, will push southeast from the Nijmegen salient, with the Rhine on its left and the Maas on the right, to clear Cleve and the Reichswald, after which there will be thrusts through rolling farming country dotted with villages, towards another forest – the Hochwald – and the town of Xanten some thirty miles distant.

The enemy front is supposed to be lightly held, but they will be fighting on their own soil for their own soil, and the main thrust of the attack must proceed through a confined corridor, no more than 5,000 yards wide between the rising floods of the Rhine polderland on the left and the dominating Reichswald ridge on the right, and in the process must surmount the strong outpost positions of the Siegfried Line, consisting of an anti-tank ditch, minefields, pillboxes, concrete gun emplacements, and barbed-wire entanglements.

Even Rhineland farmhouses are reputed to have been constructed especially for defence, with loop-holed walls and tremendously strong basements, consisting of interlocking, arched tunnels with cryptlike ceilings capable of withstanding the complete collapse of the upper storeys of the house. Towns and villages are reported to have been turned into fortress positions, and as in Normandy, defences have been constructed in depth. Some ten miles beyond the Reichswald, in front of the Hochwald, is another prepared line – the "Schlieffen Position."*

Clearly it will not be any walk-in. Fighting is bound to be more

---

* After Count Alfred von Schlieffen, nineteenth-century Prussian, whose theories of fast encirclement failed the Germans in the first days of World War I, for lack of mobile supply, but succeeded brilliantly in 1940.

severe than they would have you believe. However, victory is certain, for Allied forces are massive. For the operation Gen. Crerar's First Canadian Army will consist of some 450,000 men from thirteen divisions, nine of them British, and a vast array of Army troops – the largest force ever commanded by a Canadian. And two days after this attack goes in, February 8, Operation "Grenade," eighty miles to the south, will see 303,000 men of American Ninth Army start to cross the River Roer above Roermond, with the object of moving north along the Rhine to ultimately meet the Canadian Army driving south.

Montgomery is in overall command of these joint operations, which, as in Normandy, could lead to the destruction, between the closing jaws of two armies, of the last serious enemy resistance in the West. The plan is to catch the enemy on the west bank of the Rhine between the two armies and force him to choose between withdrawing over the river and setting up a defensive line on the east bank, or fighting to the bitter end on the west bank and ultimately losing all capacity to prevent an Allied crossing and headlong rush into the heart of Germany.

It is assumed that Hitler will require his troops to defend every metre of the Reich and that this will result in a final, bloody battle on this side of the Rhine, from which his forces on the Western Front will never recover. Not only national pride will motivate Hitler, and provide the incentive for his troops to fight on to the death to hold the west bank of the river. Strategically it is impossible for Germany to abandon the barge traffic on the river. The Rhine is the principal artery for the lifeblood of the industries of the Ruhr. Once Allied forces are in position to dominate the Rhine and entirely shut down all barge traffic, particularly that flowing to and from the mouth of the Dortmund–Ems canal halfway between Duisburg and Wesel, the German war machine must collapse.

Thus First Canadian Army, for the third time in the Allied campaign in Northwest Europe, is destined to play the crucial role in a pivotal operation having a significant bearing on the final course of the war – Operation Veritable.

The maps you've been issued for the invasion of Germany have been printed on the backs of maps of England, stored in the thousands by the Germans in a warehouse in Antwerp in 1940 for Operation "Sea-lion" (Hitler's code name for the invasion of Britain), across which the British map-makers, with a delicious sense of irony, have overprinted diagonally, again and again in satisfying repetition, "Cancelled." The ink on some of the maps is still damp enough to smudge. Some idea of the size and complications of the upcoming operations can be gained from the fact that half a million air photos and three-quarters of a million maps have been produced.

But to the gunners, the size and importance of an operation is best indicated by the build-up of ammunition, and no one has seen such mountainous deliveries of shells since Normandy. All of it has to be on gun positions before dawn February 3 so that the roads will be free for guns, tanks, and troops to move up on the last four nights before the attack. And it seems the deadline is met.

In less than two weeks more than three-quarters of a million shells have been accumulated at gun positions – 633,160 of them just to take care of the opening tasks by 1,034 guns and howitzers ranging from 20-pound missiles to 360-pound monsters.

And a further 120 lorry-loads of ammunition have been brought up for 446 more weapons (40-mm Bofors, 75-mm tank guns, 17-pounder anti-tank guns, 4.2-inch mortars, and medium machine-guns) assigned to "Pepperpot" concentrations to beat on enemy infantry and gun positions with such intensity and duration as to convince the enemy that to move above ground would be suicide.

During recent weeks only the normal traffic of 2nd Canadian Corps has been allowed to move on roads in this part of the salient in daytime. All other vehicles require special passes. But when darkness falls, many thousands of vehicles come out of hiding, filling the roads almost nose to tail as they work their loads to designated dumps.

Space has become precious, and so jammed together are the new gun positions, they encroach on each other and on existing gun positions. The Regiment will share its position with a British field regiment – 48 guns in an area no more than 600 yards wide and less than that deep. And directly behind a medium outfit will deploy. This "integration" of positions, you're told, will help to camouflage the fact new regiments are being added.

The Brits were allowed to start bringing in their guns only three nights ago (February 4) so as to reduce to a minimum the time the enemy might have to gain advance notice by air reconnaissance of the buildup. Since then, however, nights have been filled with the muffled sounds of mass movements of lorries and quads dragging guns onto positions.*

To "camouflage" the location of the offensive, 4th Armoured Division (with British commandos under its command) was ordered to wipe out a bridgehead the Germans held over the Maas, forty miles west of Groesbeek. Known as Operation Elephant, it was supported by the field guns of 4th Division, the Polish Division, the 19th Army Field Regiment, the 90th Field Regiment RA, along with mediums and heavies of 4th British AGRA. For the field guns alone, 56,000 rounds of H.E. and 33,500 of smoke were provided. Starting on the bitterly cold morning of January 26, it was to take only a few hours. It took five days and cost 236 casualties (mainly to the Lincoln and Welland Regiment and Argyll and Sutherland Highlanders) while inflicting three or four hundred on the enemy.

---

* 25,000 vehicles and 1,300,000 gallons of petrol were required to bring up the equipment and supplies. To carry this traffic, most of it moving to the extremities of the salient in the area behind Groesbeek, fifty companies of Royal Engineers, twenty-nine companies of Pioneers, and three Road Construction Units built five new bridges over the Maas and improved or replaced one hundred miles of roads. Intricate scheduling was needed to prevent traffic jams, and because all moves were carried out within the hours of darkness, with vehicles required to be off the roads and hidden by dawn, strict traffic control was enforced by 1,600 military police. Among mountains of Compo rations and other essentials accumulated in the salient were 8,000 miles of cable wire, and 10,000 gallons of fog oil for smoke screens. (Statistics from *Corps Commander* by Sir Brian Horrocks and Eversley Belfield, Toronto: Griffin House, p. 178.)

40

PREPARING FOR

OPERATION VERITABLE

✳

FOR THE PAST FOUR DAYS SUBALTERNS FROM THE GUN POSI-
tions have been taking turns going up to the OPs to take over the
watch, so that troop commanders and their crews can come back to
the guns and prepare for the days ahead, when they'll be moving
with the infantry in the attack and there will be little or no opportunity for maintenance of their equipment or their persons.

Questionable 12-volt batteries for the big 19-set radio in the
carrier have been replaced, and extra batteries scrounged for the
18-set that a signaller can carry on his back, when you must leave
the carrier and go forward on foot.

Also, a reserve supply of fresh cells have been located for the versatile little walkie-talkie 38-set, which will not only allow you to go
forward a short distance in dicey positions where a second man
might attract too much attention, but, equally important, allow you
to pick up the BBC since it operates on regular broadcast-band frequencies, which means that now and then, during lulls in the
action, you can tune in the news or pick up the familiar strains of
Eric Coates's march "Calling All Workers" – the cheerful signature
tune for "Music While You Work" that the BBC pipes to the men
and women doing their long and often boring shifts on factory
floors throughout Britain – and perhaps catch Vera Lynn earnestly
promising "We'll Meet Again."

New spark plugs are acquired, including one for the often balky, one-lung Chorehorse engine, bolted to the rear of the carrier, powering the generator, absolutely essential to maintaining a round-the-clock supply of charged batteries, without which radio communication with the Regiment and the guns would cease to exist.

Encased in freshly washed long underwear, a clean shirt, and two pairs of new socks (worn in your normal fashion, one over the top of the other) you'll at least start off clean. There's no telling how many days or weeks it will be before you get another chance for clean duds. During long periods of intense action, such as you expect in the Rhineland, equipment maintenance must take precedence over personal maintenance. Cleanliness is bound to take second place to food and sleep; and from experience you know there will never be enough time for sleep.

Still you pack extra socks to allow for a change some night when your boots and socks are sopping. Whatever else you may encounter in the Rhineland, it is certain there'll be plenty of mud and water, and by now you are well aware that dry socks are among the world's greatest luxuries. The profound comfort that comes from the sensation of dry, warm wool pulled over clammy, water-wizened feet just removed from squishy-wet socks, is beyond description.

Just when 4th Brigade, or more precisely the Royals with whom you are to move, will join the attacking forces, is not clear. Initially 2nd Division infantry will have a limited role. Les Fusiliers Mont-Royal will cut the main Nijmegen—Cleve road near Hochstrasze crossroads, four kilometres northeast of Groesbeek, and then the Calgary Highlanders will take the village of Wyler about a mile northwest along that same highway.

Since returning to 2nd Battery as commander of Baker Troop, you have bunked at Regimental Headquarters in the comfort of Rusthuis when not up at an OP, for it made no sense to dig another dug-out in the frozen ground at 2nd Battery for the short time remaining. Early in the evening you visit the guns but you don't

hang around. The command posts are still completing a mountain
of work. The details of the fire-plan for many concentrations and a
barrage, including overprinted maps and traces, accompanied by all
sorts of complicated timing-schedules and scales of fire, were only
received by command post staffs at 7:30 P.M., and the strain of deci-
phering the meaning of it all and working out the fire-plans for the
guns has put everybody in a foul mood. They all pose the obvious
question: If they could build roads and bridges, and move up thousands of tons of ammunition in the sixteen days since Monty gave
the order for the push, why the hell couldn't the arty brass have
completed their plans for the guns sooner?

You return to Rusthuis, and while you wait for the four
hundred heavies of RAF Bomber Command to arrive from
England to flatten Cleve and Goch at 11:30 p.m., and medium
bombers of 2nd Tactical Airforce, following behind, to attack
Weeze, Udem, and Calcar deep in the Rhineland to the southeast,
you pass the time glancing through carbon copies of sitreps based
on the OP logs of today's date, forwarded some hours ago by Don
R to 2nd Division Headquarters and so up the line to Corps and
Army Intelligence.

The log, about which you are most curious, and the one all "I"
officers at all higher levels will be carefully perusing tonight, is that
of Lieut. Bernie Ackerman, Able Troop GPO, who, until the last
hours of daylight this afternoon, was in "OP 45," the windmill in
Groesbeek which you've come to look upon as yours because of
the extent and frequency of your occupancy, and from which, in
fact, you were relieved only a couple of days ago.

Log OP #45 MR 756544

0800 hrs: Occupied OP. Visibility 2,000 yards.
1100 hrs: Nothing to report. Visibility 3,000 yards.
1200 hrs: Suspected enemy strongpoint. Engaged with one
           troop. Rounds in target area.

1700 hrs: Registered target with tanks. Visibility 4,000 yards.
1730 hrs: Left OP.

You visualize every "I" officer – from 2nd Division Headquarters, back through Corps to Army Headquarters – heaving a
sigh of relief, as they read this report, and proceeding to reassure
their red-tabbed bosses, who, as always, must be counting as much
on surprise as on massive fire-power to achieve success.

Obviously, reports from all artillery OPs overlooking the valley in
front of the Reichswald will receive careful scrutiny tonight by "I"
officers at all levels as they try to perceive any signs of unusual activity in no-man's-land or enemy territory that might suggest the
Germans suspect something is about to descend on them.

However, OP 45, the towering Groesbeek windmill, sitting on
the startline from which the first 50,000 men will debouch into the
valley on their predawn thrust tomorrow, is widely known as an
observation post without peer by officers of all formations involved
in "Veritable," and most particularly the officers of XXX British
Corps leading off the attack.

From personal experience you know that scores of officers, from
corps commanders down to platoon commanders in the rifle companies of the spearhead, are aware of this mill and the unrivalled
panoramic view it affords an observer. Every day, from the third
week of January until a couple of days ago, small groups of officers
visited the mill to study the land laid out below them all the way
across the broad valley to the forbidding pine-forested ridge,
slightly more than three kilometres away.

Having to put each party of officers "on the ground" (mark
identifiable landmarks on their maps), and then move out of their
way to allow them to get a good view, was at first a bore. But as time
went on, it turned into a remarkable learning experience as you
watched the visitors reveal wide differences in individual percep-
tions of war. The direct correlation between the rank of an officer
and his general attitude and approach to the coming battle would

tickle the humorist as much as it would sadden the grave-digger. In the development of a man's perspective it seems to matter a great deal whether he's been chosen to exercise vast power to plan and direct affairs from command posts and caravans well behind the lines, or go forth with those who will face the enemy in frightful intimacy.

Corps commanders, on their knees in the cupola of the mill, planning the best use of 450,000 men, swept open hands across map-boards as they talked of such and such a division going through here and another over there. Later, division commanders and brigade commanders, reviewing the role of their brigades and battalions, stroked their maps with two fingers held together. Then came battalion commanders using a single finger for similar purposes in meetings with company commanders.

But when company commanders returned with platoon commanders, maps were marked with razor-sharp pencils. Huddling over their maps before the window of your mill with their subalterns, not speaking for minutes on end as they peered out at the ground they knew they'd have to cross – where even a fold in the ground could turn out to be of ultimate consequence to their lives and to the lives of their men – they would sometimes ask, in a quiet voice barely above a whisper, questions like, "Is that a ditch out there, running left at 11 o'clock from that last glider with the broken tail?"

It's these men you remember tonight as you await the heavy bombers from England that are to hit the Rhineland towns.

About 10:30 P.M. the pulsating roar of the first wave is heard passing over on its way to bomb the first major town in the path of the attack – historic Cleve from whence had come Anne, the fourth wife of Henry VIII. You go outside to watch with the new padre, Honorary Capt. Marsh Laverty, who just arrived today to take over from Padre L. D. Begg. It is a mild night for the time of year, but intensely black, with a light drizzle of rain falling now and then.

The southeastern sky is first lit by flares, then sparkling ack-ack, as great flashes begin along the horizon. For a time there is only the sound of the planes growling overhead, but then comes the ground-shuddering string of *crump*s you've learned to associate with aerial bombing. Cleve is at least ten miles away, but the violence of the flashing explosions at times lights up the whole cloudy dome of sky; and soon the reddish glow of fires, mounting higher and higher like an early sunrise along the eastern horizon, makes it appear much closer. Not since Normandy have you seen such heavy bombing, and in your mind's eye you see the awful tumble of rubble in Caen and other Norman towns. Cleve and the Rhineland targets will look like that.*

---

* Cleve was almost wiped out by 1,384 tons of high explosives. Horrocks, Commander of XXX Corps, had decided it must be "taken out" to prevent the Germans from bringing up reserves and reinforcing that "Nutterden Feature" on the northern end of the Reichswald, the dominance of which he considered critical to the success of his advance beyond the Reichswald into the open farmland. In the postwar book *Corps Commander*, Horrocks said the bombing was "the most terrible decision I had ever to make in my life, and I can assure you I felt almost physically sick when . . . I saw the bombers flying overhead on their deadly mission . . . After the war I used to suffer nightmares and literally for years these always concerned Cleve." (Sir Brian Horrocks, Eversley Belfield, and Maj.-Gen Essame, *Corps Commander*, Toronto: Griffin House, p. 184.)

41

THE BIGGEST ARTILLERY
SHOOT OF WORLD WAR II

✳

THE THROBBING ROAR OF PLANES COMING AND GOING AND the rumble of bombs in the distance will go on for much of the night as one after another of the Rhineland towns beyond Cleve and the Reichswald are pounded. So after a few minutes you bid the Padre good night and hit the sack, knowing that at 5:00 A.M. all sleeping will end for everyone in the Nijmegen salient when 1,600 guns, heavy mortars, and medium machine-guns open up on the heaviest fire-plan of the war. But you can't sleep.

Memories of Normandy have been aroused by the scale of the bombing, and all the anxieties and tensions of those days are crawling around within you. The idea of having to leave shelter and go out into the open in an attack with the infantry as soon you must is horribly repugnant. Only now are you aware of the comparatively soft life you've been living and how thoroughly you had built up your hopes that somehow the war might end before you'd have to go back into it again – either by the assassination of Hitler, an uprising in the Reich, or an unstoppable surge by the Russians into Berlin.

Shortly before 5:00 A.M., when the great concentration of guns are to open up, you go out from Rusthuis into the dismal darkness and head across the scrubby bushland for 2nd Battery Command Post, on the rim of the deep railway cutting about a kilometre away.

It's now drizzling rain, cold and miserable – a rotten morning for the gun crews, all of whom have been at their guns for some time now completing the preparation of ammo for the big shoot, taking shells out of their cases, removing safety caps, and stacking them in piles handy to the guns. And as you slosh through mud and stumble up and down over incredibly deep water-filled ruts left by the trucks and quads pulling and winching guns into position around here during the night, you feel for the poor late-arriving British gunners, and most especially for their command post staffs. It must be wicked trying to set up under such wretched conditions for a shoot of such magnitude.

As you pass behind 26th and 14th positions, and in front of other British field and medium regiments that have been slotted into spaces behind and beside them during the night, you can see very little in the windy, wet darkness, but there are faint sounds of voices calling out orders, and brief, glowing flickers of subdued light from hooded lamps-electric hovering over dial-sights of guns getting a final check of their "parallelism" – making sure all are perfectly on line.

Silhouettes of gun muzzles poke up against the night sky where previously there were only scrubby pines. Unseen hordes of gunners, dripping with rain, are now standing to their guns as they carry out last-minute tasks. By the time you make it to 2nd Battery, ghostly faint voices from Tannoy speakers in gun pits are calling "Take Post," an order presently being given on scores of positions. You try to visualize 9,000 gunners arranging themselves in customary gun-drill positions behind their weapons awaiting H-hour, five minutes away.

Until firing gets underway you decide to stay out of the hair of Lieut. Jack Bigg, who is in charge of Baker Troop guns this morning in place of the GPO Doug MacFarlane, who is up in the Groesbeek windmill, one of twenty forward observers who, until H-hour and during a ten-minute pause by the guns scheduled for 7:30 A.M., will report any active enemy guns or mortars to Major J. M. Watson, counter-mortar officer at Division.

You stop at Battery Command Post to visit "Hutch" (Capt. Les

Hutcheon) who, like "Stevie" (Capt. W. D. Stevenson) in 14th Battery, retired from fooing last fall to assume again the duties of CPO when it was decided more experience was needed in battery command posts than could be provided by the current crop of rein-forcement officers.

When you fumble your way through the sodden tarpaulin hanging over the entrance to a log and earthen dug-out, you are blinded momentarily by the startling brightness of the electric light dangling over their artillery boards. And even before you can wipe the rain off your face and focus your eyes on anything, Ack CPO Lieut. Bill Craig has placed in your hand a tin cup and "Hutch" is slopping into it a generous dollop of a colourless, oily liquid which he guarantees "will warm the cockles of your liver!"

It's clear that you've walked into a celebration of sorts. With the intense efforts of yesterday and last night behind them, they are relaxing. And while there's still some residual cursing at the "stupid clots" in the higher echelons for not allowing them more time "to work out the most complicated fire-plan for the biggest shoot of the war on any front, from that goddamn pile of rolled-up tables, tracings, and overprinted maps lying over there," most of yesterday's bitterness has dissipated in a golden bliss induced by this firey-sweet liqueur, which, according to an unusually well-informed ack, Gunner H. Buck, resting in the shadows in a cloud of tobacco smoke, is "Danziger Goldwasser." Between puffs on his Stanley Baldwin-style pipe drooping on his chin, he explains that the little dark flecks, floating suspended in what is left of the oily liquid, are actually flakes of gold leaf.

He says that just before you came, he and fellow ack Dick Tanner were speculating on just how badly the Reichswald will be chewed up by the guns, and he calculated the 25-pounders alone will dump more than 5,000 tons of H.E. on the Germans in the forest and round about. At 0459 hours, with only a minute to go, you leave Hutch starting the countdown over his two phones to the troops and go outside to see what you can see. For a few seconds there is deep silence, broken only by the slight rustle of wind and rain lashing the surrounding trees and bushes, covering up the sounds of nearby Tannoy speakers that must now be carrying voices of countless GPOs counting down the seconds to their gun sergeants.

One faint, distant voice yells, "Fire!" And for a split second, there's a rising chorus of urgent voices on all sides yelling "Fire!" before the night is overwhelmed by furious, flashing, roaring waves of sound and concussion, rending and tearing the darkness with monstrous, theatrical effects such as only 1,500 guns, mortars, and rockets can unleash when deployed in overlapping concentrations on a narrow front – a dreadful stimulant that causes you to shiver as with a chill, even as you begin to perspire.

Most of the 1,034 guns and 12 rocket-projectors firing off the prearranged fire-plan, along with the additional 466 weapons engaged on "Pepperpot" targets, have been crowded into confined clearings in the immediate area – a narrow strip of scrubby pine plantations, about six miles long and two wide, running south from Nijmegen to Mook. The exceptions are the three AGRAs and the 3rd Super-Heavy Regiment now roaring and flashing over on the right from south of the Maas.

No fewer than forty "Heavies," 7.2-inch howitzers on their great rubber tires, are belching 200-pound shells up to 16,000 yards. Two 8-inch guns, with a range of 18,000 yards, are unloading 240-pound shells on the Reich; while the strongest concrete emplacements of the Siegfried Line are receiving the attention of four superheavy 240-mm (9.5-inch) howitzers capable of throwing their howling 360-pound missiles up to 25,225 yards (14.3 miles). During the course of the firing this morning each of these great monsters will get off 80 rounds for a total of 320 rounds – adding more than 57 tons of high explosive to the hellish cauldron the guns are creating in enemy-held territory.

What enemy outposts and first-line troops are going through is almost inconceivable. You try to imagine the stunning effects of the airbursts alone, 50,000 from ninety-six 3.7-inch heavy anti-aircraft guns firing on flat trajectories, filling the air with savage showers of shell fragments.

While unable to distinguish in the thunderous cacophony the swooshing rush of sound that marks their passage, you know the first wave of rockets, of the fifteen waves scheduled by 1st Canadian Rocket Battery, must by now be descending on the Reich – about three hundred missiles in each wave, each missile carrying a 29-pound warhead packing the destructive power of a medium shell. Fired electrically from twelve projectors, each with at least twenty-four barrels, or "rails" as they are known (some have thirty-two), in rippling salvoes a quarter of a second apart to avoid collisions in flight, they form a monstrous "flying mattress" of high explosive, which reputedly lands with remarkable accuracy on designated targets.

The 248 mediums are now booming their 100-pound shells onto their prearranged tasks at the awesome scale of 450 rounds per gun, while thirty-two 4.5-inch guns are getting off 15,000 rounds.

Of course the greatest number of shells – 433,000 on the opening concentrations alone – are being fired by the 576 Canadian and British field guns accumulated here.

Adding to the awesome din are the 466 weapons assigned to the Pepperpot concentrations, weapons not required for other tasks: 114 Bofors (40-mm) ack-ack guns, 24 17-pounder anti-tank guns, 60 75-mm Sherman tank guns, 80 4.2-inch mortars, and 188 medium machine-guns. Unequipped for precise and rapid switching on targets not visible to them, and since all the firing is "indirect," Pepperpot weapons have been given the task of beating continuously one or two areas only.

Voice communication is impossible in the Troop Command Post. The Hughes brothers, Morty and Ralph, two of the friendliest, most garrulous acks, just spread their hands as if to say, "Forget it – there's just no way you can converse." Even their booming-voiced GPO Jack Bigg, a man never at a loss for words, can only grin and point down at the troop mascot, the Louvigny hen "Hardtack," carrying on as usual, strutting about, still quite sure of herself and unperturbed by the floor shuddering beneath her feet.

And so you return to Rusthuis where you pass the time working out a breakdown of 13,000 tons of H.E. being fired on prearranged tasks:

Weapon	Rounds	Shell Weight	Tons
25-pounder	433,104	25-pounds	5,413.80
5.5-inch	111,712	100-pounds	5,585.60
3.7-inch	48,420	20-pounds	484.20
17-pounder	5,400	17-pounds	45.90
4.5-inch	14,824	50-pounds	370.60
155-mm	4,688	95-pounds	222.68
7.2-inch	8,640	200-pounds	864.00
8-inch	292	240-pounds	34.80
240-mm	320	360-pounds	57.60
Rockets	5,760	29-pounds	83.52

For the next four hours and forty-five minutes (until 9:45 A.M.), except for one pause, all known enemy localities, headquarters, and communication centres are pounded by weapons of various calibres, so arranged as to ensure at least six tons of H.E. land on each.

Concrete personnel bunkers at Materborn, southwest of Cleve, receive the attention of superheavy 8-inch and 240-mm guns, while mediums concentrate on enemy batteries. The first three "flying mattresses" of the Rocket Battery are aimed at open trenches.

Field guns, in concert with mediums, heavy ack-ack, and rockets, work over a list of ten targets at various times and rates of fire, until 7:30 A.M., when a smokescreen is fired across the whole front and all guns cease firing for ten minutes. As the silence descends it is hoped the Germans will believe the attack has begun behind the smoke, and that all their surviving guns and mortars will come alive, allowing the counter-battery people, with their sound-ranging equipment and "four-pen recorders," to get a fix on them for even more precise concentrations before H-hour at 10:30 A.M.

In the sudden quiet, only one hostile battery opens up, but nineteen mortar positions become active and are identified as gun targets.

At the end of the silent period, the guns start roaring as before and continue until they are turned onto the barrage in support of the attacking infantry and tanks. Many guns, including those of 14th and 26th batteries of 4th Field, continue with what pukka staff officers are inclined to refer to euphemistically as "artillery preparation."

The 2nd Battery guns, placed on the barrage at 9:20 A.M., fire seventy minutes on the opening line alone! At 10:00 A.M. 14th and 26th batteries join in, but without one gun, that of C Sub, Fox Troop (Bombardier Bradley in charge with Sgt. R. B. Brunton on leave). A round, left in the overheated breech when the order "stop" was given for the ten-minute pause, exploded, splitting the barrel and blowing off the dial-sight. The fact the new gun-layer, firing for the first time in action, had just slipped off the layer's seat to stretch his legs, undoubtedly saved his life. Pieces of the counterpoise whistled all over the gun position.

Smoke shells mixed with high explosive provide a frightful screen behind which the assaulting units form up. The barrage starts at a thin rate, gradually thickening until it reaches full power at 10:30, when yellow smoke is fired to indicate the barrage is moving forward. Then tanks and infantry move out, the 44th Brigade of 15th Scottish Division heading for the northern extension of the Siegfried Line, riding in Kangaroos with tanks, Flails, flame-throwing Crocodiles and AVREs.*

The barrage is fired on behalf of the assaulting troops of XXX Corps in the centre only, the 51st Highland Division on the right having chosen to use prearranged concentrations on known target areas.

It is a "block barrage" designed to consume more than 160,000

---

* Armoured Vehicle Royal Engineers: Churchill tank armed with Petard short-range heavy mortar and various devices for bridging and ditching.

shells. The "block" or depth of the concentrated shelling on each lift is 500 yards. This is accomplished by arranging for the field guns to simultaneously shell three lines 100 yards apart, while the superimposed mediums fire on two lines 100 yards apart – the whole business moving forward in lifts or "blocks" of 300 yards every twelve minutes. The slow forward movement is meant to allow time for the infantry and tanks to make it over the very difficult ground. And to help the attackers in their timing, the guns drop yellow smoke among the high explosive shells one minute before the end of each block.

In a Royals' slit trench on the railway embankment to the left of Groesbeek, Major Jack Stothers has a good view of the opening of the attack. His report will survive as an attachment to his battalion's war diary:

At 10:30 six tanks move out onto the high ground south of the railway. As the Welsh Fusiliers cross the startline, heading over the railway embankment towards the Reichswald, the tanks open up with their machine-guns. All buildings on the immediate front – houses and farms strung out along the roads leading out of Groesbeek all the way to the German border – are aflame or smoking. The infantry keep up a steady advance, and the tanks move up and join them. Masses of armour now move up in a steady stream.

Shortly after this, tanks, Kangaroos, and Flails (tanks with a revolving drum out front, to which pieces of logging chain are welded to beat the ground and explode mines) start to bog down in the soft bottom land in large numbers, but are obscured by smoke from several sources: the barrage, the burning houses, and a smoke-screen laid down on the left flank by 13th and 14th Field guns, adding to a 4,000-yard protective screen streaming out along the Rhine from mobile generators operated by the Pioneer Smoke Companies, which are moving forward as the attack progresses.

Only one Flail makes it through the mud to clear a path through the minefield, and all the Coldstream Guards' tanks following behind bog down.

All but one of the Kangaroos carrying the Argyll and Sutherland Highlanders into the attack on Kranenburg get stuck in a wasteland of mud churned up by tanks and Flails trying to clear a route through a minefield left by the U.S.A. Airborne Division last fall, and only one of the accompanying Scots Guards' tanks makes it to within sight of Kranenburg Railway Station.

Still, steady progress is reported against little resistance. And the long lines of prisoners, escorted back through the gun positions during the afternoon, offer clear evidence of the effectiveness of the stunning preliminary bombardments and the fierce barrage that rolled over them, snuffing out their will to resist. Many of the prisoners are youngsters no more than sixteen years old. Terribly shaken, they report that of thirty-six guns in their locality, thirty-two were knocked out. Their bewildered eyes and strained faces tell the story. Clearly they are still demoralized by the memory of the bombardment. Seemingly they survived because they were able to shelter in well-constructed bunkers. Those in the open were slaughtered. For the first time ever you hear a German soldier say, "*Alles kaput.*" As in Normandy some ask to see the "automatic 25-pounders"!

At the first objective of the Régiment de Maisonneuve, a tiny crossroads hamlet called Den Heuvel two kilometres northeast of Groesbeek, one officer is able to count sixty-four Germans dead from the bombardment "without examining slit-trenches" for bodies.* Survivors, still cringing in cellars from the Niagara of shells that recently descended on them, show clear signs of being in shock when flushed out, according to the commander of a leading platoon of the Maisies, Lieut. Guy deMerlis. The result is the Maisies lose only twenty-four, including two killed, taking their objective.

---

* Reported in Col. G. W. L. Nicholson's *Gunners of Canada, Vol. II,* Toronto: McClelland and Stewart, 1972, p. 407.

And while the Calgary Highlanders, in taking the town of Wyler – 2nd Division's main objective sitting astride the Nijmegen-to-Cleve road – run into more opposition and suffer 67 casualties (twenty-four of them from anti-personnel S-mines when held up in a deep minefield), the will of the defenders is so weakened by the shelling that 322 of them surrender once the Calgarians seal off the town from the rear.

Later at Kranenburg, five miles beyond Wyler and six east of Groesbeek, elements of both the Argyll and Sutherland and the Highland Light Infantry Regiment of the 15th Scottish Division report equally satisfactory results from bombardment by Canadian rockets. With their thirteenth and last salvo, 1st Canadian Rocket Battery wiped out a Moaning Minnie position on the outskirts of Kranenburg – news of the most satisfying kind to all who for the past two months have suffered spasms of agony from countless basins of these awesome missiles descending in all their hellish clamour among the ruins of Groesbeek while you were on your way up or back.

The intensity of the fire from the Pepperpot weapons, including the Bofors of 3rd and 4th Light Ack Ack Regiments, will only be known by those subjected to it, but you get some indication when you learn that eleven barrels of the twenty-four Bofors guns of 38th Battery overheated and bulged from firing their allotment of 800 rounds each, which a Bofors can do at the rate of 110 rounds a minute.

By noon the barrage has been shot, and gun crews go to work on the great mounds of expended brass cartridges – several hundred per gun – boxing and stacking them out of the way, before preparing a fresh supply of cartridges and shells for the next big shoot.

At 5:00 P.M. the guns join in another heavy fire-plan by 2nd Corps' artillery, lasting an hour and a half, on behalf of 3rd Canadian Division attacking across a now deeply-flooded plain dotted with "islands" of farmhouses and hamlets, stretching from the Rhine on the left to the Kranenburg-to-Cleve road now under a foot and a half of water in some places and rising. A sudden surge in the level of the river saw the water rise eighteen inches in only a matter of hours. You don't envy 3rd Division FOOs having to go forward in amphibious "Weasels," and the infantry in "Buffaloes." These ponderous affairs, huge steel boxes shaped like World War I tanks, may not in themselves pose any real threat to the enemy, but they surely must present a terrible façade of menace as they crawl from the water and up a bank, dripping weeds and slime like prowling, primeval monsters.

At about 6:00 P.M. some Jerry 150-mm guns come alive, rocking Able, Baker, and Charley Troop positions with sixteen wicked blasts, some of the 83-pound missiles bursting overhead and some landing with shuddering impact between the guns, sending up towering black spouts of mud and gravel. Miraculously there are no casualties, but most of the windows at RHQ's Rusthuis, which survived the winter intact, are blown out.

By late afternoon the British units have limbered up their guns and left for positions farther forward. By next morning, February 9, only a small stretch of the battlefield in front of 3rd Division on the left and an area south of the Reichswald towards Gennep remain in enemy hands within range of the guns. Nevertheless, this afternoon 4th Field guns are required to join in an Uncle target that calls for thirteen rounds from each of the division's 72 guns; and this evening they contribute to a Victor target requiring six rounds from each of the 216 field guns in 2nd Canadian Corps, drenching some desperate spot in the fluid battle in Germany with 1,296 rounds of high explosive.

Still, none of this appears to impress Regimental Clerk Sgt. A. E. Martin, responsible for the unit's war diary. His ears still humming from yesterday's stupendous shoot, he records: "A very dull day after yesterday's bustle and activity."

Next morning, February 10, the front has moved so far away, 4th Field guns can no longer reach targets even with Supercharge, and so they are taken out of action for maintenance. To be out of action while a big operation is still going on is a new experience, and while everybody is grateful for the chance to catch up on maintenance, including personal maintenance, there is a sense of being left behind.

However, things are clearly going well for the assaulting forces. The fact they have pushed beyond the range of the guns (7.6 miles) means they have not only overrun the enemy outposts and closed with the main Siegfried positions, but have penetrated them. And for the infantry to have moved so far with so many of their supporting tanks and self-propelled guns bogged down in the freshly thawed bottom land on the way to the Reichswald, speaks volumes for the effectiveness of the gun program in subduing German guns and mortars.

You are told that with comparatively low casualties to the attackers, six battalions of the German 84th Division were destroyed, and that of the more than half a million rounds fired by the guns on opening day, not a single one fell short among the attacking troops. This is to the eternal credit of gun-layers and command post staffs who prepared the gun programs, and the last-minute "corrections of the moment" (adjustments of line and range for wind and weather at various levels above the earth through which the shells looped to target) – not forgetting the accuracy of the raw material in the "meteor telegram" produced by the Meteorological Section.

For five days the Regiment does maintenance on guns and vehicles, packs up spent cartridges, and collects unspent ammunition in a central dump in readiness for the Army Service Corps. It's a humdrum time coloured by feelings of anti-climax.

Still, the hiatus provides a fine opportunity for the new Padre to get to know everybody. And very quickly all ranks come to the realization that a cheerful, genuinely supportive personality has been added to the strength of 4th Field.

On February 13 he makes the unit war diary: "Honorary Capt. A. M. Laverty, our new padre, is a going concern and all the men like him."

On the 14th the first edition of his daily regimental newspaper, *Airburst*, makes its appearance, and by the time the order "prepare to move" comes, on the afternoon of February 16, it is as though this charming man, with an amazing ability to remember names, has been around for months, firmly in position to help reduce the growing uneasiness among all ranks at having to leave familiar surroundings and move towards the distant murmuring of guns from that hostile land over there.

All want to see the war brought to an end as soon as possible, and know they can help bring this about, but these dug-outs have been home for most of three months, and memories of life in them are likely to remain vivid for the rest of their lives – particularly the humorous incidents, such as the time Gunner Lorne Galbraith was shocked by a raw 110-volt wire touching his improvised hardtack-tin stove just as he was picking up an aluminum mess-tin full of warmed-up beans. The involuntary spasm of clenched hand and arm flung the whole glutinous wad of beans up and back over his shoulder onto the back of Gunner Bruce Freelove's neck as he sat with his back to him reading a book.

"Don't move!" yelled the quick-witted Galbraith, as he grabbed a spoon, "That's our last can of beans!"

Soldiers remember mostly the humorous and the bizarre, and of all the memories of life here, the one most likely to remain forever fresh for you is the rainy night you were lost in Groesbeek. Just to think of it is to be back in the windy wet darkness, resisting panic as you try to find Riley headquarters.

After descending in the turgid gloom from the windmill to enter the village from the rear and reduce the possibility of stumbling into a Riley outpost with jittery trigger-fingers, you move at a snail's pace along a narrow street stinking with the sour odour of wet charred wood, crunching shards of window-glass underfoot at every step, and now and then startling yourself by inadvertently kicking a skittering piece of broken roofing tile along the pavement, while your hands feel for obstacles along the walls of the ruined buildings. Concerned you may wander out into no-man's-land, you keep bearing right.

Pausing at a corner to decide which way to go, you're surrounded by a teeming cacophony of water sounds, amplified from within the windowless, doorless rooms – dripping, gurgling, and splattering down from thousands of holes in cracked ceilings and shattered roofs. As you listen a pattern emerges, as though the whole thing has been orchestrated: *gurgle-gurgle, tinkle-tinkle, plop-plop, plink-plink*, repeated over and over in a weird, atonal rhythm.

A broken shutter starts clacking violently and rhythmically in the wind nearby, sending a chill up your spine, and bringing you back to reality. Now totally confused as to where the headquarters may be, you still must keep moving. You think you hear faint footsteps ahead, and it occurs to you how easy it would be for an enemy patrol to sneak into the village tonight. And at that instant you almost suffocate with panic when a sodden curtain, wafted by a draught from within a sashless window, sweeps out and envelops your face with ghastly clinging wetness. As you tear at the repulsive icy rag to clear your mouth so you can breath, there's an overpowering stench of mildew.

Now you really push forward, exercising only the over-riding precaution to keep bearing right. After what seems like an age of gloomy blackness, dripping rain, and mounting anxiety, you find yourself at an intersection, listening to a peculiar pattern of *tinkle-tinkle, plop-plop, plink-plink, gurgle-gurgle*, and a broken shutter rattling in a way that's awfully familiar. Suspicious, you hold your arm out in front of your face and move forward – and sure enough, within a few feet, an icy wet curtain curls around your wrist.

Thanking providence there's no witness to your stupidity, you go forward at an even faster pace, and after another age of blackness and rain that soaks your pants to beyond your knees, and raises your anxiety level critically, you again identify the peculiar water symphony at a certain intersection. Now you really have to struggle not to lose your cool. You are not only lost, but somehow trapped in a maze that unfailingly is bringing you back to the same point.

Before starting off a third time, you force yourself to stand still and figure out why you keep circling back here to this wretched spot. Obviously you have become completely disoriented, and while it outrages your sense of direction, you decide to try bearing left instead of right. Of course, it works.

The quads are arriving to limber up the guns when you receive an order to assemble your crew, pack in your carrier, and join the Royals at Mook for a long and roundabout move into Germany. At the same time you receive a roll of large-scale maps, reaching down to Xanten, of such recent vintage the ink is still wet enough to smudge.*

Your crew consists of a driver and two signallers. Your driver, Gunner Steve Reid, is a husky man of energy, quick of wit and quick of movement, perhaps a bit too quick, suggesting an uptight, highstrung nature. One signaller, Gunner Walter Ferry, wears glasses and the greyest complexion ever seen on a man not dying from chronic anaemia. But he is a most likeable lad, always ready with an encouraging smile and an upbeat comment at the appropriate moment. The second signaller, Gunner Mel Squissato, is a highly intelligent, self-contained, polite young man, who, you suspect has hidden reserves of strength that will make him, as time goes on, the leader of the crew. Before being posted to 4th Field, he was on his way to becoming a paratrooper by choice until someone in authority decided that, being of Italian origin, his life might be in double jeopardy if he were required to jump behind the lines in Italy. While all are strangers to you – untried quantities, as of course you are to them – in a couple of days of sharing an existence where survival is most often the prime objective, you'll know them and they'll know you better than brothers from the same womb. But for now there exists an uncomfortable diffidence in their relationship with you, and with each other.

---

* For operations in Northwest Europe forty-nine tons of maps were printed.

PART THREE: FEBRUARY 8 –

MARCH 10

The Thirty-Day
Battle for the Rhineland

42

DRIVING INTO HITLER'S
THIRD REICH

※

WHILE ELEMENTS OF 15TH SCOTTISH DIVISION WERE ABLE to surge through the northern end of the Reichswald and reach the outskirts of Cleve on the afternoon of the second day, the smashed and rubble-clogged city is not clear of the enemy until February 11.

And only after nine miserable days of bitter fighting and heavy casualties among the sodden, dripping clutter of shell-ravaged trees, booby traps, and trip wires – along narrow forest-tracks heavily mined and covered by machine-guns every inch of the way – did the 53rd Welsh Division get within sight of the far eastern edge of the Reichswald.

With the battle about to move beyond Cleve and the dismal forest into open, rolling farmland dotted by numerous villages, stretching for miles south to the next fortified line at the Hochwald forest, blocking the way to Xanten some sixteen miles away, Crerar will need all the fresh troops he can muster. By now the American Ninth Army should be threshing north, occupying the attention of many enemy divisions. Instead it is stationary and helpless behind the flooding unleashed by the enemy smashing open the discharge valves on their Roer dam, while nine additional German divisions are allowed to move north to meet the Canadian threat.

Nor have the Germans confined their tactical flooding to the American sector. To inhibit supplies and reinforcements reaching the Allied front at Cleve, they have continued to open holes in dikes on the Rhine, raising the flood waters beyond Groesbeek so that the road through Kranenburg to Cleve is now under several feet of water.

Until another road far over on the right, running from the British sector through the Reichswald to Cleve, came into Allied possession, there existed no road above water serving the Canadian Army front. While the effect of this has been somewhat overcome by all units cut off by the flood waters, taking into use a variety of amphibious vehicles (3rd Canadian Division so extensively they are becoming known as water rats), large-scale movements of fresh formations to the front have been impossible. Even now, with just that one road open, divisional moves are greatly inhibited, and when the order comes for 2nd Canadian Division to move into Germany, all convoys are forced to take a roundabout route via Mook, Gennep, and Hekkins before heading northeast over the hard-surfaced road through the middle of the Reichswald to Materborn and Cleve – a route shared with XXX Corps.

The result is a massive traffic jam in the Reichswald the like of which you have never encountered before. Tanks, covered with infantrymen laden with equipment, as many as a dozen on each tank, are moving up along the right half of the road; while on the left half, also pointed towards Cleve and jammed nose to tail, is an endless line of trucks, Jeeps, and carriers, including those of the 4th Field FOOs.

That this does not end up in impossible entanglement is some sort of miracle for which no staff officer can take credit. Only the extraordinary patience of hundreds of drivers keeps those parallel lines crawling forward all afternoon.

Somewhere in the column stretching back as far as the eye can see, and covered with infantrymen hitching a ride, are the guns that are to deploy beyond Cleve at a town with the improbable name of Bedburg.

The gunners will be grateful for the rest the slow move is providing. As your carrier was pulling out from the old positions to line up with the Royals, gun crews had to use the winches on the quads to haul every gun and limber across the boggy clearings to the nearest forest road. The balmy spring weather during the past week, so welcome while the Regiment sat in limbo, was today cursed heartily by the gunners as they manhandled the heavy winch cables to the hookeyes of guns and trailers. With the frost steaming out of the earth, bushland that had been so firm for moving guns and quads two weeks ago is now a bog. And very little better are the bush tracks that once were gravelled roads but have now deteriorated into channels of deeply rutted, slithering mud.*

There are more than 3,000 vehicles in a division (3,347 in an infantry division including supporting arms, and 3,314 in an armoured division), and all are here, crawling at a snail's pace when not stopped for minutes at a time. How anything is supposed to get back from the front is a mystery that now and then is tested by a vehicle, with ridiculous results. Fortunately casualties are being evacuated by water in various types of amphibious craft.

Once through the Reichswald the pace of movement improves remarkably. At the Siegfried Line, someone has strung some rags on a string between two posts, and placed on it a sign: "The Washing."

---

* When the author visited the area twenty-eight years later, the ruts left by 4th Field quads, leading from indentations that once had been gun pits and dug-outs, including a remarkable officers' mess, though overgrown with weeds and gorse were still deep enough to make a man stumble! Your guide, Jonkheer van Grotenhuis, wartime mayor of Groesbeek (who chose the site for the Canadian Military Cemetery for 2,335 graves overlooking the Reichswald when he discovered a "Canada" button off a greatcoat and an empty package of Sweet Caporal cigarettes in an abandoned trench), recalled that the warm weather of February 1945 aroused such awful odours of decaying flesh, you could smell Groesbeek two kilometres away. And when 2,000 of its citizens who'd taken refuge in Belgium tried to return, he was forced to set up police road-blocks to turn them back until the foul refuse of war, accumulated over the six months Groesbeek lay in the front line, could be cleared.

When finally you arrive in the devastation that once was Cleve, you can understand why traffic was backed up for miles. Cleve is a bottleneck which until a few hours ago was sealed off with a cork of rubble. They still are trying to bulldoze a second track through the mess to allow for a "Maple Leaf Down" route as well as the "Maple Leaf Up" route they have created through the mountains of rubble as bad as or worse than in Caen.

The Royals are ordered to find billets for the night. It seems the leading battalions, who are conducting a very noisy war somewhere up there beyond Cleve, have not proceeded as far as they should have. The flanks have not been been pushed forward to the point where 4th Brigade can gain a startline reasonably free of fire from which they can lead the 2nd Division's push south to the Goch–Calcar road.

The enemy is putting up fierce resistance against 7th Brigade of 3rd Division, who are trying to clear Moyland Wood, a feature on high ground on the left flank of the axis of advance, dominating even the brigade's possible forming-up areas.

However, the guns continue on to deploy at Bedburg in positions reconnoitred and surveyed yesterday by a regimental advance party, at some considerable risk, you will later learn. The guns immediately are drawn into battle in support of other units – their fire rising to the respectable level of 3,200 rounds in the twenty-four hours ending 4:00 P.M. February 18. And Sgt. Hunt's diary entries for the first three days in action in the Rhineland will suggest a return to a high-tension existence reminiscent of the bitter battlefields of Normandy and the Scheldt: "February 16: Battle really raging. Whole Regiment deployed in one field. Fire and counter-fire reverberate up and down the battle line, ebbing and flowing like heavy surf breaking on a rugged beach. Really terrific, with the earth and all therein trembling..."

43

POSTPONEMENTS OF ATTACK
ARE HARD ON THE NERVES

❋

THE BIG PUSH NOW DEVELOPING WILL SEE XXX CORPS attacking Goch, while the Canadians push southeast of Cleve down to Calcar.

Having missed the Royals' predawn "O" group called by Lt.-Col. Lendrum when the messenger failed to find you in the blackout in the dismal tumbledown clutter that is Cleve, you must learn as best you can where you are bound and what is expected of the Royals this day when you catch up with Major Bob Wedd's company leading the brigade line-of-march south through Bedburg on the Cleve–Udem road.

The attack in the centre by 2nd Division, to be led by 4th Brigade, is meant to carry south some five miles beyond Bedburg to the high ground. But before troops can form-up on a startline, Cleve Forest on the right flank and Moyland Woods on the left must be cleared of enemy, for the corridor between those woods is only about a mile in width at its narrowest point. And even as the marching troops and support vehicles, with innumerable unexplained lengthy halts, are slowly picking their way up the shell-pocked and blasted road cluttered with debris, including burned-out vehicles, the Cleve Forest is being rendered untenable by a thundering bombardment by guns of all calibres as a prelude to it being cleared by British XXX Corps. And now and then, over the tremendous racket can be heard the gut-clutching sounds of "flying mattresses" taking off in accelerating *swoosh*es from the upraised "rails" of 1st Canadian Rocket Battery deployed just to the right of the road.

Long before Cleve Forest is declared cleared it is being treated as though it is by troops moving up, including the Royals. However, the dark woods humped up on the high ground on the left is a different matter, and when the bombardment of Cleve Forest finally ends, the sounds of battle emanating from Moyland Woods make it plain the Germans are determined to remain there. Between the heavy cracks of black airbursts over the trees and the reverberating roars of Moaning Minnies ending their insane yowling flight down among them, there are sustained exchanges of small-arms fire. And before the Royals reach their 11:45 A.M. rendezvous point, they get a message from Brigade that the plan has changed; they are to assist in the attack on Moyland Woods.

But a few minutes later another liaison officer from Brigade catches up with the battalion with orders to proceed on to the original assembly area. There the troops are served a hot meal. As it is being consumed against a background of vicious sounds of battle, you can't resist the thought that for many squatting down on the muddy ground, digging into steaming mess-tins, this could be their last meal on earth. But after the meal you learn the attack has been postponed until tomorrow. The troops are to disperse and bivouac around here for the night.

Your relief on hearing of the postponement is so profound you find it discouraging. The "cellarosis," with which you clearly are infected from those long weeks of relative safety during the winter, is more deeply rooted than you thought. You expected that when you were on the move again with the infantry, the old resilience would come surging back, but this has not happened. And as you accompany the Royals dispersing among the little farms strung out along a side road within sight and sound of Moyland Woods, you find the roar of mortars landing over there very disturbing.

Normally you and your crew would occupy space in the basement of the little house where Wedd establishes his company HQ, but the basement is so small there simply is no room. Deciding it is safer in slit trenches outside than on the ground floor of the house, you dig shallow holes. And since it is threatening rain, you cover them with the green pup tents issued late last fall and never used. This turns out to be a most fortuitous move, for around midnight a cow wanders into the kitchen of Wedd's house and stumbles into the open trapdoor in the floor of the kitchen over the cellar steps — coming to rest with her generous body completely plugging the opening, her legs dangling and threshing helplessly in the dark void below, and bellowing her distress at her predicament.

When Wedd and his men awake in the inkwell darkness, it takes a little while for them to realize what has happened. Then as they try to push the beast up and out of the hole, they find her weight and her kicking a discouraging combination. Still, they can't abide this situation; they must persist and win or eventually they'll suffocate when all the oxygen in the tiny basement is used up. As they redouble their efforts, the excited animal, attacked from below by a monstrous number of hands, becomes incontinent, flooding the basement. That does it! They decide to pull the damned cow down into the cellar, climb out, and leave the problem of how to get her out to the German farmer.

Needless to say Major Wedd is late for the Orders Group called by Col. Lendrum while the cow is still plugging the trapdoor opening, and the briefing for today's push is almost over before the somewhat haggard and agitated Wedd appears in the light of the Colonel's hissing gas lantern in the quiet cellar far removed from his stressful scene.

However, he is readily excused when he provides details of the hilarious circumstances surrounding his tardiness — a welcome bit of relief from the tension that has been building ever since the Battalion entered Germany, and which has not been helped by the numerous changes in orders from on high, including yesterday's postponement of the attack.

Later when everybody is filing up out of the cellar in the predawn light, someone wonders aloud, "How in hell will that poor German farmer ever get his cow out of there?" Major Jack Stothers, never favourably inclined towards anyone wasting sympathy on the Boche, observes that while it may be a helluva problem, it hardly compares with the problems left behind for the French farmers to clean up in the sweltering heat in Normandy, recalling one particular cow, bloated and foul, decaying on the kitchen floor of a shell-ravaged house in Eterville. How would these Rhinelanders like to have that to clean up?*

And you are left thinking it is perhaps good that the war did not end in Normandy – that the Rhineland, where the Germans took their first step towards this war, should experience what war has meant to Belgium and France, something Germany escaped in the First War by requesting an armistice before the Allied armies invaded the "Fatherland."

In Cleve yesterday morning, when your crew made a joke out of "washing up" the breakfast dishes, taking turns tossing them one after another over their shoulders out a shattered window to crash onto the tiled courtyard beyond, you'd felt very uneasy. Vandalism is not your cup of tea. But then you remembered those farmhouses near Falaise in Normandy with all their drawers and cupboards dumped onto tables and beds and floors by the retreating Germans, still looking for loot even as they pulled back into the cauldron of death in the "pocket."

---

* In November 1969, Madame R. Romagne, proprietor of Restaurant des Cultivateurs, in Caen, recalled how she, as a little girl in Eterville in July 1944 (before being evacuated by the Germans), quailed with her family in their shell-wracked farmhouse, enduring the terrible odours of rotting flesh that grew worse each sweltering day from the dead cow lying in their kitchen, where her father had led it, hoping it might survive the shell-fire and provide milk for the children.

44

SPECIAL DELIVERY TO
FRONT–LINE MUDHOLE

❋

ONCE AGAIN TODAY, FEBRUARY 18, THE ATTACK BY 4TH Brigade towards the Goch–Calcar road is postponed.

This time they say it is because not enough artillery to conduct the barrage could be diverted from hammering Moyland Woods and targets called for by units attacking towards the town of Calcar, including 5th Brigade's Black Watch, Le Régiment de Maisonneuve, and Calgary Highlanders, and 7th Brigade's Royal Winnipeg Rifles, Regina Rifles, and Canadian Scottish.

But before the postponement order is received, the Royals assemble in a forward area in muddy slit trenches scattered about a forlorn stretch of soupy landscape drenched with a steady rain. Being uncomfortably close to Moyland Woods and the urgent sounds of battle, you have parked your carrier out of sight behind a barn and gone forward on foot with a signaller to occupy a sodden hole near Bob Wedd and company awaiting orders. As you wait your attention is attracted to the noisy, tortuous progress of a Don R coming up from the rear, "walking" a big, cumbersome Harley-Davidson motorbike through the deep mud. The low-slung heavy bike, designed for high-speed travel on hard-surfaced highways and issued only to despatch riders at Army or Corps Headquarters, is totally out of its element.

Now and then bike and rider pause briefly at a soldier in a slit trench, and from the pantomime of scanning the surrounding landscape and pointing, it is clear the Don R is asking and getting directions.

Spellbound, you watch the roaring, slithering bike turn in your direction, eventually pulling up and stopping with its overheated, steaming engine at eye level beside your hole. In astonishment you hear your name called out in a questioning way. And when you nod your head you hear, even over the sputtering engine, a fervent "Thank God!"

Swivelling around on his seat, he undoes some straps holding a slim, rectangular package about two feet long and some six or eight inches wide and deep, wrapped in a gas cape. As he hands it down to you, he produces a message pad on which is written "Parcel Received," explaining he needs your signature as proof of delivery.

What is it?

He has no idea, but it sure must be important. When they sent him out from Army Headquarters five days ago, his instructions were: "Find this officer and deliver this, and don't come back until you do."

Naturally he is very curious, and so are you, but there is no way you can open a parcel in the rain and mud here. So, with a resigned grimace and a shrug of his shoulders, he turns his unwieldy machine around and starts skidding and lurching back through the mud, still wondering what the hell was worth all this trouble to Canadian Army Headquarters, and to him in particular. And only after word comes up that the attack is again postponed, do you get to return to a dry farmhouse. On removal of the waterproof oilskin cover, you find the brown-paper wrapping enclosing the parcel covered with addresses overwritten with the word "Unknown." Though your last name and rank are clearly printed in capitals, the only address provided is "Canadian Army."

Totally baffled, you pry open the beautifully constructed box and find, taped securely down within it, a gorgeous doll dressed as a Dutch woman in traditional clothes and fancy headdress of the type you'd frequently seen in South Beveland Peninsula last

October – complete with brass "blinkers" and tiny wooden shoes. This could only be the doll the Mother Superior Sister Ignace didn't think could be made by her nuns and the girls at her convent school in the little village about sixteen kilometres west of Nijmegen on the Waal (the southern branch of the Rhine). For several days early last January, you had waited in vain at the convent for Operation "Heaps" to get underway to rescue the Arnhem walking-wounded British paratroopers still lurking beyond the Rhine.

Sister Ignace had assured you they could readily make a doll and costume it, but she despaired locating a china doll's head – fragile things like dolls' heads having little chance of surviving the shelling and destruction the day that the Polish tanks arrived to liberate the town, and their regular convent burned down.

The good Sister had learned of your little daughter (born Christmas Day 1942, six months after you left Canada) when you showed a wad of snapshots to her and another nun – the school's singing teacher and former opera singer – when they joined you early one evening in the music room, where you were amusing yourself at the piano before joining in the nightly vigil on the Rhine waiting for the Very light signal that never came.

You had expressed regret you had been unable to find a doll to send her for Christmas, and this had inspired the singing nun to ask if you could write down the words and music for at least one English song, explaining her girls were sick and tired of singing "It's a Long Way to Tipperary," the only song she was able to sing in English. And so a deal was struck: she and her girls would make you a doll, and you would set down the words and piano accompaniment for the George M. Cohan song that goes "For it was Mary, Mary, plain as any name can be . . ."

You had fulfilled your part of the bargain, but the doll had still not made an appearance, when suddenly, in the middle of the night, the order came to pull your guns out of action and rejoin the Regiment at Groesbeek. Now, seeing this masterpiece, you can understand why it took so long. And you visualize poor Sister Ignace walking out to the main Nijmegen road, stopping the first army truck to come along and handing up the parcel addressed simply: "Canadian Army" to a bewildered driver for delivery to you.

Obviously she believed the Canadian Army would show as much compassion for the needs of a child as the people of Nijmegen did before the war began, when they earned the profound gratitude of countless Jewish families in Germany by trying to save their children from what was coming. Nijmegen became the terminal for an "underground railroad" for Jewish children buying one-way tickets in Cleve for the regular train into Holland, which ran along those tracks through Groesbeek and on through the bush where your guns would one day be deployed.

But even she scarcely could have visualized her parcel attaining the status of special delivery by an Army Headquarters despatch rider. You can only speculate that someone with a big heart and considerable authority eventually opened it to see if it justified the trouble it was causing, and discovered the note inside from Sister Ignace, making it clear the doll was a group effort by some nuns and a lot of little girls for a child in Canada who had never seen her soldier-father.

Nailing the lid back in place and turning the brown paper inside out, you seal it up. Then, with indescribable pleasure, you address it to a little lady at "Sleepypeopledom," the name her mother had given to your little apartment in Ottawa during one of those last, incredibly beautiful weekends in another age, in another world, so perfectly described in the lyric of Hoagy Carmichael's song "Two Sleepy People . . . by dawn's early light, and too much in love to say goodnight."

When Signal Sgt. Jim Ryder comes up with the rations, it starts on its way. Before leaving, Ryder tells you that when the guns arrived at a position near Bedburg the day before yesterday, they found they were digging-in out in front of some British infantrymen hunkered down in slit trenches. Even the wagon lines, well behind the guns in the badly smashed village, were harassed by snipers, and Gunner Edgar Brown, driver of an ammunition truck, shot one out of a tree. His pal, Gunner G. Bombardier, got his wristwatch.

There may also have been a "stay-behind" artillery observer, for during the night the village and wagon lines were hammered with some really big stuff. Three were wounded – Sgt. Lawrence Cairns, Gunner David MacDonald, and Gunner John Winn. And Gunner Peter Goodz, the quiet, pipe-smoking equipment-repair man, was killed. Ryder points out it could just as well have been your batman Whitehawk. Goodz and Whitehawk were sharing the same trench. Very tired after helping to carry tons of ammunition in from the road to the guns, they slept through the subsequent German bombardment, oblivious to the shells bursting around the muddy hole they had made more comfortable with armfuls of hay. So when Goodz was awakened by a passing guard to take his turn on duty, he sat up unaware of the danger of flying shell splinters. He made no sound as he was hit and fell back. Whitehawk found him in the morning lying dead beside him as though sleeping.

Yesterday there were two more casualties: Gunner Thomas Price was wounded, and a shell fragment killed Gunner "Jimmy" Lowe, a very popular member of Fox Troop.

Already disturbed by the extent of your relief at each postponement of the attack, and struggling with even more complicated emotions since wrapping up that precious doll for your little girl, Ryder's news is extremely depressing.

It continues to rain steadily, and having discovered last night the tents are far from waterproof – distributing a spray so fine it is felt rather than seen, but wetting nevertheless – you decide to take over the living room of a nearby house. Unlike Wedd's house, this is still intact, but it is very small, so small there is not enough floor space for four bodies without moving some furniture outside. This your men are proceeding to do when the man and woman of the house appear outside the open window. The woman beseeches you not to place her red velvet settee, a stiff-backed Victorian monstrosity, out in the rain. "Nein, nein – gut für schlafen," she keeps repeating, with her hands clasped beside her head, tilted over as though resting on them.

Anger boils up in you at being placed in the position of being embarrassed at tossing this old woman's prized settee out in the rain. And you holler at your hesitating crew holding the settee on the window sill: Dammit to hell, all you are trying to do is get enough floor space so that all of you can sleep in a dry place out of the rain! You'd love not to have to clear a place on their damned floor for sleeping. You'd love to be back home in Canada sleeping in your own bed – and would be too if it weren't for these God-damned Germans!

Stunned by your fury, the couple disappears, and your men slide the settee out onto the ground. But during the night, as you hear the rain pattering down, you suffer pangs of conscience; and are greatly relieved to note, on your way to a pre-dawn "O" Group, that the settee is missing, the owners obviously having found another place to store it.

At the "O" Group, Col. Lendrum assures his company commanders that the attack is definitely on for today, February 19. There will be no postponement this time. Canadian 2nd Division must gain a deep penetration to protect the left flank of 51st Highland and 15th Scottish divisions who'll be simultaneously attacking the town of Goch. The 4th Brigade attack will, it is hoped, also reduce pressure on units of 7th Brigade of 3rd Canadian Division, held up from assaulting Calcar by the stubborn resistance encountered in dense Moyland Woods stretching along the road that leads from Cleve to Calcar.

With the Royal Hamilton Light Infantry and the Essex Scottish leading, and the Royal Regiment in close support, 4th Brigade must gain possession of a lateral road, some four kilometres distant, that runs from Goch on the right to Calcar on the left.

A massive artillery fire-plan has been arranged on behalf of the

Canadian and British attacking forces involving fifteen field regiments (of 2nd and 3rd Canadian divisions, and the British 15th, 43rd, and 53rd divisions), seven medium regiments of 5th British AGRA, and the 1st Canadian Rocket Battery.

A rolling barrage will lead the 4th Brigade battalions.

45

RHINELAND FURIES UNLEASHED

---------- ❋ ----------

IT'S 11:30 A.M. – THIRTY MINUTES TO GO. YOU ARE SITTING
with your crew in your carrier among the battalions of 4th Brigade
in an assembly area south of Bedburg, just off a main road marking
the axis of advance southeast through Louisendorf village, which,
according to the map, is laid out in a unique diamond configuration
with roads running out from each corner of the diamond, including one leading on to the brigade objective – the Goch–Calcar
highway running laterally across the front on high ground about
3,000 metres from the startline.

Over on the left mortars crash now and then in Moyland Woods
where 7th and 5th brigades are meeting fanatical resistance, and far
over on the right heavy guns rumble. But here the RHLI, the Essex
Scottish, and the Royal Regiment, with their carriers, anti-tank
guns, and vehicles, lie unnaturally quiet and motionless on the treeless slopes of this natural amphitheatre – waiting. Motors have been
turned off and although the valley is crowded with clusters of hundreds of men, there is no sound of a human voice. It is a time for
thinking, not talking.

For many, perhaps a majority, this will be their first experience in
a massive assault against a seasoned and desperate enemy, and they
are fearful and wondering how they'll do.

And for those who remember the fury of Normandy and the
horrors of the Scheldt and know only too well the meaning of that

strange charge of intensity hanging in the Rhineland air and growing stronger with each passing day, it too is a time for wondering. Those many weeks of relative safety in static positions have had their effect, and you dread, more than ever before, facing that awful feeling of nakedness when H-hour comes and you must move forward across open country among the brutal sights and sounds of battle.

Back at the beginning it looked like an easy go. The crushing bombing of all the towns in the corridor, and the overwhelming fire-plan by more than a thousand guns, most certainly did the job of cutting a swath through the Siegfried Line, and for a while it seemed that the operation would be a piece of cake.

But that was before they opened their dams on the Roer River and immobilized the American army in the south, allowing them to bring nine more divisions into action up here, supported by a great number of guns and mortars, if you can judge by the amount of stuff he's been throwing around Moyland Woods and on the British on the right.

It all sounds, looks, and feels like Normandy all over again: the bomb-smashed towns; the mass movements of tanks, recce cars, trucks, and guns; the rolling countryside, dotted with smashed farms and villages; and the strafing, rocket-firing planes and the artificial moonlight. The chief differences are that here it is cool and wet, where Normandy was usually hot and dusty; and the hard core of the enemy here is formed by paratroop divisions instead of SS divisions.

You find yourself sighing too much, and while your mouth is cracking dry, your palms are damp. You try to concentrate on the Calcar sheet of the maps they've given you to invade Germany, which have been printed on the backs of maps the Germans had printed to invade England. You turn over the map and study the "Grantham sheet of Lincolnshire" – now overprinted with the word "cancelled" – and wonder what the village of Barnaby-in-the-Willows is like, and whether you ever passed through it during schemes like "Spartan" or "Welch."

Suddenly the air is pierced with shrill screams, and you look up towards two soldiers on the opposite slope of the valley dashing hither and thither between vehicles and men after a half-grown pig. Finally they catch it, slit its throat, and butcher it on the spot. As you marvel at such an activity at a time like this, one of the soldiers starts walking across the valley towards you. How at this moment anyone could consider food, let alone raw pork, is beyond you. The soldier draws near, and you see he's carrying a bloody hunk of pig, complete with skin and bristles.

Just then the signal comes to move up and your driver starts the carrier engine. You wait for the soldier to move out of the way, but to your amazement he walks right up to the carrier and plops the pork on the fender, and looking you in the eye yells over the fanning engine, "There's the pork you wanted."

Dumbfounded and speechless you can only nod. But as he turns and starts loping back across the valley, you catch sight of his shoulder flash, "RHLI," and suddenly you remember: Major Joe Pigott's company command post in the tiny house on the forward slope to the right of Groesbeek, and a soldier (Danny Butler) who'd been a butcher in peacetime. For a week he'd provided you and the command post crowd with choice steaks from a "liberated" cow. But after the fourth steak in one day, you'd confessed to having a great desire for pork. But my lord, now? You desperately want to fire the bloody mess into the field, but your hands are helpless. Had it not been butchered, carried, and presented to you before the eyes of the entire 4th Brigade? A *beau geste* if there ever was one!

You move off with the Royals to their startline. Time only for a last cigarette and then the guns start thumping behind. In seconds shells whine overhead and flash orange and black immediately in front of the sunken road. The infantry clamber up the bank to disappear over the crest. For a moment you see Bob Suckling, with whom you've shared so much, silhouetted against the black puffs of the thunderous barrage, pistol in hand, waving his company forward, and then they are gone.

The soggy, ploughed fields will not support a carrier, so you must wheel out on the road and try to stay parallel to their advance. You hope that damned pork will fall off the fender, but a carrier is a remarkably smooth-riding vehicle and the hairy, bloody flesh sticks like glue. German airbursts are now cracking above the stunning din of the barrage, and a couple of hundred yards down the road you pass two freshly killed Canadians lying on the road. You stop the carrier, pluck the revolting obscenity from the fender, fling it into the ditch, and wipe every last drop of blood off the fender before you move on towards Louisendorf and the burning houses beyond. But the damage is done. Your legs are rubbery as you climb back into the carrier, and you find it hard to focus your eyes and find your spot on the map. You earnestly hope it doesn't show, for it will infect the crew. Already driver Reid, with his jerky starts, is showing signs of getting the wind up, stalling the carrier twice before he gets it moving.

The rest of the afternoon is a blur of dashes from farm to farm, black airbursts overhead and fountains of mud spouting in smoky fields: of cracking small-arms fire; of infantrymen peering from behind hedges and burning farmhouses; of wounded and dying men being given treatment in open ground by stretcher-bearers bent over them; and one particularly dicey moment when it appears disaster has struck the carrier.

It happens just after you spot friend Ken Mickleborough, M.D., peering cautiously out of a doorway in shell-wracked Louisendorf, and stop to ask him what the hell the MO of the Royals is doing out ahead of the battalion? He tells you he and his crew were tagging on behind the support company of the Rileys moving up on the left, until they ran into some heavy fire from the next crossroads south of the village. On hearing this you decide to shift your axis of advance over to the next parallel road leading south, even though it means moving broadside to every 88-mm they may have covering that kilometre-long stretch of road, which is without trees or cover of any kind. Leaving the earnest Doctor staring up the road after you, watching for Royals crossing in the fields, you tell Reid to "Push it to the floor and leave it there."

Quickly the carrier picks up speed and is roaring up the perfectly straight, flat, open road, when suddenly there is no road! At least that is how it appears to you, hunched over in the steel bucket, peering out through a narrow port, when a monster crater yawns across the whole road.

Later you will realize that it is fortunate Reid has no chance to apply the brakes, and so, instead of nosing over as it might have done, the carrier sails across the deepest part of the crater, slams into the far side of the great hole, and teeters up onto the road again before conking out. Then, for what seems an eternity, it has to sit there unmoving, a sitting duck, while you and Reid struggle to clear the front compartment of bedrolls, Compo rations, the 18-set and two spare 12-volt batteries, and other lesser items that cascaded forward, inundating you both in truly bruising fashion when the four-ton vehicle came to its abrupt halt.

And all the while you are clawing at the mess, recklessly tossing stuff back to the signallers in the rear, you despair the engine will ever start – and if it does, that the transmission will still be intact; surely it must have been ripped apart by that crashing, jolting stop. That the engine roars into life the moment Reid pushes the starter button, and the clinking tracks roll her along up the road with as much pep as before, seem to you an absolute miracle, equalled only by the total absence of armour-piercing shots slicing through her body during that unscheduled stop at the crater, and during the remainder of its run across that open plain.

At the T in the road where you turn left towards the front (along a road marking the boundary between British XXX Corps and 2nd Canadian Corps) a long line of slit trenches extends out across the field as far as the eye can see, filled with British troops, hunched down "standing-to" with weapons at the ready, peering ahead as though expecting a counter-attack. The sight leaves you wondering what lies ahead.

However, three hundred yards up the road at a farm on the left, you find C Company of the Royals, with Major Jack Stothers peering around the corner of the farmhouse, watching one of his platoons move with due caution among the fiercely burning out-buildings, while small arms snap and crackle in the drifting smoke that obscures the scene.

Over on the left, barely visible through the smoke, is the farm where you must join Suckling's company, but the turn-off into the track leading over there is fifty yards farther up the road, and less than three hundred yards beyond that point, German helmets can be seen bobbing in trenches dug along the verges of the road.

Not knowing how close the Essex are in the field to the left of those Germans (by now the Essex might even be behind them on their objective at the junction of this road with the Goch–Calcar highway) you cannot safely engage those trenches with the guns. But your luck holds. An Ordnance bloke drives in the farmyard with a recce car he is trying to deliver to some outfit. Surprised to learn he is in the midst of a front-line battle and that there are Germans in holes along the road just up ahead, he asks if it would be all right if he took them on with the heavy machine-gun in the car? Assured no one will object in the slightest, he climbs back up, moves the car out into a better position, and again and again sends long bursts of bullets along the ditch where the German heads had been seen. When finally the recce car turns to go back, a little reluctantly you think, and he appears to wave goodbye, he is grinning broadly, obviously quite exhilarated by his experience.

Thankful for his assistance, you lose no time getting underway for Suckling's position while the Jerries still have their heads down. But as you move up the road to where you turn left into the track across the field, you find yourself looking into the faces of Germans not fifty yards away in trenches along the ditch where you had not noticed them before. There is nothing you can do but keep on going, and though they keep their weapons pointing at you and stare intently at your carrier as it comes up and turns left within thirty or forty yards of them, they don't fire a shot. You can only reason they are getting ready to give up.

Halfway across the field, you spot Canadians lying on their stomachs, pointed in the direction of the Goch–Calcar highway about three hundred yards further on. Changing direction slightly you run over there. You discover they are Essex Scottish. Their officer was wounded or killed somewhere back there, and they don't know what to do. A corporal asks if their objective is that road up ahead. You assure him it is, and urge him and all within the sound of your voice to get moving up there to those houses as quickly as possible – that lying out here in the open is courting death. A mixture of fear, bewilderment, and distrust shows in their eyes, and you feel truly sorry for them as you leave them to continue on to where you are supposed to be, and where you can hear the snap of rifle fire and the measured staccato of a Bren.

Cutting in behind the house and stopping at the mouth of the cow stable that is just an extension of the house from the wall containing the kitchen door, you find Suckling's company preoccupied with clearing a sniper from the house across the road, who has already killed one man and wounded several others.

Unfortunately the house is less than thirty yards away, too close for shelling, and when they try to get 3-inch mortar bombs through a window, a mortar-man is shot. It is decided to whistle up a Wasp, a Bren carrier equipped with a large flame-throwing device and a huge tank of fuel. And very shortly, with a terrible roar, a huge ball of flame rolls across the road, instantly setting the house on fire. In a matter of seconds a white sheet appears at a side door, and a German soldier comes out with his hands on top of his head – then another – and another and another – until there are twenty-six strapping paratroopers, including an officer, lined up in the barnyard, grinning as though it's funny that a monstrous flame-thrower should have been used to burn them out. But the sight of their sneering faces is good for you: it arouses hate and anger – those foul twins that can sustain a man in battle when all else fails, and which, you now realize, have been missing all day. You feel the thickness disappear from your head and the jerky wobble leave your knees.

A young soldier, whose closest buddy was killed by a shot from the paratroopers' house a few minutes before the flame was used, watches soberly as others relieve the prisoners of Lugers, watches, and money. He had been promised his buddy's death would be avenged as soon as they flushed "the sniper" out, and he appeals to Major Suckling:

"Aren't we going to shoot them?"

The Major turns away. But a veteran sergeant puts his arm around the boy's shoulders and says quietly:

"We don't do that sort of thing, kid."

When the seriously wounded are taken away on a stretcher-bearing Jeep, the Royals' walking-wounded start marching the prisoners back over the muddy ploughed fields – the last two paratroopers helping to steady an elderly woman who was just brought up from the cellar of the house. Having just watched as she was tugged, groaning and gasping, up the stone steps by a younger woman (her daughter you think) and the Company Sergeant-Major, so she might be evacuated to a safer place, you marvel she is managing to move at all along those muddy furrows on her swollen, rheumatic legs and feet. Imagining your mother in such circumstances, compassion threatens to overwhelm, until you force yourself to ask aloud of no one in particular: Was she among those who cheered and applauded that day nine years ago when Hitler's legions reoccupied this Rhineland in defiance of the Versailles and Locarno treaties that had declared the left bank of the river a "demilitarized zone"?

As your mind settles down and you are able to reflect on today's events, you can only conclude that luck was with you all the way.

The Essex Scottish are still not firmly on their objectives – three farmhouses along the Goch–Calcar highway, named, according to the map, "Wilmshof, Kranenburgshof, and Schroarnenhof," the latter dominating the junction of the highway with another main road leading back to Cleve. In an on-the-air exchange between Major J. F. Brown and Regiment, you learn Ted Adams, Fox Troop Commander, assumed command of an Essex company and led them onto their objective when the company commander was hit.

The RHLI are on their objectives, but have taken heavy casualties. Among the wounded, you'll learn later, are Major Joe Pigott and his Sgt-Maj. Stewart "Pinky" Moffatt, well-remembered for the filet mignon steak (the fourth that day) he served you one night at Pigott's company HQ near Groesbeek. Today he was knocked down by a bullet smashing through his jaw, and Joe was carrying him into a house where he might shelter until he could be evacuated, when he came face to face with a paratrooper holding a grenade. The German tossed it. Joe dropped Moffatt and took the explosion on his chest. A fragment punctured his windpipe, but the worst of the blast was absorbed by body armour he'd been issued in Normandy – of which he'll say one day: "Most of the boys had discarded theirs because it was heavy. Fortunately I kept mine."*

Even the Royals, the reserve battalion, getting here and clearing this road, suffered forty-three killed and wounded, including four subalterns – Suckling's company losing twenty, seven dead and thirteen wounded.† And you surely would have added to that count had you not run into Mickleborough and been dissuaded from carrying on forward from Louisendorf and turning right into this road to pass within thirty feet of those twenty-six cold-eyed bastards in that house over there.

Now, relishing the prospect of being able to hole up for the night in relative security with a reserve company, you decide to stake out an early claim on some cellar space. As you're passing through the

---

* As quoted on p. 160, *Rhineland*, by ex-Riley Commanding Officer Lt.-Col. Denis Whitaker and his wife Shelagh. Toronto: Stoddart, 1989.
† Three officers of B Company of the Royals – Major Robert Suckling, Lieut. H. J. Harkness, and Lieut. J. H. Poole (who also was wounded) – earned Military Crosses for their "coolness and courage in the attack."

cow stable on your way to the kitchen door, you spot the upturned toes of hobnailed boots poking out of the gloom of the corner on the right. When you stop to examine their owner, a boy in muddy battledress, sitting on the cold, wet concrete floor, his back against the wall, you assume he is dead, for his eyes have the fixed stare of a dead man. But then his toes quiver.

46

BATTLE EXHAUSTION

※

FOR MORE THAN TWO HOURS THIS AFTERNOON HE'D RUN, crouched, and crawled behind the furious, flashing geysers and drifting smoke of the roaring 25-pounder barrage, across muddy fields ploughed by enemy mortars and shells, while overhead the grey sky was torn by cracking, black puffs of airbursting 88s. Although he'd been among hundreds moving forward – vaguely conscious of long, irregular lines of men extended to his right and left – he, like every man in the attack, had felt alone. And somewhere back there among those brain-numbing, raging explosions and sights of buddies falling, something inside him snapped.

And when his company reached the farm buildings that were the day's objective, he crawled into a dark corner of the cow stable and sat down on the concrete floor in a puddle of icy water. Now he stares at you with sightless eyes, completely still and unmoving except for the occasional quiver of one hobnailed, muddy boot. When you ask Bob Suckling why something isn't being done for him, he tells you the drill is to leave cases like this alone for a few hours. If it's not really authentic battle exhaustion he'll eventually get up and move around.

It's growing dark when you learn that Ted Adams, who assumed command of a company this afternoon, when the company commander was wounded, is himself wounded and missing.

Soon everybody is preoccupied with a strong German counter-attack supported by several tanks that is threatening to overrun the RHLI positions just to the left of the Essex dug-in along the near side of the Goch–Calcar highway. The guns seem to be in constant demand, and the front begins to reverberate with the roar of the shells, and the airwaves are dominated by the high-pitched Foster-Hewitt-type voice of 14th Battery signaller "Coop" (Bombardier Ralph Cooper), penetrating through the electronic babble of over-lapping frequencies to relay urgent calls for fire from FOOs as well as from his own Major Jack Drewry.

Suddenly, however, FOOs are competing for the guns, as the Essex situation deteriorates. Two and three Mike targets are called for at the same time. While the calm drawl of Col. Mac Young, now con-stantly on the air sorting out priorities, is reassuring, it is clear things are critical when Major Brown, of 26th Battery, who is with Lt.-Col. John Pangman of the Essex, calls for a Mike target on their tac headquarters, and when queried by the CO, replies: "It's our last resort . . . position overrun by tanks and infantry."

It is now 1:40 A.M.

Later you'll learn that, holed up with Brown in the cellar of the farmhouse shown on the map as "Kranenburgshof," are two FOOs, Capt. Jack Cooper and Lieut. Ernie Richardson, along with their crews, and, for a while, Sgt.-Maj. Ken Scott, who drove Richardson up to replace his Troop Commander Adams. When one day Scott gets the chance to recall for you his first and last night with the infantry in the front line, he will have no difficulty remembering the date, for this is his forty-fourth birthday, and he was just in the process of celebrating it, sharing a roast of fresh pork with some pals "sitting at a real table" in a house back at A Echelon, when about 9:30 P.M. he got a call from Lieut. Richardson to drive him up to the Essex Scottish:

We take the road up on the right flank, and when we get to within a quarter of a mile of the Goch–Calcar highway, we are stopped by some guards who won't let us go any farther. They say the Jerries are shelling the crossroads. So we park the Jeep in a farmer's lane and walk through the fields till we come to Essex Tac Headquarters, which we identify by the three carriers and trucks parked at the back of the house.

When we go in the back door we run into a lot of guys milling around, some armed with spoons and partially consumed sealers of fruit, and others with handfuls of eggs waiting for a turn to cook them. It is something of a rat race.

We find our officers down in the cellar with their crews. When I am introduced to Col. Pangman, he asks me to stay all night and be his guest. When I say I can't for no one knows where I am, he gets on the blower and calls our CO at Brigade. And so I'm stuck there for the night. Soon, about five German tanks come up the right flank. Some of the men go and get Piat launchers, but then they find they just have three bombs. They ask for volunteers to go back out there among the tanks to look for Piat bombs. That gets rid of half of the gang. Next they are to get reinforcements from the Royals, who promise to send up sixty-three men. They ask for volunteers to go back and guide them up. That's the end of the gang in the kitchen.

Left alone I start to go downstairs, but at the bottom of the stairs Col. Pangman puts his arm across in front of me and says I have to go out and help defend the building. Having no weapon, I borrow a Sten from one of the signallers and go outside.

There's a lot of tracers flying around, so I make myself scarce, landing up in the pigpen. There are four others in there already: a Lieut. Waltham, a Cpl. Hunington, and a couple of others. When it starts to get light I ask the Lieutenant if he thinks we should get out of here, as I figure the Jerries will come in and get us when it is daylight.

He says he cannot leave if anyone is alive in the cellar. So he goes out to check. When he comes back in about five minutes, he says he thinks all are done for. So that leaves it clear for him to leave. We start out the back door of the pigpen and walk right into a Jerry standing there with a submachine-gun.

When at 3:00 A.M. all communication with Major Brown goes out, you join Suckling outside, peering into the darkness ahead. At first you can make out little beyond some skittering tracers and the growling of heavy tank engines rising and falling as they move from one spot to another. But suddenly this changes when two farm-houses ("Kranenburgshof" on the right and "Wilmshof" on the left) about three hundred yards apart are set on fire by the Germans, using missiles that explode against the walls with spectacular splashes of white sparks in the manner of "hollow charge" bombs fired by Piats and Panzerfausts. As the houses blaze up, lighting the scene, things look bad. Silhouetted against the fires are tanks – three, maybe four – it's hard to tell, for they move about in the drift-ing smoke, glowing red and wavering from the flames. Now and then German soldiers pass in front of the fires. At first they scurry, bent over, but soon they are walking bolt upright, suggesting they have gained complete control of the position.

Very soon small groups of highly agitated Essex Scottish begin to materialize in the murk only a few yards in front of where you and Suckling are standing. Confronting the retreating men with the stern, confident voice of authority, Suckling inquires if there is an officer with them? They say their officer was hit going in this after-noon.

Recalling the frightened, bewildered guys you came across lying in the open field on the way over here this afternoon, you feel only deep sympathy. That they now should be ordered to return up there would never occur to you. But then you're not an infantryman. The Major, on questioning them as to what has been going on up there (Did any of them actually see anybody shot? Did any of them get a shot at a German?), clearly believes it is not as bad as they think, and he instructs their only NCO, a corporal, to collect them and lead them back up there.

Whatever he may think, the corporal makes no protest, but turning to the men, says quietly, "Sorry, fellows, but we have to go back up."

That they too respond in positive fashion, albeit slowly, turning round one after another and moving off in single file following the corporal back up towards that flaming ridge, says much for the courage and discipline of these men. But before they get halfway there, they meet an even larger group, something in the order of a platoon, coming back, and their newly found resolve dissolves.

When the combined group arrives back, Suckling gives up and orders them to dig-in to the right of his house.

Soon it is clear from the numbers arriving that the battalion has been routed. As each new group arrives they are directed to dig-in over on the right.

No one from 4th Field shows up. But as time goes on you learn that some get back to the guns. Sheltering in the cellar with their officers at Essex Tac HQ, until they are sent outside by Col. Pangman to help defend the position, are Bombardier Ray Bugden and Gunners J. J. Garrigan and Brown. Also hiding in the pigpen building until the captured Essex Scottish and Sgt.-Maj. Scott are marched away, when they get the chance to make their way back to the guns, are Gunners J. Dobson and L. Hager.

Gunners Lowe and Erickson, sheltering in slit trenches near the house all night, until they get the chance to come out under cover of one of your Mike target concentrations laid on an adjoining farm at dawn, hold out no hope for the survival of anyone up there. They say a tank circled the house and shelled it at point-blank range. (In fact, the tank crushed through the walls and ground across the main floor.) They think the foundations of the building collapsed, entombing our men.

When the last stragglers tell you there will be no more, that they saw the rest being taken prisoner and marched off, you are free at last to bring down fire on those rampaging tanks and their escorting troops. You proceed with a vengeance.

To your satisfaction the German foot-soldiers continue crossing and recrossing in front of the fires in almost leisurely fashion, right up to the instant your shells whistle overhead and flash among them. Again and again you drench the burning farms — first Kranen-burgshof, then Wilmshof on its left (east), and then Schroarnenhof on its right – with high explosive shells, each one capable of smashing a tank track or a bogie wheel, or jamming a tank turret. Your main purpose, though, is not to disable the tanks, but to destroy or drive away the screens of foot-soldiers without which tanks can't move and fight at night.

You feel remarkably secure that those flashing hurricanes of 25-pounder shells lashing the Mike targets around the burning houses up there will succeed in driving off the panzer forces that moved in with such speed and ease. It is a confidence born of having been witness to the effectiveness of similar concentrations maintained by the guns for lengthy periods along Verrières Ridge in Normandy when the Fusiliers Mont-Royal, South Saskatchewans, and these same Essex Scottish were overrun by tanks and infantry, and the guns filled the gap with curtains of shell-fire until a counter-attack could be mounted to regain the position.

When the German tanks withdraw, snarling, into the surrounding darkness, you move the shelling around, plastering every area where they might try to regroup for another attack down this way. And throughout the night, whenever the guns are not engaged in desperate support of the Rileys beating off counter-attacks, you shell the area of those smouldering farms along the road up there.*

---

* The effectiveness of the guns of 4th Field, as they consumed 8,472 rounds (established by the number of flashless NCT propellant charges used only after dark) in smashing the German attack, is confirmed by a chapter in the *History of Panzer Lehr Division* describing their involvement along the Goch–Calcar highway that night: "At 2000 hours Kampfgruppe von Hauser [special counter-attack battle group assembled under one Colonel Baron Von Hauser, commander of 901st Panzer Grenadier Regiment] launched its frontal assault on both sides supported on the right by elements of 6th Parachute Division and on the left [against Essex Scottish] by 116 Panzer Division. *As soon as the tanks rolled across the forward edge of the Canadians' position* [on the Essex front] *their artillery fired barrages which made movement difficult and separated the German infantry from their tanks. Nevertheless by midnight in the struggle for Schwanerhof* [RHLI farm] *it*

The blackness along the front is continually ruptured by roaring, flashing tornadoes of high explosive. At 0200 Major Jack Drewry lays on heavy fire in support of a counter-attack by the Rileys to retake a company position overrun by the Germans. After about an hour and a half the Rileys report that company position restored, but now another company is fighting for its life. Only gradually does the fighting in the Riley area peter out, and you keep expecting the attack by the panzers to be revived over this way. But nothing happens.

By the time the situation stabilizes and you are able to join Suckling in the cellar of your farmhouse in gulping down a scalding cup of tea and a whole sealer of preserved cherries from a well-stocked shelf under the stairs, the first sustenance you've had since breakfast almost twenty-four hours ago, it's getting on towards dawn.

Only then does someone remember the boy sitting in the puddle out in the cold, dark cow stable. They carry him down the cellar steps, still rigid in a sitting position, and put him down on a pile of potatoes. They talk to him encouragingly and try to feed him hot tea, but he doesn't respond in any way. They light a cigarette and shove it into his mouth, but they have to remove it for he makes no effort to puff it. Finally they decide to let him rest until he can be evacuated in the morning. When they try to lay him down, they have to force his torso backwards while holding his legs down. They cover him up with a blanket, but his sad eyes remain wide open, staring up at the ceiling the rest of the night, locked on some secret horror.

---

changed hands several times. But the attack was halted at the Goch–Calcar road. Access to the area beyond it was denied by concentrated fire."

47

SHELTER FROM

THE STORMY BLAST

※

AT FIRST LIGHT (FEBRUARY 20) YOU ARE OUTSIDE WITH Suckling peering at the two farms some six hundred yards away, still smouldering from the fire that consumed them last night, when a soldier in Canadian helmet and battledress appears in your glasses near the derelict farmhouse on the left front and casually starts walking this way.

While waiting for him to arrive, there is much speculation as to why the Jerries are letting him walk back here unmolested. He must be some kind of emissary. But for what purpose?

When finally he arrives no one is prepared for his question, presented in a slow Western drawl: "Where's the Essex Scottish?"

He is told that what is left of them are dug-in just over there in the field on the right. But where on earth has he been, not to know?

"Sleepin' in a trench up there," he replies.

That he slept through the whole night oblivious to roaring Jerry tank engines charging about the place, the crash of their guns firing into the houses, not to mention the deluge of 25-pounder shells you'd poured up there when you believed no more Essex Scottish were left on the position, is incredible. Nevertheless, he maintains he didn't hear a thing: "Couldn't believe it when I woke up and found I was alone!"

But how did he escape being captured by the Germans this morning? And why did they let him walk back here just now?

"Cause there aren't any Germans up there."

Is he sure?

"Positive – not a living soul up there. Plenty of dead though."

Then sensing the scepticism in his listeners' questions he says, "If anybody wants to see for themselves, come on up there with me. I gotta go back to get my 'loogur' pistol I left in my trench." And with that he turns and starts walking briskly back up.

When this astonishing bit of intelligence is transmitted through Battalion to Brigade, the Royals are ordered to reoccupy the abandoned positions as quickly as possible, and by 1030 hours your old carrier is trying vainly to follow Bob Wedd's company and a troop of tanks across the sticky, clinging mud and turned-over mats of turf of a ploughed and furrowed field, making for the skeleton ruins of the farm on the high ground on the right front that had been Essex Battalion Headquarters.

Soon you are following the example of the tanks, which give up trying to make it up that considerable slope through the gumbo to Wedd's objective, and veer off to the left to harbour on a stretch of unploughed turf lying well down behind the crest and another burned-out shell of a farmhouse. But even on the level your carrier can barely move through the mud, and it takes hours (how many will always be in dispute) to get across four or five hundred yards of ploughed field: now grinding forward a few feet – now backing up to unfold the rugs of mud rolled up in the front bogie wheels – now charging ahead again on a different tack until the engine threatens to stall or does stall – now backing up again to unsnarl the mud – and so on. And all the while shells from a German battery, deployed beyond the crest, scream in and churn the field round and about, blindly ranging on the straining sound of your carrier motor. Or so it seems, for your carrier is the only target being engaged. Those Shermans, with pennants flying arrogantly, sit unmolested up ahead.

It is shelling the like of which you've never experienced before. Always it has been one, two, or three guns firing a round at a time, but now it's a dozen or more firing together, if not salvoes, the next thing to them. Only poor ranging is saving you, and every soul in the carrier knows it. Soon the strain begins to tell on driver Reid. More and more frequently he is stalling the engine when forced to reverse direction to free the mud from the bogies, and you despair he will be able to get this gaping box to firm earth, where he can shut off its tell-tale engine, before one of those random shells drops in it and it's all over. However, their ranging-to-sound remains exceedingly inaccurate, and though, from late morning to mid afternoon, you are surrounded by violent explosions sending up black fountains of mud – now and then close enough to rock the carrier and ensure this day will register in memory as the most ter-rifying of your life – no damage is sustained by the sluggish vehicle or the white-faced men hunched down within it.

The sense of relief is indescribable when finally the carrier struggles out of the mud onto the firm pastureland where the tanks are huddled. However, it doesn't shake the shelling; if anything it grows worse. Leaving Squissato in the carrier manning the radio, you, Reid, and Ferry get down in a couple of abandoned German trenches next to the tanks. When the shelling continues, with only brief respites, you decide all would be better off in some trenches you spot along the base of the gable wall of the burned-out house up on the Goch–Calcar highway, the only remaining whole wall of what was a two-storey stone house.

During a lull in the shelling you call out to the other two trench-dwellers, that come the next lull you should all make a dash up the slope to the trenches along the base of the derelict house about two hundred yards away. But they either misunderstand or consider the idea mad, for when you call out "let's go" and gallop up the grassy slope to a trench tight against the gable wall, you find you are alone.

For a while you feel sorry for them and for Squissato, huddled down in the carrier, as you relish the sense of security provided by the towering wall, so high it seems almost to scrape the clouds passing above it. No enemy shell or mortar can reach you here. Then, incredibly, the Germans begin to cut the wall down. You know it is madness to think they are doing it to get at you, and later in a saner mood you will consider the possibility they wanted to open up a clear field of fire in case those Shermans moved up the slope. But now, as each solid-shot rips through the wall with a horrible shriek right over your head, showering you with stone chips, you cannot suppress the idea they are determined to get you regardless of what it takes. Rapidly the towering structure weakens until it quivers and sways over your head in a terribly menacing way. If it falls this way, you'll be buried alive – if you aren't squashed to pulp by chunks filling the trench. In your rising panic you abandon logic that dictates the wall must fall away from you in the direction it is being struck with such force at its base.

Often during the Caen to Falaise battles you saw men pray. Though you respected their views you didn't think it logical that a man should ask his God to redirect a shell that could kill another nearby innocent man. Now you are all alone and you wish you weren't, for the long winter lull of relative safety around Groesbeek has done something to you.

When finally you hear the wall crack, and the great mass of stone and mortar comes crashing down, your nerve cracks as well. And when the German field guns immediately start shelling with sadistic fury the newly exposed ground containing your trench, all your resilience collapses. You can take no more.

Later you'll be grateful that no one sees you like this, pushing your face deep into the mud and trying to hold onto earth that won't stand still. But now, you have nothing left to hold on to, and you have the vision of a panic-stricken kitten in the bottom of a pail while tin lids are crashed over its terrified head – on and on and on – Will they never stop? You find yourself listening to a voice mumbling, "Oh God our help in ages past, our hope for years to come, our shelter from the stormy blast..." And then you realize it's your own.

Somehow, in the long lull that follows, you manage to rally your composure sufficiently to run down the slope to your crew. There, you order an immediate move up and across the slope to the farm on the right where you know Bob Wedd will be waiting, and where you must be when the inevitable enemy counter-attack comes in. Convinced you can make it faster on foot, and at the same time lighten the load in the carrier, you decide Squissato will accompany you carrying the 18-set on his back, so you'll have communication with the guns through Ferry now manning the 19-set in the carrier if it fails to claw its way up there.

Since all will be taking advantage of this strip of solid turf to get well up the slope before turning right across the ploughed field, where you'll be under observation for the rest of the way, no one must dilly-dally. And before taking off, you lay on, through Ferry, some harassing fire on buildings you assume are infested with snipers, about four hundred yards (according to the map) beyond the highway and that forlorn cluster of burned and broken buildings that is your objective. You order "troop fire" (four guns firing in rotation), "at three-second intervals . . . for ten minutes . . . starting now."

To further reduce the carrier's weight, on Squissato's suggestion, you and he carry the 60-pound roll of remote microphone cable suspended between you on a steel bar inserted through the centre of the spool. How you manage, you will never know. To run unencumbered a three-hundred-yard dash in mud, across an uneven ripple of furrows, would be an ordeal. Encumbered it is pure hell. And Squissato has that damned 18-set on his back. Only the realization you are running for your life keeps you going – gasping for air and churning your legs that burn as though on fire from lifting boots doubling in size to monstrous globs of clay.

Just when your chest is about to burst and your legs seize up in paralyzing spasms, you reach the firm ground of the farmyard and make for the only intact building, a long, low, brick structure extending all along the left side of the laneway to the gateway at the highway.

Plunging in the first open doorway, you and Squissato stumble into a room half-filled with coal. Gasping and heaving, you flop face-down on the slithery, rasping pile, and long after you regain your breath, you lie there clutching handfuls of shiny black anthracite, relishing the strange sense of security it provides. There is about the smell and feel of the stuff an aura of normalcy that has been totally missing all of yesterday and today. And you are still there, beginning to lose a battle with sleep, when Wedd bounces in the door, calling excitedly:

"Foo! Foo! Quick – they're putting a gun in action just out front."

When you scramble to your feet, you find him backed into your doorway, cautiously peering left around the doorjamb in the direction of the gate. Urgently waving you up beside him, he points across the road:

"Look – over there in the field – see it?"

You do, not more than three hundred yards away, a 75-mm you think, when you get your glasses on it. And clearly it is being prepared for action by a crew of four or five men.

Yanking your folded map out of the front of your battledress blouse you hurriedly establish a map reference. But before you can give it to Squissato standing by with his remote mike – which he assures you is now hooked up to the radio in the carrier parked out behind – Wedd restrains you: "Look – we may not need your guns!"

Looking the way he is nodding, back in the laneway to the right, you see the crew of a Royals' 6-pounder anti-tank gun that has just been manhandled into position, frantically readying it for action. And for a few seconds you and Wedd hold your breath as your heads swing back and forth from the gun in the laneway to the gun in the field, trying to judge which gun will get off that first crucial round that will decide the outcome of this deadly duel, for neither gun could possibly miss at that range.

It happens you are bent forward looking around Wedd towards the Jerry gun when the hot smash of muzzle-blast from the snout of the 6-pounder almost bowls you both over backwards, and you barely manage to follow the tracer of the shot as it goes through the shield of the German gun. As expected there is no reply to that shot, or to two more the Royals' gun puts through the shield of the enemy weapon. Nor is there any further sign of the crew, though you search the ground around the gun in all directions with your glasses for several minutes.

Just as you are about to give up, a Bren carrier rolls into view, from the direction of the enemy, making for the disabled gun. At first you think somebody has made an error, driven into no-man's-land, and is racing to get back to the Canadian lines, but when it arrives at the disabled gun, it stops, and men in potty helmets and field-grey uniforms pile out.

With Squissato at your elbow, his remote mike at the ready and the approximate position of that gun marked on the map, in no time at all you have the guns of 2nd Battery pumping up five rounds' gun fire (40 rounds). The Jerries are still in the process of wheeling the carrier around to present its rear hook to the trail eye of the gun, when the shells start arriving. Unfortunately they fall far beyond carrier and gun.

However, when you order "North 100 – Repeat," forty rounds catch the persistent Germans still frantically throwing things into the carrier for a quick take-off, and when the shelling ends there is no sign of life in the field. Still, the Royals' 6-pounder crew, attracted back to their gun by the fuss your rounds are making, ensure that carrier is permanently disabled with a couple of well-placed solid-shot.

In the lull that follows, Wedd tells you that in the cellar of the derelict house they found three 4th Field officers and the Colonel of the Essex Scottish, badly shaken, but otherwise unharmed.[*] However, among the missing and presumed captured are a FOO, Ted

---

[*] Just how shaken is indicated by Company Sgt.-Maj. Charles Martin of the Queen's Own Rifles of Canada in his book *Battle Diary*, describing a brief encounter shortly after with Pangman, who at one time had been Martin's company commander and was chiefly remembered for being "disciplined, a good planner, but stand-offish." The Queen's Own were passing through the Essex on their way up to the Goch–Calcar startline,

Adams, and his Sergeant-Major, Scott. They say the FOO was blind from his wounds when captured.

As daylight fades on February 20, you get an urgent message from friend Suckling, inviting you to join him. His company has moved into position among the houses at the crossroads on the right, filling in the gap the Germans found last night between 2nd Canadian Corps and British XXX Corps.

(And it was some gap! The whole right flank stood empty last night when the British brigade that was supposed to have attacked simultaneously to gain that section of the Goch–Calcar highway to the immediate right of Canadian 4th Brigade inexplicably didn't budge from their trenches way back in that field, where you'd spotted them yesterday when you were making that detour on your way over from Louisendorf.)

Suckling, obviously conscious of his exposed flank and remembering the speed with which Jerry overran these positions last night, is most desirous of your company, and you are outside in the dark, considering the merits of such a move – peering in his direction, measuring the risk of driving up the road instead of using the muddy field behind the house – when you hear the sharp *bur-rup bur-rup* of Schmeissers and see streams of tracers streaking towards the crossroads.

Thus you are in position to instantly get the guns working over the darkness across the road with flashing, roaring Mike targets, Scale 10 (240 shells per target), first in front of Suckling's position, then before Wedd's, and then over on the left in front of Stothers's, before swinging the guns back to the right to plaster the road leading up from the south to the crossroads, which you believe was

---

when he saw Pangman: "He was dirty and gaunt, tears running down his cheeks. It was hard to compare this man with the major I had once known when he said, 'God bless you in this. We took terrible losses and still didn't get the objective.' He'd come to realize how war makes us all equal." See Charles Martin, *Battle Diary*, Toronto: Dundurn Press, 1994, p. 116.

the route used by the tanks last night. The ugly image of a Tiger tank crushing through the smouldering ruins of the house here last night is still vivid, and you pound that road for several minutes. When at last you let the guns rest, no more tracers are coming from anywhere out there.

Whether the guns cooled off a diversionary attack on the right wing of 4th Brigade, or snuffed out a serious attempt to retake these positions they gained so handily last night, is impossible to tell. Whatever they were trying, the guns surely soured their taste for it, for, though the Royals stand-to the rest of the night, expecting the worst as the sounds of bitter action rise about the Rileys on the left, and 4th Field shells frequently roar with grim intensity over there, the Germans leave the Royals strictly alone.

For the Rileys it is a bad night. Two companies are seriously infiltrated. This you learn from monitoring radio messages from the FOOs to the guns. At 0100 hours February 21, you identify the voice of Lieut. Gerry Corbeil, a 14th Battery GPO brought up to relieve a FOO, calling for a Mike target on his own position to flush out the Germans. There follows a terse exchange with his Battery Commander, Drewry, in that peculiar abbreviated way radio messages are passed in the heat of battle – only the barest facts, unadorned by emotion, occasionally camouflaged by facetious expressions such as "big brothers" for medium guns, and frequently punctuated by long, agonizing blanks in transmissions, during which, for minutes on end, you try in vain to distinguish something intelligible amidst the gibberish spilling from earphones.

After hearing Corbeil report "uninvited guests" are about to visit his house, you hear no more for an interminable period, though you strain your ears to identify his familiar accent in the gushing roar of static and overlapping gabble. Just as you are starting to think he must have bought it, he comes on to explain to "Sunray" he had to remain quiet while he waited with drawn pistol to get a bead on a Jerry coming in the door, so he wouldn't miss in the gloom.

Of this very grim night Riley's Col. Whitaker will recall:

Back in the milk factory [Tac Headquarters] we were swamped by reports by the FOOs and my company commanders about this extremely dangerous counter-attack. Panzer Lehr attacked Kennedy's B Company at Schwanenhof [farm] from the south and the decimated C Company from the east.

Jack Drewry and his gunner crew of two – the latter operating the 19-set from a half-track behind my HQ – swung into non-stop action that was to continue throughout the night. Jack was a big, bluff, good-looking, hard-drinking officer who never lost his cool. His gunners were an unlikely crew, both characters: Steve Pinchuk, the driver . . . and "Coop" Cooper, an excellent signaller, who was an accomplished jazz pianist. His favourite tune was "Pistol Packin' Momma, lay that pistol down . . ." Through numerous battles, those three men were responsible for saving many, many RHLI lives; the enemy laid many pistols down.

Drewry had direct call on twenty-four guns of 4th Field (for Mike targets) and on all seventy-two guns in the three field regiments of 2nd Division (for Uncle targets). He called down many Mikes and Uncles that night. It was a "Mike target Scale Five" [five rounds from each of twenty-four guns] that dispersed the enemy from C Company HQ.*

It is nearly dawn when the Germans pull back leaving scores of their dead strewn about (200 would later be counted in the vicinity of the Rileys and the Royals), and 46 prisoners from the Panzer Lehr Division in Riley hands, bringing the total POWs taken by 4th Brigade to 275. Across the front six more enemy tanks are burning, and at dawn an Air OP pilot is able to count eleven derelicts around and about the highway.†

---

* From *Rhineland*, by Col. W. Denis and Shelagh Whitaker, Toronto: Stoddart, 1989, pp. 165–6.
† *Gunners of Canada* gives 4th Field much of the credit for 4th Brigade

In an unusual document prepared for filing with the regimental war diary, the taciturn Col. MacGregor Young will write of this epic two-day struggle to gain and hold the Goch–Calcar highway:

> This operation produced the most violent German counter-attacks the Regiment has seen. On one occasion two officers with separate battalions called down fire on their own OPs at the same time. Three officers spent a whole night in a cellar with the enemy over them. Three other OP parties had the enemy throwing hand-grenades into their OPs, and got into hand-to-hand fighting on two separate occasions . . . Prisoners of war later stated at least three tanks were disabled by artillery fire, and the heaps of dead Germans in front of the various company positions were adequately satisfying.

Clearly life back at the guns remains exceedingly strenuous. Just servicing the round-the-clock demands from the FOOs for tons of shells would be enough to exhaust the gunners. But they must also contend with quagmire fields where every gun has to be winched and manhandled in and out of position, and every ton of ammunition – of the mountains consumed daily – must be

---

holding the Goch–Calcar highway, singling out for special mention Major John L. Drewry, who was awarded the DSO, and his signaller, Ralph Cooper, who received a Commander-in-Chief Certificate. However, credit for nine out of eleven kills of Panzer Lehr tanks was given to 18th Battery, 2nd Anti-tank Regiment – seven by C Troop under Lieut. David Heaps, and two by A Troop under Lieut. F. R. Ray. Both officers were awarded the Military Cross. Major Louis Froggett, who guided a 17-pounder crew from 2nd Anti-Tank into position, would never forget the satisfaction of seeing them knock out four tanks. As reported in *Rhineland* by Col. Denis and Shelagh Whitaker (Toronto: Stoddart, 1989, p. 168), those charging tanks were stopped less than one hundred yards from Battalion Headquarters. Had they made it all the way, Froggett believes they could have "rolled up the battalion."

carried in from the nearest stable road, over cavernous, water-filled ruts, especially treacherous on dark rainy nights to bone-weary gunners staggering under the weight of 110-pound shell boxes. And though the nerve-wracking tension of the front line, which can exhaust a man even when he is doing no more than crouching in a hole in the ground for survival, is less persistent back at the guns and wagon lines, life for the gunner is frequently just as fearful and dangerous. Impressive numbers of German guns and mortars maintain harassment day and night – moving their fire about from gun positions to wagon lines, to road junctions, and back again – while their new jet-propelled assault planes *swoosh* in without warning, streaking through a blur of black ack-ack puffing skyward from dozens of Bofors, to bomb and strafe whatever presents itself as a target.

All of which you must visualize by applying past experience to the bits of information garnered from Signal-Sgt. Ryder when he brings up the rations every two or three days, since you never get a chance to visit the guns. To gain the full flavour of life at the guns, you must wait the chance to peruse Bombardier Hossack's log and his revealing montage of impressions:

The front is aroar with all the guns seemingly firing in unison.

The area is literally packed with all kinds of Allied equipment, and three units divide one small smashed house. Enemy shells fall at the busy crossroads and a Don R is blown to eternity. All German houses have been well "conquered" and all civilians are evacuated to the rear, for our protection not theirs. We find sleeping space on ground floors and cellars of the broken homes, and everything from bedpans to pianos are thrown outside to give us more room. The battle is now an even–stephen affair and civilian rights are not even considered as we vie for supremacy.

Our ack-ack guns can't hit the jet-propelled planes that visit us daily. These [twin-jet M-262s] have a remarkable change of pace. We wear tin hats when ack-ack shell splinters bounce off the tile roof of our small command post. Bombs screech down and we take cover. There's a direct hit on a 14th Battery gun pit killing three and wounding four.*

The shells and mortars that come in day and night bring memories of Carpiquet, Normandy. German larders are full of choice preserves. Pork and beef roam around, and all this finds its way into our cookhouse. Pork chops used to be a memory; now they are a daily occurrence.

An enemy counter-attack gains headway overrunning Battalion HQ ... Frantic calls come in for Mike targets, and everybody goes to work with a vengeance: gunners doing their work "at the double," signallers perspiring, the officer talking himself hoarse on the Tannoy PA system, as the surveyor (GPO Ack) provides him with the data. Hours later the attack is halted, but not before sizeable losses are suffered by the infantry. In the morning (February 21) congratulations are received from the infantry commander on our efforts: the shooting was "right on the button" and the shells were "on the floor" faster than ever before recorded – just seventy seconds after the radio signal specified a map reference ...

You hear that Carrier Driver "Palm" Knight and OP Ack Eugene Bowers, who both served on your OP crew last winter, were wounded during the counter-attacks on the Rileys. The Rileys suffered 125 killed and wounded, and the Royals 64. The Essex Scottish lost 205 men and officers when they were overrun: 51 killed, 99 wounded, and 54 taken prisoner.

---

* Killed were Gunner Robert Bilodeau, Lance-Bombardier Ralph Bartlett, and Bombardier Burgess A. Porter. Wounded were Sgt. George Oleniuk, Bombardier Murray Harding, Bombardier John Homan, and Gunner James Garrigan.

48

OBSERVATIONS FROM A PIGPEN

---- ✳ ----

AT FIRST LIGHT FEBRUARY 21, YOU AND SQUISSATO REPAIR to the only place you can get an overview of enemy territory without exposing yourselves to snipers: a pigpen in the far end of this low-slung brick structure abutting the highway. Long shallow shutters, hinged along the top and raised slightly for ventilation, provide a broad view of the zone. And even though you must remain well back in the shadows, when you climb over the wooden barrier and join the grunting, half-grown pigs in the sty itself, you find you can gain a truly panoramic view when you move right and left. And so from dawn to dusk you remain among the agitated pigs while Squissato sits with his remote control outside the pen on a barrel, when he isn't rustling up tea or grub, or spewing handfuls of pig feed from the barrel to a squealing mob of porkers scrambling for position at their trough.

Though the Germans continue sporadic shelling and mortaring across the front, occasionally with awesome intensity, they launch no more counter-attacks this day against the weary battalions along Goch–Calcar highway – no more, that is, if you don't count a crazy attempt by a company of Germans to reoccupy this position late this afternoon, marching this way boldly upright, two abreast, as though on a route march, up a road that joins the highway just left of your pigpen. Obviously new troops, fresh from the south, but inexplicably ill-informed not to be aware that only some thirty-six hours ago German infantry and tanks (116 Panzer Windhund Division), after retaking this very position and inflicting heavy casualties on the Essex, were driven out by your horrendous concentrations of shell-fire; and that only last night when Panzer Lehr units hinted they wanted to return here, they too were dissuaded by another torrent of shells from 4th Field guns.

You have to be alerted to the imminent arrival of these uninvited guests by a Royals' mortar sergeant, so engrossed are you in engaging a distant target barely visible in the haze that your 10-power glasses tend to magnify excessively: a long line of tiny figures, strung out for at least two miles, interspersed with horse-drawn wagons, crawling at a snail's pace across the front from right to left along a road lined with Lombardy poplars. To reach them you are using super-charge (good for 13,400 yards), shelling first the leading end of the column and then moving back along the line of march to troops still upright, plodding along. Then back to the reformed front section and so on.

Quickly you peel off Baker Troop guns from the others working over that distant road and order "ten rounds gunfire" (ten rounds per gun fired as fast as they can) on a point just in advance of the marching column – a point easily established, for it happens to be the centre of the designated DF SOS Target area. And the Germans are still swinging jauntily up the road no more than two hundred yards away when your shells sizzle overhead, and you see them break ranks and start diving for the ditches, before the target area is obscured by a turmoil of violent orange and black puffs erupting on the road, in the ditches, and among the trees lining the road. From that moment you see no further movement out there. But assuming that most of them will have survived that initial blasting and will be crawling away along the ditches making for the farm buildings up that road, you shift the fire of the four guns in stages back along the road to where it runs past farm buildings. And while B Troop engages your latest correction, you go back to tormenting that distant column, again reformed and crawling along to a point where it will disappear from your view.

In the middle of this extraordinary business, you are suddenly conscious that another spectator has joined Squissato and the Mortar Sergeant standing on the trough and leaning on the top rail of the pen behind you. And when you get a chance to turn around to see who it is, you are astounded to find yourself looking into the smiling blue eyes and broadly grinning face of George Browne, who was your troop commander briefly after his escape from France after the Dieppe Raid in 1942, first from the Germans and then Vichy. And he is just as you remember him then, his highly polished appearance enhanced by a gleaming white set of perfect teeth and unusually high colouring, well burnished today by a frigid wind. On the epaulettes of his belted Burberry, so totally unsoiled it could have just come from the dry cleaners, are the crown and pips of a lieutenant-colonel!

Laughing at your speechless disbelief, he advises you to "Carry on – we'll talk when you finish."

But as you return to adjusting the fire on your targets, you feel increasingly uneasy about your appearance and that of Squissato, who is standing beside the impeccably turned-out Colonel. Though your nose has long since lost all sensitivity for any offensive odour a careless pig might release, you must be redolent; and while you've had no access to a mirror for days, you are fully aware that flopping down in a coal bin at night when you get the chance, and observing the zone from a pigpen inhabited by live pigs by day, is hardly conducive to good grooming.

And so you are relieved he is unable to hang around more than a minute or two when you finish – just long enough to explain he is now the CO of 14th Field (since moving over from 1st Field in Italy) and is up here with the Brigadier of 9th Brigade (John Rockingham) and the battalion commanders to recce the positions they'll be taking over tonight. Oh, hadn't you heard? 2nd Division is exchanging positions with 3rd Division on the left flank.

You tell him it has been rather a "sticky go" up here.

And he tells you it hasn't been any "piece of cake" on the road to Moyland either, but better than those first few days of "Veritable" when they were earning the title of "water rats." Maintaining arty support for units sailing forward in Buffaloes or walking through water three feet deep to clear "islands" was a trying business. But now he must rejoin the others ... He saw Mac Young for a moment at 4th Brigade on the way up ... Must get together for a drink someday. Smiling down at the pigs jostling about your legs, he expresses the hope you will find a less crowded OP where you are going – perhaps draw a luxurious upper room in Moyland Castle from whence he just came. He suggests you look out for Frederick the Great's bedroom with its canopied bed on raised platform, surrounded by curved walls covered with paintings of well-endowed nudes.

You reckon that would be rather splendid.

He wishes you good hunting, and he's gone.

So, there's to be a move tonight over on the left somewhere south of Calcar. You don't relish the idea. It means another sleepless night, and with all those hundreds of men and vehicles moving in opposite directions, the confusion could be horrendous, could draw fire, or even a counter-attack. The pigs are now snuffling around your legs, crowding for position at the trough next to your feet, thinking you are going to feed them. At least you won't be spending tomorrow in a pigpen! For this you'll not be sorry. You are heartily sick of the sight, sound, and smell of pigs, and this you remark to Squissato as you climb out of the pen to rest for a while on his pig-feed barrel.

With this sentiment Squissato heartily concurs and says he doesn't think he will ever be able to eat pork again. This morning, when he went to get something out of the carrier, parked out of sight in a notch behind the pigpen, he found a pig eating the guts out of the dead German lying there.

With that, he goes out to the carrier to rustle up some Compo tea, leaving you to revel in the prospect of a new OP – possibly in that castle that impressed Browne so much.

One day you will read a wonderful description by war correspondent R. W. Thompson of the occupation by the Maisonneuves of the great brick Schloss of Moyland, once the summer residence of Frederick the Great, pitted and scarred by shells and Typhoon rockets:

> ... a dirty white flag was hoisted above the main turret ... sunshine shone upon the dusky red bricks of its mellowed walls and revealed the desolation of surrounding lawns and parklands, laid waste by the violence of the fighting. Two antlered deer, cast in bronze and mounted on stone plinths, flanked the bridge over the outer moat. The swollen body of a dead horse lay in the drive ... Inside a vast confusion of wreckage ... In the great, principal bed chamber ... cooking stoves of a French-Canadian company roared under pans of frying fat . . . In the magnificently appointed bathrooms of the state apartments groups of soldiers washed and shaved for the first time in a week. The place had been a vast treasure house and in scores of rooms all the bric-a-brac of an exquisite home of princely wealth lay jumbled in confusion. In the cellars of the castle Ilse Marie, Baroness Steengracht von Moyland, sat upright in the midst of her white-faced servants, seeming the sole survivor of a world long since dead. It was impossible to believe that a way of life such as hers had persisted until a week ago: impossible to imagine that such a life would ever again be possible.*

But for now your thoughts are of a coarser nature, restricted, by the paucity of detail in Browne's description of the castle made of bricks, to imagining those nude-covered curved walls of the master bedroom.

---

* R. W. Thompson, *Battle for the Rhine*, New York: Ballantine Books, 1959, pp. 174–75.

49

A MOONLIGHT DRIVE
IN NO-MAN'S-LAND

❋

AS BROWNE PREDICTED, THE CHANGE-OVER WITH 3RD
Division takes place after dark. There is a moon, however, and
when not hidden by clouds it is very helpful to the long, snaking
columns of shuffling foot-sloggers feeling their way along the
rutted and shell-pitted roads, as always heavily laden with weapons,
ammunition, packs, and shovels.

During the move you lose contact with the Royals and have to
make it to their new location on your own, when you get a signal to
report to Battalion Tac Headquarters to pick up a map of the new
zone and be briefed by Battery Commander Don Cornett. Because
of the confusion of troops and support columns moving up or back
in the vicinity, it takes much longer than it should to locate
Cornett's barn.

Moyland Woods, after six days of bitter fighting, has finally been
cleared, but Calcar, two miles farther southeast, is still in enemy
hands. Thus the principal role of 4th Brigade will be to protect the
left flank of 2nd Division from attacks out of Calcar, and the
Royals, on the left flank of the brigade, will be preoccupied with
the east as much as the south.

You are to hole up in a farmhouse that will be Tim Beatty's D
Company headquarters on the brow of a hill looking southeast
over the rugged country about a mile west of Calcar. By the map
there are two routes there: a long, roundabout one which would

bring you to the rear of the house; and a more direct route which could present problems of cover as you near the farm. Not knowing which route Beatty and company are taking, you choose the shorter one. However, you have not gone far past dark and silent houses along this totally deserted road before you feel the tension rising as you spot familiar signs that no vehicles or men have passed this way recently. In the moonlight, which comes and goes with the vagaries of the drifting clouds, you see gravelly dirt, twigs, and other bits of vegetation garnishing downed power lines and other miscellaneous debris, blown across the road by past bombardments, totally undisturbed by tracks, tires, or boots.

Suppressing your anxiety that the road may be mined, you let the carrier roll on slowly until you are about three hundred yards from the house, where you should be turning left across a field sloping up to the rear of the house. This, you discover, is impossible, for the road is now passing along a deep notch cut into the hillside. You halt the carrier in the shadows of the cut, and getting down under a piece of tarpaulin, examine the map with a torch. Either you go back and circle around a couple of miles to approach the house from another direction, or you drive one hundred yards or so out into no-man's-land to the mouth of the farm lane leading up to the front of the house. You decide to chance the latter, and speaking softly to Reid, you tell him to be as quiet as he can. Within seconds of the carrier moving out into the moonlight you spot the mouth of the lane. But as you signal Reid to turn left into it, you have to jump up and direct him with hand signals so as to thread the tracks through a dozen or more German bodies sprawled face-down across the lane – the largest number of bodies you've ever seen in such a small area. Only by ingenious swivelling does Reid miss running over hands and feet.

On the way up the muddy track towards the burned-out shell of what had been a tall, white house, still largely white and glistening in the moonlight, you realize a tracked vehicle coming in from no-man's-land could arouse unpleasant action from the occupants of the ruins. So while you are still some distance away you stop the carrier and get out to walk up alone to a sashless window opening, calling out loudly as you go a stream of questions you hope will give the occupants reason to pause before letting fly at you:

"Where the hell is everybody? Are you all asleep? Why am I not being challenged? What's going on? Wake up, you lead-swinging employees of Mackenzie King, and earn your dollar-thirty a day!"

But the white skeleton remains spookily silent until you get right up to a window opening and start to lean in to examine the charred clutter. Then the ugly muzzle of a heavy machine-gun rises up level with your eyes, and a gruff voice demands: "Who the hell are you?"

You tell him you're a 4th Field FOO, and explain why you are coming in from the front. Still, he remains suspicious; nobody told *him* they were going to be relieved tonight. But when, in your best authoritarian voice (not easy with a machine-gun almost touching your nose), you suggest it might be sensible for everybody's sake to get your carrier parked in behind the house as soon as possible, he reluctantly agrees.

Profoundly relieved, you march down the hill and lead the carrier up to a spot behind a low barn untouched by shells and the fire that consumed the house a day or two ago, judging from the coldness of the debris cluttering the ground floor, and the residual heat left in the stone-and-concrete ceiling of the arched alcove that you and your crew take over in the basement, after the remote control from the 19-set in the carrier is spooled out across the barnyard and down the stone cellar steps. At first the mild heat, radiating from the floor above which had withstood the glowing embers of the whole fiery interior of the two-storey house, feels wonderfully comforting after the frigid midnight air outside. But soon you and your men are perspiring, peeling off layers of clothing, and wishing you had access to that marvellous ice-cream parlour in Antwerp.

Suddenly you remember a can of peaches and a can of creamy rice pudding out in the carrier, squirrelled away for a special occasion, on your suggestion, since carrier crews never get to see such exotic items except when errors occur in the letter of the alphabet stencilled on a Compo box to signify its contents.

Miraculously, in recent days two such incorrectly labelled boxes made it past the eagle eyes of ration despatchers at all levels of Army Service Corps and the Regiment. Could there be a better time to sample the contents of those precious cans? When the question is put to the crew, they vote unanimously for immediate consumption.

When you go out to the carrier to rummage for the cans, the mud has stiffened in the barnyard and ice has formed on the puddles. The rich, creamy rice pudding is as cold and thick as vanilla ice cream when it is spooned into mess tins. And garnished with cold sweet slices of peaches, it is the greatest dessert in the history of the world – though perhaps only mouths parched and ravenous for something cold and sweet could be expected to realize this.

When the Royals arrive space is suddenly at a premium, for though the basement is honeycombed with several arched tunnel-like rooms, all are small and some are cluttered, as yours is with a mound of potatoes. Among the stream of people who come to look in on you, checking to see if there is any extra floor space, is the friendly Mortar Sergeant who was with you and Squissato in that pigpen on the Goch–Calcar highway yesterday afternoon. Seeing two of your crew already bedded down and asleep, and another brewing up a cuppa, he wonders aloud how you made it up here so much in advance of everybody else.

You explain about the shortcut, and during the course of your explanation describe the horrific sight of all those German bodies lying in the moonlight down there where your carrier turned off the main road into the farmer's lane leading up to the house.

He is much impressed, but being pragmatic by nature, he decides that when the moon sets about 3:00 A.M. he'll go down and loot them, explaining he soon will have need of extra cash because he is getting married on his next leave.

Sometime before dawn he wakes you up and inquires rather boldly how many bodies you think you saw down there at the road. Sensing your veracity is being questioned, you turn to Squissato, now manning the radio, and ask him the same question.

"About a dozen," says he without the slightest hesitation.

"Well, there aren't any down there now!" declares the Sergeant.

Oh, but he must be mistaken. Did he go right down to the road?

"Couldn't make a mistake . . . followed the ruts left by your carrier right down to where they turned in from the road. There are no bodies down there."

The only possible explanation is that all those bodies were alive.

"And one of them at least is still down there somewhere," says the Sergeant, taking off his beret and poking a finger through a bullet hole.

The squeaking tracks of your carrier, resembling a tank, suddenly coming out of nowhere, must have surprised an enemy patrol, and they flopped face-down in the farm lane, feigning death. But then your carrier swung into the lane and they were obliged to maintain a steely coolness almost beyond belief – not moving a muscle as tracks passed within inches of their heads.

50

"NIPPING OFF" SOME ENEMY TERRITORY

❋

AT FIRST LIGHT, THOUGH IT IS FROSTY OUTSIDE, YOU ARE glad to leave that cloying, radiant heat of the cellar and pick your way through the charred trash on the roofless, ground-floor shell of what had been a very substantial house, to a position at the gaping, sashless window you'd approached with such trepidation from no-man's-land last night.

Here you look over a valley of farmland and woods, a striking field of fire for the Bren gunner with whom you share the opening. When you remark on this, he draws your attention to the para-trooper bodies dotted here and there down the slope – all face down, their weapons beside them pointing this way, just as they had fallen to a hail of bullets from this and other openings in the derelict house and barn. He tells you, "Three times, according to the 9th Brigade guys we relieved here last night, the paratroopers charged up the slope yelling obscenities in English."

Those forlorn, crumpled bodies in the dead grass out there provide melancholy testimony to a generation of young men who continue to fight and die for a lost cause. Surely the alert men of the Paratroop and Panzer Lehr Divisions have realized since late December, when their Ardennes' offensive against the Americans ground to a halt after gaining a fifty-mile breakthrough, that all hope of preventing the Allies from overrunning their homeland had disappeared. But still they fight on with an aggressiveness sometimes bordering on insanity.

But not this morning. Stand-to passes quietly.

After registering a couple of farmhouses down in the valley, dropping a ranging round through the roof of each, you retire to the cellar for breakfast. There you find the Royals engaged in an effort to gain more floor space for sleeping, cleaning out everything the farm family had stored in the interlocking, tunnel-like rooms. In the room that until now has been largely the domain of your crew, they are attacking a great mound of potatoes piled up along one wall of the room, shovelling them into burlap sacks and carrying them outside.

A soldier who has just come off duty is asleep on his back on the crest of the pile, snoring away oblivious to the fact his bed is being seriously undermined. Soon there is nothing supporting his head, but mysteriously it manages to maintain a horizontal position as though his neck is locked rigid. By the time the shoveller has undermined his shoulders without any change in his position, the phenomenon has begun to attract a crowd.

Slowly, relentlessly, the potatoes disappear from beneath the upper half of the sleeping man. Still he remains aloft as by levitation. Not until he is undermined almost to his hips does he collapse on his head in a bewildered heap in the corner.

The fact there is no accompanying roar of laughter from onlookers who crowded around to await the inevitable outcome, and are now dispersing without comment, speaks volumes for the depth of the fatigue afflicting all. Even as they marvelled at their comrade's body defying gravity, they had complete empathy with the exhausted man, understanding the capacity of a sleep-starved body to come to terms with the weirdest conditions – maintaining sweet oblivion to every filthy discomfort until the last possible moment before carrying out its next set of obligations, imposed as frequently by visits from uninvited guests from out front as by red-tabbed gentlemen studying well-lighted map-boards in the rear.

However, for the next twenty-four hours all moves, and the sleep-denying conflict they incite, are imposed from the rear, by men using sharp Chinagraph pencils to select limited company objectives designed either to straighten out the line or ensure a more secure startline for the next push: "nipping off" a dominant feature with some farm buildings over there in the valley in front of Major Suckling's B Company; "occupying" a wooded area with farmhouse south of Major Louis Froggett's Rileys company; and "clearing" Ebben, a collection of buildings at a road junction, some four hundred yards in front of A Company of the Highland Light Infantry of 9th Brigade, currently occupying your old pigpen on the Goch–Calcar highway.

But if the objectives are limited, German resistance is not, and in every case their counter-attacks equal in ferocity anything exhibited during their vain struggle to regain dominance of the Goch–Calcar highway. And sometimes you can feel, as acutely at a distance as when directly involved, the tension that exists in the frenzy of a front-line struggle, when the outcome is never certain until you suddenly become aware he is no longer coming at you. A case in point is the furious counter-attack incited by Bob Suckling's company attempting to occupy the farm buildings in front of their position, the course of which you follow squatted down on a milking stool beside Battery Commander Don Cornett, who is poring over a map-board on his lap, in the clammy, draughty cow stable that is Royals' Battalion Tac Headquarters.

Only an hour ago (6:00 P.M., February 23) Cornett, apparently becoming aware that Suckling's position, without the support of a FOO all day, was becoming increasingly vulnerable, ordered you to move over there. However, while you were still packing up, he ordered you to join him at Battalion HQ. Now, with Suckling acting as his eyes, describing as best he can where 4th Field's shells are falling, Cornett is "shooting from the map," sending appropriate corrections back to the guns.

The initial move by Suckling's company to occupy the area of some farm buildings a couple of hundred yards in front of their position began at 2:30 A.M., as a forty-man fighting patrol led by a platoon commander, Lieut. G. H. Matheson. When the rest of the company followed about 5:00 A.M., the farm buildings were still in enemy hands, and were cleared only after some tanks and flame-throwers were brought up to support a second attack about 4:30 in the afternoon. One officer and nineteen paratroopers came out with their hands high over their heads, bringing the total bag of prisoners for the day to forty.

Now with darkness covering their movement, the enemy has mounted a very strong counter-attack behind an unusually heavy and sustained box barrage. Three self-propelled guns have moved up and are smashing shells into the house and barn, and in the glaring light of flares sent skyward by the company's 2-inch mortars, some one hundred paratroopers are seen coming across the field in extended line, providing a target for the Royals' 6-pounder crew until all their H.E. shells are expended.

At this crucial point, you notice Col. Lendrum, the Royals' CO, has been drawn from behind his table and is squatting down beside you in front of Cornett, clearly recognizing that the fate of his D Company is now in the hands of this cool little man, hunched over and all but disappearing within the folds of his great sheepskin coat, in which he has virtually lived since plucking it from that great pile of discarded German winter clothing on the Merxem dock in Antwerp last September.

From the infantry 18-set earphones hanging around Cornett's neck, Suckling's voice is asking: "Can you bring your shells a bit closer?"

Cornett, still studying his map, picks up the microphone of the remote control running out to the 19-set in his half-track in the barnyard that will send his order back to the guns: "Northwest 100 – Scale 5 – Repeat!" And when again the guns can be heard thumping shells into that distant valley, he inquires, "How's that, Bob?"

In a moment Suckling is calling enthusiastically, "You're right on! They're landing right where they should! Keep them coming!"

Again and again Cornett orders "Scale 5 – Repeat," each time releasing another 120 rounds of high explosive on the target area, all the while staring intently at the map-board on his knees, as though willing the shells to land where they should: close to, but not on, that tiny dot representing Suckling's house. Only when he finally allows the shelling to subside, and the expected report from Suckling does not materialize, does he look up with worried eyes. Grasping the 18-set mike he goes on the air to request a sitrep, but when he releases the transmission switch and the gush of static returns to the earphones, no familiar voice disturbs the persistent gabble.

After the running exchange they'd been conducting, the silence is ominous, and the minutes pass slowly as further calls by Cornett fail to draw any response. Then suddenly, to the vast relief of three men huddled around Cornett's map-board, a familiar drawl comes on the air to report: "The Heinies seem to have pulled back."

Later you'll learn his long silence was due to his being fully occupied stalking a paratrooper poking around outside his back door. An amused witness will tell of his Company Commander muttering in disgust – when the grenade he bowled into the courtyard went clattering along the tiles alerting the German to take cover before it went off – "Oh hell, I should have used my pistol!" But then he got another chance when the curious German returned and poked his head in the doorway.

Understrength before the attack, D Company is now down to 20 per cent of its strength, having suffered forty-four casualties, four of them fatal. And by the time Wedd's company arrives to reinforce them, the survivors have been without food and sleep for more than twenty-four hours.

Over on the right, Major Froggett's company of Rileys runs into an equally "sticky go" in moving forward five hundred yards to some farm buildings. During a particularly tense period, their second FOO of the day, Lieut. Jim Nesbitt, GPO of Dog Troop, 14th Battery, sent up to take over from "a wounded and exhausted Troop Commander," Captain Ken Smale, calls down a Mike target on his own position when things become so bad he simply "doesn't know what the hell else to do."

Of this bitter struggle that continues off and on for seventy-two hours, one of Froggett's platoon commanders, Lieut. Ken Dugall, will one day say: "As they tried to jump through the hedge we were shooting them. There were fellows lying there with arms twisted, some shot through the knee and screaming blue murder . . . Oh Jesus, it was terrible."*

Nesbitt will remember the next night as being "a very sticky time at the farm" for him and his crew, including Gunner Al "Dutch" Plomp, his OP Ack. "Before Bren gun fire and grenades send them packing, Germans are running around the place, setting the building on fire with their mortars, and chopping the top almost completely off the 19-set in the carrier with machine-gun fire, rendering it useless."

Next morning, February 25, Capt. Don Edwards, Dog Troop Commander, is sent over to relieve Nesbitt. Thus Edwards is standing shoulder to shoulder with Major Froggett when his company is again involved in fending off a counter-attack of such fanatical intensity that many years after this intrepid company commander will still refer to it as "the grisliest day of the war for me."

Similarly, moves on the same day by battalions of 3rd Division, to improve their startline for Operation "Blockbuster," stir up a hornet's nest. Doug MacFarlane, until recently GPO of your Baker Troop, is in the thick of it, having been promoted Captain and posted to 14th Field Regiment. In fact – though it will be many moons before you learn of it – your good friend is in the process of earning a Military Cross for gallantry in his first tour of duty as a FOO, having gone forward with a leading company of the Highland Light Infantry in a predawn attack designed to clear the crossroads hamlet of Ebben, lying only about four hundred yards south of your old pigsty OP on the Goch–Calcar highway.

By first light MacFarlane has an OP in a building just cleared by

---

* From *Rhineland* by Col. Denis and Shelagh Whitaker, Toronto: Stoddart, 1989, p. 171.

the HLI. Almost immediately it is engaged by an enemy self-propelled gun from about six hundred yards away. Its first shot kills his signaller, wounds him around the face and eyes, and puts his radio out of action. Then the shelling and mortaring about the position knocks out a signal line that has just been laid to his OP, leaving him with no means of calling down fire from the guns. In spite of his wounds and the enemy fire, he traces the line back and fixes the break, returns to his OP, still under mortar fire, and shells the German SP until it goes silent. All day, he shells and disperses Germans jockeying for position to attack.

Meanwhile, the men at the guns continue their exhausting routine. From the day they took up their first position in the Rhineland near Bedburg, the gunners have had little rest. When not being called upon to produce intense fire to beat back counter-attacks, which can continue for hours and sometimes overlap, they must conduct long, drawn-out programs of harassing fire to keep the enemy on edge, especially throughout the night. Shell consumption is therefore heavy, and weary gunners have to carry most of it hundreds of yards from heavily laden trucks that can't make it to the guns through the mud. When 4th Field moves February 23 to deploy a mile northwest of Moyland, in fields from which the flood waters have just receded, the quads, wallowing through the mud, manage somehow to drop their guns off fairly near the gun markers, but then they have to winch themselves back out to the road using "ground anchors."

Bombardier Hossack's terse diary notes capture the grimness:

The Padre buries the Jerry dead near us. A bulldozer, digging gun pits, gets stuck in the heavy going. Ammo vehicles cannot get through the field . . . enemy again counter-attacks in strength . . . the guns are literally panting. Quite a few enemy shells, but none among us. . . . Army rations are practically unused as we dine regularly on [the Rhinelanders'] beef, pork, and chicken. Preserves and sugar-cured hams are also in good quantity. We now know that while the rest of Europe was nearly starved,

Germany's Rhineland, at least, fattened on the very best . . .* By treacherous roads to beyond Louisendorf, scene of heavy German counter-attack. Dead Germans are lying around – 25-pounder shells have made an awful mess of many caught out of their slit trenches . . .

Sergeant Hunt's diary for this same day will record similar reflections on the affluence of Rhineland farmers and the awful harvest their country's war of aggression is reaping:

On arrival civilians still in occupation. A white flag droops from shell-torn roof. This overly prosperous farm, which, despite its present condition, suffers a damning comparison when considered with its equivalent in France, Belgium, and Holland, has felt something of the war – something of the fire and tempest that Germany has always kept for export. In the rooms are pictures of a Nazi son in army uniform. Old-fashioned black-edged envelopes indicate a connection more impressive as from the front window may be seen the same uniform on a body sprawled and bloody. *Sieg heil!*

---

* The plight of the Dutch north of the Rhine had by then become known through Underground sources: how the Germans in late February cut off the western, highly populated regions and prevented them from scrounging life-saving food from the eastern hinterlands as a punishment for the continuing support of the population for the general railway strike that began the previous September, and how this already had caused terrible hardship in the regions of Rotterdam, The Hague, and Amsterdam. The result was widespread malnutrition and death by starvation. At one time even cardboard coffins were unavailable, and 235 bodies awaited burial in just one church in The Hague. (Facts derived from Major Norman Phillips, Canadian Army Public Relations, and J. Nikerk, Secretary, Canadian Netherlands Commission, *Holland and the Canadians* [Amsterdam: Contact Publishing, 1945])

51

FOOTNOTE TO

OPERATION "BLOCKBUSTER"

※

ON THE MORNING OF FEBRUARY 26, SOME 225,000 MUD-caked officers and men of the badly worn, casualty-riddled eight infantry divisions, along with four armoured divisions and four armoured brigades – constituting First Canadian Army – will be required to ignore their battle weariness, accumulated over days and nights of attacks and counter-attacks without number amidst demoralizing sights and smells of death and destruction, arouse their spirits, and push on with all the vigour that commanders expect of fresh troops. Though simply an extension of what has been going on for the past eighteen days, it has been given a fresh name, Operation "Blockbuster," in deference, you suspect, to the tremendous artillery "preparations" designed to get things moving.

Gen. Crerar will again be in charge, though – as in the case of Operation "Veritable" – two-thirds of the units will be British (six of the eight infantry divisions, two of the four armoured divisions, and three of the four armoured brigades), clearly indicating the extent of Field Marshal Montgomery's faith in the Canadian Army Commander.

The intention is to break through between Udem and Calcar, put two brigades on Hochwald Ridge, and exploit through to Xanten. British XXX Corps will attack on the right from about Goch, which was captured by 51st Highland and 52nd Lowland divisions, who cleared the bomb-smashed town street by street, its fanatical defenders firing from piles of rubble and loop-holed, reinforced cellars of buildings still standing.

The 52nd Division will secure the right flank of XXX Corps, and the second day (February 27) 3rd British Division will relieve 15th Scottish Division. 53rd Division, stopped two days ago short of Weeze, will resume its attack.

British 43rd Wessex Division, which took Cleve and drove south to capture the escarpment overlooking Goch during the Goch—Calcar highway struggle, will secure the left flank of 2nd Canadian Corps along the Rhine – its own flank hidden from the enemy by a smokescreen produced by mobile generators operated by the Smoke Companies of Pioneers.

In Phase One, 2nd Canadian Division, supported by 2nd Canadian Armoured Brigade, will take the high ground south of Calcar, while 3rd and 4th Canadian divisions combine to clear Udem and points south.*

As in the last days of Normandy, Canadian units are destined to play a role out of all proportion to their numbers. Attacking across open, rising ground on a narrow front from the Goch—Calcar

---

* Crerar's First Canadian Army for "Blockbuster" was grouped as follows:

Canadian 2nd Corps

Canadian 4th Armoured Division	Canadian 2nd Infantry Division
Polish Armoured Division	Canadian 3rd Infantry Division
British 11th Armoured Division	British 43rd Infantry Division
Canadian 2nd Armoured Brigade	

British XXX Corps

Guards Armoured Division	15th (Scottish) Infantry Division
6th Guards Armoured Brigade	51st (Highland) Infantry Division
8th Armoured Brigade	52nd (Lowland) Infantry Division
34th Armoured Brigade	53rd (Welsh) Infantry Division
3rd British Infantry Division	

highway, they will meet the strongest resistance from prepared positions of the reserve Siegfried Line. For this reason the assaulting
units of 6th Brigade (Les Fusiliers Mont-Royal, Queen's Own
Cameron Highlanders of Canada, and South Saskatchewan Regiment), leading off the 2nd Corps attack under cover of darkness,
will be taken forward as far as practical in Kangaroos and armoured
vehicles. Accompanied by tanks and Flails and aided by artificial
moonlight, with bursts of red tracers from Bofors ack-ack guns
pointing the way with graceful arcs across the night sky, it all will be
very reminiscent of the tactics originated by Simonds and his staff
for the great breakthrough from Verrières Ridge in Normandy.

And for good reason, for there are remarkable similarities in conditions here to those faced by Canadian Army in its drive for
Falaise: a narrow front defended in depth by the finest troops they
can muster, presenting fanatical resistance decreed by the Führer
who, as in Normandy, has forbidden commanders to contemplate
strategic withdrawal beyond a nearby, great river barrier.

Again, as in Normandy, the Americans form the southern jaw
and the Canadians the northern jaw, threatening to masticate the
Germans west of the Rhine. And precisely as in Normandy (when
the Americans were held back by orders from their General Bradley
from attacking north until the last moment of the closing of the
Falaise gap by the Canadians) the U.S.A. Ninth Army has been held
immobile by widespread flooding caused by the Germans opening
the flood valves of the Roer dam, allowing them to give their undi-
vided attention to Canadian Army – transferring north, from the
American front, nine divisions (between 135,000 and 180,000
men), equipped with the greatest concentration of mortars and
guns ever assembled by the Germans anywhere on the whole
Western Front – 1,054 guns and 717 mortars.*

---

* Army Intelligence reported the Germans assembled 451 field guns,
179 mediums, 195 anti-tank guns, 229 dual-purpose 88-mm guns, 581
heavy mortars (80-mm and 120-mm), and 136 superheavy mortars (150-

On top of this, an important change in the tactical approach to operations in the Rhineland has been imposed by the unstable ground conditions resulting from the unusually early spring weather: the use of heavy bombers in support of ground attacks has had to be abandoned. Saturation bombing, as was carried out in Normandy, could turn the low-lying, soggy fields, already treacherous to gun tractors and impossible for ammunition trucks, into a Passchendaele quagmire preventing all vehicular movement including tanks. Thus, apart from stiletto strikes by rocket-firing Typhoons and bomb-carrying Spitfires, the responsibility for destroying enemy strongpoints and neutralizing enemy guns and mortars has devolved on the guns to an even greater degree than usual.

The artillery program, as prescribed by CCRA Brig. Stan Todd (once the CO of 4th Field) will be enormous, involving about the same number of guns as were employed in support of Operation "Totalize" in Normandy. Six divisional artilleries and three AGRAs (Army Group Royal Artilleries) have been allotted to counter-battery and counter-mortar programs.

This massive counter-battery program, in which the Regiment will take part, is to open with a roar at 0345 hours and continue until H-hour at 0430.

Adding to the rolling thunder of 456 25-pounders (nineteen regiments) and 128 mediums (eight medium regiments) will be the deep bellowing of 40 heavies and the hideous swooshing of five successive "flying mattresses," looping skyward from the "rails" of 1st Canadian Rocket Battery to land with awesome violence and their distinctive long. drawn-out roars on the divisional objective before the Hochwald.

Precisely forty-five minutes later, when the counter-battery

---

mm, 210-mm, and 300-mm). Gen. Crerar, himself a former gunner officer, reporting to the Minister of National Defence declared German fire-power in the Rhineland was more heavily and effectively applied than at any other time in the Army's fighting during the present campaign.

program has been shot, 408 field and medium guns will open up on two separate barrages.

In Phase One, on behalf of 6th Brigade going forward in Kangaroos on the right, a fast-moving barrage will be fired to a depth of 4,300 yards; while on the left, in support of the walking troops of 5th Brigade,* a slower barrage will continue to a depth of 1,600 yards.

A program of "timed concentrations" on strongpoints in support of 8th Brigade,† attacking without a barrage on the right flank of 2nd Division, will be fired by 144 additional 25-pounders of 3rd Canadian and 15th British divisions, as well as by 32 mediums.

In Phase Two, on behalf of 3rd Division's attack on Keppeln and the clearing of Udem Ridge by the 4th Canadian Armoured Division, the same targets shelled in the earlier counter-battery program leading up to Phase One will be plastered for another thirty minutes. Then the guns will be switched to supporting the tanks, the M-10s, and infantry riding into action on the backs of the armoured vehicles.

Another thirty-minute artillery bombardment will open Phase Three when 9th Brigade‡ will attack south to take Udem.

Because the planners see all three phases as a continuous operation, it means exceptionally heavy going back at the guns for a day or two. Even before the guns open up, the gunners are involved in exhausting moves to positions well forward, some under enemy observation just behind the FDLs, to ensure assaulting infantry and tanks don't outrun the guns during the early hours of the attack. So limited are suitable areas for gun positions, Brig. Frank Lace, CRA of 2nd Division, does a recce by air in a little Air OP plane.

---

* The Black Watch, Le Régiment de Maisonneuve, and the Calgary Highlanders.

† The Queen's Own Rifles of Canada, Le Régiment de la Chaudière, and the North Shore Regiment.

‡ The Highland Light Infantry of Canada, the Stormont, Dundas and Glengarry Highlanders, and the North Nova Scotia Highlanders.

Slow moves over traffic-jammed roads to quagmire fields where the guns have to be winched and manhandled through the mud into place, and tons of ammo carried for hundreds of yards from trucks confined to the roads, guarantee all ranks are awake and labouring for most of the twenty-four hours before the attack.

Among the clutter of guns, tanks, and vehicles is a radar vehicle designed to pinpoint enemy mortars.* When its crew sets up shop just to the rear of your OP with Jack Strothers on the startline for Blockbuster, you mentally cringe. While you bow to their courage in situating in full view of the enemy (by necessity, if they are to pick up and trace the flight-path of the mortar bombs from source), you are sure their tall, oddly shaped radar aerial will be a beacon for enemy shells or mortars. This you know from witnessing the destruction of another radar crew yesterday morning back there in the barnyard of the Royals' tac headquarters.

It happened just at dawn, when Cornett wakened you to send you over to Strothers. As you were leaving the stable, you had to duck back inside to escape several screaming shells crashing in the barnyard among the vehicles parked there. When you went out, expecting the worst, you found your crew and Cornett's crew unharmed, but the radar crew (of 1st Canadian Radar Battery) in awful shape. The salvo caught them cooking breakfast beside their truck. Two were dead and two wounded. One had his back torn out, and the other, with his right hand dangling on its tendons, remarked with unsettling candour to Turner, the Major's Don R, who'd gone to help him:

"By Christ, I don't think I'll shoot no more crap!"

---

* 1st Canadian Radar Battery came into being near Dunkirk, September 22, 1944, under command of Capt. J. G. Telfer, 2nd Heavy Ack Ack. They taught themselves to pick up the looping bombs on their screens and do the required calculations by firing German mortars west of Dunkirk, and later at St. Leonards, near Antwerp.

52

IN A DISORIENTED
BLUR OF DREAD

※

FOR SEVERAL DAYS NOW, THROUGHOUT THIS WHOLE UGLY business in the Rhineland, you've been living every minute with the dreadful feeling that you are only a few feet away from disaster. It's not something specific you can visualize and prepare for, but the feeling is of such substance that for long periods it tends to dislocate all your other emotional responses.

At times the dread is so all-embracing, it almost disconnects your rational-thinking apparatus, turning the immediate past into a blur, and leaving you with the overpowering sense of participating in an ongoing nightmare: awakening with tremendous relief from one terrible dream, only to descend into another, worse than the one before – on and on in weird, relentless progression.

One of the most terrifying occurs in a little farmhouse on the road marking the front line and the startline for the attack by 5th and 6th brigades, during the first minutes of the barrage opening Operation "Blockbuster" and the heavy enemy counter-fire it incites.

To get a couple of hours' sleep before the guns are to open up on their preparatory tasks at 0345 leading up to H-hour at 0430, you hit the sack shortly after midnight – right after Major Jack Stothers's briefing of his platoon commanders is brought to an abrupt end by the crack of a bullet coming in through a panel of the front door of the little blacked-out living room. He'd barely had time to explain that, though 4th Brigade battalions will be in reserve for the first few hours, all ranks must be standing-to and alert (so as to ensure the startline is secure for 5th and 6th brigades), when there is the vicious slap of a bullet embedding itself in the oak drawer of the sewing machine on which you are leaning your left elbow.

Instantly the lamp is doused, and platoon commanders, fearing still another German counter-attack, rush outside to rejoin their men. But when nothing further happens, and cursory inquiries among the men in slit trenches in the front garden fail to offer any enlightenment as to the origin of the shot, suspicions develop it was only a wayward bullet from a weapon accidentally discharged – a very common occurrence these days. Satisfied this is the case, Stothers gives the order to stand-down. And after producing a generous dollop of rum, he suggests you both catch a couple hours' sleep, for "dear knows when you'll get the chance again."

Gratefully you accept his invitation to share a tiny room off the living room, for you have not staked out any territorial rights in this house or barn since moving back here late today, from a house across the road in no-man's-land where you first had established your OP.

The house over there was your first choice because of its superior view, and you and your crew spent last night over there blissfully unaware there were Germans in the cellar. Squissato had awakened you on hearing German voices coming from the kitchen across the hall. Holding up a finger to his lips for silence, he secured the Bren gun while you, with pistol drawn, joined him at the door. Flinging it open you had confronted not paratroopers, but a middle-aged farm couple, staring at your gun muzzles with anxious eyes. Embarrassed, you had gestured expansively that they should carry on preparing their breakfast. But their sudden, mysterious appearance had unnerved you. Were they really what they seemed, a farmer and wife? Somehow they hadn't shown the proper degree of fear. So when you were called back to an "O" Group at Battalion, you used the excuse to move back within the company area.

While settling down here in your bedroll (fully clothed, including your boots, of course) on the floor beside the cot on which

Stothers is rolled in a blanket, you ask him to wake you when he is getting up at 3:45 A.M. for stand-to.

At this he roars with laughter, pointing out that no one will need a wakeup call when those Tor Scots' 4.2-inch mortars behind the barn start banging away, not to mention the 7.2-inch heavies that will be blasting away somewhere back behind, adding to the din all those 25-pounders and 5.5-inch mediums will be making.

Mildly perturbed by his guffawing, you remind him that gunners are accustomed to sleeping in the midst of guns firing, and that you, having been badly shortchanged in the matter of sleep for some ten days now, will, in all likelihood, sleep through the whole damned show if he chooses not to wake you.

Waiting for sleep, you contemplate the ground-floor window just beyond his cot with suspicion. Recent mortar or shell blasts have blown out all the glass from the window sash, and the wooden shutters, drawn closed over the window from the outside, are so slashed by shell fragments you can see the night sky and feel intermittent draughts of icy air pouring down on your head. Is the German who fired that shot still out there? How easy it would be for him to sneak along the side of the house, pull open the shutters, and drop in a grenade. With such forbidding thoughts you roll over on your stomach and fall asleep.

Thus your heart-spasming horror on awakening to find the shutters wide open to the furious flashing, blasting night, and a beast, with the weight of a giant, kneeling on your back squeezing the breath out of you, as his hands seek your throat, fulfilling the fearful fantasy you imagined just as you were falling asleep.

In the split second it takes to recognize your predicament, you realize your only chance is to fake unconsciousness, while your right hand – already resting under your pillow – secures the pistol you always deposit there when you bed down.

The beast is uttering guttural mutterings as his big fingers close around your neck and begin to shake it insanely, but it's impossible to make out the words over the hellish racket of the incoming shells. Resisting total panic, you grasp the pistol butt, slip your finger over the trigger, and begin sliding it under your chin with the object of worming it up past your ear and aiming it back over your shoulder at that Germanic muttering . . . which at that moment, sounds curiously like, "Forjeesussake . . . wakeupfoo!"

Instantly the panic level drops, as you recognize the voice of Stothers's huge righthand bower – Sgt.-Maj. Hamm. Rolling him off your back, you sit up gasping for air.

"You okay, Foo? You okay? Can you walk, Foo?" Over and over he inquires of your state of health as he grabs hold of you and hoists you to your feet as he would a child. Then putting his arm around your shoulders as though to steady you, he starts guiding you towards the cellarway through the dark house fitfully lit by the flashing shells landing with horrendous crashes outside. You assure him you are just fine except where his knees landed on your back.

Apologetic, he explains that when Major Stothers sent him up to see what had happened to you, he wasn't expecting to find you still sleeping on the floor. So when he tripped over your feet in the dark and fell on you, and you didn't move, he thought you must be dead. He was feeling for a pulse in your neck, when you woke up . . .

Of course – it all makes sense. But you shudder to think how close you came to getting your pistol in place to pull the trigger.

Down in the brightly lit cellar, assembled around Stothers are all members of your crew, along with his company headquarters group, who react with cheers and applause as the towering Sergeant-Major, holding your arm solicitously as though he still believes there must be something the matter with you, triumphantly delivers you to his Major.

Stothers, while obviously pleased to see you alive and unharmed, wags his head in disbelief that Hamm could find you still asleep with the house literally rocking on its foundations from the bombardment.

He tells you that right after the guns began firing their heavy concentrations, and the Tor Scots' 4.2-inch mortars opened up behind the house, Jerry began to return the fire. And even before he could get out of his bedroll and start for the cellar steps, one round landed just outside, blowing the shutters off the window.

Naturally he took it for granted you would be following him – if you hadn't already preceded him down the stairs. But on checking heads, he found you were missing. Assuming you must have been hit, he sent the Sergeant-Major up to bring you down if you were still alive.

It's clear that henceforth he'll look upon you as a bit of a freak, but a worthy brother-in-arms. Ranking high in his estimation of the quality of a soldier, is coolness under fire – a quality in which he himself excels, sometimes to the point of foolhardiness. (Stothers was the only member of the Royals to sleep above ground at Eterville, near Caen – enduring round-the-clock bombardment by mortars and shells in a brick, two-holer backhouse that miraculously survived without a scar.)

While you know you are living under false colours, there is a certain pleasure in being thought of as "cool," so you don't revive the theme that gunners are accustomed to sleeping next to crashing guns; and though your ribs are sore enough to be cracked in spots, you are so touched by their caring actions, you decide not to share with them the churlish thought that, ordinarily, a person is awakened out of a nightmare, not awakened into one. Nor does it seem the right moment to tell Sgt.-Major Hamm that while he was in the process of scaring you half to death, he came within a hair's breadth of getting his head blown off.

As time goes on, the bombardment eases up in both directions, and you are on your way up to the attic of the little one-storey house to watch 4th Division tanks move off towards Udem Ridge in the second phase of the attack when Col. MacGregor Young arrives with the same thought in mind. Just what you expect to see, you aren't sure, but a vision of hundreds of tanks charging forward with guns blazing was implied, if not actually suggested, by the plan of attack outlined yesterday at Lendrum's "O" Group.

However, though you have a grandstand view by virtue of several holes in the roof, opened among the tiles by airbursts or mortar bombs this morning, there is nothing very dramatic about the attack. The numbers of Shermans and self-propelled anti-tank guns moving forward in ragged extended lines are impressive enough, but nothing in their stop-and-go movements would ever suggest the word "charge."

The soggy Rhineland guarantees a sluggish advance. All the tanks leave deep ruts that immediately fill with water. Miraculously few appear irretrievably bogged down as they snarl and growl across the sodden fields, meeting no opposition of any consequence. Apart from pauses to shoot up buildings in their path, and the odd steamy black fountain of mud from a Jerry shell erupting among them, they crawl forward without incident and disappear over the crest, each with a final, defiant, growling spurt. However, they don't get far before Jerry appears to bring his lethal 88s to bear. Soon, intermingled with the *crump* of shells and mortars and the whine of straining tank engines fading in the distance, are sharp *crack*s of high-velocity tank guns.

Later you will learn that while the armoured assault is effective, 4th Division units lose 100 tanks.

Also on their right flank, opposition is equally severe to the tanks of 2nd Canadian Armoured Brigade supporting an attack on Udem by 3rd Division, and as in all bitter fighting here in the Rhineland, individual courage matters greatly. Though it will be some time before you hear the story, at this very hour, just over on the right at a crossroads clump of buildings called Mooshof, a mile south of the Goch–Calcar highway, a sergeant of the Queen's Own Rifles of Canada is taking command of the survivors of his platoon, "only four in number," and, under heavy fire from a house, is climbing onto the back of a 1st Hussars' tank to direct it to punch a hole in the side of the house, where he jumps down and person-ally kills "at least twenty of the enemy" and captures "as many more" before being killed by a sniper's bullet. With the core of enemy resistance in the village broken, and his objectives secure, the twenty-three-year-old hero was on his way to report to his company commander when the sniper got him.*

As the CO is leaving your OP, he remarks that 2nd Division Headquarters (meaning Maj.-Gen. Bruce Matthews and the CRA Brig. Frank Lace), already conscious of the super way the guns have been responding to the German attacks in recent days, were very impressed by the way they routed the attack by two companies of paratroopers and tanks that hit the Rileys just before H-hour this morning – an attack which, had it been successful, would have destroyed the security of the divisional startline.

When you reveal your total ignorance of the matter, he tells you young Don Edwards, the FOO with the company attacked, put on a super show. It was another strong attack by two companies of para-troopers and some tanks. Not only did Edwards pull down shell-fire with devastating effect, but, when Company Headquarters was directly assaulted by paratroopers, seized a rifle and accounted for several of them himself.

As the minutes to H-hour ticked away and the Germans were still engaging the Rileys, everyone up to Corps Headquarters (and perhaps beyond) who remembered Normandy and the problems unsecured startlines had caused around St. Martin-de-Fontenay and Troteval Farm, began to worry. It was, according to Col. Young, "a very close thing." The startline was secure only five or ten minutes before the gunners had to lay their guns on the opening line of the barrage launching the attack. Years later, Major Froggett will recall with earnest gratitude the contribution made by the guns of 4th Field in quelling the attack:

We were almost completely overrun. There were tanks all around us, and my men were fighting hand-to-hand with the paratroops. It was the grisliest day of the war for me. Men were

---

* Sgt. Aubrey Cosens was awarded the Victoria Cross posthumously.

shouting, punching, heaving grenades, firing pistols, and swinging everything they could put their hands to. Lieut. D. D. Edwards, my FOO, was with me in the little frame cottage when all of a sudden a tank started pushing the wall down. There were forty or so German civilians in our cellar, all screaming. Edwards called down everything the artillery could send directly on our position. The Germans were above ground and they got it. We were pretty well dug-in.*

Of this morning Bombardier Hossack's diary will record: "More enemy counter-attacks precede another 'Montgomery barrage' [of long duration involving many guns]. Breeches jam on overworked guns. Number Four develops a burr in the barrel and is relegated to Ordnance for repairs."

Sgt. Hunt's diary, commenting on the guns managing to repulse this threatening counter-attack, just before having to lay on the opening fire-plan with nineteen other field regiments and eight medium regiments, will express the intriguing thought: "Jerry may not have been overly impressed by our defensive Mike targets [involving twenty-four guns], which he doubtless expected, but at 0400 hours when our Corps barrage [involving hundreds of guns] came down on the very area he'd chosen to play about in, his consternation must have been more than somewhat!"†

---

* Quoted in Col. Denis and Shelagh Whitaker's book *Rhineland*, (Toronto: Stoddart, 1989, pp. 172-3). Lieut. (A/Capt.) Donald D. Edwards was subsequently awarded the Military Cross. The citation read in part: "With complete disregard for his own safety Capt. Edwards remained at his post throughout this period of intense and concentrated fire, and coolly directed artillery fire on the advancing enemy with devastating effect."

† Sgt. Bruce Hunt's unfailingly good humour and leadership – which shone through his diary notes even during the worst days of Normandy, the Scheldt, and the Rhineland – earned him the Belgian Croix de Guerre, 1940, avec Palme.

53

A LIVING NIGHTMARE

❋

WHEN DARKNESS FALLS YOU GET A SIGNAL TO JOIN MAJOR
Bob Wedd's A Company of the Royals as it moves up to thicken up
the Rileys who suffered heavy casualties early this morning driving
off that fierce German counter-attack and restoring the startline.

Immediately you find yourself plunged into a living nightmare
among a massive movement of men and armoured vehicles. As in
Normandy the battlefield is lit mistily by artificial moonlight
created by playing searchlights on low clouds, though this is hardly
necessary, for the whole front seems to be in flames – vehicles,
houses, and barns are burning everywhere. Penetrating through the
roar of motors and a monstrous barrage they are laying down up
ahead, is the terrified squealing of pigs trapped in the flames somewhere nearby, and now and then you distinguish the *crack* of an
unseen 88 bursting overhead.

A confusion of tanks, Kangaroos, Bren carriers drawing anti-
tank guns, and marching troops slogging along the verges in single
file are on the move to God knows where, following tracks that
may have been roads once but are now churned-up watery bogs. So
deep are the ruts, vehicles of all sorts are getting stuck, forcing the
columns to keep shifting off to the left or right onto even softer
ground, and on such a detour around the rear of some buildings,
with the belly of the old carrier bottoming among cavernous,

watery ruts left by the heavier tracked vehicles, the transmission packs it in.

While this is hardly a surprise, after the beating it has taken since sustaining such shocking torque, crashing in and out of that great crater in the road back near Louisendorf several days ago, it does create a very awkward situation. By the time you recognize the seriousness of the breakdown, and realize that if you are to keep contact with the infantry you'll have to keep going on foot, a great many vehicles and marching troops have passed by. After getting off a radio signal to the Battery to send up another carrier, you leave your crew to transfer the equipment and gear into it when it arrives, and start off on foot to try and catch up with Wedd and company.

This won't be easy, for you weren't given a specific map reference for their new position. You were merely told to hook up with Wedd's company on its way up to reinforce the Rileys. Even Wedd won't know where his company is to go until he's liaised with the Rileys on the ground and been assigned a role.

All you can do is keep on tramping through the mud, stumbling over the deep ruts, and now and then leaping out of the way of a grinding line of Kangaroos or carriers dragging anti-tank guns behind them, until you catch up with Wedd or find the Rileys.

As you get out into the darkness of open country, away from the flaming farm buildings, and the traffic grows noticeably thinner, you feel the need to orient yourself before you become hopelessly lost. However, to illuminate your map you have to have some cover, for you have only a little bullet cigarette lighter and some matches. It is then you spot, just over in the field on the left a few steps from the road, what looks like the mouth of one of those one-man dug-outs the Jerries dig now and then.

Down inside, sitting on a well-sprung iron cot complete with mattress that almost fills the little dug-out, you exhaust the last of the fuel in your lighter identifying where you are. Still, satisfying as this is, you realize as you make your way back to the road that you have only a general idea where the Rileys might be and where Wedd and company are headed.

But then, just as you start up the soupy road, with your head down taking care not to stumble into a water-filled rut, you almost bump into a figure looming up in the gloom. To your relief it turns out to be Tom Wilcox, captain of the Support Company of the Royals, who is lost and doing a recce on foot to try to establish where he is.

Yes, he knows where Wedd is heading, and could show you on your map if it were possible to find some place to safely show a light.

You suggest the dug-out you've just been in and lead him back to it. Sitting side by side on the cot, lighting matches and scorching fingers, you point out his present position. He in turn points out where you can expect to locate the Rileys and Wedd. He finds it curious that you are separated from them and are walking.

You start to explain . . . and the next thing you know you awake to find yourself alone, lying on your back on the cot with your feet dangling on the floor, which is now lit by the pale light of dawn streaming in from outside.

Scrambling out of the dug-out, you start walking quickly back down the road to where you left your crew. There now is no traffic in men or vehicles in either direction, and only the odd derelict truck and the skeletons of still-smouldering farmhouses, filling the cold, misty morning air with acrid odours of smoke and charred wood, provide evidence of the juggernaut that rolled through here last night.

Apart from the faint sound of grinding trucks in the rear areas, it is now quiet, as though both sides have had their fill of attack and counter-attack, and are now willing just to stand-to this morning, listening and staring out through the mists hanging over no-man's-land.

The sound and the fury of last night now seem like a bad dream. Were you really talking to Wilcox in that little dug-out? You begin to wonder if you didn't dream the whole thing, but then the break-down of your Bren carrier is real enough. When you get back to where you left it, the weary men are just completing the transfer of all the equipment and personal gear to the replacement carrier, which only made it up a half an hour ago, they tell you.

At a late morning Royals' "O" Group, Wilcox confirms he had a map-reading conference with you in a little German dug-out just before dawn this morning – laughing at the way you stopped talking in the middle of a sentence and fell over backward as though hit in the head by a stray bullet or a piece of shell from an 88 just then airbursting above that dug-out. "In fact," says he, "I was so sure you'd bought it, I used up the rest of my matches examining your head. But you were breathing peacefully, and I couldn't find a mark on you. I was going to shake you awake before I left, but then I thought, what the hell . . . any man that exhausted should be allowed to sleep!"

And here the reality is as strange as any dream. That Wilcox – a highly disciplined veteran infantry officer with an advanced sense of duty – should leave you to sleep, simply because you appeared to need sleep, is so inconsistent as to be inexplicable.

Just back from a Brigade briefing, Col. Lendrum is able to report the attacks by the leading battalions of 3rd Division and of 5th and 6th brigades of 2nd Division were entirely successful, with all the initial objectives secure by dawn today. However, it was a rough go. In spite of our guns' extraordinary bombardment of Jerry positions before and during the attacks, seemingly very effective judging from the high number of prisoners surrendering to the assaulting platoons, attackers were still met with severe fire from surviving German strongpoints, especially camouflaged tanks and 88s around the villages and towns.

One day you will learn the details. Keppeln was only secured by the North Shore Regiment after two strenuous attacks, the last one involving a platoon riding on the backs of 1st Hussars' tanks roaring to the objective. In the attacks the North Shore suffered 28 killed and 61 wounded, and eight of the tanks involved in the charge were knocked out.

At the village of Hollen the Chaudières, after being driven back twice and suffering 17 dead and 51 wounded, finally overcame resistance and secured their objective ten hours after they began their attack.

To secure the town of Udem, surrounded by an anti-tank ditch and heavily mined, required an all-night effort by all three battalions of 9th Brigade: the Stormont, Dundas and Glengarry Highlanders, the Highland Light Infantry of Canada, and the North Nova Scotia Highlanders. Only by dawn today was the last enemy counter-attack driven off.

In comparison, the mobile attack by 5th and 6th brigades, with the support of the tanks of the Sherbrooke Fusiliers, the 1st Hussars, and Fort Garry Horse, which took the Calcar Heights, had an easier go – with units of 6th Brigade (the Queen's Own Cameron Highlanders of Canada, the Fusiliers Mont-Royal, and the South Saskatchewan Regiment) reaching their objectives with admirable despatch, even though the Queen's Own Camerons had to manage without their commanding officer. Lt.-Col. E. P. Thompson, at twenty-three the youngest battalion commander in Canadian Army, was among the first killed in the attack.

However, where tank support was not forthcoming due to squadrons getting bogged down in the mud, battalions had a stickier time.

Pinned down by heavy fire in close contact with the enemy holding firm on their objective, Le Régiment de Maisonneuve, of 5th Brigade, suffered a severe bloody nose (93 casualties including 14 dead) before their CO, Lt.-Col. Julien Bibeau, brought up flamethrowers and directed them on targets pointed out by a platoon commander (Lieut. Guy deMerlis).

54

A GUNNER'S MOST
DREADED NIGHTMARE

※

IT IS LATE AFTERNOON ON FEBRUARY 27. THE DANK CELLAR IS lit by a gasoline lantern on a table behind which sits the Royals' Colonel, who is as always looking so extraordinarily neat. Clean shaven, hair brushed smooth, his tie perfectly knotted, he is a picture of orderliness and self-assurance as he outlines the situation in a well-modulated voice. You marvel at his calmness and confidence. In the distance the guns are rumbling heavily, and you know he is perfectly aware of what it is like out there: that this, like every damned attack, will be a messy, confused, bloody terrifying affair, only partially successful on the first try, and that the plan he is outlining will be modified beyond recognition to meet the fluid fortunes of the night ahead. But right now you feel only warm gratitude that he makes the plan sound so simple and straightforward.

At the end of the "O" Group, as he passes on the official word from Corps, spelling out what is expected of the troops, he stares down at the table as though afraid it may sound like a pep talk: "We are to keep on hitting the enemy until he cracks."

But then, looking up at his rumpled, sagging, red-eyed company commanders barely able to hold open their eyelids, and who can stand upright only by leaning against the cellar walls, he adds: "But as we know, gentlemen, a well-known law of physics ensures the hammer takes as much punishment as the anvil."

No one says anything, but there is a general shifting of positions, and tiny smiles appear on drained and haggard faces in appreciation of the sardonic humour of this understanding man. And, as they file out into the night to make their way back to their companies, they go with a lighter and more confident step in the realization their CO knows the score and appreciates what he is asking of them and their men.

Battalion objectives for the attack, that will go in after dark, assigned to each of the four rifle companies of the Royals attacking in the fairly rough terrain just before the Hochwald, are: an area of gullies and scrubby bush on the left front (Bob Suckling's B Company); high ground in the centre (Jack Stothers's C Company); a crossroads on a ridge ascending on Stothers's right (Bob Wedd's A Company); and finally, on the extreme right end, on a promontory curved like a fist aimed at the Hochwald, a lone house, the objective of Tim Beatty's D Company, the company to which you are attached as it moves up to await H-hour at the startline held by the Rileys.

Just before dark, your shells start falling short.

The difference between the sound of 25-pounder shells as they sail overhead, whispering and crackling on their way to targets out beyond your OP, and the deadly sound they create when they are pouring down directly on you, is so remarkable that even when you are braced for it, it's a horrifying experience. Thus when, for absolutely no reason other than gross error at one troop gun position, shells come screaming in behind the house where you know the men of D Company are lounging above ground waiting for the signal to go forward, you are close to sobbing in your panic as you dash out to the kitchen, grab the mike from Squissato, and yell yourself hoarse, getting through to the Regiment:

"Stop! Stop! Stop! Rounds are falling short! Stop! Stop! Stop!"

When at last the shells stop coming, you have a desperate need to know the full extent of the damage they have caused. But almost paralyzed with dread, you can't bring yourself to rise from the kitchen floor and follow Tim outside. You remain kneeling on the linoleum in the gathering dusk, rocking back and forth in a state of utter despair. And this is how Beatty finds you when he comes back in to slump down on a chair at the kitchen table, reporting sadly and quietly:

"Sorry, old boy, but you just killed seven of my men."

Oh God, it could hardly have been otherwise. Without holes to get into, it's a wonder any of them survived. But hearing those dreadful words, *You just killed seven*, is almost too much to bear. You rush to absolve yourself of blame.

Tim listens patiently and sympathetically as you explain how you decided that before all the light was gone you would register the guns on that treeless hump of land about seven hundred yards out in front of here, beyond which you and the Royals will be passing tonight, so that if they come under fire from there, all you would have to do is give the target number and the scale of fire to the guns to get instant neutralizing fire. You intended just to range on it with the first troop to report ready, and let all the other troops, following the corrections on their individual artillery boards in the normal way, record their individual lines and ranges. But when your first round, landing on that barren hump, caused several Jerries to rise up and scurry back up the slope and out of sight, you went into fire for effect with all the troops of the Regiment. The first shells to come up fell precisely where they should have on the crest of that distant hill, just as the ranging round had done. But then rounds began to fall behind the house for reasons you can only guess.

Perhaps an error in passing early survey coordinates to a pivot gun . . . the Regiment had just moved. Things like that have been known to happen, but not with 4th Field – not even during training days.

One of Tim's sergeants comes in the kitchen from out back, and seeing you slumped on the floor in the darkening gloom, rocking in anguish, he inquires: "What's the matter, Foo?"

"Need you ask, Sergeant? I just killed seven of your buddies."

"No, you didn't," says he. "You wounded several, and shattered the nerves of a couple of battle-exhaustion cases who just returned from hospital, dammit. But you didn't kill anybody."

"Oh, but you're wrong, Sergeant," says Tim, "I counted seven bodies out there."

"You mean those bodies alongside the wall at the back of the house?" asks the Sergeant.

"Yes," says Tim.

"Those aren't Royals – those are Rileys killed coming in here."

The relief is like nothing you have ever experienced. It is as though a crushing physical weight has been lifted off you. With an enormous sigh you start breathing again; the nightmare is over.

However, you must make sure it won't happen again. It is now too dark to range each troop on a distant point to discover which guns are in error. So you get on the radio and tell the Regiment some guns are firing short, and until all can be checked in daylight by firing on a distant point, only the ranging troop is to be used.

Reflecting on the matter as you await H-hour, you realize a troop of four guns won't provide much support in turning back a serious counter-attack. But then you remember you can always pull down fire from the other two regiments in the Division, if it is warranted, by simply designating the task an Uncle target.

H-hour is postponed an hour to allow the moon to rise and make it easier for the companies to find their way. Of course, this also helps the enemy spot the approaching Royals. As anticipated this afternoon, the leading companies attract bursts of tracers from that bald hill. But, having registered it with the ranging troop this afternoon, you are able to squelch this fire, and the first three companies gain their objectives without serious opposition, suggesting the Germans have only outposts through here and are holding their main forces just beyond this rugged area of woods, hills, and gullies, in their "Schlieffen Position," a second Siegfried Line, reputedly stretching some twenty miles across the front before the Hochwald and adjacent Balbergerwald.

Still Beatty's company runs into strong opposition only two hundred yards from their objective, when they try to move laterally across the front through a ravine in no-man's-land and attack from the rear the farmhouse which is their objective at the extreme right end of the crescent ridge overlooking the Hochwald. This route is chosen when Beatty and company arrive at the foot of the slope leading up to Bob Wedd's position on the crest of the ridge, and find their line of advance through Wedd's position and beyond startlingly exposed to enemy view by the obscenely bright light of a great moon that has just risen to full brilliance.

This means you must part company from Tim, for your carrier cannot make it up the ravine cluttered with heavy vegetation, let alone follow men on foot when they scramble up the very high and very steep side of the ravine to assault their objective. All you can do is establish an OP along the almost clifflike edge of the ravine in the vicinity of Wedd's company and try to follow their progress in the gully below, judging as best you can when to join them on the objective, and if they run into trouble, bring fire to bear on its source.

Parking the carrier behind the farmhouse on which Wedd's company is centred, you and Squissato go forward on foot a couple of hundred yards to the cliff edge where you find a beautiful, deep slit trench, obviously of German origin, for no Canadian ever dug a trench of such proportions with such sharp sides. Thus you are sitting with Squissato on the edge of this well-constructed trench, with your feet dangling down, looking across the ravine at a house bathed in moonlight well up the slope opposite, when suddenly its interior bursts into flames. In seconds flames are licking out of every window and door, lighting up the barren slope as bright as day, and throwing into sharp relief dark figures in Canadian helmets, momentarily frozen in the glare.

Then tracers start skittering across the slope from three or four directions, and the dark figures start scattering in panic. Some go down and start crawling. Others lie in crumpled positions just as they fell. Others make it down the slope and disappear in the shadows.

When no more figures can be seen running or crawling out there, the tracers cease. And you are down in the bottom of the trench with a lamp-electric establishing a map reference for the fields on each side of the burning house where you think the tracers originated, when you hear men thumping up the slope. They turn out to be three Royals who tell you they were actually with the platoon that was sent to check out the house on the slope when it suddenly burst into flames.

They are convinced it was a well-planned ambush, that the Jerries were waiting for them, for as the Royals went in the front door, the Germans went out the back tossing a match into oil-saturated straw as they were leaving.

Did they actually see them toss the match?

No, but it had to be that way for no house could burst into flames so completely, so quickly, without being prepared with oil and straw. And there were no burp guns until the flames lit up the yard and every Royal was silhouetted against the flaming house.

Just as you begin questioning them as to whether they think you might safely shell the vicinity of the house where you saw Schmeisser fire originating (looking for reassurance that none of the wounded Royals crawled off into the darkness in that direction) there is the unmistakable hollow *plunk* of a mortar firing from over there, and immediately the whisper of its bomb descending.

Being already half in the trench with your legs dangling down, you are first to arrive on the bottom, and are instantly squashed flat under a mass of humanity scrambling to get below grade.

Though scarcely able to take even the shallowest breath with all that weight on you, for the first couple of minutes you are grateful for the extraordinary protection afforded by the mass of bodies stacked four-deep above you, as a wicked stream of mortar bombs crash and flash close to the mouth of the trench. Even a direct hit could not reach you. But when you reflect on this, the prospect of being held captive by several hundred pounds of dead flesh is not something you relish, and you are exceedingly relieved when the mortars cease, and the bodies above you unpile, allowing you to sit up.

Concerned the mortaring will start again when Jerry sees this clump of men reappear, and reasoning that Beatty and survivors of his company should by now be on their way back from the ravine, you decide to get everybody in the carrier and go back down there again to wait for them. And by the time you arrive at the bottom of the hill, they appear in the gloom, pitifully few in number, and most of them walking-wounded.

One of those being carried on stretchers is the company commander. And Tim is not at all in good shape, judging from the weakness of his voice as you bend over him to get what advice he can give you. He figures there are many more of his company back there hiding in the ravine, but he is taking what he has assembled back to Battalion where the company can be remustered under a new commander.

As the men bearing Tim's stretcher start off and you say goodbye to him, he seems so weak you despair of seeing him again. However, a veteran stretcher-bearer, bringing up the rear of the walking-wounded following in behind the stretchers, assures you the Major's wounds are more painful than life-threatening, and that it's the shot of morphine he's been given that's making him so woozy, which is good to hear. This is the third time Tim has been wounded since arriving in Normandy last July, and the second time he has been evacuated to hospital.

Watching the last of them disappear in the thick, cold mists that have begun to block out the moon, you suddenly are conscious of how vulnerable your little group has become. For half an hour or so, a strange quiet has existed along the front here that cannot last. Jerry knows he's shattered a company, and he'll be tempted to probe through the gap that may exist here. You are glad the three lads you collected up on the brow of the hill chose to stay with you instead of following the wounded to the rear as they could have. You wish it were safe to lay a heavy stonk on that ravine, but you don't dare risk it, for many Royals may still be in there crawling back.*

---

* The final casualty count was 26 — 5 killed and 21 wounded — bad enough, but not the disaster it first appeared.

Your immediate need is to make contact with another company, not only to gain local protection, but get back in the battalion picture so as to be of use to them. You recall Wedd's company was to take the crossroads a bit beyond the house where you parked your carrier while on the brow of the ravine watching D Company get shot-up. Being on the right flank, closest to the objective still remaining to be taken, makes it your logical choice: either his company will be ordered to go for it, or you can hook up with whoever it is that passes through him.

But before you move off, heavy small-arms fire, punctuated by the reverberating *wham* of a high-velocity gun, starts up in the wooded area on the left. Taking over the signaller's radio headset, you listen to an exchange between Cornett at Royals' Tac Headquarters and Col. Young at Brigade, which make it clear Royals' Headquarters is seriously threatened by a fighting patrol; and just over on the left among folds in land congested by brush and trees, B Company (Suckling's) is being shelled at close range by a German SP (self-propelled gun). When Cornett reports that B Company is under heavy machine-gun fire and the Germans appear to be getting into position to close in, the Colonel decides to take a hand in proceedings.

Coming on the air, he asks you: "Are you in a position to see where the SP fire is coming from?"

You report you can't see its muzzle-flash, but it certainly is close by.

"Do you have a map reference?"

Anticipating the question, you already have your head under the tarp in the front compartment of the carrier and the dismal glow of a lamp-electric shining on the area of the map just to the left of where the Royals' ravine bends this way, broadening out and flattening as it passes almost on a level with where you are now sitting. You give him the map reference of a point about four hundred yards away.

Nothing happens for a few seconds, then you hear, "Shot SOS." The map reference you gave appears to have coincided with the

designated, precalculated DF SOS target, always placed on the most
vulnerable route. Immediately you hear the guns thumping behind
– all of them, you fear. And seconds later shells are screaming and
bursting all around your carrier in a repeat of their ghastly afternoon performance. With your radio mike readily at hand, hanging
from your earphones, you are yelling, even as the first shells are
landing: "Stop! Stop! Stop!"

When they do, you blow your stack. You address your remarks to
your Commanding Officer in such a way as to give him the benefit
of the doubt, referring to unnamed "boneheads" and levelling
charges of "criminal stupidity" at whoever is responsible for shooting all those guns after you had made it crystal clear at last light that
only the original troop of ranging guns (14th Battery) should fire
until daylight when a proving-shoot can be made on a distant point
to discover which troop or troops are in error. You finish off your
tirade by stating, in the most deliberate and forceful voice you can
muster, that you "will not be held responsible for what may happen
if those guns are fired again before daylight." Precisely what you
mean by this, you are not sure, but your intention is to imply dire
consequences to anyone disregarding your solemn warning.

For a while there is no comment from Sunray. Minutes go by,
and as your overwrought nerves relax and reality returns in the
form of a cold fog seeping through your garments so that you
shiver violently, you start to worry. Perhaps you went too far with
your intemperate comments; after all, no one was wounded.
Eventually, to your great relief, he comes on the air, and in his
calm, slow drawl assures you arrangements have been made for
another regiment to provide "supplementary fire" as may be necessary for the rest of the night.

As you prepare to move off up the hill to Wedd's company, you
are suddenly aware that the *bur-rup bur-rup* of Schmeissers and the
crack of the SP, which brought all this on, are no longer with you.
Short rounds notwithstanding (and perhaps even because of them),
the Colonel's shoot produced a most beneficial effect.

It's after midnight when you and your little raggle-taggle group, now grown to nine including your own crew, check in at A Company HQ in a shallow cellar underneath Wedd's farmhouse where you earlier had parked the carrier.

With the very low ceiling and the vague light from one candle resting on an upturned wooden box, the cellar seems vast, and although there must be a dozen men lying here or there on the hard-packed, wavy, earthen floor, or propped against the walls, there's still lots of room for your group. However, crowding such a large number into a company headquarters doesn't seem quite the thing to do, and you feel obliged to provide the sergeant, squatting beside the box with the candle on it, with an explanation.

Of course he's already guessed, and speaking softly for your ears only, he says: "Most of these other guys in here are from D Company. They've had a bit of a rough go, sir. We'll let them rest for a while, and then get them digging-in outside."

55

THE NIGHT A STEN
GUN DOESN'T JAM!

❋

THE SERGEANT EXPLAINS MAJOR WEDD HAS BEEN CALLED back to Tac Headquarters. He expects he'll arrive back soon with orders for A Company to renew the attack on the objective D Company failed to take. This being the way things tend to develop for the P.B.I. (poor bloody infantry) he's probably right. It looks like it's going to be a long night.

As you wait, sprawled against some sacks of potatoes, you pass the time listening to a couple of the still-agitated survivors of D Company compare notes on how they escaped the wicked crossfire of tracers sweeping that bald slope across the ravine when they were caught in the glare of the burning house.

One soldier confirms the earlier report: "They were waiting for us – had to be – for when our guys were goin' in the front door, they were goin' out the back throwin' lighted matches over their shoulders into the straw and petrol they'd scattered around."

While you had been too far away to see anybody going or coming from the house before the flames lit up the landscape, the startling suddenness of the fire – from total darkness one moment to flaring flames enveloping every room behind every window the next – would seem to bear out the young soldier's contention.

His buddy, however, couldn't care less how the fire started; he is interested only in describing what happened when the Jerry machine-guns opened up, and he was caught like everybody else right out in the open kneeling down on one knee:

"Everybody starts scattering in all directions looking for cover, and I am pounding down the slope, when I spot this partially covered trench. I make a running dive head-first into the nearest open end. Then followin' good old infantry drill of never reappearing where you're last seen disappearing, I roll over a couple of times along the bottom before coming up at the other open end, face to face with a Heinie! I don't know who is more surprised – him or me. But my Sten is almost poking him in the belly, so I squeeze the trigger and hope to God something'll happen. And guess what?"

"She jams," volunteers his friend in ho-hum fashion.

"No, by damn," says he with a real sense of awe in his voice, "she fires!" And he starts to laugh as though he suddenly sees this as being very funny.

Immediately his buddy joins him in hearty laughter, and suddenly the cellar is full of laughter from others who have been listening and who obviously also consider it hilarious when a Sten gun actually fires when the trigger is pulled.

You can't believe your ears. Is it possible you were not listening properly? You question the narrator. Surely he meant he was afraid his Sten might jam from dirt in the mechanism, picked up when he rolled along the bottom of the trench?

"Dirt, hell! There doesn't have to be any dirt, for right after you've cleaned and oiled it, the bastard takes the notion. You never know..."

As if to underline the truth of this, the Sergeant says, "Reminds me of something that happened back at Louvigny in Normandy. Just after we'd jumped into the orchard through a hole in the stone wall blown by the tanks, my pal surprises a German in a trench. And when his Sten doesn't fire, he clubs the guy across the face with it, jumps on him, and strangles him with his bare hands."

Again, everybody roars with laughter.

This is beyond belief. While the meaning is clear, common sense argues they are exaggerating the Sten's unreliability. But when you suggest that surely Stens can be made reliable by proper maintenance, snorts and guffaws on all sides provide you with your answer. Still you persist: Do they mean to say that men will go into the attack carrying a weapon they can't be certain will fire when they pull the trigger?

"Of course, what else," calls out a bitter voice from the far end of the cellar, "the bastards made us turn in all the Schmeissers and Berettas we'd captured and were using last fall back at Groesbeek."

At this there are growls of agreement from many quarters, and the Sergeant quickly jumps in, "It's true, sir, they don't always work the way they should." Then lowering his voice he says, "I think it's time we changed the subject." And in the cunning way all effective sergeants are able to manipulate men under their command, he quickly changes the subject to sex, recounting a crazy story, with suitable embellishments, about a guy on leave in Brussels who was stranded in a hotel room for several days without money or uniform, when the "biddy he shacked up with made off with both his pants and his wallet while he was asleep."

But the subject of the Sten gun doesn't readily leave your head. You recall the first time you ever saw one in the spring of 1943 when they issued them to replace the tommy-guns taken away to give to 1st Division, rumoured to be going into action in the Mediterranean. You and your Troop Commander, Capt. Bill Graham, had been given the job of trying out a couple of them in a chalk pit on the northern outskirts of Worthing, Sussex, where the Regiment had been temporarily posted to relieve a 1st Division unit (3rd Field) leaving for Scotland for special training for landing on a hostile shore.

You remember your initial reaction was shock at its primitive appearance, looking for all the world as though the plumber down the street had improvised it from what he could find in his bin of cast-off pipe; a perfect monstrosity when compared to the sleek gun it was meant to replace, especially the part that rested against your shoulder – a skinny piece of piping with a flattened shoe welded on the end of it, in place of the highly polished wooden stock of a tommy-gun.

There was a stubby barrel crudely welded to a bulgy piece of pipe with slots cut in it. One accepted a long, slender magazine of bullets, sticking out at right angles; another roughly cut opening allowed for the ejection of spent cartridges, if and when the gun felt so inclined; and still another notch was meant to provide a safety catch, accepting the knob attached to the bolt mechanism, when it was pulled back to cock the gun. Turned upwards and hooked in the shallow notch in the casing, accidental discharge was prevented as long as the gun wasn't dropped or otherwise jarred.

While the magazine fitted well enough, neither of you could get your gun to fire a burst of more than three rounds without jamming. Whether the problem was in the magazine or in the ejection mechanism, it had been impossible to discover, since unexpended rounds as well as expended cartridges combined to jam the ejection system. When you'd reported this mulish behaviour to the battery commander, he'd assured you all new weapons had to be worked on by the artificers, and as soon as the sharp edges were filed off, the thing would work perfectly.

While very suspicious of the effectiveness of the so-called safety-catch arrangement, you didn't mention it, for you hadn't yet seen a Sten, on being accidently dropped on its butt end, fire off its entire magazine of bullets, pinwheel fashion – while revolving slowly on its side on the floor – causing everyone in the room to leap into the air as the barrel swivelled in their direction.

At any rate you had accepted the battery commander's assurances, and not having had occasion to fire a Sten from that time on to prove him wrong, you never, at any time during the past eight months, felt any special concern for the hundreds of young infantrymen you'd seen slogging along with Stens slung over their shoulders.

But now – my God – this is really unbelievable. How on earth could a condition like this be allowed to exist? You try to recall all you know of the origins of the Sten gun. You remember being told that the manufacture of these primitive gadgets had been undertaken primarily to satisfy the need for cheap, easy-to-produce weapons that could be dropped to the underground Resistance fighters, that the Sten was chosen because it was of German design and could use 9-mm rimless ammunition which the Resistance fighters could steal from enemy dumps.

In the desperate days of 1941 and 1942, the Sten may have been a justifiable compromise for securing arms for the Resistance, who otherwise would have been weaponless during their brief, infrequent hit-and-run encounters with the Germans. But to supply these totally unreliable weapons to regular troops, who must face the enemy in mortal combat for days, weeks, and months on end, must surely rank among the foremost criminal acts perpetrated on Allied troops in World War II.

The more you think about it, the worse it seems. How many hundreds or even thousands of Canadian and British soldiers have died because Stens failed to fire when they were face to face with the enemy? The numbers will never be known, for dead men cannot recount the circumstances of their death. But these soldiers here tonight, and countless others like them who have managed to survive after being let down in a crisis by its fickle mechanism, would surely agree that the Sten is among the most successful booby traps planted in the way of Canadian and British troops.*

---

* When the British War Office ordered the Sten into production in 1941 they were aware that the design from which it was derived had already been rejected in scorn by the German Wehrmacht. In a rare defence of the freakish Sten, and not one to give the user any real confidence, Lieut. F. Matthews of the South Saskatchewan Regiment reported that in the muddy conditions brought on by torrential rain during the attack on Verrières Ridge, July 20, 1944, they were more reliable than the normally highly dependable Bren. Their Stens worked okay if they were fired "holding the mags vertical and the ejection slot to the bottom, so that if the force of the ejection was insufficient, gravity would push the spent casings out."

56

THE CONDUCT OF
SUPERIOR MEN IN A CRUCIBLE

───────────── ✳ ─────────────

YOU WILL NEVER GET USED TO THE ASTOUNDING CAPACITY of infantry officers to resist despair, and in the confused, clamorous conditions of battle, to think clearly and coolly – assessing situations which appear to you absolutely hopeless, formulating plans even as the roaring battle ebbs and flows about them, and issuing clear, precise orders in such a calm, quiet style, and in such confident tones, that they breed confidence in all who must carry them out and who, in turn, must persuade others to follow their leadership. Surely this capacity to maintain a constant, positive posture, regardless of how bad things get, must be the ultimate expression of true and enduring courage.

And even as you know you will carry forever the image of the eternally calm and resolute battalion commander, so dramatically displayed by Col. Lendrum at his "O" Group yesterday, the wise and understanding leadership shown by Company Commander Bob Wedd when he returns to this dank and smoky basement at around 3:30 A.M. with orders to attack at 4:00 A.M. is, in a way, more impressive.

Spirits and energy are ebbing to their lowest point as he calls his "O" Group to lay on the attack which must go out through that same defile in which Tim Beatty's company was lacerated. His company has been so reduced by casualties he has only one subaltern, veteran Lieut. "Mo" Berry, and two sergeants to lead his other two platoons.

Thus he must have been grateful to have appear at his "O" Group a subaltern from Beatty's devastated company, who'd come back with the survivors gathered here in the basement. As always, he speaks quietly and confidently in his deep, musical voice as he explains that one platoon (Berry's) will move in against the front of the house while another goes up through the ravine and hits it from the rear, emphasizing that the platoon moving up the ravine will concentrate on the final objective, staying clear of any involvement with the Germans in the area of the smouldering house. The young subaltern from Beatty's company, still shaking from the awful ambush, and assuming he is to go back down there and lead a platoon up through that dark valley of shadows, starts to weep – not sobbing, but sighing deeply and brushing tears from his eyes and cheeks.

Wedd gives no indication he is aware of this as he continues in his calm way. But as he finishes, seemingly without having to pause to consider possibilities, he assigns the leading role for the ravine sortie to one of the sergeants. And the sergeant, to his eternal credit, accepts the assignment without hesitation, as though an obvious decision, and proceeds to get himself organized with such noisy gusto he covers up everybody's embarrassment and diverts attention from the agitated young subaltern who turns away, blowing his nose and sighing with relief.

He'll be LOB on this attack, and by tomorrow night he'll have regained his resilience and be "right as rain," as Harvey would say. You liked Bob Wedd from the first hour you were with him, admiring his cool decisiveness under fire. But now, warmed with admiration for his kind and generous heart, you feel real affection for him as you and Signaller Ferry, with the 18-set on his back, move out on foot with him and the remainder of his company around the rim of the ravine towards the objective, now hidden in fog just over the brow of the easterly end of the promontory, to be in position to rush the burned-out house from the front as soon as the sergeant's platoon hits it from the rear.

And his plan works wonderfully well. With your guns methodically dropping shells on the slope beyond the ravine for fifteen minutes by way of "troop fire – three seconds" (guns of one troop firing in rotation at three-second intervals) to cover sounds of stumbling boots and rattling equipment, the sergeant is able to lead his platoon up the ravine without attracting attention, climb the steep incline, and attack with such surprise that the defenders offer little resistance. The objective is secure before you and Wedd know it is happening, diverted as you are by the startling effect of the muzzle-blast of a Royals' anti-tank gun getting off a couple of rounds at the house. "Mo" Berry will never forget his chagrin at having his "whole platoon bolt for the rear when the gun opened up, just as we were passing it in the dark."

Expecting to be ordered to push on at dawn, it is a relief to be left in place, even though you are forced to remain reasonably alert throughout most of the day, which begins in vastly irritating fashion shortly after dawn. The CO, in an obvious attempt to put you in your place after your undiplomatic outburst on air last night following his bombardment of your carrier with short rounds, sends up "Mac" McDonald (Regimental Quartermaster since last November) to conduct the "proving shoot" to uncover which guns are firing short. And your mood is not improved when the well-rested, "bright-eyed, bushy-tailed" McDonald digs you out of your warm cellar to guide him to a place where he can safely observe the fall of shot on a distant map reference – or "datum point," as he would have it.

It is not a simple matter of leading him upstairs to a spot among the ruins and "putting him on the ground." You don't know how far over this way the heavy enemy fire you've been hearing may have diverted the 4th Division infantry (Argyll and Sutherland Highlanders) attacking the gap in the "Staats Forst Xanten" – between the Hochwald (high woods) on the north and the Tuschen Wald (black woods) on the south – through which a railway line runs east to Xanten. Before dawn there was much high-pitched whining of straining tank motors over there, rising and falling again and again, suggestive of mud-wallowing tanks vainly struggling to extricate deeply embedded tracks.

Then at first light a series of vicious, cracking booms, peculiar to high-velocity tank or anti-tank guns, attracted your attention to some Shermans (South Alberta Regiment) sitting helter-skelter about the soggy landscape down below you to the right, immobilized by mud or enemy fire. There is no infantry in sight.

To be safe, you lead McDonald and Signaller Ferry, again carrying the 18-set, back around the hill to the deep slit trench you occupied briefly last night on the lip of the ravine.

Convinced that whatever was wrong at the guns will have been corrected by now, and anxious to get back to your warm cellar for a bit of shut-eye, you suggest that only the pivot gun of each troop be fired. However, with his sense of mission as inflated as your ego is deflated by the CO selecting him to carry out the shoot, he insists on every one of the guns of 2nd and 26th batteries being fired individually, and that each round be observed and its accuracy noted on the neatly ruled paper clipped to his map-board, before the next round is fired.

Thus the business takes more than an hour, and by the time it is done, you are slumped down in the bottom of the trench sound asleep, totally oblivious to a light dusting of snow then falling, and he has to shake you awake (rather more vigorously than necessary you think) to tell you he found no guns firing short, and to complain of your inconsiderate cluttering of the floor of the trench during the shoot.

You will never know who or what caused those short rounds, but of one thing you are certain: the guns of at least one troop were in error, suggesting an error in communicating survey coordinates or an error in plotting an artillery board. Clearly it was not a gun-laying error, though you can only imagine the fatigue bordering on exhaustion the gunners are enduring at this time: moving in the mud, digging gun pits in the mud, carrying tons of ammunition from the road to the guns through the mud, living day after day in the mud.

Hossack will write in his log: "More rain has made the roads all but impassable, but the vehicles bump and slither their way forward to deploy at Todtenhügel. The command post is dug in deeply and our stoves make it quite comfortable. The Rhine River is far over to our left, and the CO calls for a special target to be fired across the headline waterway. The range required is 11,525 yards. Fierce fighting is taking place at the Hochwald and we fire regularly. Enemy shells land regularly on the road before 26th Battery guns, but the road is used sparingly and there are no casualties."

The succinct Sgt. Hunt records: "Quiet. The slaughter continues."

The diarist at regimental headquarters, equally blasé about the contribution of guns to the progress of the war, will report of this day: "Shot in 2nd and 26th batteries on datum point. Eleven Mike targets engaged. Otherwise NTR (nothing to report)."

Next day, however, the war diary will recognize, "The guns are fairly busy most of the day ... on Mike targets for our own FOOs and small fire-plans in support of 5th and 6th brigades as they move in to attack the Hochwald."

As 4th Brigade (Essex Scottish leading) joins in the attacks March 3 on the northern half of the forest, 4th Field is again busy firing: two defensive fire targets, twenty harassing-fire targets, a quick barrage, and eighteen Mike targets called for by the FOOs, one of them killing many of the enemy. According to Major Brown, 26th Battery Commander, the deluge of 4th Field shells "caught a German company at change-over. The three prisoners of war taken claimed to be the sole survivors."*

---

* Major J. F. Brown was subsequently honoured by being officially Mentioned-in-Despatches. Other members of 4th Field who were cited for outstanding and/or gallant efforts beyond the call of duty, on one or more occasions, were: Major Wm. P. Carr, Major Don Wilson, BSM E. Blodgett, BSM P. Oleniuk, Gnr. R. Cardinal, Gnr. J. Grenier, Bdr. C. S. May, and Sgt. D. R. Pratt.

57

MURDEROUS FIRE IN

THE HOCHWALD GAP

✳

AT A ROYALS' "O" GROUP, CALLED TO LAY ON AN ATTACK
through the Rileys to clear the extreme northern end of the
Hochwald at 6:30 tomorrow morning, March 3, Col. Lendrum,
just back from a briefing at Brigade, is able to put his company
commanders in the picture as to what has been happening in the
confused and ugly fighting around and about the mouth of that
two-mile-long corridor between the forests.

On the map the gap is about a mile wide at its far eastern end, but
only 250 yards wide at its western mouth near here. Through it runs
a railway right-of-way, but no road. Simonds wants to secure the
railway so the tracks can be ripped up and the firm roadbed used as
a direct supply route for the upcoming battle for Xanten.

It seems that two days ago, when 2nd and 3rd divisions and supporting armour punctured the outer defences of the Schlieffen
Position (the reserve position of the Siegfried Line) with a break-in
near the clearing just in front of here at the mouth of this corridor,
Simonds ordered them to push on and clear the forest flanks of
Germans: 2nd Division, the Hochwald, lying north of the gap; and
3rd Division, the smaller forest, south of the gap. However, before
either division got started, 4th Armoured Division was ordered to
push along the railway line.*

---

* First the Algonquins with South Alberta tanks in support tried it. They
barely got started when they were forced back. Of nine Shermans and

With the woods on both sides of the gap still full of well-camouflaged anti-tank guns and machine-guns, every courageous attempt by 4th Division tanks and infantry to run this horrific gauntlet has been stymied.

When the high-profile Shermans, to avoid getting stuck in the soggy fields, attempted to use the railway, crawling out along the embanked portions of the track, they were potted like ducks in a shooting-gallery. And when they tried the fields, they bogged down and are left at the mercy of whatever Jerry chooses to throw at them and their accompanying infantry.

Clearly no combination of forces can secure the Hochwald gap until the flanking woods are cleared of the enemy. Thus the importance of the attacks that got underway in earnest yesterday, March 1, starting with 6th Brigade (FMRs, Queen's Own Cameron Highlanders of Canada, and SSRs) relieving 10th Brigade and carrying the battle into the Hochwald at the northern shoulder of the gap, while the Essex Scottish led off 4th Brigade's attempt to penetrate the forest on their left flank.

---

twelve carriers trying to do a hook through a railway underpass, only one carrier made it back. Then the Canadian Argyll and Sutherland Highlanders, with another squadron of South Alberta tanks, tried it under cover of darkness. Some elements made it to the eastern end of the gap, but with the dawn they were attacked with murderous fire from all sides and though severely weakened by casualties, they could not be reinforced. Still the Lincoln and Welland Regiment was ordered to pass through them. The attack quickly petered out when all the tanks bogged down, and foot-soldiers came under drenching artillery and mortar fire in fields swept by streams of tracer bullets from both flanks. Similarly an attempt by the Lake Superior Regiment, supported by the tanks of the Grenadier Guards, ended in disarray with the armour bogged down, and the infantry forced to withdraw. On February 28, two squadrons of the Grenadier Guards had only three tanks not disabled 600 yards from their startline. And 4th Canadian Armoured Division (British Columbia Regt., Governor General Foot Guards, Canadian Grenadier Guards, South Alberta Regt.) on February 27 and 28 lost more than 100 tanks.

German resistance aroused by the Essex Scottish was particularly severe. But clearly the recently reconstructed battalion did a super job – driving the Germans from an exceptionally strong log-revetted trench system, and then holding off a succession of fierce counter-attacks by paratroopers determined to regain the security of their deep trenches and spacious, wood-lined dug-outs – some even outfitted with table and chairs.

At the outset the Essex, leading off from the Royals' positions in the rain and sleet and even the odd flutter of snow, were accompanied by a squadron of tanks of the Sherbrooke Fusiliers that took turns pumping H.E. shells at suspicious points up ahead – their high-velocity *wham*s penetrating over the roaring furore of the 25-pounder barrage designed to carry the Essex up to the rim of the Hochwald.

But when the tanks bogged down, and the poor foot-sloggers had to carry on alone, you wondered how those poor lads, going into battle for the first time, would make out. Would they again be driven back into the Royals' position as they were the last time you saw them in the attack on the Goch–Calcar highway?

Though Lendrum doesn't refer directly to the fact that the Essex had only a week to rebuild their fighting strength with large numbers of raw reinforcements fresh from Canada (including some of the first conscripts to be sent up to the line), it clearly is on his mind as he recalls in great detail what Brig. Cabeldu reported earlier today about the inspiring leadership of one company commander (until recently the battalion adjutant) who was handling his first attack ever with a rifle company.

He knocked out a machine-gun post with grenades, and though wounded twice, refused to be evacuated when his company was immediately subjected to a succession of counter-attacks. Several times he left cover to cross and recross open spaces to carry ammunition to his hard-pressed platoons, boosting their confidence that the company could hold on, even as it was reduced to fewer than thirty desperate men gathering what ammunition they could from the bodies of dead comrades.

Hit a third time, and lying in the mud and water of a shell crater, barely conscious, one leg blown off and the other so badly mangled it will have to be removed, he refused to be evacuated until he issued firm orders for defending the position to his one surviving officer.*

---

* The summation sentence of the citation for the Victoria Cross awarded Major Frederick Albert Tilston read "By his calm courage, gallant conduct, and total disregard for his own safety, he fired his men with grim determination and their firm stand enabled the Regiment to accomplish its object."

58

FAREWELL TO ARMS
FOR NINE DAYS

❋

STAFF OFFICERS BACK AT CORPS OR ARMY MAY SEE THE clearing of the Rhineland as a series of well-defined operations to which they attach stirring names. But for those directly participating, it surely will be remembered as one long, continuous messy business of attacks and counter-attacks without respite, with never a sense of having arrived anywhere in particular or having decided anything of consequence, as another road, another bit of high ground, another burned-out farm or derelict village is taken.

It's enough you've survived the night, or the last hour, or even the last five minutes. And all the while, you lust for sleep. Denied sleep for outrageous periods, it has become the most desirable objective of life. Every chance you get, regardless of where you are, you sleep, if only for a few minutes: usually sitting up and leaning against something, seldom stretching out flat, and, of course, always fully clothed with your boots on. Your body aches arthritically for sleep, your joints are stiff and painful for sleep, your voice is hoarse for sleep, and your brain dull and insensitive to all needs except the oblivion of sleep.

As an officer you have learned to expect a special kind of torture each night, particularly in the wee hours of the morning. Whenever the Battalion is not engaged in an attack, beating off counter-attacks, or exchanging sectors with other units, they allow you to get to sleep and then send up a signal to report back to Battalion Headquarters for an Orders Group briefing on the next attack.

While chronic fatigue has the virtue of dampening down fear and anxiety, it cannot eliminate the conviction, which you must continually suppress, that the only way out of this is on a stretcher or under a mound of earth at the roadside. So when newly promoted Capt. Don Patrick suddenly appears this afternoon and tells you he is taking over your crew so that you can go back and get ready for seven days' leave in England, it sounds like a joke, and not a very good one at that.

You and your crew are just finishing off cleaning out your arched cellar room – not in the interests of good housekeeping, but to rid the windowless cell of a mild but persistent odour of a repulsive nature that all fear will ultimately "do in" the thin, grey-faced Signaller Walter Ferry who is cursed with an overly sensitive stomach. Assuming the vegetables and hams stored in what normally would be a cool cellar were deteriorating from the radiant heat still beaming down from the thick, concrete ceiling, which, the night you arrived, still carried a load of glowing embers from the collapsed and burned-out upper storeys, it was decided everything should be thrown outside. But with every last potato bagged and removed, every last cabbage leaf swept up, and every ham removed from its ceiling hook and deposited outside, that insidious, nauseating odour still persists.

This is maddening because only in the last twenty-four hours, with much encouragement from the rest of the crew, Ferry had begun to keep a little food down long enough to gain a modicum of nourishment. Now everyone is on edge he will start upchucking again if the nauseating odour persists. Only one thing remains on the floor over in a dark corner – a German jackboot – ignored until now as not being a possible source of the odour. But when Squissato picks it up to fling it out, he finds it grossly heavy, and looking inside discovers the stump of a man's foot and leg. Ferry, gagging, barely makes it outside.*

---

* Gunner Ferry was wounded two days later, and Capt. Patrick March 8.

Somehow this repelling incident strikes an appropriate note for your exit from these wretched Rhineland battlefields, or so it seems to you riding back in the Jeep that brought up Patrick, as you try in vain to account for fifteen days and nights since you last saw the guns. You don't remember shaving, and seldom washing, for sleep took priority over everything else. You must have managed to get a hot meal sometime, but you remember only an endless diet of glutinous M & V Stew and Steak-and-Kidney Pudding spooned icy-cold from the can; chips of Compo cheese on slices of sultana pudding; and oily sardines speared from the tin with concrete-brittle hardtack crackers.

Back at Baker Troop gun position the churned-up mud and ruts are so deep you dispense with Jeep and driver at the road and make your way on foot to the Troop Command Post, visiting each gun pit on the way to tell the gun crews how much the infantry appreciate the speed and accuracy of their shells in breaking up counter-attacks. Knowing how the gunners take pride in such messages from the foot-sloggers they admire so much, you find the total lack of reaction on haggard faces and in red-rimmed weary eyes disconcerting until, arriving at the Troop Command Post, you are reminded by your GPO Lieut. Jack Bigg and his acks (the brothers Hughes, Bombardier Morty, and Lance-Bombardier Ralph) of the heavy-going they've been enduring twenty-four hours a day for days on end.

Your barrel-chested GPO, of rich baritone voice, describes how the guns on occasion have glowed red from intense fire on overlapping targets called for by you and other FOOs. His acks tell how Jerry has maintained a nerve-wracking schedule of random shelling, along with aerial bombing and strafing attacks by jet-propelled planes, including the one that killed the 14th Battery gunners. While they are giving you a lively description of an attack the day before on the woods behind the guns by bomb-carrying Spitfires – which were supposed to knock out a Jerry self-propelled gun that had been harassing the guns all day from somewhere in the rear, but mistakenly knocked out six of our tanks instead – you find yourself going to sleep standing up.

Rousing yourself, you ask Bigg if by any chance there is anything left of the monthly ration of officers' booze – officially a bottle and a half per officer per month, normally shared unofficially with the NCOs when there is no officer's mess in action. To your astonishment, he produces a bottle of champagne he had set aside. Thus equipped you ask where you might bed down for the night.

He suggests the battery cookhouse, a reasonably intact house a couple of hundred yards on the road behind the guns, and offers to guide you. While this hardly seems necessary, he insists, taking hold of your arm to steady you when he notices you stagger a little as you turn to make your way across the muddy field deeply rutted by the quads that hauled the guns in here yesterday.

Aware for some time that you are inclined to stagger a bit now and then, you had no idea it was so obvious to others until now. And while it is disturbing to be treated like a doddering old man, you are very touched by the obvious concern of this big, powerful man, and grateful for the support of his firm grip on your elbow, which he does not release until he has deposited you at the door of the cookhouse.

Inside some gunners sit at the kitchen table lit by an oil lamp, playing cards. You open the champagne and offer to share it with them, but they decline. And when it is gone you ask if any of them has anything to drink, assuring them that you will replace whatever they can turn up the first chance you get. One of the gunners pulls out of his pocket a little medicine bottle in which he has been saving his daily rum ration. As he hands it to you, he says you need not replace it for he doesn't touch the stuff.

Gratefully you consume the strong liquor, a sip at a time, sitting on a wooden chair drawn up close to the stove glowing and clicking with delicious heat.

It's only 6:00 P.M., but you know you should hit the sack. Still you go on sitting there, luxuriating in the smell and taste and feel of the heat, as you carry on a desultory conversation with the card players at the table. It is the first hot stove you have been near for more than two weeks, and you fairly drink in the delicious heat.

You could not have dozed off more than a few seconds, leaning against the hot stove, before the smell of burning flight-jacket alerts your companions at the card table and you wake up as they drag you away and beat out the smouldering sleeve of your jacket. But the experience is sufficiently shocking you decide to relax on the floor on your back, with your hands locked under your head.

And this is how you remain, without turning over or changing the position of your hands for twelve hours, until you awake with a line of men stepping over you on their way to pick up their breakfast. Some kind soul has thrown a greatcoat over you, and a good thing too, for the fire is out and the stove is stone-cold.

Relocating yourself out of the way over in a corner, you again go to sleep until suppertime when good old Whitehawk arrives with clean shirts, clean underwear, and clean socks, and your bedroll, which he located still in the back of a Jeep at RHQ. Gratefully you crawl into it and sleep until awakened next morning to get ready for the leave truck that will carry you and several others, including friend Bob Grout, now with 26th Battery, to the Channel ferry dock at Ostend.

59

FOOTNOTE TO

RHINELAND FINALE

*

WHEN THE NORTHERN PART OF THE HOCHWALD IS CLEARED
by the Royals and the Rileys on March 4, and the guns are ordered
to move up through the mud, the landscape is so churned up by
tanks and shell-fire that Bombardier Hossack will write in his diary:

Roads are just guesswork as we go forward to Neu Louisendorf
at the edge of the Hochwald. The woods are strewn with German dead, presenting a grotesque sight. The area is well mined,
and we avoid all white-taped places. At midnight the barn containing Regimental Headquarters burns, illuminating the whole
area nicely.

Engineers employ bulldozers to knock down damaged
houses, producing rubble to maintain roads. An afternoon move
(March 6) through mined areas of the Hochwald sees us passing
more dead and torn Jerries alongside burned-out tanks and vehicles. We dig-in in a pasture near the badly damaged village of
Labbeck [beyond the eastern end of the Hochwald Gap, five
kilometres from Xanten]. The new 32-barrel mortars [rocket
projectors] are deployed beside us. When they fire, a terrific
explosion rends the air and a swish says they are on their way.
Toronto Scottish machine-guns, in line behind us, fire frequently. . . . The wagon-lines area is being shelled repeatedly, and
our vehicles move to a quieter area.

We are afforded an excellent view of the enemy battling strongly for . . . a ridge on our right front. Shells from our lines can be seen to land among them and beat them back.

Hossack is describing a counter-attack on the British struggling to maintain a foothold on Boenninghardt Ridge on the right flank that overlooks the whole German bridgehead – taken by a small band of 3rd Battalion Irish Guards, and reinforced during two days of bitter fighting by the 4th Grenadier Guards and the 5th Coldstream Guards.

On the left flank of the Canadian drive now threatening Xanten, the leading battalions of the British 43rd Wessex Division, fighting southeast this way along the Rhine, are now within six miles of this fortified town, which provides the anchor for the German rear-guard action to maintain intact the bridge at Wesel, their only escape route. Their encirclement on this side of the Rhine is now complete, for three days ago, March 3, a powerful American spearhead (the other half of the pincer movement planned by Montgomery back in February and long delayed by flooding) driving northwest along the Rhine sealed off the right end of the Wesel pocket, when they made contact near Geldern with XXX Corps then doing a right hook beyond the Hochwald battle.

The American Ninth Army – 375,000 strong – immobilized for fifteen days while waiting for the flooding to subside from the open valves on the Roer dam, on February 23 had begun crossing the still swollen Roer river, the infantry in assault boats, and the tanks on rapidly built bridges. Safely across they swung northwest, well behind the German defences that were designed to protect the Rhine from attacks from the southwest, and drove (if they were tankmen) and walked (if infantrymen) some fifty miles in eight days, now and then confronting and overcoming pockets of resistance, accepting casualties in hastily prepared attacks that were sometimes inadequately supported, so as to carry on "relentless pursuit" of territory thinly held by badly confused and disorganized enemy troops.

Pushing on, along hard, dry roads with remarkable boldness, on occasion with what staff officers like to call "dash and verve," six infantry and three armoured divisions with almost 1,400 tanks had, by March 1, gained half the distance to the Rhine from the Roer. In one week the 13th Corps (made up of 84th, 102nd, and 5th armoured divisions) had taken more than six thousand prisoners. And the 29th Division had "swept a path 20 miles wide and 25 long, containing some 40 towns, the largest being the textile centre of Muenchen-Gladbach with a population of over 300,000," providing "34 accredited newsmen" with great stories of triumphant American troops winning the Rhineland.

However, when they hit the outer perimeter of the German bridgehead near Wesel, soon after making contact with the British right wing of First Canadian Army, they got some inkling of the quality of the enemy troops confronting the Canadian and British troops these past three weeks. Schlemm's forces severely punished the American tank units pushing forward in reckless fashion. Spoiled by the ease with which they had pushed along against weak or non-existent opposition, they were clobbered on March 5 by Panzerfausts and 88-mm guns, as they approached the southern bastion of the bridgehead bunched up (according to 1st Parachute Army General Alfred Schlemm's postwar testimony) in a "wedge-shaped formation of several hundred tanks with little dispersion."

The 8th Armoured Recce Battalion had 50 tanks knocked out in five minutes. Their 36th Battalion lost 41 of their 54 tanks. And their supporting infantry battalion (49th Armoured Infantry) had 343 casualties. According to Lt.-Col. M. G. Roseborough, commander of the 49th, they had no idea what they were getting into:

We were barrelling along against minimum resistance when we ran out of maps and intelligence . . . Our armour [going on alone] just ploughed headlong into a prepared defence the Germans had put in to protect the Wesel bridge. They had a number of their dual-purpose 88-mm ... ringing the town, and they had a field day ..."*

Now with their shrinking bridgehead under fire from Allied guns on three sides, Germany's battered First Parachute Army is headed for total disaster if it continues to try to hold territory on this side of the Rhine, particularly if the weather clears enough to allow Allied bombers to locate targets, including the bridges at Wesel, something they've been unable to do.

Nevertheless, with their only escape route at stake, they will make the Allies pay dearly before they withdraw or surrender. They have managed to remove most of their guns and mortars to the far bank of the Rhine and can still reach any point on the perimeter of their holding on this side. And they constantly underline this fact with impressive counter-fire whenever Allied guns pour shells into Wesel, Xanten, and nearby fortified villages Veen and Alpon.

Observing this finale to the awesome struggle for the Rhineland, British war correspondent R. W. Thompson will capture indelible images observed from an artillery OP on the ridge east of the Hochwald Gap:

... in a magnificent and terrible panorama ... the battle raged with frightful intensity on a front no more than eight miles wide ... the pounding by artillery and bombing within the confines of that narrow triangle [of villages Xanten, Veen, and Alpon] was awe-inspiring ...

Thursday, March 8th, had the feel of a day of reckoning ... the 43rd, 52nd [British] and 2nd, 3rd and 4th Canadian divisions ... gathered themselves for major attacks ... supported by an immense weight of artillery ...

---

* This and the preceding quotes are from pages 251, 252, 255, and 272 of *Rhineland*, Toronto: Stoddart, 1989, by Col. Denis and Shelagh Whitaker.

A white smokescreen streamed across the northern flank . . .
shells from batteries of 5.5s crashed into the town of Xanten so
that the dark shroud in which the town was hidden flickered
incessantly . . . The lovely church and spire . . . seemed to be
riding the heavy cloud banks as the battle swathed its base . . .

Crocodiles, Flails, tanks, and men moved in eccentric fashion
. . . in the midst of a great turbulence of smoke and flame, Veen
lay hidden at the very vortex of the tremendous struggle . . . The
whole middle distance was lit hour after hour with the constant
flicker and flare of running fires and explosions and the flash of
guns.

At intervals farmsteads and ammunition dumps blew up in
billows of heavy smoke shot through with flames, and men like
ants ran and fell . . .

But even as he recorded this picture of the fighting for Xanten,
"the undoubted key" to the wiping out of the German bridgehead,
he recognized that "it was easy to see everything and yet see
nothing," and there was "no way of knowing reality . . . without
going down on that terrible stage."*

---

* From R.W. Thompson, *Battle for the Rhine* (New York: Ballantine
Books, 1958), pp. 200-201.

60

SHADES OF SIEGFRIED
AT XANTEN

❋

ON MARCH 7, 1945, GERMAN TROOPS ARE SAID TO HAVE begun pulling back over the Rhine at Wesel, nine years to the day in 1936 Hitler, in pointed defiance of France and her allies, sent two battalions of his élite personal guard, SS Leibstandarte Adolf Hitler, marching through cheering crowds over the Hohenzollern Bridge at Cologne, symbolically reoccupying the Rhineland's left bank that had been demilitarized by the Locarno Treaty of 1925.

However, few of the soldiers engaged in attempting to take Xanten and nearby villages – squeezing the last fight out of paratrooper rearguards holed up in previously prepared positions behind mine fields and anti-tank ditches – will have the time or inclination to dwell on such matters, even if by chance they hear the historically conscious BBC remarking on this remarkable coincidence. German resistance, born of desperation, is just too severe. Their searing machine-gun fire from slits in fortified barns and thick bunkers and emplacements rakes the attackers, while hundreds of German guns and mortars of all calibres pound them with unabated fury from across the Rhine.

Xanten, the legendary birthplace of dragon-slayer Siegfried, is the linchpin of the German bridgehead centred on Wesel. Obviously it must be held at all costs if the remnants of their badly mauled paratroop formations (some reduced to half-strength and others to quarter their original number) are to make it back across the river.

For those who remember the wicked confrontations day and night from Caen to Falaise in Normandy last July and August, the Rhineland fighting seems on occasion to reach comparable levels of intensity. Certainly this was so during the struggle for the Goch–Calcar highway when massive concentrations of shells, resembling those dropped by the 25-pounders and mediums on Verrières Ridge, were needed again and again to stabilize the front. And no resistance anywhere along the Rhine is more severe than that encountered during the first days of March, when the words "Hochwald" and "Xanten" become synonymous with flaming battle and remorseless killing by men nearing exhaustion from three weeks of almost continuous attacks and counter-attacks.

A battalion attack by 6th Brigade having failed to take Xanten on March 6, a set-piece attack, involving three brigades (4th and 5th Canadian and 129th British of 43rd Wessex Division), is mounted March 8, to take the town, while 4th Armoured Division captures nearby Veen.

The Wessex units are to capture the main part of Xanten and a hamlet named Beek east of there, while 5th Canadian Brigade secures the high ground south of the town between the railway and the Alter Rhein, and 4th Canadian Brigade clears the western edge of the town. Assaulting units of 4th Brigade are the Essex Scottish on the left and Royal Hamilton Light Infantry on the right, supported by tanks of Fort Garry Horse.

The attack opens at 5:30 A.M. with a sudden rising whine of many tank engines and great splashes of light across the dark skies, as seven regiments of field guns and four regiments of mediums open up with mighty roar from all sides on the shrunken German bridgehead. OP Signaller John Cooper, who, with his Troop Commander, Capt. Gordon Lucas of Fox Troop, is going into the attack for the first time in the turret of a tank supplied by the squadron of Fort Garry Horse supporting the Essex, and will remember every minute of that grim morning:

The enemy position consists of farmhouses and barns built as bunkers with thick, steel-reinforced concrete walls and cellars built in the shape of air-raid shelters – very formidable. The ground leading up to the bunkers, that form part of the northern end of the Siegfried Line, is devoid of all trees and brush – a bare, upward grade without cover. A barrage by our guns is to precede the attackers, but it will be of short duration. The tanks will then take over close support.

We are awakened while it is still dark. Climbing up into the Sherman tank that has been allotted to us as a mobile observation post during the attack, I "net in" the 19-set radio transmitter and receiver to our Regiment. Down in the hull of the tank, there is a driver and a co-driver. Capt. Lucas and I take over the turret. Just after first light, we move off over a ditch onto a road, and carry on for a mile or two, until we turn right into a field that is to be our startline for the attack.

Grave misgivings arise when our wireless goes dead as we are running up to the startline. However, to our relief it turns out we are merely passing through a wireless "dead zone," and soon we regain radio contact with our troop and Regiment.

I feel immensely safe in the tank in comparison with the Bren Gun Carrier we usually use, until the thought of 88-mm anti-tank guns passes through my mind. Still, I think, if a person has to go into battle, there's no better way than sitting down in comparative floating comfort surrounded by thick steel.

All of a sudden our guns open up and the Essex Scottish start forward. Almost immediately a German counter-barrage comes down right on our position. The crashing concussion of each shell is so great, I can only guess they're firing something quite heavy at us – 105-mm or heavier – and I am truly thankful for the protection of the tank, as I look out the periscope and catch sight of some stretcher-bearers attending the wounded among some obviously dead men. It is truly shocking. It all happened so quickly.

The tanks now move up into the clearing close to the enemy

positions and begin firing their 75-mm guns into the bunkers, but without much effect. It is then I notice two or three extended lines of Essex Scottish charging up the incline past our tanks. I'd seen our infantry attack before, but in this case they are attacking across open ground against a very strong position held by German paratroopers armed with many automatic weapons and heavily backed by mortars and artillery. The attacking lines of men are being hit and knocked down by machine-gun fire and well-aimed mortar bombs. I see an infantryman hurled at least ten feet in the air. And the same explosion takes out three or four other men. After taking many casualties, the first line of infantry goes to ground, while the second line charges up the hill with the same result. By this time our barrage has stopped.

Our shells – like those from the 75-mm tank guns – aren't all that effective against these deep bunkers, and for a time the attack is stalled. With our infantry digging in, covered by the tanks continuing to fire on the German positions, the German artillery attempts to knock out individual tanks by firing heavy concentrations on them, and though none are set on fire that I see, they may disable some. The tank in front of us was violently rocked by a heavy shell exploding under the front of its hull.

Now the Essex try to outflank the German positions, and are, to a point, successful. But the main bunkers are still being defended very aggressively, when more German troops are seen coming forward from their rear areas, to dig-in behind the bunkers. Capt. Lucas immediately gives me fire orders to transmit to the guns laying down a Mike target on them. After this they disappear and we never see or hear from them again.

But the stalemate is not broken until about 1500 hours when Crocodiles [flame-throwing Churchill tanks towing trailers of fuel] appear and begin to burn the paratroopers out of their bunkers. The position is finally taken after about an hour of shooting flames and taking prisoners from one bunker after another. As batches of prisoners are being escorted to the rear, some are laughing and some are crying . . .*

The Crocodiles also deal effectively with a small, ancient stone fort that "looks as though it could have been built in the Middle Ages."

The Royals' leading companies (Stothers's C and Wilcox's D) are under shell- and mortar fire from the moment they leave their forming-up place, and the closer they get to Xanten, the worse it gets. When they come under machine-gun fire from the old fort on the right and a windmill on the left, they have to resort to crawling up a ditch until they get close enough to rush their objectives in the town.

By now the Rileys are in serious trouble on the right flank of the brigade: two company commanders are dead, and another, the indomitable Major Froggett, in command of a company cut off by counter-attacking Germans, has been taken prisoner.

At noon Brig. Cabeldu, 4th Brigade commander, orders the Royals to renew their attack to help the British 129th Brigade on the left, and take some pressure off the desperate Rileys. They attack with two companies up (Wedd's A and Stothers's C).

Aided by Wasp flame-throwers, Stothers's men quickly gain their objective, but Wedd's company is soon in a very bad way, with his forward platoon pinned down in a group of buildings by such severe fire it is impossible for his other two platoons to move up.

After both of his remaining lieutenants (R. S. Beckley and veteran "Mo" Berry) are wounded and evacuated, Wedd himself is wounded in one leg. Being the only surviving officer in the company, he rejects evacuation and carries on. As he limps towards the factory that is his company's objective in Xanten, he is hit in the

---

* This description of the fighting at Xanten was prepared by John Cooper at the author's request.

other leg, and this time so seriously he can no longer walk. However, until he can get another officer forward to take over the company, he refuses to be evacuated, even though he can't gain shelter in a trench, but must lie on a stretcher above ground in a shallow declivity.

Only when he is hit a third time, the mortar splinters inflicting mortal wounds to his head, neck, and chest, making it impossible for him to protest, are his stretcher-bearers allowed to evacuate him. The delay in evacuation will prove fatal, and he will die in a hospital in England a couple of days later, clearly the victim of devotion to duty.*

By nightfall victory is assured. With 129th Brigade dominating at least half of Xanten, and the rest of the terribly smashed town, where less than 10 per cent of the buildings still stand, dominated by 4th Brigade, the enemy withdraws – even as they keep two companies of RHLI pinned down and inflict 134 casualties on them. The Essex suffer 108, and the Royals 46 while taking 110 prisoners. During the night 5th Brigade passes through to take the high ground south of Xanten, and by early March 10 the last enemy resistance is liquidated.

In clearing the Rhineland a significant Allied victory has been achieved, and there is an appealing ring of honest understanding about the signal from the Supreme Commander Eisenhower to General Crerar to be passed on to the Canadian and British troops under his command: "Probably no assault in this war has been conducted under more appalling conditions of terrain than was that one. It speaks volumes for your skill and determination and the

---

* At a dinner with the author in London after the war, Col. Lendrum of the Royals expressed his earnest regret he had not recommended Major Bob Wedd for the Victoria Cross instead of a medal that could not be awarded posthumously. He certainly would have, he said, had he known the seriousness of Bob's wounds, which at the time, though serious, were not considered life-threatening.

valour of your soldiers, that you carried it through to a successful conclusion."

And XXX Corps Commander Horrocks, a veteran of the mud of Ypres and Passchendaele of the First World War, and who, but for fourteen months recovering from life-threatening wounds suffered in 1943 in North Africa, served continuously in battle zones in this war since before Dunkirk – will one day feel obliged to declare in his book *Corps Commander*: "This [the Rhineland] was the grimmest battle in which I took part during the war. No one in his right senses would choose to fight a winter campaign in the flooded plains and dense pinewoods of Northern Europe, but there was no alternative. We had to clear the western bank of the Rhine if we were to enter Germany in strength and finish the war."*

As in Normandy and along the Scheldt, the vastly superior fire-power of Canadian and British field guns had guaranteed success. The unique fire-control system embracing all field regiments in all the divisions in the corps, developed in late 1942 by a British officer, Brig. H. J. Parham, to allow FOOs of lowly rank to concentrate the fire of many widely dispersed regiments on a "target of opportunity" – twenty-four guns on a Mike target, seventy-two on an Uncle target, and two hundred and sixteen on a Victor target – had, throughout the Rhineland, delivered massive concentrations with a speed and accuracy beyond the wildest dreams of even field marshals and five-star generals of other nations.

"A very impressive technical achievement," will be the grudging tribute paid by German General Schlemm to the weight and accuracy of the concentrations regularly laid down by the guns of First Canadian Army on his First Parachute Army units, as they were decimated and driven back over the Rhine. While remaining scornful of Allied tactics, which he will claim during postwar interrogation "never surprised" him – that he could always "determine from the kind and location of artillery fire, and from the assembly

---

* Sir Brian Horrocks, *Corps Commander*, Toronto: Griffin House, p. 204.

positions of the tanks, where and when the attack would take place" – he will admit Canadian Army gun fire was so intense at times, he marvelled any German soldier managed to survive.

He concluded: "Two qualities are necessary if troops are to stand this *Hell Fire* – energy and resistance. Deep and narrow foxholes for one or two men have to be dug. The men have to have nerves of steel."*

Though the Germans had managed to assemble almost 1,800 guns and mortars to drench the muddy fields with storms of flashing geysers, and fill with shattering airbursts the woods through which white-faced, wincing men had to pass, they never came close to matching the hurricanes of high explosive which Canadian and British FOOs regularly called down on them from 25-pounders and their slower, but heavier cousins, the 5.5-inch mediums.

For the month ending March 7, shell consumption by just the field guns and the mediums – the work-horses of every battle – tell the story: almost 2,000,000 rounds by the 25-pounders and almost 360,000 by the mediums.

During twenty-one days, from February 17 to March 9, 4th Field alone fired 84,072 rounds, averaging 4,000 rounds per day.

In just the last two days (March 8 and 9) 4th Field consumed 15,288 rounds (637 per gun), representing almost eight tons of shells per gun crew, participating in 22 Mike (regimental) targets, one Uncle (divisional), and two Victor (Corps) targets, a small barrage, two counter-battery shoots, and a harassing fire-plan, all one night.

---

* 1st Fallschirmtruppen (paratrooper army) report of commander, prepared by General Alfred Schlemm at #11 POW Camp Wales. (MS #B-084, National Archives, Washington, U.S.A.)

61

THE BILL

✳

GERMAN LOSSES IN THE THIRTY-DAY BATTLE FEBRUARY 8
to March 10 were estimated at more than 89,000: 38,000 killed and
wounded and more than 51,000 taken prisoner. Their 116th Panzer
Division that had confronted 2nd Canadian Division on the
Goch–Calcar highway alone lost almost 3,000 men.*

But the "butcher's bill" was also very high for the Allied armies:
22,934 – the American Ninth Army suffering 7,300 casualties
during its seventeen-day campaign, and First Canadian Army
accounting for double that, with 15,634 killed, wounded, or
missing, 5,414 of them Canadians.

Almost half the Canadian casualties were suffered in only
twenty-one days by just one division – 2nd Canadian Infantry
Division. As in Normandy the previous July and August, the men
wearing the dark blue shoulder patch had the highest rate of casualties of all Allied divisions engaged in the clearing of the Rhineland:
2,307 killed and wounded, surpassing the 2,243 suffered by the 53rd
Welsh Division with thirty days' strenuous service that began in the
Reichswald on February 8.

---

* German casualty figures from Col. G. W. L. Nicholson, *Gunners of
Canada, Vol. II*, Toronto: McClelland and Stewart, 1972, pp. 420-1.

Casualties by Divisions Under Command Canadian Army
February 8 to March 11, 1945

Canadian		British	
2nd Cdn Inf Div	2,307	53 Welsh Inf Div	2,243
3rd Cdn Inf Div	1,530	51st Highland Inf Div	1,583
4th Cdn Armd Div	1,117	15th Scottish Inf Div	1,495
2nd Cdn Armd Bde	88	43rd Wessex Inf Div	1,244
2nd Cdn Corps Tps	177	3rd Brit Inf Div	945
1st Cdn Army Tps	84	52nd Lowland Inf Div	681
	5,303	11th Armd Div	679
		Guards Armd Div	587
		30th Brit Corps Tps	254
		6th Guards Armd Bde	197
		8th Armd Bde	194
		49th West Riding Div	172
		34th Armd Bde	46
		1st Brit Corps Tps	18
			10,348

(National Archives Records RG 24 Vol 18502 File 133.009 D-6)

PART FOUR: MARCH 11–MAY 15

Crossing the Rhine to
Sever Holland from Germany

62

A THIRTY–MILE–LONG

SMOKESCREEN

✳

OPERATION "PLUNDER," AS THE RHINE CROSSINGS ARE TO be known collectively, requires the assembly and camouflage of stupendous quantities of supplies – particularly bridging stores amounting to some 22,000 tons for the use of 8,000 Royal Engineers, including Royal Canadian Engineers who will build near Emmerich the last of the five bridges to be thrown across the swift-flowing river.*

No fewer than 260 miles of steel-wire rope and 80 miles of cable (originally designed for tethering barrage balloons) will be needed: first, by RAF volunteers of 159 Wing to winch ferries and rafts back and forth; and second, by the engineers stringing together and holding in place some 25,000 wooden pontoons under the bridges, and sustaining an anti-mine boom strung across the river upstream by the Royal Navy in case the Germans try floating down explosive charges to blow up the bridges. Then there are 2,000 assault boats, 650 storm boats, and 120 river tugboats, as well as mountains of ammunition to be brought up.

And with the far bank of the Rhine somewhat higher than this side, exposing most of the rolling open country to enemy observation, it is necessary to lay down, right up until D–Day on March 24,

---

* 155 Engineers were killed or wounded while bridging the Rhine.

a dawn-to-dusk smokescreen along a thirty-mile stretch of river. To maintain the white blanket, billowing from hundreds of smoke generators using 200 tons of zinc chloride and fog oil a day, without leaving any gaps to expose Allied activity, is a tremendous engineering feat requiring constant adjustments for wind and atmospheric conditions.

Canadian Army's Meteorological Group's special "Met Officer," Capt. M. E. Comfort, the only one of his kind in the British–Canadian forces, provides Smoke Control with reliable forecasts of atmospheric and wind conditions, advising on the best beaming points for fog-oil generators to meet changing conditions, and moving them as necessary.*

For twelve days, until March 23, when artillery units are allowed to move up into positions prepared in advance by discreet work parties, the Regiment, along with the rest of the Division, bivouacs in the southeast corner of the Reichswald, which escaped the worst of the "Veritable" bombardments that smashed or denuded 70 per cent of the trees in the great forest.

It is here, far from the sounds of battle, with a degree of relief you find embarrassing, you catch up with them when you return from seven days' leave in England. All the way back you had been plagued with dread at the thought of having to return to action. In vain you had tried to suppress the sickening feeling you were returning to your doom, a feeling that deepened with each passing mile as the racing train from London closed on Dover and the ship that would carry you back across the Channel.

---

* In the planning and distribution of smokescreens that moved up the Rhine as the front moved from near Nijmegen to Wesel, blocking the enemy view of the left flank during the thirty-day campaign, and for two more weeks before the Rhine Crossings, other key officers were: Lt.-Col. W. R. Sawyer, GSO 1 Chemical Warfare; Major J. T. Hugill, RCA; and Capt. J. C. Bond, Chemical Warfare, awarded a Military Cross for his gallant and dangerous work of reconnaissance for deployment of generators often in front of the FDLs, and sometimes in mined areas.

From the outset of your leave, you were totally ill at ease. Finding yourself in London, only hours after being pulled back from an OP at the Hochwald, was a shock. The contrast between survival in the muddy, shell-swept Rhineland and life "laughing onward" in the West End – callously indifferent if not totally oblivious to what was going on over in the Rhineland – was almost too much to bear as you studied every edition of the papers trying to picture what was happening to comrades left behind.

While fully appreciating the British must be sick to death of war news – and that Londoners, of all people on earth, surely had earned the right to ignore the war for a while now the rocket blitz had ended – you still were unable to restrain your temper when a churlish hotel clerk or snotty headwaiter treated with cold disdain your request for a modicum of service. And this was particularly so the day you learned, through a chance meeting with Royals' Major Tom Whitley on Piccadilly, that Bob Wedd had died of wounds in a Limey hospital and been buried that day in Tom's presence in Brookwood Cemetery south of London.

Time and again good old Bob Grout (invited to accompany you on a visit to your wife's relatives in Birmingham) dragged you away from situations in the West End before they developed into something really serious, but in the process further enraged you by begging the offended parties to make allowances for his slightly unbalanced companion. Of course, on cooling down each time, you knew it to be true; you had never really recovered from the unwitnessed but very real breakdown in that isolated Jerry slit-trench on the Goch–Calcar highway. And as your leave was drawing to an end, you took to worrying that under similar conditions another breakdown was not only possible, but entirely likely, placing at risk the infantry depending on you to deliver the support of your guns at a time of desperate need.

And when two attractive, young ladies, volunteer hostesses at the regular Saturday night dance for officers at the Overseas League, where you and Bob had spent the previous evening, arrived uninvited at Victoria Station to see you off, it seemed clearly an ill omen.

After years of coming and going from British station platforms without greeting or farewell from a living soul, this gesture by these two young women from two of the best families in London, with bags of other things to occupy their Sunday afternoon, was just too remarkable.

Then, just as the train was about to pull out, and all the doors along the platform were *thunking* closed, one of the girls reached up and kissed you. You knew it meant no more than "Cheerio – take care – sorry you have to go back there – best wishes for a safe return, for you seem a decent enough chap." But deep feelings you had almost forgotten existed stirred within you. And as the train tore for Dover, you felt your mind, body, and soul surrendering to a rebellion you had suppressed all the time you had been in the U.K., and you unloaded your worries on Bob.

You told him about breaking up in that hole, and of your continuing fear that when you'd be most needed by the infantry, you'd cower in a hole. You swore that if there was an honourable way to get out of it all, you'd take it in a minute – that you'd do almost anything, short of a self-inflicted wound, to get out of going back.

An officer sitting opposite you in the compartment, a total stranger, incensed by your desperate talk, which he clearly felt was unbecoming to one holding a King's Commission, undertook to give you a pep talk, pointing out the obvious disadvantage of allowing the mind to dwell on something that might never happen, while advising against any course of action for which your conscience would never forgive you.

While not helping in the slightest to solve your dilemma, he at least shut you up, as you realized that only someone who'd been driven to the brink could really understand what you were talking about.

Over many months, observing those around you, you have to believe that though men have an extraordinary capacity to absorb and manage fear in all its shades, from breathtaking anxiety to shivering terror, every man has his limits. By suppression or repression, or whatever, a man can appear to carry on indefinitely, holding fear at bay if conditions are not too severe. But even as he blotters it up and puts on a brave front, fear is relentlessly taking its toll. And one day he finds he's had his fill: he can take no more.

It's clear you've lost your resiliency through cumulative effects of having lived too long with fear, cowering too often under shell and mortar blasts, and, on too many occasions, steeling yourself to go forward when every part of your being ached to remain hidden in a hole.

So when you read in a letter from your wife (the first of several awaiting you) that Gen. McNaughton, Minister of National Defence, has approved of an application, made by her father (senior naval member of the Dependants Allowance Board) that you are to be flown home on compassionate grounds to aid in the convalescence of your mother recovering from a serious illness (until now hidden from you), it seems heaven sent.

But the next letter (in chronological order) tells how your dear mother, persuaded she shouldn't let her needs interfere with the war effort, assured a bewildered nurse from Defence Headquarters, filling out a routine form at her bedside, that your return was not necessary.

At first you feel only crushing disappointment. But then you are overwhelmed by the realization you now have an obligation to stay alive even greater than before: if you buy it now, your mother will surely die of anguish, believing she condemned you to death. You've no choice but to go begging. At RHQ you find the CO is up at Division acting as CRA, and the second-in-command has left on long service leave to Canada.* So it's to Adjutant Sammy Grange you confess your plight, holding back nothing.

To your amazement, he reveals your removal from front-line duty is already in the works! He wasn't supposed to tell you in case

---

* Major Gordon Savage, who by then had earned a DSO for his aggressive reconnaissance and forward planning of regimental moves to ensure continuous support of the infantry.

it didn't work out, but the Colonel has recommended you for a job back at the reinforcement depot in Ghent in Belgium. Why? Well, it seems he discovered, through an investigation he undertook from his elevated position at Division, of the longevity records of current FOOs (no doubt inspired by an inquiry from McNaughton's office) that you've survived as a FOO longer than anyone else in the Canadian Army. And to make sure you get the job, he saw to it that only your name went forward. Still, knowing the ways of the military, the appointment could be weeks coming through. Meanwhile, do you think you can hang in there?

In your happiness you assure him that knowing relief is nigh you will have no difficulty. However, later, when the euphoria wears off, you decide you are not going to die twice – that when the time comes to move out with the infantry again, you'll have one of those rum-filled water-bottles, now cluttering the floor of the carrier, always buttoned into the front of your battledress blouse where it'll be handy whenever you feel you are getting the wind up.

With remarkable satisfaction all ranks welcome the news that when 1st Canadian Army goes back into action across the Rhine, it truly will be an army of Canadians – 1st Canadian Corps (including 1st Infantry Division, 5th Armoured Division, 1st Armoured Brigade, and all their Corps and Army Troops) having been brought up from the Italian front, where they'd been fighting since the summer of 1943. This is first learned from Gnr. "Babe" Hughes (kid brother of Bdr. Morty and L/Bdr. Ralph, of Baker Troop, 2nd Battery), who, about a year ago, was posted from 4th Field to Italy. He says all 1st Division arty regiments are now bivouacked in the Reichswald.*

---

* Entering battle in Holland for the first time over the Rhine, 1st, 2nd, and 3rd Field Regiments answered calls for fire from 7th Brigade, of 3rd Division, moving against Deventer.

63

MORE FIRE SUPPORT
THAN FOR D-DAY

✳

WITH THE REGIMENT OUT OF ACTION AND AT EASE FOR THE
first time since those four days last November at Rumst after the
Scheldt, and blessed with sunny days and balmy spring nights, the
gunners enjoy a lazy period of maintenance and recreation. Daily a
certain number are trucked into Nijmegen where wet canteens and
a "hamburger joint" have been set up, and some forty-eight-hour
passes to Brussels are issued.

With the war seemingly far away from the peaceful security of
this bushland, the tragic death of Gunner T. E. Brydges, of 26th
Battery, by a mine on the second day the Regiment is here, seems
monstrously unfair.

A few days later, Gunner E. F. Fyles, an RHQ Don R, narrowly
escapes death when he's swept from his motorbike by the concussion wave of an awesome explosion that rocks the Reichswald and
blows to eternity several Engineers attempting to disarm two huge
piles of mines that had been lifted from the forest floor and stacked
beside the main road.

All ranks are warned against wandering off routes established by
white tape, and you find yourself examining every inch of ground
you are going to pass over, as you recall the advice of an infantry
pioneer officer: If you hear a pop underfoot, leave your foot there,
pressing down, for it could be an "S" mine designed to pop up in
the air about three feet before exploding. Held down, it will

explode underground – blowing off your foot perhaps, but saving your life.

"Long Service Leave" comes through for nine Other Ranks and your GPO, Lieut. Jack Bigg, who leave immediately for England en route to Canada. How wonderful for Jack, and for his wife and seven-year-old daughter who was only a babe of seventeen months when, just before Christmas 1939, he left Winnipeg as a newly enlisted gunner with C Battery RCHA for Halifax and England.*

Again assigned to Baker Troop – Don Patrick having been wounded by a sniper near Xanten – you are ordered to go up beyond the smokescreen and establish an OP overlooking the Rhine and the sizeable town of Emmerich across the river. Collecting your old crew, which now includes Gunner L. R. Cunningham, replacing Ferry who was wounded in the Hochwald, you go forward after dark to an infantry outpost in a lonely farmhouse, sitting out in the open fields about four hundred yards from the river and a couple of hundred yards in from the main road leading to a ferry dock. There you park the carrier out of sight in the barn which, like so many in Holland and Germany, faces the road as an extension of the house.

Of course no one must be seen outside the house in daylight. Thus, next afternoon, when two Provost Corps types in a Jeep, followed by a water truck, casually start down the road past the

---

* Even after fifty years, Gladys Bigg would recall with painful clarity "the empty, lonely feeling of every single minute of those five and a half years Jack was away" that began with the agony of parting in the Winnipeg Railway Station on December 4, 1939: "There was such a crowd, you couldn't move. I was trying to hold baby Phyllis up so she wouldn't be hurt. People were like maniacs. I lost my hat. And there was such weeping and wailing! I look back on it as a scene from hell. When Jack left, I had fifteen dollars to look after myself and Phyl, and his assigned pay [$30 of the $39 a month earned by a gunner] and dependants' allowance [$35 for wife and $12 for the child a month] did not come through for another six weeks. Christmas, shared with the wife of another C Battery gunner, was unforgettable – broke and desolate."

farm, stopping now and then to nail up on a telephone pole another directional sign to the "Water Point," you are restricted to shouting yourself hoarse while they ignore your frantic arm-waving from your obscure position in the shadows of the open barn doors screening you from the windows of Emmerich. Helplessly you watch them drive right down to the dock, get out, and stand talking and pointing at Emmerich in total unconcern, until shells begin to flash and crack around them, and they disappear in the smoke and dust. In a couple of minutes they reappear, running bent-over back down the ditch along the road. More shells burst on the road and they drop out of sight again. From there on they must crawl, and you see them no more, but their vehicles remain at the dock – monuments to poor intelligence, and not just in the military sense.

Still they proved there is at least one artillery OP in Emmerich. Until now your dreary vigil in the smoky mists – nauseatingly oily when the wind shifts this way – studying the dead city had produced nothing. During March 19 and 20, behind the smoke, 4th Field work parties prepare gun and ammo pits near Cleve, while regimental "ammunition numbers" dump 700 rounds per gun.

On March 22, you are pulled back for an officers' briefing by the CO on the Rhine crossings – Operation "Plunder" – scheduled for 9:00 P.M. next day. Units of Ninth U.S.A. Army will cross on the right flank of British 21st Army Group, whose units will cross between Wesel and Rees. Curiously, Wesel and Rees were the first towns in Germany hit by Allied bombs in World War II, when in May 1940 the RAF tried to prevent the Germans reinforcing their *blitzkrieg* in the Low Countries. And Wesel will be flattened by bomber Command dropping 1,100 tons of bombs on it tomorrow night.*

---

* During the last three days leading up to Plunder, Bomber Command dropped 10,000 tons of bombs on enemy airfields, bridges, along supply routes, and on gun positions. And 2,500 heavy bombers of the U.S.A. 9th and 15th Airforces have daily added to the distant, heavy rumbling beyond the Rhine.

Tomorrow's assault, over a twenty-mile stretch of river, is being made with heavier artillery fire support than was provided for the D-Day Landings in Normandy (*see* Appendix A).*

The only Canadian infantry taking part in the initial crossing will be 9th Brigade attached to the 51st Highland Division, the assault division of XXX Corps. Once on the far bank, the rest of 3rd Canadian Division will cross to extend the bridgehead westward through Emmerich. However, though few Canadians will be involved in the crossings, all the Canadian guns including 4th Field's will add their voices to the roar that will rise from more than 3,400 barrels and rocket projectors – 766 more than used in support of Operation "Veritable."

Of this total, 1,780 are field guns, mediums, heavies, heavy ack-ack (in a ground role), and rocket projectors. Together they will engage in a complicated plan of diversionary fire, counter-battery fire, and incredibly heavy neutralizing bombardments – one of which will be maintained continuously for three days!

---

* Operation Plunder, planned and controlled by Field Marshal Montgomery, was really five major operations: "Turnscrew," at 9:00 P.M., March 23, led by 51st Highland Division crossing at Rees, followed by the 43rd Wessex Division, the 3rd British Infantry Division, and the Guards Armoured Division; "Widgeon," at 10:00 P.M., involving five Commando brigades (1st Army Commando Brigade leading, and 3rd and 6th Army Commandos following, along with 43rd and 46th Royal Marine Commandos) landing near Wesel to surprise the Germans from the rear; "Torchlight," at 2:00 A.M. next morning, led by the 15th Scottish Division, crossing from Xanten; "Flashpoint," at about the same hour, by American 9th Army, led by 79th and 30th Divisions, crossing at two points near Rhineburg, south of Wesel; and finally "Varsity," at 10:00 A.M., involving landings among the German gunlines by 14,000 British and American airborne soldiers from U.S.A. 17th Airborne and British 6th Airborne Divisions, dropping by parachute or sailing down in gliders after being unhooked from tug planes. Of 6th Airborne's nine battalions, six parachute in and three arrive in gliders.

The remaining guns – anti-tank guns, tank guns, and light ack-ack guns, along with medium machine-guns and heavy mortars (not included in the totals) – will fire on selected targets across the Rhine a series of "Pepperpot" concentrations of awesome intensity.

At 11:00 A.M., March 23, the Regiment begins its move into the prepared positions near Cleve, and by 1:00 P.M. all three batteries have reported ready. Command posts receive traces and task tables for the operation, but the Regiment's involvement is not great.

During the afternoon an Air OP observer registers five targets over the Rhine utilizing one 4th Field gun – swooping his little Auster back and forth over the batteries, gunning his motor to climb up to observe the fall of each shot, and quickly dropping down again to pass over the guns with motor shut down in a long, whistling glide almost at ground level. All of which is part of a deception plan, you are told.

Precisely at 5:00 P.M. the guns of 3rd Division, over on the left, open up on their counter-battery work that will last sixty-five minutes.

At 6:00 P.M. on the right of XXX Corps, where XII Corps is to move early tomorrow, another bombardment by 700 more guns begins.

And during the evening, with horrific swooshes, salvoes from 1st Canadian Rocket Battery loop overhead towards targets north of Rees.

At 8:30 P.M. the Canadian guns switch from counter-battery work to direct support of the assault.

Pepperpots are now being fired across the Rhine at rates of fire that cannot be sustained by the 40-mm Bofors ack-ack guns. Designed for very rapid fire, but in short bursts, their barrels soften and bulge from the white heat accumulated from sustained fire, and only by stripping parts from other guns do some remain in action to complete the required expenditure of 750 rounds per gun.

At H-hour and again at H plus-45, 2nd Corps guns fire a counterbattery program designed to neutralize all enemy batteries.

Then they engage on call all batteries that can be identified as still active.

Early next morning, March 24, after firing the prescribed bombards, 4th Field, along with the other field regiments of 2nd Division and 4th Division, joins 2nd AGRA in firing a diversionary plan on Emmerich.

At 10:00 A.M. all the guns go silent as the great air armadas of planes and towed gliders of 6th British Airborne Division (including 1st Canadian Paratroop Battalion) and 17th U.S. Airborne Division stream over ahead. The first waves are the 1,795 transport planes carrying 8,000 paratroopers, and soon, far beyond the Rhine, myriads of white parachutes blossom in the clear blue sky. And as they drift down and disappear, amidst heavy flak, hundreds more planes come over from the direction of Belgium, towing over a thousand gliders (1,305) filled with troops and fighting equipment (109 tons of ammo, 695 vehicles, 113 light artillery pieces).

While the smoky mists lying across the landscape beyond the Rhine swallow up parachutists and gliders as they descend in the distance, the great amount of cracking and booming, though distant and faint, suggests they have aroused a storm of fire from 88s on the ground. You shudder for those poor guys descending through tornadoes of flak, hanging on parachutes or buckled in flimsy wooden gliders, as you remember the broken gliders lying askew in front of your windmill at Groesbeek, including one laden with dead paratroopers still sitting in the open-mouthed glider with a Jeep half in and half out.

Very high casualties would seem to be guaranteed among the 8,000 British, Canadians, and Americans who dropped over there today.*

That they accomplished their tasks is a miracle. But by noon there are reports of success by all assaulting formations, although

---

* 1,100 parachutists, glider men, and aircrew died, and 1,800 were wounded.

fighting continues, and Canadian 3rd Division units are meeting resistance in Emmerich.

By the time darkness falls, there are reports that the airborne troops have linked up with the assaulting ground forces expanding the bridgehead inland from the river, and that in the process have taken 3,500 enemy prisoners.

For the next three days the guns of 2nd Canadian Corps fire Victor targets every ten minutes, and the three batteries of the 2nd Heavy Ack Ack Regiment each contribute 5,000 rounds of 3.7-inch airbursting shells, as an uninterrupted program of harassing fire is conducted on behalf of XXX Corps expanding the bridgehead north and west.

Counter actions by German guns and planes is not great, but for four nights (March 24–27) there is some shelling, and nightly a few planes arrive on schedule, growling in the darkness overhead in a menacing way before dropping their bombs and strafing the area.

Fortunately, though this action is nerve-wracking, no 4th Field personnel are injured by the bombs or strafing – at least, no *human* personnel.

However, Baker Troop's beloved mascot, "Hardtack," the long-legged hen that has travelled with them since Louvigny eight months ago, is found dead under a truck on the morning of March 25.

64

GUNNER HARDTACK

---　❋　---

"HARDTACK" MAY HAVE BEEN ONLY A HEN, BUT ON A GREY March morning just south of Cleve, she is tendered a soldier's burial by the men of Baker Troop, 2nd Battery, 4th Field Regiment. In the midst of heavy gun fire rolling over the Rhineland, a sound to which she'd long become accustomed, appropriate words are murmured over her grave marked by a wooden cross, inscribed: "Hardtack B Troop 42 [4th Field unit sign] – Died March 25, 1945." And on the mounded sod they leave a china nesting-hen.

What exactly caused her death is not known, though it's assumed to have been enemy action. German bombers were over last night dropping flares and anti-personnel bombs close by, and though it was thought they missed the guns, one of those lightly fuzed missiles that leave no crater could have been the cause. At dawn she was found dead without a mark on her under a vehicle where she'd taken shelter. Nearby was a broken jam jar that some gunners suspect played a role in her death.

She will be sorely missed. During the past nine months, she not only won the complete affection of everyone who knew her, but there was a widespread belief throughout the Troop and Battery that Hardtack possessed an uncanny ability to foretell the arrival of enemy shells. And now their little sentinel is no more.

While you followed the Hardtack saga from way back at Fleury-sur-Orne in Normandy, first as a neighbour and nodding acquaintance while still with Able Troop, and then as her troop commander after your posting to Baker Troop before the Rhineland attack, you never were back at her gun position long enough to witness a demonstration of her clairvoyance. But there is no shortage of witnesses, and Gunner "Buck" Saunders will testify in no uncertain terms to her eerie capability:

That bird was the greatest living air-raid warden . . . She could sense something was pointed in her direction long before anybody else heard anything coming, and just take off and run for cover, like down in the command post if it was dug, or back under a truck still on the position. On the outside of TL vehicle the boys had built a box for her and whenever they were going to move, they'd open the door of the box, slap their hands a couple of times and say "let's go," and that bird would head over and hop up into her box. Then, when they got to the next position, they'd open the door and let her jump down and wander.

But if you watched that damned bird, you could get a warning something was coming. You wouldn't hear a sound . . . absolutely quiet . . . then all of a sudden she'd look up and start to wander around looking . . . you know . . . poking around looking for cover, like under GA or in a hole. And if you were on your toes and didn't want to run any risk, you'd follow that bloody bird and take cover yourself! That bird would go and take cover twenty seconds before anything came in. I am sure she could hear the breeches closing on the German guns! And when she took off to one side there . . . oh-oh . . . you knew something was coming!

Among the chief witnesses to her extraordinary conduct were the bird's principal guardians: Gunner W. J. Brewster, who drove the TL vehicle, and Lance-Bombardier Ralph Hughes, a Baker Troop Command Post ack.

According to Hughes they'd found a scrawny, woebegone half-starved pullet, wandering aimlessly in the rain among the dripping ruins of Louvigny, her bedraggled feathers filthy with rubble dust. By some miracle she had survived a succession of hellish days of torment, beginning with the stupendous concussions from Allied bombs tumbling down on the village and cratering the surrounding fields from early morning of July 18, followed by horrendous concentrations of shells later in the afternoon from 4th Field guns, only to be subjected all next day to periodic bombardments by Moaning Minnies, whose arrival in the village was heralded by blood-chilling wailing and screeching so loud it penetrated even over the continuous roar of your 25-pounders in the field across the road. Finally on the afternoon of the 20th, the sky really fell on her when torrential rain began pelting down, continuing all night and well into the next day, making life entirely miserable for all living creatures forced to survive without shelter.

And she had looked even worse after her first night at the gun position, tethered by a string on one leg to a stick stuck in the floor of Sgt. Morley Jeffries' gun pit, only slightly less close to the crashing gun than the gunners attending their weapon and serving up an endless stream of shells on targets called for by the FOOs.* At dawn she was a pitiful sight, having dropped all her feathers in a premature moult. (While Gunner Hank Prentice, who grew up on a farm, would not rule out the possibility the shedding of her feathers was caused by her terrifying introduction to the unholy racket of a 25-pounder gun position, he thought it more likely it resulted from having her feathers saturated by the torrential rain that fell that night, for hens are known to moult after a thorough soaking.)

At first it was thought the long-legged skinny bird was a rooster, and the only reason to rescue it was to fatten it up for a future feast somewhere down the road. But by the time she'd earned her name "Hardtack" from her principal diet of those brittle biscuits (if not her favourite food, certainly the most consistently available), and

---

* The heaviest twenty-four-hour consumption of shells by 4th Field ever – 1,000 rounds per gun.

had learned to live without fear down among a world of restless boots and dusty gaiters in the Command Post dug-out, which shuddered day and night with the concussion of the guns firing away just outside, no one would have dared suggest a chicken dinner.

A coop was built on the tool box on the side of the TL vehicle (the vanlike HUP), and each time orders came to move, it became part of the command post drill to scoop up Hardtack and button her into her coop, to bump along through dust or rain or darkness until released at the new position.

One dark and stormy night a fast move was called for, and they neglected to pick up Hardtack, each member of the command post thinking the other had put her into her travelling cage. However, it didn't worry them too much. They knew she would not wander far, and they would go back for her in the morning. But when they arrived at the new position, to their astonishment Hardtack jumped down from her coop, having hopped up into it herself when the truck was pulling out, and ridden all night with the unbuttoned door flapping open – determined to stay close to these men of gentle hands.

As days turned into weeks, and weeks into months, and the troop moved through dozens of new positions, farther and farther north, deeper into Europe, Hardtack became "one of the boys" while still retaining a distinctly individual personality.

First, she went through the whole Caen-to-Falaise maelstrom, and crossed the Seine to drive in triumph through Rouen up to Dieppe – saw a couple of Channel ports – lived a placid life on the docks of Antwerp before suffering the mud and water along the whole length of South Beveland peninsula. All winter in the Nijmegen salient she'd put up with the rain, the sleet and snow, including a brief move south over icy roads to hole up in reserve at Boxtel for a few days during the Battle of the Bulge – all the while laying soft-shelled eggs, demanding her share of tidbits from the parcels the boys got from home, and fuzzing up her wings and cackling like a fighting-cock when a brash newcomer to Baker

Troop, Lieut. Jack Bigg, tried to shoo her out of the way in the crowded Troop Command Post.

To the sad gunners who leave their little pal under a mound of fresh earth this day, it is only right that she lived long enough to pass through the Siegfried Line into Germany for the last big battle on the Western Front that crushed all resistance west of the Rhine.

For the next three days, as XXX Corps expands the bridgehead west and north, the guns of 2nd Canadian Corps fire Victor targets every ten minutes, and three batteries of British 2nd Heavy Ack Ack Regiment each contribute 5,000 rounds of 3.7-inch airbursting shells to an incredible uninterrupted program of harassing fire.

By March 28 all three brigades of 3rd Canadian Division are across the Rhine, and after a two-day battle, rubble-clogged Emmerich is cleared of the enemy.

At noon, wicked Pepperpot concentrations blanket the eight-kilometre stretch from Emmerich west to the village of Elten. Again the intense firing is hard on the thirty-six Bofors of 8th Light Ack Ack, wearing out a total of forty-three barrels in expending 2,400 rounds per gun.

At the same time the guns on the tanks of four regiments, firing intermittent salvoes that use up two and a half rounds per gun per minute, expend 1,600 rounds per gun, the heaviest concentration ever fired by any army's tanks anywhere.

And rattling away periodically, at the rate of thirty rounds per gun per minute, thirty-six medium machine-guns of the Toronto Scottish Regiment beat their assigned target areas across the river.

But the target singled out for heaviest treatment by the massed 2nd Corps artillery – a Victor target involving every gun in the Corps every ten minutes – is Hoch Elten, a heavily forested hill shaped like an overturned soup bowl, rising dramatically out of the otherwise flat terrain north of the Rhine halfway between Emmerich and Elten village. Only 1,500 metres from 4th Field gun positions just north of Cleve, it clearly would dominate both banks of the Rhine for miles, providing superb observation for enemy guns and mortars, if left unmolested.

When the three-day continuous bombardment of the hill begins, it is thickly covered by forest. Gradually barren spots begin to appear. By the time the last instalments of some four million shells are exploding on it, Hoch Elten resembles the badly shaved head of a female collaborator. At the beginning of the bombardment, each of the field guns is required to fire only eight rounds an hour, but with each gun crew in the Corps firing at their own discretion during each hour, some shells are always landing on that tortured hill.

Then, after twelve hours of this, the procedure is changed to massive time-on-target salvoes. This means the firing of each troop of guns is so timed that, regardless how far away or how near they are to the target, their shells will land at the same time as the shells from all the other guns in 2nd Corps.

And when finally it comes time for the Regiment to pull out to go over the Rhine, to be replaced by a British regiment, only two guns at a time are allowed to go out of action during the change-over. Thus the relentless pounding of the dismal hill with time-on-target Corps salvoes is allowed to continue without interruption.

At 1030 hours on March 31 the change-over is complete, and 4th Field guns cross the Rhine near Wesel at 1530 hours via the rumbling, spongy planks of a floating bridge called Blackfriars. Rolling east through the smashed and smouldering ruins of Emmerich, the guns pass just below the giant shaven mound that was Hoch Elten.

Seen close-up, the ravaged hill reveals a few shattered buildings jutting bleakly up from a barren expanse of stumps and blasted tree trunks. It's hard to believe there could be any resistance left in those still alive on that hill when 3rd Division units moved in, but it will not be reported clear of the enemy until later today.

Poor roads, heavy traffic, and blown bridges combine to make it one of the slowest moves ever, and it's midnight before the guns get into position near Ulft in Holland.

65

A DASH FOR THE TWENTE CANAL

※

FOR A COUPLE OF DAYS AFTER CROSSING THE RHINE, 4TH Brigade units and their supporting arms muck about in aimless fashion, moving hither and yon around a rural landscape from farm to farm, until you move back across the border into Holland and arrive at a town called Doetinchem, the occupation of which (by 5th Brigade) is still being disputed.

There, in a quiet part of town on the night of April 1, you learn the Royals have been assigned the task of securing an objective sixteen miles farther north, a bridgehead over the Twente Canal said to be vital to the future progress of the whole Canadian Army and the ultimate success of its attempt to cut off all lines of retreat for the German occupying forces in Holland.

A significant assignment indeed, but Doetinchem to you will always be the place where the mundane demands of the military combine to deny you the chance to sleep the night through in an exotically perfumed bed billowing with pastel eiderdowns in the front bedroom of a beautifully furnished but mysteriously unattended modern home.

At the outset the night seems blessed. Even as you and your crew explore this delightful billet (using a candle, for there is a power blackout in the town) and you sit down to try out the shiny, black grand piano bathed in bright moonlight spilling in through the filmy curtains on the living room window, Bob Suckling's driver

NIJMEGEN TO MEPPEL
23 MARCH - 06 APRIL 1945

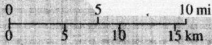

N

0 5 10 mi

0 5 10 15 km

4 RCA gun positions .... ///

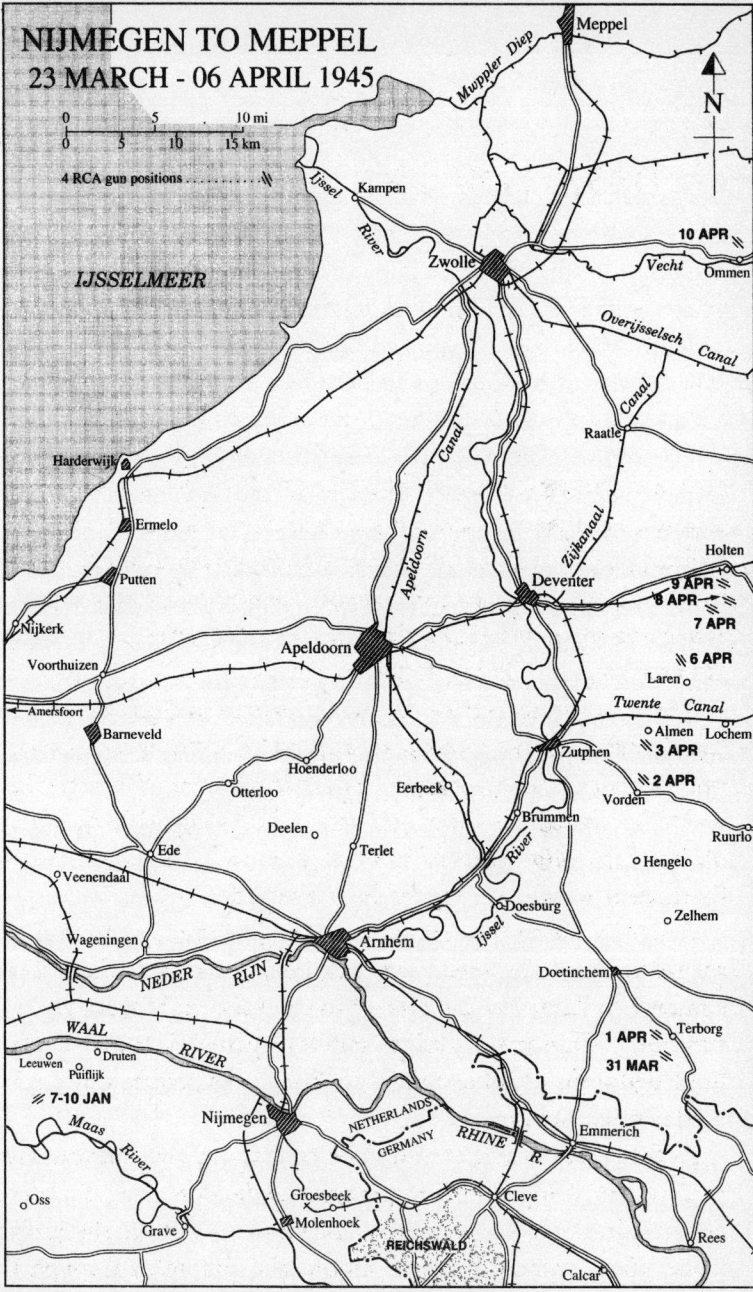

IJSSELMEER

Meppel

Muppler Diep

Ijssel River

Kampen

Zwolle

10 APR ///

Vecht

Ommen

Overijsselsch Canal

Raatle

Apeldoorn Canal

Zijkanaal

Canal

Harderwijk

Ermelo

Putten

Nijkerk

Voorthuizen

Holten

Deventer

9 APR ///

8 APR ///

7 APR

Amersfoort

Barneveld

Hoenderloo

Otterloo

Apeldoorn

Eerbeek

Brummen

6 APR ///

Laren o

Twente Canal

o Almen   Lochem

Zutphen

3 APR ///

2 APR ///

Vorden

Ruurlo

Deelen o

Terlet

Ijssel River

o Hengelo

Ede

Veenendaal o

Doesburg

o Zelhem

Wageningen

NEDER RIJN

Arnhem

Doetinchem

Terborg

WAAL

RIVER

Leeuwen o   o Druten

Pijflijk

/// 7-10 JAN

Maas River

1 APR ///

31 MAR ///

o Oss

Grave

Nijmegen

Groesbeek

o Molenhoek

NETHERLANDS

GERMANY

RHINE R.

Emmerich

Cleve

Rees

REICHSWALD

Calcar

comes over from next door to tell you the battalion won't be moving until dawn.

Alas, you should know by now that the order "no move before dawn" never applies to officers, and that you should not squander precious sack time playing the piano. But that extraordinary instrument, in such fine tune – something totally lacking in most pianos in Western Europe – is irresistible. And so when finally you ascend the stairs to the sweet softness of your elegant bower, it is close to midnight.

You are just drifting off, snuggled down in the rustling, white, linen sheets from which arise the most exotic of scents, suggestive of a beautiful woman, when you hear a distant voice, calling, "Foo . . . Foo . . . Foo . . ."

At first you think it is part of your dream. But the voice persists and finally draws you to the open casement window, where, from the street below, you are informed by Suckling's driver that the co has called a "balls" at battalion . . . that Major Suckling is already there . . . and that he's been sent back to collect you.

"Balls" being the unique, if irreverent, label currently in vogue for Royals' orders groups (springing from the universally popular expression of exasperation "Oh balls!" uttered with profound feeling most frequently by exhausted company commanders on being aroused from deep sleep to attend "O" groups), you wake your crew and tell them to pack up the carrier and be ready to move immediately you get back. But then a few minutes later, at the briefing, you learn the actual move won't get underway until dawn. Imagining the feelings of your crew when you inform them, you involuntarily mutter, "Oh balls!" – arousing chuckles among the company commanders, and even drawing a smile from the concentrated and earnest Colonel.

The Royals' objective is a bridge over the canal six kilometres east of Zutphen. The Royals are to form part of a "jock column" riding on the backs of tanks of the Fort Garry Horse, the Royals' carriers, and in the quads of 4th Field (in that order), following a prodding screen of armoured scout cars of 8th Recce Regiment's A

Squadron. You and Able Troop Capt. Bob Haig, a newcomer, will attach yourselves to the spearhead of five scout cars commanded by a Lieut. Lorne Mackenzie.

Lendrum, with long experience with middle-of-the-night "O" groups, wastes no time in laying on the operation, and you are looking forward to still getting a goodly stretch of shut-eye, when on the way out of the meeting, Major Jack Cooper (now battery commander, replacing Don Cornett who is now counter-mortar officer at Division) tells you to pick up from the CO at 4th Brigade, somewhere on the south side of town, a roll of maps covering the move, withdraw what you and Haig require, and deliver the rest to him. Cursing your luck, but still optimistic you can get a couple of hours' sleep if you hurry, you start out on foot.

However, as you discovered long ago in Antwerp, nothing is harder to find than a military headquarters in a built-up area in a blackout. By the time you make it back to your demoralized crew slouched around the kitchen table, staring at you with reproachful eyes from under drooping eyelids, the dawn is arriving overcast and dismal. Then as you pile in the carrier to join other vehicles grinding out of town to the forming-up point on a road leading north to Vorden, Hengelow, and a hamlet called Almen, rain begins to fall and bone-chilling gusts of wind swirl across the open carriers and the Royals shivering on the backs of tanks and vehicles. From this point on it's to be a "dash" to the bridge, or bridges to be exact, for there is another small bridge over a narrow stream at Almen a kilometre before the canal. Clearly whatever chance there is of "bouncing a bridgehead over the canal" (Corps Headquarters' dainty way of putting it) will depend entirely on the degree of surprise achieved during the final run for the canal, for certainly all bridges over the canal will be blown the instant they spot the first armoured car rushing up the road.

As your carrier takes its place in the column behind the last armoured car, just before H-hour (6:00 A.M.), you begin to experience the familiar symptoms of rising anxiety – the shallow breathing, the frequent deep sighs, and the desire to urinate – which occupants of armoured cars must experience every time they set forth along uncleared roads to feel out the opposition, presenting themselves as bait for enemy outposts, inviting them to fire and expose their presence and position.

Just before the column moves off, you and Haig get an unusual signal from Sunray. Because your carriers may not be able to keep up with armoured cars (capable of 50 mph), you are to hitch rides with them, taking along your 38-sets for communicating with your carriers when they fall behind. As Haig passes your carrier on the way to climbing up on a recce car, he stops a moment to grin broadly and stare quizzically at you as though asking, "Is this really happening?"

Suppressing your misgivings as you leave your own familiar, steel cocoon – telling yourself that at least you'll be warmer and drier inside the turret of an armoured car – you scramble up onto the rear deck of one of the rumbling monsters, a map stuffed in the front of your jacket and your 38-set hanging from your neck, competing in a clashing-duel on your chest with your dangling field-glasses. Though the deck is only about five feet above the ground, it seems much higher, and you are looking forward to getting inside, when to your dismay you discover a hitchhiker on a Daimler armoured car rides *on* the car, not *in* the car, there being no room for an extra body within.

It takes more than four hours to traverse the sixteen miles to the canal – sometimes rumbling along at a steady pace, sometimes halted while field-glasses scan farms far across the fields ahead in an attempt to identify distant figures as welcoming Dutchmen or Germans, and sometimes spurting ahead with what seems total abandon. But mostly the lead vehicle moves with timid caution, particularly along confined roads through bushland of sinister aspect. And never once do you cease wondering what kind of fire you may attract. Will it be the *bur-rup, bur-rup* of an MG 42, the *pom-puh, pom-puh, pom-puh* of a hopper-fed ack-ack gun, or the ungodly *whack* and *ee-ow* of an 88?

However, apart from a gun nest at a crossroads barn early in the drive, from which one survivor, devastated by the death of a close comrade, is flushed by an awesome burst of fire from the leading car's coaxially-mounted Besa machine-gun and 2-pounder gun, there is no opposition along the road. Emboldened, the Daimlers increase their speed to a level that might properly be called "a dash" as they draw near the bridge over the narrow little Berkel Beek at Almen.

Then, just as the road breaks out of a large forest into a recently cut-over area full of stumps and piles of brush, and Almen can be seen some seven hundred yards away, the recce cars pause to lace with machine-gun fire two figures standing suspiciously close to the far end of the bridge as though preparing to blow it up. As tracers streak at them, one disappears and the other goes down and does not move again.

Your carrier having just caught up, and the Twente Canal less than two kilometres away, you decide to drop off your precarious perch on the recce car and proceed the rest of the way in your own steel bucket. At this moment two of the recce cars, including the one to which Bob Haig is still clinging, roar forward to the bridge where they pause to check if it has been mined or booby-trapped.

Days later Haig will still be marvelling at the courage of the 8th Recce man he watches jump down in the water and swim across the little stream to dismantle explosive charges wired to the bridge abutment, never knowing whether or not a hidden German sentry is about to push down a plunger detonating them.

At the bridge, they discover to their profound regret the corpse on the roadway, killed by their bullets, is of a Dutch civilian, while the German sentry, with whom he'd been conversing, is able to arise unharmed, hands over his head, from a roadside round "pothole" trench. However, many of his comrades in the vicinity are not so lucky. By now the guns are deployed back at Vorden, and you are able to bring down fire on points where you think the enemy may be concentrating.

Haig will later report coming across Germans killed by fire from 4th Field shells, or by bursts of MG fire sprayed in likely places by

8th Recce while they lift some twenty mines from the roadway
and dump them in the river, along with the explosive charges from
the bridge, a brand new MG 42, and five Panzerfausts, one of them
dropped by a German cut down by a burst from the Besas of a
recce car as he approached with the thing resting on his shoulder
ready to fire.

Then revving their engines the cars roar over the bridge and disappear up a road that wiggles left between trees and houses in the
direction of the canal bridge, with the rest of MacKenzie's troop
and your carrier following. As the first car approaches the canal
there is a monstrous explosion, and a black cloud billows up full of
debris from the bridge, which spatters down, pelting the ground in
all directions.

Obviously they were prepared and waiting. And now surely
they'll be waiting for anyone foolish enough to try a water crossing
within sight of that destroyed bridge, and this thought haunts you
late into the afternoon as you join Suckling's company, designated
the first to cross. And as you wait with him for canvas assault boats
to be brought up to an isolated, dockside warehouse on the canal
bank about a kilometre east of the blown bridge, the knowledge
that, on orders from Lt.-Gen. Simonds, the Royals will not be reinforced until a bridge is built, is equally disquieting. As Lendrum
explained at a Royals' "O" Group, the Corps Commander is prepared to sacrifice one of his battalions securing the bridgehead, but
no more until a bridge is in place.

Late in the day the skies clear and the winds drop, and as the sun
is going down and the crossing gets underway, there is not a breath
of air rippling the water in the canal.

Though clearly every man in the boat you are in is white with
apprehension, having waited so long for the boats to be brought
up, no shots ring out, no mortars flutter down to crash about the
boats, and no airbursting 88s crack overhead. It is uncannily quiet
since the 72 guns of 2nd Division finished firing the smokescreen
and the diversionary shelling on the left near where the bridge
used to be.

Paddling over the still water, glowing blood-red from the stunning sunset now in progress, with only the gentle sound of dipping paddles and gurgling water breaking the silence of the balmy spring evening, it is as though there are no Germans anywhere within miles. And when you walk half a mile with Suckling and company, directly into the blinding rays of the setting sun, across quiet green meadows and pastures lined with trees and hedges, without arousing any enemy fire, everybody relaxes. It would seem the Corps Commander was unduly concerned.

Even after dark as you and Suckling stand outside the little farmhouse that is to be his company headquarters, listening to nearby sounds of horses and wagons and guttural voices, which, to your untutored ear could be German or Dutch, you don't worry. That you drew no enemy fire getting here encourages you to conclude the sounds are of a Dutch family removing themselves and their belongings to a less dangerous place. And as darkness deepens, it all seems so peaceful, friend Suckling decides to treat himself to a real night's sleep in a real bed in the house, even donning a new pair of silk broadcloth pyjamas he recently received in a parcel from home.

That the sounds of horses and wagons might be associated with guns and mortars being deployed does not occur to you until dawn when Jerry begins counter-attacking with such force, and shelling and mortaring with such intensity, it becomes clear he means to wipe out the bridgehead. His bombardment is particularly heavy back at the crossing point on the canal where overnight the Engineers put into service a heavy rafting operation using a section of Bailey bridge on pontoons, which brings over your carrier, Bob Haig's, the Royals' Carrier Platoon, and some tanks of the 10th Armoured Regiment. But it's a hazardous crossing, and Gunner W. H. K. Locke, of Able Troop's carrier crew, is killed on the way.

Becoming aware of the mounting aggressiveness of the enemy, but unable, because of clumps of trees and dense woods on the right, to observe anything of the early attacks on the centre of the bridgehead – against the companies manning the east–west railway embankment and a group of houses (Boschhouk) on the extreme right flank – you take advantage of the arrival of your carrier to wheel over that way.

On the way, wearing your signaller's helmet, passed up to you from the rear compartment, you listen to the boyish, high-pitched voice of the sixteen-year-old signaller Bill Knox, passing orders back to the guns from Bob Haig, with Wilcox's D Company. They are obviously under heavy shelling, and Haig calls down a roaring Mike target on the German infantry and tanks attacking them.

Just before the road you are following east bends left towards a railway crossing, you are attracted to a tall, nobly proportioned house that turns out to be Major J. K. Shortreed's B Company headquarters. You barely have time to establish yourself at the third-storey landing of a tower with a circular staircase before rifle shots snap from a couple of Royals snipers stationed at the lower tower windows and you are calling for fire on the field north of the railway embankment behind the house, helping to beat off a counter-attack by infantry that manages to get within fifty yards of the rail line. Accompanying tanks are growling about, menacing Haig's position on the left, but you can't see them because of the bush, which is a worry until you are told a couple of self-propelled anti-tank guns of 2nd Anti-Tank are now positioned over that way.

66

THE WAR CORRESPONDENTS'
VIEW OF BRIDGEHEAD

✳

ONE DAY YOU'LL BE SHOWN CLIPPINGS OF STORIES FILED BY war correspondents about the crossing of the Twente Canal, including the front page of the Toronto *Telegram* of April 5, 1945, carrying an eight-column banner line: TORONTO'S ROYAL REGIMENT WINS GATEWAY TO NORTH HOLLAND.

In the story, filed by Allen Kent, there'll be a picture of a smiling Major Bob Suckling, who led the first company across the canal in "canvas assault boats." While Kent's story will be as confusing as the actual events, subheadings manage to summarize with reasonable accuracy what went on from the evening of April 2 to dawn April 4: "Vital Holland Bridgehead Won by Toronto Royals . . . Held Under Heavy Attack . . . First Real Fight Since the Rhine was Crossed Carries Unit Across the Twente . . . What First Appeared a Push-Over Turned Into Grim Struggle to Remain."

And John Clare in the Toronto *Star* will tell how the Royals held the bridgehead "through 15 counter-attacks," quoting company commanders:

"They seemed to be using about a battalion of infantry, although they never did use them all at one time," said Major Stothers. "One counter-attack would have 80 Germans in it, and another of our platoons would report 10 or 12 taking a poke at them, and that is how it was." The major looked fresh and full of bounce after a night spent fighting off the Germans.

The Canadians killed many of the attackers. Bodies of the enemy lie thick on the ground before Major Stothers's company. Among them is the body of a German officer, who led his men right up to the Canadian foxholes. Lieut. George Ackhurst dropped him with one shot (through his eye) . . .

The whole bridgehead area was lashed with artillery fire. The Colonel [Lendrum] of the Toronto regiment described it as "intense and accurate." It was so heavy and intense that Canadian Engineers bridging the canal were forced to take cover, and field engineers, ferrying the vehicles and tanks across the narrow strip of water on rafts, were subjected to a hail of metal.

The Germans also threw tanks at Major Stothers' company, and when two of them bore in on the Canadian infantrymen, tanks from a western regiment [10th Armoured] scored a hit on one of them . . . All Tuesday night (April 3–4) the Canadians could hear the screams of the wounded and dying Germans lying where they fell in their desperate rushes at the Canadians.

They threw tanks at Major Shortreed's men too. His Piats went into action and when one of the two tanks moving in was hit in the turret they both fled . . . The second attack on Major Shortreed's positions was the biggest one of the day, as a company of Germans, walking beside two tanks, moved in on the Canadians. What Major Shortreed called "a beautiful piece of shooting" . . . A succession of barrages [concentrations] were laid down virtually on the infantry's (Royals) own position by the forward observation officer . . . *

---

* The war diary of 4RCA for April 4 will refer to the extraordinary overnight demands on the guns: "Altogether we fired 11 Mike targets, two Victor, and two Uncle targets in addition to a harassing fire program."

Targets from FOOs may have been upgraded by the 4RCA Colonel, but more likely the Victor targets, at least, were fired by the CRA to cool down enemy shelling holding up the bridging operation.

67

OVERRUN

——————————————— ✳ ———————————————

JUST AS THE SUN IS GOING DOWN, THEY COME – IN EXTENDED
line across the grassy meadow towards the railway embankment
along which two platoons of Shortreed's B Company are dug in,
about three hundred yards behind the house. From your third-
storey window, in the tower on the east wall of the house, you
could count them if you had time, for the setting sun, casting dark
shadows, makes each of them stand out sharply. Having helped
abort a morning attack from this direction, you're able to bring
down fire quickly. Instantly they disappear in the tall grass, and all
you can do is work over the field for a while to persuade them to
crawl back rather than forward.

Just as you are becoming smugly satisfied that once again the
guns have snuffed out an attack, staccato bursts of machine-gun
fire draw your attention sharply right to a small copse five
hundred yards away on this side of the railway, just after the road
comes over the crossing and turns this way for a short distance,
before turning to its left and swinging in behind trees and houses
on your right in a long curve that will bring it this way again past
the front of the house.

Tracers lace the trees and undergrowth only a few yards from the
snout of a beige-coloured German tank, the first of two sitting on
the road with their guns pointing to their right at the copse. Soon
all firing ceases, and for the first time ever you watch, with a sick

heart, men in Canadian battledress, their hands held high over their heads, surrender to German soldiers now appearing in numbers around the tanks. Then, as though taunting you – knowing you can't fire on them – the Heinies take their time searching their prisoners, and dusk descends before they march them away. You are still studying the darkening scene with your glasses, held helpless by concern that more Royals may be lying doggo in the bushes up there, when the muzzle of the gun on the first tank swings around to point directly at you. Instantly there's a flash and a horrible rip as a solid-shot passes through the tower just beneath where you and Squissato are standing, and two more tear through the tower as you and he scramble to a lower level.

With darkness closing in, and guided only by muzzle flashes and the sound of straining tank motors suddenly rising and abruptly falling off as though proceeding in stop-and-go fashion up the road this way, all you can do is estimate how far they and their accompanying infantry may have come, and call down Mike targets.

Your shells set fire to a barn four hundred yards east of your house. By the light of the flames, you can see cows standing facing into the open barn doors, close enough to be singed by the heat, but drawn to seek sanctuary in their familiar barn. Two actually stand inside the barn amidst flames and smoke. Confused and paralyzed, the poor beasts bellow in terror, but remain, swaying slightly, right next the fire. It's only a passing image, as you vainly try to see beyond the drifting smoke that is now providing cover for the advancing German tanks and their infantry screen, but you know it will remain forever vivid.

When a few survivors from the overrun platoon manage to crawl back, Shortreed is reminded his anti-tank gun at the railway crossing is out of action, and sends his 2 IC, Capt. Ross Newman, rushing back up the road in a Jeep to where Sherman tanks are harbouring, to lead a couple up for anti-tank protection. When the frustrated Captain returns to report the tanks refuse to come forward in the dark, Shortreed suddenly shouts: "B Company

Headquarters, follow me!" And out the side door he goes, leading every last man from the house except your crew.

Watching them, hastening back in the dusk towards the woods three hundred yards away, you are tempted to follow. However, you must be able to communicate with the guns if you are to be of any help in restoring the situation, and the only way is through the big radio now removed from the carrier and resting on the tiled floor of the entrance hall before the front door which, like the side door, is wide open to the gathering gloom that suddenly takes on sinister aspects.

Too late you realize you should have sent your crew back with Shortreed. They must be hidden in the crawl-space under the back kitchen. Advising them to grab their greatcoats from the carrier near the side door, for it will be cold lying on the damp earth under there, you lead them behind the house. Removing a section of the latticework skirting, they crawl in. You join them long enough to utilize a lamp-electric under a greatcoat to memorize the map reference of the house so you may use it as a reference point for any target you may have, since from now on it will be suicide to show a light.

Cautioning them to remain hidden until the position is retaken, as it's bound to be in the morning, you replace the lattice skirting and start back through the garden for the side door. Heavy small-arms fire is now snapping along the railway embankment. Clearly the attack from the field beyond the track has been renewed. Gaining the front hall, you follow the hissing gabble from the earphones to locate the radio mike. Gratefully you get through to the guns on your first try.

You give them the target you registered during the earlier attack in the field beyond the tracks "south 400" so the shells will drop four hundred yards closer to, and you hope, just beyond the embankment where skittering Schmeisser tracers are originating. Since the shells will land close to the infantry, you start with "Scale 1." But when the flashing storm erupts where it should, you order

"Scale 20 Repeat," and go outside and up the garden to judge its effectiveness. Halfway to the embankment you meet the Platoon Sergeant on his way back to Company Headquarters, which he thinks is still in the house. With remarkable aplomb he receives the news. He assures you, that with the support of your guns, his platoon will hold: "But please move your fire away a bit – no sense wasting rounds on us on the embankment!" It was to deliver this droll message that he was on his way back.

In the silence following your shelling, the absence of Schmeisser fire suggests the attack from this quarter has been extinguished, at least for now. Assured he will continue to have your support "a bit farther out," the Sergeant returns to his platoon and you turn back towards the house. Just short of the side door your heart almost stops when a dark figure materializes in the gloom – another survivor from the overrun platoon. Weaponless, having thrown his Sten away when expecting capture, he'd be of no use to the platoon on the embankment. You lead him into the house to shelter in the cellarway, opposite the side door, which descends into inky blackness you've not had time to explore.

Leaving him there, you feel your way towards the tower staircase to see what you can by the light of the burning farm, now reduced to the odd flickering flame among glowing ruins. Before you reach the stairs, the hall is lit by a tremendous flash accompanied by a shocking *wham!* And for a split-second through the open front door you see the hulking outline of a German tank opposite the gate firing down the road to the right. That you are being subjected to muzzle-blast only is a relief. But the feeling is shortlived when it occurs to you the tank is leaving the clearing of houses to the infantry.

You can expect visitors at any moment. That tank would not have come this far in the dark without its screen of foot-soldiers you'd seen moving with it at last light. Again it fires into the darkness down the road, as you kneel on gritty fragments of plaster and shards of glass, fumbling for the microphone – guided by the hissing storm of static and garbled voices from the earphones. Locating it you call for acknowledgement, and after several attempts, you hear the high-pitched squeak of "Coop" (L/Bdr. Ralph Cooper) back there somewhere over the canal with Rileys in reserve, but always alert to the needs of the FOOs.

You call for a Mike target "Scale 10" giving the map reference of the house "south 25" yards. As you transmit your fire orders, you are grateful for the racket the tank is making, its engine rumbling when it isn't firing, for you are no more than thirty yards from it as you kneel at the radio, and though you hold the rubber mouthpiece of the mike right up against your lips as you speak, you still must speak sharply to cut through all that electronic interference and be understood.

Since intruders may prevent you from getting back to the radio for a while, you order: "Fire until you're told to stop." Then, dropping the mike, you head for the cellarway, certain that shells will airburst among the trees out front and some may hit the house itself.

On reaching the door to the stairs, you find there is barely enough room to back in with the infantryman occupying the top step. Breathing down the back of your neck, he tells you all available space in the cellarway is filled with Dutch people, and when your howling shells start flashing and crashing among the trees out front you hear children, down in the dark behind you, whimpering in terror and women reassuring them. For a moment you are plagued with the thought you may drive the Germans to take cover in here with awful consequences.

A shell strikes on or near the front of the house, sending a hurricane of dust and debris flying past your doorway, and a child starts screaming inconsolably, setting off the others.

Trapped in your shallow alcove by your own fire, you wonder how you are ever going to get out to the radio to stop the guns pouring shells up here, when suddenly, mysteriously, they stop.*

---

* The CO of 4th Field caused the guns to stop. Though all FOOs were not aware of it, the order "Fire until told to stop" had been outlawed, for

In the silence, the infernal babble of voices and static spewing from the radio earphones out there, amplified by the echoing emptiness of the tiled hall, seem horribly loud – a perfect beacon to draw the Germans into the house to investigate. You easily imagine them creeping stealthily this way, stopping now and then to listen. Still standing in the mouth of the cellarway opposite the side door leading to the garden, you draw your pistol and hold it in readiness, pointing at the darkness beyond the open doorway. A Browning automatic may be no match for a Schmeisser, but you'll get the first one.

As you strain all your senses, trying to pick up anything that could give warning, you resign yourself to the fact that death is both imminent and inevitable, for no quarter can be expected in the dark. This, then, is how it must happen: a shattering burst from a Schmeisser or the blinding flash of a grenade flung in from an open door. And with the sense of resignation comes an extraordinary sense of calm; gone is all the inner turmoil and panic you've been resisting ever since you heard Shortreed call out, "Company headquarters follow me!"

From the earphones on the hall floor comes a high-pitched insistent voice, penetrating through the unintelligible cacophony, but so strained and garbled you can't quite make out what it is saying. Could it be, "Message for Baker One . . . Are you receiving me?" You think you hear, "Describe your situation?" But are they calling "Baker One?"

Oh, God, if only the children would be quiet!

To hell with the radio! You must concentrate on the gloom out there beyond that open doorway to the garden. All you'll get is a fleeting glimpse of a moving silhouette against a patch of night sky that now is only slightly lighter than the surrounding blackness.

---

the sound reason that if a FOO were killed or his radio blown up after giving the order – a distinct possibility in such circumstances – the guns would keep on firing until they ran out of ammunition.

Then suddenly one of those unaccountable surges in the strength of wireless transmission that occur periodically allows you to clearly distinguish your call signal, and the high-pitched, strident voice of "Coop" passing on "a request from Sunray for a sitrep."

Let him call . . . there's no way you can take your eyes off that doorway. They'll get their situation report in due course . . .

But now, with uncanny perception, the soldier standing behind you starts patting you on the back and talking to you in a low-pitched, soothing voice, barely above a whisper: "That's you they're calling, ain't it, Foo? Yuh have to go, Foo. They need to know we're still here. You have to answer them, Foo. We're all depending on you, Foo."

Unquestionably the weaponless man is just trying to help in the only way left to him. But his hand patting your shoulder is enraging, and his preacherlike intonations, obviously meant to be reassuring, going on and on as you try to listen for the faintest stir of stealthy footfall on the gravel outside, are intolerable. You turn on him, hissing fiercely, "Shut up!"

The very instant you turn your attention back to the gloom outside a dark silhouette looms up in the doorway. And as you are raising your pistol to take aim, the hulking form comes directly towards you – making it impossible to miss. Just as your finger starts its fatal pressure on the trigger, you discern the outline of a British-style helmet.

Assuming it's another survivor of the overrun platoon who has managed to make his way back, you whisper hoarsely, "Who goes there?"

"Squissato," comes the reply.

For a moment you are speechless, knowing how close you came to pulling the trigger – a split-second less hesitation and he surely would have died. You are at once thankful and furious: "My God, Squissato, I almost shot you! You were told to stay put with the others out there under the kitchen."

"Yes, sir, I was. But I don't think it's right that you should be up here alone. I can at least help you by handling the radio."

Instantly your anger fades away. He knows perfectly well you can handle the radio by yourself. He has left a perfectly safe hiding place to take his chances out here with you, purely out of compassion. You know you should send him right back into hiding, but you can't. Your need for the company he offers is just too great.

On many occasions throughout the Normandy campaign last summer, along the Scheldt last fall, and recently in the Rhineland, you have been humbled by the courageous conduct of men under fire, but never more so than now when you are the beneficiary of the selfless action of this brave man. Until dawn he will lie on the floor beside the radio, clutching his microphone, stretched out among the scattered shards of glass and chunks of brick and plaster from the front wall of the house, much of it blasted over him by one of the first basin of shells you have him call up after he takes over the set: "Scale 10 – repeat" of that last Mike target on the tank whose idling motor still mutters menacingly at the front gate. The wayward shell, striking just above the front door, not ten feet from where he is lying, sends a shower of jagged fragments and debris whipping past him. Miraculously he suffers only a minor cut on the back of his neck.

In the quiet that follows, you discover the tank is no longer out front. During the shelling you thought you heard its engine rising to a roar, indicating it was removing itself from the hurricane of shells, any one of which could blow off a track, jam its turret, or set it on fire. But in the confusion of screaming shells, blinding flashes, and stunning concussions, you were unable to maintain the wits to tell if it was going forward or back. You assume it was back, for it would be extremely vulnerable going forward in the dark without its infantry screen; and the tank commander would be as convinced as you that no foot-soldier could possibly remain alongside the tank and survive the torrent of high explosive poured down on the road around it out there.

At a window high up in the circular staircase, you listen for receding tank engines, and move your shelling in graduated corrections back up the road as it curves north towards the railway crossing and the copse where you first saw them in the dusk last night.

Then, still nervous there may be survivors lurking near the house, you move your shelling around and about, a few rounds here and a few there, with longer and longer listening periods between your bombards. During this sweeping process, a cumulative error in your calculations results in your shells dropping farther west than you wished. Again some strike the trees and house, showering the front hall and Squissato with bits of brick and mortar, once more leaving him shaken, but otherwise unharmed.

Eventually it becomes obvious that the tanks, abandoned by their infantry, have gone and will not be heard from again.

By first light, the whole bridgehead is completely quiet. The Germans have even ceased shelling their favourite target, the crossing point at the canal where the engineers have been trying to erect a Bailey Bridge to replace a rafting operation blown to bits by hostile shells yesterday afternoon.

You send Squissato out to release Reid and Cunningham from their cramped and clammy crawl-space, while you take up vigil on the third-floor landing in the circular stairway in the tower, sweeping the zone beyond the railway track with your glasses for any movement. But all is still. The blackened skeletons of buildings at the farm across the field on the right, set on fire by your shells at dusk last night, still smoulder, glowing and smoking in the pale, dawn light. Otherwise the landscape is one of peace.

Presently the women and children from the cellar can be heard assembling in the kitchen, where they create the friendly sounds of cutlery and china plates being set out on a table and a steel spatula scraping a frying pan. When the smell of frying potatoes drifts up to you, you realize, that with all the counter-attacks and other concerns, you and your crew have had nothing to eat since early yesterday.

As you descend into the hall, you discover you have a visitor, a tank captain. He tells you he has a squadron of Shermans on the road out front, and wants to know where you think he should place them. You are greatly tempted to tell him precisely where, but restrict yourself to asking how tankers have the gall to show up now that the enemy has withdrawn? Why weren't they up here last night when they were needed – when all the infantry anti-tank guns were overrun?

He makes no attempt to answer your insulting charge, but listens patiently until you tell him it's a good thing you weren't the one that went back to bring him up last night, for you think you might have shot him dead when he refused to bring his tanks up the road in the dark.

This arouses him to protest that he and his tanks were not even on this side of the canal last night. His squadron crossed over only a few minutes ago with orders to join you up here – immediately after the Engineers got the Bailey Bridge in place.

Flustered and sorry for your mistake, but still bitterly critical of his fellow tankers lurking somewhere back in the woods, you are left mumbling incoherently in embarrassment. Fortunately, Shortreed and his company HQ gang are now clumping in through the side door and down the cellar steps to set up shop; and you lead the tank captain down and turn him over to the weary Major, who looks particularly haggard by candlelight as he bends over the tanker's map spread out on a table improvised on a vegetable-storage bin.

Leaving them to sort out where the tanks should be placed, you are amusing yourself looking over rows of dusty bottles of wine lying on shelves beyond a wire grill, when a remarkably cheerful woman, coming down the stairs with a basin to get more potatoes, catches you staring covetously at the bottles. Instantly, in perfect English, she invites you to, "Help yourself if you see anything you fancy."

You pick out a bottle of German brandy and a bottle of Black and White Scotch with the date 1936 pasted on it, and head upstairs to the master bedroom at the front of the house on the second floor. Shaking the bedspread vigorously to rid it of layers of broken window glass, you pile into bed with a bottle cradled in each arm, and sleep until late afternoon. By the time you awake, the whole Canadian Army seems to be on its way up the road past the house, which, you discover on descending to ground level, is now both Battalion and Brigade headquarters. Your crew requests a twenty-four-hour rest back at the guns, and you approve as soon as they can get up a temporary replacement crew.

Finding all four Royals' company commanders assembled in the front yard, fresh from a battalion "O" group at which they were informed they will rest in reserve at least until tomorrow, you make the mistake of offering them a taste of your 1936 Black and White whisky. Instantly you become the object of a fierce competition as each tries to entice you to spend the evening at his headquarters. Stothers wins hands down with the offer of a well-tuned piano. But then the losers, expressing a desperate need to partake in a musical evening, follow along anyway.

You had forgotten the invigorating strength of prewar whisky. One bottle is more than enough to turn the evening into a heady event for four company commanders and one arty captain. And there is still a respectable heel of the bottle left when the three visiting majors – Caldwell, Suckling, and Shortreed – sensibly decide they should return to their own company headquarters while they still can find their way.

Fortunately for all concerned there are no Germans left anywhere within miles of the Royals' positions, a point Stothers proceeds to prove in a most original fashion immediately his guests depart. Irritated by the stream of persistent requests he has been getting all evening from Battalion Headquarters to supply them with "a precise disposition of his troops," he lurches out behind the house to where his Jeep is parked in the misty darkness, closely followed by his Sergeant-Major Hamm who signals you in an urgent way to follow him.

Stothers, brushing aside the protests of his devoted sergeant-major, climbs behind the wheel, starts the engine, and turns on full the high-beam headlights over which no blackout screens have been installed.

Appealing to you to bear witness to the necessity of his action, the giant Hamm leans over Stothers to turn off the ignition. Stothers, recognizing he is about to be physically restrained, pulls out his pistol and threatens to "hold a field court martial on the spot" if either of you lays a finger on him.

With that, Hamm, totally disgusted, waves you back, growling: "To hell with him — let him get himself killed if that's what he wants."

And so, with headlights blazing, Stothers wheels the Jeep around the yard and roars off towards what last night was no-man's-land. And for the first and only time in the war, you see the headlights of a Jeep bouncing about the front like miniature searchlights, as you walk back to a dimly lit slumbering house of big maps, signallers speaking in subdued voices, and sleepy duty officers — the whole building exuding a sense of confidence and security so very different from the way it was here last night for you and Squissato.*

It seems hardly possible it was only last night. Already the whole business is taking on the fuzzy outline of a bad dream, from which you recall only certain moments with gut-clenching clarity.

However, of one thing you are certain: until your last hour on earth, the name Mel Squissato will have a special place in your heart, along with "Coop" — the indefatigable Bombardier Ralph Cooper — without whose timely intercessions, relaying your target information to the guns, you and Squissato might well be lying out there in the garden tonight under two more mounds of freshly turned earth.†

---

*   The 21st Army Group Commander-in-Chief's Certificate, signed by Field Marshal B. L. Montgomery, awarded Gunner A. Mel Squissato, February 8, 1946, read as follows: "It has been brought to my notice that you have performed outstanding good service, and shown great devotion to duty during the campaign in North West Europe. I award you this certificate as a token of my appreciation, and I have given instructions that this shall be noted in your Record of Service."

†   "Coop" survived the war and became widely known as the perennial

jazz piano-player and hilarious commentator on life and people at the old Hotel Metropole in Toronto, where, between his musical numbers, he interspersed jokes and original skits commenting on the passing parade. Unfortunately, like many other veterans, he brought home from the war an unusual attachment to an enemy that eventually did him in – booze. One night he fell to his death trying to escape from an upstairs bedroom in which he'd been locked to sober up. New York *Variety* ran the following obituary:

Damon Runyon would have felt right at home in the "guys and dolls" impromptu wake held last Tuesday at the Metropole Hotel for veteran pianist Ralph Cooper who plunged from a fourth-storey hotel window to his death the night before. Cooper, 44, a Toronto native, had been a regular at the hotel's dining room for 17 years. He had been "performing" after hours for several cabdrivers on the street when he tied two bed sheets together and attempted to swing out of the window down to them. The sheets came apart and he landed headfirst on the pavement. The next night prominent city lawyers, racetrack habitués, cabdrivers, veteran newspaper reporters – all without previous arrangement – congregated in the dining room for the city's first such wake. Hotel owner Sid Straus arrived and the mourners gathered at his table, drinking, smoking and only occasionally passing a remark about Cooper. For most of the evening Cooper's piano stand was empty. But several mourners bought drinks and ordered them to be placed on the piano. One wry incident marked the wake and it was repeated throughout the evening . . . A lawyer asked a waitress to place a drink on the piano. "He's dead, you know," she replied. "Yes, I know. Come to think of it you'd better make that a double – he always drank doubles," the lawyer said. "Well, that will be $1.30 – if you really want a double," she answered without the slightest tinge of sentimentality.

68

YOUR CREW IS OFFERED A CHANCE ON A UNIQUE POOL

✳

GUNNER ANDY TURNER, WHO SERVED AS THE BATTERY Commander's Don R from when he joined 4th Field last July in Normandy, is now your carrier driver, thanks to several happenings only tenuously related.

First, there was one of Turner's unauthorized junkets on his old Norton motorbike, in which he seems to have an uncontrollable urge to indulge whenever "the war stops for a while" – to use his own words. This he had decided was the case back at Cleve. The guns were back in action firing across the Rhine, but 4th Brigade infantry were still holed up in the Reichswald. He'd headed for Nijmegen to get a haircut (or so he told the Provost), not knowing that town had been declared out of bounds. No longer protected by a tolerant battery commander (Don Cornett having become counter-battery officer at Division), Turner was paraded before the CO, who gave him fourteen days' C.B., "Confined to Barracks," having no meaning in action apart from being confined to 2nd Battery gun position. His only real punishment derived from being divorced from his beloved motorbike, and being denied the life to which he'd become accustomed at Royals' battalion headquarters. But this was enough to make him "chafe at the bit."

Then there was the overrunning of your OP position at the Twente Canal, which, according to witnesses at the guns that night, became of great personal concern to Sgt. Ryder, a concern that deepened as the crisis over the canal deepened, until he was charging about "like a man possessed," from gun to gun, and into command posts, exhorting everybody to respond "faster . . . faster" to your calls for fire – as all off-duty acks and signallers carried hundreds of shells to guns glowing red in the dark.*

The strain of that night caused your crew to ask for a rest back at the guns, which was supposed to be only twenty-four hours but became a great deal more when on arrival back there, they were offered the chance to buy into a pool which, they were told, would be won by the man who most correctly foretold the day and hour Baker Troop FOO "got it."

While agreeing it was certainly a unique contest, they felt obliged to ask why their particular FOO.

Oh, didn't they know? He'd acquired the reputation of having outlasted all other FOOs in the Canadian Army. Now, obviously a FOO with that reputation has long since outlived his luck, and will be buying it any day now. The only question was when. All they had to do was write down on this piece of paper the day and the hour . . .

To your frazzled crew, this was a most disturbing revelation, and an immediate vote was taken, resulting in a majority decision to split from your carrier while the splitting was good.

While disappointing news, you were not greatly concerned until you discovered, just as you were suddenly ordered to move off with the infantry, that no one in your replacement crew knew how to

---

* Ryder's unusual involvement was explained by diary notes of Sergeants Johnston and Foley: "Had helluva time getting guns in. Very deceptive ground which broke as soon as quads drove onto position – a freshly cleared area full of stumps and very boggy. Opposition counter-attacked and gun fire targets came thick and fast. Ammo vehicles got stuck. Help sent for in order to feed the guns. Sigs and Acks appeared . . .")

drive a tracked vehicle. Thus you were forced to take over the job yourself until you could get a driver, and it is at this point that a relationship among the foregoing happenings shows up. Bringing up the rations, Ryder caught up to your carrier grinding along a road behind a column of infantry. On seeing you driving with a map spread out on your lap underneath the steering wheel, his sense of fairness was so outraged, he threatened to go back and "shoot the bastard responsible for sending you up a crew without a driver." But then he remembered Turner eating his heart out back at the guns. Would you take him?

Of course you would. But could he drive a carrier?

"Don't worry," he shouted, over the roar of his motorbike as he took off back down the road, "we'll see he can before he comes up!"

This morning, April 9, he arrives in a Jeep accompanied by Turner, the two of them smiling from ear to ear – Ryder, happy he's able to do something for you, and Turner, pleased as punch to be back up with the infantry, even if he won't be riding his beloved Norton.

With equal pleasure you turn over the steering wheel to Turner, exchanging the righthand bucket seat for the left, where you can ride standing up – a preferred way when studying the road ahead for mines.

Obviously an apt pupil, with an affinity for tracked vehicles, Turner turns out to be surprisingly smooth in nursing the old carrier around sharp corners and through narrow gateways and the like, and by noon you've relaxed and have almost forgotten you have a rookie driver. But then during a pause at a nondescript farmhouse with Jack Stothers's Company awaiting orders, you discover life with Turner will be full of surprises.

Just as you are about to partake of a feast of scrambled eggs the infantry are whipping up in the kitchen from a basket of eggs found under a bed, a Royals' sergeant comes in and asks you a ridiculous question that sounds like, "Are you aware your driver has both tracks off your carrier?"

Preposterous of course – obviously a crude device for getting you to come outside for some sort of surprise. But when you go out in the barnyard, there, before your incredulous eyes, hang the naked bogie wheels of your carrier. Lying flat on the ground beneath them are two pathetic-looking tracks, while Turner whales away with a sledgehammer at a great rivet holding one of the links at one end of a track, aided by your other crew members – Signaller Sam Kotyk and Signaller H. L. Doherty, an American from Dearborn, Michigan.

Spotting you, Turner calls out cheerfully: "Don't worry, Skipper, we'll have her ready to go when you have to move!"

Just how the hell he would know when that will be, when no one else has a clue, is beyond you, and you tell him so, adding some well-chosen comments you think are appropriate to the situation. Unabashed by your obvious displeasure, this overnight-expert on Bren carriers declares the tracks were getting much too loose and needed to have a link or two removed to tighten them up.

To save your sanity you go back in the house to finish your mess of eggs, leaving him under a threat of dire consequences if the carrier isn't ready to move when you are. As it turns out, it isn't ready when the infantry move off up the road, and by the time you finally are moving, they are out of sight. However, the road is hard-surfaced and there is no fear of mines, so Turner is able to press the accelerator to the floor. Soon you are sailing along full-out through a wooded area, where along the left side of the road, every hundred yards or so, sit camouflaged stacks of huge, black aerial bombs. Just as you are approaching one of these dangerous-looking piles, there's a shocking bang under the carrier, announcing the separation of one of Turner's newly formed track links.

Desperately you yell: "Don't touch your brakes or try to steer!"

Instantly grasping your meaning – that applying the brakes to the one surviving track will send the carrier into an uncontrollable spin – he lifts his hands off the steering wheel and lets the carrier roll to a perfectly peaceful stop, riding on bogie wheels on one side and track on the other, still in the middle of the road.

When you look back, stretched out on the road like a flattened boa constrictor, lying right opposite a big pile of those black, bulbous bombs, is the wayward track. Thoughts of what might have happened, and *didn't*, help suppress most of the irritation at this new predicament, as you walk back with Kotyk in the balmy air that has turned almost sultry, to drag the track up the road to the point where Turner can back the carrier's bogie wheels onto it. This is accomplished much more easily than you imagined it could be, and with equally astonishing speed he links up the open ends of the track with a bolt from the toolbox, and you're again on your way.

Fortunately the infantry meets no opposition until late in the afternoon, and then it is very light; and by the time you catch up with them, they've been ordered to consolidate for the night. Stothers has established his headquarters in a barn and house combination, typical of these parts: the "front" of the house facing into the fields, and the barn doors facing the road, obliging you to pass through the cow stable on the way to the kitchen door.

The few Jerries they'd encountered appear to have withdrawn, but they've left behind a very disturbed Royals' company, not knowing whether their revered stretcher-bearer, Pte. Faubert, has been killed or taken prisoner. Faubert's reputation for fearless service to the wounded is special even among his peers, all of whom daily exhibit out-sized courage. When he disappeared, he was conducting an errand of mercy far out in front of the Royals' lines checking on German casualties.

By the time it grows dark it is raining heavily, and you are most grateful for the dry comfort of the farmhouse kitchen. The infantry has just received a large shipment of parcels from home, and Stothers and Company Sgt.-Major Hamm are in the process of opening boxes addressed to boys long dead. To facilitate dividing up the goodies among the living, the contents are sorted into appropriate piles: chocolate bars here, packages of peanuts there, and gumdrops, jelly beans, and candy kisses in still another pile. Brownies, fruit cake, and other crumbly homemade cookies make up a special pile; while canned goods, razor blades, each have their own pile – as do home-knitted socks, scarves, and sweaters.

In each parcel (strictly against regulations of course) is a one-page letter from the sender. Jack, you notice, carefully unfolds each note and reads it, and then spreads it out on the table in front of him – carefully, gently, almost reverently flattening out the wrinkles before placing it on top of the growing pile of letters.

Becoming aware you are watching with interest, he hands one across the table to you without comment. It is a hand-written note of only a few lines: "Dear Son," it begins, and the words blur as you read of a mother's deep concern for her boy – she sounds so much like your own mother. "The papers tell us that it is very wet where the Canadians are fighting now. So please, Dear, always be sure to wear your rubbers and keep your feet dry."

When you look up at Stothers, he tells you that her boy is the one lying dead outside the back door, face-up in the rain.

For a long while you sit with him at the table, consuming a goodly amount of over-proof "issue rum" as you discuss homes and families. This becomes truly absorbing when you discover that he, like you, has never seen his firstborn, and you take turns imagining what it will be like meeting for the first time a child already in her third year: what she will expect of you, and what might you reasonably expect of her? But neither of you, of course, can visualize the mental development of a three-year-old, and you are forced to conclude that what you don't know about the early stages of child development would fill a football stadium, and are left with an uneasy feeling that life has been rushing onward while you have been standing still.

When, well sedated with rum, you finally bed down out in the clammy hay in the draughty loft over the cows, with the cold rain drumming the roof, sleep comes slowly. Try as you will, you can't shake the image of that boy lying outside there in the rain, and a loving mother back in Canada, perhaps at this very moment writing him another letter of concern for his welfare. And fuelling your melancholia is the nagging thought that a lottery is still being run back at the guns on the day and hour you are to "buy it."

69

LIBERATING A
CONCENTRATION CAMP

*

PUSHING NORTH BEYOND HOLTEN, THE GUNS OCCUPY SIX
positions in four days, maintaining support for the swiftly moving
infantry and inspiring the regimental war diarist to record: "Sleep is
becoming a memory."

This apparent ease of passage by the Brigade could be traceable
to confusion sown among the enemy by a drop of French paratroopers across the axis of advance of 2nd Division five nights ago.
Though the front line is lit each night by artificial moonlight, and
mysterious fires sometimes flare up in no-man's-land, you see or
hear nothing of them until today (April 12), when you are told that
some turned up at 2nd Battery gun positions claiming the Germans
had captured and shot some of their comrades.*

On April 12 the objective is Assen, the last sizeable centre before
Groningen, in the upper reaches of the map of Holland, the ultimate
objective in the Canadian drive to sever Holland from Germany.

---

* From the 2nd and 3rd Régiment de Chausseurs Parachustistes of the
Special Air Service, they were trained to operate in small groups. They
were dropped on a wide area between Zwolle and Groningen, to secure
bridges. First ground contact was made with them on morning of April 9,
by 18th Armoured Car Regiment (12th Manitoba Dragoons) near
Meppel.

At about 4:00 P.M. the Essex Scottish encounter the enemy in strength at Hooghalen. To help reduce enemy resistance, the Royals are ordered to utilize the Kangaroo troop carriers for a flanking movement northeast, through the tiny village of Rolde, three kilometres to the right of Assen, on a plunge deep into no-man's-land, that is to curl left, some three or four kilometres behind Assen, through the village of Loon, to cut the Germans' main supply road from Groningen at the tiny crossroads hamlet of Peelo. So it is that you and your crew find yourselves roaring up a sandy track across flat moorlands in your carrier, trying to keep up with a column of Kangaroos carrying Bob Suckling's A Company but falling farther and farther behind with each passing kilometre.

Coming towards you along the right side of the road, silhouetted against the red April sky, are the watch towers of a huge prison camp surrounded by a high, barbed-wire fence and a very deep ditch. As the Kangaroos, far up ahead, roar past the camp and disappear, you see people running out of the huts and massing at the barbed-wire gates halfway along the fence parallel to the road you are following.

And as you pull abreast of the camp, they have the gates open and some of them are running down the road right up to the front of your carrier. In a moment you are surrounded by men and women of all ages yelling and whimpering, their eyes full of pure, raw joy. Skinny arms reach out to touch you. Weak hands clutch at the sleeve of your battledress and stroke the side of the carrier as though reassuring themselves you are real, even as you and your crew throw them chocolate bars, cigarettes, and bread. After handing out all the canned goods you can spare, you realize you must leave immediately if you are to catch up with the others. But how? You are hemmed in by a dense crowd of delirious people that is growing larger with each passing moment. In desperation you pull out your pistol and wave it in their faces.

The men standing immediately in front of you fall back groaning in dismay, wagging their heads and spreading their open hands in supplication, as if to say: "Oh no, not now . . . after all we've been through!"

Suddenly you are aware of the unfeeling harshness of your pistol-waving to people who until only moments ago were surviving in cruel bondage at the whim of brutal SS masters. Still it has the effect of bringing a deep hush to the crowd, and you are able to ask, "Does anyone here speak English?" One man, holding up his hand, says, "A little."

You tell him to explain to the others they must clear a corridor and allow you to move on. The war is not over – you must catch up with your comrades on their way to fight the Germans up ahead.

The Dutchman takes over like a sergeant-major, and in a minute the road ahead is magically clear, though you notice as you race past the gate, men and women, ill or weak from hunger, still shuffling slowly out, obviously intent on greeting a liberator. Turner says one of them told him they are all Jews.*

The Kangaroos are by now completely out of sight, but their tracks are easily followed. Shortly after pulling away from the camp, they took off, bearing right, across country, a boggy moor laced with deep drainage ditches. While these ditches presented no problem to the Kangaroos with their powerful tank engines, it is very tough going for your old carrier, and before long, it bottoms

---

* Westerbork was the most notorious of the concentration camps in Holland, being a collection centre for Jews. From there 100,000 men, women, and children, including Anne Frank, were deported in boxcars for extermination. Today there is a telling memorial at the spot where all left on their final journey to the gas chambers and ovens. Behind the bumpers of the railway siding is a plaque with a quotation from Lamentations: "They hunt our steps, that we cannot go in our streets; our end is near, our days are fulfilled, for our end has come." The rusting steel rails, still bedded on their worn ties and oil-stained gravel, run out in the direction of Germany for about fifty yards, and then are twisted up in grotesque and tortured fashion as from intense heat.

out coming out of a ditch. For a while it looks like you are destined to spend the night on the moor – an uninviting prospect as the gathering dusk deepens across the gloomy, forbidding landscape.

But suddenly you hear tank motors coming up from behind, and soon another troop of Kangaroos come roaring up. One of them wheels around in front of you and stops, and a sergeant piles out and hooks a chain from the Kangaroo into a ring welded on the front of the carrier for this purpose. With remarkable ease the carrier is hauled across the spongy land where all previous Kangaroo tracks now glisten with water. You are not set adrift until you are on an established, gravel road leading to Rolde.

At Rolde you find Suckling and Company have already taken off in their Kangaroos on a four-kilometre sweep through no-man's-land, north and then west towards a bridge over a canal west of the village of Loon, from which Tom Wilcox's company will later attack the Royals' final objective, the crossroads at Peelo north of Assen, thereby cutting the German's main supply route from Groningen.

A few minutes after leaving Rolde, you see, far up ahead, about where the village of Peelo should be, a great many tracers, a sure sign of German machine-guns. While they'll do little harm to the thick-skinned Kangaroos, you fear for you and your crew when you start passing there. Unquestionably they were taken by surprise by the Kangaroos roaring up the road, but they will be alert now, with their Panzerfausts armed and ready when you come along.

Worried, you have Turner halt the carrier while you get down under a piece of tarpaulin and study the map with the aid of a lamp-electric, searching for another route that would bypass that hornet's nest. But there is only one way to get to that bridge, up the road through Peelo. Advising your crew to unlimber the Bren gun, and get their personal arms, you are about to tell Turner to start the engine, when you hear the whine of the now-empty Kangaroos coming back down the road.

Here of course is your answer: get one of them to take you and your signallers up to Suckling's canal house. But when you stop the leading Kangaroo, the lieutenant says he can't, that he has to go right back to collect more troops for transport elsewhere.

They pull away and you and your crew are left alone in the dark and eerie silence. But only momentarily, for suddenly you hear up ahead the sound of boots running this way on the paved road, getting louder and louder as the runner comes closer. Bewildered, you wait for whoever it is to appear out of the gloom. Finally a hatless soldier, dripping wet from head to toe, staggers up and flops exhausted over the front of your carrier, oblivious to the muzzle of the Bren pointed at him by Doherty from a rear compartment.

Gasping for air and shuddering violently from the effects of the icy night air on his wet clothing, he is totally incoherent. And for a while his overwrought condition appears to border on madness as he rocks from one foot to the other, moaning and wringing his hands.

Kotyk produces a blanket and Turner huddles it around his shoulders, as you haul up one of the water-bottles full of rum from the floor and persuade the shaking man to take a couple of really long belts of the fiery liquid.

And shortly you make out the words: *I killed my Sergeant!*

What does he mean – killed his sergeant? A couple more slugs of rum and the story comes gushing out:

He was the driver of the last Kangaroo in the troop, concentrating on the vague outline of the one ahead of him. He got too close to the edge of a culvert over a creek . . . his right track slipped over the edge and the thing toppled upside down in the water. His Sergeant, standing upright and peering ahead when the thing went over, was caught and pinned under the water by the rim of the open body of the Kangaroo. He tried to pull him free but it was impossible. With the water rising around him up to his chin, he grabbed a rifle and was about to shoot himself in preference to drowning, when he noticed the water had stopped rising. Remembering there was an escape hatch in the floor, he felt around on what was now his ceiling until he found it, undid the catches, and climbed out.

You suggest he climb aboard and come with you – eventually there'll be a farmhouse with a nice warm stove where he can dry out. With this he readily agrees, but asks you to stop for a moment at the dark creek culvert. There you accompany him on a silent pilgrimage to where you can look down on the scene of his recent ordeal.

There, just as he described it, is the upside-down Kangaroo with the dark, glistening water swirling gently around it, filling the quiet night with little bubbling and chuckling sounds so cheerful and so out of harmony with the horrible death of the poor man down there somewhere under the water. At last your companion turns away wiping his eyes.

As you are returning to the carrier, you ask him about the prospects for a German ambush in Peelo up ahead. Of this he is entirely unconcerned, believing they have pulled out of Peelo, since they didn't fire at them on their way back. And he may well be right, for not only does your carrier draw no fire on the way through the dark, silent streets of Peelo, but the village remains sound asleep when Tom Wilcox's company tramps through it an hour or so later, in contrast to the fields a couple of hundred yards past the farmhouse at the canal where Bob Suckling has set up his company headquarters. Wilcox's leading platoon suffers some casualties from heavy small-arms fire – sufficiently heavy, you decide, to bring the guns to bear on the source, Kotyk having just gotten through to the guns by adding so many extensions to the short whip aerial of the 19-set that the unwieldy thing towers above the house.

At dawn, April 13, Wilcox, moving up to the crossroads where he can dominate the road and deny its use to all German movement in and out of Assen, ambushes three truckloads of Germans stopped right at the crossroads for a break. Machine-gun fire combined with a blast from a flame-thrower, which sets the trucks on fire, kills almost all of them. The few who are captured are old men called up to fill the ranks of Hitler's "people's army." One white-haired man sitting on a log with his head in his hands, tells Turner, who can manage some German, that he was a bank manager until a few days ago.

Why the death of these old men seems so awful would be difficult to explain. After all, they had a chance to fulfil their lives in many ways, something the youngsters, who make up the bulk of the dead of the war, will never have. But you cannot shake off the sense of tragedy hanging over this smoking crossroads and the burned-out trucks with forty-five charred bodies strewn about. And you are glad when you get busy shelling distant enemy troops retreating north along another parallel road. The target is at 13,800 yards, requiring super charge, the greatest range fired by 4RCA.

While so engaged you spot a German tank crawling forward on that same road towards Assen, and point it out to the crew of a 17-pounder just then putting their gun in action at the crossroads. They knock it out with three shots, easily followed by the streaking bright tracers.

Kangaroos, carrying Rileys, pass up the road, and in some astonishment you look up to see your own guns rolling by.

70

THE FINAL SEVERING OF

HOLLAND FROM GERMANY

※

"GENTLEMEN, WHEN WE HAVE SECURED GRONINGEN, WE effectively will have severed Holland from Germany."

That impressive opening sentence of Col. Lendrum's briefing of his company commanders on the situation that will be confronting the Royals at dawn when they join in 2nd Division's attack on this, the most northern of Dutch cities, is the last you consciously hear before you fall asleep with your head on your arms, leaning on the rug-covered table behind which he sits in the dining room of a farmhouse on the southern outskirts of the city.

When you awake about 3:45 A.M. (April 14) the room is dark, Lendrum has disappeared, and the company commanders, who were lining the walls of the little room when you fell asleep, are stretched out snoring here and there on the floor. The almost total denial of sleep the last two days and nights, while the unit was either moving or fighting, has clearly overtaken everyone. As you are wondering what the plan is and where you are to fit in, their Adjutant comes in and starts waking everybody up.

From Majors Suckling and Shortreed you learn there is to be a canal crossing in assault boats at 4:15 A.M. in a southern section of the city not far from the principal railway station, which is the ultimate objective of the Battalion. Two companies (Stothers's and Wilcox's) will cross first and secure a base for the assault on the station by Shortreed's company. You will go with Shortreed.

He says they've been warned to be on the alert for suspicious civilians. Lendrum at the "O" Group reported that the RHLI, in the southeast outskirts of the city yesterday afternoon, were sniped at by Dutch SS posing as civilians. Apparently Dutch SS units exist here, and many of them, afraid of what their fellow countrymen will do to them when their German masters are no longer in control, have changed into civilian clothes. But some seemingly can't resist sniping from apartment-building windows.

A walkie-talkie 38-set being totally inadequate for this crossing, you take along "Junior" – as Signaller Kotyk is now affectionately known by his buddies Turner and Doherty – to carry an 18-set. After walking with the infantry for some time, Shortreed's company is broken off in the shadow of a building a block or so short of the canal.

Hunched down beside you as you sit on your heels with your back against a dark building, Shortreed says that if you were asleep throughout the whole "O" Group, you probably didn't hear that President Roosevelt is dead. This is sad news indeed, for FDR was a stalwart friend of Canada and Britain, and the only U.S.A. president during your adult life. But for the moment you are more concerned with the coming canal crossing, which you earnestly hope will be in the dark, for you've come to hate crossing water obstacles in assault boats. As it turns out, the first companies over the canal run into sniper fire from some apartment buildings over there, and are forced to systematically check out every suite, and it is after first light before Shortreed gets the signal to move up to the canal and the boats.

Before rising from the shadows to move with the Royals down the street, now plainly visible in the grey light of the coming dawn, you take a deep pull from the water-bottle of rum you now always carry buttoned into the front of your battledress, hoping to head off the mounting dread. You know from past experience with canal crossings that it will threaten you as you crowd into that bobbing boat cluttered with men humpbacked with small packs dangling cups and trenching-tools, bulging in front with bandoliers of ammunition draped over webbing pouches jammed with extra Bren magazines, but still cossetting their weapons as best they can as they paddle with desperate strokes, knowing they are totally vulnerable to unseen hostile muzzles.

At this crossing snipers could be taking aim from a hundred windows, and choking tension persists until you arrive on the far side, scramble up the high canal bank, and, with Shortreed, cross the street that runs parallel to the canal for a prearranged rendezvous with Stothers in front of a substantial housing block.

He warns that accepting coffee from civilians over here could be hazardous ... that it could be poisoned ... a couple of guys in the first company over became deathly ill from coffee given them by civilians who, according to the Dutch Resistance, could have been Dutch SS posing as friendly civilians. Apparently there are Nazi sympathizers in this area, and some of them have been active collaborators. Until they are rounded up by the Resistance, it will pay to be very careful.

While all is peaceful here in the street during the brief meeting, as soon as Shortreed's men start moving left along the canal bank in single file, they attract small-arms fire that seems to originate from a row of shaggy bushes stretching across the far end of the street and marking the boundary of railyards containing several tracks, separated by raised passenger-platforms, which will constitute a formidable obstacle course on the final dash from the hedgerow to the main station platform.

Instantly all the infantrymen drop down below the edge of the roadway, and henceforth move forward with care, keeping their heads down and sidling crablike along the sloping bank – all except your old friend the intrepid Mortar Sergeant, who chooses to join you and Kotyk in going forward in spurts from doorway to doorway up the line of row housing abutting the narrow sidewalk on the right-hand side of the street. Recessed deeply, the doorways provide good shelter from the bullets buzzing down the street, as you pause in your periodic dashes to stay parallel with the bobbing helmets of the infantry appearing and disappearing along the opposite curb.

Suddenly a door opens behind you and a smiling Dutch youth hands you steaming coffee in a delicate china cup, complete with saucer. Only ten minutes ago you were warned against accepting coffee offered by the civilians who could be Dutch SS with poisonous intentions. But the general air of innocence in the joyous eyes of the young man, and the effect of the odour of coffee on taste buds that have had nothing to work on but undiluted slugs of issue rum since yesterday noon, is irresistible. Just as you raise the cup, the leading soldiers of the leading section, of the leading platoon, of the leading company, of the leading battalion of the leading division of the Canadian Army, spot you. A howl of protest goes up that must surely be startling to the Germans up ahead:

"Look at that! Coffee yet! Leave it to the bloody artillery – they always get the best of everything . . ."

The young Dutchman looks worried: "What do they say?"

Raising your cup in a mocking toast to the hooting soldiers, with your little finger extended in the best provincial fashion, you facetiously tell the Dutch lad, "They want one too."

To your astonishment he rushes into the house for two more cups, complete with saucers, and dashes across the roadway, leans down, and serves the two leading soldiers their morning coffee. Then oblivious to the bullets that buzz down the street, he waits to retrieve the cups, kneeling on one knee like a waterboy at a football game.*

You wonder what the generals and their earnest staff officers

---

* After thirty-two years, through the curiosity of Groningen's war historian, Menno Huizinga, author of two books on the liberation of northern Holland and assiduous collector of wartime memorabilia, and the help of a Groningen newspaper, you learn the "Koffiejongen" – J. E. Spakman – dared not return to the flat of his future mother-in-law (Mrs. Narold) without her precious porcelain. While sternly rejecting his suggestion that "ordinary mugs would be easier to carry" – preferring to follow the tradition that one "must always stay polite to foreigners and

back at Army Headquarters, or the newspaper editors back in Canada plotting their black arrows on maps showing the most forward advance of the Allied Armies, would say if they knew why the tip of the arrow of the great war machine had stopped moving this morning.

Further along you are again peering out of another recessed entry, when the door opens behind you and a most pleasant-looking woman, doing her best to smile in a reassuring way, while warning you with her eyes full of distress, points discreetly over her shoulder into the house, and whispers so softly you have difficulty, with her Dutch accent, making out what she is saying. It sounds like "the Boche – the Boche," but it could be "the Deutsch – the Deutsch." At any rate you do make out, "I think they will surrender."

As you follow her inside, you come face to face with two German soldiers, who immediately drop their rifles and raise their hands. This is fortunate, for, when you feel for your pistol, you find you have dropped it – holster, web-belt, and all – somewhere back there during the canal crossing. However, the alert woman, realizing you are unarmed and brazening it out, passes unobtrusively by you into the kitchen and out the back door, as you order the Germans, with suitably aggressive gestures, to undo their black leather tunic belts, on which dangle potato-masher grenades, and let them slide to the floor.

Presently you'll learn that the first Canadian soldiers she meets up with are your signaller Kotyk and the Royals' Mortar Sergeant. She tells them, "Your officer has just been captured by two Germans!"

This brings them crashing through the front door, with their Sten guns ready to spray the room, only to find you intent on

---

give them the best you have" – the good woman's hospitality did not extend to having her best china abandoned on a muddy canal bank, war or no war, liberation or no liberation!

counting thick wads of guilders and marks from two billfolds, while the Germans, with their hands clasped behind their heads, stand quietly watching.

Tipping back their helmets, your "rescuers" dissolve into laughter, and for the moment the nobility of their instant, unhesitating gallant response to the woman's report that you'd been captured, is lost – overwhelmed by the comic opera aspects of the real situation. But as they usher the prisoners out into the street, and you have a chance to reflect on their actions, you are swept with a wave of immeasurable gratitude. When they rushed in here, they didn't know they wouldn't be met by a hail of bullets. That two men were willing to risk their lives on your behalf will remain forever a treasured memory.

The prisoners, sent running on the double down the street towards the rear where someone will eventually take charge of them, need no urging. Obviously fearing they may be shot by their own men, they run as fast as men can with their hands clasped behind their heads. Their passage arouses a storm of contemptuous hooting from a long line of helmeted heads that pop up along the rim of the roadway, as far back as you can see, causing you to wonder how much action these current Royals have seen, that the sight of a couple of Germans would excite them so.

Returning to the business of moving along from doorway to doorway, you find you must hustle, for the leading section of the Royals has reached the end of the street and several men are kneeling down along the bushes from which the German snipers appear to have withdrawn.

By the time you and Kotyk join the Royals clustering at a gap in the bushes, they are taking off, a couple at a time, on a weird obstacle race over that succession of tracks and waist-high platforms raked by machine-gun fire from a signal tower bridging the tracks on the right, but far enough away that none of the galloping Royals are knocked down as far as you can make out.

At last you take off followed by Kotyk. Unencumbered, as he is with an 18-set on his back, you gain the first set of tracks and, prancing over them, clamber up onto the platform where you dash across and jump down on the next set of tracks as fast as you can, only to gallop across the next set of tracks to climb out again on the next platform – and so on for four or five of them (you lose count) – until at last, with lungs threatening to burst, you crawl exhausted up onto the main station platform, and huddle among a long line of infantrymen pressed tight against the station wall.

Everybody around you is gasping for breath. When you are capable you call for Kotyk, but there's no answer. He must have been hit. Weighed down by that damned radio – no wonder. You call again and again, and just as you are becoming certain he bought it, a voice calls out:

"He's here – he's okay – he just hasn't got the breath to answer."

An empty passenger train stands at the platform, with all lights on in the coaches, its air-brake compressor thumping away. Luggage sits on the platform.

As you move through the various empty offices, telephones are ringing incessantly, and in one office a switchboard is lit up with winking white lights. Baggage sits on counters and floors just as it was dropped. Suddenly there is a tremendous explosion. Dust and smoke roil out of one of the doorways. They assure you that it is not enemy action – the Pioneers have blown the safe and are unloading thousands of guilders from it.

Somehow this seems perfectly natural. For the moment the idea that they are safecrackers and thieves doesn't occur to you. Assuming all public services like railroads have been operated for the benefit of the Nazis, you can readily understand why the Pioneers would consider them fair game. However, as you go looking for a spot in the station to establish an OP, you remain mildly astonished at the priorities of some people in the middle of a battle.*

In a baggage room, a Dutchman (the only visible member of the

---

* Shortly after VE-Day, the chief safecracker was easily traced and the

station staff still on the premises) helps you push open the sliding truck-doors a crack, just wide enough to allow you to observe north across the turning basin of another broad canal (Verbindingskannal) running off at right angles west from the north–south one you crossed.

Immediately you spot, in a tree-lined street just beyond the canal, two German camouflaged staff cars sitting in front of a large house. As you give the map reference to Kotyk for transmittal back to Doherty manning the big 19-set in the carrier, who will send it back to the guns as a Troop target, you see a German rush out to the car with a package and rush back in. Obviously this is some sort of headquarters and they are packing up to leave.

After much shouting into his 18-set, twisting of dials, banging on the microphone, and changing positions here and there in the station, Kotyk gets through, and shortly you hear shells whining in from the left. Instantly the tree-lined street is filled with flashes and dust, and when it settles, a whoop of delight goes up from the infantrymen who have collected to watch, for one car is burning fiercely (maybe both), sending up columns of black smoke.

It will be your only effective target in Groningen, for though you try to hit single German vehicles periodically appearing on an overpass that loops north over the tracks a kilometre west of the station, you are unsuccessful, though you have perfect observation from the Station Master's bed-sitting room on the second floor of the station. Even when you lay the guns on the overpass, well in advance of the appearance of each prospect for destruction, your shells always manage to arrive too late.

Around noon your carrier arrives – Turner grinning from ear to ear in that unique way you have come to expect whenever he has

---

money recovered through the fact the naïve fellow inexplicably had deposited it all in a Groningen bank in his name. When the Dutchmen most directly concerned with the matter learned the safecracker had already volunteered to fight in the Pacific, all charges were dropped.

been through a dicey period, and Doherty frowning and wagging his head in wonderment that they managed to escape being potted by an ack-ack gun covering the wooden drawbridge (Parkwegbrug) they used to cross the canal some seven hundred yards south of the station.

However, though you get the impression the trip up was a bit of a shocker, with Turner joking about it and the reserved Doherty exhibiting his usual reticence, you get no real picture of what was involved until much later when you're given a vivid description by 26th Battery Signaller Gunner John Cooper, who, with Gunner B. S. Laycox, comes up via the same bridge in Gordon Lucas's carrier driven by Gunner L. E. Erickson:

Capt. Lucas is the FOO moving up with the Essex Scottish carriers, to pass over the canal and through the Royals to attack west from the station and secure an important bridge over another broad east–west canal. Fortunately the Jerry ack-ack gun covering this first little drawbridge is only a 20-mm and not an 88, for the carriers draw its fire, as well as fire from machine-guns, resulting in three casualties, including an Essex Scottish stretcher-bearer riding on our carrier. After crossing the bridge, the carriers turn off to the right for the protection of some buildings. One carrier, carrying a Toronto Scottish machine-gun officer, fails to make this turn, and drives right up the street into the face of all this fire. Somehow, it manages to get turned around and gets back, intact, but smoking badly from direct hits.

The Germans respect the red cross on the ambulance Jeep that comes up, and stop firing while the wounded are being picked up and transported back over the canal. But immediately after, when the Essex try to deploy a 6-pounder anti-tank gun in the street to knock out the opposition, the gunners become casualties.

Now a 17-pounder is brought up and positioned to shoot up the street. We, on the other side of the canal, almost directly in front of its muzzle, don't realize that before it can lay on its target, a nearby five-foot-high stone wall, running along the canal, has to be shot away with H.E. shells.

The double, almost instantaneous, smashes of sound – first the violent muzzle blast of the gun and then the shattering roar of the shell exploding only twenty-five yards in front of its muzzle – make us dive for cover, and cause near panic among the civilians in the houses around there, especially the children, as the tiles from the roofs in the vicinity lift and slide to the ground like snow. Once the German gun is visible, the 17-pounder makes short work of it, and we are able to move up to the railway station.*

Next day, with 5th Brigade moving in from the west and 6th Brigade passing through the bridgehead secured over the canal by the Essex Scottish, 4th Brigade is pulled back for a rest in a rather posh neighbourhood in the southern suburb of Haren. Fighting in the flaming, smoking city goes on street by street, and in some cases building by building, for another three days. The tanks of Fort Garry Horse punch shells into strongpoints, and the infantry moves cautiously forward to escape the snipers' bullets, attempting to get a shot at a sniper at a basement window, or at a window high up – sometimes creeping along the walls and hedges in the street in front, but most often through the shrubbery and fences of back gardens to hit the buildings from the rear.

Late in the afternoon of April 14, the leading company of FMRs, commanded by Major Elmo Thibault, pushing north along the main artery from the Essex bridgehead over the canal – with the SSRs clearing streets on their left flank, and the Queen's Own Cameron Highlanders of Canada winkling out snipers and machine-gunners along the streets on their right – reach their objective, the

---

* Lieut. H. P. Croome, 2nd Anti-tank Regiment, who, when his six-pounder was knocked out, went back over the canal under fire to bring up the 17-pounder, was awarded a Military Cross.

central city square. There the veteran Thibault, who has managed to survive with a rifle company since early last August in Normandy, is peering around the corner of a big building where his street meets the square, when he hears his name called from across the street. Looking over he sees Colonel Jacques Dextraze, now in command of the battalion, waving an envelope at him:

"Major Thibault," he calls, "a telegram from Southampton."

"Please open it," Thibault calls back, "and tell me what it says."

A slight pause, and Dextraze shouts: "Congratulations! You are the father of a nine-pound-eleven-ounce boy!"

And good fortune continues to smile on Thibault next morning, when he goes forward to inspect his platoon positions and spots a number of Germans up ahead with rifles slung on their shoulders, milling about in front of the big University of Groningen building – a number of them rushing in and out of the noble edifice. To Thibault's astonishment, one of the Germans, on spotting him, doesn't unsling his rifle and bring it to a menacing position, but walks over to him. When Thibault asks him what is going on, the German tells him in good English that they are trying to decide whether to give up. Asked about his excellent English, the soldier explains that before the war he worked for Ford in Detroit.

Thibault advises him to tell his comrades they are surrounded and have no future – that they should follow him back to his battalion headquarters. This turns out to be a persuasive argument, for soon after the German carries it back to his comrades they begin to form up three-abreast in a column, which grows until it numbers 375 men, with several officers in the lead, and then they follow Thibault back to where Dextraze takes charge.*

In the meantime the southeastern part of the city is being cleared by the Camerons, and the northern half of the city by the Black Watch, the Maisonneuves, and the Calgary Highlanders.

---

* Dextraze survived the war, fought in Korea, and eventually became Chief of the General Staff of the Canadian Army.

The German garrison commandant surrenders on April 16, but some pockets continue to resist for another day. In all, the four days of fighting cost 2nd Division a mere 209 casualties, while causing the Germans considerably more casualties and capturing 2,400 prisoners. In eighteen days 2nd Division advanced 195 kilometres and captured 165 officers and 6,031 Other Ranks, at a cost of 44 officers and 768 Other Ranks killed, wounded, or missing. More than 15,000 miles of signal wire had been laid, and divisional engineers had constructed eighteen bridges.*

And in twenty-six days, 3rd Canadian Division thrust from the Rhine to the North Sea, clearing the northwest of Holland from Deventer to Leeuwarden, building 36 bridges and capturing 4,600 prisoners.†

---

* Major D. J. Goodspeed, *Battle Royal* (Toronto: Royal Regiment of Canada Association, 1962), p. 558.

† Col. C. P. Stacey, *Six Years of War, Part II,* the official history of the Canadian Army in the Second World War (Ottawa: Queen's Printer, 1955), p. 557.

71

IT'S AWFULLY
WINDY IN A TANK

❋

EVERY NOW AND THEN A FOO IS INVITED TO USE A TANK IN
an attack that is closely supported or led by tanks. Usually you
decline the offer, preferring to take your chances in your carrier –
even though its roofless box is an open invitation to anything
descending from the heavens, and its relatively thin sides (12-mm of
armour plate) provide puny protection compared to the thickly
armoured tanks. The lower profile of a carrier offers less of a target
for an 88, while guaranteeing you an independence of decision and
movement not possible in a tank that's part of a group of tanks
subject to their own peculiar set of controls, habits, customs, tactics,
and disciplines associated with the steel cavalry.

However, this morning (April 23) you set aside these considerations and accept the reassurances of the thick hide of a Sherman at
the rear of a troop of Fort Garry Horse, moving with Tom Wilcox's
company towards Falkenburg and Kirchkimmen along the road
west from Delmenhorst to Oldenburg.

You need all the reassurance you can get these days. In spite of
the frequently replenished water-bottles of rum, carried day and
night buttoned into the front of your battledress, you are beginning
to "get the wind up" more and more frequently. You know the war
is going to end soon . . . you've made it this far . . . you've got to
make it the rest of the way. Shell fragments and Spandau bullets

can't penetrate the turret of a tank, and apart from mines (which you think a tank can more readily absorb) these are the chief hazards these days.

The war has degenerated into crossroads ambushes, with the Germans showing no tendency to form a line along here. They appear interested only in delaying the advance to Oldenburg, and Wilhelmshaven about thirty miles north of there. Rumour has it they'll make a stand at a formidable water barrier, the Ems–Jade Kanal, just south of the big naval base.*

And they have been able to slow the advance to a crawl with very small expenditures of ammunition and manpower simply by mining all the major crossroads, and blocking them by exploding collars of explosive around the huge trunks of living trees (lining many of the roads along here), only partially severing them in such a way as to drop the massive trunks and branches over the roadway, while leaving the splintered butt-ends still firmly attached to stumps standing several feet above the ground. Then when your column comes up to the tangled mess, a hidden ack-ack gun starts punching airbursts overhead, and one or two Spandaus open up from the flanks, making it very uncomfortable for the halted infantry and their arty carrier crews waiting for the pioneers to come up with their saws to sever the tree trunks into manageable pieces that a tank can tow out of the way.

Usually you drop some shells around and about where you think the gun might be, judging from its barking, and now and then they seem to be effective for the firing ceases abruptly. But then you find it along with the Spandaus waiting for you at the next crossroads, and you suspect you merely encouraged them to withdraw a little

---

* That this could be a real bloodbath was indicated by their stand two days before at the Küsten Canal when they absorbed 1,700 casualties in suicidal counter-attacks against the Algonquin Regiment, who were holding the bridgehead while a bridge was built for 4th Division tanks.

sooner. Casualties are not high, but there are enough that one will be able to follow the route of each brigade by the sad mounds of fresh earth with their lonely new wooden crosses, left along the verges near crossroads lined with the splintered and ragged stumps of trees.

And you are far from feeling reassured up in the turret of your tank as it rumbles down a hard-surfaced road through rather close country, your nerves stretched taut as a drum. You had forgotten the awful sense of confinement that exists in a tank, and how windy it is from air sucked into the turret by fierce ventilation fans, which must be welcome in summer, but which today, with its frosty air, is bone-chilling.

Soon your teeth are chattering and you are wishing you had worn your tank suit, a recent issue to all personnel moving in tracked vehicles – a light beige affair with hood, made of dense, denimlike cloth thickly lined with khaki wool, large enough to be worn as a coverall over battledress, but, unlike the sad-sack look of coveralls, presenting a rather dashing front covered, from chest to thighs, with zippered pockets and special crevices to hold Chinagraph pencils and other necessities not easily recovered from interior pockets when the two long, heavy-duty zippers are run up from ankles to collarbones.

You seem to be occupying the position of the gun-layer, and would be delighted to stay down in the turret amusing yourself looking out through the telescopic sight as you revolve turret and gun, but you immediately realize that if you are to continue to keep track of your precise location on the map – absolutely essential for an artillery FOO – you'll have to ride with your head out the top of the turret. And it is then you are struck by the arrogant height of these vehicles – you must be at least ten feet up in the air – a big target for an 88-mm gun, or for a Panzerfaust for that matter. You've seen what the "hollow charge" of a Piat or Panzerfaust bomb can do to a tank and its crew.

Early on in Normandy you'd peered inside burned-out tanks,

and been shocked by the charred remains of the crew still sitting there in position, reduced to skinny black cinders, their white teeth showing in the grin of death, though the only visible damage to the turret of the tank had been a tiny hole on the outside, leading to a funnel-shaped hole on the inside. However, those concave, brassière-like depressions represented, you were told, the amount of steel that had been instantly turned into white-hot, molten pellets and been sent careening around inside the turret killing all the occupants and setting the tank on fire.*

Now you find yourself studying the ditches on either side of the road, particularly where thick bushes are growing, and each time the column stops, you crawl down onto the road. After a while it appears your nervousness is transmitted to your signaller Kotyk, for he also begins to vacate the tank each time it stops, climbing back up again when the column starts to roll.

Thus when a sparkling explosion suddenly puffs up on the roadway, just to the left of the tracks of the leading Sherman, inducing it to reverse direction with a roar, its heavy machine-gun almost cutting in two the young German still standing upright in a slit trench holding the Panzerfaust projector that had missed its target, you drop down on the verge of the road. And there you are standing, right of your tank, next to the ditch, as some very young prisoners come marching back down the road with their hands behind their heads.

Just as they are coming close enough for you to study their faces

---

* The Panzerfaust was a hand-held, one-shot, throw-away German anti-tank weapon, weighing only 11 pounds, capable of piercing 80 mm of armour at up to 80 metres. The British Piat was effective up to 100 yards and could be used as a crude mortar, but weighed twice as much and was awkward to carry, cock, and fire. The American Bazooka fired a projectile too light to penetrate the frontal armour of German tanks.

and discover they are mere boys (cadets from a naval academy you'll later learn), a rapid snapping of rifle-fire starts up from across the field on the left, apparently from a bordering hedge-row that runs diagonally across the field towards the road up ahead, meeting it just about where the Panzerfaust incident had taken place.

As you jump into the ditch to the right of your tank, the Royals already deployed along the ditch start firing across the road at the puffs to be seen in the hedgerow. The prisoners, caught between the two lines of fire, drop their hands and start running towards the Royals. Immediately some Royals' rifles are turned on them, and several are dropped in squirming heaps on the pavement before you, and a bellowing Royals' sergeant further up the ditch, can get them stopped.

Calling on Kotyk to follow, you scramble up into your tank, and get him loading an H.E. shell in the breech of its 75-mm gun as you squat on the gun-layer's seat and start the gears whirring to swing turret and gun in the direction of the hedge. Though you hadn't expected to actually fire the thing, you had, before setting out this morning, sought instruction in loading and aiming. When the middle of the offending hedgerow swings into your eyepiece, you lower the crosshairs onto it and pull the firing lever. As Kotyk will always remember: "It damned near blew my ears off."

The numbing crash of the gun in that confined space, the sting-ing whack of the rubber-cushioned eyepiece on your cheekbone, and the rather unspectacular single puff of black smoke on the hedgerow combine to inspire the question: With two dozen 25-pounders at your disposal, why the hell are you playing around with this one gun?

Giving Kotyk the map reference of a point midway along the hedgerow for transmittal to the guns, you order a Mike target, going into fire for effect without ranging. The rounds arrive promptly, but most plough the field in front of the hedge. However,

"Northwest 100 – Repeat" brings them bang on the hedge, and before you can "repeat" the order again, several snowy-white pillow cases or sheets are thrust forth to festoon the greenery of the hedge in a way you have never seen before. It is as though someone in authority – loyal to the Führer, but not wanting inexperienced boys slaughtered – instructed them to come prepared to surrender rather than face such an eventuality.

The Royals will record they took 180 prisoners today – a most satisfactory bag – but the image of those young boys running to your trench for safety with terror in their eyes, and being shot down and left squirming on the roadway, will haunt you for days, and perhaps never will be blotted from your memory. At least one of them was shot by the young Royal next to you, before you could knock down the barrel of his rifle. And when you yelled at him, "Why are you shooting them – can't you see they're just trying to take cover?" he'd replied remorsefully, "I don't know ... everybody else was shooting ... I guess I thought they were taking advantage of the situation to make a break for it."

Like the burning of the truckload of white-haired businessmen in ill-fitting uniforms back at the Loon crossroads, this is something else to feed your hatred of Hitler and his Nazi gang – sending kids, untrained and ill-equipped, to be slaughtered for no useful purpose.

But soon your concern for German schoolboy cadets and elderly Volkssturm troopers wanes as you learn, by way of BBC broadcasts, of the death by starvation threatening 40 per cent of the Dutch men, women, and children in the heavily populated western part of the country – shut off with the strong military forces of their German masters in "fortress Holland" (as the Germans call it) by the 1st Canadian Infantry and 5th Canadian Armoured Divisions. The Canadians are halted somewhere west of Appledorn by orders from Einsenhower while negotiations proceed with Seyss-Inquart, the Reichskommissar in the Netherlands, for a truce to allow truckloads of food and fuel to be brought to the desperate people of Amsterdam, Rotterdam, and The Hague. The citys' inhabitants are reduced to eating tulip bulbs, if they are lucky enough to have some, and burning furniture and cupboard doors for fuel to cook them.*

---

* An average working man requires three thousand calories a day. In the last week, before foodstuffs began to drop from the skies from Allied bombers on April 28, the daily ration dropped to 250 calories, and insiders knew there would be no bread at all by May 5. Malnutrition and starvation oedema (dropsy) touched hundreds of thousands, killing tens of thousands. And when the Allied food convoys finally got to roll through the lines on May 4, thousands were too weak even to feed themselves. Facts from Maj. Norman Phillips, Cdn. Army P. R. Services, and J. N. Kerk, Secretary, Canadian-Netherlands Committee, *Holland and the Canadians* (Amsterdam: Contact Publishing, 1945), p. 27.

72

YOUR DRIVER GETS A LETTER
FROM A MAJOR-GENERAL

※

THE SULLEN, DOWNCAST, WITHDRAWN GERMAN TOWNS and countryside are in great contrast to the joyous, festive, flag-bedecked, liberated Dutch towns you passed through as you retraced your route south from Groningen, down through Assen, Beilen, Hoogeveen, and Hardenberg, and then turn east and re-enter Hitler's Reich towards Lingen, before turning northeast to Haselunne and Lahden past Meppen and the Krupp's vast testing range for all the various weapons spawned by those vile merchants of death for both world wars.

You hear all actions by 1st and 5th (Canadian) divisions, who have been pushing northwest through Arnhem and Appeldoorn, have been halted to allow for negotiations to proceed with Nazi Reichskommissar Seyss-Inquart to allow Canadian–British convoys of food to move across no-man's-land to the starving people of Western Holland; that 3rd Division has swept clean Northwest Holland from Deventer to Leeuwarden; that the Brits are in Bremen; and that thousands of German troops are being taken prisoner by the Russians in the outskirts of Berlin.

Obviously the war could end any hour now. And each day, as a few more Canadian helmets are left hanging on wooden crosses along the verges, it becomes a little harder to suppress the growing anxiety that you may get it just before it's all over.

By all rights, it should have happened yesterday. For some inexplicable reason you were standing up in your carrier, which had barely begun to move, grinding along with the leading platoon as it led off into the day's action. Maybe the carrier dipped a little, or jerked forward, but that first shot from the hedge didn't miss by much. It passed so close it stung like a hand slapped across your left ear, leaving it deaf and ringing for a good hour.

When the infantry attacked the hedge, running recklessly at the black, raging puffs of your exploding shells, they captured the lot without a casualty. They were a motley gang in ill-fitting uniforms, and you wondered which of them had been assigned to start the firing by picking off that stupid officer standing up in that carrier. The incident so bothered Turner (B Company Sergeant-Major later told you) that when you and Kotyk, carrying an 18-set, went ahead on foot with Shortreed's company through the thick bush, leaving him and Doherty behind in the carrier, he'd stewed and fussed like a "wet hen," particularly when the inevitable light ack-ack gun started pumping airbursts into the trees where he saw you and "Junior" disappear.

That he is a man of large and tender heart, who would like you to think otherwise, was further exposed when he was able to bring the carrier up at dusk to the farm where company headquarters was set up for the night just beyond the bush. Full of remorse, he immediately sought you out to describe how the arrival of his carrier had indirectly resulted in the death of a Royals' lad, who, at the moment of his arrival, was coming from the barn with an armful of straw:

"Jerry has the road covered right where it leaves the woods and I have to make a right turn into the laneway to the farm. So as we come out in the open, we are hit by machine-gun fire. And when I make my turn and start up the driveway, the fire follows me. Just as I am coming up to the barn, this soldier with an armful of straw is walking towards me from the barn on my right. And as he gets close to me, his forehead just opens up from a shot through the back of his head."

Of course you assure him he was in no way to blame, but all last night he was tormented with regret, and repeated again and again:

"All the poor bastard wanted was a bit of straw to make the bottom of his trench a little more comfortable for the night. And if we hadn't pulled in just then and attracted that machine-gun . . ."

Turner is the best thing that could happen to a carrier crew with a FOO who'd begun to lean too heavily on a water-bottle of rum buttoned into the front of his battledress. He's always grinning, even when the going is at its roughest. The briefest pause and he whips up a pot of steaming tea. Chicken stew, fried eggs, and German sausages appear from nowhere. And at the end of a long day he'll pack you and the others off for sack time while he takes an extra long shift on the radio set.

A few nights ago waiting for dawn on the side of a bald hill in a lonely listening post, he told you about himself. Of Hungarian birth, he'd run away from his home in Toronto, changed his name to Turner from Spirnyak, and gone to sea at the age of fifteen. Christmas 1939 he'd piloted a Canadian tugboat bound for Siberia, through the Panama Canal, when all other crew members, with the exception of the captain, were drunk. He'd learned to speak German in a Hamburg jail shortly before the war, when he missed his ship and was held for months before release to the British.

And just before coming to 4th Field in Normandy he rounded out his experience by doing time in the infamous "Glass House" (detention centre) after being picked up in London in civilian garb on his way to shipping out with the merchant marine on the North Atlantic run – where he felt he'd be "doing something useful" instead of endless training in an army that never seemed to be anywhere near the fighting.

While claiming he harbours no resentment for the severity of his sentence, fully realizing how foolish he'd been, he understandably will never forgive the sadistic treatment meted out by the guards on him and his fellow prisoners. According to him, men sent to the Glass House are completely at the mercy of their guards, without resort to any form of appeal, and those attracted to the job of guarding prisoners (some of whom, admittedly, are deemed incorrigible) enjoy bullying them.

For instance, frequently at morning inspections, a burley NCO would grind the sole of his muddy boot on the gleaming toes of the boots of a helpless prisoner standing rigidly at attention, daring him to protest as he snarled, "Do you call them boots polished?" And if a prisoner's endurance broke, and he lashed out at his tormenter, he was thrown in "the hole" – a totally blacked-out, tiny cell – and kept on a diet of bread and water until released some days later, temporarily blind from his eyes having become accustomed to living without light.

And now and then, in the middle of the night, the lights would come on in the barrack room and a roaring voice would demand to know "Who's been smoking in here?" Getting no answer, since smokes were impossible for prisoners to come by, the inquisitor would proceed with a kit inspection. Finding nothing in the kit he'd spewed all over the floor, he would dump the contents of each straw palliasse-mattress out onto the helter-skelter of each man's kit, on the pretext of examining the straw for hidden cigarettes. On finding none, he would then order the prisoners to return every last piece of straw and bit of chaff to their palliasse bags, without the aid of a broom or dustpan. And when, hours later, the last man had picked up the last bit of straw, returned the last bit of kit to his kit bag, and settled down for some sleep, the lights would go on again, and the roaring order for kit inspection would bring Turner and his fellow prisoners standing again at attention at the foot of their bunks to watch, with grinding teeth, their unsated inquisitor proceed with exactly the same routine as before.

Last winter his kid brother, Frank (who'd retained the family name of Spirnyak), died from a sniper's bullet while serving with the Royals at that island position you once occupied by boat in the area of Mook. He'd gone looking for brother Frank as soon as he heard he was wounded, and had caught up with him at a Casualty Clearing Station:

"Too late – he was already wrapped in a blanket. And there was this Sergeant who was just too damned casual – I nearly punched his goddamn head off! I know he had his hands full, but he knew what I was looking for. Throwing a thumb over his shoulder he said, 'There he is – over there.' Over there was a whole line of bodies sewed up in blankets awaiting burial."

In recent days Turner has been carrying clippings from several London papers – photographs taken at the recent liberation of Bergen Belsen and Dachau concentration camps – showing piles of unburied, naked, emaciated bodies, and hordes of hollow-eyed, hollow-cheeked living-skeletons in prison suits. And at the first sign of arrogance or resentment by German civilians, particularly those who are using Polish slave labourers at the time of your arrival, Turner pulls from his breast pocket a double-page spread of horrifying pictures.*

After carefully opening it on a table, he demands in German they look at the naked bodies stacked up in their tangled repulsive piles, and study the faces of the freed prisoners, distinguishable from the dead only by the fact their mouths are not quite as noticeably agape. Invariably the reaction of the Germans is disbelief, charging the newspapers with propaganda. This, of course, always sends Turner into a rage, causing him to smash his fist on the table and shout that Hitler and his Nazi swine are the liars, not the pictures. Whether or not they believe him, at least they are impressed with his fury and never pursue the argument, thereafter speaking very little, and always in low tones.

In one farmhouse yesterday a Pole, wearing a jaundice-coloured P in a circle of faded purple cloth on his shirt, denoting his slavery status, driven slightly mad either by past treatment or by the intoxication of his liberation – or a combination of the two – went completely berserk after telling you in German (with Turner translating)

---

* While front-line soldiers seldom saw newspapers, tons arrived daily in the theatre of operations – 946 tons from 6 June 1944 to 8 May 1945.

how he'd been denied the means of writing home to his family during all his years of slavery. As you followed his rampage through cupboards, desks, and bureau drawers, you thought at first he was after loot. But soon it was clear he had in mind the singular objective of destroying every piece of writing paper he could lay his hands on – shredding it and scattering it like confetti as he laughed and danced in childish glee.

At another farm, Turner saw to it that the woman of the house mopped the kitchen floor under the supervision of her ex-slave, a young Polish woman who, having exchanged her rags for her former mistress's best clothes, sat with her feet up enjoying a cup of coffee she'd been regularly denied.

Yesterday, he shook you awake in a haymow over a cow stable, and spilled on your chest the contents of an envelope he'd just received. A strange multicoloured ribbon fluttered down with a letter from Maj.-Gen. Bruce Matthews, Commander of 2nd Division, informing him that he'd been awarded the Croix de Guerre With Bronze Star for wheeling his old Norton motorbike back and forth over shell-pocked roads keeping communications open in some foul spot on the road to Falaise.

Grinning from ear to ear – ready to deprecate the gallantry that had brought him this high honour, claiming that "Fred Brohman [another member of the Major's crew] should have had it or one just like it" – he still saw some practical advantage arising from it and could hardly wait until you'd finished reading, before proposing:

"Wouldn't a bit of leave to wet my gong be in order, Skipper?"

Totally in agreement, of course, you were able to get approval from RHQ for a forty-eight-hour pass, and helped him sew the colourful ribbon on his chest beside the faded and crushed CVSM ribbon (Canadian Volunteer Service Medal), borrowed from your chest, he having lost his own somewhere along the way (probably during events leading up to his trip to the Glass House).

And after a couple of stirrup cups with Doherty, Kotyk, and Major Suckling, you packed him off to Antwerp where he figured that ribbon would be worth a lot of free booze at his favourite watering-hole. But just in case, he took along an impressive piano accordion he'd picked up along the way, which could readily be converted into several hundred Belgian francs.

73

YOUR LAST DAY IN
A UNIVERSAL CARRIER

———————————— ✳ ————————————

DAWN THE LAST DAY OF APRIL BREAKS MISTY AND COLD, AND all parts of the carrier are clammy and wet as you and your crew climb into it to move out with the infantry.

Everything in an open carrier including its passengers, being completely exposed to the elements at all times when on the move, cannot escape accepting whatever weather the elements choose to deliver – from baking sun and sudden cloudbursts in summer, to the drenching, cold rains of fall, and the black frosts and freezing snows of winter. Moreover, the coarse and unfeeling characteristics of the thick steel box in which you are immersed for hours on end tend to magnify the discomfort of all the extremes of weather – radiating suffocating heat at bake-oven levels in July, and in January doing its best to freeze you stiff by drawing from your shuddering frame, shrinking from its frost-biting touch, the last bits of precious body heat.

Usually when you stop for the night, or are in a static position in foul weather, the rear compartments and the equipment carried on top of the engine amidships are covered by a tarpaulin, and this was in place last night. However, the old tarp has so many slits in it from mortar and shell splinters, including some from your own shells air-bursting in the trees around your house on the Twente Canal, that everything is miserably cold and wet, including the thin slabs of sponge rubber that pass for upholstery on the metal bucket seats.

The Royals, with whom you are to move, are to provide protection to the left flank of 4th Brigade as it moves up to the outskirts of Oldenburg, preparatory to taking this major centre. During the day it is expected you will run into enemy outposts.

Setting off at 0800 hrs, with D Company leading, you roll slowly up a bleak secondary dirt-road, and while there is no sign of the enemy, it takes an hour to cover two kilometres because of the enemy's cratering and the muddy condition of the road.

During the morning there is a steady drizzle of icy rain, and by mid-afternoon this has turned to snow. Though most of it melts as fast as it falls, the thickness of the flurries swirling around the carrier makes it seem even colder than it is.

By late afternoon, as a result of all the rain and snow, the unpaved road you are following with Bob Suckling's A Company, now leading the advance, is very muddy.

From the ruts your carrier is leaving in it, these roads are bound to deteriorate fast with the passage of all the trucks and other wheeled vehicles coming behind, including the quads and their heavy ammunition limbers and guns. You pity the drivers who'll be coming up later along this stretch of road. It is distinguishable from a mere farmer's lane only by the deep ditches running along both sides, which make it imperative your driver steers carefully along its crown so as to not slither off and get bogged down.

Clearly your carrier is the first vehicle to use this road for some time, for there are no tracks in the soft mud before you pass along. Thus you ride standing up to better study the roadway for any sinister signs of mines.

One day you must try to calculate how many thousands of square feet of road surfaces you have peered at in nervous fear, on many occasions walking in front of the carrier to get a closer look at cobblestoned roads and unpaved tracks like this one when it has been obvious your vehicle was the first to pass that way. And though you have never spotted a single mine in all those hundreds of miles of studying every foot of the ground before you, the process has become second nature, as have all survival habits of importance.

Lately you have become exceptionally wary, having seen a number of vehicles blown up by mines, and frequently piles of mines, lifted from roadblocks, stacked up beside the road.

Just this morning you learned that the legendary former sergeant ack of 2nd Battery, Emile Dalgas (an officer in World War I and militia major at the outset of this war, who resigned his commission so he might serve overseas) was killed when his Jeep ran over a mine on his way up to visit 4th Field. Overage for "the field," he'd got his commission back as an instructor at the Canadian School of Artillery

Now as you are coming up to a crossroads – some forty or fifty yards short of it – you spot a very faint, rectangular indentation in the wet, undisturbed soil of the road, lying at right angles to your carrier's left track, no more than twenty feet from it. Thrusting your clenched hand down in front of the driver, you yell, "Stop!"

Immediately he brings it to a rocking halt, and you jump out and go forward to the indentation. It is the exact shape of a box mine, obviously planted when the ground was dry. The rain has settled the thin layer of soil that was smoothed over it – just enough to allow you to see the outline. And no more than fifteen feet further on, in line with the right track, is another indentation of identical size and shape.

When Suckling comes up and examines the indentations, he agrees with you and sends a message back to the Pioneers to come up and lift the mines. He tells you his company will go ahead and consolidate around the farmhouse at the crossroads, and will try to get permission to give his troops a breather while the mines are being lifted. They have been walking since early morning and have had nothing to eat since breakfast. And that is how it works out. By the time the Pioneers come up with their mine detectors, lift and stack almost three dozen of the deadly devices at the crossroads, and it is safe for your carrier to proceed, Suckling and company are back on the road, trudging forward again. Now the countryside changes from bleak, open fields with few trees and even fewer buildings, to a more tree-lined road along which are distributed a succession of respectable-looking farms.

A few hundred yards past the crossroads, the leading platoon comes under small-arms fire from somewhere up ahead – the first contact with enemy rearguards the battalion has had in three days. Fortunately your carrier at that moment is just approaching a farm-house close to the road on the right, and as the infantry jump over the rain-swollen ditch and run, crouched over, to take up defensive positions around the house and barn, you are able to spot a culvert a bit farther along, that allows your driver to swing the carrier into the laneway and get it out of sight behind the house in a matter of a few seconds.

Joining Suckling under a dripping, shaggy hedge on the far side of the house, in the midst of several of his riflemen, you sweep the glistening fields and bushes with your field-glasses, but can spot no movement of any kind. He decides the firing probably came from the vicinity of the next farm, partially hidden by trees, a few hundred yards further along the road up ahead, and leaves you to go to his Company's 18-set, somewhere behind the barn, to exchange views with Battalion Headquarters and receive fresh orders.

As you focus in on the distant house, vaguely outlined in the grey mists now forming over the sodden fields, its yard and gardens appear as innocent as hundreds of others you've passed in the past few days. But as you continue to study them, their very deadness presents a sinister aspect. And as the minutes drag by, and your arms grow tired holding the glasses to your eyes, you ponder how many hundreds of hours you've spent studying dead buildings and dead landscapes in the past ten months since Eterville and St. Martin-de-Fontenay – without losing one iota of your sensitivity to the lurking menace suggested by unnatural stillness and absence of movement.

Before it grows dark, which will be very soon with all this fog, you want to register those buildings as a potential trouble spot, and at the same time intimidate the opposition round and about here, with the tremendous fire-power available to the sparse and weary column they tried to shoot up as it was trudging up the muddy road towards them a few minutes ago. So you call down a stormy

Mike target on them, and while you ask only for "Scale 3" (three rounds for each of the regiments's twenty-four guns) the seventy-two roaring explosions are so concentrated in space and time, they can't help but be impressive, particularly if the enemy troops in the target area are anything like those poorly-equipped inexperienced "Volkssturm" (people's army) you have been running into in recent days.

At any rate there's no more fire from there. Now C Company, which was diverted to the left from the crossroads (where the mines were lifted this afternoon) to move north on a road parallel to this one, has bumped the enemy. Judging by what you can pick up from radio exchanges, their skirmishing is no more serious than what has been going on here. However, upper echelons seem to suspect these are enemy outpost positions in the first line of defence of the city of Oldenburg which, according to intelligence reports, will be defended vigorously as the main anchor in their defensive plan for the region leading up to Wilhelmshaven. With darkness falling and visibility worsening by the hour, the Royals are ordered to consolidate and dig-in here until daylight.

The snow has stopped, but with the darkness a real pea-soup fog descends, cutting visibility to zero. The very clean, cosily furnished farmhouse, immediately taken over for company headquarters, looks exceedingly comfortable after the long, cold, wet day; and you look forward to spending the night here, as do the infantry.

With luck, Jerry will keep his distance, so that all but the sentries will be able to take advantage of the shelter of the house and barn. But before you get settling down in one of those comfortable chairs, Bob gets a signal to be on the lookout for a wayward Panther tank spotted by C Company somewhere over beyond their line of march just before it grew dark.

This is most disturbing news. You recall hearing a distant motor over that way and wondering what it meant. All the fears you've been trying to suppress are aroused. With all that fog out there, it would be so easy for them to overrun this position before you could fire a round.

You go outside and listen for the whine of a motor and squeaking tank tracks, but all you can hear is the rustle of the cold air through the trees and bushes.

When you finally decide that Jerry is probably just as uneasy as you are, and has grounded his tank or tanks for the night, and return inside, there's a signal waiting for you: you and your crew must report back to Battalion Headquarters immediately.

This turns out to be the house you'd noticed this afternoon back on the northeast corner of the mine-cleared crossroads. When you report in, you find Col. Lendrum and Major "Paddy" Ryall, his 2 IC, waiting for you. They tell you that you've been called back to take the place of your battery commander, Jack Cooper, who it seems got stuck in the mud somewhere back there this afternoon and then got lost in the snowstorm. Now with this dense fog, he has sent up a message that he is not going to try to find his way up tonight.

As you listen, you find their manner a little strange — leaning towards a chummy, man-to-man manner — not at all typical of either of these officers who normally are inclined to hold themselves politely aloof except when conducting military business with you. And when well-filled tumblers of good whisky are poured all round, they broach the subject they really want to discuss with you. It seems they are not satisfied with Don Cornett's replacement, and intend to approach Mac Young with a request that you be made battery commander in his place.

You hasten to point out that, while you are flattered, in the artillery promotions are made on the basis of total service seniority, not just within the Regiment, and the new major has bags of seniority built up in coastal defence in Canada from early in the war.

However, Lendrum will not be put off. He says Don Cornett showed just how effective a first-class artillery rep at the battalion level can be, and he is not prepared to accept anything less. He says you must have noticed that for days now at "O" Groups he has been addressing his questions to you on the most effective application of the guns in each move, and to which company you think you should be assigned. And tonight was the last straw. He intends to approach MacGregor Young forthwith, but before doing so, he wanted to get your blessing.

It is such a staggering idea, holding out such possibilities, that for a moment your head swims and you are tempted to say, Yes, why not? But before you can commit yourself, there's a rap on the door, and in comes a remarkably cheerful, young anti-tank officer looking for advice as to a safe route to C Company on a parallel road over on the left.

It seems he is responding to a call for a 17-pounder anti-tank gun to be brought up and positioned with C Company on that parallel road over there where a Panther tank was roaming around before dark. He needs to know if the connecting road, leading from the crossroads outside the house here to that other road, has been cleared of mines?

While no one can answer that for certain, you are able to tell him that the Pioneers cleared a big stack of mines out of the crossroads while you watched this afternoon. You don't know if they cleared the side roads, but surely they would have cleared the connecting road to the left knowing that C Company was going to use it. And the Royals' RSM, who came in with the anti-tank officer, says at least one Royals' carrier must have pulled a 6-pounder up that connecting road late this afternoon.

Finding all of this reassuring he is about to leave when Paddy Ryall suggests a tot of whisky for the road, and the very likeable, outgoing chap seems grateful for the suggestion. After only a brief discussion of the atrocious weather that has now turned to drizzling rain – during which he describes the gargantuan disgust of his gunners at being yanked from a warm farmhouse to come up and stand-to all night in the fog and rain – he tosses off the whisky and goes out into the filthy, black night.

The conversation is slow to pick up again on the subject at hand, and you are still recalling what a pleasant, refreshing chap he was, when there is a heavy, dull boom that rattles the windows.

All look at each other questioningly as the Sergeant-Major goes out to investigate. Shortly he returns to report: the 17-pounder only started up the side road – got no more than twenty-five yards – when the carrier towing the gun hit a mine. The whole crew bought it.*

Oh God . . . he was such a pleasant fellow! And you visualize him riding along in the front of the carrier unable in the dark to see the tell-tale indentation in the soggy roadway that had saved you and your crew from a similar fate this afternoon . . .

For a while no one speaks, and when Lendrum and Ryall resume the discussion of your accelerated promotion, you find your taste for the subject has vanished. When they suggest that if there was any sense or logic to the artillery promotion system, you would have your majority by now through your long experience as a FOO, you find yourself pointing out the guy didn't invent the seniority system – which is the way he put it the day he informed you, almost apologetically, he had become your battery commander.

It wasn't his fault he built up his long service as a captain in Canada where no one is killed, wounded, or promoted, and he clearly had paid his dues as a FOO since joining the Regiment back on South Beveland last November – a good long stretch – a lot longer than most.

You can see your infantry friends, who have never had to contend with such broad seniority rules when making promotions in the field, have mixed feelings when you tell them you could never give your blessing to their plan.

Later in the day you are given cause to wonder if they went ahead anyway, and thus triggered a sequence of events that sees your position suddenly change drastically to one where you have no further regular regimental duties in the front line or at the guns.

---

* Lieut. H. P. Croome, who, the week before at the canal bridge in Groningen, won the Military Cross for going back under fire and bringing up a 17-pounder; and his gallant crew that had faced the German ack-ack gun at point-blank range, and subdued it.

Mid-morning Capt. Don Patrick, who only recently came back from hospital after recovering from a wound suffered at Xanten, suddenly appears, just as he had back in the Rhineland in front of the Hochwald, and announces he is to take over your crew again, so you can report back to Regimental Headquarters for a "special assignment."

Your first thought is that the job back at the Reinforcement Depot in Ghent has finally come through. But when you locate RHQ in a working windmill, Adjutant Grange tells you it has nothing to do with the Ghent posting; the 2 IC, Major Wilson, has asked to see you.

And where is he, this morning?

"Standing behind you," says a familiar, well-modulated voice.

When you turn, to face him, expecting to be warmly greeted, you are bewildered by his cool demeanour. Dammit, you haven't seen each other since he was your troop commander in Easy Troop way back at Barnham Junction in the fall of 1942! But he hasn't changed one iota. After a perfunctory greeting he is all business, getting on with what he wants to say in those abrupt, abbreviated sentences you remember so well – expressed in the low, restrained tone he always affected when his great barrel-chest was about to burst with indignation.

At first he gives the impression he is disgusted with you for having survived so many months as a FOO – a matter that has come to his attention only this morning.

But then it becomes clear his complaint is not with you, but with those "strange souls" who left you up there so long. Then, after pointing out "your fooing days are over," he proceeds, in all seriousness, to appoint you "third-in-command" of the Regiment, stating that while it is beyond his capacity to improve your rank, he can, and will, see you benefit from all the privileges and respect due a "3 IC."

When you go along with the joke to the extent of asking him just what a "3 IC" is expected to do, he replies with such sober intensity, he almost has you believing that there is such a job. "The

3 IC will be attached to A Echelon, but will have no duties or responsibilities except one: he will take advantage of every opportunity to live like a king – always comfortably, and in luxury wherever possible. And I warn you, I shall be checking up on you, and if I find you are not carrying out this responsibility to the best of your ability, it will be back up to the front line forthwith."

Tonight, May 1, the BBC reports Hitler is dead. You hear it in a cold, stinking cow stable, as you are stretching out to sleep beside a pigsty adjacent to the kitchen door in a barn chosen by someone as a billet, wondering how you'll ever gain the elevated lifestyle expected of a "3 IC" if this is the way A Echelon lives. In the morning when you decide to treat yourself to some hot water for shaving from the warming reservoir on the kitchen range, and the German farmer and his wife make no effort to hide their resentment, you find yourself wishing you had those London newspaper clippings of Belsen that Turner's been carrying.

For a couple of days you follow Wilson's instructions, taking no responsibility for anything, except responding to a request to all officers to come up with names of persons who may have been overlooked or turned down for medals for outstanding or gallant efforts beyond the call of duty.* But when life continues to revolve around dismal cow stables, you decide you must take a hand in the selection of billets if ever you are to fulfil your obligation in the matter of securing a princely lifestyle. So on the afternoon of May 4, you take over the job of reconnoitring billets for the night.

The move is north of Oldenburg, its surrender having been arranged by telephone calls involving Major Jack Drewry and Col. Whitaker from Riley's Tac HQ on the south side of the canal to the

---

* Members of 4th Field who subsequently were awarded Commander-in-Chief Certificates from Field Marshal Montgomery were: Capt. P. C. Voloshin, M.D., L/Sgt. W. J. Neill, Bdr. Ralph H. Cooper, Gnr. E. L. Bowers, Gnr. J. L. Dobson, Gnr. L. J. O'Connor, and Gnr. J. P. Pelletier.

Bürgermeister on the north side, warning him that his beautiful, old city (until then largely unscarred by war) would be reduced to rubble starting at midnight if he didn't persuade the garrison commander to remove his troops. The phone call was simply following up on propaganda leaflets, printed in nearby Delmenhorst and showered by the thousands across the ancient city by 26th Battery guns airbursting smoke shells from which smoke canisters had been removed to take wads of pamphlets. At first the *Bürgermeister* said he couldn't influence a military decision. And with negotiations at an impasse, the seventy-two guns of 2nd Division were laid on to deliver a city-rocking salvo on the town's central square at thirty minutes after midnight. With only four minutes to go, the *Bürgermeister* phoned to say the military had agreed to withdraw all troops from the city by dawn.

And there is more good news: Captain Ted Adams, blinded and captured on the Goch–Calcar highway when the Essex were overrun, is in a hospital in North Holland, his sight restored by German doctors; and L/Bdr. Ken Munro and Gunner Hans Neilson, captured last July in Normandy, have been released by an American spearhead.

74

JOURNEY'S END

---- ❋ ----

ABOUT 10:30 A.M. (MAY 4) THE REGIMENT IS WARNED OF A move to new positions north of Oldenburg on the road to Wilhelmshaven. This time you move with the advance parties as they make their way through the narrow, winding, medieval streets of a city that apparently held little attraction for RAF bombers on any of their frequent nocturnal visits to the Reich, including nearby Wilhelmshaven and Bremen, though residents had provided for such eventualities by constructing a truly massive concrete bunker several storeys high just outside the city centre.

The sergeant driving your Jeep, who speaks some German and is able to talk to the people he encounters, concludes that the lack of major scars in the city is due to Oldenburg's being utilized as a hospital and convalescent centre for the wounded from larger cities, and, as a consequence, the number of buildings with red crosses painted on their roofs.

On reaching the allotted area, well out in the country, you turn right up a lane to a clutch of buildings, set back some distance from the road, which you selected before setting out simply from their designation on the map as "Distillery." The name suggests affluence of more than one kind, but especially substantial buildings attached to an enterprise that rates identification on a map. And your assumption proves correct: while the distillery itself is a gloomy, dusty, cavern of pipes and vats, there is a row of spacious warehouses, and quite a splendid house providing both office and residence for the manager of "Hullman Korn" distillery.

Though the yard is uncannily reminiscent of a farmyard with its arrangement of out-buildings, no one in A Echelon will sleep with stinking cows or pigs tonight. When you check out the distillery it appears long dead, full of dust and cobwebs. In the basement, in behind a floor-to-ceiling grating formed from heavy industrial-fencing and securely padlocked, is a huge rectangular galvanized tank, which you presume is empty though you can't check it, for the two-inch pipe, protruding from the bottom rim, is fitted only with a plug, not a tap.

You take over the main part of the house for officers and NCOs. And using your sergeant-interpreter to communicate with the mistress of the house, you lay on "a chicken dinner with all the fixings to be presented on her best dinner service at 8:00 P.M.," promising that on the basis of the quality of the dinner, a judgement will be made whether the family will be allowed to occupy the servants' quarters or be forced to find accommodation elsewhere.

It is, of course, your intention to show off your high standard of living while at the same time getting the chance to have a chinwag with Don Wilson over dinner. And as soon as the Regiment comes up and the telephone line is laid to RHQ, you intend to invite him, Adjutant Sammy Grange, and Padre Marsh Laverty to share in the feast.

But within minutes after the arrival of the main body of troops, they've discovered that a dusty 2,400-gallon tank in the basement is full of alcohol, have shot the padlock off the barrier, knocked the pipe off the bottom, and are carrying away pails full of the stuff. Of all this you are blissfully unaware until one Sgt. G. Whitley comes in the house seeking advice on what you think should be done about it. When you go rushing out to see for yourself, and are striding across the yard, you are accosted by a laughing pair who offer to pour you a tin cup full from a teakettle they are carrying. Brushing them aside, you make for the stone stairs leading down into the basement. As you descend in the gloom you note the bottom step has disappeared under a glistening, dark lake of alcohol that is being fed by an unimpeded *glug-glugging* flow out of the ruptured tank. As you stand there wondering how you are going to maintain sober guards at this cistern of alcohol – the fumes of which are enough to make you dizzy – a gunner comes down the stairs with a pail: "Excuse me, sir," says he, as he bends down to dip his vessel in the pungent pool and lift out all it will hold.

Guards are placed, but they have to be changed frequently.

When you phone RHQ to invite Wilson and the other two for dinner, you are told to call a muster parade of your group immediately and call back when it's ready.

Why, for gawd's stake?

You needn't know! Simply report when every last man is on parade.

Just then the mistress of the house passes on a warning from her husband lurking in the background: the alcohol is not meant for human consumption, but was manufactured to pep up the fuel in V-2 rockets! Frantically you call the MO, Dr. Veloshin, and ask him if he can test it to see if it's poisonous? He tells you he can't test for higher forms of alcohol – that "they all may be blind in the morning."

It begins to drizzle rain as the men start mustering in the yard. Most of them can still walk, but some cannot, and those who cannot are dragged out and laid face-down in the line. After every nook and cranny of the premises has been searched, there are still a couple missing. You try to get Grange to release the others, for it's now raining steadily, but he tells you they must remain until you locate every last man.

Surprisingly, the men take it all in good humour as the minutes crawl by and still the remaining two can't be turned up. Finally Adjutant Grange arrives with a military policeman and two women – a young woman and an older woman who appears to be her mother – who go down the line peering at each soldier's face, including the faces of those lying in the mud, whose heads must be raised for examination. "Nein ... nein ... nein ..." is heard over and over as they pass on from one to the other.

When you spot the Padre, you ask if he knows what this is about. He does. Shaking his head and grimacing in disgust, he tells you it is a revolting tale of rape involving men with 4RCA on their shoulders.

Though relieved the culprits are not found among these men, when permitted to break off the parade, you keep them standing a few more minutes to tell them what the parade was about and how damned lucky they are not to have been picked as a rapist. How could they have defended themselves in their condition? You tell them to take their sodden comrades and themselves out of sight, and to remain out of sight until morning. You tell them you are taking the guards off the alcohol, but if you see a drunk out in the yard, you'll beat his brains out with a rifle butt ... might as well, for he'll probably be blind or dead in the morning anyway! The intemperance of your lecture – most of which would have sounded silly under normal conditions – impresses, and where they were giggling and simpering before you spoke, they leave the parade supporting their limp comrades in a very subdued and reflective mood.

What they don't know is your decision to remove the guard from the alcohol in the distillery is no gamble at all, for you learned from Sgt. Whitley, just before you spoke, that soldiers are now coming from far and wide to take away jerrycans full of the stuff from railway tank cars sitting on a siding over in the field.

Inside the library of the house, a little 38-set on the mantel plays "Workers' Playtime" from England. You wait until all the goblets are full of Mosel from the case you'd had brought in from a large cache in one of the warehouses, and then you ask the Padre to propose a toast. But before he can speak, the music ceases abruptly and a woman's voice says: "We interrupt this program to bring you a very important announcement. Field Marshal Montgomery's 21st Army Group Headquarters has just announced the surrender of all German forces in Holland, Northwest Germany including the Frisian Islands, Heligoland, Schleswig-Holstein, and in Denmark.

The cease fire will take place at 0800 hours tomorrow, May 5th. We repeat this very important announcement . . ."

You sit stunned and speechless with relief and thankfulness. The Padre rises as though on cue and gives a beautiful toast to peace, to loved ones at home, and to the memory of comrades who have died helping to bring about this moment. Silently you drink this toast, and for a long time no one speaks. Then Paymaster J. D. Macdonald turns to you and in his kindly fashion says earnestly: "Well, it's all over."

Overwhelmed with relief that you are going to live and will actually be going home, you can find nothing to say. Nor can anyone else. In the silence, there is a knock at the door and you hear a woman's voice: "Dinner is served."

Silently, you all move into the dining room and sit at a table of polished silver and crystal, sparkling in the light of a candelabra. Dishes are passed and plates are filled before Sgt. Whitley breaks the spell – "How in hell did you know the war was going to end tonight, sir?" A roar of laughter, and then as though a dam has broken, everyone starts talking at once.

There's a tapping on the hall door behind you, and when you open it, the woman of the house reports they have just discovered a casket of valuable jewels has been stolen, and can you help them get it back. Ten minutes ago you would have told her "tough luck" and closed the door, but it is no longer "spoils of war," but theft – criminal and punishable. And so you get Whitley to go out and spread the word that if the jewels are returned, no charge will be laid. In a few minutes a gunner delivers a heavy metal casket to you after getting you to come out in the hallway to the foot of the stairs.

Standing alone in the dark hallway after he leaves, staring at the tiaras, bracelets, and necklaces sparkling in the shaft of light coming through the crack of the door, you are greatly tempted to take something for your wife. But the splendid reverent feeling for the gift of life itself, presently flooding your being, forbids it and you deliver the casket intact to the grateful woman in the kitchen.

As you undress for bed in the unnatural silence, you relish the strange, almost-forgotten feeling of safety. There'll be no orders group tonight, or any other night. If only there was some way of notifying your wife that you have made it safely to the end. And you go to sleep imagining how wretched it must have been for her, and all the other wives and families, never knowing...

In the morning you are awakened by the unmistakable crashing of 25-pounders firing nearby, and you dress hurriedly, cursing that it has started again.

But when you go over through the bush to RHQ in the great mansion that is the home of the owner of the distillery, they tell you it was just some rounds of red, white, and blue smoke, fired first by the three field regiments of 2nd Division, and then by selected 4th Field "1939 gunners" – a crew from each of the original four batteries – so timed as to land at precisely 8:00 A.M. and stream victory hues across no-man's-land as the last rounds fired on the Western Front in World War II. And you were not the only one disturbed by the sound of the guns. Grange hands you a signal just received from Army Headquarters:

"First Canadian Army will cease fire. Fourth Field Regiment will cease fire!"

There are no boisterous victory celebrations on this north German plain. It is enough to relish the deep relief and gratitude that the fighting is over and that you have survived – that you have been spared a final battle with well-armed enemy forces concentrated north of a formidable canal before Wilhelmshaven. (Just how well-armed will become known when 4th Field helps collect 1,400 artillery pieces from the Germans north of the canal for towing to the Krupp gun park at Meppen.)

On Sunday, May 6, in barns and sheds for miles around, thousands of men in stained battledress kneel on rough concrete floors to utter genuine prayers of thanksgiving as they participate in regimental memorial services. The men of 4th Field assemble in the barn beside the regimental headquarters' mansion, and listen with profound sadness as the Colonel reads the names of their dead.

Word also comes that the officers and men captured at Dieppe in August 1942 have been released.*

On May 8, officially declared VE-Day (Victory Europe Day), the unit assembles in a nearby field to hear a broadcast from the King. Still there is no celebrating. Everyone is tired, emotionally drained, and with unlimited opportunity for sleep many find it difficult to drop off in the disconcerting stillness. While others, who haven't been conscious of having dreamt in months, start having dreams and nightmares.†

There is an unreal, aimless quality to these first few days. Free of censorship and those personal restraints you imposed on your letter-writing when you thought you might not live to get a reply, you can now write long letters home and say exactly what is in your heart. And every time you get a chance to be alone, you study snapshots and try in vain to recall the sound of her voice.

Now and then you experience a wave of exultation combined with profound thankfulness that you survived – death passed so close so many times. Then you hear friend Capt. Jimmy Else, formerly of 4th Field, who landed on D-Day as a 13th Field FOO with the Chaudières (Major Michel Gauvin's company), and was wounded twice – once on the beach and again farther on, and had to be ordered three times to seek medical treatment before he did so – was killed on VE-Day. His Jeep ran over a mine.

---

* See Appendix B.
† Some were unable to grasp the full reality of peace for months. Major Elmo Thibault, who, from when he joined the FMRs in Normandy, projected the image of the cool, confident, self-possessed company commander, was so uptight by the time peace came that, for months after, to go to sleep he had to have his loaded pistol under his pillow – even on leave with his wife in Southampton. And bad dreams pursued many for years – some up to the present. One very common recurring dream is of being back in action, with the sense of having awakened from a sweet dream of peace into the reality of a war still going on.

75

THE RESTING OF THE GUNS

--- ✳ ---

THE DREAM OF GOING HOME WILL NOW ACTUALLY COME true. The thought is intoxicating. But try as you will, it is impossible to suppress the feeling that this is only a temporary pause before another push, or at least another training scheme – there has always been another. So it is a striking day of truth when at an isolated spot along a tree-lined, sun-dappled country road near Oldenburg, you take part in a solemn ceremony, "Resting of the Guns," preparatory to handing them over to the Dutch Government.

The reviewing stand, on which the commanding officers of all nine infantry battalions and their brigade commanders assemble with the Corps Commander, the Divisional Commander, and the CRA to salute the guns, is quite a noble affair – or so it seems to you who, with Major Don Wilson, are responsible for its design and manufacture. Erected on the steel girders of a Bailey Bridge, the platform is backed by three great billboards painted by an Oldenburg artist and paid for by that wad of marks you took from those two German prisoners delivered to you by the Dutch woman back in Groningen. The outer two boards resemble 2nd Division shoulder-patches with golden "C-IIs" on royal blue. The middle board is a great stylized maple leaf crowned by a huge artillery crest. Finally, as a reminder of the origins of these regiments, Major Don Wilson and Major Geoff Brookes, of 6th Field – suitably attired in forage

caps, serge jackets, Sam Brownes, riding breeches, and highly polished riding boots – sit stiffly on horses flanking the stand.

Except for the officers, NCOs, and drivers conducting the guns
past Lt.-Gen. Guy Simonds, flanked by Maj.-Gen. Bruce Matthews,
and CRA Brig. Frank Lace, all personnel of the five gunner regiments
(4th, 5th, and 6th Field, 2nd Anti-tank and 3rd Ack Ack) line both
sides of the road leading up to the stand. Then, following the
example of 4th Field's CO, all officers riding in Jeeps at the head of
each battery, after passing the reviewing stand, dismount and join a
growing line of officers at the side of the road saluting the slowly
passing guns.

No drums roll. No voices call out orders. Each gun sergeant,
standing proud and tall, his head and shoulders protruding through
the roof-opening of his quad, automatically does eyes-right as his
gun, glistening with new paint, oil, and polish, approaches the
reviewing stand. Still there is something about the simple, quiet
solemnity of the affair that affects you deeply.

As the first gun rolls slowly by, chuckling and clinking on its
limber hook, there's a growing awareness of just how deeply these
cold, steel machines have endeared themselves to you. It's as though
you're saying goodbye to old friends you shall never see again.

Remembering the revulsion you felt on first being introduced to
the death-dealing capacities of an old 18-pounder by an enthusiastic lieutenant at summer camp, you marvel at your feelings. Has
time, training, and experience perverted you? Can it be right for a
man to look with affection on killing machines?

But as you stare at those passing guns, you decide a man would
truly be perverted if today he was unable to feel gratitude for those
trustworthy old weapons that subdued countless counter-attacks
and unquestionably saved the lives of many, many men, including
your own.

D Sub's gun is going by, and you look for the holes in the shield
through which the bullets came that killed Sgt.-Major "Lefty"
Phillips. Its breech shines like silver in the sunlight. What a mountain

of cotton waste and oily rags must have been consumed over the years in the tender care of each gun – of each tiny part of the breech and firing mechanism. Inexplicably you recall in every detail one particular day in a gun shed in the sheep and cattle market at Barnham Junction, Sussex. It's December and it's raining. A chilly wind blows through the open-sided shed, but gun crews have the breech mechanisms spread out on oily canvas breech-covers on the ground, and are rubbing each little piece with a bit of oily cotton waste . . .

Now you see those breeches, in blasting recoil, splashing in the reddish, muddy water of the gun pits of Louvigny as the gunners, stripped to the waist, respond to calls from desperate FOOs for overlapping fire: "40 rounds gunfire – enemy tanks . . . 50 rounds gunfire – SS attacking . . . 60 rounds gunfire . . . Fire until you're told to stop!"

Then you hear a voice, as though from a great distance, saying: "Well now . . . let's go and find something to drink." And you realize the ceremony is over.

The last gun muzzle is disappearing around a bend in the road on the right, followed by the two majors on horseback. And when they disappear, the road is deserted except for a solitary German soldier walking barefoot up from the south, making his way home – dusty and unshaven, his unbuttoned, rumpled tunic flapping open, and his jackboots inexplicably slung around his neck on a piece of string.

Col. Lendrum of the Royals comes down from the platform and joins you to walk over to the refreshment marquee in a nearby orchard.

It is obvious he too has been much affected by the ceremony. His voice is husky with emotion as he earnestly expresses his regret that all the infantrymen of 2nd Division were not invited to turn out and line the road to salute the guns.

Then he stops and proceeds to read aloud with great feeling from the printed program entitled "Farewell Review of the Guns" issued to platform guests, Rudyard Kipling's famous words of gratitude from a surviving front-line soldier:

Ubique means that warnin' grunt
The perished linesman knows,
When o'er his strung and sufferin' front
The shrapnel sprays his foes,
And when the firin' dies away
The husky whisper runs
From lips that haven't drunk all day
"The guns, thank God, the guns."

APPENDIX A

GUN STATE FOR OPERATION "PLUNDER"
MARCH 23–24, 1945[*]

(A) In support of the 2nd Canadian and the VIII, XII, and XXX British Corps:

3.7"	75-mm	105-mm	25-pr	4.5"	5.5"	155-mm	7.2"	8"	240-mm	Totals
30	–	–	912	48	320	76	40	4	6	1,436

Rockets	3.7"AA	40-mm	37-mm	20-mm	17-pr	6-pr	
24	144	870	–	54	675	–	1,767
						sub total:	3,203

(B) In support of XVIII U.S. Corps:

75-mm	105-mm	25-pr	6-pr	17-pr	37-mm	
60	12	12	80	12	32	208
					Total:	3,411

If each of the 32 firing "rails" on the 24 rocket projectors is counted a "barrel," another 744 barrels (768 minus the 24 already included above) could legitimately be added: 744

Grand Total: 4,155

Not included in this total are 2,000 additional guns firing on behalf of Ninth U.S.A. Army crossing southwest of Wesel at 10:00 A.M. that same day.

The monstrous fire-power represented by these totals can best be placed in perspective when compared to other remarkable assemblages of guns:

El Alamein (N. Africa)	980	guns
Hitler Line (Italy)	786	guns
Gustav Line (Italy)	1,060	guns of all types
Operation "Veritable" (NWE)	2,645	guns[†]

---

[*] Derived from a chart attributed to AEF: 45/Second Army/G/D Docket II, Appendix "H," Ch. VII p. 406.
[†] Includes 17-pounders, 20-mm and 40-mm Bofors engaged in a ground role firing neutralizing Pepperpots.

APPENDIX B

4TH FIELD POWs TAKEN

AT DIEPPE AND LATER FREED

The *only* field gunners on the Dieppe raid for the purpose of taking over a troop of German guns and turning them on the enemy at Puys, these officers and men of 4th Field were prisoners from August 19, 1942. They were manacled with steel handcuffs, joined by a chain only fifteen inches long, from December 2, 1942 to November 21, 1943. They were released on May 1, 1944 by British tanks:

Capt. Thomas D. Archibald
Lieut. Tait M. "Moose" Saunders
Sgt. Leonard Joseph D'Arcy
L/Sgt. Irving Heller
L/Sgt. James George Potter
Bdr. Deans Cummings Lansing
Bdr. George Leslie Gow
Bdr. Harry Hancock
L/Bdr. Morris Allen Demeray

Gnr. Fulton James Adams
Gnr. M. D. C. Eager
Gnr. Charles Stanley Gray
Gnr. Joseph Krawda
Gnr. J. Carl Killeen
Gnr. David Brown McIntosh
Gnr. Archie Mills
Gnr. Horden J. Phillips
Gnr. Wm. Mortimer Scott
Gnr. Wm. Egill Sveinson

Also captured (up on the Puys headland with Lt-Col. D. E. Catto of the Royal Regiment of Canada), Capt. George Browne, within hours, managed to escape and make his way, with the help of the French Underground, to "Unoccupied France." When, soon after, it was "occupied" by the Germans, he was jailed by the Vichy people. But again he escaped and got to England via Lisbon with information of crucial importance to the planning of the Normandy invasion, for which he was awarded the DSO (Distinguished Service Order).

Sgt. John W. Dudley, L/Bombardier F. H. Lalonde and Gnr. Donald McLean, along with eight officers and 201 Other Ranks of the Royal Regiment of Canada, with whom they went ashore, died on "Blue Beach" at Puys — a skinny stretch of sea-lapped gravel, which for Gnr. Carl Killeen, a signaller with Browne that morning, will forever be "littered with dead bodies."

INDEX